PARTIES AT WAR

Parties at War

Political Organization in Second World War Britain

ANDREW THORPE

OXFORD

UNIVERSITY PRESS

OXFORD

UNIVERSITY PRESS

Great Clarendon Street, Oxford OX2 6DP

Oxford University Press is a department of the University of Oxford.
It furthers the University's objective of excellence in research, scholarship,
and education by publishing worldwide in

Oxford New York

Auckland Cape Town Dar es Salaam Hong Kong Karachi
Kuala Lumpur Madrid Melbourne Mexico City Nairobi
New Delhi Shanghai Taipei Toronto

With offices in

Argentina Austria Brazil Chile Czech Republic France Greece
Guatemala Hungary Italy Japan Poland Portugal Singapore
South Korea Switzerland Thailand Turkey Ukraine Vietnam

Oxford is a registered trade mark of Oxford University Press
in the UK and in certain other countries

Published in the United States
by Oxford University Press Inc., New York

© Andrew Thorpe 2009

The moral rights of the author have been asserted
Database right Oxford University Press (maker)

First published 2009

All rights reserved. No part of this publication may be reproduced,
stored in a retrieval system, or transmitted, in any form or by any means,
without the prior permission in writing of Oxford University Press,
or as expressly permitted by law, or under terms agreed with the appropriate
reprographics rights organization. Enquiries concerning reproduction
outside the scope of the above should be sent to the Rights Department,
Oxford University Press, at the address above

You must not circulate this book in any other binding or cover
and you must impose the same condition on any acquirer

British Library Cataloguing in Publication Data

Data available

Library of Congress Cataloging in Publication Data

Data available

Typeset by Laserwords Private Limited, Chennai, India
Printed in Great Britain
on acid-free paper by
the MPG Books Group

ISBN 978–0–19–927273–0

1 3 5 7 9 10 8 6 4 2

For Rhodri Thorpe

Preface

This book is the result of a double curiosity. On the one hand, it arose from a hunch that the local-level records of political parties could be used in an integrated fashion to offer a new level of insight into twentieth-century British history. On the other, I wanted to try to understand what had happened to Britain's major parties during the Second World War, and how those experiences affected their longer-term development.

This was, to say the least, a challenge: starting at the Dorset Record Office in Dorchester on 23 March 2000, and finishing with the East Sussex Record Office at Lewes on 28 May 2004, I visited ninety-four record repositories. This would simply not have been possible without generous financial support from the British Academy, via one of its Small Research Grants, the Arts and Humanities Research Council, via one of its Research Leave Awards, and also the University of Exeter. The research would not have been possible, either, without the excellence of British archivists and archives. The archivists with whom I dealt were unfailingly helpful, some going well beyond the call of duty in hunting out their holdings. Mention must also be made of the Archon Directory, hosted on the website of The National Archives, which enabled me to locate holdings with relative ease.

I am also grateful to those constituency parties and associations whose specific permission I needed to consult their collections, and to Sir Michael Spicer for permission to consult the papers of the 1922 Committee. Quotations from the Chartwell papers are reproduced with permission of Curtis Brown Ltd., London, on behalf of The Estate of Winston Churchill, and are Copyright Winston S. Churchill. I am also grateful to the holders of copyright in material quoted in the book. Every effort has been made to identify and seek permission from copyright holders; any omission in this regard is deeply regretted.

I am of course grateful to the Oxford University Press for publishing the book: Seth Cayley, Mikki Choman, Rupert Cousens, Anne Gelling, and Ruth Parr were all unfailingly helpful, tolerant, and encouraging. The anonymous readers of the original proposal and the final typescript offered extremely useful and important comments, all the more helpful for being far from uncritical at times. Various aspects of the research were tried out on audiences at the University of Birmingham (2001), the European Social Science History Conferences at The Hague (2002), Berlin (2004), and Lisbon (2008), the first Rethinking Social Democracy conference in London (2004), Anglia Polytechnic University in Cambridge (2004), the Political Studies Association conference at the University of Bath (2007), Durham University (2007), the University of Strathclyde (2007), and Yaroslavl' Pedagogical State University (2008), and I am grateful to all those who made those presentations possible and who attended them. In particular, on this matter and for more general encouragement, help, advice, and criticism, I would also like to thank (in alphabetical order) Stuart Ball, Lawrence Black, Gidon Cohen, Paul Corthorn, Nick Crowson, Jon Davis, Dominic Fenech, Steven Fielding, Nina Fishman, Clare Griffiths, Larisa Kuzmitcheva, Kevin Morgan, Neil Riddell, Evgeny Sergeev, Andrei Sokolov, Duncan Tanner, Richard Toye, Garry Tregidga, Jim Tomlinson, and Matthew Worley. Naturally, I take full responsibility for the contents of the book; its failings probably result from my failure to take the advice of others more seriously.

The University of Exeter has been an exciting place to pursue historical research. Heads of school/department and directors of research, in the form of Jonathan Barry, Michael Duffy, Tim Dunne, Jo Melling, Mark Overton, and Alex Walsham were unfailingly supportive. Jane Whittle helped me considerably in formulating my early ideas. I am also grateful to Jeremy Black, Henry French, Tim Rees, Mark Rothery, Sarah Toulalan, and Alex Walsham for the support they gave me when I needed it; I also appreciated very much the help and advice of Steve Smith and Roger Kain at a crucial time. Much of the writing was completed while I was Head of Department between 2004 and 2007, and it is a pleasure to thank Maggie Bishop, Rachel Cardew, Debbie Freeman, and Dee Freer, who in various support roles eased my workload considerably. My students were always a source of good ideas and difficult questions, and I am happy to thank, in particular, those excellent people—they know who they are—who took my Special Subject on this topic in 2002–3, 2005–6, and 2008–9.

Outside academia, I am grateful as always to my parents, Chris and Shirley Thorpe, for their continuing support, and for regularly updating me on their most recent—and usually sobering—visits to sit beside a certain field in Sheffield 6. They also accommodated me, on numerous research trips, in Dronfield which, among its many other virtues, is an excellent base from which to reach numerous northern and Midlands record offices. My grandfather, Arthur Barratt (1912–2003), was a key figure in my life and was still very much around at the start of this project; I am sorry that he is not still here to see it completed. On a happier note, it is impossible to imagine better friends than Roger Fisk, Andrew Jay, and Philip Telford, all of whom have once again supported me through interesting times. The book is dedicated, with love, to my son, Rhodri Thorpe, for whom the word 'party' rightly conjures up the very different images that it should do in the mind of a young boy.

Contents

List of Tables

List of Abbreviations

ABB	Active Back-Benchers group (Conservative)
AEU	Amalgamated Engineering Union
ARP	air raid precautions
ASW	Amalgamated Society of Woodworkers
BLP	borough Labour party
CA	Conservative association
CCO	Conservative Central Office
CPGB	Communist party of Great Britain
CRD	Conservative Research Department
CW	Common Wealth
CWS	Co-operative Wholesale Society
DLP	divisional Labour party
DR1AA	Defence Regulation 1AA
ETU	Electrical Trades Union
ILP	Independent Labour party
ISTC	Iron and Steel Trades Confederation
JIL	Junior Imperial League
LA	Liberal association
LCA	Liberal Central Association
LCC	London County Council
LCNWLF	Lancashire, Cheshire, and North-Western Liberal federation
LF	Liberal federation
LLP	local Labour party
LPACR	*Labour Party Annual Conference Report*
LPO	Liberal Party Organization

LPP	Liberal parliamentary party
MFGB	Miners' Federation of Great Britain
MoI	Ministry of Information
MP	member of parliament
NEC	national executive committee (Labour)
NFU	National Farmers' Union
NLF	National Liberal federation
NPB	National Publicity Bureau (National government)
NSCUA	National Society of Conservative and Unionist Agents
NUAW	National Union of Agricultural Workers
NUCC	National Union central council (Conservative)
NUDAW	National Union of Distributive and Allied Workers
NUEC	National Union executive committee (Conservative)
NUGMW	National Union of General and Municipal Workers
NULOEA	National Union of Labour Organizers and Election Agents
NUR	National Union of Railwaymen
NUTGW	National Union of Tailors and Garment Workers
PLP	parliamentary Labour party
PPS	parliamentary private secretary
PWPCC	Post-War Problems Central Committee (Conservative)
RACS	Royal Arsenal Co-operative Society
RAF	Royal Air Force
RCA	Railway Clerks' Association
RCL	regional council of Labour
SCALA	Society of Certificated and Associated Liberal Agents
TC	trades council
TCLP	trades council and Labour party
TGWU	Transport and General Workers' Union

TLC	trades and labour council
TRC	Tory Reform Committee
UA	Unionist association (Conservative)
UTFWA	United Textile Factory Workers' Association
VfS	Victory for Socialism (Labour)
WLF	Women's Liberal Federation
WVS	Women's Voluntary Service

Introduction

Political parties formed the cornerstone of the liberal democracy for which Britain claimed it was fighting in the Second World War. Paradoxically, however, that war represented the most sustained challenge to the British party system during the twentieth century. It placed serious obstacles in the way of the normal functioning of politics. Parties faced the suspension of normal electoral politics, and considerable extra demands on the time of their activists and organizers. This book examines how parties responded to the challenge, at all levels, and considers the war's effects on the long-term development of 'party' in Britain.

The outlines of British politics before and during the Second World War are well known. Britain was taken into war on 3 September 1939 by a Conservative-dominated National government under Neville Chamberlain, following the failure of the attempt to appease Nazi Germany. Chamberlain had been the dominant figure in this government, originally formed by Ramsay MacDonald in 1931: first as Chancellor of the Exchequer, and then, from May 1937, as Prime Minister. MacDonald's original anti-Labour combination had been intended as a temporary administration, but had achieved apparent permanence as a result of sweeping victories at general elections in October 1931 and November 1935. Partly because of the nature of the government's origins, its relations with the Labour party had generally been very poor, and there was little enthusiasm on any side for Chamberlain's rather cursory proposal of a coalition government to Labour and the Liberals when war broke out. The three parties did, however, agree that they would not oppose each other at parliamentary by-elections, the idea being that vacancies would be filled by the party already in possession. This electoral pact did not apply to minor parties, however, which left it open for contested elections to take place. (There was no such latitude with local elections, which were prohibited by law: vacancies on councils were to be filled by co-option.)

But a realignment of political forces was not long delayed. Chamberlain's government appeared reasonably secure at the start of 1940. If anything, it was Labour and the Liberals whose problems were magnified as a result of the war, whereas some Conservative cracks had at least been concealed by Chamberlain's appointment of his erstwhile critics, Winston Churchill and Anthony Eden, to ministerial positions in September 1939. The government's strategy was to plan for a three-year war of economic attrition, which would see Germany bled dry and eventually suing for peace before it collapsed altogether. However, doubts about the strategy grew, and by April 1940 it was looking threadbare. It became increasingly clear that the government needed to claim the support of the industrial workers upon whose productivity success in the war was likely to depend. Symbolically, this meant the formation of a government in which organized labour was represented. This gave Labour—among other things, the party of the trade unions—significant purchase, despite its parliamentary weakness (it had won only 154 out of the 615 seats in 1935). When Chamberlain's majority collapsed from the usual 200 to 80 as a result of Conservative defections in the Norway debate on 7 and 8 May, he sought to shore up his position by a renewed appeal to Labour leaders to form a coalition. But he was rebuffed. Even the German invasion of the Low Countries on 10 May did not save him: if anything, it merely underscored the need for change. After some preliminary shuffling on behalf of the Foreign Secretary, Lord Halifax, Churchill became Prime Minister later that day.

Churchill's Coalition war cabinet of five included Labour's leader and deputy leader, Clement Attlee and Arthur Greenwood. The other members were Halifax and Chamberlain; the latter, who remained leader of the Conservative party, served as Lord President of the Council, effectively in charge of the home front. There was no place for the Liberals: their leader, Sir Archibald Sinclair, had to be satisfied with the position of Secretary of State for Air outside the war cabinet. Churchill's own political past was chequered, and he remained deeply suspect to many Conservatives, among whom Chamberlain remained popular. However, when Chamberlain died later in the year, it was Churchill who took over as party leader. He was to remain in the position until April 1955, when he was finally ousted at the age of 80.

The British war effort underwent many vicissitudes before victory was finally won in 1945. The fall of France in June 1940 suggested to some people that the war was lost, although many of them volunteered for active service all the same. Towards the end of May, the war cabinet had discussed the possibility of responding to peace feelers coming from Berlin, with Halifax showing an interest in keeping the door open. However, he was defeated, not least because Chamberlain lined up with Churchill and the Labour ministers against him. Paradoxically, the defeat of France, attended as it was by the heroic British evacuation from Dunkirk, probably helped morale, especially so as no German attempt at invasion followed. The winter of 1940–1 was that of the 'big Blitz' when London was bombed nightly for months, and most major port cities and provincial centres were also attacked, often with devastating results. Without allies of any significance, Britain appeared to be hanging on, waiting desperately for a change that would kick-start a recovery. Many on the left believed that this change could only come about through some kind of moral and political rebirth: in late 1940, the socialist intellectual George Orwell wrote that, while the British could not establish socialism without defeating Hitler, neither could they defeat Hitler while remaining 'economically and socially in the nineteenth century'.[1]

June 1941 saw Britain's isolation ended as the Soviet Union, which had been observing a benevolent neutrality towards Germany, was invaded by three million Axis troops. Britain and the USSR soon agreed a mutual assistance pact. One result of Soviet involvement was that the British Communist party was now free to state its support for the British war effort: the 1939 Nazi–Soviet pact had severely limited its scope for giving such support, and the party's official line had been strongly critical of the war. Now, they became some of the most bellicose advocates of the British war effort, allied as it was with the struggle for survival of the 'workers' state' that they supposed the Soviet Union to be. At first the Soviet Union was not much of an ally, as German troops advanced relentlessly, but in December 1941 the Red Army held Moscow in the face of a German assault, while in the Pacific, the Japanese attack on the United States' fleet at Pearl Harbor brought the USA into the war on the same side as Britain and the USSR.

From this point onwards, it can be argued, the Axis was doomed. Although Germany fought a strong and long rearguard action, its chances of prevailing against such a powerful alliance in the long term were meagre. However, victory was not easily won. In Britain, the travails of 1942, in particular, led to some criticism of the Churchill Coalition. One manifestation of this was that the electoral truce came under pressure. The three main parties kept the bargain, but could not prevent other candidates coming forward. In 1939 and 1940, a number of anti-war candidates had run for election, but had usually polled dismally; the Independents of 1941 did not fare much better. From early 1942 onwards, however, a series of Conservative seats were lost to Independents (some of them socialists), or, later, to representatives of the new ethical socialist party, Common Wealth (CW). Combined with continuing military reverses during 1942 (Singapore fell in February, and Tobruk in June), this increased the pressure on the government. There were parliamentary manoeuvres against the Coalition, and the former Labour, but now Independent, MP Sir Stafford Cripps—recently returned from a two-year spell as Ambassador to the USSR—grew in public stature: he entered the war cabinet that February, and was soon being touted in some quarters as a potential rival to Churchill as the head of a non-party government. The apparent progress of this 'movement away from party' has tended to be seen as a symptom of the extent to which the organizations of the three main parties—but especially the Conservatives—had collapsed in the early part of the war. The degree to which this was, in fact, the case will be a central theme of this book.

The end of 1942 and beginning of 1943 saw significant developments in wartime politics. First, the British victory at El Alamein (October 1942) and

---

[1] G. Orwell, *The Lion and the Unicorn: Socialism and the English Genius* (1941), 88.

the Soviet victory at Stalingrad (February 1943) can be seen as the turn of the military tide: increasingly thereafter, the question was not whether the Allies would win the war, but when. This was confirmed by what proved to be victory in the battle of the Atlantic in May/June 1943, the German failure to win the battle of Kursk that July, and finally the success of the June 1944 D-Day landings in Normandy. At that stage there were hopes that the war in Europe would be won in 1944, but unexpectedly strong German resistance delayed the end until May 1945. In the meantime, they had used their flying bombs (V-1s) and rockets (V-2s) with some success against the British mainland, and particularly London and the South-East. The last V-2 was launched as late as March 1945.[2] Japan appeared likely to take much longer to defeat, but the deployment of atomic bombs at Hiroshima and Nagasaki in August 1945 soon prompted unconditional surrender there, too.

The period around the end of 1942 and the first two months of 1943 was also a major turning point in domestic British politics. In December 1942, the publication of Sir William Beveridge's *Report on Social Insurance and Allied Services* set out something like a blueprint for a 'better' post-war Britain, with stronger and more comprehensive welfare provision than had been the case before 1939. The war cabinet agreed with Churchill's line that reform would have to await the end of the war. However, the parliamentary Labour party (PLP) divided the House of Commons in a vote for early implementation, so symbolizing continuing Conservative–Labour divisions over welfare issues. Such conflict over the post-war world became increasingly obvious, as all three parties began to revive in spirits and activity.

By the time the European war ended in May 1945, both Labour and the Liberals had made it clear that they were not prepared to remain in the Coalition. Churchill therefore formed a 'Caretaker government', which presided over the holding of a general election—the first for almost ten years—in July 1945. After a delay to gather in the votes of service personnel, Labour emerged victorious, a swing of 12 per cent from the Conservatives giving it 393 seats to the 210 held by the Conservatives and their allies, and a mere 12 for the Liberals.[3] Attlee went on to form Labour's first majority government, which was re-elected by a narrow majority in 1950, but defeated in 1951, when Churchill returned as head of a Conservative administration: the Conservatives were to remain in office until 1964.

The above outline of wartime politics will strike familiar chords with most readers of this book. And if it was just going to be another exercise in recounting those familiar landmarks, then the reader might well be forgiven for putting it aside. In fact, however, something different is intended: a book

    [2] R. M. Titmuss, *Problems of Social Policy* (1950), 323; F. Sheppard, *London: A History* (Oxford, 1998), 338.
    [3] R. B. McCallum and A. Readman, *The British General Election of 1945* (1947), 264.

which, by using neglected sources and focusing on what is usually seen as the 'unfashionable' question of party organization, will shed new light on wartime politics.

Where the Second World War is concerned, it is more than usually diffi-cult to draw a definite dividing line between contemporary commentary and historiography. In a sense, the attempt to provide a dominant narrative of wartime politics began at a very early stage, almost as soon as the Chamberlain government fell. In the best-selling *Guilty Men* (1940) and a series of similar books, left-wing journalists, politicians, and commentators attempted—with some success—to fasten the blame for the outbreak of war, and for military failure in it, onto the Conservative party; they then used military defeat to broaden the attack to all aspects of the record of the mostly Conservative or Conservative-dominated governments of the inter-war period.[4] This was, to say the least, a tendentious view: in a sense, it was no more nor less than the construction of a political myth.

Given that fact, most Conservatives were sure to want to challenge it, although their ability to do so in wartime was compromised, first by the fact that Churchill subscribed to most of its foreign policy and defence aspects and, secondly, because of the need to keep Labour—most of whose members accepted the *Guilty Men* myth with alacrity—working inside the Coalition government. However, as the Coalition approached its end in 1945, a more robust response finally burst forth from the Conservative MP for Oxford, Quentin Hogg, in the provocatively titled book *The Left was Never Right*. Appropriating a view that had already gained currency in Conservative circles, Hogg claimed that the *Guilty Men* thesis had held the Conservative party up to 'hatred, ridicule, and contempt', and offered an alternative narrative, which would form part of a powerful Conservative counter-myth of patriotism and self-sacrifice. Hogg argued that the Conservatives had made a disproportionate contribution towards actually fighting the war. Taking members of parliament (MPs) as his sample, he showed that 136 Conservatives had served in the armed forces, and that 10 of them had been killed and 57 decorated; this compared with 14 Labour MPs serving, none of them killed and only 5 decorated, and 3 Liberals serving, of whom 1 had been killed and 3 decorated. The authors of *Guilty Men*, Hogg pointed out, had not served in the war although of military age, and he concluded that 'whilst some of the poor derided Tories were fighting the enemy, these egregious pamphleteers were sowing discord in the ranks at home behind our backs and attacking our sincerity and personal honour'.[5] This line was further developed by Churchill, in his six-volume *History of the Second World War* (1948–54). Churchill noted

---

[4] 'Cato' [M. Foot, P. Howard, and F. Owen], *Guilty Men* (1940); see also e.g. 'Cassius' [M. Foot], *The Trial of Mussolini* (1943); idem, *Brendan and Beverley* (1944); 'Gracchus' [T. Wintringham], *Your MP* (1944); 'Celticus' [A. Bevan], *Why Not Trust the Tories?* (1944); 'Licinius' [authorship uncertain], *Vote Labour? Why?* (1945).

[5] Q. Hogg, *The Left was Never Right* (1945), 7, 11–14, 15.

especially that, whereas Conservative agents had gone off to fight, the 'core' of the Labour party's constituency-level personnel was in reserved occupations, and so exempt from military service; and that once Britain's 'mortal danger had passed' they had become increasingly partisan in pushing Labour's interests forward. 'Thus on the one side there had been a complete effacement of party activities, while on the other they ran forward unresisted.' This, he concluded, was 'not a reproach, but a fact'.[6] Subsequent Conservative memoirs certainly took it as such, while some Liberals also saw themselves as having suffered politically for their patriotism when compared with Labour.[7]

It was only in the 1960s that a serious historical view of the politics of the Second World War began to emerge. In 1965, A. J. P. Taylor's volume in the Oxford History of England presented the war as a heroic struggle, at the end of which the British people came into their own by electing the first majority Labour government.[8] A more detailed study followed in 1969 with the publication of Angus Calder's *The People's War*. While Calder's focus was far from being exclusively political, the book was full of insights for the political historian. His extensive use of Mass-Observation data offered new insights into wartime by-elections, and into popular attitudes more generally, while the fruits of his own (vast) doctoral thesis on Common Wealth were widely in evidence.[9] If Calder broke new ground at the level of popular politics, then Paul Addison did so at the level of high politics in *The Road to 1945* (1975). Using recently released public records as well as the numerous collections of private papers that had by then become available, Addison argued that the war years saw the development of a degree of consensus at the top of British politics, and that this consensus was then carried on into the post-war period. While the notion of consensus has been contested, Addison's book was, and remains, a classic volume.[10]

In the three decades since the publication of Addison's book, there has been much further work on British wartime politics, falling, for the most part, into one of three categories. First, there have been further studies of the high politics of the Coalition. Two works stand out here. One, J. M. Lee's 1980 study of the Churchill government, was a useful but rather slight thematic treatment of the main areas of policy. The work of a political scientist rather than a historian, it made little use of primary sources beyond the cabinet minutes, and could not be said seriously to have rivalled Addison.[11] A more ambitious work was

---

[6] W. S. Churchill, *The Second World War* (6 vols., 1948–54), v. 509.

[7] See e.g. Earl Winterton, *Orders of the Day* (1953), 315; P. Donner, *Crusade: A Life against the Calamitous Twentieth Century* (1984), 311; Sir P. Harris, *Forty Years in and out of Parliament* (n.d. [1947]), 184–5.

[8] A. J. P. Taylor, *English History, 1914–1945* (Oxford, 1965), 600.

[9] A. Calder, *The People's War: Britain 1939–45* (1969); A. L. R. Calder, 'The Common Wealth party, 1942–45', University of Sussex D.Phil. thesis, 1968.

[10] P. Addison, *The Road to 1945: British Politics and the Second World War* (1975).

[11] J. M. Lee, *The Churchill Coalition, 1940–45* (1980).

Kevin Jefferys' *The Churchill Coalition and Wartime Politics, 1940–1945* (1991). Building on the growing scepticism about the nature of 'consensus politics' that had accompanied the increasing political polarization of the 1970s and 1980s, and on his own earlier work on the 1944 Education Act, Jefferys demonstrated the extent to which Coalition policy remained contested and controversial, and poured doubt on the notion that any kind of consensus emerged from the war.[12] Since his book was published, however, much less has appeared in this area. Secondly, the question of popular politics and attitudes also continued to arouse interest. Steven Fielding, in particular, has offered a vigorous critique of the 'myth' that the British population swung to the left during the war. In *England Arise!* (1995) Fielding, Peter Thompson, and Nick Tiratsoo made use of a wide range of sources, including Mass-Observation, to argue that popular attitudes did not change all that significantly. At most, there was an increased desire to be rid of the Conservatives. This had a positive impact on the Labour vote, but only by default: Labour's victory in 1945 was not a positive vote for 'socialism' but a realization that voting Labour offered the only prospect of removing the Conservatives.[13] The book was, perhaps unsurprisingly, controversial; but, read soberly, it offers a valuable antidote to the wilder claims for 1945 as some kind of revolution. Thirdly, valuable work has continued to be done on the development of individual parties. Such work has tended to focus on issues of leadership, ideology, and policy. Much of this work has appeared in article form, although an obvious exception would be Stephen Brooke's 1992 book on the Labour party. Brooke made extensive use of national-level party records, plus the papers of the relevant politicians, to present a compelling account of Labour's political and policy development between 1939 and 1945.[14] For the Conservatives, John Ramsden's volume in the Longman History of the party offers a great deal in these respects, and also in terms of the organizational side of the party.[15] The best work on the Liberals in the period remains unpublished, except in the form of brief articles.[16]

Even as cursory a summary as this shows that there has not exactly been a dearth of high-quality work on British politics and political parties during the Second World War. The main primary sources for the high politics of the war and the development of popular attitudes have been very largely mined, although

---

[12] K. Jefferys, *The Churchill Coalition and Wartime Politics, 1940–1945* (Manchester, 1991); idem, 'R. A. Butler, the Board of Education and the 1944 Education Act', *History*, 69 (1984).

[13] S. Fielding, P. Thompson, and N. Tiratsoo, *England Arise! The Labour Party and Popular Politics in 1940s Britain* (Manchester, 1995); see also e.g. S. Fielding, 'What did "the people" want? The meaning of the 1945 general election', *Historical Journal*, 35 (1992).

[14] S. Brooke, *Labour's War: The Labour Party during the Second World War* (Oxford, 1992).

[15] J. Ramsden, *The Age of Churchill and Eden, 1940–1957* (1995).

[16] M. Baines, 'The survival of the British Liberal party, 1932–59', University of Oxford D.Phil. thesis, 1990; see also idem, 'The Liberal party and the 1945 general election', *Contemporary Record*, 9 (1995), 48–61.

gaps remain, not least in the need for a modern study of the 1945 general election itself. However, although there have been some good studies of individual parties, these tend to focus only on certain aspects of the respective parties' development; they have little comparative angle as regards other parties; and there are severe gaps even at this level of analysis.

And, for all the work that has been done on British politics during the Second World War, there is one huge gap: party organization. Despite a handful of articles, and the work of Ramsden on the Conservatives, the essential question posed by Churchill more than half a century ago remains largely unanswered, and indeed to a large extent unasked: did the experiences of the parties *in organizational terms* vary considerably during the war? The aim of this book is to answer that question.

Contrary to many common assumptions, the history of political organization is not an old-fashioned subject that has been repeatedly covered in the scholarly literature. It has in fact been seriously neglected by historians of twentieth-century British politics. This claim might surprise the reader: after all, strong studies of nineteenth-century organization have been with us for many years, and continue to appear.[17] But there is far less for the twentieth century. Two major collections of essays, published for the centenary of the Labour party in 2000, contained between them more than thirty essays by eminent scholars, but hardly touched on the matter.[18] Furthermore, studies that have looked at organization have tended to pass over the Second World War period. Robert McKenzie's classic study of *British Political Parties* (1955) is a case in point.[19] While it would be churlish to be over-critical of a path-breaking work, it is nonetheless illustrative that McKenzie, while saying a great deal about the inter-war period and the period after 1945, virtually ignored the war years: it was as though the party system had simply gone into cold storage in 1939, to re-emerge in much the same state in 1945, rendering discussion of the intervening years otiose. Subsequent studies by political scientists took 1945 as year zero, and moved on from there.[20] Historians have not really made good the lag. Neither Addison nor Jefferys offered detailed analysis of organizational matters. Brooke did refer to the issue, but found that '[t]he state of the [Labour] party's organization [was] a . . . difficult question', although in the two pages devoted to the subject he made some characteristically shrewd comments.[21] Nor do more general works, even where they take some

[17] See e.g. N. Gash, *Politics in the Age of Peel: A Study in the Technique of Parliamentary Representation, 1830–1850* (1953); H. J. Hanham, *Elections and Party Management: Politics in the Time of Disraeli and Gladstone* (1959); P. Salmon, *Electoral Reform at Work: Local Politics and National Parties, 1832–1841* (2002).
[18] B. Brivati and R. Heffernan (eds.), *The Labour Party: A Centenary History* (Houndmills, 2000); D. Tanner, P. Thane, and N. Tiratsoo (eds.), *Labour's First Century* (Cambridge, 2000).
[19] R. T. McKenzie, *British Political Parties: The Distribution of Power within the Conservative and Labour Parties* (1955).
[20] S. H. Beer, *Modern British Politics: A Study of Parties and Pressure Groups* (2nd edn., 1969).
[21] Brooke, *Labour's War*, 320.

interest in organizational matters, have much to say about the war years.[22] There are some exceptions. Ramsden's work stands as a model, while Fielding et al. asked important questions about organization in *England Arise!*[23] But these have remained rather isolated examples of engagement with the subject.

If this book's first claim is that it is important to study party organization at all, the second is that we can only gain anything like a true picture of the state, nature, and development of party organization through analysis of all levels of a party's activities. It is not enough to focus solely on headquarters. In the research for this book, an attempt has been made to interrogate an unusually wide range of sources for evidence about parties at all levels. Certainly, the national level is important: hence the attention to the papers of the various parties' leaders, and the detailed study of the records of the respective party headquarters. But to complement all this work on the national level, considerable research has been undertaken on the records of the three main parties at the regional and constituency levels. When the present author published his study of the 1931 crisis and general election in 1991, it was possible to claim his use of local party records as virtually pioneering: up to that point, only Ramsden and Stuart Ball, both working on the Conservatives, had used them extensively in national-level studies.[24] Since the early 1990s, however, more and more historians have recognized the value of the often neglected, and sometimes mouldering, minute books, annual reports, accounts, and ephemera that are available.[25]

The aim in researching this book was to study in detail all the extant collections of local party records for the Conservative, Liberal, and Labour parties from the period between 1939 and 1945 that were available in publicly accessible record repositories. This meant immediately that a number of collections that are retained in the offices of the local parties concerned were omitted from consultation. Ultimately, a handful of—mostly minor—collections in public repositories also had to go unconsulted. No historian is immortal, and in any case it was clear that the law of diminishing returns was beginning to operate: the sample as represented in the bibliography to this volume is sufficiently large to allow serious historical conclusions to be drawn. At regional level, the records of 11 Conservative, 8 Labour, and 9 Liberal bodies were consulted; at constituency level, those of 96 Conservative associations, 106 divisional or borough Labour parties, and 26 Liberal associations. Some collections yielded more than others, but few had little to offer, and overall the quality of the evidence garnered was

---

[22] See e.g. M. Pugh, *The Making of Modern British Politics, 1867–1939* (Oxford, 2nd edn., 1993).

[23] J. Ramsden, *The Age of Balfour and Baldwin, 1902–1940* (1978); idem, *Age of Churchill and Eden*; Fielding et al., *England Arise!*

[24] Ramsden, *Age of Balfour and Baldwin*; S. Ball, *Baldwin and the Conservative Party: The Crisis of 1929–1931* (New Haven, 1988).

[25] See e.g. N. J. Crowson, *Facing Fascism: The Conservative Party and the European Dictators, 1935–1940* (1997); N. Riddell, *Labour in Crisis: The Second Labour Government, 1929–31* (Manchester, 1999).

impressive. Like Fielding, I have decided that it is best to use the evidence garnered qualitatively: as he has argued, 'it is virtually impossible to assemble a statistically "representative" selection, even if it could be agreed on what grounds sampling might be conducted'.[26]

Finally, and implicit in the above, it has, from the outset, been taken as axiomatic that this book must try to *compare* parties. Philip Williamson has warned against 'a common snare in studies of a particular party: forgetting that whatever it did had meaning and purpose only within a party system, by contrast and struggle with other parties'.[27] Indeed, it will be one of the contentions of what follows that one of the reasons for the obstinate survival of the 'Conservative myth' regarding organization is the fact that the people who subscribed to it were only able to compare the Conservatives in, say, 1942 with the pre-war and post-war Conservative party. Not surprisingly, they found that it was a good deal less active then than it was beforehand or afterwards. If, however, they had been comparing with Labour in 1942, they might have seen that there was a good deal less about which to be pessimistic. On the other hand, of course, we do need to be sensitive to the differences between parties. Maurice Duverger warned many years ago that parties of the right and the left usually differ in form, raising the prospect of trying to make comparisons which are not really valid, while Ball has rightly cautioned against the tendency for the Conservative organization to be 'crudely measured' against a Labour 'template'.[28] Nonetheless, applied sensitively, a comparative approach can tell us a great deal about parties at war.

Organization has not been interpreted in too narrow a sense, however. The aim has not been to produce a dry, depopulated volume with endless tables of 'facts'. Indeed, the volume sheds considerable light on political myth making; it will be seen that all three parties relied to some extent on their carefully constructed myths. It demonstrates the strength of party ties, both in the considerable ongoing commitment that individuals at all levels continued to make to their parties, and also in the fact that people appear to have remained partisan even when their party seemed, organizationally, to be disappearing from view. A considerable amount emerges about grassroots attitudes and views on policy, not just with regard to reconstruction, but also on issues like the internment of aliens, bombing, and the Soviet Union. It will be seen that, Coalition or no Coalition, issues continued to separate and divide the parties. In that sense,

---

[26] S. Fielding, 'Activists against "affluence": Labour party culture during the "Golden Age", circa 1950–1970', *Journal of British Studies*, 40 (2001), 248.

[27] P. Williamson, review of S. Ball and I. Holliday (eds.), *Mass Conservatism: The Conservatives and the Public since the 1880s*, in *English Historical Review*, 119 (2004), 738–40, at 740.

[28] M. Duverger, *Political Parties: Their Organization and Activity in the Modern State* (1954), 426; S. Ball, 'The national and regional party structure', in A. Seldon and S. Ball (eds.), *Conservative Century: The Conservative Party since 1900* (Oxford, 1994), 220.

the book also says much about the finite nature of the wartime Coalition. Issues of gender are also addressed, and it is shown, in particular, that women often became more prominent at the grassroots in wartime, but that those gains frequently proved to be only temporary as they were once again marginalized after the war.

The Second World War offered a serious challenge to party organization. But it also seemed, at times, to offer a challenge to 'party' itself. Parties of a kind existed in Britain as early as the seventeenth century; by the mid-eighteenth century 'party' was central to British politics. What might be termed 'modern' political parties began to emerge with the franchise extensions of the nineteenth century, by the later part of which many of the elements of modern party politics were in place. These organizations had their parallels in other parliamentary or semi-parliamentary regimes, such as the United States or Imperial Germany. Many admired them, or at least saw potential virtue in them. But others were more critical. At the start of the twentieth century, the Russian thinker Moisei Ostrogorski launched a fierce attack on the development in Britain of the 'Caucus', a kind of party politics that allowed 'a little coterie which monopolized power by pulling the strings behind the scenes' to crowd out '[i]ndependent and thoughtful people', and leading to a lamentable 'dwindling of individuality'.[29] His hope was that ultimately party would decline and that it would be replaced by a system wherein political allegiances would form and re-form in 'leagues' as issues arose. In 1915, the German sociologist Robert Michels criticized the development of organization particularly within social-democratic parties as demonstrating the 'iron law of oligarchy', with the then-current war having 'further accentuated the oligarchical character of the party leadership'.[30] For Michels, the person '[w]ho says organization says oligarchy'.[31] He found this a pessimistic conclusion, but an inescapable one.

However, Britain between the wars offered little succour to those who believed that party needed to be reined in: rather, it demonstrated what J. C. D. Clark has described as the 'immensely durable' nature of party in British politics.[32] If anything, the development of the Labour party helped to encourage all parties towards a tighter, more centralized structure. There were many critics of party, but party survived all the same: writing in 1930, the American political scientist James K. Pollock Jr. stressed that British political organization had become 'more mechanical, more strongly controlled from the center [*sic*]' and that party

---

[29] M. Ostrogorski, *Democracy and the Organization of Political Parties*, i: *England*, ed. S. M. Lipset (New York, 1964), 293, 299.

[30] R. Michels, *Political Parties: A Sociological Study of the Oligarchical Tendencies of Modern Democracy* (New York, 1962), 342, 361.

[31] Quoted in S. M. Lipset, 'Introduction' to Michels, *Political Parties*, 15.

[32] J. C. D. Clark, 'A general theory of party, opposition and government, 1688–1832', *Historical Journal*, 23 (1980), 295.

remained of crucial importance.[33] It recovered to sweep aside David Lloyd George's efforts at charismatic government above party between 1918 and 1922; it survived the assaults of the press barons and the petulance of Sir Oswald Mosley; it even survived the establishment of the supposedly non-party 'National' government in 1931. Yet criticism continued. In the 1930s, the National government was often seen, and certainly portrayed, by its critics as nothing more than a Conservative government in thin disguise, while many people saw Labour as little more than a front for the sectional claims of trade unionists.

Conversely, as seen above, the war years were to see much talk of a 'movement away from party'. Indeed, it might be argued that, if there was ever an opportunity for an alternative basis for politics to be established, it was in the years after 1939. With the established parties facing a potential crisis of survival, surely here was the chance for something else to take their place. Yet it did not happen. By 1945 'party' was as firmly entrenched as ever. This book attempts to explain why this was. It does not seek to do so, primarily, by focusing on the would-be challengers to the system. The premiss of the book is that, short of military defeat and the imposition of an alien political system by triumphant Nazis and their collaborators, the established parties were the only ones who could cause a change, by opening up political space through their own disintegration and decay. The focus, therefore, is on the Conservative, Labour, and Liberal parties. If they remained strong enough to resist, none of the movements that grew up was likely to be strong enough to oust them, although the main wartime challengers, the Communist party and Common Wealth, are addressed where necessary.[34] The Fascists, who had hoped that war would bring them political opportunity, found that it brought, instead, bans and, in the case of many individuals, internment without trial.[35] It would also have been possible to discuss other minor parties, both those in opposition to the government inside and outside parliament, and the Liberal Nationals and National Labour that supported it and still had a number of MPs at the outbreak of war. There are fascinating stories to be told of the development of all these organizations during the conflict. National Labour ceased to exist, although in a way rather different from that usually repeated in the books.[36] The Liberal Nationals failed to reunite with the Liberal party

---

[33] J. R. Pollock Jr., 'British party organization', *Political Science Quarterly*, 45 (1930), 180.

[34] See J. Callaghan, 'Common Wealth and the Communist party and the 1945 general election', *Contemporary Record*, 9 (1995), 62–79; A. Thorpe, *The British Communist Party and Moscow 1920–1943* (Manchester, 2000), 256–76; N. Redfern, 'Winning the peace: British Communists, the Soviet Union and the general election of 1945', *Contemporary British History*, 16 (2002), 29–50; Calder, 'The Common Wealth party'; M. Hilson and J. Melling, 'Public gifts and political identities: Sir Richard Acland, Common Wealth, and the moral politics of land ownership in the 1940s', *Twentieth Century British History*, 11 (2000), 156–82.

[35] See R. Skidelsky, *Oswald Mosley* (1975), 447–64; R. Thurlow, *Fascism in Britain 1918–85* (Oxford, 1987), 188–232; J. Gottlieb, *Feminine Fascism: Women in Britain's Fascist Movement, 1923–45* (2000), 227–65.

[36] See esp. Nicolson papers, diaries 1939–46 *passim*; Chartwell papers, CHAR 2/551, S. F. Markham to Churchill, 14 June 1945.

proper and gravitated ever closer towards merger with the Conservatives.[37] The Scottish National party won its first-ever parliamentary seat (Motherwell, in April 1945).[38] The Independent Labour party (ILP) shifted from an anti-war and anti-Labour position in 1939 to seeking reaffiliation to the Labour party in 1945.[39] But the wartime experiences of all these organizations are essentially tangential to the really big questions at the core of this book.

The organization of *Parties at War* itself is determined by the desire to offer as much direct comparison between the parties as possible. The first three chapters focus on the role of groups of key individuals within the parties. In Chapter 1, the focus is on the parties' leaders and headquarters. While this is not primarily a book about high politics, it is important to assess the role of party leaders and headquarters officials, and the nature of the relationship between them. The chapter analyses how they reacted to the war, how their responses varied between parties and over time, and how their role and position had changed by 1945. In Chapter 2, attention turns to MPs and, to a lesser extent, prospective candidates, investigating the extent to which they maintained a relationship with their constituency organizations; differential levels of military and other service; the extent to which MPs at Westminster maintained 'party'; and how far constituency organizations were concerned with maintaining a relationship, or with adopting new candidates where vacancies existed. Then, in Chapter 3, the focus is upon constituency agents, with a series of questions about what happened to the agents of the respective parties, the effects of the decline in the number of agents, and the extent to which the position was recovered later in the war. Chapter 4 is about party membership. Here, the bulk of the hard evidence comes from Labour, and it is with that party that the analysis starts and is primarily concerned; however, there is sufficient material on the Conservatives and Liberals to offer comment on them, too. Overall, the chapter shows the extent of the commonalities of experience, although it does not neglect to point out the variations that also existed. The next three chapters look in turn at the constituency-level activity of each of the three major parties. These chapters focus on the extent to which local parties and associations did, or did not, remain active, the nature of their activity, and how far there were variations between the

---

[37] See G. Goodlad, 'The Liberal Nationals 1931–40: the problems of party in a "partnership government"', *Historical Journal*, 38 (1995), 133–43; D. Dutton, 'William Mabane and Huddersfield politics, 1931–1947: "By any other name a Liberal"', *Northern History*, 43 (2006), 137–53; Lloyd George papers, LG/G/25/1, Sylvester to Lloyd George, 20 Mar., 23 Dec. 1942.

[38] R. J. Finlay, *Independent and Free: Scottish Politics and the Origins of the Scottish National Party, 1918–45* (Edinburgh, 1994), 199–242; P. Lynch, *SNP: The History of the Scottish National Party* (Cardiff, 2002), 45–60; I. G. C. Hutchison, *Scottish Politics in the Twentieth Century* (Houndmills, 2001), 83–5.

[39] G. D. H. Cole, *A History of the Labour Party from 1914* (1948), 373–4; R. Stevens, ' "Rapid demise or slow death?" The Independent Labour party in Derby, 1932–1945', *Midland History*, 22 (1997), 113–30; G. Brown, *Maxton* (Edinburgh, 1986), 297–306; LPNEC papers XXI, elections subcommittee 4 June 1945.

parties. Social activity is noted as well as political, and the relationship between the two is investigated closely. There is also some discussion of changing—or unchanging—political attitudes at constituency level. In Chapter 8, attention turns to the financial impact of the war on the parties, and it will be seen that the effects were not quite as expected, and also that significant long-term developments had their roots in the war years. Finally, in the Conclusion, there is an attempt to draw out some broad themes, and to assess the extent to which the war made a difference to the development of political party organization in twentieth-century Britain. Overall, it will be argued that historical neglect of the war years has been unwarranted, and that the events of the years between 1939 and 1945 played a significant part in the long-term development of British party politics.

1

National-Level Party Management

INTRODUCTION

Any study of political parties in Second World War Britain must start at the centre: at the level of leaders and managers. The Conservative, Labour, and Liberal parties each had a leader, each of whom had to negotiate his position within a leadership group. In addition, management of the wider party was the business of professionals at the party headquarters. In order to understand the resilience of the three main parties in wartime Britain, we need to focus, not just on the big names like Churchill and Attlee, but also upon the officers and headquarters officials whose job it was to keep the parties going. Ultimately, it will be seen that, in these areas at least, Labour had a better war than either of its rivals.

THE CONSERVATIVE PARTY

In the spring of 1939 the Conservative party could look back on more than two decades of almost uninterrupted office, and it was looking forward to winning the next general election, planned for autumn 1939. Its leader since 1937, Chamberlain, was a formidable and experienced politician, and his leading lieutenants—Halifax (Foreign Secretary), Sir John Simon (Chancellor of the Exchequer), Sir Samuel Hoare (Home Secretary), and Sir Kingsley Wood (Minister of Health)—were widely respected. There were, admittedly, some question marks—there was no obvious successor to the 70-year-old Chamberlain, the second tier of ministers was not terribly impressive, and long-term critics like Churchill were being joined on the back benches by less idiosyncratic opponents of Chamberlain, such as Eden, the former Foreign Secretary. By and large, however, the government seemed secure, and Chamberlain enjoyed a close relationship with Conservative party headquarters at Central Office. His own brief tenure as party chairman in 1930–1 gave him an unusually close appreciation of the problems that faced the party's professional organization, and especially the chairman, Sir Douglas Hacking, and the general director, Sir Robert Topping. Central Office was generally regarded as being efficient at this time, although, privately, party officials had some concerns.[1] Hacking's virtues were solidity and loyalty rather than dynamism, while Topping seemed to be loosening his grip somewhat as he entered his early sixties: a sense of drift was being detected by some senior Conservatives in 1938–9, notably in the failure to see through plans for reform of party finance and youth organization.[2] However, the Conservatives would have done well at an autumn 1939 general election, where they planned to campaign on a choice 'between an irresponsible and inexperienced Labour Party and the known sense of responsibility for the prosperity of the country and for the future of democracy which has been the key-note of the National Government'.[3] This would have been enough to cover a perhaps rather threadbare set of policies.[4]

Events immediately following the outbreak of war tended to support the views of some of Central Office's pre-war critics. The initial reaction was to close down activity and cancel events, in the way that cinemas and other places of entertainment were closed down when the war started. This was, in some ways, understandable, given expectations of imminent aerial bombardment. Furthermore, there was general agreement that Conservatives should feel free to serve their country, and party officials did not want to confuse matters by urging the claims of party at such a juncture. But there was also a more calculating consideration. The Conservatives had done very well in the 1920s and 1930s as the 'national' (and latterly 'National') party, portraying themselves (especially in 1931) as having sacrificed 'mere party concerns' to 'the national interest'. Many saw the war as a further opportunity to establish the party's credentials in this area: the more the party was closed down, the more it would benefit at the end of the war.

There were certainly signs of run-down and closure. Headquarters were moved immediately from Westminster to Ealing, in the west London suburbs; that October's party conference was cancelled, the publication of party literature was suspended, and the National Society of Conservative and Unionist Agents (NSCUA) decided to cease all its activities.[5] On 6 September, Hacking sent a circular to Conservative association (CA) chairmen, which stressed the importance of their organizations' cooperating with local Ministry of Information (MoI) committees, to the exclusion of all else, giving some the strong impression that associations should effectively close for the duration.[6] Some members of staff left for active service, or were seconded to other duties, and the Conservative

---

[1] S. Ball, 'Local Conservatism and the evolution of the party organization', in Seldon and Ball (eds.), *Conservative Century*, 309.

[2] See e.g. Davidson papers, DAV/273, Davidson memo, 25 Jan. 1940; Sir J. Ball to Davidson, 30 Jan. 1940.

[3] CRD 1/7/37, 'Draft election manifesto', n.d. [1939].

[4] Ibid., D. K. Clarke to Sir J. Ball, 4 Aug. 1939.

[5] Derby papers, 920DER(17)/31/6, Topping to Derby, 4 Sept. 1939; NSCUA papers, Acc. 485/5, council meeting, 6 Oct. 1939.

[6] CCO 500/1/9, Hacking circular, 6 Sept. 1939.

Research Department (CRD) was closed down, despite the urgings of some senior Conservatives.[7] Although it soon reopened, it was on a very attenuated basis, and its revival would only really begin after the 1945 election.[8] No plans were made to reschedule the cancelled conference, and the next would not be held until 1943. The National Union's executive committee (NUEC) and central council (NUCC), representing the voluntary side of the party, did continue to meet regularly. But the National Society of Conservative and Unionist Woman Organizers (NSCUWO) held no executive meetings between October 1939 and November 1945.[9]

All this seems to confirm the notion of Conservative closure on the outbreak of war, and so to work with the grain of the subsequent formulations of Hogg, Churchill, and others. But things were not that simple. Central Office rapidly recognized that too total a closure might give the party's opponents potentially insuperable advantages: Topping feared that unless the party remained well organized it might find itself unable to resist possible demands for damaging wartime changes like electoral reform.[10] In the same way that the cinemas were soon reopened, therefore, they sought to revive constituency associations. On 12 September, Hacking wrote again to constituency chairmen. This time, the message was to carry on: he enclosed press cuttings showing Labour and the Liberals' intentions of doing so, and called on associations to sustain themselves. 'The Conservative and Unionist Party', he emphasized, had 'a great and stabilising influence in this country which should be exerted to the full in these days of anxiety'. While reiterating Chamberlain's advice that the overriding priority was to win the war, he stressed that CA participation in MoI, air raid precaution (ARP), and charity work could play a part in this.[11] These views were endorsed a week later by the NUEC.[12] On 26 October, Hacking sent detailed instructions out to constituency officials on the types of work that their associations might undertake, while pressure from Topping led the NSCUA to rescind its earlier decision to suspend activities.[13] Central Office realized that it needed a regular publication if it was to rally the party, and so publication of the *Onlooker* as an eight-page monthly was resumed.[14] The response from the wider party was mixed, but, by the end of the year, Hacking felt that the threat of wholesale closure had been averted, and as late as June 1940, Topping could report privately

[7] Davidson papers, DAV/273, Davidson memo, 25 Jan. 1940.

[8] J. Ramsden, *The Making of Conservative Party Policy: The Conservative Research Department since 1929* (1980), 95–105.

[9] CCO 170/1/1/2, central women's advisory committee minute book 1939–49; CCO 170/2/1/1, NSCUWO minute book 1939–49.

[10] CCO 4/1/86, Topping to Hacking, 14 Nov. 1939.

[11] CCO 500/1/9, Hacking to CA officers, 12 Sept. 1939.

[12] NUA 4/1, NUEC 20 Sept. 1939.

[13] CCO 500/1/9, Hacking to CA and women's chairmen, 26 Oct. 1939; NSCUA papers, Acc. 485/5, council meeting, 6 Oct. 1939.

[14] NSCUA papers, Acc. 485/5, annual general meeting, 24 Nov. 1939.

that there were 'not many constituencies' in which the party had been 'unable to preserve an organization'; even in the minority 'where none exists' there were 'responsible individuals' with whom he could communicate.[15]

The early months of the war saw no serious challenge to Chamberlain. In some ways, the outbreak of war actually reinforced his position, by getting people to rally around the leadership and by bringing into government Churchill and Eden, whose sting was therefore drawn, at least for the time being. Some criticism and grumbling remained.[16] But this, and Chamberlain's inability to get Labour and the Liberals to join him in a coalition, did not matter too much so long as the war was not going badly and the government's attritional three-year war strategy remained credible. Chamberlain himself remained supremely confident of his position until spring 1940. However, increasing doubts as to the efficacy of the blockade which underpinned the three-year strategy were then compounded by the fiasco of the Norway campaign.[17] The collapse of the government's majority in what was effectively a vote of censure at the end of the Norway debate on 8 May 1940 made Chamberlain's position unsustainable. Initially, he refused to accept this, and tried to use the German attack in the west the next day as a reason to stay on.[18] But that very onslaught finally discredited the attritional strategy, while Labour's refusal to contemplate serving under him finished him off. The result, ultimately, was Churchill's accession to the premiership. Halifax, whom Chamberlain initially preferred and encouraged, decided that he would be better placed serving as a restraint on Churchill, and as a potential successor should he come unstuck. For Halifax, the alternative—trying to contain a restless subordinate constantly intriguing and angling for the premiership—lacked appeal.[19]

Chamberlain's swift and unexpected fall winded the Conservative party. Even so, he remained party leader, and joined Churchill and Halifax in the five-member war cabinet. He remained more popular than Churchill among Conservatives for some time; indeed, as Andrew Roberts has shown, there was considerable Conservative resentment at the change of government.[20] (Then again, even anti-Chamberlainites could occasionally be rattled by Churchill's behaviour as Prime Minister.[21]) Churchill welcomed Chamberlain's remaining

[15] NUA 4/1, NUEC 13 Dec. 1939; Chamberlain papers, NC 8/21/19, Topping to Hacking, 26 June 1940.

[16] See e.g. Emrys-Evans papers, Add. 58262, R. K. Law to Emrys-Evans, 13 Sept. 1939; Eden to Emrys-Evans, 8 Jan. 1940; Templewood papers, XI/5, Hoare to Lothian, 8 Jan. 1940; XII/3, Hoare diary 2 Apr. 1940.

[17] T. C. Ismay, 'A reassessment of Anglo-French strategy during the Phony War, 1939–40', *English Historical Review*, 119 (2004), 333–72.

[18] J. Reith, *Reith Diaries*, ed. C. Stuart (1975), 250, entry for 10 May 1940.

[19] A. Roberts, *'The Holy Fox': A Life of Lord Halifax* (1991), 198–203.

[20] A. Roberts, *Eminent Churchillians* (1994), 142–210; and see e.g. Crookshank papers, MSS Eng. hist. 360, diary 27 July 1944, 13 Dec. 1944, 26 July 1945; Elliot papers, Acc. 6721/10/F4, Walter Elliot to Katharine Elliot, 1 Mar. 1944.

[21] See e.g. Emrys-Evans papers, Add. 58262, R. K. Law to Emrys-Evans, 8 June 1941.

in the government for this reason, and also because it meant he did not have to waste time overseeing domestic policy or trying to thwart Labour attempts to do so.[22] Chamberlain himself continued to hope for 'another Premiership after the war' until an operation for bowel cancer in July 1940, which left him 'practically crippled', convinced him otherwise.[23] But he remained loyal to the new premier. He continued to carry out the functions of leader in relation to the wider party. On 27 June 1940, he offered the NUEC a strong and rather partisan vindication of the role of the party, urging Conservatives to keep their organization going, rather than allowing it 'under the pressure of the War to fall into disorganization in the way it did in the last War'. They 'should not allow [them]selves to fall into a condition of false confidence similar to that which was created in the French by the existence of the Maginot Line'.[24]

Most Conservatives were concerned, above all else, to win the war: and if Chamberlain was supporting Churchill to that end, then they should have no compunction in doing so, too. It was possible, after all, to support both men, even though private carping at Churchill continued. Churchill himself pursued a double policy. On the one hand, he sought to reassure his erstwhile enemies within the party that they were part of his team. Thus in June 1940, the widespread press agitation against the 'Men of Munich' was 'turned off like a tap' at his behest.[25] He remained quick to react against overt attacks on erstwhile enemies like the chief whip, Sir David Margesson, and was rewarded when the latter eased his succession as party leader that autumn; indeed, Margesson would be his first choice to succeed Thomas Dugdale as party chairman in 1944.[26] But he also picked off old enemies when he could do so: Hoare and Simon were dispatched very quickly indeed (to the British Embassy in Madrid and the House of Lords respectively), and he remained alert to opportunities to remove others. Once Halifax had burnt his boats with Labour's representatives in the war cabinet by nibbling at the bait of a negotiated peace in late May 1940, for example, his days were numbered, and he was eventually dispatched as British Ambassador to Washington that December, with Eden taking over as Foreign Secretary. By that time, Churchill's public persona had developed to such an extent that he was in any case the only conceivable premier.

A Churchill–Chamberlain partnership might have worked effectively for some time: each man filled a vital role, but neither craved the position of the other.

[22] Templewood papers, XIII/17, Bracken to Hoare, 4 Aug. 1940, Churchill to Chamberlain, 16 May 1940, quoted in M. Gilbert, *Winston S. Churchill*, vi: *Finest Hour, 1939–1941* (1983), 347–8.
[23] Chamberlain papers, NC 2/24A, diary 9 Sept. 1940.
[24] Ibid., NC 4/4/1, 'Report of a speech by Mr Neville Chamberlain at meeting of National Union Executive Council', 27 June 1940; NUA 4/1, NUEC meeting, 27 June 1940.
[25] Chamberlain papers, NC 2/24, diary 5, 7 June 1940.
[26] Adams papers, 1/2/1, Churchill to Vyvyan Adams, 16 Nov. 1940; S. Lawlor, *Churchill and the Politics of War, 1940–1941* (Cambridge, 1994), 109–11; Margesson papers, MRGN 1/4, Churchill to Margesson, 2 June 1945.

However, Chamberlain's cancer ruled it out in anything but the shortest of terms. Churchill was initially reluctant to see Chamberlain retire, but by October there was no alternative, and Chamberlain died the following month.[27] He was widely mourned within the party. Central Office printed a twelve-page booklet, *Neville Chamberlain: Tribute to a Revered Leader*, which praised 'one of the greatest figures in the history of the Conservative Party', 'a great Englishman', whose work 'w[ould] long remain an inspiration' to all Conservatives.[28] Churchill himself was sorry to lose his colleague, although this did not prevent him later launching occasional private tirades against him, or from strong criticism of his policies in his subsequent writings.[29]

Churchill now faced a dilemma. There were powerful arguments against his taking the party leadership: it might make him seem less of a national leader, damage his relations with Labour, and give the Conservative party more of a hold over him. His wife was adamantly hostile.[30] But two factors seem to have overridden such considerations. He realized that, failing him, the party would have to select someone else as leader, which might lead to friction and tension.[31] Secondly, while he did not make a fetish of the Conservative party, he did believe that it was a vital element in sustaining the kind of political, economic, social, and international order in which he believed. As he told the executive of the National Union a few days after his election as leader, he felt that the party had 'an absolutely vital and indispensable part to play in the future turn of events', and therefore he was 'most anxious that there should be in our Country a strong Conservative Party. . . . It would be disastrous if the Conservative Party were to disappear or its structure to fall into decay.' To avoid this, Conservative organizations should pursue war work vigorously.[32] If, for the remainder of the war, he sometimes exasperated party officials, it was not because he could not care less about the party. He offered strong criticism, for example, of its lacklustre by-election efforts in July 1941.[33] The problem was that he was usually too preoccupied with other matters to sustain close attention, and was also aware of the need to avoid alienating his Labour and Liberal colleagues. This meant, however, that there was frequently no strong lead given to a party that had experienced severe trauma. Peace was lost, the National government ousted, Chamberlain dead, and the established social order in mortal peril. What many Conservatives believed the party needed was a rallying cry. What it got was a leader whose main priority was to appease all colleagues in a wide-ranging government as the prerequisite to winning the war.

---

[27] Chamberlain papers, NC 2/24A, diary 30 Sept. 1940.
[28] Butler papers, G11, *Neville Chamberlain: Tribute to a Revered Leader* (1940).
[29] J. Stuart, *Within the Fringe: An Autobiography* (1967), 87; J. Colville, *The Fringes of Power: Downing Street Diaries, 1939–1955* (1985), 406, entry for 22 June 1941.
[30] N. Rose, *Churchill: An Unruly Life* (1994), 267.
[31] Churchill, *Second World War*, ii. 439.   [32] NUA 4/1, NUEC 13 Nov. 1940.
[33] Chartwell papers, CHAR 2/428A, Churchill to Hacking and Stuart, 26 July 1941.

Before 1940, Churchill's relationship with the party machine, and not least Hacking and Topping themselves, had been poor. Churchill realized this, but had little interest in a wholesale purge of Central Office while the Blitz was raging, and realized replacements would be hard to find; so he asked all leading officers to remain in post.[34] The first significant change did not come until June 1941, when he dismissed Lord Windlesham as party vice-chairman in charge of vetting prospective parliamentary candidates; Hacking survived until February 1942, when he was replaced by Dugdale, while Topping was to hold out for the duration of the war.[35]

Churchill's unwillingness to focus on party policy making aroused more adverse comment. By 1941, some Conservatives, including Topping, were beginning to agitate for some forward planning, and this eventually led to the establishment, that May, of a Post-War Problems Central Committee (PWPCC) chaired by the Conservative minister R. A. Butler.[36] It soon had eight subcommittees, and by 1945 it would have sixteen.[37] But although a number of reports were produced, most notably on education, Butler would feel by late 1942 that most of the subcommittees were ineffectual, while his attempt to get an updated version of 'a Conservative Faith' ran up against headquarters indifference and resulted only in the publication, in July 1943, of a 'rather pedestrian document' by David Stelling of Central Office.[38] The fact that the latter sold out its first print run of 10,000 within a week suggested potential for further activity, but Butler's own interests were increasingly focused on his ministerial work on education, and that same month he resigned the PWPCC chairmanship, to be succeeded by Sir David Maxwell-Fyfe, who had no more success in pushing things forward.[39] Churchill's indifference, shading into hostility, did not help: Butler had been his particularly bitter opponent in the 1930s over both India and appeasement. At best, the PWPCC kept the party's thought processes on policy in motion, and laid some foundations for post-war changes.

The perceived shortcomings of the PWPCC led some 'progressive' Conservatives to take matters into their own hands. In March 1943, the Tory Reform Committee (TRC) was formed under the MP for South Dorset, Lord Hinchingbrooke, as a result of the government's halting response to the Beveridge report.

[34] Ibid., CHAR 2/402, Churchill to Lady Hester Bourne, to Lord Windlesham, and to Lord Marchwood, all 14 Oct. 1940.
[35] Ibid., CHAR 2/426, Windlesham to Churchill, 18 and 20 June 1941; CHAR 2/450, Hacking to Churchill, 21 Feb. 1942.
[36] See e.g. NUA 3/1, NUCC 27 Mar. 1941; 1922 Committee papers, 1922/4, meeting 25 Mar. 1942; A. Howard, *RAB: The Life of R. A. Butler* (1987), 140–1.
[37] Ramsden, *Making of Conservative Party Policy*, 97–8.
[38] Butler papers, H61, Butler, memo, 'Subjects for discussion at chairman's lunch', 3 Dec. 1942; Butler to W. S. Morrison, 30 Oct. 1942, Butler to Dugdale, 20 Feb. 1943, Butler to W. S. Morrison, 22 June 1943; D. Stelling, *Why I am a Conservative* (1943).
[39] NUA 4/2, NUEC report to NUCC, 7 Oct. 1943; Butler papers, H61, Butler to Miss M. G. Cowan (Scottish Unionist Association), 30 July 1943; NUA 4/1, NUEC 13 Jan. 1944, 8 June 1944.

Claiming the allegiance of about three dozen backbenchers, it was better financed and more glamorous than the PWPCC, and showed that some Conservatives were not afraid to be seen as 'progressive' or to embrace what would later become known as 'consensus politics'.[40] When Churchill broadcast in March 1943 about his ideas for 'what might be called a Four Years' Plan' regarding home policy, Hinchingbrooke was greatly encouraged; but Churchill's intention had been to close a debate, not open one, and his message to Hinchingbrooke that the priority was victory in the war gave the Tory Reformers scant comfort.[41] But the TRC did at least help to galvanize Central Office and others into action. Butler, believing that the Tory Reformers would 'give the Country rather a funny conception of what Conservative policy may be', decided to return to the chairmanship of the PWPCC in 1944, once his Education Act was on the statute book.[42] But any distinctly Conservative statement of future policy remained elusive, and it was significant that when Ralph Assheton first met the NUEC as party chairman in November 1944 he could say nothing more definite than that he was 'very keen on getting a declaration of policy which the Party could put forward at the forthcoming General Election'.[43]

The difficulties that some Tory Reformers had with their local associations showed that many Conservatives felt that the drift to the left had already gone far enough. In December 1942, Churchill put Assheton in charge of a committee to investigate the Beveridge report, and its findings, which it claimed were shared by the majority of Conservative MPs, were very hostile.[44] The non-party, free-market group Aims of Industry, which was formed in autumn 1942, took a similar line, and by 1944, industrialists would be becoming increasingly strident in demanding a retreat from wartime state controls.[45] The 'secretive' Progress Trust, formed by a group of about twenty Conservative MPs in November 1943 to defend private enterprise and individual liberties, although not terribly successful, was another manifestation of Conservative 'anti-Beveridgism', which could also be seen in backbench revolts against the Catering Wages Bill in February 1943 and the Town and Country Planning Bill in October 1944. It also helps explain the positive reception accorded to Friedrich von Hayek's *Road to Serfdom* when it appeared in 1944.[46]

[40] Butler papers, H61, Butler to Dugdale, 23 Dec. 1943; P. Addison, *Churchill on the Home Front, 1900–1955* (2nd edn., 1993), 368; Ramsden, *Age of Churchill and Eden*, 42–3.

[41] *The Times*, 22 Mar. 1943; Chartwell papers, CHAR 2/480, Hinchingbrooke to Churchill, 25 Mar. 1943, Churchill to Hinchingbrooke, 28 Mar. 1943. Significantly, Churchill does not mention the broadcast in his voluminous war memoirs.

[42] Butler papers, H61, Butler to Dugdale, 23 Dec. 1943; NUA 4/1, NUEC 14 Sept. 1944.

[43] NUA 4/1, NUEC 8 Nov. 1944.

[44] Addison, *Road to 1945*, 221; R. Cockett, *Thinking the Unthinkable: Think-Tanks and the Economic Counter-Revolution, 1931–1983* (rev. edn., 1995), 60–2.

[45] Addison, *Road to 1945*, 231; G. Wootton, *Pressure Groups in Britain, 1720–1970* (1975), 92; L. Johnman, 'The Labour party and industrial policy, 1940–45', in N. Tiratsoo, *The Attlee Years* (1991), 30, 42, 47.

[46] Cockett, *Thinking the Unthinkable*, 67.

These divided counsels help explain why Churchill and other leading Conservatives were reluctant to commit themselves too clearly, too early, on policy. Another was the Conservative view of the electoral truce, signed in September 1939. Modelled on an agreement of 1915, it only covered parliamentary by-elections and, unlike the ban on contested local government elections that followed, it had no legal force.[47] Many Conservatives, however, believed that the truce involved a much wider agreement to abandon purely 'party' concerns in the national interest (hence the common Conservative usage of the terms 'political truce' or 'party truce'). When Ernest Bevin, newly promoted to the war cabinet, was pictured at his desk on the front cover of the magazine *Picture Post* in October 1940, the words 'Labour Party' were visible on some headed notepaper in front of him. 'So much for the Party Truce,' railed one Devon Conservative.[48] But it was not only backwoodsmen who were confused. When, in November 1942, the Central Office agent for the East Midlands was asked by a constituency official about 'the terms of "the Party Truce"', he was unable to answer, and wrote to Topping for enlightenment.[49] That one of the senior figures within the party organization could not answer the question was, to say the least, worrying. But the fact was that, when Conservatives discussed what the truce meant, their views often varied.[50] Topping's view, as expressed in reply, was that, although the *formal* truce was only an agreement covering electoral arrangements in the event of parliamentary vacancies, there was much more to it than that:

There existed, however, at the outbreak of war a feeling throughout the country that it was not in the national interest to engage in political controversy and that view is still held very strongly by many people, particularly in the Conservative Party. It is this general understanding, I think, that most people have in mind when they refer to the Party Truce and not simply to the document which was signed by the Whips.[51]

In part, of course, this line was due to Churchill. His main aim was victory in the war. He reckoned that the best means to achieve that end was for his government to remain in office, and a generous interpretation of the truce seemed most likely to help avoid the kind of petty squabbles which would bring the government down. In addition, however, it appears that Conservatives at all levels expected this approach to pay political dividends. In 1943, Dugdale privately praised the party's 'forebearance [*sic*] over a long period and in the face of very considerable provocation', and the fact that this had 'saved the country from being involved in acute political strife at a time when the national effort should be wholly concentrated on the war'.[52] The clear implication was that

[47] CCO 4/1/84, G. R. Shepherd to Topping, 14 Sept. 1939.
[48] Ibid., Sir Samuel Harvey (Totnes) to Miss Palmer (Western Area agent), 16 Oct. 1940.
[49] CCO 4/2/142, J. W. Lancaster to Topping, 30 Nov. 1942.
[50] See e.g. ibid., Muriel Borron (woman organizer, Darlington CA) to Topping, 27 Feb. 1943.
[51] Ibid., Topping to Lancaster, 1 Dec. 1942.
[52] Ibid., Dugdale to Kenneth Glenny (Romford CA), n.d. [between 3 Mar. and 30 July 1943].

neither he nor his party would be slow to tell this story once the war was over, and the Coalition at an end. This attempt to demonstrate fusion between 'the nation' and the Conservative party was nothing new; and, in the absence of more positive policies, it was to be expected that party managers would fall back on the kind of appeals that had previously served them so well. By the autumn of 1943, however, Dugdale was starting to signal a slightly more partisan approach. Under pressure from his officials and grassroots Conservatives alike, he decided to push the truce closer to its limits, signalling that constituency associations could legitimately do more than they had been doing, and telling them that they should try to hold public meetings addressed by their MP or another speaker, although these should avoid 'pointed criticism of other parties'.[53]

Conservative mutterings against Churchill were at their height in 1942.[54] It was hoped that the appointment of Dugdale as party chairman, and Harold Mitchell (the backbenchers' choice) as vice-chairman, would help to restore unity.[55] But continuing military disappointments periodically opened Churchill to attack, and a series of embarrassing by-election defeats, which saw four seats lost to Independents between March and June, made matters worse. On 1 and 2 July, many criticisms were made in a lengthy parliamentary debate. Thanks to effective whipping and the lack of an obvious alternative premier (other than the problematic Cripps), Churchill easily won a vote of confidence, and his public opinion poll rating remained high. Indeed, the establishment of a Committee on Electoral Machinery under Sir Sylvanus Vivian in January 1942 may well have been aimed at opening up the possibility of a wartime election at which Churchill—who remained very popular in the country—could have gained a clear mandate and cleared many of his critics out of parliament.[56] In the event, of course, victory at El Alamein in October 1942 added immensely to the government's prestige, and allowed Churchill to dish Cripps and stabilize his own position once and for all. By March 1943 the Prime Minister would be able to reassure the war cabinet that they would need to take note of the findings of the Vivian committee, 'not because we want a Genl. Election in war, but because responsible Govts. must be ready for contingencies'.[57] In the event, the main outcomes of the committee were a mild redistribution of seats (the first since 1918), which broke up some of the largest constituencies into smaller units, increasing the number of seats from 615 to 640 at the 1945 election, and new restrictions on claiming the business franchise.

---

[53] Norwood CA papers, IV/166/1/16, emergency committee 18 Oct. 1943.

[54] See e.g. Hannon papers, Hist. Coll. 189/59/1, Sir Patrick Hannon to Churchill, 17 Feb. 1942; 1922 Committee papers, 1922/4, meeting 18 Feb. 1942.

[55] Templewood papers, XIII/19, Butler to Hoare, 6 Mar. 1942.

[56] Mander papers, DM 668, Sir Geoffrey Mander draft autobiography, 'A Back-Bencher Looks Back', n.d., fo. 75; J. C. Ede, *Labour and the Wartime Coalition: From the Diary of James Chuter Ede, 1941–1945*, ed. K. Jefferys (1987), 86, 13 July 1942.

[57] CAB 195/2, war cabinet minutes 29 Mar. 1943.

There was some talk of whether a deputy leader might be appointed to offer clearer leadership to the party. Eden, described by Beaverbrook in June 1942 as 'Winston's right hand man', was the obvious candidate, but Halifax and Margesson had successfully resisted the suggestion in 1940, and he remained unpopular with many orthodox Conservatives for his perceived 'disloyalty' in resigning in 1938; he was in any case already overworked as Foreign Secretary and Leader of the Commons, and nothing came of the suggestion.[58] Wood, who as Chancellor of the Exchequer was the last remaining orthodox Conservative in the upper echelons of the government, was also too busy, and died suddenly in September 1943. Others had high hopes of Butler, who remained closely concerned with purely party affairs; he clearly had high hopes of himself.[59] But it was inconceivable that Churchill would allow so prominent a role to so bitter a former opponent. With no deputy leader in sight, others turned to the idea of establishing a Conservative 'opposition' front bench, to rival the Labour one that had been set up in May 1940 to help with the conduct of parliamentary business, but Churchill vetoed the suggestion.[60]

Meanwhile, Central Office ticked over. It had little choice in one sense: by May 1942, it only employed a fifth as many staff as before the war.[61] Dugdale was more sympathetic towards Churchill than Hacking had been, but did not prove particularly energetic. However, headquarters was not totally inert. Area agents' reports were used as the basis for a survey of popular attitudes in the autumn of 1941.[62] Topping continued working towards the development of his scheme for the central employment of agents after the war (see Chapter 3) and pressing for reform of party finance (see Chapter 8). Lack of progress in these areas was frustrating; the defeat of the former was a particular blow.[63] The National Union did what it could to cheer up the activists. The first party conference of the war, in May 1943, 'went off quite well, giving a vague and amiable impression of progressive spirit', according to Butler.[64] A three-day conference of Central Office area agents was held that September to discuss the state of the party and plan for the future.[65] However, little was done to push CAs and MPs along. Associations needed to be cajoled into action, but the centre brought little sustained pressure to bear, which meant that levels of activity varied greatly, and those few interventions that did come were sometimes poorly received. This was

---

[58] Templewood papers, XIII/19, Beaverbrook to Hoare, 12 June 1942; Ramsden, *Age of Balfour and Baldwin*, 375; Crookshank papers, MSS Eng. hist. 360, diary 26 Aug. 1942; D. Dutton, *Anthony Eden: A Life and a Reputation* (1997), 254.

[59] Templewood papers, XIII/18, Hoare to Butler, 30 July 1941, Butler to Hoare, 29 Aug. 1941.

[60] 1922 Committee papers, 1922/4, meeting 3 Feb. 1943.

[61] Ramsden, *Age of Churchill and Eden*, 73.

[62] CCO 4/2/162, Topping to Stuart, 24 Nov. 1941.

[63] NSCUA papers, Acc. 485/5, annual general meeting 2 Oct. 1942, council meeting 30 Mar. 1943.

[64] Templewood papers, XIII/19a, Butler to Hoare, 31 May 1943.

[65] CCO 500/1/11, report of staff conference, 18–20 Sept. 1943.

in stark contrast to the Labour party, whose more active headquarters set a clear standard to its constituency organizations (see below).

Film propaganda, an area where the Conservatives had been pre-eminent prior to 1939, ceased, and the party handed its cinema vans over to the MoI, many of whose films tended, ironically, to be of a leftish hue.[66] Publications other than the *Onlooker* remained suspended. The PWPCC published *Politics in Review*, a digest of recent press material plus book reviews, from late 1942 onwards, but it was aimed at a limited readership: Topping said it was 'of a strictly confidential nature'.[67] Also arising from the PWPCC were the 'Looking Ahead' pamphlets, published from September 1942 onwards and intended, *inter alia*, as a focus for discussion in local party organizations, although Churchill refused to read them, claiming lack of time.[68] Meanwhile, the Signpost Press had published thirteen pamphlets on post-war problems by July 1944, by authors including the Tory Reformer Hogg, and the chairman of the 1922 Committee, A. G. Erskine-Hill.[69] As will be seen, however, this output did not really match that of Labour's headquarters. In addition, whereas left-wing publishers continued to produce new books, the 10,000-strong Right Book Club had folded on the outbreak of war.[70]

Tensions between the leadership and Central Office remained. In part, they explained Churchill's wartime closeness to Lord Beaverbrook, the proprietor of the *Daily Express* and wartime minister who was heartily distrusted by most orthodox Conservatives.[71] Beaverbrook periodically infuriated him, by his threats to resign and constant intriguing, but he was a valuable counterpart to the party machine, telling Churchill what he wanted to hear about Central Office, such as that it was favouring party worthies over war heroes when it came to candidate selection.[72] These tensions between leaders and managers came to a head due to a further series of by-election reverses. In December 1943, Darwen (Lancashire) was only held by a tiny majority against an independent Liberal, while in January 1944, Skipton (West Yorkshire) was lost to Common Wealth. Topping believed these results proved the need for 'a positive policy on home affairs', as opposed to 'vague promises': at the very least, Conservatives ought to be allowed to take a more partisan line. Dugdale endorsed Topping's

[66] T. J. Hollins, 'The Conservative party and film propaganda between the wars', *English Historical Review*, 96 (1981), 366; J. Fyrth, 'Days of hope: the meaning of 1945', in idem (ed.), *Labour's Promised Land? Culture and Society in Labour Britain 1945–51* (1995), 8.

[67] Chartwell papers, CHAR 2/450, Topping to Harvie Watt, 27 Nov., 3 Dec. 1942.

[68] Ibid., Topping, circular, 4 Sept. 1942, Dugdale to Stuart, 27 Aug. 1942, Stuart to Churchill, 28 Aug. 1942, with Churchill minute, 29 Aug. 1942.

[69] Q. Hogg, *The Times We Live In* (1944); A. G. Erskine-Hill, *The Future of the Small Trader* (1944).

[70] E. H. H. Green, *Ideologies of Conservatism: Conservative Political Ideas in the Twentieth Century* (Oxford, 2002), 140–1, 155.

[71] See e.g. Crookshank papers, MSS Eng. hist. 360, diary 24 July 1941.

[72] Beaverbrook papers, BBK/D/423, Beaverbrook to Churchill, 5 Apr. 1945; BBK/D/420, Beaverbrook to Churchill, 3 Nov. 1942; BBK/D/422, Churchill to Beaverbrook, 3 July 1944.

comments, and sent them on to the chief whip, James Stuart, so that he could show them to Churchill. Stuart duly did so, though entering the caveat that Topping's suggested solutions would probably hasten the collapse of the truce. This game of Chinese whispers suggested real problems with the way the party was managed. Furthermore, the advice, when it finally arrived, was disregarded. Churchill agreed with Beaverbrook that candidate selection was largely to blame: there were too many ageing businessmen and the like, whose 'virtues consist[ed] entirely in what happened in the past', while Beaverbrook agreed with Churchill that the party did not need firmer policy commitments, which would simply be 'an embarrassment', although Central Office did need to produce better propaganda.[73]

It was in an attempt to win this argument that Beaverbrook and Churchill hatched the plot to use the impending by-election in West Derbyshire, where the current MP was about to resign, to test a new strategy. West Derbyshire was seen as a safe Conservative seat, dominated by the interests of the Duke of Devonshire; the Duke's son, the Marquess of Hartington, was able to get leave from the army for a period in January and February 1944. Churchill and Beaverbrook ensured the writ was moved quickly so that a snap election could be held. They expected that Hartington would be elected; his election would 'prove' their point that young, 'manly' candidates could defeat Common Wealth and other stay-at-home leftists in a way that superannuated worthies could not.[74] And, of course, such a victory would stem demands for more specificity on policy. However, vindication depended on Hartington's winning the seat, which was very much in doubt by polling day on 17 February.[75] Immediately after the poll closed, and even before the count confirmed the Conservatives' defeat by an Independent Labour candidate, a council of war, comprising Churchill, Eden, Dugdale, Stuart, Beaverbrook, and Churchill's loyal lieutenant, the MP Brendan Bracken, convened at 10 Downing Street. Churchill was extremely upset; indeed, his initial reaction had been to call a general election.[76] He soon changed his mind, but the Downing Street meeting belied notions that he had no interest in the party. It was agreed to employ 'every endeavour' to revive the party organization 'at Headquarters and throughout the country'. Where possible, agents would be recalled from other work, or new ones appointed. Further by-elections would be avoided wherever possible. A special group of expert organizers and canvassers would be established to travel to by-elections in order

[73] Chartwell papers, CHAR 2/509A, Topping to Dugdale, 12 Jan. 1944; Dugdale to Stuart, 13 Jan. 1944; Stuart to Churchill, 13 Jan. 1944; Beaverbrook to Churchill, 19, 20 Jan. 1944; 2/507, Beaverbrook to Churchill, 15 Feb. 1944.

[74] Ibid., CHAR 2/509, Stuart to Churchill, 24 Jan. 1944; G. H. Bennett, 'The wartime political truce and hopes for post-war coalition: the West Derbyshire by-election, 1944', *Midland History*, 17 (1992).

[75] *The Times*, 17 Feb. 1944.

[76] G. S. Harvie-Watt, *Most of my Life* (Windlesham, 1980), 141–2.

to oppose 'the "travelling circus" run by Common Wealth', and propaganda would be produced discrediting Common Wealth's policies and leaders. All CAs should try to adopt candidates as soon as possible; Churchill stressed that he would only support candidates of whom he approved in future by-elections, and Dugdale undertook to try to ensure that candidates were 'suitable' people, especially 'young men, preferably with outstanding military records'. Propaganda was to be improved, and closer links developed between the party and the press. As the meeting ended, Churchill 'expressed a desire that meetings of this nature should be held from time to time to consider the political position and to discuss any further questions which might arise', and suggested that they might try to meet monthly.[77]

This episode has been considered at length because it was the point at which the 'new' party leader really came together with his closest personal advisers and party officials for the first time. Churchill still distrusted Central Office, but realized that he needed to work with it. Initially, things went well. Improved relations seemed to be continued by the following month's successful party conference.[78] Central Office began in March 1944 to issue cyclostyled information circulars to CAs on issues like nationalization, education, and the House of Lords.[79] Plans began to be laid for an autumn campaign of ministerial speeches.[80] Though unable to pursue an all-out counter-attack on the party's critics, Central Office now felt it had the authority to sharpen up Conservative politics. But it had taken more than three years for Churchill as party leader to hold such a meeting. The contrast with the Labour leadership could hardly have been greater (see below). Furthermore, the crisis mood soon passed, as Churchill once again became fully absorbed in military matters, planning that June's Normandy landings; and, once military success became increasingly apparent, he moved towards the idea that a charismatic appeal, rather than strong organization, would prove the key to post-war victory. The V-1 attacks on England, which started in mid-June 1944, dampened Conservative effort at just the point when it might otherwise have begun to take off, while Beaverbrook and Bracken continued to hold Churchill back from too enthusiastic an embrace of Central Office. All these factors militated against the crystallization of the developments that might have been expected in the aftermath of West Derbyshire. Butler's return to the PWPCC led some to urge him to develop a 'shadow' programme for the next election, but he realized the scale of the task faced, and it remained impossible to find a new head of research.[81]

---

[77] Chartwell papers, CHAR 2/507, minutes of meeting held at 10 Downing Street, 17 Feb. 1944, 10 p.m.

[78] Ibid., CHAR 2/545, Churchill to Topping, 18 Mar. 1944; Topping to Churchill, 20 Mar. 1944.

[79] CCO 4/2/13, circulars Mar.–Dec. 1944; 4/2/14, Jan.–Dec. 1945.

[80] Chartwell papers, CHAR 2/507, Churchill to Assheton, 7 Nov. 1944.

[81] Butler papers, H62, 'Dick' [Proby] to Butler, 9 Sept. 1944, Henry Brooke to Butler, 6 Sept. 1944.

The reform of the party's youth organization provides one example of what could be achieved, given the right circumstances. Plans to reform the party's Junior Imperial League (JIL) had been developed before the war, but not implemented.[82] Since young people were most likely to be under pressure of military and other kinds of national service, most JIL activity closed down in 1939–40. But some younger Conservatives, as well as party officials, continued to desire change, and felt that it would be easier to effect at a time when the organization was to a large extent in limbo, and its members in no position to resist. In May 1943, following urgings from Topping, a new committee was established under the MP for Winchester, Gerald Palmer, and in December 1943 the committee recommended that the JIL should be replaced by a new organization; unlike the League, it would be an integral part of the party organization. Its upper age limit would be 30, but its members would automatically become members of the senior CA at the age of 21.[83] There was some opposition, but strong support from Dugdale and others outweighed it.[84] The first branch of the new 'Young Conservatives' (YC) organization was established in Newcastle West on 8 September 1944; the movement was flourishing even before the end of the war, and by 1949 it would have 149,000 members, and would soon be claiming to be 'the largest voluntary political youth Movement of its kind in the free world'.[85]

In other areas of the party's work, however, reformers saw headquarters as a significant obstacle to progress. By September 1944, Butler felt its inertia 'ha[d] to be seen to be believed', with Topping increasingly seen as a problem, and Dugdale in poor health and looking to resign.[86] The prospect of an early end to the war finally forced Central Office's hand. Paris was liberated on 25 August; Brussels, nine days later. On 11 September Allied troops entered German territory. Victory in Europe seemed close, even imminent; a general election might be only weeks away. On 22 September Dugdale circularized all CA chairmen, MPs, and prospective candidates, urging them to call meetings of their associations urgently, to begin to harness the 'remarkable revival of interest in politics' seen in recent months.[87] This appeal received a somewhat mixed reception, but it did at least show that Central Office was gearing

---

[82] CCO 506/4/2, 'Report of the Junior Imperial League Survey Committee, 1937' [Frazer Report], 19 July 1939.

[83] CCO 506/4/4, Topping to Dugdale, 3 Dec. 1942; CCO 500/1/10, 'Report of the Youth Committee' [Palmer Report], 14 Dec. 1943.

[84] CCO 500/1/10, Sir Herbert Williams to Dugdale, 24 Jan. 1944; Dugdale to Lord Dunglass, 4 Jan. 1944; Sir Eugene Ramsden to Dugdale, 24 Jan. 1944.

[85] Ibid., memo, 'New Young Conservative organization', n.d. [Sept. 1944]; Z. Layton-Henry, 'The Young Conservatives, 1945–70', *Journal of Contemporary History*, 8 (1973), 148; Young Conservative and Unionist Organization, *Notes for Speakers—1955: The Year of Great Opportunity* (1955), 2.

[86] Butler papers, H62, James Stuart to Butler, 26 May 1944; Butler to Henry Brooke, 8 Sept. 1944; Proby to Butler, 5 Oct. 1944; 19 May 1944.

[87] Ibid., Dugdale to Butler, 22 Sept. 1944.

itself up for the fight. Meanwhile, a central panel, comprising Eden, Stuart, Beaverbrook, Bracken, and Butler, was sitting to vet potential candidates, with a view to selecting ones acceptable to Churchill.[88] Considerable efforts also began to secure the release of candidates and agents from the armed forces.[89]

But even as Dugdale was sending out his circular, Allied troops were struggling at Arnhem, and the revival stalled once it became clear that an election was no longer imminent. Indeed, Churchill began to speculate on the possibility of continuing the Coalition, or at least of delaying any election until after the defeat of Japan. All this impeded Central Office planning. One consolation was that it did allow the leader to replace Dugdale as party chairman that October. Once Margesson had declined the position, a group comprising Beaverbrook, Bracken, Butler, and Stuart nominated the 43-year-old Assheton who, although initially reluctant, proved energetic and receptive.[90] A partisan Conservative, he was keen to reverse the collectivizing tendencies of wartime. He had been considerably influenced by Hayek, and was to try, in vain, to use a significant portion of the party's paper ration to reprint *Road to Serfdom* as part of the Conservatives' 1945 election campaign.[91] He got on quite well with Churchill, and certainly saw more of the leader than either of his predecessors had; and, although he could not overcome all his party's failings, he did bring a new edge to its work.[92] However, Churchill also continued to pay heed to Beaverbrook and Bracken, who, as newspaper owners, he assumed to be experts 'on public opinion'.[93] It certainly seems that the Conservative strategy of focusing so much on Churchill in the 1945 campaign was at least buttressed by Beaverbrook, who was in turn encouraged in his views by information from his editors and journalists.[94] He was also encouraged by opinion polling, which showed Churchill's overwhelming popularity by the spring of 1945, and this further reinforced the notion that a charismatic appeal by Churchill was the likeliest way to bring success at the polls.[95] Victory in Europe, and the praise for Churchill that surrounded it, were hardly likely to dent such a view.

[88] Chartwell papers, CHAR 2/545, Beaverbrook and Bracken to Churchill, 16 Dec. 1944; Harvie-Watt, *Most of my Life*, 143–4, 182–4; Chartwell papers, CHAR 2/547, Assheton to R. K. Magor (Chelmsford CA), 18 Jan. 1945.

[89] See e.g. CCO 4/2/2, Topping to the Labour and Liberal chief agents, 25 Oct. 1944.

[90] Harvie-Watt, *Most of my Life*, 141; Chartwell papers, CHAR 2/507, Churchill to Eden, 6 Oct. 1944, Beaverbrook to Churchill, 13 Oct. 1944; MSS Simon 95, fo. 17, Assheton to Simon, 2 Nov. 1944; Davidson papers, DAV/273, Assheton to Davidson, 7 Feb. 1945.

[91] Cockett, *Thinking the Unthinkable*, 92–4.

[92] Chartwell papers, CHAR 2/507, Assheton to Churchill, 14 Nov. 1944; 2/547, Churchill to Assheton, 10 Jan. 1945; 2/554, T. L. Rowan, minute, 8 June 1945.

[93] Beaverbrook papers, BBK/D/423, Churchill to Beaverbrook, 29 Apr. 1945.

[94] Ibid., BBK/H/115, Arthur Christiansen (*Daily Express*) to Beaverbrook, 13 Apr. 1945.

[95] See e.g. Chartwell papers, CHAR 2/548B, Centre of Public opinion, 'Report on question no. 3', 12 June 1945.

When the election came, Central Office was confident. The evidence of (relatively) new-fangled opinion polls to the contrary was treated with scepticism: in any case, as Ramsden has argued, Conservatives had long believed that victory in the war, once achieved, would transform the 'electoral landscape'.[96] Assheton told Eden that the party now had 'a fine lot of candidates and some excellent literature and posters'.[97] The reports of the party's area agents were mostly very positive: their predictions, when aggregated, suggested an overall majority for the government in excess of two hundred.[98] Topping was sceptical that a victory on *such* a scale—in effect, a near-repeat of 1935—was likely, and asked the agents to think again. But even these more pessimistic projections foretold an overall majority of 108, with the Conservatives and their allies winning 380 of the 640 seats.[99] There were, of course, problems and uncertainties. There was general agreement that the votes of service personnel and first-time voters were particularly unpredictable, while in a handful of seats, like Manchester Exchange, changes to the business vote made Conservative losses almost inevitable.[100] By and large, though, organization was not seen by Central Office agents to be particularly defective at this time, whatever their subsequent claims.[101] Assheton himself, although recognizing the uncertainties, did feel that the agents' predictions were 'reasonably cautious estimates', and as late as 24 July he was reported as believing firmly that the Conservatives would have 'a considerable majority' when the votes were counted.[102] But it was not to be. The election results, when declared on 26 July, showed that the party had lost heavily in its worst result since 1906.

The Conservative party had been in reasonable shape at national level in mid-1939. It was looking forward to victory at an autumn general election, under a competent and united leadership, which was itself working closely with Central Office, which remained the best-equipped headquarters in British politics. But this equilibrium was seriously disturbed by the war. Churchill, understandably, prioritized winning the war.[103] He was not indifferent to his party, but his distrust of leading Conservatives made him reluctant to support their plans for

[96] Ramsden, *Age of Churchill and Eden*, 74.

[97] Avon papers, AP 11/4/68, Assheton to Eden, 15 June 1945; see also Emrys-Evans papers, Add. 58263, Marjorie Maxse to Emrys-Evans, 29 May 1945.

[98] CCO 4/2/61, memo [by Topping], 'General election 1945: summary of reports by area agents', n.d. [early July 1945].

[99] Ibid., memo [by Topping], 'Revised forecast for general election 1945', n.d. [mid-July 1945].

[100] See e.g. ibid., J. W. Lancaster (East Midlands) to Topping, 17 July 1945; H. H. Little (West Midlands) to Topping, 28 June 1945; Miss Palmer (Western Area) to Topping, 7 July 1945.

[101] See e.g. ibid., Brigadier Rawcliffe (Yorkshire) to Topping, 11 July 1945.

[102] Chartwell papers, CHAR 2/548B, Assheton to Churchill, 10 July 1945; T. L. Rowan to Churchill, 24 July 1945.

[103] For contrasting views of Churchill's leadership, see (for the prosecution) J. Ramsden, 'Winston Churchill and the leadership of the Conservative party, 1940–51', *Contemporary Record*, 9 (1995), and (for the defence) S. Ball, 'Churchill and the Conservative party', *Transactions of the Royal Historical Society*, 5th series, 11 (2001).

change; it was a reluctance that the influence of people like Beaverbrook did little to mitigate. Meetings of minds, such as that which followed the West Derbyshire by-election, were all too rare, and once he began to sniff imminent military victory in 1944–5, Churchill moved towards the notion of a charismatic personal appeal to the electorate, a view reinforced by the fact that the party organization was rather hamstrung that winter by V-weapon attacks and continuing concerns about Central Office.

The electoral disaster that greeted the Conservatives in July 1945 was primarily about politics, not organization. But it had far-reaching effects on the party's organizational, as well as political, approach for the future. The old ways had not brought success. Faced with the reality of a 'socialist' government, most Conservatives were able to set aside old grudges at least sufficiently to reform the party. It was generally agreed that there must be a move away from Churchill's failed 'charismatic' approach, and a return to a more orthodox 'party' stance. Some wanted to be rid of Churchill altogether. Butler was among those who seem to have assumed that he would rapidly retire in favour of Eden.[104] But Churchill did not want to go; and given his war record, this meant that the Conservatives were stuck with him until old age and infirmity finally forced his departure, to the general rejoicing of his cabinet colleagues, in 1955.[105] Proxies like Beaverbrook, who was widely blamed for the defeat, were more vulnerable: he was attacked repeatedly at a meeting of 200 Conservative ex-candidates in October 1945, and Churchill's attempts to continue using him as a trouble-shooter after the war received short shrift from other senior Conservatives, hastening his retirement from front-line politics.[106] With the party in opposition, Churchill could not resist more power returning to Central Office; but it was to be a different Central Office that would take the Conservatives forward into peacetime, with a new chairman, Lord Woolton (a wartime 'non-party' minister recruited by the leader), and a new general director in Stephen Piersenné.[107] Woolton and Piersenné were left to get on with the job, in collaboration with reformers like Butler and Maxwell-Fyfe. In return, Churchill was allowed to carry on as the charismatic leader of the party. In the end, as John Ramsden has argued, the wartime dichotomy between organization and charisma had found a virtuous resolution: a charismatic leader would be backed by a powerful machine. In this way, the synchronicity between leaders and managers, so rudely interrupted by the war, was restored in its aftermath, albeit in a new blend.[108]

[104] Emrys-Evans papers, Add. 58263, Richard Law to Paul Emrys-Evans, 25 Aug. 1945.

[105] J. Ramsden, *An Appetite for Power: A History of the Conservative Party since 1830* (1998), 316–17.

[106] Emrys-Evans papers, Add. 58263, J. P. L. Thomas to Paul Emrys-Evans, 5 Sept. 1945.

[107] Woolton papers, MS Woolton 21, Churchill to Woolton, 21 May 1946; M. D. Kandiah, 'Lord Woolton's chairmanship of the Conservative party, 1946–51', University of Exeter Ph.D. thesis, 1992.

[108] Ramsden, *Appetite for Power*, 316–17.

THE LABOUR PARTY

By mid-1939 the Labour party had spent almost eight years in opposition, and was facing a third successive general election defeat.[109] The 1930s had seen some recovery from the depths of 1931, but the party remained some distance from power. Its leader, Clement Attlee, was out of action through ill health. Labour continued to be affected by splits, most recently the expulsion of Cripps, Aneurin Bevan, and others in February 1939 for advocating alliances with other parties. It is possible to offer too negative a view—Attlee had proved a more effective leader of the opposition than many had anticipated, and he had with him able colleagues. The party machine, based at Transport House, was reasonably efficient, but underfunded, and some of its employees left something to be desired.[110] The key officials—James Middleton (party secretary since 1934) and George Shepherd (national agent since 1928)—were experienced figures. The party's ruling national executive committee (NEC) was largely made up of experienced and able figures, mostly of the centre and right; Harold Laski, and the MPs Ellen Wilkinson and D. N. Pritt, made up a weak left group which was unable to seriously challenge the essential underlying unity at the top of the party on a wide range of strategic questions. Although the war would see changes to the personnel of this inner group, it was to remain in existence, with much the same philosophy, throughout the conflict. Unity would be challenged, but it would not be destroyed.

Party headquarters coped reasonably well with the initial challenge posed by the outbreak of war. By 29 August, party and TUC departments were being evacuated to Market Bosworth in Leicestershire, and preparations were being made to lay off staff in anticipation of a considerable reduction in party correspondence.[111] The NEC voted on 2 September that constituency or, as they were still known, divisional Labour parties (DLPs) should participate in the work of the Ministry of Information, despite protests from Pritt and Wilkinson.[112] However, the letter conveying this view to DLPs on 4 September also made clear the 'vital urgency' of 'keeping the Party fully in being and as active as circumstances permit', ready for a post-war election: as the only alternative to the National government, its policies 'must be kept continuously before the electorate'.[113]

The electoral truce made no difference to this attitude. Indeed, Transport House sent DLPs the text of the agreement to prove that it was limited in

---

[109] LPNEC papers XVII, 'Report on campaign activities: municipal election campaign', n.d. [Nov. 1938].
[110] Ibid., XVIII, memo, 'Financial position of the party', June 1939.
[111] Ibid., J. S. Middleton circular to NEC members, 29 Aug. 1939.
[112] Ibid., NEC 1–2 Sept. 1939.
[113] Ibid., A. Greenwood, B. A. Gould, and Middleton circular to DLP officials, 4 Sept. 1939.

scope and that parties should remain active, although this did not stop it soon becoming the subject of protest and controversy (see below).[114] The annual conference of Labour MPs and candidates went ahead on 7–8 October as planned.[115] Within six weeks of the outbreak of war, headquarters had also issued a detailed questionnaire to DLPs about their activities, leaving them in no doubt that they were meant to be carrying on, and efforts were made to improve pamphlet propaganda.[116] In March 1940 it was agreed to bring staff back to Transport House from Market Bosworth (some returned there due to the Blitz later in 1940; the Market Bosworth operation was eventually mothballed in 1943).[117]

Party officials could not have relaxed even if they had wanted to. Labour had spent the inter-war period trying to keep the Communist party of Great Britain (CPGB) isolated and marginalized. Fears that the war might open up political space into which the Communists could move at Labour's expense became more real when the CPGB changed its line in early October 1939. The signature of the Nazi–Soviet Pact a few weeks earlier was deemed to require western Communist parties to shift position: from supporting a war against Germany and fascism, to regarding the war as a struggle of rival imperialisms that was of no concern to the working class. The prior existence of anti-war feeling in the Labour party meant that a close eye had to be kept on potential rebels. Circulars were sent out, attacking Communist perfidy and laying down with great clarity what was, and what was not, acceptable.[118] Fear of the far left was also seen in February 1940, when the Trotskyite entryist organization the Militant Labour League, which had been quite prominent in anti-war agitation within the party, was added to the party's list of proscribed organizations.[119]

The party leadership was united on entry to the war. On 1 September, the executive committee of the parliamentary Labour party (PLP) agreed to support the government's extension of conscription, but was unanimous that the party should refuse to join the government if invited. The PLP supported both decisions the next day, although a small group of pacifist MPs did make their voices heard for some time. The spectre of Nazi Germany enabled most Labourites to combine patriotic, ideological, and party feelings in support of the war effort. This essential unity on the justice of the war allowed the leadership to meet grassroots calls for a statement of war aims in December

---

[114] LPNEC papers XVII, Middleton and Shepherd, circular to DLPs, n.d. [Oct. 1939].

[115] *Report of the Twentieth National Conference of Labour Women, 15–16 October 1940* (1940), 6.

[116] LPNEC papers XVIII, Middleton and Shepherd, circular to DLPs, 13 Oct. 1939; press, publicity, and campaign subcommittee 31 Oct. 1939.

[117] Ibid., NEC 20 Dec.1939, finance and general purposes subcommittee 18 Mar. 1940; organization subcommittee 22 Oct. 1940; XIX, finance and general purposes subcommittee 16 Oct. 1941; XX, NEC 20 Dec. 1942.

[118] Labour party, *Stalin's Men: About Turn* (1940); LPNEC papers XVIII, Middleton and Shepherd, circular, 'Disloyal attacks on the party', 25 Jan. 1940.

[119] LPNEC papers XVIII, NEC 28 Feb. 1940.

1939.[120] Indeed, Bevan was readmitted that autumn, following pressure from his union, the South Wales Miners' Federation, although Cripps resisted pressure to rejoin, only coming back in February 1945.[121] The biggest challenge to this cohesion during the Phoney War period came from the Russo-Finnish 'Winter War'. Most of the leadership took the view that, whatever the moral questions involved, Britain could not afford to alienate the Soviets by offering material support to Finland, but a much stronger anti-Soviet line came from a minority including the TUC general secretary Sir Walter Citrine and the MP Philip Noel-Baker, the latter of whom favoured arming the Finns.[122] Pritt, on the other hand, took so stridently a pro-Soviet line that he was expelled from the party in March 1940, never to be readmitted, although he was to retain his North Hammersmith seat in 1945 as a Communist-backed Independent.[123] Meanwhile, Labour's leaders remained firmly opposed to serving under Chamberlain. They did, however, begin to forge new relationships with the other side, as members of the PLP executive shadowed particular government ministers and had mostly amicable one-to-one briefings which in some cases paved the way for closer cooperation in the Churchill Coalition: indeed, Churchill was to appoint his shadow, A. V. Alexander, as his own successor at the Admiralty in May 1940.

The fall of Chamberlain in May 1940 could be seen as vindicating the line taken by Labour's leaders over the preceding eight months. In biding their time, and not launching into extravagant partisan assaults on the government, they had maximized points of contact with its Conservative and other critics, rather than allowing Chamberlain to unite his party against shrill opposition rhetoric. Labour's firm line against the Communists had helped establish its own patriotic credentials. The responsible way in which it had handled its links with ministers had also helped confirm the growing impression that Labour was once more 'fit to govern'. Furthermore, the leadership's careful tactics in the Norway debate on 7–8 May—allowing Conservative critics of the government to build up a head of steam before announcing the party's intention to call for a vote of censure—helped maximize the anti-government vote. Then, the leadership's firmness about the need for a new government under a new Prime Minister, allied to its flexibility as to whether that person should be Halifax or Churchill, meant there could be no last-minute reprieve for Chamberlain. The underlying strength of Labour's position should not be underestimated—in a war of production, it

[120] Dalton papers, II 3/2, fo. 10, Dalton note, 'The international subcommittee of the national executive', n.d. [*c*. Dec. 1939].

[121] Laski papers, DLA/15, Cripps to Laski, 14, 28 Sept. 1939. Bevan was only readmitted on a vote of 4 to 3 in the NEC's relevant subcommittee: see LPNEC papers XVIII, organization subcommittee 13 Dec. 1939.

[122] H. Dalton, *The Fateful Years: Memoirs 1931–1945* (1957), 293; W. M. Citrine, *My Finnish Diary* (Harmondsworth, 1940).

[123] For more on Pritt's war see *Forward*, 6 Apr. 1940; Pritt papers, esp. 1/3, 1/4, diary notes 1941–2, 1941–5.

was obvious that the party of the trade unions needed to be given some kind of role—but, even so, its leaders' keen sense of priorities allowed them to exploit the situation to the full. It also meant that, although the NEC 'boggled a bit' at first about some of the terms of the coalition, the party as a whole could easily be carried on the question at the party conference that followed shortly afterwards.[124]

Some things changed dramatically with Labour's entry into government in May 1940, of course. Attlee (as Lord Privy Seal) and Arthur Greenwood (Minister without Portfolio) joined the five-member war cabinet. Ernest Bevin, leader of the Transport and General Workers' Union (TGWU), became Minister of Labour and National Service, with the role of mobilizing the workforce. Other leading Labourites appointed to ministerial positions were Alexander (Admiralty), Dalton (Economic Warfare), and Morrison (Supply), and there were further junior appointments. Bevin soon joined the war cabinet; Morrison moved to the Home Office in October 1940 and joined the war cabinet two years later. The dangers of a rift opening between ministers and the PLP were recognized, but Labour's leaders were strongly committed to the party. They had, after all, spent almost a decade trying to revive its fortunes from the severe decline which, they believed, had come as a direct result of Ramsay MacDonald's moving too far from the party and its interests, even before his 1931 'betrayal'. They remained imbued with a powerful Labour ethos, and continued to attend PLP meetings. Significantly, the PLP, unlike the Conservative 1922 Committee, included all the party's MPs, and not just backbenchers. Similarly, the decision to establish a kind of shadow parliamentary opposition, first under H. B. Lees-Smith and later Frederick Pethick-Lawrence and then Greenwood, was to prove important in allowing Labour MPs the illusion, and sometimes the reality, of distance from government policy without the need to disown their leaders in the government.

As with the Conservatives, though to a lesser extent, the political and military events of May 1940 had a somewhat depressing effect on the extent of party activity. But the NEC and its subcommittees continued to meet regularly. Continuing Communist activity meant that Labour had to go on functioning as fully as possible: in June 1940 the mere publication of the CPGB leaflet *The People Must Act* was sufficient to provoke a flurry of meetings to plan steps against what was seen as growing Communist influence.[125] Furthermore, the whole structure of the Labour movement—regular meetings, accountability downwards, affiliation fees, and the rest—pushed the party to remain active. And while Labourites were overwhelmingly committed to winning the war, they found it harder than many Conservatives did to see this as an end in itself. There

---

[124] H. Dalton, *The Political Diary of Hugh Dalton, 1918–40, 1945–60*, ed. B. Pimlott (1986), 345–6, 11 May 1940.
[125] LPNEC papers XVIII, emergency committee of NEC 3 July 1940.

was a sense, very much pronounced in the left's somewhat apocalyptic mood in 1940–1, that it would be little better than defeat simply to return to the *status quo ante* once Germany had been beaten.[126]

Entry into government helped to entrench Attlee's leadership of the party. Early in the war, he had appeared vulnerable: in October 1939, Dalton, Greenwood, and Morrison had been nominated against him for the leadership, and their withdrawal probably meant little more than that the timing was wrong.[127] By May 1940 such considerations seemed long past. Criticisms of him continued, of course, and his public profile was lower than that of some colleagues.[128] In 1942, Laski urged Bevin to come forward as 'a fighting leader', but Bevin recognized Attlee's strengths, and ignored Laski.[129] In contrast with Churchill, Attlee was closely concerned with party management. As a minister—and deputy Prime Minister from 1942 onwards—he carefully avoided public partisanship.[130] But his work behind the scenes, and his networking, meant that people in the party's higher echelons were left in no doubt that he was still 'one of them'.

This work took a variety of forms. He attended PLP meetings 'frequently', was assiduous in trying to clear dead wood among the Labour MPs, made sure that the Labour ministers consulted each other regularly, liaised with leading party officials, and intervened to try to resolve points of conflict between colleagues.[131] When Morgan Phillips was appointed secretary of the party's research department in October 1941, Attlee had a detailed discussion with him; Churchill would not have dreamt of holding such a meeting with anyone from the CRD (which was virtually moribund anyway).[132] Attlee remained an ex officio member of the NEC and its subcommittees throughout the war; although time-consuming, this brought him physically into Transport House and kept him at the heart of the machine. Nor was such membership merely honorific. It was at Attlee's instigation that the NEC launched its review of parliamentary candidatures, which led to a moratorium on new selections, in October 1941, and he was particularly active on the elections subcommittee throughout the war.[133] He maintained relations with ancillary and related bodies, such as the Society of Labour Candidates and the Co-operative Wholesale Society.[134] He also took

[126] For a taste of this mood, see e.g. Orwell, *The Lion and the Unicorn.*

[127] Dalton, *Political Diary*, 311–13, 'November 1939'.

[128] See e.g. C. H. King, *With Malice toward None: A War Diary*, ed. W. Armstrong (1970), 82, 12 Oct. 1940.

[129] Bevin papers, BEVN 3/2, Laski to Bevin, 9 Mar. 1942.

[130] See e.g. MS Attlee dep. 10, fos. 12 ff., Attlee, speech at Carmarthen, 3 Sept. 1943.

[131] J. Parker, 'After a year of coalition', *Fabian Quarterly*, 30 (1941), 5; MS Attlee dep. 2, fo. 22, Attlee to Shepherd, 20 Dec. 1940; dep. 4, fo. 140, Ede to Attlee, 19 Dec. 1941; Bevin papers, BEVN 3/1, Attlee to Bevin, 30 Sept. 1941.

[132] MS Attlee dep. 4, fos. 1–2, Phillips to Attlee, 1 Oct. 1941; Attlee to Phillips, 2 Oct. 1941.

[133] Ibid., fo. 3, Shepherd to Attlee, 3 Oct. 1941; 14, fo. 124, Shepherd to Attlee, 1 June 1944; LPNEC papers XIX, elections subcommittee, 15 Oct. 1941.

[134] See e.g. MS Attlee dep. 6, fo. 44, Attlee to Shepherd, 8 Sept. 1942; fos. 171–2, Miss E. J. Emery to J. H. Dunford, n.d. [Dec. 1942]; dep. 10, fos. 239–41.

the lead in organizing social events that brought together ministers, MPs, NEC members, trade union leaders, and party officials in convivial surroundings, as with the reception held at Admiralty House on 24 November 1942, just a week before the publication of the Beveridge report.[135]

Transport House continued to see its role as being to exhort and assist the party at all levels towards greater levels of activity. Coordination of public meetings remained a major responsibility. The onset of the Blitz in the autumn of 1940 did not stop a nationwide series of forty-six conferences, and the publication of the interim party policy report, *The Old World and the New Society*, in February 1942 was marked by a vigorous three-month campaign of no fewer than thirty-two 'highly successful' and well-attended conferences all over Britain.[136] Labour ministers were reminded to ensure some contact with local activists in the areas they visited on government business.[137] The pre-war network of DLP literature secretaries had been disrupted, because most had been younger members, most likely to be called up, but publicity material continue to sell well, even so.[138] *Labour in the Government*, published in May 1941, sold 70,000 copies in seven months, while the MP and NEC member George Ridley's pamphlet on social services sold out its first edition almost immediately on publication in October 1941.[139] In September 1942, the party had three new pamphlets in production, and was considering suggestions for six more, in contrast to the lacklustre efforts of the Conservatives in this field.[140] Headquarters also made special efforts, as in August 1942, when it organized a conference on town planning and reconstruction for representatives from fifty-one DLPs in blitzed areas.[141] Staffing remained problematic. Ironically, the major pre-war constraint—money—became less of a concern (see Chapter 8): the problem now was one of staff retention and recruitment in the light of military call-ups, illness, and so on. Labour, however, remained committed to sustaining its staffing levels wherever possible, and even at a low point, in November 1942, with 12 members of staff in the armed forces, working in civil defence, or seconded to government departments, 79 active employees remained.[142] Wartime stresses

---

[135] See e.g. MS Attlee dep. 6, fo. 106, Attlee to Bevin, Dalton, Thomas Johnston, W. A. Jowitt, and Morrison, 6 Nov. 1942; fo. 122, A. L. Scott to Miss E. J. Emery, 18 Nov. 1942; fos. 171–2, C. Wallworth to Miss E. J. Emery, 18 Nov. 1942.

[136] LPNEC papers XIX, organization subcommittee 15 Jan. 1941; central committee on reconstruction problems 10 Feb. 1942; memo, 'Condition of the party', n.d., to NEC 25 Mar. 1942; memo, 'Regional conferences on interim report: "The Old World and the New Society"', n.d., to NEC 22 Apr. 1942.

[137] MS Attlee dep. 3, fo. 229, Shepherd to Attlee, 29 Sept. 1941.

[138] LPNEC papers XIX, memo, 'Condition of the party', n.d., to NEC 25 Mar. 1942.

[139] Ibid., press, publicity, and campaign subcommittee 28 May, 21 Oct. 1941; memo, 'Condition of the party', n.d., to NEC 25 Mar. 1942.

[140] Ibid., press, publicity, and campaign subcommittee 15 Sept. 1942.

[141] Ibid., XX, NEC 23 Sept. 1942; 'Summarised report of the conference of representatives from blitzed areas', 29–30 Aug. 1942.

[142] Ibid., memo, 'The Labour party staff', Nov. 1942.

did affect some staff, of course. Middleton suffered a 'breakdown' in July 1942, which necessitated a lengthy period of convalescence in Cornwall, and even when he did return, that October, it was initially on a part-time basis.[143] Middleton's chief assistant, the long-serving A. Luckhurst Scott, spent most of the war off work with physical and nervous ailments of one kind or another. In July 1944, two days before he was finally due to return to work after a long absence, a flying bomb hit his house, killing his sister and leaving him hospitalized. It was only in October 1944 that he was finally able to resume his duties.[144]

By late 1942, though, there were concerns that the party was not fully exploiting the prospects opening up before it.[145] Ridley feared that 'although there is undoubtedly a body of leftish opinion, thinking largely in our terms, it is not at the same time thinking about *us*'; Labour was being 'contemptuously disregarded'.[146] It was this sense that made Labour so keen to capitalize on the Beveridge report. Labour had already begun to take steps to do so even prior to its publication in December 1942, running a series of six big 'experimental' meetings addressed by leading speakers and including a film show. The campaign's success encouraged plans for a much larger programme of meetings to welcome the report once it was published.[147] On 12 December 1942, the NEC broadly welcomed the report, and called for early implementation, while a joint meeting of the NEC and the PLP executive established a special committee to plan eight regional and forty-four area conferences on Beveridge.[148] When almost all non-ministerial Labour MPs voted for the report in parliament in February 1943, it sent out a strong signal that Labour was now looking to move to the head of the radical propaganda that had hitherto, in the words of Addison, been led mainly by the 'leftish intelligentsia'.[149]

Intensifying Communist activity provided another incentive towards revival. Boosted by the Soviet Red Army's resistance to Hitler's armies, CPGB membership in December 1942 reached 56,000—about a quarter of Labour's individual membership. Concurrently with the epic battle for Stalingrad, the CPGB applied

---

[143] Ibid., NEC 22 July, 12 Oct. 1942; Middleton papers, MID 68/37, Scott to Middleton, 16 Sept. 1942.

[144] Middleton papers, MID 63/35, Middleton to Mr and Mrs A. O. Roberts, 11 Mar 1940; 68/12, Scott to Middleton, 12 Aug. 1942; 68/23, Scott to Middleton, 1 Sept. 1942; 70/82, Middleton to Ernest Whitfield, 28 Mar. 1944; LPNEC papers finance and general purposes subcommittee 15 May 1944, NEC 26 July, 13 Sept. 1944, finance and general purposes subcommittee 26 Oct. 1944.

[145] See e.g. *Labour Organiser*, Oct. 1942.

[146] MS Attlee dep. 7, fos. 198–200, Ridley to Shepherd, 10 Mar. 1943.

[147] LPNEC papers XX, 'Report on experimental demonstrations and suggestions for extended series', n.d., to NEC 28 Oct. 1942.

[148] Ibid., NEC 15 Dec. 1942; joint meeting, NEC and PLPAC, 15 Dec. 1942; social insurance conference arrangements subcommittee, 5 Jan. 1943.

[149] Addison, *Road to 1945*, 143; and see H. Dalton, *The Second World War Diary of Hugh Dalton, 1940–45*, ed. B. Pimlott (1986), 575–6, 7 Apr. 1943, quoting Attlee.

formally for affiliation to the Labour party for the first time since 1936, aiming to capitalize on the Soviet war effort. Labour's leaders and managers believed that Communist affiliation would be a political, electoral, and moral disaster, and the NEC rejected the application, although not without some questioning from Laski and the MP Emmanuel Shinwell.[150] Party managers were initially confident that this rejection would be endorsed by that June's party conference. The anti-affiliation campaign included the publication of pamphlets attacking the Communists and especially their links with the Moscow-based Communist International (Comintern), such as the less than conciliatory *The Communist Party and the War: A Record of Hypocrisy and Treachery to the Workers of Europe*, and they also coordinated action with the editor of the pro-Labour *Daily Herald*.[151] In no mood for half-measures, the NEC made short shrift of proscribing the recently formed Common Wealth; and by early May, the position seemed to be under control, and Shepherd reported that conference would vote against affiliation.[152] But there was a flaw in Transport House's strategy. It rested, more than ever before, on the existence of the Comintern as an external body whose orders the CPGB had to follow; and this rather lazy approach was exposed when Stalin rather inconveniently abolished the Comintern in May 1943. This created panic at Transport House, and it was only after a 'prolonged' meeting that the NEC agreed to argue that, Comintern or no Comintern, Communists would still be a disruptive force, taking orders from abroad. However, Shinwell and Laski's intensified pressure for a more conciliatory approach showed that there were other viewpoints, which might be stronger at the party conference than they were on the NEC.[153]

When the party conference met in London on 14 June, therefore, party leaders and managers were probably more nervous than they had ever been before about the issue of Communist affiliation. In the event, even though the vote for affiliation had never been higher, and despite the support of the Miners' Federation of Great Britain (MFGB), it was still defeated by a large margin (1,951,000 to 712,000). In a powerful speech winding up the debate, Morrison was careful to distinguish between Soviet Communists like the 'great man', Stalin, and British Communists, and then between 'decent' British Communists like the party secretary, Harry Pollitt, and 'sinister' characters like its leading ideologist, Rajani Palme Dutt. There was nothing to stop people in the former group coming into the Labour party, but they must join as individuals and not as members of a rival organization.[154] This commonsense view was calculated to appeal very widely among those who respected the hard work of individual Communists, especially in the trade unions.

[150] LPNEC papers XX, joint meeting of international and organization subcommittees, 26 Jan. 1943; NEC 27 Jan. 1943.
[151] Ibid., NEC 24 Feb. 1943.   [152] Ibid., NEC 24 Mar., 5 May 1943.
[153] Ibid., NEC 28 May 1943.   [154] *LPACR* 1943, 165–8.

Under Labour's 'three-year rule', Communist affiliation could not be discussed again at a party conference until 1946. During late 1943 and into 1944, however, Communist pressure on DLPs and trade unions continued. The Amalgamated Engineering Union (AEU), where Communist influence had grown significantly since 1939, was particularly affected. In spring 1944 it rebuffed Communist advances for formal unity, but demanded that the Labour party should further investigate the possibilities of closer cooperation. The NEC agreed to investigate, but there was no doubt as to the outcome, and in fact the joint meeting of the elections and organization subcommittees that resulted took the opportunity to declare in July 1944 that Labour would fight the post-war general election as an independent party.[155] This line, which was reiterated more publicly that October, ruled out continuing Coalition as well as 'progressive unity'. Although the Communist party continued to call for united action and the joint selection of 'progressive' candidates, and to threaten to add to its claimed figure of fifty candidates at the next election if Labour did not yield, the Communist challenge seemed, by the last months of the war, to have been contained.[156]

The electoral truce also excited controversy. Many Labourites opposed it from the start, but the leadership remained firmly for it, believing that, as Attlee put it in January 1940, '[a]n election in most constituencies to-day would mean the practical disenfranchisement of a big proportion of the workers'.[157] Strong action, including expulsion, was taken against members who stood as, or actively supported, independent candidates.[158] But the danger of a revolt remained if the leadership went too far towards accommodating the Conservatives. Attlee saw this in September 1941, when he rejected Churchill's plea to write personal letters of support to all government by-election candidates. Instead, it was agreed, at Attlee's suggestion, that the party leaders would issue a joint statement supporting 'the Government candidate' at all by-elections.[159] This limited the potential for damaging criticism of the leadership. But even this proposal was only narrowly approved by the NEC.[160]

The upsurge of serious by-election challenges to Conservative candidates in the first half of 1942 led to heightened controversy within the Labour party. In April 1942 Attlee asked reliable South Wales Labour MPs to go to Cardiff East to speak for the 'entirely non-party' (but in fact distinctly non-Labour)

[155] LPNEC papers XXI, special NEC 16 May 1944, joint meeting of elections and organization subcommittees, 5 July 1944.

[156] See e.g. ibid., elections subcommittee 24 Feb. 1944, NEC 22 Mar. 1944, though see also Ede, *Labour and the Wartime Coalition*, 196–7, 29 Nov. 1944.

[157] LPNEC papers XVIII, elections subcommittee 12 Dec. 1939; MS Attlee dep. 1, fo. 57, Attlee, speech, 17 Jan. 1940.

[158] See e.g. LPNEC papers XIX, 'Report on the principal features of the King's Norton by-election', n.d. [May 1941].

[159] MS Attlee dep. 3, fo. 215, Attlee to Churchill, 24 Sept. 1941.

[160] LPNEC papers XIX, NEC 24 Sept. 1941.

Secretary of State for War Sir James Grigg, in his campaign against the 'Pacifist' ILPer Fenner Brockway.[161] But there was significant Labour hostility, and on the NEC, Laski called on the leadership to demand immediate reforms.[162] The NEC continued to back Attlee loyally, but Laski was articulating concerns that were felt widely within the Labour movement. Increasing worries about the post-war world, crystallized in early 1943 by the Conservatives' obvious reservations about the Beveridge report, inflamed matters further. In the months before the June 1943 party conference there were fears of a serious challenge to the truce, although, ultimately, that gathering endorsed the truce by what Ridley called 'an astonishing majority' of 2,243,000 votes to 374,000.[163] In some ways, the margin, if not the fact, of the victory was surprising, but as Fred Peart, the prospective candidate for Sunderland, put it, 'Our task is to win this war. Our task is to defeat Fascism. Our task is to defeat Nazism.' Ending the truce would handicap that fight by weakening, if not destroying, the Coalition. Besides, the truce did not mean a 'political truce', and parties could still carry on with 'Socialist propaganda'.[164] At this stage, it seemed, much could still be gained from the Coalition, and Labour's machinery was not ready for a general election. All told, it was a time for careful planning and avoiding adventures.

Labour's leaders were relieved to have got through the 1943 party conference with their strategy intact.[165] A successful challenge on either Communist affiliation or the truce would have been very damaging. Even a close result on either issue would have been a major blow, stimulating further grassroots pressure. As it was, the votes were sufficiently convincing to allay the worst fears. That July, propaganda material was planned for the coming year, with a major pamphlet on *The Labour Party and the Future* to be complemented by others on issues like health, housing, and international affairs.[166] A major policy campaign was initiated, and between 25 September 1943 and 29 January 1944, thirty-three 'quite successful' policy conferences on Labour and post-war reconstruction, each addressed by an MP or candidate, were held across the country.[167] Meanwhile, moves were also set afoot to move the party towards 'mass' individual membership, and to encourage a higher affiliated membership by increasing the proportion of trade unionists 'contracting in' to the political levy.[168]

---

[161] MS Attlee dep. 5, fo. 42, Attlee to William John, James Griffiths and D. R. Grenfell, 3 Apr. 1942; LPNEC papers XIX, NEC 9 Apr. 1943.

[162] Middleton papers, MID 67/45, B. W. Best (Hornchurch Labour party) to Middleton, 29 Apr. 1942; LPNEC papers XX, Laski, memo, 3 May 1942.

[163] *LPACR* 1943, 153, 132.   [164] Ibid. 128.

[165] Dalton, *Second World War Diary*, 606–7, 15 June 1943.

[166] LPNEC papers XX, press, publicity, and campaign subcommittee 20 July 1943.

[167] Ibid., memo, 'The Labour party policy campaign', n.d., to NEC 28 July 1943; 'Report on policy conferences on Labour and post-war planning', n.d. [Nov. 1943].

[168] Ibid., memo, 'Mass individual membership', n.d., to NEC 22 Dec. 1943; memo, 'Contracting-in membership of trade unions', Oct. 1943; joint meeting of finance and general purposes subcommittee and trade union representatives, 12 Nov. 1943.

As military events moved still more in the Allies' direction, thoughts turned increasingly to the post-war world. In January 1944, Labour's elections subcommittee scrutinized the list of Labour MPs and agreed to press for the retirement of ageing or ineffectual MPs when parliament was dissolved. There was also discussion of further tightening the procedures for the selection of candidates, although practical considerations—especially military service abroad—were held to rule out the most radical option of cancelling all existing candidatures and selecting candidates afresh. It was also felt that some DLPs were currently in no fit state to undertake a selection process, and, in any case, it was still unclear how extensive the much-discussed redistribution of seats would be.[169] It was partly for this reason that 'A Year of Party Development' was launched in February 1944, calling on all Labourites to work hard to recruit new and active individual members.[170]

But the truce remained problematic. DLPs in by-election constituencies continued to criticize Attlee for signing messages of support to Conservative candidates, while the August 1943 electoral victory of the Australian Labor party whetted the appetites of many British Labour supporters.[171] West Derbyshire (see above) was an important catalyst. Grassroots pressure was worrying, but more immediately so were fears that a highly agitated Churchill might use any weakness in Labour's support for Hartington as a pretext to do Labour down within the Coalition, or even break it up altogether. Two right-wing Labour MPs, George Muff and Alec Walkden, were sent to the constituency to speak for Hartington against the independent Labour challenger, Charles White. This led to a predictable outcry within the party. Bevin had to threaten resignation to bring some Labour ministers into line, while even the normally loyal *Labour Organiser* denounced the party leadership's line as 'flagrantly stupid'.[172] Only White's victory prevented a stronger reaction. A lesson was learnt, and when, shortly afterwards, Dugdale tried to get Attlee to accept an essentially Conservative view of the truce, he got a very dusty response.[173] It was generally realized that there could be no repetition of the Muff-Walkden experience.[174] Fortunately for the leadership, the postponement of the party conference due in June 1944 (see below) meant that there was no opportunity for the increasingly strong opposition to the truce to make itself felt. By the time conference did convene, that December, the end of the war in Europe was obviously approaching, and the NEC was, in any case, formally committed to

[169] Ibid., XXI, elections subcommittee 13 Jan. 1944; NEC 26 Jan. 1944.
[170] Ibid., Shepherd circular, 'A year of party development', 24 Feb. 1944.
[171] See e.g. MS Attlee dep. 8, fo. 248, Shepherd to Attlee, 29 June 1943; *Labour Organiser*, Sept. 1943.
[172] Ede, *Labour and the Wartime Coalition*, 174, 1 Mar. 1944; *Labour Organiser*, Mar. 1944; see also e.g. Noel Baker papers, NBKR 1/126, H. J. T. Russell to Noel Baker, 16 Feb. 1944.
[173] MS Attlee dep. 12, fo. 203, Attlee to Dugdale, 2 Mar. 1944.
[174] Noel Baker papers, NBKR 1/126, Noel Baker to H. J. T. Russell, 23 Feb. 1944.

Labour fighting the post-war election as an independent party seeking a majority Labour government.

Rebellions against the truce continued to make people vulnerable to expulsion.[175] As the end of the war approached, however, the party became rather more open to applications for membership from erstwhile opponents or critics. Indeed, the NEC positively bullied Cripps back into the party by threatening him with the adoption of an official candidate in his Bristol East constituency.[176] In early 1945, Jennie Lee, expelled for her anti-Conservative candidacy at Bristol Central in 1943, was readmitted, along with the independent MPs White and Tom Driberg.[177] For some, though, the door remained closed. Pritt's attempts to rejoin were rebuffed, while R. W. G. Mackay was also rejected so long as he refused to renounce Common Wealth, of which he was still chairman.[178]

This last response showed that Labour was now seeking to asset-strip Common Wealth. On 15 November 1944, the NEC's organization subcommittee met a five-strong delegation, which included Mackay and CW's leader, Sir Richard Acland. Although the meeting was amicable, the NEC had ruled out in advance CW's preferred options of affiliation or an electoral pact: the aim was simply to find out whether CW had unexpected levels of support or membership, and when it became apparent that it did not, Labour declared its clear preference as being for CW to dissolve itself and advise its members to join Labour as individuals.[179] The CW leadership ruled this out; but CW members were already heading in that direction: the CW MP for Eddisbury (Cheshire), J. W. Loverseed, who had already applied and signified his willingness to leave CW, was admitted in January 1945, while Mackay moved so fast that he was able to stand as the Labour candidate at Hull North West at the general election.[180] At the general election, there were few direct clashes between candidates of the two parties; CW mostly ran candidates in seats that were hopeless for Labour. It is by no means inconceivable that this was the result of an informal agreement, and when, in the aftermath of the election, CW imploded, it was agreed to admit its former members, including Acland, who went on to become a Labour MP in 1947.[181] By the start of 1945, even the ILP was close to reaffiliating to the Labour party.[182]

Election preparations had been made in February 1944, when the NEC had met Attlee and Morrison for a discussion of the current, and likely future, political

[175] LPNEC papers XXI, elections subcommittee 24 Feb. 1944.
[176] Ibid., elections subcommittee 14 Nov. 1944; organization subcommittee 21 Feb. 1945.
[177] Ibid., elections subcommittee 21 Mar. 1945.
[178] Ibid., organization subcommittee 21 Feb. 1945, elections subcommittee 9 Feb. 1944.
[179] Dalton, *Second World War Diary*, 791–2, 14 Sept. 1944; LPNEC papers XXI, NEC 30 Nov. 1944; organization subcommittee 15 Nov. 1944.
[180] LPNEC papers XXI, NEC 22 Nov. 1944, 28 Feb., 25 Apr. 1945; elections subcommittee 23 Jan. 1945.
[181] Ibid., NEC 30 May 1945; organization subcommittee 19 Sept. 1945.
[182] Ibid., elections subcommittee 14 Feb., 21 Mar. 1945; notes of discussion between Labour officials and ILP delegation, 31 May 1945.

situation, at the end of which it was agreed that the party should continue to support the Coalition until the end of the war in Europe, but that it could not entertain any notion of a post-war 'Coalition "Coupon" Election'.[183] In April, serious discussions about propaganda for the election campaign began, and that May the party's press and publicity department drew up detailed plans to spend £150,000 on election propaganda when the time came.[184]

Labour's annual conference was planned for June 1944, but on 12 May Attlee told Middleton that the government was discouraging unnecessary use of the railway system ahead of D-Day, and four days later the NEC agreed, after 'brief discussion', to postpone it.[185] This decision had ulterior motives. Issues like the electoral truce and the government's failure to do more in the direction of implementing Beveridge would have loomed large at a June 1944 conference; the Communists would have been pressing for 'progressive electoral unity'. Postponement allowed those controversies to be sidelined; and, if the Normandy landings were successful, there might not be time for another party conference before the end of the war. A few protests were received at headquarters from DLPs and union branches, but these were probably muted because of the renewed interest in the military effort that followed D-Day; it was, in fact, Bevin's promulgation of Defence Regulation 1AA (DR1AA) against unofficial strikes that aroused most controversy at this point (see Chapter 6).[186] Middleton himself was delighted. He was due to retire at the 1944 conference: its postponement postponed his retirement. When the NEC decided on 13 September that the annual conference would be held in the week commencing 11 December, it was still just about possible to believe that it would be conducted close to, at, or even after the end of the war in Europe, and hence be little more than a pre-election rally.[187] 'Parties Must Get Busy NOW' screamed the headline of the September 1944 *Labour Organiser*.[188] The autumn saw a series of well-attended regional conferences on election preparations, where Labour agents and voluntary workers received guidance from leading officials.[189] The final eighteen months of the war also saw some rejuvenation at headquarters. Scott Lindsay (PLP secretary) was replaced by the 39-year-old Carol Johnson in September 1943, and Middleton by the 41-year-old Morgan Phillips in December 1944, while Phillips was himself replaced as head of the research department by Michael Young, the 30-year-old secretary of the progressive think-tank Political and Economic Planning.[190]

[183] Ibid., NEC 26–7 Feb. 1944.

[184] Ibid., press, publicity, and campaign subcommittee 18 Apr. 1944; 'Memorandum on election services', 5 May 1944.

[185] Ibid., special NEC 16 May 1944. [186] Ibid., NEC 28 June 1944.

[187] Ibid., NEC 13 Sept. 1944. [188] *Labour Organiser*, Sept. 1944.

[189] LPNEC papers XXI, organization subcommittee 18 Oct. 1944.

[190] Dalton, *Second World War Diary*, 725–6, 22 Mar. 1945; K. O. Morgan, *Labour People: Leaders and Lieutenants from Hardie to Kinnock* (Oxford, 1987), 232; LPNEC papers XX, finance

It would be wrong to paint too rosy a picture, however. The continuing potential for conflict was demonstrated dramatically when the party conference convened in December 1944, shortly after British troops had stood by while Greek police had fired on unarmed demonstrators in Athens. This brought to a head Labour fears that Churchill did not share its desire to create a 'better' post-war world, and Labour ministers' apparent complicity added to earlier fears that had arisen at the time of Morrison's release of the Fascist leader Mosley from prison in October 1943, and Bevin's introduction of DR1AA in May 1944. With some difficulty, and helped by a strong speech from Bevin, the NEC was able to secure the passage of a bland resolution on Greece, but the party's mood was ugly, Communist agitation on the matter a further unwelcome complication, and conference, anxious to hold the leadership to account, passed a resolution proposed by Reading DLP, which demanded definite commitments to nationalization by any post-war Labour government, despite NEC opposition. Events in Greece moved on, and by mid-January 1945 Labour's Greek crisis had been overcome. But it had shown how unlikely it was that a united Labour party could have remained in any post-war coalition.[191]

Labour leaders now began to introduce a more partisan tone into their speeches: at Woolwich on 11 February 1945, Attlee stressed that 'the problems of the peace . . . [could] only be met by the application of Labour's principles'.[192] Eight days later, Morrison chaired the first meeting of a high-powered campaign subcommittee, which began to determine budgets and staffing, and to prepare propaganda material, not least attacking Communist candidates; by the end of March, preparations for the election were 'well under way'.[193] They included the publication of an illustrated magazine, *Straight Left*: an expensive full-colour edition was ruled out because of printing difficulties, not on grounds of cost. It was also agreed to print a first edition of 100,000 copies of the election manifesto, *Let Us Face the Future*, as well as two pamphlets on the ministerial work of Bevin and Morrison and a *Speaker's Handbook*, while plans were also laid for election training courses for activists.[194]

The end of the European war concentrated Labour minds. For all their careful preparation, some leaders, at least, appear to have had second thoughts when the prospect of a break actually came, but Labour rank-and-file attitudes, plus Churchill's increasing bellicosity, ruled out any last-minute reconciliation. Many

---

and general purposes subcommittee 18 Feb. 1943, special subcommittee 16 Sept. 1943; XXI, subcommittee on party secretaryship 23 Feb. 1944, NEC 22 Mar. 1944, policy subcommittee 23 Jan. 1945.

[191] A. Thorpe, ' "In a rather emotional state"? The Labour party and British intervention in Greece, 1944–45', *English Historical Review*, 121 (2006), 1075–1105.

[192] MS Attlee dep. 16, fo. 247, Attlee, speech at Woolwich, 11 Feb. 1945.

[193] LPNEC papers XXI, campaign subcommittee 19 Feb., 19 Mar., 11 Apr. 1945, NEC 28 Mar. 1945; B. Donoughue and G. W. Jones, *Herbert Morrison: Portrait of a Politician* (1973), 331.

[194] Ibid., campaign subcommittee 11 Apr. 1945; Labour party press and publicity department, 'General Election, July 1945: report on campaign publicity services', 23 July 1945.

Labourites called for the election to be delayed until October, but this was mainly the cautious reaction of people accustomed to losing elections for too long. By 18 May, the NEC was reiterating its view that Labour must fight the election independently, and that the party conference, due to open three days later, must be told that 'there was no desire or intention to enter a Coalition with the Conservative Party'; meanwhile, Attlee was careful to ensure that the executive approved his correspondence with Churchill on these matters.[195]

By the end of May, Labour was putting its detailed election plans into operation. Morrison, Phillips, and Laski (now party chairman) were to run the campaign, although Attlee would be consulted on 'major matters of policy'. Continuing transport difficulties ruled out major national speaking tours by Labour leaders, but speakers' meetings were to be 'zoned' to ensure a good and reasonably even coverage of the country as a whole.[196] Producing sufficient printed propaganda for the campaign was a challenge: initially, it was expected that the parties would get only 200 tons of paper each, but eventually they were allowed a ton of paper per constituency fought, which proved sufficient. Printing remained more problematic, because of labour shortages. Here, however, Labour's union links were helpful—the leaders of the two major print unions helped to smooth the party's way with their members—and probably gave it a competitive advantage over its rivals. Even so, fourteen different printing firms had to be used. But the ultimate results were impressive. As well as two million copies of *Straight Left*, the party managed to produce 1.3 million copies of *Let Us Face the Future*, more than 500,000 copies of other pamphlets, 12.5 million copies of seven different leaflets, almost 400,000 posters, and almost 1.3 million copies of a four-page election special, *The British Elector*.[197]

Labour headquarters had a good campaign; its leaders 'worked as a team, backed by an excellent organization and a detailed plan of action'.[198] They remained 'seriously handicapped by a shortage of staff' at first, but many gaps were filled by volunteers.[199] One innovation was the holding of four press conferences, three briefed by Morrison and one by Phillips.[200] Attlee and other party leaders put forward the Labour programme and attacked the Conservatives while trying to avoid the appearance of excessive partisanship towards the still-popular Churchill. During the campaign, Transport House was rumoured to be expecting to win 265 of the 640 seats, with a majority of 36 for the government; this would chime in with Attlee's comment that, while he expected to see 'a fine lot of new Members' to be elected, the 'chief difficulty' was 'to credit the

---

[195] Ibid., NEC 18, 20 May 1945.   [196] Ibid., NEC 30 May 1945.
[197] Ibid., campaign subcommittee 24 July 1945.
[198] J. E. D. Hall, *Labour's First Year* (Harmondsworth, 1947), 2.
[199] LPNEC papers XXI, 'General Election, 1945: interim report by the secretary', n.d. [Aug. 1945].
[200] Ibid., XXI, press and publicity department, 'General Election, July 1945: report on campaign publicity services', 23 July 1945.

optimism of all our people'.[201] But they were right to be optimistic, and on 26 July Attlee was to form the first majority Labour government.

Indeed, the size of Labour's majority—146—gave its leaders and managers ample opportunity to plan for the future. On 26 September, Phillips produced a report on party development that outlined the steps he believed necessary to restore the party to a full peacetime footing. These included improved organization at all levels, a membership drive, the revival of publications suspended in wartime, and improvements in the production and distribution of party literature. More innovatively, there would be better training for radio broadcasting and further work on film propaganda. Such activity was especially urgent because of the need to consolidate Labour's general election gains at the first peacetime municipal elections, to be held in November 1945.[202] Much of this would be acted on in the years that followed. However, in retrospect it is hard to avoid the view that there was, perhaps, a degree of complacency at, and about, Labour headquarters in the years immediately after 1945. That year's electoral success tended to mask the extent to which Labour's advantage was temporary, and began to end once Central Office started to re-staff and revive after the war. It seems likely that Transport House lost it wartime competitive advantage relatively quickly, even if it was not perhaps to be quite as incompetent by 1955 as Harold Wilson's notorious report would imply. An early indicator was Labour's laggardly development of its youth organization. Whereas by 1945 the Young Conservatives were already expanding impressively in some places, the Labour League of Youth had been largely ignored by Transport House; by October 1945, few League of Youth branches were operating, and there was no imminent prospect of improvement.[203]

At that point, however, the fate of the League of Youth was small beer beside the immediate fact of a majority Labour government. That Labour had come to power at all was due to numerous factors, but the wartime unity of Labour's leaders and managers was of particular importance. That unity allowed Labour to overcome what could have been serious difficulties. Had they been less single-minded and less closely integrated, any one of a number of issues could have become major crises. As it was, however, they were overcome, and settled largely on terms with which the leadership could be content, without fundamentally altering the party's strategy. The extent to which this unity was sustained, certainly until the end of the 1940s, was also impressive. Once again, however, there would be some unravelling in the early 1950s, by which point 'unity' was not the most obvious concept with which to associate the Labour party.

---

[201] Chartwell papers, CHAR 2/548B, Beaverbrook to Churchill, 15 July 1945; Dalton papers, II 8/1, fo. 13, Attlee to Dalton, 13 July 1945.

[202] Phillips papers, GS/1945/37, 'Party development: report by general secretary', 26 Sept. 1945.

[203] LPNEC papers XXI, Alice Bacon, memo, 'League of Youth', n.d. [Oct. 1945].

THE LIBERAL PARTY

By 1939 the Liberals were very much the third party in British politics. In 1935, less than three decades after their 1906 landslide victory, they had been able to run only 161 candidates and elect only 21 MPs; more pro-National government Liberal National MPs were elected than 'official' Liberals. After 1935, a new leader, Sir Archibald Sinclair, offered a rather more youthful feel, although he was sometimes seen as a rather lightweight figure. In 1936 the party's president, the former Indian civil servant Lord Meston, implemented a package of reforms aimed at modernizing the party's organization, finance, and membership, with a new body, the Liberal Party Organization (LPO), established to oversee the party machine; the old National Liberal Federation (NLF) was abolished, and its conference replaced by an annual Liberal assembly. The institution of a Liberal Book Club in 1939 was a further positive sign: three volumes had been published by the time war broke out.[204] Even so, a general election in 1939 or 1940 would not have seen a major Liberal breakthrough: indeed, many constituencies lacked formal Liberal organization.

On the outbreak of war, the Liberals were invited into the government, but without a seat in the war cabinet.[205] After some deliberation it was recognized that there could be no real 'coalition' without Labour, and the offer was rejected.[206] Meanwhile, the LPO responded quickly to the outbreak of war. Plans for an autumn campaign by Sinclair were scrapped immediately. Headquarters were moved from central London to Sutton, in Surrey. But the Women's Liberal Federation (WLF) stayed put, the continuing presence of the whips' office at Westminster offered a *pied à terre*, and the party was quick to rebut the idea that it was closing down: in a message issued on 6 September, Meston stressed that it was 'the paramount duty of the Liberal party not only to help in the prosecution of the war but also to lay the foundations of a just and durable peace', which could only be done by 'maintain[ing] the existence of every Liberal organization now in being'.[207] The LPO supported the electoral truce, but only as such: as Meston put it in February 1940, Liberals remained 'free to criticise the conduct of the Government as long as that criticism was honest and constructive, and they were in complete possession of their own independence', and Liberal association offices should be kept open, 'and the name-plates polished'.[208] Although the

---

[204] WLF papers, DM 1193, WLF, 'Twentieth Annual Report', May 1939.
[205] *Manchester Guardian*, 5 Sept. 1939.
[206] Crookshank papers, MSS Eng. Hist. d. 360, Crookshank diary, 29 Dec. 1939; J. Vincent, 'Chamberlain, the Liberals and the outbreak of war, 1939', *English Historical Review*, 113 (1998), 367–83.
[207] WLF papers, DM 1193, WLF, 'Report, 1942', n.d. [Sept. 1942]; Liberal Party Organization, *Report to Assembly, 1941* (1941), 6; *Manchester Guardian*, 7 Sept. 1939.
[208] *Liberal Party Organisation Bulletin*, 6, Apr. 1940; *Manchester Guardian*, 12 Feb. 1940.

1940 Liberal assembly was cancelled, the party's council and executive were to continue to meet regularly except in the very worst periods of bombing in late 1940.[209]

Some Liberals played a significant role in the events leading to the Norway debate, but their leaders' initial reaction to the vote that ended it was equivocal. Deeply shocked by news of the German invasion of Holland and Belgium on 10 May, they agreed that 'in light of this new threat Neville [had] better carry on', and agreed to send a statement to the press to say that although 'radical change of Govt. [was] wanted' now was 'not the time for it'.[210] Whether or not as a result of this equivocation, the Liberals reaped scant reward when the Churchill government was formed. Sinclair, who had entertained dreams of the Foreign Office, had to settle for being Secretary of State for Air. Worse still, and despite his express wish, he was not appointed to the war cabinet; the inclusion therein that August of Beaverbrook, the Minister of Aircraft Production, merely added insult to injury.[211] The only other Liberals to gain significant ministerial positions would be Dingle Foot, Gwilym Lloyd George, and Harcourt Johnstone. This lack of Liberal representation was much resented, because Liberals felt that the size of the Liberal parliamentary party (LPP) severely under-represented their support in the country at large. The brutal reality, though, was that the LPP was weak in quality as well as in numbers. Perhaps the ablest to be omitted was the chief whip, Sir Percy Harris, who was enraged that Sinclair overlooked him in favour of Johnstone, 'a fat overfed self indulgent batchelor [*sic*] who [was] dinning [*sic*] & wining Archie all the time'.[212] Crucially, though, Sinclair needed Harris to remain as chief whip and deputy leader, since that meant that Sinclair did not have to worry too much about leading his party in parliament. Indeed, the positive views of Sinclair often presented by historians sit somewhat at odds with many contemporary sources.[213] He was probably too easily manipulated by Churchill over ministerial appointments and his own exclusion from the war cabinet. He also became too deeply absorbed in the Air Ministry, to the exclusion of party matters. True, ministerial duties did keep him very busy; but Attlee was no less busy, while remaining far more involved in the management of his party. Indeed, it is hard to avoid de Groot's conclusion that Sinclair was 'a slow and over-meticulous worker disinclined to delegate authority'.[214] When he attended

[209]	LPO, *Report to Assembly, 1941* (1941), 8–10.
[210]	Harris papers, HRS/1, diary, 10 May 1940.
[211]	Ibid., 6, 11 May 1940; Elliot papers, Acc. 6721/7/F1, Elliot to Katharine Elliot, 4 Aug. 1940.
[212]	Ibid., 14, 16 May 1940, and *passim*; Dalton, Johnstone's ministerial superior, described him variously as 'rather a ridiculous person with not quite enough brains or energy', 'that damned fool Harcourt Johnstone', and 'a queer man, and not a satisfactory or loyal colleague': see Dalton, *Second World War Diary*, 464, 813, 839, 6 July 1942, 6 Dec. 1944, 2 Mar. 1945.
[213]	See e.g. R. Douglas, *The History of the Liberal Party 1895–1970* (1971), 237.
[214]	G. J. de Groot, *Liberal Crusader: The Life of Sir Archibald Sinclair* (1993), 156.

an LPP meeting in December 1940, it occasioned comment, because it was so long since his last attendance.[215]

One result of all this was the development of Radical Action (see below); another was persistent incoherence within the LPP, as its members continued to give the impression of a party divided by, for example, voting in different lobbies.[216] Many felt that Sinclair wanted to continue the Coalition after the war: in the middle years of the war, at least, this appears to have been the case. This was not just, or even mainly, hunger for office; Sinclair might well have seen a post-war Coalition, under Churchill and including Labour, as an essentially 'liberal' administration in contrast to inter-war 'Tory' hegemony. But such thinking sat uneasily with the views of many Liberals. By February 1943, he was seen as being 'out of touch with Liberal thought', and the senior Liberal peer, Lord Rea, was planning a deputation to demand a more active approach to the party leadership: as Harris put it, 'feeling [was] running high in both right & left circles against Archie's refusal to take any part in politics or give the party a lead' when Morrison, Eden, and others were 'making excellent speeches on general politics'.[217] At that July's Liberal assembly, Cardiff East Liberal association (LA) proposed a motion calling on Liberal leaders to renounce any post-war coalition. Sinclair declared that the assembly had no right to tell him, or the LPP, what to do, but was clearly uncomfortable.[218] In early 1944, leading Liberals were carping privately about 'Archie's lack of leadership & its results', while that October, the chairman of the LPO organization committee, Wilfrid Roberts, told the leader that 'Liberals everywhere' were hoping he would 'be able to give more of a lead in future'.[219] But the overthrow of Sinclair was unlikely, if only because there was no obvious alternative: the fact that Gwilym Lloyd George's name was the one most commonly mentioned served mainly to show how meagre the field was.[220]

In part, these worries about Sinclair reflected wider concerns about the party's wartime role. In July 1941, Johnstone was appointed to the government's Home Policy Committee after complaining to Eden about the party's lack of influence, but it made little difference.[221] Many Liberals believed that their claim to represent individual freedom against excessive state power was as strong as Labour's claim to represent organized labour. When the government was considering banning the *Daily Mirror* in 1942, for example, Foot was 'trouble[d]' that it did not recognize 'that the Liberal Party ha[d] any particular standing in relation to

---

[215] Harris papers, HRS/1, diary, 4 Dec. 1940.   [216] Ibid., 26 May 1943.
[217] Ibid., HRS/2, diary, 12 Jan., 24, 25, 26 Feb. 1943.
[218] LPO, *7th Report to the Assembly* (1944), 10–12.
[219] V. Bonham Carter, *Champion Redoubtable: The Diaries and Letters of Violet Bonham Carter, 1914–1945*, ed. M. Pottle (1998), 293, 25 Jan. 1944; De Groot, *Liberal Crusader*, 216.
[220] Harris papers, HRS/2, diary, 26 Feb. 1943.
[221] Treasury papers, T172/1952, Johnstone to Eden, 8, 15, 29 July 1941.

questions of th[at] kind'; but this 'special interest' was not widely recognized, and Sinclair refused to push the point.[222]

There was more progress in the area of post-war policy making. As early as autumn 1940, Harris established a Liberal reconstruction committee to enquire into post-war policy; it eventually had sixteen subcommittees.[223] The 1941 Liberal Assembly demanded that something be done to counter trends towards retail monopoly, and to help small traders, who often faced ruin if they themselves were conscripted to the armed forces. The result was the Independent Trader Committee, chaired by Elliott Dodds, editor of the *Huddersfield Examiner*. The committee's extensive proposals were eventually published in June 1943: further important reports included those on full employment and pensions in September 1944.[224]

Some Liberals were soon demanding more. Frustrated by the electoral truce and the refusal of party managers to allow it to be debated at the party's assembly, a number of them formed the Liberal Action Group (later Radical Action) in November 1941.[225] They were progressive Liberals who chafed under Coalition, and wanted the party to develop a distinctive Liberal leftism. They were helped by the party leadership's lacklustre response to the Beveridge report, when many Liberals felt that Sinclair fell in too readily behind Churchill's 'wait and see' line.[226] For much of 1943, the leadership was nervous about Radical Action, which supported Independent Liberal candidates at by-elections at Chippenham (Wiltshire) in August 1943 and Darwen (Lancashire) that December. The fact that both were only very narrowly defeated spurred Radical Action into greater activity and fund-raising. In this context, talk of future coalitionism was anathema, and on 15 March 1944 the party council finally declared that the Liberals would fight the next general election 'as an independent Party, free from entanglements with any other political Party', and on 'an advanced Liberal programme'.[227] This averted a head-on clash between Sinclair and Radical Action, but the latter remained active, tapping Lloyd George for funds and making a beeline for Beveridge once he came into the party (see below).[228] Significantly, Sinclair's own acceptance of Beveridge into the leading group of the party following his election to parliament in October 1944 helped reconcile Radical Action to his own leadership.

On the centre and right of the party, conversely, some Liberals still had lingering hopes of reunion with the Liberal Nationals. Many of the latter

---

[222] Foot papers, DGFT 1/3, Foot to Sinclair, 30 Mar. 1942; Sinclair to Foot, 1 Apr. 1942.

[223] Harris, *Forty Years*, 158–9, 167.

[224] *Fair Play for the Small Man: The Report of the Liberal Independent Trader Committee* (1943); Harris papers, HRS/3, diary, 8 Jan. 1943; LPO, *Supplement to the 7th Report to the Assembly* (1945), 7.

[225] D. Dutton, *A History of the Liberal Party* (Houndmills, 2004), 145.

[226] Harris papers, HRS/2, diary, 19 Feb. 1943.

[227] LPO, *7th Report to the Assembly* (1944), 15.

[228] Lloyd George papers, LG/G/25/2, A. J. Sylvester to Lloyd George, 15 June 1944.

were seen as essentially Liberal in outlook, their parliamentary numbers were relatively impressive, and they remained quite well resourced. Before the war, they had more real existence as a party than is usually recognized, their London headquarters presiding over a full-blown party machine, including annual conferences, professional area organizers, individual membership, and an active Liberal National League of Youth.[229] In wartime, however, their future looked murky, as the organization was run down, Simon went to the Lords and was replaced as leader by the lacklustre Ernest Brown, and the parliamentary party fragmented.[230] In 1943, Churchill, a great enthusiast for reunion, seized on news of grassroots demands for Liberal unity to press Sinclair and Brown to discuss the matter. Some initial progress was made; and Churchill's interest, Sinclair's deference towards Churchill, and the position of the Liberal Nationals as clients of the Conservative party all helped avert a complete breakdown.[231] However, Churchill's desires alone were not sufficient to achieve success, especially given that his attention to the matter could only be spasmodic at best, and talks continued mainly because neither side wanted to look 'unreasonable', either to Churchill or to broad Liberal opinion.[232] In October 1944, however, Labour's declaration that it would fight the next election independently left the Liberals with no alternative but to reiterate their own intention of doing so; and, because this was a step the Liberal Nationals obviously could not follow, wartime hopes of Liberal reunion came to an end.[233] Liberal National resentment against the Liberals would intensify at the 1945 election, and although some correspondence between the two parties followed in July–October 1946, this was very much for the record, with the Liberal Nationals merging with the Conservatives shortly afterwards; Clement Davies's refusal of office under Churchill in 1951 would finally end hopes of reunion.[234]

Maintaining the Liberal machine in wartime was easier said than done. At the end of 1940, when Harris took over the Liberal Central Association (LCA) from Johnstone, he found it in a very poor state (see Chapter 8). The LPO struggled to cope, although the appointment of the energetic Roberts as chairman of its organization committee in summer 1941 in place of Johnstone helped, as did the return of head office to London that December, albeit with

[229] See e.g. MSS Simon 87, fo. 17, Evans to Simon, 17 Oct. 1940; ibid., adds. 2, fos. 112–13, Magnay to Bernard Musgrave, 10 May 1939; fo. 229, Douglas Ganter to Musgrave, 10 May 1939; fo. 52, Sir Alfred Svenson-Taylor to Evans, 3 July 1939.

[230] Harris papers, HRS/1, diary, 15 Jan., 18 July 1940; Morris-Jones papers, D/MJ/21, diary 22 May, 5 June, 16 Oct. 1940, D/MJ/24, diary 24 Feb. 1943; Lloyd George papers, LG/G/25/2, Sylvester to Lloyd George, 13 Mar. 1944.

[231] *Liberal Party Organisation Bulletin*, 44, July 1943; Lloyd George papers, LG/G/25/2, A. J. Sylvester to Lloyd George, 30 July, 24 Sept., 10 Dec. 1943.

[232] Ibid., A. J. Sylvester to Lloyd George, 14 Feb. 1944.

[233] LPO, *Supplement to the 7th Report to the Assembly* (1945), 9–10; CCO 3/1/64, Topping to Assheton, 9 Nov. 1944.

[234] See e.g. Mabane papers, DD/WM/1/9, Mabane to T. S. Hickman, 10 Aug. 1945; LPO, *9th Report to the Assembly* (1947), 51–7.

a 'much depleted' staff.[235] Eighteen area conferences were held between August
1941 and August 1942, while the party's leading committees were streamlined
in December 1943.[236] But, on the whole, headquarters remained far weaker
than in peacetime. Meanwhile, the party tried to keep up its production of
propaganda. On the outbreak of war, the Liberal Book Club was abandoned,
the *Liberal News* and the *Liberal Yearbook* were suspended, and the monthly
Liberal Magazine became bimonthly. To fill the gap, a new monthly journal, the
Liberal Party Organisation Bulletin, was launched in November 1939. Initially, it
included news from the party nationally, and also from constituency associations
across Britain, but it struggled once the war intensified, being cut from eight
to four pages; for some months it did little more than report Sinclair's work
as Air Secretary, and although it reverted to eight pages at the end of 1940,
it was only in early 1942 that news about the party in the country began to
return.[237] The *Bulletin* helped bind the party together, as did the reversion of
the *Liberal Magazine* to monthly publication in 1942. Like Labour, the Liberals
also continued to publish significant numbers of pamphlets and leaflets: two
reports by the Dodds committee in 1941 and 1942 sold a total of 35,000
copies, mostly to shopkeepers.[238] Paper controls often meant restricted print
runs, however, while by 1943, strong sales of some publications meant that the
party had to begin to reduce them in size in order to make better use of its paper
ration.[239]

By 1944, then, the Liberal party had not collapsed at national level; in
many ways, it had coped surprisingly well with the challenges it had faced.
But as far as many Liberals, particularly Radical Action, were concerned, it
needed a boost. What it got was Sir William Beveridge. Beveridge had been
on the fringes of politics for much of his career, as journalist, civil servant, and
academic. Although he had shown no obvious party allegiances for many years,
public celebrity had turned his thoughts to a parliamentary career, and by the
summer of 1944 he was contemplating becoming prospective Liberal candidate
for Watford (Hertfordshire).[240] But when the Liberal MP for Berwick, George
Grey, was killed in action in France, local Liberals invited Beveridge to stand,
and on 17 October he was elected, despite the misgivings of senior Liberals like
Sinclair and Gwilym Lloyd George.[241]

---

[235] *Liberal Party Organisation Bulletin*, 22, Aug. 1941, 26, Dec. 1941; LPO, *Report to the Assembly, 1942* (1942), 23.

[236] LPO, *Report to the Assembly, 1942*, 11–13; LPO, *7th Report to the Assembly* (1944), 21–2.

[237] LPO, *Report to Assembly, 1941* (1941), 17; *Liberal Party Organisation Bulletin*, 6, Apr. 1940, and *passim*.

[238] LPO, *Report to Assembly, 1942* (1942), 16.

[239] LPO, *Report to Assembly, 1941* (1941), 17; LPO, *Report to Assembly, 1943* (1943), 19–20.

[240] J. Harris, *William Beveridge* (rev. edn., Oxford, 1997), 443; Lloyd George papers, LG/G/25/2, A. J. Sylvester to Lloyd George, 27 Jan. 1943; Beveridge papers, VI/1, J. Kearns to Beveridge, 14 Sept. 1944.

[241] Bonham Carter, *Champion Redoubtable*, 316, diary 29 Aug. 1944.

For the Liberal party at large, the election of Beveridge was a sensation.[242] After more than two decades of high-profile defections, it was a welcome reversal of fortunes, and the rather feeble LPP was boosted by a notable figure of legendary energy and zeal. Despite his reservations, Sinclair gained a colleague who could share the burdens of leadership, and shore him up against Radical Action critics.[243] Radical Action itself was delighted, seeing Beveridge as a kindred spirit. As one Radical Action leader told him, there was 'not a more urgent task in Liberal propaganda than that of associating your name and personality as closely as possible with the Party's policy', and Beveridge's presence would hopefully guarantee a more radical manifesto, including, for example, public ownership of 'transport, land and power'.[244]

Not all Liberals were in political agreement with Beveridge, however. Indeed, Jose Harris has shown that, far from being 'a fairly straightforward and orthodox reformist liberal', Beveridge had come to the view 'that the free market itself had . . . proved unworkable, and that not merely social but economic policy needed large-scale intervention by a centralized collectivist state'.[245] For many Liberals, such views were anathema. Ultra-traditionalists like F. W. Hirst and Ashley Mitchell, chairman of the Liberal Liberty League, with its slogan of 'Free Land, Free Trade, Free Men', remained.[246] But even less hidebound figures, like Dodds and the party treasurer, the banker Sir Andrew MacFadyean, had spent much of the war railing against state infringements of individual liberty and demanding better protection for small traders.[247] Indeed, the publication of the Dodds report in June 1943 had been hailed at the time as a key moment in the party's wartime history.[248] Two years earlier the LPO had commissioned and published a report bemoaning *The Drift to the Corporate State* by 'a young Cambridge economist', Arthur Seldon, which was very much against the kind of statist biases shortly to be advocated by Beveridge.[249] In early 1945, Dodds wrote privately that it was 'not at all reactionary' to see 'arbitrary government' as 'a real danger'.[250] These people were not insignificant, and their views were echoed in the highest councils of the party. Percy Harris worried about the expansion of the 'dead hand' of the state, feeling that '[l]ife is an adventure & if it is to

---

[242] Lloyd George papers, LG/G/25/2, A. J. Sylvester to Lloyd George, 1 Dec. 1944.

[243] Beveridge papers, VI/1, Sinclair to Beveridge, 22 Sept. 1944.

[244] Ibid., VI/13, A. Everett Jones to Beveridge, 19 Apr. 1945.

[245] J. Harris, 'Beveridge's social and political thought', in J. Hills, J. Ditch, and H. Glennerster (eds.), *Beveridge and Social Security: An International Retrospective* (Oxford, 1994), 26, 28. This view is disputed in M. Freeden, *Liberalism Divided: A Study in British Political Thought, 1914–39* (Oxford, 1986), 366–8.

[246] Harris papers, HRS/1, diary, 12 July 1940; Beveridge papers, VI/103, Hon. Sec., Liberal Liberty League, to 'Fellow Liberal', 27 Jan. 1945.

[247] For MacFadyean, see A. Howe, *Free Trade and Liberal England 1846–1946* (Oxford, 1997), 307–8.

[248] LPO, *Report to the Assembly, 1943* (1943), 21.

[249] *Liberal Party Organisation Bulletin*, 24, Oct. 1941.

[250] Beveridge papers, VI/103, Dodds to Beveridge, 28 Jan. 1945.

mean anything, there must be some risk'.[251] And, when the Beveridge report had been published, Sinclair had warned the LPP against giving it too uncritical a reception, while Johnstone had suggested industrial revival would have to come before welfare politics after the war.[252] For the time being, however, people like Dodds and MacFadyean were happy to welcome Beveridge, in part because they did not recognize the full extent of his collectivism, but also because they allowed their partisan delight at recruiting a celebrity to override any doctrinal doubts: Percy Harris's subsequent reflection that he 'satisfied [him]self that [Beveridge] was a good Liberal' was rich with meaning.[253] Sinclair, to his credit, realized the gap between Beveridge and others, but his efforts to steer a middle path were not very successful.[254]

In the period between October 1944 and July 1945, Beveridge was effectively the joint leader of the Liberal party. Within a week of his election, he was planning meetings with senior Liberals like Foot, Harris, and Lady Violet Bonham-Carter (but not Sinclair) to discuss 'what we mean by a Liberal Party with a Radical policy'.[255] He rapidly became the driving force behind the party machine. He chaired the Liberal Election Campaign Committee, giving 154 speeches—exactly half of them outside his own constituency, and 'practically none' of less than thirty minutes' duration—between 20 April and 18 July 1945; the only major centre where he did not speak was Birmingham.[256] In early May, he also took over as chairman of the LPO organization committee from Roberts, who was now to concentrate on candidates and candidatures.[257] It was perhaps no wonder that Foot worried privately about how they were going to control 'this Frankenstein [*sic*]'.[258]

Despite Beveridge's efforts, Liberal headquarters struggled as the party moved from Coalition to general election. It proved impossible to find the money or candidates to mark a step-change from earlier campaigns. Beveridge's own celebrity was diminishing: people were interested to hear him speak, but he was past the political peak of 1942–3.[259] The Liberals were only able to run 306 candidates for the 640 seats, and so could not have formed a majority government even if all their candidates had won; this meant in turn that electors had to vote Labour if they wanted the kind of welfare state he had advocated then. In the same way that people appear to have cheered Churchill for winning the war, before voting Labour, they appear also to have cheered Beveridge for

---

[251] Harris papers, HRS/1, diary, 19 Feb. 1940.   [252] Ibid., HRS/3, diary, 17, 18 Feb. 1943.
[253] Beveridge papers, VI/13, Dodds to Beveridge, 18 May 1945; Harris, *Forty Years*, 186.
[254] Harris, *William Beveridge*, 450; de Groot, *Liberal Crusader*, 221–3; see also R. F. Harrod, *The Prof: A Personal Memoir of Lord Cherwell* (1959), 244–8.
[255] Beveridge papers, VI/20(1), Beveridge to Bonham-Carter, 23 Oct. 1944.
[256] Ibid., VI/13, Beveridge, notes re 1945 general election, n.d.; VI/103, Beveridge, election diary, n.d. [July 1945].
[257] Ibid., VI/13, Liberal party press officer, circular, n.d. [May 1945].
[258] Bonham Carter, *Champion Redoubtable*, 321, 10 Dec. 1944.
[259] McCallum and Readman, *British General Election of 1945*, 166.

outlining post-war welfare politics, before doing the same. It is hard to avoid Jose Harris's verdict that excessive focus on the Beveridge report probably damaged the Liberals in 1945.[260]

During the campaign, though, the party expressed considerable optimism. Some of this was bravado, but many Liberals genuinely believed that they stood on the verge of a Liberal renaissance, both in Britain and the wider world. Victory in the war was seen as a victory for freedom; the Conservatives seemed discredited; Labour was looked down upon. The Liberals also believed they were the party of youth, with many young candidates, especially from Radical Action, and with a travelling team of Liberal-supporting students giving the party's campaign a lively feel in the twenty or so constituencies they visited.[261] Beveridge himself was swept up in the enthusiasm he met.[262] Of course, the party could not hope to form the next government, but in mid-1944 Radical Action had hoped for 50 MPs, and that December Percy Harris had spoken privately of getting between 50 and 60 MPs, who would form 'a big wedge' in parliament and so increase the party's prestige, enabling it to expand and put up a stronger fight at the subsequent general election.[263]

But Harris had also opined that, if it came back with fewer than twenty seats at the election, then 'the Party, as a Party, was finished'.[264] And when the results were declared on 26 July, it had only 12 MPs, one of whom, Gwilym Lloyd George, was already moving towards the Conservatives. Sinclair, Beveridge, and Harris himself were all defeated. Among those elected were some patently unsuited for any role other than that of backbencher. Ultimately, Clement Davies emerged as the new leader, despite the misgivings of senior Liberals, one of whom had described him in 1944 as one of 'too many lunatic & pathological cases in the Party'.[265] But in 1945 there was no alternative.

Meanwhile, the party machine was in for further periods of turmoil. The initial reaction was that 1945 had been an aberration, and that more money, more candidates, and more propaganda would have brought greater success.[266] Hopes that peace would provide, and something of a siege mentality, helped to keep spirits up: the defeated candidates were decidedly upbeat when they met that September.[267] A committee on party reconstruction, appointed shortly after the election, met forty-six times from October 1945 onwards, and reported to the

[260] Harris, *William Beveridge*, 449.
[261] *Liberal Party Organisation Bulletin*, 49, Dec. 1941; LPO, *8th Report to the Assembly, 1946* (1946), 13.
[262] Beveridge papers, VI/17, Beveridge to Brian Goddard, 4 June 1945; to Joan Gaved, 27 June 1945.
[263] Lloyd George papers, LG/G/25/2, Sylvester to Lloyd George, 15 June, 1 Dec. 1944.
[264] Ibid.   [265] Bonham Carter, *Champion Redoubtable*, 294, diary 15 Feb. 1944.
[266] Beveridge papers, VI/103, anon. memo [Dodd], 'The future of the Liberal Party Organization', n.d. [29 July 1945]; anon. memo, 'Main points emerging from LPD election campaign', 31 July 1945.
[267] Samuel papers, SAM/A/155(XI), Violet Bonham-Carter to Samuel, 12 Sept. 1945.

1946 Liberal assembly. Recognizing that 'the world is faced with the eclipse of British Liberalism', it offered detailed proposals for organizational and financial reforms.[268] Meanwhile, the publisher Herbert Joseph Ltd. was persuaded to risk £4,000 on a series of eight books proselytizing Liberalism, the first of which, Enid Lakeman's hopeful *When Labour Fails*, was published in 1946.[269] However, these early signs of progress would ultimately be crushed by the party's humiliation at the 1950 general election, when, despite running 475 candidates, it would win only 9 seats.

Essentially, the Second World War had had a steadily deflating effect upon the Liberal party's leadership, because of the essential opting out of Sinclair, and the lack of profile gained by Liberal leaders due to their lowly position in the Churchill Coalition. The sudden prominence of Beveridge late in the war said much about the weakness of the leadership team he was joining. But he could not resolve all the problems; indeed, insofar as he quite possibly put off many traditional Liberal voters, and inhibited erstwhile Conservative voters from defecting to the Liberals, he might well have been part of the problem by the time the country went to the polls. His rapid departure from the chair of the LPO organization committee after the election then created further short-term difficulties.[270] Ultimately, therefore, a weak Liberal party was weakened further by the war, at the national level at least. The independent Liberal party would be kept alive after 1945, but there was to be little concrete to show for the Liberals' efforts until the mid-1950s at the earliest.

CONCLUSION

What difference did the war make to the leadership and management of the three major parties? It clearly had a significant impact on the Conservative party leadership. It is inconceivable that, but for the war, and more precisely the turn it took in the spring of 1940, Churchill would have been able to succeed Chamberlain. Conversely, most former Chamberlainites were out of the picture by 1945. Many of the 'Conservatives' in the war cabinet, like Beaverbrook, were scarcely regarded as such by more orthodox party members. Out of the sixteen-strong Caretaker cabinet of 1945, only two (Sir John Anderson and Oliver Stanley) had been in the cabinet in August 1939. Churchill, and his eventual successors Eden (1955–7) and Macmillan (1957–63), had looked most unlikely future leaders of the party in 1939, but they were to lead it for almost a quarter of a century: it was only with Macmillan's retirement that a

---

[268] *Coats off for the Future! The Report of the Committee on Party Reconstruction* (1946), 3.
[269] Thurso papers, THRS VII 1/2, J. Ward Daw to Sinclair, 12 Feb. 1946.
[270] LPO, *Report to the Assembly, January 1945–March 1946* (1946), 12.

former appeaser (Sir Alec Douglas-Home, who, as Lord Dunglass, had been Chamberlain's parliamentary private secretary (PPS) at the time of Munich) once again took over the leadership.

Leadership changes were less seismic within the other parties. Labour's 1945 leadership was recognizably similar to that of 1939, with Attlee still the leader of the party, and key figures like Morrison and Dalton still in place. Overall, the war cemented the centre-right coalition of forces that had come to dominate the party in the later 1930s. Indeed, insofar as it kept issues like cooperation with the Communists on the agenda, the war actually helped this group to retain its shape and coherence; it was only in the early 1950s that it faced a significant challenge, culminating in the wholesale changes to the constituency section of the NEC that occurred in 1952. However, the war did propel Bevin into parliament and thus into the party leadership, while Bevan and Shinwell owed their appointment to cabinet office in 1945 at least partly to their wartime prominence as left-wing goads to the Churchill Coalition.

So far as the Liberals were concerned, the war did not topple Sinclair from the leadership, but it did weaken him to the extent that Beveridge was able to emerge as *de facto* joint leader in late 1944. However, the vulnerability of them, and others, to electoral defeat meant a severe rupture in the party leadership after the 1945 general election, with Davies emerging, *faute de mieux*, as leader, where he was to remain until 1956. Although there would be few obvious signs of revival under his leadership, the mere survival of the party after 1945 was an achievement for which he deserves some credit.

The headquarters of all three parties were adversely affected by the war, especially in the period to 1942, as staff shortages, travel restrictions, paper rationing, and the like all hit hard. Around the end of the war, and shortly afterwards, there were also significant changes of personnel. The Conservatives saw Topping replaced by Piersenné, and Assheton being succeeded by Woolton. The rejuvenation of Transport House, under way by late 1944, continued after the war with Denis Healey taking over Labour's international department, while R. T. Windle succeeded his old boss, Shepherd, as national agent in 1946. There were, however, fewer immediate changes at Liberal headquarters. Overall, Labour's head office had a better war than its rivals. From 1940 onwards, it was the only one that enjoyed close relations with its party's leadership. It did not suffer the consequences of ill-advised flirtations with closure, as did Conservative Central Office; and it maintained its staffing levels better than either the Conservatives or the Liberals. By the last winter of the war, Central Office was starting to make impressive moves towards revival, but by then a well-resourced Transport House was moving forward as never before. The Liberal machine, for its part, was not as amateurish as might be thought, but it was unable to develop in such a way as really to rival Labour or the Conservatives. At the national level of leaders and party management, then, the Conservatives started the war in the strongest position, but Labour ended it there. However, the latter's new-found ascendancy was to prove far from invulnerable in the years that were to follow, and it may even be that, whereas the experience of the war years pushed Central Office towards change in the post-war years, it drew Transport House away from it.

2

MPs and Candidates

INTRODUCTION

Party leaders and headquarters were the most obvious sources of leadership within wartime political parties. But they were not parties' sole founts of authority, guidance, and identity. Two further important groups were members of parliament (and, in some cases, prospective candidates) and professional agents. In the next chapter, attention will turn to the role of the agents, and the ways in which the war affected them. In this chapter, however, the focus will be on the role of MPs and, to a lesser extent, prospective candidates. The chapter will assess how far they continued to play a role in the maintenance of 'party', and investigate the ways the war obstructed them from doing so. It will also discuss some of the problems caused by the long period between elections (1935–45), and will also attempt to assess the extent to which these factors varied between the different parties.

Many MPs—Churchill included—had fought in the Great War. It was in response to pressure from MPs wanting to fight in 1939 that, on 2 September, the government introduced a parliamentary motion to the effect that military service would not be a bar to becoming or remaining an MP.[1] Those affected were more likely to be Conservatives than Labour, if only on demographic grounds: although most Labour MPs were firmly behind the war effort, the PLP's median age in 1935 had been 54, as opposed to 49 for the Conservatives; 53 per cent of Conservative MPs had been under the age of 50, as opposed to only 29 per cent of Labour members.[2] There was also far less likelihood of Labour MPs having the kind of military backgrounds which would predispose them towards volunteering.[3] For its part, the Liberal parliamentary party was so small that it could not have been expected to do very much in this direction. The figures given by Hogg in 1945—165, comprising 136 Conservatives, 6 other 'Nationals', 14 Labour, and 3 each from the Liberals, Common Wealth, and Independents—are broadly accurate, although they were not, of course,

---

[1] *HC Deb*, 5th ser., vol. 351, col. 277, 2 Sept. 1939.
[2] T. Stannage, *Baldwin Thwarts the Opposition: The British General Election of 1935* (1980), 223.
[3] LPNEC XXI, Labour party Research Department, 'Parliamentary Labour party (at 21 March, 1944)', n.d. [Mar. 1944]; McCallum and Readman, *British General Election of 1945*, 81.

all serving at the same time.[4] Conservatives like Jack Macnamara (Chelmsford) and Lord Halifax's son, Charles Wood (York), joined up immediately war broke out; Hogg (Oxford) himself soon followed, while Patrick Donner (Basingstoke) joined RAF Fighter Command.[5] By January 1940, 85 National government MPs were in the forces, and a second wave of recruitment followed the German invasion and fall of France.[6] Of course, joining the services did not always mean front-line action: in January 1940, 63 of the army's 71 MPs were serving at home, and when the lawyer Maxwell-Fyfe joined up that month he was placed in the Judge-Advocate's Department.[7] Later that year MPs of all major parties joined the Home Guard.[8]

Many MPs did get experience of battle, though. Wood served in France until Dunkirk, and later in the Middle East; Roger Conant (Bewdley (Worcestershire)) participated in the Sicily landings in 1943.[9] Twenty-one MPs died while serving. The first was Richard Porritt, the Conservative MP for Heywood and Radcliffe (Lancashire), who was killed in France on 26 May 1940.[10] Five days later, Sir Arnold Wilson, who had joined the RAF at the age of 56 despite his previous admiration for Fascist Italy and Nazi Germany, was reported missing, presumed killed.[11] The authoritative list was that published in the *House of Commons Debates* (see Table 2.1). It was chronological in the order in which people were declared dead: in some cases, this was some months after they had been reported as missing.[12] Indeed, a year elapsed between Baldwin-Webb being reported missing at sea due to enemy action and the by-election in his Shropshire constituency. Ten died in action; Maxwell died of wounds inflicted in action, and Duggan and Russell both died on service as well. Six died in accidents: Cazalet, Whiteley, Bernays, Campbell, and Brabner in air crashes, Heilgers in a train crash at Ilford. Munro had a heart attack while serving with the House of Commons Home Guard.[13] All but two were Conservatives: the exceptions were

---

[4] Hogg, *Left was Never Right*, 13; see also Ramsden, *Age of Churchill and Eden*, 49.

[5] Chelmsford CA papers, D/Z 96/3, executive committee 7 Mar. 1941; York CA papers, Acc. 156.22, executive committee 14 Sept. 1939; Lord Hailsham, *A Sparrow's Flight: The Memoirs of Lord Hailsham of St Marylebone* (1990), 131–2; Donner, *Crusade*, 251.

[6] Addison, *Road to 1945*, 69; Lennox-Boyd papers, MSS Eng. 3459, Somerset de Chair to Alan Lennox-Boyd, 17 May 1940; Hailes papers, HAIS 1/4 , E. J. Deane to Patrick Buchan-Hepburn, 18 June 1940.

[7] *HC Deb*, 5th ser., vol. 357, cols. 438–9, 8 Feb. 1940; Earl of Kilmuir, *Political Adventure: The Memoirs of the Earl of Kilmuir* (1964), 56.

[8] Ramsden, *Age of Churchill and Eden*, 50; H. Morris-Jones, *Doctor in the Whips' Room* (1955), 129; G. G. Eastwood, *George Isaacs: Printer, Trade-Union Leader, Cabinet Minister* (n.d.), 147.

[9] York CA papers, Acc. 156.22, annual general meetings, 14 Mar. 1940, 7 Mar. 1942, executive committee 29 July 1942; Bewdley CA papers, BA 956/8, annual meeting, 14 Apr. 1945.

[10] M. Stenton and S. Lees, *Who's Who of British Members of Parliament* (4 vols., Brighton, 1976–81), iii. 285.

[11] Ibid. 382.

[12] There was some debate as to when MPs should be presumed dead: see *HC Deb*, 5th ser., vol. 368, cols. 1088–9, 6 Feb. 1941; 377, cols. 425–6, 22 Jan. 1942.

[13] Ibid., vol. 407, col. 509, 19 Jan. 1945; Stenton and Lees, *Who's Who*, iii, *passim*.

Table 2.1. MPs dying while on active service, 1939–1945

Name	Constituency	Party	Service	Date
Richard Porritt[a]	Heywood & Radcliffe (Lancashire)	Conservative	Army	26 May 1940
Peter Eckersley[a]	Manchester, Exchange	Conservative	RNVR	13 August 1940
Sir Arnold Wilson[a]	Hitchin (Hertfordshire)	Conservative	RAF	31 May 1940
John Rathbone[a]	Bodmin (Cornwall)	Conservative	RAF	December 1940
Ronald Cartland[a]	Birmingham, King's Norton	Conservative	Army	May 1940
Dudley Joel[a]	Dudley	Conservative	RNVR	May/June 1941
James Baldwin-Webb	The Wrekin (Shropshire)	Conservative	Army	17 September 1940
Patrick Munro	Llandaff & Barry (Glamorgan)	Conservative	Home Guard	3 May 1942
Somerset Maxwell	King's Lynn (Norfolk)	Conservative	Army	December 1942
Lord Apsley[a]	Bristol, Central	Conservative	Army	17 December 1942
Edward Kellett[a]	Birmingham, Aston	Conservative	Army	March 1943
John Whiteley	Buckingham (Buckinghamshire)	Conservative	Army	4 July 1943
Victor Cazalet	Chippenham (Wiltshire)	Conservative	Army	4 July 1943
Hubert Duggan	Acton (Middlesex)	Conservative	Army	25 Oct. 1943
Stuart Russell	Darwen (Lancashire)	Conservative	Army	October 1943
Frank Heilgers	Bury St Edmunds (Suffolk)	Conservative	Army	16 January 1944
George Grey[a]	Berwick (Northumberland)	Liberal	Army	30 July 1944
John Macnamara[a]	Chelmsford (Essex)	Conservative	Army	22 December 1944
Robert Bernays	Bristol, North	Liberal National	Army	23 January 1945
John Campbell	Antrim	Conservative	Army	23 January 1945
Rupert Brabner	Hythe	Conservative	RNVR	27 March 1945

[a] Died in action.

Source: *HC Deb*, 410, col. 1871, 8 May 1945; Stenton and Lees, *Who's Who, passim.*

the Liberal National Bernays and the Liberal Grey, whose death was to allow Beveridge to start his own brief parliamentary career.

The death of so many Conservative MPs could be used as a sign of the party's patriotism, and some Conservatives did try to use it, and the lack of Labour casualties, to cast aspersions on the 'socialists'. Donner later suggested that '[s]ome leading Socialists, such as the late Aneurin Bevan, though of fighting age, so managed things that they never fought in either war. To be a "squalid nuisance" was, for Bevan, apparently enough.'[14] However, such attacks did not

[14] Donner, *Crusade*, 249.

always go down well in wartime: when in early 1945 the Conservative MP for Worcester, Crawford Greene, made a series of speeches along similar lines, he infuriated his local association, which believed his effusions were damaging its prospects at the forthcoming general election.[15] Even so, Labour fears on the subject could be seen by the attempts it made to counter Conservative claims.[16]

Combining the roles of serviceman and MP could be difficult. As one army MP put it privately, 'I do not know that it is a good thing to play Box and Cox with the H[ouse] of C[ommons] and Army. The H of C position requires, like anything else, concentrated attention & study if one is to be of use there.'[17] But the perception of neglect was not all one way. MPs serving in the army were granted leave to attend to their parliamentary duties 'as freely as the exigencies of the Service permit[ted]', but there was occasionally a sense that they were getting the balance wrong.[18] Vyvyan Adams, the Conservative MP for Leeds West, was strongly criticized by a senior officer in 1944 for neglecting his military duties by spending many hours each day on constituency correspondence, and the matter was only resolved by his being given a less demanding posting.[19] Most Conservatives were proud of the number of their MPs on active service, and when Thomas Galbraith offered to resign his seat if his local association in Glasgow Pollok felt that he could no longer represent his constituents effectively, he was told firmly that 'his naval duties must come first'.[20] Many activists were genuinely excited by their MPs' exploits. In July 1941, members of Blackpool CA reached the end of their annual general meeting disappointed that their MP, J. R. Robinson, had not been able to attend due to his RAF duties. As they were about to disperse, however, Robinson strode in dressed 'in flying kit', having flown himself to the meeting. It was perhaps little wonder that his subsequent half-hour speech on the progress of the war was received 'with the utmost enthusiasm'.[21] This sort of thing clearly helped bind associations closer together.

But other Conservatives were more critical, particularly of the fact that MPs could opt to draw both their parliamentary salary and their service pay.[22] Some Conservative activists felt neglected: in August 1940, Mrs Western of Chelmsford CA criticized Macnamara, on the grounds that it was 'not possible for an Electorate to be properly represented by an Absentee Member in the

[15] Worcester CA papers, BA 10925/3, annual general meetings 21 Apr. 1944, 5 Apr. 1945; executive committee 18 Apr. 1945.
[16] See e.g. *Labour Organiser*, Feb. 1945.
[17] Elliot papers, Acc. 6721/7/F1, Walter Elliot to Mrs Katherine Elliot, 27 June 1940.
[18] Cabinet papers, CAB 65/8/193(40), war cabinet conclusions 4 July 1940.
[19] Adams papers, 1/1/2, Major V. Adams to Colonel i/c Administration, South Midland District, 20 Sept. 1944; Lt. Col. Dennistoun to Adams, 17 Nov. 1944.
[20] Glasgow UA papers, Acc. 10424/75, general council 28 Apr. 1941.
[21] Blackpool CA papers, PLC 5/1/3, annual general meeting 4 July 1941.
[22] *HC Deb*, 5th ser., vol. 358, col. 212, 5 Mar. 1940.

Army', and claimed that voters 'felt themselves to be disenfranchised and felt also that if a Member of Parliament were not necessary in War time [*sic*] then he could be dispensed with in peace'.[23] Hogg, on returning to Oxford from active service, found that his 'absence abroad had been more lastingly resented' than his vote against Chamberlain in the Norway debate, and at one constituency dance was harangued by a partner for not doing more to represent Oxford while serving in the Middle East.[24]

Indeed, Conservative party managers became increasingly concerned as to whether active service was the best way for the party's MPs to employ themselves. By 1941, the whips were saying privately that, with so many Conservative MPs away in the forces, MPs who could attend parliament regularly were at a premium.[25] The rules allowed MPs to leave the forces at any reasonable time. So, in 1942, when the government was under pressure, the Conservative whips discreetly asked a number of MPs to resign their commissions and return to parliament. Around twenty, including Donner, did so, although claiming that they were returning of their own volition.[26] Of course, being released from the services did not necessarily make MPs more attentive to the claims of their constituents or the party whips: the release of Robert Boothby (East Aberdeenshire) from the RAF in late 1942 was said to be less about devoting himself to parliamentary and constituency duties than about finding time in which to earn the £1,200 a year he was receiving from a commercial firm.[27]

Conservatives believed that the disproportionate participation of their MPs on active service would bring political dividends. But these were not as rich as had been hoped, for a number of reasons. It was not possible, by 1945, to claim that only Conservatives had served in the forces: although there was a large imbalance among MPs, it was less marked in terms of 1945 election *candidates* (see below). The party in parliament was weakened, some activists were disgruntled, and the by-elections that resulted from heroic deaths could have less than heroic results, for the Conservatives at least. It seems, as well, that people in general were less impressed with martial vigour in this war than they had been a generation earlier. At least, other contributions, like employment in reserved occupations, were probably valued more highly than previously. In trying to play on the military prowess of their own MPs, therefore, the Conservatives may have underestimated voters' sophistication.

Other areas of public service for MPs were, potentially, more problematic. The long-standing ban on them holding offices of profit under the Crown was an early casualty. By the summer of 1939 it was becoming clear that some civil

[23] Chelmsford CA papers, D/Z 96/3, ways and means subcommittee 9 Aug. 1940.
[24] Hailsham, *Sparrow's Flight*, 226.
[25] West Dorset CA papers, D399/3/1, war emergency executive committee, 19 May 1941.
[26] Donner, *Crusade*, 295–6; *HC Deb*, 5th ser., vol. 376, col. 1684, 11 Dec. 1941.
[27] MS Woolton 3, diary 17 Oct. 1942.

defence operations would need MPs' input. That August, the Labour MP Jack Lawson (Chester-le-Street (Durham)), only agreed to a request to serve as Deputy Regional Commissioner for the Northern Region after gaining an assurance that he would not have to vacate his seat.[28] Further appointments included that of the Labour MP Thomas Johnston (West Stirlingshire) as Regional Commissioner for Scotland. Soon after coming to the premiership, Churchill appointed the National Labour MP Malcolm MacDonald (Ross and Cromarty) as High Commissioner to Canada, the Independent Cripps (Bristol East) as Ambassador to the USSR, and the Conservative Hoare (Chelsea) as Ambassador to Spain.[29] To meet the problem that, technically, all should have resigned their seats, the war cabinet introduced the House of Commons Disqualification (Temporary Provisions) Act, despite some backbench fears that ultimately all MPs would be in the pay of the government and so lose their independence.[30] The fact that the legislation had to be renewed annually kept some pressure on the government, which was forced in February 1942 to pledge that the number of certificates under the Act, which then stood at 18, would never exceed 25 at any one time.[31] It was with some relief that the war cabinet realized in January 1945 that it did not need to renew the legislation, and so could avoid a further round of parliamentary criticism.[32]

The MPs thus exempted worked for the government in a wide range of positions. By April 1941, for example, Ben Smith (Bermondsey Rotherhithe, Labour) was acting as labour adviser to the Ministry of Aircraft Production; J. P. Maclay (Paisley, Liberal) was working for the Ministry of Shipping; Major J. S. Dodd (Oldham, Liberal National) was Tank Production Adviser to the Ministry of Supply; and Sir Isidore Salmon (Harrow (Middlesex), Conservative) was advising the War Office on catering.[33] The more important positions were usually held by Conservatives, partly perhaps because they were more trusted, but partly as well because there were simply more of them from whom to choose. Some served with reluctance. Hoare had expected only a brief sojourn in Spain, but his adeptness at handling the Franco regime, combined with Churchill's determination to prevent his return or to give him the job he really wanted—the viceroyalty of India—kept him in Madrid; ultimately, pressure from his constituency association in Chelsea, tacitly encouraged by Downing Street, ensured that he was forced to resign his seat in return for a peerage in 1944.[34] MacDonald, for his part, was reluctant to go to Canada; by 1944,

---

[28] Lawson papers, box 3, John Anderson to Lawson, 27 Aug. 1939.
[29] *HC Deb*, 5th ser., vol. 369, cols. 769–72, 4 Mar. 1941.
[30] Cabinet papers, CAB 65/17/15–19(41), war cabinet conclusions 10–20 Feb. 1941.
[31] *HC Deb*, 5th ser., vol. 377, col. 1822, 18 Feb. 1942.
[32] Cabinet papers, CAB 65/49/10(45), war cabinet conclusions 26 Jan. 1945.
[33] *HC Deb*, 5th ser., vol. 370, cols. 1721–4, 10 Apr. 1941.
[34] See Templewood papers, XII/3, diary 'Sunday' [12 May 1940]; XIII/17, Hoare to Beaverbrook, 29 Aug. 1940; XIII/18, Hoare to Beaverbrook, 14 June 1941; XIII/19a, L. S. Amery to Hoare,

he was desperate to return ready for the post-war general election. But he was compelled to remain, and so ultimately could not stand in 1945.[35] There were also complaints about the length of time that MPs on government service spent away from parliament. In 1944, the town council in Rawtenstall in the Rossendale (Lancashire) constituency protested against the continuing absence of its MP, Ronald Cross, regardless of the fact that his service as High Commissioner in Australia was undoubtedly 'patriotic'.[36] Harold Macmillan's already challenging task in trying to retain Stockton (Co. Durham) in 1945 was certainly not helped by the fact that he had to spend much of the war abroad, visiting only once in the last thirty months of the conflict, in contrast to his assiduous pre-war nursing of the constituency.[37]

Ministerial responsibility could also inhibit MPs' attention towards their constituency organizations, leading to strained relations.[38] And, as the wartime state grew, the number of ministers rose, twenty-two new ministerial posts being created by February 1941, with the number of parliamentary private secretaries (PPSs) growing in parallel.[39] Since PPSs were meant to remain silent, and act as loyal followers of their minister and the government, complaints about these developments escalated.[40] Geoffrey Mander's appointment as Sinclair's PPS in March 1942 effectively silenced one of the most vocal Liberal backbenchers, and PPSs' relations with their constituency organizations could also become more distant.[41]

MPs could also be prevented from participation at Westminster and in their local parties by other responsibilities and interests. For example, Fred Messer, the Labour MP for Tottenham South, was criticized by his constituency party in June 1940 for not voting against the Chamberlain government in the Norway debate; but he had arranged a 'pair' that night, so that he could attend to vital work on the Middlesex County Council, of which he was a leading member. With the benefit of hindsight this seems a strange choice; in context, much less so.[42] Mander found that his support for the Zionist cause took up increasing amounts of his time, especially as the scale of Nazi atrocities against the Jews

---

10 June 1943; XIII/8, Hoare, 'Letter to Chelsea, 29 May 1944'; CAC CHAR 2/509, B. Bracken to J. H. Martin, 5 June 1944.

[35] Harvie-Watt, *Most of my Life*, 157.

[36] *HC Deb*, 5th ser., vol. 397, cols. 974–5, 24 Feb. 1944.

[37] H. Macmillan, *Tides of Fortune, 1945–1955* (1969), 30; idem, *Winds of Change, 1914–1939* (1966), 163.

[38] See e.g. A. Duff Cooper, *Old Men Forget* (1953), 282; Noel-Baker papers, NBKR 1/97, Noel-Baker to H. J. T. Russell, 9 Oct. 1939.

[39] *HC Deb*, 5th ser., vol. 369, col. 286, 20 Feb. 1941.

[40] See e.g. ibid., vol. 380, cols. 26–7, 19 May 1942.

[41] Mander papers, DM 668, 'A Back-Bencher Looks Back' fo. 85; Clitheroe CA, DDX 800/1/3, annual general meeting 23 Mar. 1942; Harborough CA, DE 1170/4, annual general meeting 26 June 1943.

[42] Tottenham South DLP papers, BLPES Film 211A, reel 97654/2, general committee 26 June 1940.

became clearer.[43] Meanwhile, the usual 'outside' responsibilities of MPs, such as business, legal practice, or trade union work, still took up their time, in some cases increasingly so.[44] Various other official or quasi-official responsibilities also impinged on MPs' time, as when the Conservative MP for Maidstone, Alfred Bossom, went on a lengthy trip to the USA in 1943 as a member of the British Building Mission.[45]

Broadcasting helped many MPs to raise their public profile. Radio was almost universal to British homes by 1939, and played an important part in the war effort. The MoI was keen to use MPs' communications skills, and in the first three years of the war, 176 MPs gave 1,321 broadcasts; the only parties represented in parliament not to get a broadcast were the ILP and the CPGB. In that period, the Independent Progressive MP and experienced broadcaster Vernon Bartlett made the most, with 176. Other leading figures in terms of numbers of broadcasts made were Noel-Baker (Labour, 75), Stephen King-Hall (National Labour, later Independent, 61), Walter Elliot (Conservative, 51), and Leo Amery (Conservative, 39). Perhaps surprisingly, given 'memory' of wartime broadcasting, Churchill only broadcast 33 times in the period.[46] Between October 1942 and October 1943, 57 MPs other than ministers broadcast a total of 174 times, with Hogg (Conservative, 21) and Megan Lloyd George (Liberal, 14) doing so most frequently.[47] During 1944, 78 MPs, 22 of them Labour, broadcast.[48] A number of MPs, including James Griffiths (Labour), Clement Davies (Liberal), and Sir Henry Morris-Jones (Liberal National), broadcast in Welsh.[49] MPs were also used widely by the MoI to address public meetings all over Britain.[50]

Most MPs continued to take their parliamentary role seriously. Indeed, the absence of significant numbers of MPs did place upon those who remained a consciousness of the importance of their own role in maintaining the functions of the legislature against the wartime expansion of executive power. Members also remained keen to protect their own rights over issues like the integrity of their mail, their own freedom of movement, and their ability to intercede with service departments on behalf of constituents serving in the forces.[51] As Sir Percy Harris

---

[43] Mander papers, DM 668, 'A Back-Bencher Looks Back', fo. 85.
[44] B. Criddle, 'Members of Parliament', in Seldon and Ball (eds.), *Conservative Century*, 147; Emrys-Evans papers, BL Add. 58262, Richard Law to Paul Emrys-Evans, 13 Sept. 1939; Miners' Federation of Great Britain papers, MNA/NUM1/1/42, 'Annual Volume of Proceedings for 1944', executive committee 7 Jan. 1944.
[45] Maidstone CA U1634/A3/1/2–3, emergency subcommittee 13 May 1944.
[46] *HC Deb*, 5th ser., vol. 383, cols. 1983–5, 21 Oct. 1942.
[47] Ibid., vol. 393, cols. 203–4, 27 Oct. 1942.
[48] Ibid., vol. 404, col. 2154, 16 Nov. 1944.
[49] Ibid., vol. 393, cols. 203–4, 27 Oct. 1942; 397, col. 845, 23 Feb. 1944.
[50] Ibid., vol. 383, col. 76, 8 Sept. 1942.
[51] See e.g. *HC Deb*, 5th ser., vol. 380, cols. 913–14, 9 June 1942; vol. 378, cols. 1980–1, 25 Mar. 1943; cabinet papers, CAB 65/27/130(42), war cabinet conclusions, 28 Sept. 1942; Sir H. G. Williams, *Politics Grave and Gay* (1949), 217–18.

stated when welcoming the Coalition, 'the House of Commons ha[d] still great duties to perform'.[52] There was adverse comment about MPs' failings, though: Labour's NEC complained repeatedly about poor attendance in parliament, and demanded that Labour MPs should try to speak regularly at public meetings.[53] Conservative and Liberal headquarters were much less insistent in this regard, but in July 1940 the Conservative MP Alfred Denville suggested that the salaries of absentee MPs should be stopped, unless they were ill, on government business, or fighting. Churchill refused to act, however, claiming somewhat disingenuously that '[p]ractically all' MPs were, unless otherwise occupied on the war effort, 'carrying out their Parliamentary duties to the full', and the government stuck to this line, refusing requests for a formal register of attendance.[54]

Parliament was not supine, but the government could count on parliamentary support at most stages of the war. The vote on the Norway debate of 7–8 May 1940 was such a shock in large part because there had been few portents of it in the previous eight months. Only two ILP MPs recorded their opposition to the formation of the Churchill government.[55] There were periodic revolts thereafter, but none came close to bringing down the government. Perhaps the best-known division came in July 1942, after the fall of Tobruk, when the Conservative backbencher Sir John Wardlaw-Milne moved a resolution of no confidence in the government. Although the government won easily, by 475 votes to 25, the fact that 25 MPs (plus two tellers) were prepared to go on the record against the Churchill government at this point in the war was significant, particularly since the 27 included 8 Conservatives and 8 Labourites.[56]

Bevan claimed that ministers expected MPs 'to listen, like the Reichstag, to a long speech by the Prime Minister and say "Amen", and then go home'. However, the government needed to keep a wary eye on parliament.[57] Some of the issues raised, such as the suppression of the *Daily Worker* (January 1941) or the continuation of detention without trial (July 1942), were essentially minority tastes.[58] But some rebellions were more significant. In February 1943, 121 MPs (97 of them Labour) voted against the government's cautious response to the

[52] *HC Deb*, 5th ser., vol. 360, col. 1505, 13 May 1940; P. Norton, 'Winning the war but losing the peace: the British House of Commons during the Second World War', *Journal of Legislative Studies*, 4 (1998), 33–51.

[53] LPNEC papers, XVIII, NEC 22 Nov. 1939, XX, NEC 22 Dec. 1943; Ede, *Labour and the Wartime Coalition*, 84, 7 July 1942; LPNEC papers, XVIII, 'Memorandum on platform propaganda under war conditions now prevailing' considered by organization subcommittee, 16 Dec. 1941; XXI, NEC 26 July 1944.

[54] *HC Deb*, 5th ser., vol. 363, col. 603, 23 July 1940; 388, col. 1821, 22 Apr. 1943; Eastern Conservative area council papers, CPA ARE 7/1/8, finance committee 12 Nov. 1940; 10/1/3, Wessex Conservative area council papers, executive committee 26 Nov. 1941; ibid., finance and general purposes committee 4 Nov. 1942.

[55] *HC Deb*, 5th ser., vol. 360, col. 1522, 13 May 1943.

[56] Ibid., vol. 381, cols. 609–10, 2 July 1942.   [57] Ibid., vol. 365, col. 1299, 5 Nov. 1940.

[58] Ibid., vol. 368, cols. 463–5, 28 Jan. 1941; 381, cols. 1517–20, 21 July 1942; 383, cols. 885–8, 1555–8, 30 Sept., 13 Oct. 1942.

Beveridge report, and there was also a Conservative rebellion, led by Hacking, in which over a hundred MPs voted against Bevin's Catering Wages Bill.[59] Further rebellions, like those against the release of Mosley (December 1943) and DR1AA (April 1944), also showed many people in the country at large that their own dissenting positions were not going unrepresented.[60] Controversial backbenchers like Bevan could—and did—really make their name during the war period, precisely because they were willing and able to offer a critical commentary on the government's performance.[61]

On the whole, however, party discipline, and hence identity, were maintained. Labour fared best here, because its institutional structures were well suited to wartime. All Labour MPs were members of the PLP, which met weekly while parliament was in session, as in peacetime. Once Labour entered government, Attlee ceased to chair the meetings, and a PLP chairman was elected instead, but ministers were still expected to attend.[62] Discipline was periodically a cause for concern, but the appointment of a new chief whip (William Whiteley) in 1942 improved matters, as did the decision to restrict the number of ministers who could be on the PLP's administrative committee following the debacle over the Pensions Bill that June when 49 MPs voted against the decision of the party meeting.[63] The tightening of the PLP's standing orders in 1943–4 also sent out a clear signal to potential rebels, although Bevan came close to expulsion over DR1AA.[64] Busy ministers might moan about the meetings—Dalton, for example, found them variously 'deplorable', 'chaotic', and 'preposterous'.[65] Yet the fact that all Labour MPs, of whatever rank, could meet regularly was worth the irritation. It gave the PLP an *esprit de corps* that was to prove important in keeping it, and the wider party, together, both during the war and as Labour emerged from the Coalition at its end.

The main group for Conservatives MPs, the 1922 Committee, also continued to meet weekly when parliament was in session. Attendances were respectable: in the period for which minutes are available (September 1939 to May 1943), 148 meetings were held. The highest attendance, of 200, was to hear Halifax talk about the international situation in October 1939, but 150 listened to Beveridge in late 1942, and attendances of over 100 were not unusual; they rarely fell below 70.[66] Unlike the PLP, however, the 1922 Committee was for

---

[59] Addison, *Road to 1945*, 225; Ramsden, *Age of Churchill and Eden*, 46–7.

[60] *HC Deb*, 5th ser., vol. 395, cols. 475–8, 1 Dec. 1943; H. A. Clegg, *A History of British Trade Unions since 1889*, iii: *1934–51* (1994), 266, 1299, 5 Nov. 1940.

[61] Harris, *Forty Years*, 165.

[62] MS Attlee dep 1, fo. 222, Attlee to Labour ministers, 3 Oct. 1940.

[63] Dalton, *Second World War Diary*, 388, 527, 4 Mar., 28–30 Nov. 1942; PLP papers, minutes 3 June 1942.

[64] Woodburn papers, Acc. 7656/3/4, Carol Johnson to Arthur Woodburn, 22 May 1944; PLP papers, minutes 27 Apr., 3, 10, 17, 24 May 1944.

[65] Dalton, *Second World War Diary*, 498, 552, 677, 30 Sept. 1942, 12 Feb., 1 Dec. 1943.

[66] 1922 Committee papers, 1922/4, meetings 20 Sept. 1939 to 12 May 1943, *passim*.

backbenchers only, and there was no forum where all Conservative MPs could meet regularly; and Churchill's dislike for, and reluctance to meet, the 1922's chairman, Sir Alexander Erskine-Hill, did not help.[67] Attempts were made to improve matters. From November 1941 onwards, Churchill gave a series of dinners to select groups of around a dozen Conservative MPs at the Savoy Hotel; but such events could not really compare with the cheek-by-jowl relationship that Attlee had with his backbenchers at weekly PLP meetings.[68] Matters improved somewhat from early 1943 onwards, though. The 1922 Committee approved Oliver Stanley's proposal to allow ministers to attend, while regular meetings of Conservative ministers also began, with Churchill attending when he could.[69] As political controversy developed over the next two years, these various meetings proved useful in organizing Conservative opinion; the 1922 revived significantly during the second half of the war.[70] The year 1942 also saw the revival of the pre-war Active Back-Benchers (ABB) group, comprising around twenty Conservative MPs like Sir Herbert Williams who were a self-appointed 'awkward squad' who aimed to keep the government close to Conservative principles; their activities at least helped to lift grassroots spirits.[71]

The LPP was far smaller, and had long lacked discipline. In January 1942, Churchill was so agitated that he complained formally to Sinclair about its inability to get all Liberal MPs to vote for the government, and threatened to reduce the number of Liberal ministers if there was no improvement; but little changed, and the continuing inability of the LPP to act as a unit did little to improve the party's image or profile.[72]

To an extent, then, MPs were able to continue to perform a useful function in wartime, both as legislators and as beacons for their parties. Despite all the difficulties they faced, they did manage to keep the government more or less accountable. If they did not often succeed in forcing major changes in government thinking, they did win minor victories, and even when they were heavily defeated—as they often were—the government's critics were, at least, able to remind ministers that they could not simply have everything their own way. Even the most loyal of backbenchers could continue to play a useful role in British political life. Notions of an attenuated parliament, rotting away, are inaccurate.[73] Most fundamentally, MPs continued to offer party a public face.

---

[67] Ede, *Labour and the Wartime Coalition*, 103, 26 Oct 1942, reporting Butler; Harvie-Watt, *Most of my Life*, 131.

[68] Harvie-Watt, *Most of my Life*, 64–5.

[69] 1922 Committee papers, 1922/4, meetings 21 Oct. 1942, 24 Feb., 3 Mar. 1943; L. S. Amery, *The Empire at Bay: The Leo Amery Diaries 1929–1945*, ed. J. Barnes and D. Nicholson (1988), 848, 883, 975, 1042, 30 Nov. 1942, 20 Apr. 1943, 5 Apr. 1944, 22 May 1945.

[70] S. Ball, 'The 1922 Committee: the formative years, 1922–45', *Parliamentary History*, 9 (1990), 146–51.

[71] Williams, *Politics Grave and Gay*, 163, 166–8.

[72] Churchill, *Second World War*, iv. 63; Harris papers, HRS/2, diary 26 May 1943.

[73] Norton, 'Winning the war'.

There was enough open difference between MPs of rival parties to ensure that, for the most part, the continuing significance of party in British politics could not easily be ignored.

That said, it must also be noted that some MPs were very far from covering themselves in glory. Indeed, some became scandalously neglectful of their duties. A few 'drew their salary and scarcely bothered to turn up at all', and people who neglected their parliamentary duties in this way were rarely, if ever, assiduous in their constituency work.[74] By 1939, a number of MPs were well past their best, and many were looking to retire. Some Conservatives had, by now, been serving for long continuous periods, following the party's run of relative success since 1918. But Labour also faced problems. Its partial recovery in 1935 had been large enough to allow significant numbers of old-timers defeated in normally safe seats in 1931 to return, but not sufficient for it to win the more marginal seats where many of its younger and most promising candidates had been concentrated. The next general election (due by the end of 1940 at the latest) would have seen many of these older members retire, but its indefinite postponement meant that it was up to individuals to take the initiative to resign. One Conservative backbencher, Sir Thomas Moore, was to try to establish a power of recall so that unhappy electors could petition for their MP's immediate removal, but he attracted little support and was effectively ignored by the government.[75]

In this situation, some MPs were much slower than they ought to have been to vacate their seats. Middleton outlined some of the worst Labour examples as they stood at the start of 1940: Jack Jones (West Ham, Silvertown) was infirm and had 'practically lost his sight'; Will Kelly (Rochdale) 'c[ould] not transact any business of any kind'; David Williams (Swansea East) was 'past any active work'. Most of those identified were soon prevailed upon to resign their seats: Williams did so in January 1940, and Jones that February, while another invalid, William Sanders (Battersea North), agreed to retire in April 1940.[76] But it took an NEC intervention to finally persuade Kelly to go in July 1940.[77] F. O. Roberts, the Labour MP for West Bromwich, was even more recalcitrant. A severe heart attack in 1937 had left him totally incapacitated for well over a year. Then, in the autumn of 1939, any prospect of his ever returning to work was ended by a severe stroke.[78] However, pressure from Middleton, the NEC, his union, and even Attlee himself could not force him out, given his wife's reluctance to forgo Roberts's parliamentary salary; it was only in April 1941 that he finally retired, to die seven months later.[79] A similar situation arose with the Conservative MP for

[74] Sir L. W. B. Teeling, *Corridors of Frustration* (1970), 110.

[75] *HC Deb*, 5th ser., vol. 365, col. 1332, 6 Nov. 1940; 367, col. 664, 5 Dec. 1940.

[76] Middleton papers, MID 63/35, J. S. Middleton to Mr and Mrs F. O. Roberts, 11 Mar. 1940; MS Attlee dep 1, fo. 111, Attlee to G. R. Shepherd, 21 Mar. 1940.

[77] LPNEC papers, XVIII, NEC 20 Mar. 1940.   [78] *Northampton Independent*, 31 Oct. 1941.

[79] Middleton papers, MID 63/35, J. S. Middleton to Mr and Mrs F. O. Roberts, 11 Mar. 1940; LPNEC papers, XVIII, NEC 20 Mar. 1940; MS Attlee dep 2, fo. 22, Attlee to G. R. Shepherd,

Edinburgh Central, James Guy, who had had a severe breakdown in 1937, and whose parliamentary career had clearly been over by 1939, but who remained MP until Conservative officials, under pressure from Transport House which was itself being pressed by the local DLP, finally forced his resignation in November 1941.[80] Such cases were extreme, but they showed how difficult it could be to remove even a complete invalid if he or she refused to budge.

In less extreme cases, it could be harder still. In November 1942, for example, Glasgow Maryhill DLP made a formal complaint about the failure of its MP, J. J. Davidson, to fulfil his obligations on health grounds, but the national party backed the MP, not least because the decayed state of the Glasgow party made it keen to avoid a by-election.[81] The following year, Leek (Staffordshire) DLP complained to the NEC about its MP, William Bromfield, who at the age of 75 was incapacitated by illness and unable to do any serious work; but again, no action was taken, and Bromfield, like Davidson, continued to draw his salary for doing very little.[82] Lord Dunglass, the Conservative MP for Lanark, became very ill in the autumn of 1940, and only really returned to regular front-line politics in 1944.[83]

Age and illness were not the only reasons why some MPs failed to discharge their duties satisfactorily. In March 1939 the MP for Bury (Lancashire), Alan Chorlton, announced that he would not fight the next election, so the local association adopted a new candidate, William Teeling.[84] But the war allowed Chorlton to remain *in situ*. Teeling pressed hard for Chorlton's retirement, but the latter clearly disliked Teeling (who among other things was a Catholic), and would not be moved.[85] In desperation, Teeling wrote to Churchill in October 1940 asking him to act, but the premier's staff kept the letter from him, on the understandable grounds that he had more pressing concerns at that point than Bury, and advised Teeling 'to wait, like Mr Micawber, in the hope that something will turn up'.[86] By 1941, Bury CA was trying both to force out Chorlton and to deselect Teeling, by now an absentee candidate serving in the RAF, who was also a liability.[87] It failed in the former respect, despite Chorlton's virtual parliamentary torpor throughout the war, but succeeded in the latter,

20 Dec. 1940; fo. 40, Attlee to G. R. Shepherd, 31 Dec. 1940; ibid., fo. 37, C. W. Roberts to John Fletcher (Typographical Association), n.d. [Dec. 1940]; LPNEC papers, XIX, NEC 26 Feb. 1941.

[80] *The Times*, 11 Oct., 16 Nov. 1937; Mass-Observation Archive, FR 1015, 'Report on Edinburgh by election', 16 Dec. 1941; LPNEC papers, XIX, NEC 30 May 1941, organization subcommittee 14 Oct. 1941.

[81] LPNEC papers, XX, NEC 25 Nov. 1942.

[82] Ibid., elections subcommittee 11 Mar., 4 Aug. 1943.

[83] D. R. Thorpe, *Alec Douglas-Home* (1997), 102–3, 121.

[84] Bury CA papers, GCP/C/1/3, executive committee 7 Dec. 1938, 15 Mar. 1939.

[85] Ibid., executive committee 27 Sept. 1939, William Teeling to Kenyon, 1 Aug. 1943; Derby papers, 920DER(17)/31/7, Douglas Hacking to Lord Derby, 11 Mar. 1940.

[86] Churchill papers, CHAR 2/403, Teeling to Churchill, 8 Oct. 1940, John Colville to Teeling, 18 Oct. 1940.

[87] Bury CA papers, GCP/C/1/3, Rothwell to Teeling, 22 Aug. 1942.

with Teeling going on to be elected for Brighton in February 1944 after a bitter by-election campaign characterized by vitriolic anti-Catholic propaganda.[88] In 1945 a new candidate held the seat by a tiny minority despite Labour criticism of Chorlton's wartime record.[89]

In June 1940, the constituency of Peebles and Southern Midlothian was effectively disenfranchised by the action of the state, when its rampantly anti-Semitic and allegedly pro-fascist Conservative MP, Captain Archibald Ramsay, was detained without trial under Defence Regulation 18B (DR18B).[90] Few MPs had much sympathy for Ramsay's views, but some of them did raise the question of his detention without trial at regular intervals. These were mainly Conservatives, but they were joined by others on the broader issue of DR18B, as when thirty-one MPs of various parties voted for the reconsideration of the regulation in June 1944.[91] The Labour MP for Ipswich, Richard Stokes, usually joined them, a fact for which he received some criticism in his constituency party.[92] Ramsay was, however, able to table written questions to ministers from Brixton Prison, and continued to do so after his release in September 1944.[93] Shortly before the dissolution of parliament in 1945 he placed a motion on the House of Commons order paper calling for the reintroduction of the anti-Jewish laws of King Edward I (1272–1307), including the expulsion of all Jews from England.[94]

Scandal affected a few MPs. Some of it was war related: for example, the Conservative MP for St Marylebone, Alec Cunningham-Reid, aroused fury in July 1940 when it emerged that he had sailed to Canada, accompanied by his mother and two children.[95] The Conservative MP Mavis Tate demanded that MPs 'who ha[d] run away' from Britain at a time of peril 'should forgo for ever' the right of sitting in parliament, and the war cabinet got as far as preparing a bill to declare such MPs' seats vacant, but the need for it passed and it was dropped.[96] Cunningham-Reid flew back to Britain in October 1940, but was deselected by his constituency association, later had the Conservative whip withdrawn, and would never quite manage to escape the charge of having run away.[97] The act

[88] Bury CA papers, GCP/C/1/3, anon. memo, 'Alan Chorlton, MP', n.d. [*c.* July 1945], executive committee 19 Aug. 1942, 3 Mar. 1943; Teeling, *Corridors of Frustration*, 70.

[89] *Bury Times*, 25 Apr. 1945.

[90] Gottlieb, *Feminine Fascism*, 63; Morris-Jones papers, D/MJ/21, diary 18 Jan. 1940; Roberts, *Eminent Churchillians*, 159.

[91] *HC Deb*, 5th ser., vol. 400, cols. 2417–18, 16 June 1944.

[92] Ipswich TCLP papers, GK400/1/1/3, delegate meeting 11 Aug. 1943. There would have been even more comment had it been generally known that Stokes had made an interest-free loan to Ramsay to tide him over financial difficulties consequent upon his internment: see Stokes papers, box 1, R. R. Stokes to Oswald Hickson, solicitor, 26 Feb. 1942.

[93] *HC Deb*, 5th ser., vol. 403, cols. 41–2, 26 Sept. 1944.

[94] Thurlow, *Fascism in Britain*, 228.   [95] *The Times*, 13 July 1940.

[96] *HC Deb*, 5th ser., vol. 362, col. 1076, 9 July 1940; Cabinet papers, CAB 65/8/200(40), 205(4), war cabinet conclusions 11, 16 July 1940.

[97] *The Times*, 16, 28 Oct. 1940; *HC Deb*, 5th ser., vol. 391, col. 1931, 30 July 1943.

of sending one's child abroad could be interpreted as unpatriotic, as was the case with the Conservative Minister of Information, Duff Cooper.[98] Meanwhile, money, sex, and drink continued to claim victims. There was financial scandal in late 1940 when it emerged that Boothby—hitherto a protégé of Churchill—had been charging commission on any Czech assets that he was able to help recover. Condemned by a parliamentary inquiry, his ministerial career was effectively ended.[99] Sexual scandal also arose. In July 1941 Sir Paul Latham, Conservative MP for Scarborough and Whitby (East Yorkshire), who was serving as a captain in the Royal Artillery, was found in a compromising position with three gunners and a male civilian. He then crashed his motorcycle in an attempt to kill himself, and a charge of attempted suicide was added to the fourteen counts of 'disgraceful conduct' under the Army Act that he was already facing.[100] He had no choice but to resign his seat and, in the first court martial of an MP since 1815, Latham was found guilty of eleven of the fourteen charges, cashiered, and sentenced to two years' imprisonment.[101] Another Conservative, Crawford Greene (see above), abandoned London once the bombing began in 1940, and settled with relatives in their house in the provinces, where he reputedly slept until 5 p.m. and sat up drinking all night, somewhat ironically given his splenetic attacks on Labour cowardice. Unsurprisingly, he was not asked to stand again in 1945.[102]

Specifically in relation to their constituencies, MPs took a variety of attitudes. It was no doubt a problem that MPs who were looking forward to retirement, or otherwise occupied, during the war years became less attentive to constituents' problems at just the point when those problems were intensifying. Admiral Sir William James, Conservative MP for Portsmouth North from 1943, failed to visit the constituency at all once elected and, unsurprisingly, was not selected to fight it in 1945.[103] But others who looked to continue a parliamentary career were also sometimes quite cavalier. The Labour MP for Wrexham, Robert Richards, although in contact with his DLP, attended hardly any of its wartime meetings, while Foot was a largely ephemeral presence where his Liberal association in Dundee was concerned.[104] The Conservative Walter Elliot wrote to his wife in September 1940 that he felt 'light and happy' knowing that he did not, that year, have to start a 'horrible' autumn campaign in his Glasgow constituency:

---

[98] Templewood papers, XIII/17, R. A. Butler to Hoare, 29 July 1940.

[99] Roberts, *Eminent Churchillians*, 190, 200; *HC Deb*, 5th ser., vol. 368, cols. 447–62, 28 Jan. 1941; 'Report from the select committee of the conduct of a Member with the proceedings of the Committee, minutes of evidence and appendices', House of Commons Sessional papers 1940–1, vol. ii (1941).

[100] *The Times*, 5 Sept. 1941; F. Wheen, *Tom Driberg: His Life and Indiscretions* (1990), 193.

[101] *The Times*, 1 Aug., 24 Sept. 1941; Mass-Observation Archive, FR 902, 'Scarborough and Whitby by-election', 6 Oct. 1941.

[102] Roberts, *Eminent Churchillians*, 202–3.

[103] CCO 4/2/61, Mr Homan (Wessex area agent), to Sir Robert Topping, 27 June 1945.

[104] Wrexham TCLP papers, DD/DM/344/5, executive committee 18 Mar. 1942, council 15 Dec. 1943; Dundee LA papers, GD/DLA 1/1, 1/2, minutes, *passim*.

'Wars and [army] staff-work are simply nothing in comparison.'[105] Then again, even conscientious MPs for south and east coast constituencies struggled to maintain a profile given transport restrictions, evacuations, and so on.[106] The Conservative party did try to counter such problems. In November 1940, its Eastern area asked Central Office to stress to MPs how important it was that they should stay in touch with their constituents, while a year later the Wessex area chairman, Sir Austin Low, demanded that the NUEC should take action against those MPs who were 'running the risk of losing their seats through neglect'; however, headquarters continued to prefer a subtler approach via the whips, whose quiet words appear to have had only a limited effect.[107] The whips, after all, could tell who was failing to attend parliament, but not who was neglecting their constituency work. Labour's NEC and national agent's department kept a closer eye on its MPs; perhaps the Conservatives should have risked injuring MPs' *amour propre* by taking a blunter approach. But the nettle was not grasped. Of course, it was not always a problem. Dalton sat for Bishop Auckland in the Durham coalfield, but he worked in London and his main home was in Wiltshire.[108] He was able to go for months without visiting his constituency and yet there would be 'no suggestion that [he had] left them too long'.[109] Of course, Dalton was widely respected in the constituency, no one could fault his commitment to the Labour cause either locally or nationally, and he had a strong constituency organization in a relatively safe seat. The Conservative George Harvie-Watt was able to use the fact that he was Churchill's PPS to carry him along with his constituents, but he was also fortunate in the proximity of his Surrey constituency (Richmond) to London, although having to look after the Prime Minister's Epping (Essex) constituents as well was a headache.[110]

Absentee MPs often got someone else to take on some of their constituency work. The Conservative MP for Twickenham, E. H. Keeling, acted for Macnamara's Chelmsford constituents in any matters requiring parliamentary action.[111] In York, all Wood's constituency concerns—including speaking at CA annual meetings—were looked after by the Bradford South MP, Sir Eugene Ramsden.[112] MPs' wives continued in their traditional role of liaising with women's associations, but they also filled in for their husbands in more

[105] Elliot papers, Acc. 6721/7/F1, Walter Elliot to Katherine Elliot, 4 Sept. 1940.
[106] Chelmsford CA papers, D/Z 96/3, E. H. Lea, 'Report on general election: 1945. Eastbourne division of East Sussex', 17 July 1945; Teeling, *Corridors of Frustration*, 112.
[107] Eastern Conservative area council papers, ARE 7/1/8, finance committee 12 Nov. 1940; Wessex Conservative area council papers, ARE 10/1/3, finance and general purposes committee 26 Nov. 1941, 4 Nov. 1942.
[108] Dalton, *Second World War Diary, passim*.   [109] Ibid. 467, 17 July 1942.
[110] Harvie-Watt, *Most of my Life*, 120, 125, 168–70, 180–1, 196; W. S. Carroll, *Years in Richmond and Barnes: A Chronicle of the Richmond and Barnes Conservative Association, 1880–1972* (Richmond, 1972), 80–1.
[111] Chelmsford CA papers, D/Z 96/3, ways and means subcommittee 15 Sept. 1939.
[112] York CA papers, Acc. 156/22, executive committee 14 Sept. 1939; 156/53/114–23, annual reports 1939–42.

traditionally 'masculine' roles, too.[113] When Duncan Sandys was away on military service, his wife filled in for him extensively in his constituency of Lambeth, Norwood: this went down well with the activists, not least because she was Churchill's daughter.[114] In October 1944, Amery—too busy for his constituency given his ministerial duties regarding India—recorded gratefully that his wife was 'the real Member for [Birmingham] Sparkbrook'.[115] In places where the MP was going to retire but his or her putative successor was otherwise engaged on military service or the like, the MP often stood in for the candidate at party functions.[116]

Numerous MPs did remain active on behalf of their constituents, and not just because they wanted to avoid London's bombs, as a rather cynical Dalton put it.[117] After all, MPs could play positive roles in highlighting politics and party in their own constituencies. Churchill believed that it was 'of the utmost importance' for members 'to visit their constituencies as much as possible', especially at times of distress.[118] Inevitably, there were considerable variations, but many MPs did expand their constituency role in the war years, and there was, overall, an increase in what constituents expected of their MPs. Some constituency associations and parties began to raise their expectations of how far their MP should be 'one of them'. This meant dealing with growing numbers of individual cases. The upward trend did not start with the war: the longer-term growth of the state was the key factor. But the considerable extension of state power in wartime and the more general disruption to everyday life intensified the process. People had more reason than ever to seek advice, assistance, or reassurance from their member of parliament. For their part, MPs sometimes found that this was one area where they could continue to have a meaningful relationship with their constituencies: for example, even though the Waterloo (Lancashire) CA was one of those that effectively closed for the duration in 1939, its MP, Malcolm Bullock, stated in June 1945 that 'except for a few letters lost in the blitz, he had answered all correspondents'.[119]

The result could be a huge increase in an MP's workload. Morris-Jones (Flintshire) found that constituency problems were 'much more numerous than in peace times'; his postbag doubled within a few weeks of the outbreak of war,

[113] See e.g. Derby papers, 920 DER(17)/16/4, Manchester CA, annual report to annual meeting 26 Apr. 1940; York CA, Acc. 156/22, executive committee 29 July 1942, annual general meeting 26 Mar. 1943.
[114] Norwood CA papers, IV/166/1/16, executive committee 2 Feb. 1940, annual report for 1940–1.
[115] Amery, *Empire at Bay*, 1018, 26 Oct. 1944.
[116] See e.g. Clitheroe CA papers, DDX 800/1/3, executive committee 21 Feb. 1945; Northwich CA papers, LOP 1/1/4, executive committee 23 May 1940, Lord Colum Crichton-Stuart to Mrs Newell, 17 July 1942.
[117] Dalton, *Second World War Diary*, 760, 27 June 1944.
[118] Woodburn papers, Acc. 7656/1/1, Churchill to Arthur Woodburn 25 Nov. 1940; see also NUA 4/1 card 60, national union executive committee 20 Sept. 1939.
[119] Waterloo CA papers, DDX 806/1/4, annual meeting 8 June 1945.

and had trebled by 1945, which meant 'terrific work' given that he had no secretary.[120] William Nunn dealt with 750 individual cases between his election as Conservative MP for Newcastle West in July 1940 and the end of the war, while in 1942 alone the Labour MP for Doncaster, Evelyn Walkden, dealt with 'a record number of cases'.[121] The approaching end of the war brought a fresh assault: in early 1945, the Liberal National MP for Huddersfield, William Mabane, was inundated with letters about the release of personnel from the armed forces, and also about the proposed new health service.[122] MPs received little support to deal with this work. They were paid an annual salary of £600, but their only perquisite was free rail travel between Westminster and their constituency. The increase in workload led to demands (especially from the PLP) for free postage and an expense allowance, as well as better pay, but the government ruled out such a move in March 1945.[123] It was left to the subsequent Labour government to increase salaries to £1,000 and allow free travel between Westminster and MPs' homes; a secretarial allowance would not be introduced until 1969.[124] Not all MPs were hard up, of course: when the Conservative MP Ronald Tree entertained Driberg to dinner one night in his 'spacious suite' at the Ritz, he claimed that he 'honestly' found living there 'the cheapest way to live in wartime', while the Conservative minister Oliver Lyttelton lived at the Dorchester.[125]

Further ways in which MPs could serve their constituents, and raise the profile of their parties, included morale-boosting and fact-finding exercises. The activities of the two MPs for Bethnal Green illustrate the point. In late 1939 the Labour MP for the North-East division, Dan Chater, drove almost a thousand miles with the DLP secretary in visiting thirty towns and villages and seventeen schools to which children and mothers from the borough had been evacuated, while his Liberal counterpart in the South-West division, Percy Harris, paid numerous visits to people in the area's air raid shelters during the blitz.[126] Some MPs continued to write regular columns for the local press.[127] The member for Fylde

[120] Morris-Jones papers, D/MJ/20, diary 7 Dec. 1939, 18 Dec. 1945; idem, *Doctor in the Whips Room*, 114.

[121] Newcastle West CA papers, 1579/4, annual general meeting 25 May 1945; Doncaster DLP papers, DS 7/1/5, 'Annual report and balance sheet for 1942'.

[122] See Mabane papers, DD/WM 2/1 (re health service), 2/2 (re armed forces).

[123] Parliamentary Labour party papers, meetings 31 Jan., 10 May 1945; *HC Deb*, 5th ser., vol. 409, cols. 629–30, 20 Mar. 1945.

[124] D. Butler and G. Butler, *Twentieth Century Political Facts, 1900–2000* (Houndmills, 2000), 221–2.

[125] T. Driberg, *Ruling Passions* (1977), 186; Viscount Chandos, *The Memoirs of Viscount Chandos* (1962), 197.

[126] Bethnal Green North-East DLP papers, TH/8488/16, management committee 19 Dec. 1939; Harris papers, HRS/1, diary 10 Sept., 10 Oct. 1940.

[127] See e.g. *Bermondsey Labour Magazine*, Apr. 1940; Reigate CA papers, 353/3/1/1, special meetings 6 May 1940, 25 Apr. 1941, 8 May 1942.

(Lancashire), Claude Lancaster, continued to attend every Conservative club in the constituency at least once a year.[128] Less positively, MPs could also queer the pitch of any proposed MoI speakers in their constituencies. At a relatively early stage of the war it became a complaint on the part of local Labour parties that their Conservative MPs were blocking public meetings being held under MoI auspices and, despite such protests, the power of veto remained.[129]

Some MPs played a very significant direct role in keeping their constituency organizations active. Many Conservatives, in particular, made crucial interventions to prevent closure. In December 1939, for example, the MP for Horncastle (Lincolnshire), Henry Haslam, stressed to his CA that it was vital that their organization was kept going, not least because Labour 'hoped to use the War to introduce Socialism'.[130] Other parties' MPs also stressed the need to carry on: Labour's Messer in Tottenham South and the Liberal Nationals' Mabane in Huddersfield both urged explicitly the need to maintain their party organizations intact.[131] Contact with constituency organizations was vital in this, of course: it was maintained in a number of ways. One of the most obvious was to speak at the annual meeting which, at least for the Conservatives and Liberals, was traditionally a major event with a high attendance, and even MPs serving in the forces could often manage such a yearly morale-boosting speech.[132] Some MPs, and particularly Labour ones, attended virtually all party meetings: in Yorkshire alone, H. E. McGhee and Edward Dunn made speeches at practically every monthly meeting during the war of the Penistone and Rother Valley DLPs respectively, while the MPs for Sheffield Brightside (Fred Marshall), Colne Valley (Glanville Hall), and Batley and Morley (Hubert Beaumont) all attended and spoke regularly at meetings.[133] Most Conservative MPs were less assiduous attenders, but there were exceptions. Bossom attended Maidstone CA's meetings religiously, and remained very active on behalf of his constituents, as did Sir Frank Sanderson at Ealing, while a city party like Birmingham—with twelve MPs to

---

[128] Fylde CA papers, DDX 1202/1/1, annual general meetings 25 Mar. 1944, 28 Apr. 1945.

[129] See e.g. Halifax DLP papers, TU28/1, executive committee 21 Nov. 1940, general committee 26 Nov. 1940; *HC Deb*, 5th ser., vol. 371, col. 150, 23 Apr. 1941.

[130] Horncastle CA papers, Misc. dep. 268/1, finance and general purposes committee 18 Dec. 1939; see also e.g. Clitheroe CA papers, DDX 800/1/3, executive committee 21 Sept. 1939; City of London CA papers, Acc. 487/34, women's branch, annual report for 1939 (Mar. 1940).

[131] Tottenham South DLP papers, BLPES Film 211A, reel 97564/2, general committee 3, 8 Oct. 1939; Mabane papers, DD/WM 1/3, Mabane to T. S. Hickman, 5 Oct. 1939.

[132] See e.g. Cardiganshire LA records 1, annual general meeting 31 Oct. 1942; Horncastle CA papers, Misc. dep. 268/1, annual general meetings 20 May 1940, 19 May 1941, 18 May 1942, 7 June 1943; Norwood CA papers, IV/166/1/16, annual general meeting 20 Mar. 1943.

[133] Penistone DLP papers, BLPES Film 211, reel 56, minutes, *passim*; Rother Valley DLP papers, 290/G1/1, minutes, *passim*; Sheffield Brightside DLP papers, LP (B) 8, executive committee 12 Apr. 1942; Colne Valley DLP papers, BLPES Film 211, reel 5, minutes, annual report 1943; Batley and Morley DLP papers, MS 146/2, annual meeting 15 Mar. 1942.

choose from—was usually able to find a member to attend and address a meeting when required.[134] Attendance at social events also performed a useful function.

MPs sometimes pressed their constituency organizations to think about post-war challenges. As early as December 1941, Dunn instigated an enquiry into Rother Valley DLP's organization, resulting in major changes, and by early 1944 many other MPs were doing likewise, in some cases explicitly because of the threat posed by the Communists.[135] By then, the Conservatives were also coming to see the role that MPs could play in reviving party organization: that June, Henry Brooke emphasized privately the centrality of MPs and candidates to effective organization, and argued that if they were 'capable but idle', then 'a personal friend must be detailed to talk to [them] and remind [them] that the Party cannot afford to see seats thrown away'; three months later Dugdale reiterated the same point more publicly.[136] Some Conservative MPs did valuable service in this way: at Ealing, for example, Sanderson held a 'very successful' cocktail party for younger Conservatives in January 1945 to enable them to meet him and join the party.[137]

Finally, prospective parliamentary candidates could also play a significant role in maintaining and developing their parties' profiles during the war. The fact that a general election had been widely anticipated for the autumn of 1939 meant that an unusually large number of prospective candidates had been adopted by the time war broke out. In more than five years of war, inevitably, some fell by the wayside. In the early months of the conflict, in particular, some Labour candidates resigned on principle. A. E. Hunter, the prospective candidate in the double-member borough of Derby, disagreed strongly with the party's line on the war, and resigned his candidature, although he went without fuss, asking that the party announce he was leaving on health grounds; the candidate in Taunton also resigned because of his opposition to the party's support for the war.[138] Pro-Communist Labour candidates in Sheffield Hallam, West Ham Upton, and Hendon were all expelled from the party in 1940, and four more followed in February 1941 as a result of their support for the People's Convention.[139]

---

[134] Maidstone CA papers, U1634/A3/1/2–3, minutes, *passim*; Ealing CA papers, Acc. 1338/2, minutes, *passim*; Birmingham UA papers, management committee 4 Oct. 1940, 20 Nov. 1941, 18 Dec. 1942, 29 June 1944, central council 14 Sept. 1944; management committee, 25 Jan. 1945.

[135] Rother Valley DLP papers, 290/G1/1, executive committee 20 Dec. 1941; conference of all affiliated trade union organizations 14 Feb. 1942; conference of local Labour parties and women's sections 28 Mar. 1942; conference of Labour councillors 16 May 1942; and see e.g. Sheffield Brightside DLP papers, LP(B) 8, executive committee 19 Mar. 1944; Wrexham TCLP papers, DD/DM/344/5, executive committee 31 Jan. 1945.

[136] Butler papers, H62, H. Brooke, memo, 'Organizing to win elections', 8 June 1944; Dugdale, circular, n.d., enclosed with Dugdale to R. A. Butler, 22 Sept. 1944.

[137] Ealing CA papers, Acc. 1338/2, executive committee 17 Nov. 1944, 8 Feb. 1945.

[138] Derby DLP papers, DL 116/1/1, executive committee 9, 22 Sept. 1939, 12 Jan. 1940; Taunton DLP papers, DD/TLP/1/1, general committee 20 Jan. 1940.

[139] LPNEC XIX, elections subcommittee 10 Apr. 1940; Sheffield Hallam DLP papers, LD 1564/2, management committee 8 July 1940; Hendon DLP papers, BLPES film 211A, reel

Some departed for more mundane reasons, like poor health or because they moved from the area.[140] Others entered the armed forces and saw little point in maintaining a relationship with a local party organization into an unforeseeable future. Some took the view that other priorities came first, or were unable, or unwilling, to keep up pre-war levels of financial commitment: the fact that, unlike MPs, they drew no salary in respect of their political role meant that they were less able to weather these storms. Some departing candidates were rapidly replaced, but in other cases there was a long delay. Windsor DLP deselected its candidate in November 1939 but then had to wait until October 1944 before it was able to adopt a replacement, while Bedford, which ousted its prospective candidate in the quest for a more 'active' person in March 1942, had to wait until June 1944.[141] The DLP in Derby—a highly winnable marginal—had to hammer away at Transport House for more than four years until it was allowed to start the selection process to replace Hunter in August 1944, the new candidate finally emerging only in early 1945.[142]

Labour was the only party to produce regular summaries of the number of candidates currently adopted (see Table 2.2). These figures suggest that the number of constituencies without a candidate actually fell in 1940, but then rose dramatically in 1940–1 and again, though less dramatically, in 1941–2. In the

Table 2.2. Constituencies without a prospective Labour candidate, 1939–1945

Year	Month	Constituencies without Labour candidate
1939	May	126
1940	May	115
1941	June	148
1942	May	161
1943	June	163
1944	December	152
1945	May	28

Source: *LPACR*, 1939–45, *passim*.

97559/1, special executive committee 24 July 1940; LPNEC XIX, organization subcommittee 19 Feb. 1941, regarding Henley (Oxfordshire), Lonsdale (Lancashire), Newbury (Berkshire), and Wirral (Cheshire).

[140] See e.g. London LF papers, Acc. 1446/7, general purposes committee 6 Sept. 1939; Wimbledon DLP papers, 1/2, Merton and Morden LLP, executive committee 2 Apr. 1940.

[141] Windsor DLP papers, D/EX 832/3, executive committee 16 May 1941; special general committee 29 Oct. 1944; Bedford DLP papers, X494/3, annual meeting 17 Mar. 1942, executive committee 14 Apr., 11 Aug. 1942, 13 Apr. 1943, 11 Apr. 1944; LPNEC XXI, elections subcommittee 7 June 1944.

[142] Derby DLP papers, DL 116/1/1, executive committee 14 June 1940, 10 Apr. 1942, 10 Dec. 1943, 10 Mar., 9 June, 11 Aug., 21 Dec. 1944.

eighteen months from June 1943 onwards there was a marginal overall improvement: in reality, numerous new candidates were adopted in that period, but a large number of withdrawals and retirements masked the fact. The six months after December 1944 saw a rapid movement towards the filling of remaining vacancies, a performance made all the more impressive when it is remembered that there were now twenty-five more constituencies following boundary changes.

Earlier in the war, though, things had been more difficult. Even where local party organizations retained their prospective candidates, and where those candidates were happy to remain, it was not always possible for the candidate to do much political work. Active service accounted for some, especially among the Conservatives. Employment in government posts was another obstacle to political activity. People who became temporary civil servants were not forced to relinquish their parliamentary candidatures, but it was made clear to them that their public activities must be cut to an absolute minimum, with the result that Labour candidates like Richard Crossman (Coventry), who worked for the Political Intelligence Department, Hugh Gaitskell (Leeds South East), who was employed by the Ministry of Economic Warfare and the Board of Trade, and Arthur Skeffington (Lewisham West), who worked at the Board of Trade and Ministry of Supply, were reduced to attending occasional private party meetings and corresponding with the local party agent or secretary.[143] There was a civil service move against even this level of activity late in 1940, although Attlee acted rapidly to thwart it.[144] By 1944, however, with the pace of adoption and the pulse of politics quickening, it was expected that, while temporary civil servants could seek candidatures freely, they must resign their civil service positions once adopted, although this did not apply to existing candidates.[145] Most DLPs were prepared to accept the limitations on their candidates that these restrictions brought, although there were those, like Wansbeck (Northumberland), which deselected their candidates as a result.[146] A few Liberal candidates were affected in the same way. In East Dorset, D. Graham Hutton, adopted as prospective candidate in May 1939, took on a government post in January 1940, and did nothing in the constituency thereafter, although his failure formally to withdraw until October 1944 then left the association rushing to find a candidate.[147]

Despite all this, however, many prospective candidates did remain close to their constituencies. Some Labour candidates were especially active. Even

[143] A. Howard, *Crossman: The Pursuit of Power* (1990), 106–9; P. M. Williams, *Hugh Gaitskell: A Political Biography* (1979), 93, 123; Lewisham West DLP papers, A89/100/9, general committee 19 July 1941; A89/100/10, annual general meetings 14 Mar. 1942, 11 Mar. 1944.

[144] MS Attlee dep 2, fo. 38, G. R. Shepherd to Attlee, 31 Dec. 1940; fo. 73, Attlee to Shepherd, 2 Jan. 1941; fo. 74, Attlee to Kingsley Wood, 2 Jan. 1941.

[145] P. Ziegler, *Wilson: The Authorized Life* (1993), 40.

[146] Wansbeck DLP papers, 527/A/3, executive committee 4 Sept., 2 Nov. 1943, special general committee 18 June 1944.

[147] East Dorset LA papers, D1512/A1, annual meeting 24 Jan. 1940, finance and general purposes committee 5 Oct. 1944.

though he worked for the MoI throughout the war, the candidate for Cleveland, O. G. Willey, stayed 'in constant touch' with his DLP; Sidney Dye in South-West Norfolk and J. R. Battley in Clapham were also highly active.[148] Others, like Moss Turner-Samuels in Gloucester, maintained their candidatures and were occasionally seen at meetings, but were, on the whole, less involved.[149] But even these candidates could form a point of reference for DLPs, and help them remain focused on the post-war world.

It was worse where candidates effectively gave up the ghost while nonetheless remaining, officially, the candidate. The veteran Labour ex-minister Margaret Bondfield hung on ineffectually as prospective candidate for Reading until 1942, when her retirement opened the way for the rather more lively Ian Mikardo to take over.[150] F. A. P. Rowe, who had fought South Derbyshire unsuccessfully in 1935, remained the candidate there until 1944, but was reported in 1941 to have been 'seen very little in the Division since the War started'.[151] Such candidates could be very difficult to move, and, where Labour was concerned, the NEC's ban on new adoptions in the middle years of the war offered DLPs little incentive to do much about them. But even when new candidates were adopted in, say, 1942, it did not always lead to an increase in activity, given the prevailing conditions.[152] Once the end of the war came into view in 1944, however, there was a new drive to remove unsuitable candidates.[153] At this point, candidate replacement and adoption began to operate as a major factor in promoting constituency-level activity in all three parties, but perhaps especially Labour and the Liberals.

Labour's efforts were helped by the existence of the Society of Labour Candidates, which was unlike anything possessed by its rivals. This coordinating body remained active during the war: its bulletin *Labour Candidate* was still published, and it continued to meet annually, at each year's party conference.[154] It would be wrong to exaggerate its significance, but it did provide assistance to its members and allow them to share ideas and concerns. Conservative and Liberal candidates tended to be more atomized unless, perhaps, they were leftish Liberals involved with Radical Action.

[148] Cleveland DLP papers, U/CDLP 1/1, annual report to annual meeting 15 Feb. 1941, and *passim*; South-West Norfolk DLP papers, Acc. 2001/145/1, annual meeting 6 Apr. 1940, 29 Mar. 1941, 25 Mar. 1944, executive committee 9 Sept. 1944; Wandsworth Clapham DLP papers, IV/156/2/2, annual report 1943.
[149] Gloucester TLC papers, D3128/5/7 minute book 1939–45, *passim*.
[150] I. Mikardo, *Back-Bencher* (1988), 62; *LPACR* 1942, 68.
[151] Noel-Baker papers, NBKR 1/107, Russell to Noel-Baker, 30 May 1941.
[152] See e.g. Newbury CA papers, D/EX 409/3, finance and general purposes committee 9 June 1942, on local Liberals.
[153] See e.g. Warwick and Leamington DLP papers, MSS 133/1/1/4, special general committee 30 Apr. 1944.
[154] D. E. McHenry, *The Labour Party in Transition, 1931–1938* (1938), 177–9; and see e.g. Dalton, *Second World War Diary*, 218, 3 June 1941; LPNEC XX, elections subcommittee 23 Feb. 1943; MS Attlee dep 14, fo. 2, Helen Keynes to Attlee, 2 May 1944.

It is also worth noting that the differential between the Conservatives and their rivals in terms of war service narrows when the focus is moved from MPs to all 1945 election candidates. Of course, Conservative candidates, as well as MPs, served in the war. To take just three examples, the candidate for Northwich, John Foster, rose to the rank of brigadier in 1944; Graham Guest (Kirkcaldy Burghs) served in the army for five years; and when Captain Roy Lowndes was adopted as candidate for Clapham in February 1945 he was still detained in a German prisoner of war camp.[155] But at the 1945 general election, a higher proportion of Liberal candidates than Conservatives had served in the armed forces during the war.[156] In part, of course, this reflected the Liberals' desperation and the fact that they had had so few candidates in place earlier in the war: it was possible for Major Paul Wright, 'an absolute babe in the wood politically' as he later put it, to be adopted as Liberal candidate in Bethnal Green North-East, for example, because there were no other, more suitable, contenders.[157] Even so, a number of those who had been Liberal candidates on the outbreak of war had gone off to fight: by February 1940 four of the candidates in the Western Counties region had enlisted.[158] And, where candidates were serving in the forces, their associations clearly expected to be able to capitalize on the fact.[159]

The proportion of Labour's 1945 candidates who had served in the forces was 'very much' smaller than for the Conservatives or Liberals.[160] However, *Labour Organiser* described the notion that the Conservatives had 'a monopoly of courage and the patriotic virtues' as 'arrant rubbish', numerous Labour candidates did serve in the army, navy, and air force, and, after the election, Transport House listed 68 'servicemen' among the 393 Labour MPs elected.[161] Indeed, as seen above, many Conservatives found it embarrassing when members of their own party started talking about Labour 'cowardice', and the Conservatives in Buckingham were worried that the Labour candidate, Aidan Crawley, had 'the glamour of a released Prisoner of War [he had served four years after being shot down in the desert], while our Candidate's military record is not very impressive'.[162] Harold Laski was keen to adopt more service candidates in order to provide similar embarrassments to the Conservatives on a wide scale.[163]

[155] Northwich CA papers, LOP 1/1/4, executive committee 23 Jan. 1945; Kirkcaldy Burghs UA papers, MS 36621, executive committee 17 May 1945; Clapham CA papers, BLPES microfilm 548 (reel 3), council 14, 21 Feb. 1945.
[156] McCallum and Readman, *British General Election of 1945*, 86.
[157] A. Mitchell, *Election '45: Reflections on the Revolution in Britain* (1995), 35.
[158] Western Counties LF papers, DDM 1172, executive committee 17 Feb. 1940.
[159] See e.g. Walthamstow East LA papers, Acc. 10208/4, executive committee's report for 1945, to annual general meeting 28 Mar. 1946.
[160] McCallum and Readman, *British General Election of 1945*, 86.
[161] *Labour Organiser*, Feb. 1945; LPNEC XXI, memo, 'Servicemen returned as Members of Parliament, general election 1945', to elections subcommittee 18 Oct. 1945.
[162] CCO 4/2/61, R. Homan (Wessex area agent) to Topping, 27 June 1945; Lord Pakenham, *Born to Believe: An Autobiography* (1953), 150.
[163] I. Kramnick and B. Sheerman, *Harold Laski: A Life on the Left* (1993), 472.

Where they had candidates who were still in the forces, DLPs were often keen that they should be depicted in uniform in their campaign literature, and it was significant that when the London Labour party held a conference on organization in November 1944, the first item on the agenda was the availability of candidates currently serving in the forces.[164]

Individual examples of Labour candidates serving abound. Woodrow Wyatt was selected as candidate for Birmingham Aston while en route from Normandy to India; Cledwyn Hughes, serving in the RAF, flew himself to Anglesey to be adopted there.[165] Denis Healey, who had been a beachmaster at Anzio, was adopted by the DLP in the safe Conservative seat of Pudsey and Otley (West Yorkshire) while in Italy planning a landing in Yugoslavia; his sole communication with the DLP up to that point was by letter.[166] However, some were not so fortunate, Anthony Crosland being especially peeved that his army service overseas precluded him from attending selection conferences.[167] James Callaghan, serving in the Royal Navy, was selected as candidate for Cardiff South in 1943, but remained on naval service and was serving in the Indian Ocean *en route* to Japan when the election date was announced. Although he was entitled to release from the navy for the duration of the campaign (and permanently if elected) he had to make his own way home, and covered the last leg of the journey 'in the baggage compartment of an RAF bomber'.[168]

One key theme that emerged across British politics in 1945 was rejuvenation, and this applied with regard to candidates—one of the most public faces of party—as much as anything. The idea of a House of Commons 'enfeebled by . . . its own old age' may be overdone,[169] but there were concerns in all parties about the need for a significant infusion of fresh blood at the next election. On the Labour side, efforts began at an early stage. Dalton's efforts on behalf of his young protégés particularly deserve note, but in fact the problem was recognized by most party leaders and officials; some unions, like the Durham Miners' Association, introduced age limits (typically 65) for their own sponsored MPs.[170] The NEC tried to avoid bullying people into retirement, but some of the more obvious people were approached.[171] According to one Labour minister, the result of this, and of the unexpectedly large number of seats Labour won at

---

[164] Wolverhampton Bilston DLP papers, D/LAB/3/1, general meeting 21 Apr. 1945; London LP papers, Acc. 2417/A/27, conference on organization and electoral matters, 4 Nov. 1944.

[165] P. Hollis, *Jennie Lee: A Life* (Oxford, 1997), 116.

[166] D. Healey, *The Time of my Life* (1989), 66.   [167] S. Crosland, *Tony Crosland* (1982), 40.

[168] K. O. Morgan, *Callaghan: A Life* (Oxford, 1997), 51–3; J. Callaghan, *Time and Chance* (1987), 61–2.

[169] Driberg, *Ruling Passions*, 178; for the alternative view, see Norton, 'Winning the war'.

[170] Dalton, *Second World War Diary*, 586, 799, 831, 23 Apr. 1943, 27 Oct. 1944, 14 Feb. 1945; *Labour Organiser*, Feb. 1942; LPNEC papers, XX, elections subcommittee 3 Sept. 1942; Dalton papers, II 8/1, fo. 44, John Swan to Dalton, 15 Sept. 1942; City of Leeds Labour party papers, WYL 853/4/21, annual general meeting 20 Feb. 1944.

[171] LPNEC XXI, elections subcommittee 21 Mar., 23 Apr. 1945.

the subsequent election (which brought in candidates who had been thought to have little chance of success), was that the new PLP was 'a great change from the old . . . teem[ing] with bright, vivacious servicemen', while 'superannuated' trade unionists were far less in evidence than before.[172] In fact the extent of the change can be overdone — there were still plenty of union MPs, for example, but they were proportionately fewer than in the 1935 parliament, and even here there was something of a shift in generations. Nonetheless, about two-thirds of Labour's 1945 MPs were new to parliament. The party's concern for rejuvenation had had some effect, and many of those elected for the first time in 1945 would serve into the 1970s or even, in some cases, beyond.

The Conservatives were also concerned. As early as 1941, Eden was writing privately that the party needed to get 'as many younger men into the House as possible, untainted with the recent Tory past'.[173] Churchill and Beaverbrook's concern to see young men with fighting records selected has already been noted (see Chapter 1); indeed, Wing Commander P. B. 'Laddie' Lucas, who was the party's candidate at Fulham West in 1945, was recruited not by the local association, but by the editor of Beaverbrook's *Sunday Express* in early April 1945.[174] Towards the end of the war, a Central Office directive discouraging candidates over the age of 70 allowed Churchill — himself 70 in November 1944 — to pull a few legs at headquarters.[175] According to Ramsden, some of the more decrepit Conservative MPs were 'forcibly removed' immediately prior to the general election, and, increasingly, associations did look for younger candidates.[176] The large number of retirements in 1945 meant that even though the party only returned 213 MPs, 76 of them were new to the House of Commons.[177] Furthermore, Piersenné lost little time, when he took over from Topping, in identifying around fifty young candidates, mostly under the age of 40, who had been defeated but nonetheless done well at the general election: the resulting list included, among others, future ministers like Julian Amery, Reginald Bevins, and Reginald Maudling.[178] The Liberals were also concerned to present a youthful face, although in their case the lack of older candidates meant that there was not much of a battle to be had.[179]

Another theme which became more significant in candidate selection at this time was the desire for local candidates, or at least a feeling that, once selected,

[172] Chuter-Ede papers, BL Add. 59701, diary 28 July 1945.
[173] Emrys-Evans papers, BL Add. 58262, Eden to Paul Emrys-Evans, 6 Nov. 1941.
[174] Mitchell, *Election '45*, 37–9.
[175] Wolverhampton West CA papers, D/SO/27/4, 'Notes by S[amuel] B[ower] [Secretary and Agent]', n.d. [1944]; M. Gilbert, *Winston S. Churchill*, vii: *Road to Victory, 1941–1945* (1986), 1316.
[176] Ramsden, *Age of Churchill and Eden*, 42; and see e.g. Horncastle CA papers, Misc. dep. 268/1, finance and general purposes committee 6 Mar. 1944.
[177] Howard, *RAB*, 150.   [178] CCO 4/2/8, Sayers to Piersenné and Assheton, 24 Sept. 1945.
[179] See e.g. Glasgow Hillhead LA papers, TD 480, annual meeting 2 Mar. 1945.

candidates should live in, or at least near to, the constituency. This appears to have been especially marked among Conservatives. The war gave a boost to ideas already developing in the 1930s against the kind of 'carpet-bagger' MP 'who lived in London and visited his constituency twice a year'.[180] However, it seems that the war also gave them a further push. From mid-1942 onwards, Conservative associations preparing to select candidates often stipulated a strong preference for a local person.[181] When selecting a new candidate in 1944, Worcester CA asked applicants whether they were 'willing to reside . . . in the Constituency or at a place not more than twenty-five miles from Worcester'.[182] Defeat in 1945 did little to change views: in seats that were lost to 'outsider' Labourites, like South Derbyshire and Winchester, there was a feeling that the Conservatives could gain an advantage by choosing a local next time.[183] During the war, Harborough CA (Leicestershire) had declared itself broadly happy with the extent of Ronald Tree's involvement in the constituency; but he lost to Labour in 1945, and when the association rather unenthusiastically re-adopted him as its candidate in 1946, it did so with a demand that he should 'work in the Constituency more than heretofore'.[184] This was not really Tree's style, and he withdrew.

It was perhaps significant that, when associations and local parties spoke of local candidates, they often employed gendered terminology: 'a local man', 'a Bradford man'.[185] While it would be crass to make too much of this, it did nonetheless betray a continuing gendered view of political activity which the war did not disturb very deeply, despite the role that women had played in all parties in keeping constituency organizations going. Most ironical of all was the fact that the Conservatives, who probably benefited most of all from women's efforts during the war, actually ran fewer women candidates in 1945 than ten years earlier (14 as opposed to 19).[186] Labour ran 45 women candidates, as opposed to 35 in 1935; the Liberals, 20 as opposed to 11. Overall, the number of women candidates only increased from 67 to 87; and while this increase of 30 per cent outstripped the overall rise in the number of candidates (25 per cent), the figures for the total number of candidates—1,348 in 1935 and 1,683 in 1945—showed what a small percentage of the candidates women

[180] G. L. Reakes, *Man of the Mersey* (1956), 73.

[181] See e.g. City of Cardiff CA records 26, Llandaff and Barry CA special finance and general purposes committee n.d. [c. May 1942]; Worcester CA papers, BA 10925/3, officers' conference 22 Sept. 1944; Chelmsford CA papers, D/Z 96/7, executive committee 6 Jan. 1945; Horncastle CA papers, Misc. dep. 268/1, finance and general purposes committee 15 May 1945.

[182] Worcester CA papers, BA 10925/3, officers' conference 22 Sept. 1944.

[183] Emrys-Evans papers, BL Add. 58250, South Derbyshire CA, annual report 1946–7; Winchester CA papers, 73M86W/5, central executive committee 1 Dec. 1945.

[184] See e.g. Harborough CA papers, DE 1170/4, annual reports 1940–1, 1943–4, constituency council 11 May 1946.

[185] Sheffield Central CA papers, LD 2104, finance committee 28 May 1945; Bradford Central CA papers, 36D78/18, parliamentary committee 1 Mar. 1945.

[186] Butler and Butler, *Twentieth Century Political Facts*, 261.

comprised (5.0 per cent in 1935 and 5.2 per cent in 1945). Overall, women made up 7.5 per cent of Labour candidates, 6.5 per cent of Liberal ones, and only 2.3 per cent of Conservatives. Of the 24 women elected—as opposed to 9 in 1935—21 were Labour, with one each for the Conservatives, Liberals, and Independents.

This was despite the efforts of the Women for Westminster movement, which had been set up by the feminist Women's Publicity Planning Association in January 1942.[187] Women for Westminster aimed to campaign across all parties for the adoption of more women candidates. This was its first problem, because it meant that those who opposed its objectives could use party discipline as a stick with which to beat it. There was some initial Conservative interest, for example, but this was withdrawn once it supported Jennie Lee's Independent Labour candidature at the Bristol Central by-election in early 1943, and soon Conservative women were being warned to have nothing to do with what was now seen as a 'completely unsatisfactory' body.[188] In Labour eyes, it was seen as either a rightist deviation in the direction of permanent coalitionism, or a leftist one in the direction of the Communists: the latter was a predictable charge, but it was given added ballast by the prior existence of the (entirely unrelated) 'Communist-inspired' Women's Parliament, which had sparked a mild Transport House propaganda campaign in 1941.[189] Thus headquarters declared Women for Westminster *ultra vires* in April 1942, and called for its two most prominent Labour proponents, Edith Summerskill (MP for Fulham West) and the LCC councillor Freda Corbett, to desist.[190] They ultimately agreed to do so; and although the movement continued to appeal to DLPs for support, its card had been well and truly marked.[191] The NEC promised that the whole question of women candidates would be reviewed as part of the general review of parliamentary candidatures that was taking place, but it was an empty pledge.[192] At the 1942 Labour women's conference, a motion urging selection committees to look favourably on potential women candidates was defeated by 211 votes to 192 on the grounds that women did not want special treatment, while at the following year's event NEC veteran Barbara Ayrton Gould, though stressing the need to remove 'prejudice' against women

[187] A. Oram, ' "Bombs don't discriminate!" Women's political activism in the Second World War', in C. Gledhill and G. Swanson (eds.), *Nationalising Femininity: Culture, Sexuality and British Cinema in the Second World War* (1996), 54, 64–5.

[188] CCO 170/1/1/2, central women's advisory committee 30 Sept. 1942, 13 Apr., 6 Oct. 1943.

[189] J. Hinton, *Women, Social Leadership, and the Second World War: Continuities of Class* (Oxford, 2002), 195; LPNEC XIX, organization subcommittee 19 Feb. 1941.

[190] LPNEC XIX, elections subcommittee 15 Apr. 1941.

[191] Ibid., elections subcommittee 13 May 1941; Peterborough DLP papers, BLPES film 211, reel 131, annual meeting 25 Apr. 1942; Norwich DLP papers, SO 198/1/3, executive committee 9 June 1942.

[192] LPNEC XX, standing joint committee of working women's organizations 14 May 1942; elections subcommittee 21 July 1942.

candidates, also stressed that 'the women of the Labour Party did not want women as women in Parliament. They wanted Labour women.' Women for Westminster fizzled out of existence towards the end of that year.[193] This is not to say that there was no impact: some DLP women's sections did become more assertive in the later years of the war, often demanding that at least one woman be placed on shortlists.[194] However, it was one thing to be placed on a shortlist, and another to be adopted. All in all, attitudes did not change as far as might have been expected: Labour conferences were still often chaired by men 'born and bred to notice only men', while the likeliest context in which Conservative selection committees would meet women was as wives to aspirant candidates, perhaps making 'a charming little speech' while they were there.[195] The Liberals, for their part, had some prominent women: Megan Lloyd George was an MP, while Violet Bonham Carter became president of the LPO in 1944, Lady Glen-Coats virtually ran the Scottish Liberal federation (see Chapter 7), and Margaret Corbett Ashby was chairman of the Women's LF executive and a great grassroots favourite. But even though Lady Denman gave the party £400 towards running women candidates in rural seats at the 1945 election, the party only managed to increase its number of women candidates to 20.[196]

The Second World War did not see a revolution in the nature of the British parliament or its members. It was an exceptional time, even so. Parliament faced the challenge of a much more powerful executive. But the latter continued to take parliament seriously, and MPs were able to fulfil their function of oversight. At the same time, however, the periodic or regular absence of numerous MPs did place pressure on those who remained. By 1945—with no general election having taking place for almost a decade—many MPs were no longer fit for their work, and parliament was in desperate need of rejuvenation. Meanwhile, the potential demands on MPs grew. Yet the fact that many of those faced with these challenges met them served to ensure that the party system was not fatally undermined. MPs and, to a lesser extent, prospective candidates played a significant role in the resilience of party in wartime Britain. In party terms, Conservative MPs were most likely to see, and hence die on, military service, although the gap narrows when attention is switched from wartime MPs to candidates at the 1945 election. The party clearly hoped to capitalize on that record, but it proved harder to do so than they had anticipated. However, the Conservatives' pre-eminence in the military field would prove useful as the party began to explain its 1945 defeat and rebuild, because it allowed Conservatives of all stripes to explain that defeat as being a by-product of the selfless patriotism of

---

[193] *Report of the Twenty-First National Conference of Labour Women* (1942), 40; *Report of the Twenty-Second National Conference of Labour Women* (1943), 24–5.

[194] B. Castle, *Fighting All the Way* (1993), 121.

[195] Ibid. 116; Horncastle CA papers, Misc. dep. 268/1, general committee 1 May 1944.

[196] Women's LF papers, DM 1193, annual reports, Jan. 1945, May 1946.

Conservative MPs. In other words, they had put country before party, as against 'stay-at-home' Labourites who had shirked their duty. This was a distortion of reality, but it would serve as a powerful myth with which to unite the party in the aftermath of defeat in 1945 and steel it for the struggle to regain power in the years that followed.

3

Agents and Organizers

INTRODUCTION

The fate of full-time party agents is a central element in established narratives of political organization in Second World War Britain. Conservatives' memoirs are replete with claims about the war's adverse effects on their party's agency, as those of two of the party's most prominent post-war reformers show. Lord Kilmuir (David Maxwell-Fyfe), writing in 1964, argued that during the war 'the Conservative Party in the constituencies was not functioning', that, unlike Labour, it did not have 'a hard core of Trade Unionists, organized in active branches, whose jobs prevented them going to the war', and that '[a]ll except the elderly Conservative agents were in the Services, and the same applied to constituency officers'.[1] R. A. Butler, meanwhile, argued that, by early 1945, the Conservative organization was in a 'parlous' state, 'much harder hit than that of our opponents by the absence of agents and organizers on war service'.[2] Such concerns had been expressed in wartime. 'I cannot understand', wrote A. J. Gibbs, Eden's agent in Warwick and Leamington, in mid-1942, 'how the Labour Agent, Wright, is avoiding Military Service for he is quite a young man working on the railway.'[3] But less sympathetic observers have tended to downplay such claims. The Liberal Jo Grimond, a candidate in 1945, claimed that 'the Tories' were 'not . . . much worse organized than anyone else', while Kenneth O. Morgan has pointed out that there were still more full-time Conservative than Labour agents.[4] There is, therefore, clearly scope for comparative study of the fate of the political agents of the three main parties in wartime. However, it is important that the comparison should be a true one: it must compare, not just what happened, but also the impact of those developments according to each party's perception of normality.

---

[1] Kilmuir, *Political Adventure*, 76.   [2] Lord Butler, *The Art of the Possible* (1971), 127.
[3] Avon papers, AP 11/1/10, A. J. Gibbs to Anthony Eden, 20 July 1942.
[4] 4 J. Grimond, *Memoirs* (1979), 130; K. O. Morgan, *Labour in Power, 1945–1951* (Oxford, 1984), 29–30; idem, *Labour People*, 232.

THE CONSERVATIVES

Most Conservative associations had an agent in 1939, and most of the others aspired to do so: as Stuart Ball has shown, they were 'the linchpin of the organization'.[5] Out of 512 English and Welsh constituencies, Ramsden suggests that 352 had a qualified agent in 1937, and Ball claims that in 1938 'only 128 English and Welsh seats lacked a certificated agent', which would place the number that had one at 384.[6] The agent (usually male) would often have paid assistance, such as a full-time woman organizer and a typist or office clerk.[7] The agent would normally have a car or, if not, a travel allowance. Although employed and paid by constituency associations, and not employees of Central Office, agents were expected to have passed the party's rigorous examination and qualification system (unless they were among the diminishing number who qualified by seniority alone), the introduction of which had been a hard-fought victory for party modernizers in the 1920s.[8] They also had their own professional body, the National Society of Conservative and Unionist Agents (NSCUA). Their functions included running election campaigns, organizing meetings, presiding over campaigning and fund-raising, and coordinating and encouraging party activists. They also liaised with other organizations, and with the local Conservative clubs. A working week of up to 65 hours was far from unusual, but they were quite well paid, with salaries averaging around £400 a year plus expenses.[9] Financial commitments of this magnitude might well leave Conservative associations in fear of bankruptcy if, as expected, war led to a significant fall in income; and so from early 1939 onwards, some associations were planning redundancies should war break out.[10]

Speculation became reality on 3 September 1939. Many agents who had previously served in the forces were reservists who were rapidly recalled to the colours and had little choice but to go.[11] Four of Birmingham Unionist association's eleven constituency agents were called up immediately. Even so, this still left the association with a large number of clerical and other staff. So the chief agent, fearing the financial consequences of having so many staff at a time when party politics appeared to be of little importance, arranged for the remaining seven—along with a junior organizer and nine typists—to transfer

[5] Ball, 'Local Conservatism', 281.
[6] Ramsden, *Age of Balfour and Baldwin*, 239; Ball, 'Local Conservatism', 284.
[7] See e.g. Reigate CA papers, 353/3/2/3, emergency committee 22 Mar. 1945, with agent reminiscing about situation prior to 1935 general election.
[8] Ramsden, *Age of Balfour and Baldwin*, 238–9.
[9] Henley CA papers, S. Oxon. Con. I/3, executive committee 26 Jan. 1938; Ramsden, *Age of Balfour and Baldwin*, 240; see also Ball, 'Local Conservatism', 282.
[10] See e.g. Chelmsford CA papers, D/Z 96/7, executive committee 29 Mar. 1939; East Norfolk CA papers, SO 92/1, joint executive committee 29 Apr. 1939.
[11] Ball, 'Local Conservatism', 279–80.

en bloc to the Food Control office, and a further four typists and the caretaker to go to the Fuel Control office. Shortly afterwards, the chief agent himself went to work for the Fuel Controller, leaving just the association secretary, R. G. Hewins, and a single typist to do all the association's work.[12] Chichester CA (Sussex) encouraged its agent, Mr Ablewhite, to seek alternative employment, despite a pre-war decision to retain him in the event of war.[13]

Hacking's first letter to associations, on 6 September, made no specific reference to agents, and certainly did not encourage their retention.[14] However, Central Office's rapid realization that the party machine must be kept intact meant that Hacking's next communication, on 12 September, urged associations explicitly to retain them wherever possible.[15] Meanwhile, Topping—the agency's chief advocate and supporter in Central Office—worked hard to bolster agents' resistance to CAs' efforts to dismiss or downgrade them.[16] The NSCUA continued to publish the *Conservative Agents' Journal*, albeit on a quarterly, rather than the pre-war monthly, basis. It published long lists of useful work that agents could continue to perform, such as fund-raising, arranging meetings, and trying to keep in touch with association members; helping the Ministry of Information; acting as a contact point between MPs and their constituents; helping convey the views of farmers; establishing information bureaux and wartime savings groups; keeping a close eye on Communist activities; and cooperating with war emergency measures and other organizations such as Rotary Clubs and the Red Cross.[17] In Birmingham, there was a prime ministerial intervention in November when Chamberlain (MP for the city's Edgbaston constituency) told the chief agent to return to work for the association after the death of Hewins.[18]

Some associations began to take a softer line towards their staff thanks to one or more of Central Office advice, MP or candidate pressure, or an awareness that opponents remained locally active. Many continued to employ their agent, but encouraged him or her to look for other work, on the understanding that if such work was taken he or she would continue to have some oversight of constituency business; in return, the association would make up any shortfall in pay.[19] Chichester revised its earlier decision about Ablewhite—keeping him on, at two-thirds his pre-war salary of £600—on the advice of its MP, although ultimately the army settled the matter by recalling him to the colours in

[12] Birmingham CA papers, uncat., officers' subcommittee 19 Sept., 12 Nov. 1939.
[13] Chichester CA papers, CO/1CH/Add. MS 12,088, finance subcommittee 19 Jan. 1939; emergency general purposes and finance committee 5 Sept. 1939.
[14] CCO 500/1/9, Hacking circular to associations, 6 Sept. 1939.
[15] Ibid., Hacking circular to associations, 12 Sept. 1939; Ramsden to CA chairmen, 23 Sept. 1939; Hacking to CA and women's chairmen, 26 Oct. 1939.
[16] See e.g. ibid., Topping to agents, 6 Oct. 1939; Topping to agents and women organizers, 13 Nov. 1939; also Maxse to agents 14 June 1940.
[17] *Conservative Agents' Journal*, July 1940.
[18] Birmingham CA papers, uncat., officers' subcommittee 19 Sept., 12 Nov. 1939.
[19] See e.g. Hertford CA papers, Acc. 3258/unclassified, executive committee 25 Nov. 1939.

February 1940.[20] Clitheroe (Lancashire) was told in no uncertain terms by its MP, Sir William Brass, that it must retain the agent to help him deal with constituents' wartime problems and to keep him informed of local opinion in the constituency, although when Roger Conant in Bewdley (Worcestershire) tried a similar argument, he received short shrift, his association feeling that 'transport restrictions and other war difficulties' made it impossible for an agent to function effectively.[21] In a handful of cases, such as Flintshire, area bodies offered subsidies conditional on the continued employment of an agent, which helped to force matters, but such assistance could only be afforded in a limited number of cases.[22] Some associations, however, were not to be moved. North Cornwall CA, meeting on 11 September 1939, reiterated its pre-war decision to give the agent and woman organizer a month's notice, and remained largely inert until it appointed a new agent in May 1945.[23] Ealing, which was to prove more active, nonetheless gave its agent three months' notice at the outbreak of war, although it did fulfil its promise to take him back at the end of the conflict.[24] And decisions made in the early months of the war to retain agents could later be reversed when it became clear that there was, in the event, little for the agent to do.[25] It was not solely the decision of the associations as to whether their agents should stay or go, of course. The agents themselves were often keen to do something more directly related to the war effort. For example, Mr Hicks, the agent for Llandaff and Barry, was kept on at the start of the war, but was desperate to secure war-related employment, finally being appointed as the divisional salvage officer for the Ministry of Food in early 1941.[26] The state, for its part, was quick to make the decision for some of those concerned, and there was no protection for agents from the call-up for military or other service.[27]

The result was that, by early spring 1940, many Conservative agents had left. Once the war intensified that May, there would be a further cull, despite the increasingly vain urgings of Central Office officials.[28] Many maintained a relationship with their constituency body, some a close one. The agent for

---

[20] Chichester CA papers, CO/1CH/Add. MS 12,088, emergency general purposes and finance committee 12 Sept. 1939, general purposes and finance committee 12 Feb. 1940.

[21] Clitheroe CA papers, DDX 800/1/3, executive committee 21 Sept., 16 Oct. 1939; Bewdley CA papers, BA 956/8, officers' meeting 29 Mar. 1940.

[22] Flintshire CA papers, D/DM/307/4, management committee 11 Sept. 1939, executive committee 25 Nov. 1939, management committee 11 Apr. 1942, annual general meeting 29 Sept. 1945; City of Cardiff CA records 26, Llandaff and Barry CA special finance committee 2 Oct. 1939.

[23] North Cornwall CA papers, DDX 381/5, special finance and general purposes committee 28 Aug. 1939, executive committee 11 Sept. 1939, 2 June 1945.

[24] Ealing CA papers, Acc. 1338/2, executive committee 30 Sept. 1939, 2 Mar. 1945, council meeting 1 June 1945.

[25] See e.g. Crookshank papers, MSS Eng. Hist. d. 360, diary 29 June 1940.

[26] City of Cardiff CA records 26, Llandaff and Barry CA finance committee 29 Jan. 1941.

[27] See e.g. East Norfolk CA papers, SO 92/1, joint executive committee 24 Feb. 1940.

[28] See e.g. CCO 500/1/9, Maxse to agents 14 June 1940.

York, E. Bland, moved from part-time to full-time civil defence work in 1941; this meant that the association office was closed for much of the time, but he continued to supervise the association's business, with the help of the honorary secretary, Councillor Wright.[29] Ipswich CA agreed in October 1939 to pay off its agent, George Sisam, with three months' salary. However, it also agreed that Sisam would continue to receive a retainer of £100 a year, and that—given that the party's offices were closed down—association business should be conducted from his house. Although the association showed little activity during the war, it clearly maintained a close relationship with Sisam, and reappointed him as its full-time agent in May 1945.[30]

Even when they were in the armed forces, some agents—if stationed on home territory—could continue to oversee their association's affairs. In Warwick and Leamington, Gibbs served in the army throughout the war, but he was stationed in Britain, in the pay corps. As the war progressed, he moved closer and closer to his home base, ending up in Kidderminster, about 35 miles west of Warwick, which meant that he could spend his periods of leave in the constituency performing his agent's duties.[31] This is not to claim that Conservative claims of the wartime sacrifices of their agents were mythological, of course: among others, E. C. Kennedy and H. J. Murray, the agents for Aylesbury (Buckinghamshire) and Plymouth Drake respectively, were killed in action in 1940–1, while R. J. Willey, the agent for Houghton-le-Spring (Co. Durham), was a prisoner of war.[32] Nor is it to impugn for a moment the contribution to the war effort made by people like Gibb. Nonetheless, it is worth bearing in mind that service in the army, for all that it represented in terms of a contribution to the war effort and personal sacrifice, was not necessarily as heroic, nor as distinct from service on the home front, as it might initially seem. A few agents, on the other hand, found the allure of a new career too much, and turned their backs on agency altogether. The agent for Middleton and Prestwich (Lancashire) left permanently in September 1940, having been appointed as personnel and welfare manager by a local engineering firm.[33] In 1941, the agent for Peckham (London) resigned, giving up political work in order to take up a job with an insurance company, while in 1942 the agent for Clitheroe became a factory welfare officer.[34]

[29] York CA papers, Acc. 156/53/121, annual report for 1941;/ 123, for 1942; 156/22, annual general meeting 7 Mar. 1942.

[30] Ipswich CA papers, GK 401/1/1, executive committee 5 Oct 1939, 14 May 1945.

[31] Avon papers, AP 11/1/14, A. J. Gibbs to Eden, 27 Apr. 1943; 16, 8 Aug. 1943; 26, 17 Jan. 1945.

[32] National Union papers, NUA 4/2, card 148, NUEC report to NUCC 4 Apr. 1940; card 149, 27 Mar. 1941.

[33] Middleton and Prestwich CA papers, PLC 1/2, finance and general purposes committee 19 Sept. 1940.

[34] Clapham CA papers, vol. 5, microfilm 546, Metropolitan Association of Conservative and Unionist Agents, executive committee 2 July 1941; Clitheroe CA papers, DDX 800/1/3, executive committee 4 Mar. 1942.

The war placed severe obstacles in the path even of those Conservative agents who remained thoroughly committed to the political life, however. Restrictions on travel (especially in coastal areas), petrol shortages, the requisitioning of association offices by the military and civil authorities, and a lack of meeting halls all inhibited the activity of even the keenest, most stickable agents. Petrol rationing was a particular obstacle. It was introduced shortly after the outbreak of war and tightened progressively thereafter, culminating in the withdrawal of the basic ration from private motorists in July 1942.[35] Agents continued to be eligible for small amounts, but they were woefully inadequate. In September 1940, the agent for Fylde (Lancashire) CA, which had 90 branches spread across over 100,000 acres, estimated that his normal political activities required him to cover 550–660 miles a month, which would use around 22 gallons. The failure to get sufficient supplies led in part to the association suspending most of its activities and laying the car up over the winter of 1940–1.[36] When the agent once again began to use the car in spring 1941, his new, lower, ration enabled him to travel only about 200 miles a month; and this was then further reduced that May.[37] This was not an isolated example. By 1943, petrol shortages were severely hampering the work of the agent in the Hertford division.[38] By late 1944, the agent for Chichester was calculating that the monthly ration of seven gallons allowed to political agents was only enough to drive about 140 miles—totally inadequate for serious purposes in a large county division.[39] Another problem was 'the great increase in prices for all car accessories and repairs' since the outbreak of war.[40] Many associations' cars were sold soon after the outbreak of war, disposed of once the war intensified in mid-1940, or laid up off the road pending the end of the war.[41] Just as Brian Harrison was right to suggest that transport improvements, by 'enlarg[ing] what was regarded as the viable community', were a key element in the development of British politics in the twentieth century, so the sudden and quite drastic impact of the war upon transport had a significant and deleterious effect on the ability of political parties to organize on their accustomed scale.[42] And, in this context, the disappearance of an agent—often the key individual holding a Conservative association's

[35] D. J. Payton-Smith, *Oil: A Study of War-Time Policy and Administration* (1971), 288–93.

[36] Fylde CA papers, DDX 1202/3/7, J. R. Almond to Divisional Petroleum Officer, Manchester, 2 Sept., 7 Nov. 1940.

[37] Ibid., Almond to B. A. Warner (Divisional Petroleum Officer, Manchester), 2 Apr. 1941; Warner to Almond, 23 May 1941.

[38] Hertford CA papers, Acc. 3258/unclassified, annual report 1943 to annual general meeting 6 May 1944.

[39] Chichester CA papers, CO/1CH/Add. MS 12,088, organization subcommittee 20 Nov. 1944.

[40] Stafford CA papers, D1289/1/3, finance committee 19 May 1942.

[41] West Fife UA papers, MS 36593, annual general meeting 19 Mar. 1940; Stone CA papers, D1289/1/12, women's divisional committee 30 Sept. 1940; Maidstone CA papers, U1634/A3/1/2, emergency subcommittee 16 Oct. 1939; U1634/A3/1/3, emergency subcommittee 5 May 1945.

[42] B. Harrison, *The Transformation of British Politics, 1860–1995* (Oxford, 1996), 120.

different branches together, especially in rural constituencies—had a significant impact.[43] Meanwhile, the extensive wartime movement of population—a civilian population of 48 million recorded around 60 million changes of address during the conflict—meant that even full-time agents who remained in post found their areas increasingly alien and difficult to reach politically, even if not geographically.[44]

A number of expedients were employed to combat the increasing shortage of agents. One was grouping (first employed in the 1920s), whereby a number of neighbouring constituencies were placed under the control of a single qualified agent or woman organizer. This was employed in parts of London and the Midlands, with some positive results.[45] In Birmingham, the city association formed its eleven constituencies into five groups—each with its own paid organizer—from May 1941 onwards.[46] Secondly, associations could share their agent with a neighbouring constituency. In October 1939, the organizing secretary in Glasgow Camlachie was deputed to cover the work of his counterpart in neighbouring Bridgeton, who had gone on military service.[47] West Dorset shared its agent, A. G. Edwards, with North Dorset for a year until September 1940, when North ended the agreement on cost grounds; he was later shared with Salisbury (Wiltshire) from September 1942 until his departure for a Buckinghamshire agency in April 1944.[48] A third option was to employ a lesser-qualified individual. In April 1941, for example, Bristol West CA appointed the secretary of its women's branch as acting agent and secretary while the agent was serving in the army.[49] Agents' wives took over in Tynemouth and Bury, while in Chichester, Ablewhite's daughter took over until she herself joined the Land Army.[50] Lay constituency officials could also take on some of the burden. When he became chairman of the party in October 1944, Assheton found that there was almost always someone, usually an officer or group of officers, keeping even the most

---

[43] A. H. Birch, *Small-Town Politics: A Study of Political Life in Glossop* (Oxford, 1959), 47.

[44] I. C. B. Dear (ed.), *The Oxford Companion to World War II* (rev. edn., Oxford, 2001), 885; Titmuss, *Problems of Social Policy*, 101; and see e.g. Winchester CA papers, 73M86W/5, finance and general purposes committee 5 Nov. 1945.

[45] National Union papers, NUA 4/2, Card 148, NUEC report to NUCC 4 Apr., 2 Oct. 1940; *Conservative Agents' Journal*, Apr. 1940.

[46] Birmingham CA papers, uncat., officers' subcommittee 26 May 1941.

[47] Glasgow UA papers, Acc. 10424/74, executive committee 9 Oct. 1939.

[48] West Dorset CA papers, D399/3/1, meeting of officers 17 Oct. 1939, war emergency executive committee 27 Sept. 1940; 3/2, war emergency executive committee 25 Sept. 1942; executive committee 25 Mar 1944; 4/1, finance committee 29 Apr. 1944; and see also e.g. East Norfolk CA papers, SO 92/1, joint executive committee 24 Feb. 1940, 13 Jan. 1945; Northampton CA papers, NCCA 29, annual report Mar. 1944.

[49] Bristol West CA papers, 38036/BW/2(b), annual general meeting 4 Apr. 1941.

[50] Tynemouth CA papers, Acc. 1633/2, executive committee 18 July 1941, Acc. 1633/6/1, finance committee 6 Nov. 1943; Acc. 1633/2, special executive committee 4 May 1945; Bury CA papers, GCP/C/1/3, executive committee 19 Aug. 1942; GCP/D/2/1, women's CA annual report, 26 Mar. 1945; Chichester CA papers, CO/1CH/Add. MS 12,088, general purposes and finance committee 12 Feb. 1940, 24 Sept. 1945.

inert associations going to some extent.[51] However, lay officials, unless middle-aged or older, were themselves liable to be called up. In Winchester, for example, the agent, H. T. Worlock, joined the army soon after the start of the war.[52] But the chairman, vice-chairman, and secretary also served, in the War Office, Royal Navy, and RAF respectively; and the women's branch secretary and the CA clerk were also called up for national service. Although the Treasurer, General A. J. F. Eden, and a Mrs Murray managed to keep things ticking over, they had no clerical help and were desperate, by early 1945, to get professional assistance.[53]

Finally, of course, the work could simply go undone. The loss of the agent could be part cause, and part effect, of closure for the duration. In Denbigh (North Wales) the agent joined the RAF on the outbreak of war; there were then no recorded meetings of the association or its committees until 21 June 1945, when he was welcomed back to the constituency after his war service.[54] In West Fife, the association declared its intention of carrying on as best it could in October 1939, but felt it had no alternative but to dismiss its organizing secretary (as agents were known in Scotland); the result, perhaps unsurprisingly, was that there was virtually no activity for years to come.[55]

Statistical precision is difficult to achieve, but the available figures are very suggestive. By June 1940, 193 agents and 69 women organizers were in the forces or on other forms of national service, and by March 1941, these figures had risen to 275 and 76 respectively.[56] By any standards, such levels of engagement with the war effort had a major impact on the Conservative party's professional organization in the constituencies. In Manchester, a comprehensive reorganization plan in March 1939 had left all ten constituencies with a full-time agent, but on the outbreak of war, three were called up, and another two volunteered, for military service.[57] The party's Scottish western divisional council covered 38 constituencies, 28 of which had employed organizing secretaries at the outbreak of war, but by June 1941, only 9 remained in full-time employment with their associations, and by June 1944 it was reckoned that no more than 13 of the pre-war 28 would be working for their associations by the end of the war.[58] Even so, it is important not to go too far: in London, towards the end of the Blitz in March 1941, there were still 15 full-time and 8 part-time agents

    [51] Addison, *Road to 1945*, 259.
    [52] Winchester CA papers, 73M86W/52, women's branch annual report for 1939 (Feb. 1940).
    [53] Ibid., 73M86W/5, Eden to branch officials, 12 Sept. 1939; finance and general purposes committee 12 June 1945; central executive council 1 Dec. 1945.
    [54] Denbigh CA papers, DD/DM/80/6, finance and general purposes committee 21 June 1945.
    [55] West Fife UA papers, MS 36593, central council 23 Oct. 1939, annual general meeting 19 Mar. 1940, annual general meeting 11 Mar. 1947.
    [56] Chamberlain papers, NC 8/21/19, Topping to Hacking, 26 June 1940; National Union papers, NUA 4/2, card 149, 27 Mar. 1941.
    [57] Derby papers, 920DER(17)/16/4, Manchester CUA, report of the emergency committee to the annual meeting, 26 Apr. 1940.
    [58] Scottish Conservative and Unionist association papers, Acc. 10424/27(viii), western divisional council, annual reports for years ending 30 June 1941, 30 June 1944.

in employment, while at that time even the party's weak Northern area still had 7 agents between its 34 associations.[59] But the Eastern area was hit very hard, reflecting its position close to the front line: by January 1945 there were only 5 agents still working in the area; and even by mid-April, there were only 10, plus 3 women organizers.[60]

The attenuation of the pre-war agency was a problem, but Topping also saw it as an opportunity. He had long believed that Conservative agents were poorly distributed, with the best tending to be employed, not by financially hard-pressed CAs in the marginal seats where they were most needed, but by the wealthiest associations, which could afford to pay the most generous salaries, in utterly safe seats. He told Hacking as early as November 1939 that 'a central service must be established' for the employment of agents and women organizers, so that the party could 'place in the key constituencies those men and women who possess the best qualifications, and remove the present anomalies which permit of the best salaries being paid in Divisions with majorities so large that a mere novice could conduct an election campaign'.[61] By early 1941, he believed that his chance had come. With no prospect of an early end to the war, reform could not be opposed on the grounds of potential electoral disruption. At the same time, the weakness and/or inactivity of many associations, for which local autonomy was 'a powerful totem', and the absence of so many agents on war duty, meant that key elements of possible resistance were weakened significantly.[62] Topping also believed that Churchill's preoccupation with the war effort would prevent him from being a major obstacle. More altruistically, Topping also claimed that pooling agents under a Central Employment Board run by Central Office would ensure that those who had gone to war could be assured of re-employment after they were demobilized.[63]

If ever there was a time to launch a campaign to centralize the agency, therefore, this seemed to be it. At first, Topping seemed to be making progress. In January 1941, the NSCUA council agreed to elect a war emergency council to consider his plans, and although the latter did not commit itself fully, it did not rule the scheme out.[64] That November, the NUEC reacted with similar caution, but agreed to appoint a committee to confer with NSCUA representatives.[65]

[59] Clapham CA papers, vol. 5, microfilm 546, Metropolitan Association of Conservative and Unionist Agents, executive committee 6 Mar. 1941; Northern area Conservative council papers, NRO 3303/2, annual report for 1940 to annual meeting 3 May 1941; annual report for 1941 to annual meeting 18 Apr. 1942.

[60] Eastern area Conservative party papers, ARE 7/1/8, annual report to annual meeting 18 Apr. 1945.

[61] CCO 4/1/86, Topping to Hacking, 14 Nov. 1939.

[62] Ball, 'Local Conservatism', 262.

[63] National Union papers, NUA 6/2/1, memo, 'Draft post-war scheme for the employment of agents, 1942', n.d.; NSCUA papers, Acc. 485/5, war emergency committee 26 Mar. 1941.

[64] NSCUA papers, council meeting 23 Jan. 1941, war emergency committee 19 Sept. 1941.

[65] National Union papers, NUA 4/1, card 62, NUEC 12 Nov. 1941.

Ultimately, in February 1942, it was agreed to place the issue before NSCUA branches, and that area chairmen should also be consulted.[66] But resistance emerged. Many people objected to change taking place while agents were away on active service. There was also considerable hostility towards centralization from constituency associations jealous of their autonomy. The agents themselves expressed concern about the prospect of being moved around the country on the say-so of Central Office. The NSCUA area branches offered very mixed views, and in May 1942 its national council voted against the scheme.[67] That July, the women organizers' society, and then a well-attended meeting of the 1922 Committee, also failed to come out in their favour, and most of the constituency associations that discussed the proposals were also hostile.[68] The area meetings that were called, typically comprising CA chairmen in the area, came up with mixed responses, but there was certainly no groundswell of opinion in favour: it was perhaps to be expected that the party's two weakest areas, Northern and Wales, were the most supportive.[69] The scheme was now dead. Although Topping still believed that 'time would prove him right', he was a beaten man.[70] On 11 November 1942, the NUEC finally rejected his proposals, although it did agree to look into the whole question of party finance.[71] Even an attempt to pool some limited resources to help key constituencies came to nothing, and the post-war Maxwell-Fyfe report, harbinger in other areas of significant organizational change, did not revive the agency scheme.[72] Only the early 1970s would see the party actually attempt to implement something like it, and then with disappointing results that tended retrospectively to vindicate the views of Topping's critics.[73]

The failure of Topping's scheme meant that, as the party began to revive from early 1944 onwards, the agency was recognizably similar in form to that which had prevailed in the later 1930s. In one way, though, this represented an achievement for Topping, because there remained considerable stress on the maintenance of professional standards. This was no mean feat. The agents' training scheme had been suspended at the outbreak of war and therefore there

---

[66] NSCUA papers, Acc. 485/5, war emergency committee 24 Feb. 1942.

[67] Ibid., council meeting 29 May 1942.

[68] CCO 170/2/1/3, National Society of Conservative and Unionist Woman Organizers, meeting 17 July 1942; 1922 Committee papers, CPA 1922/4, meeting 22 July 1942; and see e.g. Maidstone CA papers, U1634/A3/1/2, special emergency subcommittee 28 July 1942; Monmouth CA records 10, finance and general purposes committee 31 Aug. 1942.

[69] National Union papers, NUA 6/2/1, memo, 'Post-war agents' scheme: summary of chairmen's reports arranged in the order in which the meetings were held', n.d. [c. Sept. 1942].

[70] NSCUA papers, Acc. 485/5, annual general meeting 2 Oct. 1942.

[71] National Union papers, NUA 4/1, card 63, NUEC 11 Nov. 1942. This was the genesis of what was to be the 1944 Proby report on party funding.

[72] NSCUA papers, Acc. 485/5, council meeting 30 Mar. 1943; National Union papers, NUA 6/2/7, Maxwell-Fyfe committee, 'Interim report', 1948; J. D. Hoffman, *The Conservative Party in Opposition, 1945–51* (1964), 93–4.

[73] J. Ramsden, *The Winds of Change: Macmillan to Heath, 1957–1975* (1996), 409–10.

were no new qualified people coming through, but for Topping, it was axiomatic that the party must avoid the situation at the end of the Great War, when large numbers of 'unqualified people' had been acting as agents.[74] Where unqualified, or partially qualified, staff were employed, it remained the expectation that their job titles and remuneration would reflect the fact, and in 1944 Topping established a Guild of Party Workers to represent, regulate, and ultimately restrict the role of, uncertificated agents and organizers.[75] Significantly, it was to be a temporary body: there was no sense that the party should seek permanently to accommodate a non-professional agency.[76] Although Central Office's search for people who had been invalided out of the forces to train as agents met little success, calls for the employment of unqualified staff continued to be rejected; and, after the war, it was still expected that agents would be fully qualified.[77]

The push to release agents had begun earlier in 1944, in part as a response to the by-election defeat at West Derbyshire, but had stalled as military matters once again took Churchill's full attention. On 28 June, the war cabinet discussed the possibility of seeking the temporary release from the forces of party agents for constituencies in which by-elections were pending, but decided not to act.[78] With the end of the war apparently in sight, the release of *all* agents now seemed more important than the issue of *ad hoc* releases for by-elections. But this was a bigger issue to tackle, and progress was slow.

It was clear, though, that the Conservatives had much to gain from making the effort. In October 1944, the party had 163 agents and 25 women organizers serving in the forces, and 53 agents and women organizers on other forms of national service, a total of 216 agents and 76 women organizers.[79] Topping therefore joined forces with the chief agents of the Labour, Liberal, and Liberal National parties to impress upon government the need for agents to be released as soon as possible.[80] The war cabinet referred the issue to Bevin, the minister responsible, and on 22 December he chaired a meeting of ministers, civil servants, and party officials on the matter.[81] They agreed that, 'subject to overriding military considerations', people who had been agents prior to joining the forces should be released early, and that 'key staff' of headquarters and regional

[74] Birmingham CA papers, uncat., management committee 20 Apr. 1945; CCO 170/2/1/3, National Society of Conservative and Unionist Woman Organizers, meeting 17 July 1942.
[75] See e.g. Clapham CA papers, vol. 5, microfilm 546, Metropolitan Association of Conservative and Unionist Agents, executive committee 26 Apr 1940; CCO 500/1/11, report of Central Office staff conference, 23 Apr. 1944.
[76] NSCUA papers, Acc. 485/5, war emergency committee 21 Sept. 1944.
[77] National Union papers, NUA 4/1, NUEC 27 July 1944; Ramsden, *Age of Churchill and Eden*, 71; CCO 170/1/1/2, Conservative party central women's advisory committee 26 July 1944; and see e.g. Bodmin CA papers, DDX 385/1, executive committee 12 Jan. 1946.
[78] Cabinet papers, CAB 65/41/83(44), war cabinet conclusions 28 June 1944.
[79] CCO 4/2/2, untitled memo, n.d. [*c*. Oct. 1944].
[80] Ibid., Topping to G. R. Shepherd (Labour party), Sir R. Evans (Liberal National party), and Raymond Jones (Liberal party), 25 Oct. 1944.
[81] Cabinet papers, CAB 65/41/164(44), war cabinet conclusions 11 Dec. 1944.

organization should be treated similarly. There would be no such favours for people who had not formerly been agents but had now been appointed as such, or for former agents who were now required for headquarters or regional work. It was felt that releases from industry 'would be easier to arrange': the Ministry of Labour and National Service (MLNS) would deal with such cases on their merits. It would be for the respective party headquarters to apply for agents to be released. Agents and others who were released and then did not act in that capacity would be recalled to the forces. Finally, it was accepted that 'Cabinet authority w[ould] be necessary before releases c[ould] begin'.[82] The government was slow to respond, but Conservative pressure in parliament grew, with Hacking playing a leading role, and finally, on 29 January 1945, the war cabinet accepted the decisions of the 22 December meeting.[83] Even now, though, the MLNS and forces ministries were sometimes slow to act. Agents had often attained important positions in military or civil bodies.[84] It must have seemed perverse to, say, the Ministry of Food that it was losing some of its ablest administrators to party politics at a time when it was still in urgent need of their services in the face of serious ongoing problems.

By spring 1945, large numbers of Conservative agents were starting to return; ultimately, 187 would be released temporarily from the forces or war work.[85] If an association had appealed for its agent's release in January or February, he or she was usually back by May.[86] On 10 May 1945, Assheton could tell the NUEC that 65 agents had been released from the forces in the last month alone.[87] By April 1945, meanwhile, Birmingham had full-time organizers in all twelve of the divisions covered by the city's Unionist association, although only six were qualified agents, one being partly trained and five being 'young trainees'.[88] However, things were still not going as smoothly as they might. Releases remained slow in many cases, and were only speeded up when Churchill intervened directly with Bevin in May.[89]

Associations that had no continuing commitment to an individual began to advertise for agents in the summer and autumn of 1944.[90] By February 1945,

[82] CCO 4/2/2, notes of meeting to consider release of candidates etc. from the forces, 22 Dec. 1944.

[83] *HC Deb*, 5th ser., vol. 407, cols. 343–4, 18 Jan. 1945; col. 945, 25 Jan. 1945; cols. 1599–601, Bevin, 1 Feb. 1945; Cabinet papers, CAB 65/49/12(45), war cabinet conclusions 29 Jan. 1945.

[84] See e.g. Ealing CA papers, Acc. 1338/2, executive committee 27 Nov. 1939, 17 Nov. 1944, 2 Mar., 11 May 1945; council meeting 1 June 1945; Fylde CA papers, DDX 1202/1/1, emergency committee 3 Oct. 1939, 16, 28 Apr. 1945.

[85] Ramsden, *Age of Churchill and Eden*, 71.

[86] See e.g. Newbury CA papers, D/EX 409/3, finance and general purposes committee 26 Feb., 10 May 1945; Gravesend CA papers, U1795/AD3/1, women's advisory council 11 May 1945; Maidstone CA papers, U1634/A3/1/3, emergency subcommittee 9 Dec. 1944, 7 Apr. 1945.

[87] National Union papers, NUA 4/1, NUEC 10 May 1945.

[88] Birmingham CA papers, uncat., management committee 20 Apr. 1945, officers' subcommittee 18 July 1945.

[89] Chartwell papers, CHAR 2/545, T. L. Rowan to Churchill, 9 May 1945.

[90] See e.g. *Conservative Agents' Journal*, July, Oct. 1944.

the area organizer for the South-West was able to report that eight of the area's associations had appointed new agents, while three more were in the process of doing so.[91] But even where associations were keen to make appointments, they often faced great difficulty. As stated above, the pool of qualified agents was shrinking: as the chairman of Salisbury CA put it in frustration at their failure to find an agent in 1944, the demand for agents 'far exceed[ed] a very limited supply'.[92] Although by early 1945 larger numbers of people were applying for organizing posts, it was by no means unusual for an association to be unable to appoint an agent ahead of the 1945 election, or to appoint from a thin field only to discover that their appointees were incompetent.[93]

In many cases, the former agent simply returned to duty. In April 1944, Central Office had laid down that, where an agent had been promised reinstatement, it must be given unless there were 'insurmountable difficulties': conversely, any agent receiving a retainer from a CA should not try to leave that association before the next general election.[94] When dormant associations began to be revived from September 1944 onwards, therefore, former agents were contacted to see whether they wished to return, and in some cases the response was a swift and straightforward affirmative.[95] In Kirkcaldy Burghs, where the constituency association had remained inactive for most of the war, the pre-war organizing secretary, David Paxton, returned to work in March 1945 and was soon galvanizing the organization.[96] In associations that had remained more active, similarly, the former agent often returned to his post. In Salisbury, F. J. Tucker, who had joined the army at the end of 1939, finally returned to work on 14 May 1945, although whether he knew that his association had been seeking full-time agents during his absence in Italy, where he had been wounded in action, is unclear.[97] However, many expected a substantial increase in their pay: in Warwick and Leamington, for example, Gibbs's salary was increased from the pre-war £500 to £750, and that of the woman organizer from £250 to £375.[98] Birmingham's chief agent told the city's association that, unless pay increased significantly after the war, the agency as a profession would die; this helped secure increases in the pay of constituency agents from £400 to £500 a year, while his own remuneration also rose to well over £1,000.[99] But in other cases,

[91] Western provincial area council papers, ARE 11/7/3, annual report to annual meeting 9 Feb. 1945.
[92] Salisbury CA papers, 2639/1, annual general meeting 22 Apr. 1944.
[93] Maidstone CA papers, U1634/A3/1/3, special emergency subcommittee 17 Feb. 1945; Middleton and Prestwich CA papers, PLC 1/3, finance and general purposes committee 1 June 1945; Mitchell, *Election '45*, 50.
[94] CCO 500/1/12, report of staff conference, 2–3 Apr. 1944.
[95] Louth CA papers, Misc. dep. 250/1, reorganization committee 7 Dec. 1944.
[96] Kirkcaldy Burghs UA papers, MS 36621, executive committee 15 Mar. 1945.
[97] Salisbury CA papers, 2639/1, annual general meeting 27 Apr. 1940; 2639/13, finance and general purposes committee 15 Jan. 1946.
[98] Warwick and Leamington CA papers, CR1392, finance committee 3 Nov. 1945.
[99] Birmingham CA papers, uncat., officers' subcommittee 31 Mar. 1944, 18 July 1945.

the previous agent did not return.[100] And some returning agents did not remain long with their old associations.[101]

As seen above, after their general election defeat the Conservatives were to make great play of the wartime attenuation of their agency. But far less concern was expressed before the election results were declared than afterwards. Central Office area agents' reports on the election made *prior* to the declaration of the results contained very little adverse comment on the subject of agents, beyond occasional derogatory references to individuals.[102] Even in the immediate aftermath of the election defeat, when the area agent for Yorkshire, Brigadier Rawcliffe, identified ten reasons for the Conservative defeat, he made no reference to agents at all, while the East Midlands area agent went so far as to say that he '[could] not speak too highly of the way the Agents ha[d] carried on, particularly . . . the untrained ones. . . . I have had no trouble at all with any of them.'[103] More and better agents in 1944–5 might have made some difference: it was widely agreed, for example, that the electoral register compiled in 1945 was far from perfect, and experienced Conservative agents might have been able to do more to challenge their validity; a stronger agency would almost certainly have secured better registration of business votes.[104] But the latter were only significant in a handful of constituencies, and anyway the Conservatives did not lose the 1945 general election because of the state of the register.

After the war, recovery was not slow to come. By December 1945, every constituency but four in the party's Eastern area (which had had only five agents in post at the start of the year) had a full-time, certificated agent, and, of the four, two had uncertificated full-timers and the remaining two were in the process of making appointments.[105] By early 1946, attempts to recruit agents were eliciting significant interest. Thirty-eight applications were received for the agency at Harborough (Leicestershire), for example.[106] However, shortages of agents did persist into 1946 in some places, with the Northern area and Yorkshire both reporting difficulties: at the end of 1945, 15 of the 34 Northern associations were still without an agent.[107]

---

[100] Henley CA papers, S. Oxon. Con. I/3, finance and general purposes committee 16 Sept. 1939, finance and general purposes committee 13 Feb. 1945, 6 Apr. 1945.

[101] See e.g. Bury CA papers, GCP/C/1/3, executive committee 22 May 1945, emergency committee 27 Aug. 1945; Newbury CA papers, D/EX 409/3, finance and general purposes committee 2 Feb. 1946.

[102] CCO 4/2/61, Major H. H. Little to Topping, 28 June 1945.

[103] Ibid., Brigadier Rawcliffe to Topping, 3 Aug. 1945; J. W. Lancaster to Topping, 17 July 1945.

[104] McCallum and Readman, *British General Election of 1945*, 30–1; Hutchison, *Scottish Politics*, 71.

[105] Eastern area Conservative party papers, ARE 7/1/8, finance meeting 12 Dec. 1945.

[106] Harborough CA papers, DE 1170/4, executive committee 23 Mar. 1946.

[107] Northern area Conservative council papers, NRO 3303/7, annual report for 1945 to annual meeting 4 May 1946; Yorkshire provincial area council papers, WYL 1856/1/3, half-yearly report of executive committee to area council, 22 Sept. 1945.

The effects of the war upon Conservative agency were significant, but essentially transient. Without a doubt, the agency was hit hard by the war. There was always, however, a sense that—finances permitting—associations would once again employ full-time agents and organizers after the war and, ultimately, associations were often more, rather than less, likely to do so after 1945 than they had been in the later 1930s. But the defeat of Topping's plans for centralization meant that, in many ways, the post-war agency was very similar in form to that of the 1930s, not least in meaning that associations in marginal seats were often much less well organized than completely safe ones.[108] But if that was a defeat for Topping, his legacy was the maintenance, despite the pressures of war, of a professional standard for agents, rigorously enforced. It was significant that the NSCUA was quick to declare, at its first post-election meeting, that members of what was now known as the Guild of Conservative Workers should be encouraged to take the agents' examination as soon as possible; and it was also partly to ensure the maintenance of professional standards that the NSCUA and the NSCUWO were merged after the war, and the position of women organizers generally improved.[109] The Maxwell-Fyfe report, while leaving the issue of central employment closed, would defend, and reinforce, the principle of a professional agency, and seek to improve the lot of agents more generally; and in post-war Britain, the Conservatives would continue to have far more full-time agents than their rivals.[110]

LABOUR

Labour's agency was relatively weak in 1939, but the fact that it had full-time agents in just under a fifth of constituencies meant that its agents were far from an irrelevance to the party's wartime experience. The appointment of full-time constituency agents had been an intended outcome of the new party constitution adopted by Labour in 1918, but over the next two decades the party's attempts to establish a full-time agency had achieved only mixed results. The number of agents had not expanded as far as had been hoped: it had peaked at 189 in 1928, and in the eighteen months to May 1939 fell by 14 per cent to only 115.[111] As with the Conservatives, agents were not always located where they were most needed, some of the best working in safe seats

108 J. E. Johnson, 'From defeat to victory: the Conservative party in the constituencies, 1945–59', University of Oxford D.Phil. thesis, 2001, p. xiv.

109 NSCUA papers, Acc. 485/5, war emergency committee 12 Sept. 1945; J. Lovenduski, P. Norris, and C. Burness, 'The party and women', in Seldon and Ball (eds.), *Conservative Century*, 622; CCO 170/2/1/2, National Society of Conservative and Unionist Woman Organizers, 'Report covering period June 1939–May 1946', n.d. [May 1946].

110 National Union papers, CPA NUA 6/2/7, Maxwell-Fyfe committee, 'Interim report', 1948.

111 *LPACR* 1951, 11.

while marginals were all too often neglected. This situation could only have been changed if Transport House had had enough money to force DLPs' hands, but its grants were too small to have this effect. Furthermore, Labour had not professionalized its agency as early or as thoroughly as the Conservatives. A 1919 conference decision to introduce formal examination and certification of agents was only put into effect in 1930, and the scheme itself had shortcomings, being very much based on electoral law and the party constitution to the exclusion of wider skills more useful in agents' work.[112] Although the later 1930s saw some improvement, the Conservatives' level of professionalization had not been reached by 1939.[113]

Labour had tried to improve the terms and conditions of its agents. In 1925 a model contract was introduced, which included a recognized pay scale of between £260 and £310 a year.[114] But this scale was not revised before 1939, despite rising prices in the later 1930s. The lack of a pension scheme also rankled. A Labour party superannuation fund was introduced in January 1937, but it only covered headquarters employees, despite the protests of the National Union of Labour Organizers and Election Agents (NULOEA).[115] The NEC did put a scheme for a new Labour Agents' Superannuation Society to the 1939 party conference, but added that 'the financial liability imposed on Party funds by the Scheme outlined . . . [was] quite beyond present available resources'.[116] The conference agreed that attempts should be made to raise the required sum, but in reality there appeared little immediate prospect of establishing the fund in a context where the party as a whole was in financial crisis. Here, as in many other areas of party organization between the wars, Labour found that the solution to its problem depended upon the expenditure of money that the party lacked (see Chapter 8).

Some DLPs sought to dismiss their agents when war broke out. Seven weeks into the conflict, NULOEA reported that 37 out of the 115 agents employed by DLPs on the outbreak of war were detrimentally affected in some way or other, with 9 having been made redundant and others facing big pay cuts. In response, the NEC relaxed party rules to allow unions and candidates to increase their payments to DLPs, and itself paid modest grants to some parties, although setting its face against indiscriminate largesse.[117] NULOEA's early attention to the problem had prevented a wholesale cull taking place; its secretary, Herbert Drinkwater, was justifiably self-congratulatory.[118] By the time of the party conference in May 1940, the number of full-time agents, at 117, was actually slightly higher than it had been a year earlier.

---

[112] *LPACR* 1920, 19; *LPACR* 1930, 7–8; 'Wanted: a new crop of organizers: why and when and how', *Labour Organiser*, June 1941.
[113] *LPACR* 1936, 64; 1934, 25.   [114] *LPACR* 1921, 205–6; 1922, 175–7; 1925, 33–4.
[115] *LPACR* 1936, 56–9; 1937, 35.   [116] *LPACR* 1939, 99–101.
[117] LPNEC papers XVIII, finance and general purposes committee 14 Dec. 1939.
[118] *Labour Organiser*, Nov.–Dec. 1939.

At that very point, however, the intensification of the war threatened to disrupt the situation considerably. Matters took a definite turn for the worse from September, as the Blitz began in earnest. Naturally, London was most affected. The bombing was terrifying, and the agent for Lewisham West, H. N. Silver, fled London shortly after the air raids had started. Silver had left a card on his desk saying simply that he had gone away for a few days. He stated later that he had taken the chance, which might be 'now or never', to get his children out of the city. En route to Liverpool, he claimed, their car was bombed and machine-gunned, and he had had some kind of nervous breakdown as a result. The discovery of financial irregularities sealed his fate, and he was dismissed.[119]

This was an extreme example, but party leaders and managers realized that more needed to be done to ensure that agents were retained. The NULOEA had urged from the outset that party agents should be exempt from military service, but Transport House had decided not to press the suggestion.[120] When Bevin was appointed Minister of Labour in May 1940 there were hopes that he would help, but the efforts of headquarters officials to influence him from July 1940 onwards proved largely fruitless.[121] Ultimately, only one of the 27 Labour agents of military age in May 1940 was helped: the call-up of Harry Russell, the agent in Derby, was delayed long enough to allow him to reach 41, the age beyond which he would no longer be liable for military service.[122] Elsewhere, DLPs read the signs and started advertising for agents who were beyond military age.[123]

Nonetheless, some positive steps were taken to improve the position of Labour agents. In March 1940, leading union representatives told the party treasurer, George Lathan, that they would support the launch of the superannuation scheme (as well as an increase in affiliation fees), and the TGWU, the MFGB, the National Union of Distributive and Allied Workers (NUDAW), the National Union of Railwaymen (NUR), and the Railway Clerks' Association (RCA) were as good as their word, supporting a levy of 3*d*. a member to contribute to the start-up costs, which were estimated at £23,807.[124] Some DLPs grumbled about being asked to pay a share, but in fact 94 per cent of the £26,284 eventually raised came from the unions.[125] When the scheme was launched

[119] Lewisham West DLP papers, A89/100/9, general committee 13 Oct. 1940, executive committee 13 Oct. 1940, annual report for 1940, to annual general meeting 15 Mar. 1941, general committee 19 Jan. 1941.

[120] LPNEC papers XVIII, organization subcommittee 18 Oct. 1939.

[121] Ibid., NEC 26 June 1940; organization subcommittee 17 July, 20 Nov. 1940; executive committee of NEC 21 Aug. 1940.

[122] NULOEA papers, uncl., annual conference, Bournemouth, n.d. [May] 1940; LPNEC papers XVIII, organization subcommittee 14 Oct. 1941.

[123] *Labour Organiser*, May 1940.

[124] LPNEC papers XVIII, NEC 20 Mar. 1940; MFGB papers, MNA/NUM/1/1/39, executive committee 30 May 1941; *LPACR* 1941, 131, 36.

[125] *LPACR* 1942, 29; *Labour Organiser*, Oct. 1941; *LPACR* 1943, 48. The final total was £26,611. For DLP complaints, see e.g. Warwick and Leamington DLP papers, MSS 133/1/1/4, executive committee 9 Aug. 1941.

on 1 July 1941, it was warmly welcomed by Labour agents, all but two of whom immediately applied to join it.[126] Only the war had made it possible, especially on such a generous scale. Moves were also made to revamp the training programme. NULOEA's sixteen-page monthly, *Labour Organiser*, edited by Drinkwater, made a significant contribution, as a valuable conduit of advice and encouragement to agents and officials across Britain. Although its tone could be didactic and, at times, patronizing, it offered plenty to sustain the work of even the most hard-pressed officials; and it was a testament to its value to the party that, when Drinkwater retired in 1944, Transport House agreed to take over its publication.[127] Despite the fact that Drinkwater considered the year to May 1941 'the most difficult and anxious of the last 20 years' so far as the paper was concerned, its circulation held up remarkably well at around 1,800 a month.[128]

Despite all this, the prospects for the agency were looking rather bleak by mid-1941. The number of agents fell sharply from 103 in June 1941 to 62 in May 1942; where there had been 17 full-time agents in the 88 Midlands constituencies in 1939, there were only 7 by June 1942.[129] At a crisis meeting at Transport House in January 1942, various regional organizers expressed alarm at the decline of the agency, and the following month, partly to improve staff retention, the NEC agreed that all agents should receive a war bonus of fifteen shillings a week (£39 a year).[130]

Agents who remained in post often did valuable work. They were vital in maintaining a good relationship between an MP or candidate and their constituency and DLP. In South Shields, A. E. Gompertz was an unfailingly loyal servant to the Labour front-bencher (and, from May 1940, junior minister) Chuter Ede, arranging Ede's visits to County Durham from his Surrey home with military precision, meeting him off the train, driving him around the constituency, and fixing up meetings for him.[131] In Derby, Russell was the eyes and ears for Noel-Baker, who lived in London, regularly warning his MP of 'uneasiness and criticism of the Government', and acting as his sounding

[126] NULOEA papers, uncl., annual conference, London, 1 June 1941; *Labour Organiser*, July 1941.
[127] LPNEC papers XIX, NEC 25 June 1941; 'Wanted: a new crop of organizers: why and when and how', *Labour Organiser*, June 1941; LPNEC papers XIX, memo, 'Condition of party', n.d. [*c*.25 Mar. 1942]; NULOEA papers, uncl., executive report to aborted annual conference, London, 28 May 1944; supplementary report, n.d. [Dec. 1944].
[128] NULOEA papers, Drinkwater, 'Report of the *Labour Organiser*', 23 May 1941, 5 May 1942, 23 May 1943.
[129] Ibid., annual conference, London, 1 June 1941; LPNEC papers XIX, memo, 'The Midland counties and proposals for the establishment of regional councils of the Labour party therein', 30 June 1942.
[130] LPNEC papers XIX, 'Notes on the discussion at the individual membership consultation between subcommittees of the National Executive and members of the organizing staff', 19 Jan. 1942; adjustments board 3 Feb. 1942.
[131] See Chuter-Ede papers, Add. 59690–59701, diaries 1941–5, *passim*.

board.[132] Agents also found that the war brought new responsibilities and roles: for example, they were usually nominated by their DLPs to serve on MoI local committees.[133]

The number of agents fell for a number of reasons. Death was one factor. Seamless transitions did occasionally take place, as at Woolwich in 1941; but Woolwich was exceptionally well organized, and the experience of DLPs like Sheffield Park and Barrow in losing long-standing agents and being unable to find replacements due to a lack of suitable applicants or funds was more common.[134] In Leeds South, the agency was only saved for the impoverished DLP when a local Labour-sympathizing clothing manufacturer agreed to put the agent on his company's payroll.[135] Some agents were replaced when they retired, as in early 1943 at Leigh (Lancashire) and Leeds Central.[136] But it could prove difficult: even a well-organized and prosperous party like Ipswich found it impossible to make a full-time appointment in late 1942 because none of the applicants could obtain release from war work, and it had to appoint the party president, Reg Gray, at £3 a week on a part-time basis; in the event he proved a competent organizer and was duly appointed full-time agent in January 1945.[137] In July 1941, Doncaster DLP found itself unable to appoint a new agent due to the poor quality of the few applicants for its agency; when it re-advertised, it received no applications at all.[138] In April 1943, the appointment of Ian Dean as secretary of the Glasgow City party was made with some reluctance by people unimpressed by his work as organizer of Rutherglen (Lanarkshire) DLP, but it was Dean or no one, even after the post had been re-advertised.[139]

Problems could follow if an agent was promoted within the party. In 1940 the agent for Frome (Somerset), Harry Wickham, was appointed secretary-agent of Birmingham BLP. This was a significant promotion for Wickham, but it left Frome with a vacancy it could not fill.[140] Then, in 1942, Wickham was appointed as Labour's West Midlands regional organizer; but this left Birmingham without

[132] See e.g. Noel-Baker papers, NBKR 1/107, Russell to Noel-Baker, 24 Apr. 1941; 1/126, Noel-Baker to Russell, 15 Dec. 1944.

[133] See e.g. Salford BLP papers, BLPES film 211A, 97555/2, executive committee 17 Sept. 1939, 29 May 1940; Scottish Labour party papers, TD 1384/1/2, Scottish executive committee 23 Dec. 1939.

[134] Woolwich BLP papers, WLP 40.3, annual report for 1941, to annual general meeting 11 Apr. 1942; *Labour Organiser*, Jan. 1941; Barrow DLP papers, BLPES film 211A, reel 97566/1, general meeting 29 Oct. 1942.

[135] Williams, *Hugh Gaitskell*, 124.   [136] *Labour Organiser*, Feb. 1943.

[137] Ipswich TCLP papers, GK 400/1/1/3, delegate meeting 12 Aug. 1942, executive committee 2 Sept. 1942, 12 Jan. 1945; annual meeting 11 Feb. 1945.

[138] Doncaster DLP papers, DS 7/2/7, executive committee 9, 16 July 1941, general management committee 8 Sept. 1941.

[139] LPNEC papers XIX, organization subcommittee 20 Apr. 1943.

[140] Frome DLP papers, A/AAW 28, special executive committee 11 Feb. 1940, general committee 16 Mar. 1940.

a full-time agent until the 1945 election.[141] Jim Simmons, an experienced organizer and former MP, stood in as part-time secretary in the meantime: but he was also a member of the City Council and seven of its committees, secretary of the council Labour group, editor of the local Labour newspaper the *Town Crier*, and, until October 1944, prospective candidate for Wolverhampton West.[142] Elsewhere, the outstanding work of Sara Barker as agent for Halifax DLP was recognized in early 1942, when she was appointed as woman organizer for the Yorkshire region, but her replacement lasted only seven months before he was poached by the National Union of Seamen, and Halifax was then forced to make do with a part-time secretary until February 1945.[143]

Some agents took on other work, or found that other existing responsibilities grew dramatically. Alderman William Asbury was agent for Sheffield Brightside DLP; but he was also leader of Sheffield City Council and chairman of the local emergency committee. Once war began, he had no time for the DLP, which as a result held no meetings at all for a year after October 1940. He was appointed as Deputy Civil Defence Regional Commissioner for the Southern area, based in Reading, in early 1942, and, as 1944 drew to a close, confirmed to Brightside that he would not be returning to the city after the war.[144] In Greenwich, W. F. Shepherd, who had been appointed agent shortly after the outbreak of war, became the borough's rehousing officer in December 1940. Ultimately, despite his protestations that he would have no time for party work, he was prevailed upon to remain agent on a part-time basis. He was not able to do as much as he would have liked for the party; but the latter recognized that even this was better than no agent at all. So it was that, even when he went to work at Transport House in April 1943, he was still retained on a part-time basis, and it was only when he was appointed the party's regional organizer for the Home and Southern Counties in September 1944 that the DLP finally let him go: it helped that they were now in a position once again to appoint a full-time agent, who duly arrived that December.[145]

Indeed, it was in London that the decline of the agency was particularly marked. Of the 60 DLPs in the London County Council area, 31 had had full-time agents on the outbreak of war, but only 7 remained by January 1942, and even they often had 'additional onerous duties'.[146] Of the others, a number

---

[141] *Labour Organiser*, Dec. 1942; Birmingham BLP papers, uncl., BLP meeting 13 Dec. 1942, 11 July 1945.

[142] Wolverhampton West DLP papers, D/LAB/1/8, special executive committee 2 Oct. 1944.

[143] Halifax DLP papers, TU 28/2, special executive committee 6 Feb., 28 Mar. 1942; general meeting 30 Apr. 1942; special executive committee 17 Aug., 1 Sept. 1942, 18 Feb. 1945.

[144] Sheffield Brightside DLP papers, LP(B)8, executive committee 19 Oct. 1941, 3 Dec. 1944; *Labour Organiser*, May 1942; T. H. O'Brien, *Civil Defence* (1955), 675.

[145] Greenwich DLP papers, GLP 2.4, executive committee 8 Dec. 1940; GLP 1.3, general committee 22 Apr. 1943, 28 Sept. 1944, special general committee 3 Dec. 1944.

[146] London Labour party papers, Acc. 2417/A/25, Herbert Morrison to G. R. Shepherd, 11 Sept. 1939; A/26, H. Atkinson, 'Report on individual membership', 11 Feb. 1942.

had been evacuated at the outbreak of war, one was in the army, and others were working full-time in a number of roles, including ARP controller, Food Officer, Fuel Officer, Registrar, Ministry of Information employee, council rehousing officer, and air raid shelter inspector.[147] Matters then deteriorated further, and by July 1942, only two of the six agents who now remained were reckoned not to be 'immersed on [*sic*] other duties concerning the municipality or civil defence'.[148]

As with the Conservatives, a variety of people filled the gaps when agents left. In some cases, a spouse came to the rescue. In Cleveland (North Yorkshire), the agent, Stan Nicholson, remained very active once war broke out: in the year to February 1941, he attended 138 party meetings and functions in the constituency, as well as MoI meetings, and spent a lot of time helping constituents with individual cases. When he was called up to the Royal Artillery in August 1941, his wife stepped into his shoes. She stood down once he returned in early 1945, but when he died a year later, she was appointed agent in his place.[149] The agent's wife also took over the work in Lewisham East and Bristol East.[150] Otherwise, work fell upon the party's lay officials and members. In Southampton, for example, the gap created by the appointment of the agent as an MLNS Welfare Officer in April 1941 was filled by a trade union official who was able to combine the work with his existing job quite effectively, while in other cases, the work of the agent was taken on by ordinary members of the DLP executive.[151]

DLPs were particularly reliant on their secretaries.[152] But many were seriously affected by wartime conditions. Life on the home front did not always allow much time for politics. In a war of production, many of Labour's officials, in reserved occupations and out, found themselves too busy for serious party work. In Sheffield, for example, the secretary of the Attercliffe DLP wrote in April 1942 that he had been 'working such funny hours' that he had not been able to 'really get down to' party business.[153] He was by no means unique. The prospective candidate for Plymouth Sutton, Lucy Middleton, lived in Wimbledon, so she relied heavily on the party's secretary, F. Lyndon. But immediately war broke out, Lyndon was working at the Royal William Victualling Yard six days a week from 7 a.m. to 7 p.m., 'and sometimes much later'. Only occasional Sundays

[147] Ibid., Atkinson, 'Report on individual membership'; *LPACR 1942*, 76–9.

[148] London Labour party papers, A/26, D. H. Daines and H. Atkinson, 'Individual membership of the party in London, 1941–42', 7 July 1942.

[149] Cleveland DLP papers, U/CDLP 1/1, annual report to annual meeting 15 Feb. 1941, 14 Feb. 1942, 15 Mar. 1945; annual meeting 9 Mar. 1946.

[150] *LPACR 1941*, 94; Bristol East DLP papers, 39035/19, special general committee 8 Nov. 1939, general committee 30 Sept. 1942.

[151] Southampton DLP papers, D/LAB/box 2, executive committee 17 Apr., 4 May 1941; and see e.g. Darlington DLP papers, D/X 922/5, special executive committee 16 July 1940; Sheffield Brightside DLP papers, LP(B)8, executive committee 19 Oct. 1941.

[152] McHenry, *Labour Party in Transition*, 92.

[153] Hynd papers, HYND 2/4, E. Mulligan to J. B. Hynd, 17 Apr. 1942.

were available for any kind of party work or meetings.[154] Even before the end of October 1939, Lyndon was telling Middleton testily that he had 'not the time to organize public meetings as I have to consider my home life and family and employment'. Protesting that he got 'no support whatever' from the rest of the party in Plymouth, he carried on as best he could, but by January 1940, he was working until 7 p.m. seven days a week, and that March, he collapsed at work and had to be taken home in an ambulance.[155] By June 1940, his working hours were so long that it was not worth his going home between shifts, and he was sleeping at his workplace, which made him extremely difficult to contact.[156] Although things then eased a little, the destruction of the party headquarters in the Plymouth blitz in early 1941 meant that Lyndon's house had to become the temporary base, and this added complications especially once the intensification of the North Africa campaign in 1942 increased his workload at the victualling yard once again.[157] Lyndon's contribution was therefore severely limited, but he remained secretary until February 1945, simply because there was no one else to do the job.[158]

Lay officials were as liable as agents to be called up, or to volunteer, for military service. Within six weeks of the outbreak of war, two members of the executive committee of Sheffield Brightside DLP, as well as the secretary of its League of Youth branch, had joined the forces.[159] Epsom (Surrey) DLP lost its treasurer, voluntary organizer, and prospective candidate to military service in the first year of the war, and the resignation of its assistant secretary in June 1940 'due to his disgust with Labour's official policy' just made matters worse.[160] In Bedford, the secretary elected in June 1939 was called up to the army soon after the outbreak of war, which meant that the previous secretary had reluctantly to resume his duties, not helped by the resignation of the assistant secretary in January 1940 because he 'differed very widely from the party's attitude in the war'.[161] Between 1941 and 1944, successive secretaries of West Derbyshire DLP died, resigned due to overwork, joined the forces, and resigned to plan a post-war move to Canada.[162] No wonder *Labour Organiser* inveighed against too high a turnover of constituency party secretaries.[163]

[154] Middleton papers, MID 62/61–3, F. Lyndon to Lucy Middleton, 13 Oct. 1939.
[155] Ibid., MID 62/64–5, F. Lyndon to Lucy Middleton, 29 Oct. 1939; 63/20, C. Townsend to Lucy Middleton, 17 Jan., 11 Mar. 1940.
[156] Ibid., MID 63/62, C. Townsend to Lucy Middleton, 14 June 1940.
[157] Ibid., MID 65/51, F. Lyndon to Lucy Middleton, 27 Apr., 27 Nov. 1941.
[158] Ibid., MID 74/8, F. Lyndon to Lucy Middleton, 12 Oct. 1944; 76/3, Ted Perry (secretary, Plymouth Sutton DLP) to Lucy Middleton, n.d. [Apr. 1945].
[159] Sheffield Brightside DLP papers, LP(B)7, executive committee 21 Oct. 1939.
[160] Epsom DLP papers, 2141/1, annual report 1939; general committee 6 July, 23 Aug. 1940; executive committee 7 June 1940.
[161] Bedford DLP papers, X494/2, executive committee 13 June, 28 Nov. 1939, 9 Jan. 1940.
[162] West Derbyshire DLP papers, DS1650 G/M2, divisional meeting, 13 Sept. 1941, executive committee 20 Dec. 1941, divisional meeting 5 Aug. 1944.
[163] *Labour Organiser*, July 1943.

Some secretaries showed formidable dedication. In 1942, A. T. Grindley, the septuagenarian secretary of Cardiganshire DLP, put in over thirty hours a week as a volunteer, and walked 861 miles as well as travelling 1,430 miles by train, visiting members and collecting subscriptions, helping the party increase its membership against the national trend.[164] S. R. South, honorary secretary of Windsor DLP (Berkshire) since 1935, planned to retire in November 1939, but changed his mind due to war pressures on the party, and eventually remained in office until the DLP appointed a full-time agent, with strong financial backing from its local parties and affiliated trade unions, in February 1945; his parting shot was to donate a car for the new agent to use.[165]

By early 1944, minds were turning to the post-war agency. That May, NULOEA demanded an immediate increase in the war bonus from 15s. to 25s. a week (they got 20s. (£52 a year)). It also made a series of detailed demands about the post-war situation: these included an improved pay scale of £320–400, the establishment of a development fund, partly funded by a tax on DLPs, to allow the NEC to be more proactive in developing the agency, and improved grants and more flexibility in their payment.[166] These suggestions were not accepted, but headquarters responded with two proposals: first, that NEC grants to DLPs for new agents' salaries should be increased, at a cost of £13,000 for 100 agents, £19,500 for 150 agents, and £26,000 for 200 agents, chargeable to the General Election Fund; and, secondly, that the amount that unions and candidates could pay towards DLP agents' salaries should be increased from £150 to £200 in borough constituencies and £200 to £250 in county seats.[167] The war bonus was finally increased to 25s. (£65 a year) in January 1945.[168] This all represented a significant improvement, reflecting the party's financial prosperity, but it fell short of a revolution in the position of agents.

The NEC also began to have qualms about any hint of headlong expansion. They demanded more information about the agents they were being asked to approve, a sure sign that they were concerned about the prospect of pro-Communists being appointed; and they refused to endorse the appointment of agents in a number of weak areas, like Chippenham (Wiltshire), where the DLP appeared to have no real prospect of electoral success or of maintaining the agency.[169] More emphasis was also placed on training, and by October 1944 plans were being laid for correspondence courses and regional classes for full-time

[164] Ibid., Apr. 1943.
[165] Windsor DLP papers, D/EX 832/3, annual general meeting 22 Apr. 1945, general committee 18 Nov. 1939, annual general meeting 27 Apr. 1940, special general committee 3 Feb. 1945, executive committee 9 Mar., 16, 22 Apr., 27 May 1945.
[166] Ibid., XXI, joint meeting of finance and general purposes committee and NULOEA representatives, 1 May 1944.
[167] Ibid., finance and general purposes committee 15 May. 1944.
[168] NULOEA papers, uncl., executive report to annual conference, Blackpool, 20 May 1945.
[169] LPNEC papers XXI, NEC 10 Jan. 1945; and see e.g. Stafford DLP papers, divisional management committee 28 Apr. 1945.

agents as well as part-timers.[170] Around the same time, the Lancashire and Cheshire regional council of Labour (RCL) was one of the first to hold a series of refresher courses for agents which aimed 'to rub off the rust of the war years'; other areas followed, while in Scotland, a weekend school for election agents in February 1945 was attended by representatives from about half the Scottish DLPs.[171]

Meanwhile, like Central Office and partly in league with it, Transport House was seeking the release of agents from the forces and war work.[172] But, as seen above, release was slow, although there was a little acceleration as the end of the war approached.[173] Progress regarding London agents was particularly lacking, although the return of the agent for Lewisham East was a factor in Morrison's decision to move from Hackney South to fight that seat at the general election.[174] In terms of overall national numbers, recovery was partial and very late indeed. As we have seen, the number of agents slumped from 103 in June 1941 to 62 in May 1942. It then hovered around that very low figure for the rest of the war: 58 in June 1943, and 65 in December 1944. The figure reported to the May 1945 conference was only 64.[175] This, and the fact that only 100 DLPs had agents even in June 1946, would suggest that the party went into the 1945 election with fewer full-time agents than at any general election since 1918.

The overall picture at the 1945 election was certainly not very favourable to Labour. Labour fought all thirty-nine constituencies in the six counties covered by the East Midlands region (Derbyshire, Leicestershire, Lincolnshire, Northamptonshire, Nottinghamshire, and Rutland), but it had only seven full-time agents; and, of those seven, only four were in post prior to the calling of the election. This meant that most election agents were amateurs, many doing the job for the first time. Most did fairly well, but there were criticisms, and notions that Labour had a finely tuned machine going into the campaign in the constituencies were wide of the mark.[176] J. P. Connolly, an experienced former regional organizer, worked as election agent in Chichester, but found the job in

---

[170] LPNEC papers XXI, organization subcommittee 18 Oct. 1944.

[171] *Labour Organiser*, Oct. 1944; Wansbeck DLP papers, NRO 527/A/3, executive committee 10 Feb. 1945; Labour party Wales records 5, meeting of election agents and constituency party secretaries 3 Feb. 1945; Scottish Labour party papers, TD 1384/1/2, Scottish executive committee 6 Jan., 17 Mar. 1945.

[172] LPNEC papers XXI, organization subcommittee 21 Feb. 1945.

[173] See e.g. Frome DLP papers, A/AAW 26, executive committee 23 Mar., 4 May 1945.

[174] London Labour party papers, Acc. 2417/A/27, H. Atkinson, 'Party organization and electoral preparations', 13 June 1944; ibid., H. Atkinson, 'The work of the London Labour party, 1943', Feb. 1944; Donoughue and Jones, *Herbert Morrison*, 336.

[175] LPNEC papers XXI, organization subcommittee 18 Apr. 1945; Belper DLP papers (Derby), uncl., annual report to annual general meeting 31 Mar. 1946.

[176] Labour Party East Midlands Woman Organizer's papers, DD/PP/14/8/5, unsigned memo [Constance Kay, East Midlands Woman Organizer], 'From the East Midlands front', n.d. [Aug. 1945]; Labour Party East Midlands Regional Organizer's papers, DD/PP/14/7/5, J. T. Baxter to B. Taylor, 15 Jan.. 1945; J. T. Baxter, memos, 'Mansfield', 28 Apr., 4 June, 7 July 1945.

such a large constituency all but impossible, given the lack of either a telephone or a car.[177] For those agents who had cars, the easing of petrol restrictions did at least help.[178]

After the war and the general election, Labour's unprecedentedly positive financial position (see Chapter 8) seemed to augur well for the future employment of agents. As early as September 1945 Morgan Phillips was talking about the need to review the whole scheme under which agents were employed in the light of 'changed conditions', and arguing for 'specialist training' and a 'properly directed educational scheme' to develop an able party membership which could provide a 'reservoir' of potential future agents.[179] Cambridge TCLP's decision to seek a full-time agent in August 1945 was followed by 'enthusiastic singing of the Red Flag'; two years later, the recently formed Southern RCL left its affiliates in no doubt that '[t]he appointment of full-time Agents would, in a number of cases . . . transform minorities at the 1945 General Election into Labour gains'.[180] And, indeed, the later 1940s saw a significant advance in the number of agents employed, to peak at 296 in 1951. However, this progress was not to be maintained, and although the decline was not precipitate, it was, by the mid-1950s, unmistakable. By the early 1960s, the Conservatives' superiority to Labour in the matter of agents—never overcome, but challenged briefly—was beyond question, and Labour was on the path to a situation wherein, by the late 1970s, the number of full-time constituency agents would not be much higher than it had been in the direst days of the Second World War.[181]

The war clearly had an impact on the Labour party's agents. Contrary to mythology, the Labour machine did not carry on regardless. Indeed, both in numbers and quality of agents, Labour was seriously affected, and the impact was especially significant in London. Labour had fewer agents in 1945 than it had had in 1939. Because the great majority of DLPs had not had an agent before the war, however, the impact of the decline was less than it was for the Conservatives. But, then again, lay officials and voluntary workers were often themselves affected by wartime conditions. Finally, there was no revolution in the nature of the Labour agency. Local employment and lack of centralization remained key characteristics, and arguably prevented the most rational deployment of finite resources. The introduction of the agents' superannuation fund, however, was a major advance in professionalizing the Labour agency, and in that respect, at any rate, the war did make a significant difference.

[177] Chichester DLP papers, LA/1CH/1/1/2, general committee 10 June, 27 July 1945.
[178] See e.g. East Grinstead DLP papers, LA/2 MS/1/2/2, executive committee 27 Jan., 19 Mar. 1945.
[179] Phillips papers, GS/1945/37, 'Party development: report by general secretary', 26 Sept. 1945.
[180] Cambridge TCLP papers, 634/08, monthly meeting 3 Aug. 1945; Southampton DLP papers, D/LAB/box 1, Southern regional council of Labour, 'Report of the provisional executive committee to the first annual meeting', 20 Sept. 1947.
[181] The figure fell to 199 in 1967, the first time it had been below 200 since 1948; it later fell from 131 in 1973 to just 77 in 1978.

THE LIBERALS

Like the Conservatives, the Liberals had traditionally made great use of salaried agents at constituency level.[182] Unlike the Conservatives, however, the Liberals had found it difficult to retain a widespread paid agency during the inter-war period for financial reasons, and because potential agents became thinner on the ground. But accounts that imply that the full-time Liberal agency collapsed completely are exaggerated.[183] Limited headquarters subsidies assisted some constituency associations and regional Liberal federations (LFs) to employ agents and organizers. Secondly, in constituencies with lively associations, or where the MP or candidate was reasonably well off or apparently secure, there was every possibility that an agent would be found. It was just that there were fewer such seats for the Liberals than for the Conservatives. Indeed, some Liberal associations were looking to expand their paid staff during the later 1930s. Westmorland LA took on a new agent in 1938, and a scheme was launched across the north-west in March 1939 whereby Liberal agents would earn commission by securing subscribers for the Liberal *Manchester Guardian*: this would expand that newspaper's readership while subsidizing party agents' salaries.[184] However, it could be difficult to recruit staff, and was sometimes even harder to retain them, given the often uphill nature of their struggles.[185]

The outbreak of war curtailed expansion, including the *Guardian* scheme. As with the Conservatives, initial signals from headquarters were discouraging, and implied a bleak future for agents; although Meston's 6 September message told associations to remain active, his silence about agents led to some redundancies.[186] In Chester, Leonard Smith, who had achieved a great deal in ten years to turn the LA into 'a model Association', resigned and joined the ARP on the grounds that the association would not be able to afford to keep him on, when a stronger lead from the centre might have persuaded him to remain, and made his association keener to keep him.[187] Some Liberal agents joined the forces: J. Wallace Carter,

---

[182] K. Rix, 'Hidden workers of the party: the professional Liberal agents, 1885–1910', *Journal of Liberal History*, 52 (2006), 4–13.

[183] For an example, see C. Cook, *A Short History of the Liberal Party, 1900–2001* (6th edn., Houndmills, 2002), 112.

[184] Westmorland LA papers, WDSo/174/2, finance and general purposes committee 25 June 1938; Society of Certificated and Associated Liberal Agents (North-West district) papers, M392/1/4, branch meeting 17 Mar. 1939.

[185] See e.g. Dundee LA papers, GD/DLA/1, executive committee 10 Feb. 1938, 9 Mar. 1939.

[186] London LF papers, Acc. 1446/4, chairman, Liberal party organization (LPO) and treasurer, Liberal Central Association (LCA), to Harold Glanville, London LF (circular), 31 Aug. 1939; *Manchester Guardian*, 7 Sept. 1939, 6 Nov. 1939; LPO, *Fourth Report to the Assembly, 18–19 July 1941* (1941), 8.

[187] Chester LA papers, CR159/5, emergency meeting of officers 5 Sept. 1939; for Chester as 'model', see ibid., council meeting 21 Sept. 1939.

the agent for Yeovil (Somerset), joined the RAF and was killed in action in the winter of 1940–1, while the clerk of the Home Counties LF, J. Doel, escaped from Dunkirk in 1940 'without a scratch'.[188] Others took on work of national importance, such as the Scottish LF secretary, Ronald Findlay, and the organizer of Paisley LA, Mrs Crawford.[189]

There was soon a reaction, however. Some area federations offered a clearer lead from the start: the Lancashire, Cheshire, and North-Western LF (LCNWLF) circularized its associations on 4 September to tell them to retain their agents for as long as possible, and to maintain contact with any that were called up for national service.[190] Walthamstow East and West LAs merged for the duration of the war, allowing their depleted staff to cover work in both areas where necessary.[191] In some cases, retention was very much on the understanding that people would find alternative employment if possible, as in Westmorland, although there the agent was still paid a retainer of ten shillings a week to carry on the association's correspondence and 'do any other work in Liberal Interests that came his way'.[192] Other associations coped by sharing their agent, as when Knutsford (Cheshire) retained its official, Frank Clegg, on a part-time basis from late 1940 onwards by sharing him with Manchester LF.[193] When, in early 1942, William Phipp was appointed as secretary of the Western Counties LF (WCLF), he continued to help his old association at Westbury (Wiltshire) by dealing with its correspondence and collecting its subscriptions, making it the only association in the whole of the federation area to have an agent during the middle part of the war.[194]

Occasionally, it was possible to plug the gaps that emerged. The regional federations were particularly important here. Initial reactions to the outbreak of the war in the federations had been grim—some had made staff redundant—but the LPO had moved rapidly to forestall collapse, offering them a headquarters grant to enable them to continue to employ a secretary, so long as current levels of activity were maintained.[195] This was a godsend to hard-pressed federations: by June 1941, the WCLF was noting that the LPO grant was 'making all the

[188] *Liberal Party Organisation Bulletin*, 6, Apr. 1940; Western Counties LF papers, DDM 1172, finance and general purposes committee 17 Feb. 1941; Home Counties LF papers, DM 668, report for period 1 Apr. 1940–30 June 1941.

[189] Paisley LA papers, ARC67, executive committee 26 Feb. 1940.

[190] LCNWLF papers, M390/1/11, John Ormerod (chairman), circular, 4 Sept. 1939.

[191] Walthamstow LA papers, Acc. 10126/2, meeting of Walthamstow Liberal and Radical council, 28 Aug. 1939.

[192] Westmorland LA papers, WDSo/174/2, executive committee 28 Oct. 1939.

[193] Manchester LF papers, M283/1/3/7, executive committee 18 Dec. 1940.

[194] Western Counties LF papers, DDM 1172, finance and general purposes committee 26 Jan., 18 Apr., 16 Nov. 1942.

[195] Yorkshire LF papers, WYL 456/3, executive committee 25 Nov. 1939; London LF papers, Acc. 1446/7, general purposes committee 6 Sept. 1939; Home Counties LF papers, DM 668, report for period 1 Mar. 1939–31 Mar. 1940; Western Counties LF papers, DDM 1172, finance and general purposes committee 8 Dec. 1939. The threat to reduce or stop payments was carried

difference between "carrying on" and "closing down" '.[196] Yorkshire was able to retain its secretary and, when he died in late 1940, to replace him, while London was able to replace its retiring secretary in 1943.[197] By then, the LPO was also making small additional payments to some federations to help them pay honorariums to part-time organizers.[198] Federations were thus able to cover at least some of the work that would normally have fallen to constituency-level organizers. In the Home Counties, for example, the federation secretary revived the associations in Newbury (Berkshire), Watford (Hertfordshire), and the boroughs of Richmond and Bournemouth in 1942–3 virtually single-handedly.[199]

The Scottish LF lost its secretary at the outbreak of war. But it then had two strokes of luck. First, its former secretary, William Webster, agreed to return to do routine work in return for his pension, money the LF would have had to pay out in any case; and, secondly, Lady Glen-Coats volunteered, 'with the assistance of her private secretary', to take on an impressive amount of work on the federation's behalf.[200] She was to prove almost indefatigable: as the SLF chairman remarked in March 1941, after one of her regular reports of extensive travels and numerous visits to constituency organizations all over Scotland, her activities were 'very satisfactory, if not even marvellous for one single lady'.[201] But even she could be discouraged: as she recognized in October 1942, '[i]t was very trying and disappointing work, because, while she had managed to get a few Associations to meet, whenever her effort had passed nothing further was done'.[202] However, the publication of the Beveridge report a few weeks later lifted her out of her gloomy mood, and launched three more years of intense activity on behalf of the party, which culminated anticlimactically in her own crushing defeat at Paisley in 1945.[203] Sadly for the Liberal party, Glen-Coats was unique.[204]

As the end of the war approached, constituencies which felt they could afford to employ paid officials tried to secure them, either full-time or part-time. As early as February 1944, the WCLF had found a part-time organizer willing to

out on occasion: see e.g. London LF papers, Acc. 1446/7, general purposes committee 18 May, 18 July 1944.

[196] Western Counties LF papers, DDM 1172, executive committee 7 June 1941.

[197] Yorkshire LF papers, WYL 456/3, executive committee 25 Nov. 1939, 16 Nov. 1940; LPO, *Sixth Report to the Assembly, 15–17 July 1943* (1943), 17.

[198] See e.g. LCNWLF papers, M390/1/11, W. R. Davies (LPO) to Councillor Ernest Kenyon (treasurer, LCNWLF), 24 Dec. 1942; London LF papers, Acc. 1446/7, general purposes committee 6 May 1940.

[199] Home Counties LF papers, DM 668, report for period 1 July 1941–30 Apr. 1943.

[200] Paisley LA papers, ARC67, executive committee 26 Feb. 1940; Scottish LF papers, Acc. 11765/14, joint finance committee 20 Dec. 1939, 24 Jan. 1940.

[201] Scottish LF papers, Acc. 11765/14, executive committee 26 Mar. 1941.

[202] Ibid., executive committee 28 Oct. 1942.

[203] Ibid., meeting of office-bearers 13 July 1943.   [204] Hutchison, *Scottish Politics*, 80.

go into the Thornbury and Stroud divisions of Gloucestershire 'to work up the old Committees'.[205] That March, new headquarters, with a full-time agent, were opened in Liverpool—long a weak spot for the party—after a strong fund-raising campaign by local Liberals.[206] In September 1944, the LCNWLF told all its eighty-three LAs that they should be aiming to employ an agent, and that those which were planning to run candidates would be paid sufficient to allow them to employ one full-time for three months; by December Southport, Bury, and Wirral had all appointed full-timers, while the Manchester LF was about to do so.[207] Constituencies were further encouraged by the agents' body, the Society of Certificated and Associated Liberal Agents (SCALA), which declared in January 1945 that all Liberal candidates needed at least a part-time organizer, and preferably a full-time agent, because otherwise the party would fail to capitalize on 'the undoubted trend towards Liberalism at the present time'.[208] By March 1945, meanwhile, London Liberal party was advertising for agents in the press, presumably in the belief that it would be easier to appoint agents centrally and then try to place them with constituencies than to have dozens of LAs all doing their own thing.[209] East Dorset LA advertised for an agent in the local press, and, when nineteen applications were received, a number of the association's wealthier members agreed to subscribe £25 each towards the salary of the appointee.[210] The optimism of the time could be seen in the aspirations of an association like Stockport, which had only re-formed in 1944 after seven moribund years, but which was seeking to employ an agent by May 1945.[211]

Like the other parties, however, the Liberals found new agents elusive. As one leading figure in the LCNWLF said in August 1944, 'there was more difficulty in obtaining agents than Prospective Candidates'.[212] One solution was training eager but inexperienced volunteers, a process that began in some areas as early as the summer of 1944.[213] Although the number of agents in the WCLF area expanded from two in November 1944 to nine in March 1945, this was still considered inadequate, especially as many were only part-time, and it was agreed that a series of training classes for new agents would be held.[214] And, like their

---

[205] Western Counties LF papers, DDM 1172, finance and general purposes committee 2 Feb. 1944.
[206] LCNWLF papers, M390/1/12, executive committee 17 Mar. 1944.
[207] Ibid., executive committee 29 Sept., 1 Dec. 1944.
[208] Society of Certificated and Associated Liberal Agents papers, WYL 456/16, annual meeting 31 Jan. 1945.
[209] London LF papers, Acc. 1446/7, general purposes committee 24 Apr. 1945.
[210] East Dorset LA papers, D1512/A1, finance and general purposes committee 2 Nov. 1944.
[211] Stockport LA papers, B/NN/2/10, executive committee 21 Nov. 1944, 4 May, 5 June 1945.
[212] LCNWLF papers, M390/1/12, executive committee 25 Aug. 1944.
[213] Ibid. 28 July 1944.
[214] Western Counties LF papers, DDM 1172, finance and general purposes committee 4 Nov. 1944, 3 Mar. 1945.

rivals, the Liberals also faced difficulty in getting people released from the forces or war work.[215]

In February 1945, the LPO organization committee decided to appoint eight organizers whom it would send out into the constituencies.[216] By the time of the election, five were in place (three in London and the Home Counties, and one each in the Midlands and the Western Counties).[217] Also in February 1945, a Miss Ruckstuhl started work as full-time organizer for the WLF, with the task of helping the party's female candidates. But this was a hard task: the five prospective candidates at the time of her appointment had increased to twenty at the election itself, and she had to spread herself quite thinly. In the event, the only woman Liberal MP elected in 1945 was Megan Lloyd George at Anglesey, and her fate owed nothing to Ruckstuhl, whose campaign journeys did not take her to Wales at all.[218]

The position at the 1945 election, therefore, was mixed at best. Rasmussen's statement that the Liberals' organization 'was totally unprepared for a resumption of politics in the summer of 1945' is too sweeping, but some delay in the date of the election might at least have helped the party to find more agents.[219] Of course, it was not hard to find Liberals after the election developing a self-justificatory narrative that rivalled that of the Conservatives in essentials. The secretary of the WCLF, which covered twenty-seven constituencies of which only one (North Dorset) had been won, was quick to develop and employ this approach:

[I]n the West we entered the fight badly armed. Our Agents were either brought out of retirement, or new and inexperienced, and in no case had they had sufficient time to get to know their Constituencies properly. Organization in most Divisions was scanty, and helpers generally scarce. In spite of these handicaps, however, there was a spirit of optimism in all Divisions, and the result was a great disappointment.[220]

This was not wholly fictitious, but it is hard to avoid the conclusion that it was a good way for the secretary to deflect some of the criticism that might otherwise have come his way. What is clear is that some areas had seen progress in the months prior to the election. In the north-west, there had been only 2 or 3 agents at work at the beginning of 1945, but 22 (4 of them women) were

[215] Manchester LF papers, M283/1/3/7, executive committee 2 Jan. 1945, 6 Feb., 6 Mar., 24 Apr., 29 May 1945.

[216] LPO, *Report to the Assembly, January 1945–March 1946* (1946), 12.

[217] Beveridge papers, VI/13, fo. 52, unsigned memo, 15 May 1945.

[218] Women's Liberal federation, 'Report of Women's Liberal federation, July 1943–January 1945', n.d. [1945].

[219] J. S. Rasmussen, *The Liberal Party: A Study of Retrenchment and Revival* (1965), 10.

[220] Western Counties LF papers, DDM 1172, finance and general purposes committee 9 Aug. 1945.

working full-time before and during the general election, and a further 19 part-timers were taken on for the campaign itself.[221] In the Home Counties, where two-thirds of constituencies had a Liberal candidate (the highest proportion for any federation area), 26 agents were trained prior to the election, and their work was supplemented by the three travelling organizers taken on by the federation shortly before the campaign began, who did 'excellent work'. This would suggest that it was now possible to recruit agents in reasonable numbers. But the numbers were still insufficient, and the quality very variable.[222] Whether having more agents would have made much difference is another question, of course: a story of Liberal party decline stretching back to at least 1918 was not going to be arrested dramatically by the employment of a couple of dozen more constituency agents in 1945.

After 1945, as before it, the Liberals continued to aspire toward the employment of more paid agents. Some associations were successful in doing so: Cambridgeshire was able to appoint a full-timer on 28 July, despite its disappointment at having come a poor third in the poll, while Westmorland LA, which had shied away from retaining its full-time agent after the 1945 election, reversed its position in 1947.[223] But, in most cases, it remained an uphill struggle. Within a few months of the election, two of the five organizers appointed by the LPO organization committee had resigned, and could not be replaced due to lack of funds, leaving just three out of the originally projected eight, while a 1947 scheme whereby the WLF pledged £50 to help regional federations start a fund to employ a woman organizer had a 'somewhat disappointing' take up, with only four areas adopting it.[224]

In the matter of agents, therefore, the Liberals' wartime experiences were not too dissimilar to those of the Conservatives and Labour. The party's agency came under many of the same stresses and strains. However, it was starting from a lower base, and the war therefore provided a particularly severe challenge to agencies where they existed. All the same, however, the Liberals still had some professional agents in 1945, which was no slight achievement in itself. And the fact that they had had so few agents in 1939 meant that the majority of Liberal associations were not affected directly by the attenuation of the agency during the war. In the years that followed, Liberals would continue to aspire to the employment of full-time agents; by 1963 sixty-four associations, or approximately one in ten,

---

[221] LCNWLF papers, M390/1/12, Arthur D. Worsley (Secretary), 'Report on the election July 1945', 26 July 1945.

[222] Home Counties LF papers, DM 668, report for year ended 31 Dec. 1945; London LF papers, Acc. 1446/7, general purposes committee 25 Jan. 1945.

[223] Cambridgeshire LA papers, R93/73, selection committee 28 Apr. 1945; association meeting 28 July 1945; Westmorland LA papers, WDSo/174/2, executive committee 11 June 1947.

[224] LPO, *Report to the Assembly, January 1945–March 1946* (1946), 12; Women's Liberal federation, annual report, Apr. 1948.

would have one.[225] This would not have been possible without the survival of the Liberal agency through even the darkest years of the war.

CONCLUSION

The Second World War had a significant impact on the agency arrangements of all three parties. All suffered a fall in the number of agents early in the war, and found it difficult to restore numbers prior to the end of the conflict. There were changes in the nature of each party's agency, but the changes were not dramatic, on the whole. The Conservatives retained a highly professionalized agency, but attempts to centralize employment failed. The Liberal party was unable to effect a major change in the scale and scope of its agency. Perhaps things changed most in relation to Labour agents, where increasing professionalism was demonstrated and enhanced by the establishment of a superannuation scheme. But here again, there was no centralization of the agency. After the war, the absolute and relative positions of the parties' agents would be largely similar to that pertaining before it. By 1963, the Conservatives would have 520 full-time agents to Labour's 208 and the Liberals' 64.[226]

The war therefore had a short-term adverse effect on all the parties' agencies. But it would be misleading, simply for that reason, to discount Conservative claims that their party suffered particularly on this account. As Michael Kandiah has pointed out, the key point was that the Conservatives had been accustomed to being much better endowed with full-time agents and other staffers than their rivals.[227] It was this loss of *relative* superiority that so affected the Conservatives, both practically and emotionally, in 1945. Labour was far more accustomed than the Conservatives to fighting election campaigns and functioning effectively between elections without the ministrations of a professional. Thus more Conservative associations than Labour parties were hit, and hit harder, by the lack of a full-time agent both during the war and in 1945. The Conservatives were further from pre-war normalcy than Labour, and in this sense they were at a relative disadvantage. This does suggest that there was something in the argument that, in respect of agents at least, wartime conditions had damaged the Conservative party machine more than they had the Labour one.

But we need to be sceptical here, too. In the context of 1945, it suited most Conservatives to blame organizational decline for political failure and electoral humiliation, and move on. It suited Churchill, whose shortcomings as party leader were thereby obscured; it suited party reformers like Maxwell-Fyfe and

[225] R. L. Leonard, *Elections in Britain* (1968), 33.   [226] Ibid.
[227] M. D. Kandiah, 'The Conservative party and the 1945 general election', *Contemporary Record*, 9 (1995), 24–5.

Butler as giving them a mandate for change; and it suited Conservatives more generally because it set their apparent patriotic self-sacrifice against the perceivedly 'party first' mentality of Labour. In this sense, established Conservative narratives about party agents in wartime tell us as much about the post-war party as they do about the parties at war.

4

Party Membership

INTRODUCTION

Analysis of party membership figures during the Second World War can lead to some stark conclusions. For example, we know that the Labour party's individual membership fell to less than 220,000 in the period to 1942 and that, conversely, the membership of the Communist party grew exponentially to almost 60,000 in the same year. This can be taken as indicative of a move against established party politics. Yet this presupposes that the main reasons for changes in party membership were political: that people joined and left parties because they agreed or disagreed with their policies and stances. In fact, however, these were not necessarily the prime motivating factors in determining whether people joined, or remained members of, political parties. The majority of members were not active: they simply paid their subscriptions when asked, and if their membership was essentially passive, then we should not, perhaps, seek active reasons for their departure from it.[1]

Comparative analysis of the three main parties' membership is difficult. No national totals were published, or even compiled, by the Conservatives and Liberals. In these cases, indeed, it seems that what constituted membership could vary from constituency to constituency. An attempt has been made, therefore, broadly to accept the definitions of membership given in CA and LA records, and then to try to assess what happened during the war, and why. For Labour, the position is in one sense less complex—there are masses of statistics, for affiliated as well as individual membership, divided by affiliated organizations (mainly trade unions) and DLPs respectively. These figures are themselves somewhat problematic, but they are suggestive, and can be used to identify important trends, particularly when used in conjunction with other national and local party records. Because the bulk of the evidence is from the Labour side, the chapter starts with a discussion of that party, before investigating, so far as is possible, the Conservatives and Liberals.

---

[1] J. Blondel, *Voters, Parties and Leaders: The Social Fabric of British Politics* (Harmondsworth, 1963), 93; S. E. Finer, *The Changing British Party System, 1945–1979* (Washington, DC, 1980), 134.

LABOUR

Labour had two categories of membership. 'Individual' members joined a divisional Labour party directly by paying a subscription to it. 'Affiliated' members were members of another organization—usually a trade union—who paid a 'political levy', covering their subscription to the party, in addition to their ordinary union dues. These levies went to their union's political fund, out of which the union paid its annual affiliation fee to the party. All of this led to the publication, in the Labour party's annual report, of seemingly precise membership figures for each DLP and affiliated union. However, the figures need to be treated with some caution. First, where individual membership was concerned, DLPs bought a number of cards from headquarters at the start of each year, based on an estimate of how many they thought they would need. This number was reflected in the official figures, but in some cases the cards would go unsold, thus overstating the party's membership.[2] In addition, parties were not allowed—except in unusual circumstances, such as where a DLP had just been formed in a particularly weak area—to affiliate with fewer than 240 members. This meant that any DLP with between 1 and 240 members would be recorded in the annual report as having a membership of 240. Indeed, wherever a DLP's membership was recorded as 240, it is usually safe to reckon that the real figure was lower. Secondly, unions' affiliated membership was often calculated back from the amount contributed to the party, and it was not unusual for unions to underpay in relation to the actual number of members paying the political levy. Finally, it should be remembered that the majority of members were not very active, if at all, and this was particularly true of affiliated ones, unless they were also individual members. However, it should be noted that some accounts of the Labour membership's passivity are too gloomy, in part because of Panglossian readings of the nature of social democratic parties in other countries.[3]

Labour's individual membership had risen quite impressively for much of the inter-war period. The first figure published, in 1928, was 214,970; by 1937 it had risen to 447,150. But small decreases in 1938 and 1939 were disappointing (see Table 4.1). Headquarters exhortation towards a target of one member for every eight Labour voters in each constituency continued, but the abandonment, in November 1938, of a major membership drive planned for 1939 suggested

[2] LPNEC XVII, memo, 'Individual membership', to organization subcommittee 19 July 1939.
[3] For a gloomy view, see C. Howard, 'Expectations born to death: local Labour party expansion in the 1920s', in J. M. Winter (ed.), *The Working Class in Modern British History* (Cambridge, 1983), 65–81; this appears to develop the themes of B. Hindess, *The Decline of Working Class Politics* (1971). For a valuable corrective, see S. Berger, *The British Labour Party and the German Social Democrats, 1900–1931: A Comparative Study* (Oxford, 1994).

Table 4.1. Labour party membership, 1935–1945

Year	Individual	Affiliated		Total
		Trade union	Socialist societies etc.	
1935	419,311	1,912,924	45,280	2,377,515
1936	430,694	1,968,538	45,125	2,444,357
1937	447,150	2,037,071	43,451	2,527,672
1938	428,826	2,158,076	43,384	2,630,286
1939	408,844	2,214,070	40,153	2,663,067
1940	304,124	2,226,575	40,464	2,571,163
1941	226,622	2,230,728	28,108	2,485,458
1942	218,783	2,206,209	28,940	2,453,932
1943	235,501	2,237,307	30,432	2,503,240
1944	265,763	2,375,381	31,701	2,672,845
1945	487,047	2,510,369	41,281	3,038,697

Source: LPAR 1946, 35.

that parts of the party hierarchy were becoming almost resigned to a failure to recruit.[4]

In 1939, only 14 seats, mostly in far-flung agricultural areas, lacked a divisional Labour party; 6 others from similar areas were so fragile that they were being permitted to affiliate on fewer than 240 members. A further 99 affiliated on the minimum figure of 240 members. Again, many of these were from areas of acute electoral weakness, although some, like Barnsley and parts of Glasgow, were places where the seat was so safe for Labour that there seemed little incentive in developing a thriving local party, especially given financial support from local union branches. At the other end of the spectrum, the DLPs in 27 single-member, and 5 double-member, constituencies had more than 2,000 members. Of the former, the champion was Romford (Essex), admittedly a huge constituency, with 8,591, and in all 23 of the 27 were situated in the greater London area. In all, 112 DLPs—only 2 of them in Scotland—reported a membership of 1,000 or more. The majority of parties, though, reached neither extreme, 351 parties having between 241 and 999 members.

Initially, Shepherd and others believed that the outbreak of war gave the party a chance to increase its membership.[5] By early 1940, however, many DLPs were reporting real difficulties in maintaining contact with their members. Labour party membership rested, to a very large extent, on the collection of subscriptions

---

[4] See e.g. Cambridgeshire TCLP papers, 416/0.22, Labour party to Cambridgeshire TCLP, n.d. [1938 or 1939]; *Labour Organiser*, Nov.–Dec. 1939; LPNEC XVII, memo, 'Individual membership', to organization subcommittee 19 July 1939, campaign committee 18 Nov. 1938.

[5] *Labour Organiser*, Sept.–Oct. 1939, Nov.–Dec. 1939; Lambeth North DLP papers, 1/3, special general committee 15 Sept. 1939; Hendon DLP papers, BLPES film 211A, reel 97559/1, executive committee 13 Sept. 1939, executive committee 13 Sept. 1939.

from members on a regular—usually weekly—basis.[6] If people were not called on, they did not usually seek the party office out; and if they did not subscribe, they ceased, by definition, to be members.[7] The war posed a serious challenge to this system. First, increasing numbers of people moved. If they moved away from the area, for work or military service, they were often lost to the party altogether; but even moves within the local area could be too much trouble for collectors to trace. Secondly, the blackout exacerbated the exceptionally cold winter to make collecting an extremely unattractive pastime.[8] Finally, and partly as a result, there was an increasing shortage of collectors: as the party secretary in Swansea put it, the fall in membership was not solely due to 'the War, blackout, or slum clearance'; instead, 'the difficulty [was] mainly that of collectors'.[9]

Some DLPs, though, were better placed, and remained able to cover their collecting, retaining (and indeed recruiting) members.[10] This meant that optimism did not entirely disappear. The secretary of West Derbyshire DLP felt they would be able to increase their membership because 'the War was shocking the minds of people to make them more receptive to ideas which had been locked out by traditional beliefs'.[11] In some areas, like Barrow and Gloucester, there was hope that an influx of workers from outside would increase party membership.[12] Halifax (West Yorkshire) ran a successful membership drive in the final quarter of 1939, and many DLPs were planning to follow suit: in Greenwich, hard work on collecting early in 1940 at least postponed a big fall in membership until 1941.[13] But recruitment and retention became increasingly difficult. As DLPs' orders for membership cards arrived at Transport House in January 1940, it became clear that individual membership was falling.[14] Meanwhile, the youth organization in many areas had disintegrated.[15]

Labour did not simply give up. Headquarters responded by sending each DLP a detailed questionnaire on its activities, membership, and finance, as well as a 'membership history' outlining the DLP's past achievements and present

[6] McHenry, *Labour Party in Transition*, 98; J. Gould, 'Riverside: a Labour constituency', *Fabian Journal* (Nov. 1954), 14.

[7] *Labour Organiser*, Nov.–Dec. 1939; Stockport TCLP papers, B/MM/2/19, executive committee 4 Sept. 1939.

[8] See e.g. Sheffield Hallam DLP papers, LD 1564/2, management committee 12 Nov. 1939; Greenwich DLP papers, GLP 8, 22nd annual report, 1939, 3 Feb. 1940; Doncaster DLP papers, DS 7/2/7, executive committee 20 Nov. 1940.

[9] Swansea LP papers, BLPES film 211A, reel 97580/11, Swansea Labour Association annual report to annual meeting 18 Apr. 1940.

[10] Lewisham West DLP papers, A89/100/9, general committee 22 Oct. 1939; Newport DLP papers, MNB/POL/6/A/22, Malpas ward League of Youth, meeting 8 Dec. 1939.

[11] West Derbyshire DLP papers, D1650 G/M2, annual meeting 20 Jan. 1940.

[12] *Labour Organiser*, Jan., Mar. 1940.

[13] Halifax DLP papers, TU 28/2, executive committee 24 Oct. 1940; *Labour Organiser*, Mar. 1940; Greenwich DLP papers, GLP 2.4, executive committee 15 Feb., 21 Mar., 18 Apr. 1940.

[14] LPNEC XVIII, organization subcommittee 21 Feb., 17 July 1940.

[15] London LP papers, Acc. 2417/A/25, Hinley Atkinson, circular to London DLP secretaries, 2 Apr. 1940; *Labour Organiser*, Jan., Mar. 1941.

position, and setting a target membership based on the 'one-in-eight' formula. In May 1940, officials of the largest DLPs were called to headquarters to discuss membership issues, and propaganda was issued stressing the need for party members to maintain their membership.[16] Many DLPs continued working hard. That summer, Lewisham West ran a membership canvass, and the South Wales RCL ran a widespread membership campaign in response to an impassioned plea from Shepherd, one of whose themes was to appeal to the middle class: if Labour was eventually to form a government, it must attract 'those administrative and other workers who occupied key posts in commerce and industry', so it 'should not only think of approaching the manual workers'.[17]

But the onset of the Blitz severely hampered efforts. The regular and frequent collection of dues became less and less feasible, for all the urgings of headquarters and its staff.[18] Lewisham West's high hopes collapsed, and by December collections were proceeding in only one of the constituency's wards.[19] This explains why the party had a membership of 1,495 in 1940, but only 474 in 1941. The DLP in the double-member constituency of Southampton was held up early in the war as a model party, its membership of 3,000 sustained by a strong network of 143 unpaid collectors making a total of 1,600 calls a week in late 1939.[20] But from September 1940 onwards, as a series of air raids hit the city, the number of collectors fell to 93; the party's individual membership, which had fallen to 2,248 in 1940, was to be only 692 in 1941.[21] Air raids disrupted party membership in many other places too (see Chapter 6). Bright spots—as at Sheffield Hallam, where three collectors in one ward managed to recruit twenty new members to the party in November 1940—were increasingly rare.[22] Berwick (Northumberland) found that special efforts did bring in recruits, but also discovered that the collecting and other work involved in retaining them was too much.[23] All this meant that 1941 saw individual membership fall by 25 per cent, from 304,124 to 226,622 (see Table 4.1), with the great majority of DLPs losing members and only really well-organized parties like Halifax and Woolwich able to buck the trend (Halifax recruited 514 new members in the year).[24]

Initially at least, this precipitous decline appears to have been taken for granted by Transport House. Indeed, it spent more energy over the winter of

[16] LPNEC XIX, memo, 'Individual membership', to organization subcommittee 18 Nov. 1941.

[17] Lewisham West DLP papers, A89/100/9, general committee 12 Aug. 1940; Labour party Wales records 2, South Wales regional council of Labour, individual membership subcommittee 20 June 1940; executive committee 9 July, 10 Sept., 11 June 1940.

[18] See e.g. the comments of the North-Western organizer, J. W. Kneeshaw, reported in *Labour Organiser*, Mar. 1940; see also 'War-time collecting problems: some hints and suggestions', *Labour Organiser*, Feb. 1940; 'Some collecting and membership problems', ibid., Aug. 1940.

[19] Lewisham West DLP papers, A89/100/9, general committee 15 Dec. 1940.

[20] *Labour Organiser*, Jan. 1940.   [21] Ibid., 'Blitz 1940' [*c*. Nov. 1940].

[22] Sheffield Hallam DLP papers, LD 1564/2, management committee 10 Nov. 1940.

[23] Berwick DLP papers, NRO 544/1, special conference 1 Feb. 1941.

[24] Halifax DLP papers, TU 28/2, executive committee 23 Oct. 1941; *Labour Organiser*, Apr., July 1941.

1940–1 seeking out members to expel. Heresy hunting had begun in earnest the previous winter, in relation to the CPGB's change of line, and over the Russo-Finnish war, when Pritt had been the highest-profile casualty (see Chapter 1).[25] Others, either pro-Communists or just ordinary Labourites sympathetic to the 'imperialist war' line, had followed; a number of local parties, including Sheffield trades and Labour council (TLC) and Pritt's own at Hammersmith North, had been disbanded and re-formed without their 'disloyal' members.[26] However, the Communist-led People's Convention (see Chapter 6) took things to a new level. In October 1940, any association with it was declared *ultra vires*; by February 1941, head office had expelled 33 members and was still investigating 30 others, while DLPs had expelled a further 55, and expulsions continued until the end of May.[27] In these circumstances, headquarters placed little emphasis on fresh recruitment, perhaps for fear of drawing in 'unreliable' elements, although the NEC allowed the erstwhile pro-Communist John Strachey to join Maldon (Essex) DLP in April 1941.[28]

By the second half of 1941, concern about membership was growing. Fewer members meant less money. It might also mean a weaker campaign at the post-war general election. And anti-Communists at all levels, and not least at Transport House, realized that the entry of the Soviet Union into the war in June 1941 offered huge recruitment potential to the CPGB. It was also recognized that recruiting new members was a good way of diverting existing members' attention from supporting cooperation with the Communists or attacking the electoral truce. For all these reasons, headquarters was reawakened to the need to recruit members; so, at the end of 1941, new membership leaflets and forms were issued to DLPs, who were also exhorted to help, or to re-establish, their League of Youth branches.[29] Some DLPs were already showing what could be done—membership of Epsom (Surrey) DLP, which had fallen from 2,052 in 1939 to just 968 in 1941, recovered to 1,490 in 1942 thanks to a campaign launched in November 1941, for example.[30] Results were not always, or even usually, very impressive at this stage, however, and parties like Exeter, which had managed to retain 75 per cent of their pre-war membership, felt that they were doing very well.[31] And the broader reality was grim. The number of

---

[25] LPNEC XVIII, elections subcommittee 11 Jan. 1940; Middleton and Shepherd, circular to CLP secretaries, 25 Jan. 1940.

[26] Ibid., organization subcommittee 17 July 1940.

[27] Ibid., Walter Citrine and Middleton, National Council of Labour circular to secretaries of affiliated organizations, Oct. 1940, organization subcommittee 19 Feb. 1941, 22 Apr., 28 May 1941.

[28] Ibid., XIX, NEC 23 Apr. 1941.

[29] Ibid., organization subcommittee 18 Nov. 1941; Huddersfield DLP papers, BLPES film 211, reel 143, executive committee 28 Oct. 1941; *Labour Organiser*, Oct. 1941.

[30] Epsom DLP papers, 2141/1, executive committee 16 Nov. 1941.

[31] Middleton papers, MID 66/66, T. A. Hendy (general secretary, Exeter DLP) to Lucy Middleton, 21 Nov. 1941.

constituencies without a DLP had risen each year of the war, from 14 in 1939 to 26 in 1940, 39 in 1941, and 45 in 1942. Meanwhile, the number of DLPs affiliating on 240 members rose dramatically, from 99 in 1939 to 167 in 1940, and 247 in 1941. The rate of increase then fell off, but the fact that, in 1942, no fewer than 251 DLPs were 'on the minimum' was very worrying. When added to the constituencies that no longer had a DLP, and the two DLPs that were being allowed to continue affiliation with fewer than 240 members, this meant that Labour organization in 298 constituencies—just over half the 586 constituencies outside Northern Ireland—was in serious difficulty.

London faced some of the greatest problems. The 60 DLPs in the London County Council area had totalled 63,888 members in 1939. This fell to 43,283 in 1940, and only 22,200 in 1941. In 1939, 53 of the 60 parties had exceeded 240 members, but only 31 had done so in 1941. Hinley Atkinson, the London organizer, reckoned current circumstances ruled out a recruitment campaign: his DLPs could not be expected to do more than try to contact their lapsed members.[32] When pressed further by Shepherd and Morrison in June 1942, Atkinson replied testily:

In many constituencies the records of Labour supporters (even where such records still exist) have been rendered almost useless. In many a good Labour division which formerly maintained a big membership large numbers of houses have been made uninhabitable; many of the still-functioning collectors lost track, almost overnight, of large numbers of their members (not to mention potential members) with little hope of tracing the bulk of them easily while present conditions last, and perhaps until a new electoral register is available. Many other of our members or supporters whose houses remain intact have removed either outside of London altogether, or . . . to the suburbs of Outer London.

Furthermore, '[t]he demands of the forces for men and women, the call of the civil defence services, of the Home Guard, of war-time employment, of the various agencies for voluntary war service' had all 'played havoc with the field of potential Labour Party membership', as well as with the existing membership, while the fact that local government had become far less partisan had removed an important source of Labour recruitment, since Labour's work in local councils in the 1930s had been a major factor inspiring people to join the party.[33] Almost all the DLPs did at least remain in existence, though, largely due to the hard work of local party organizers, and the relative ease of transport and communication that prevailed there in all but the worst periods of enemy action.

The issues affecting London Labour were replicated in a minor key in many of the great provincial cities. While DLPs fell back to the minimum membership in

[32] London LP papers, Acc. 2417/A/26, Hinley Atkinson, memo, 'Report on individual membership', 11 Feb. 1942.
[33] Ibid., Acc. 2417/A/3, executive committee 4 June, 15 July, 27 Aug. 1942; A/26, D. H. Daines and Hinley Atkinson, memo, 'Individual membership of the party in London, 1941–42', 7 July 1942.

Table 4.2. Number of big-city DLPs with 240 members or fewer, 1939–1945

City	Seats	1939	1940	1941	1942	1943	1944	1945
Glasgow	15	12	14	14	14	12 (+2)	14	13
Birmingham	12	3	5	9	8	6	7	9
Liverpool	11	3	7	8 (+1)	6 (+2)	8	5 (+1)	2
Manchester	10	1	1	3	3 (+1)	5	3	1
Sheffield	7	2	3	4	3	4	4	4
Leeds	6	0	0	0	0	0	0	0
Bristol	5	0	0	0	1	2 (+1)	1	1
Edinburgh	5	1	3	3	3	3	3	3
Nottingham	4	0	0	1	1	1	0	0
Hull	4	0	2	1	3	2	2	2
Bradford	4	2	3	4	3	1	2	2
Newcastle	4	3	4	4	4	4	3	1
Totals	87	27	42	51(+1)	49 (+3)	48 (+3)	44 (+1)	38

Note: +1, +2 indicate additional number with no functioning DLP at all.
Source: LPACR 1940–46, passim.

many cases, they usually managed to remain in some form of existence, although there were some problems in some seats in Glasgow, Liverpool, Manchester, and Bristol. However, membership did fall sharply in some cities, and recovery was slower here than in most other places. Well over half the constituencies in the twelve largest provincial cities were 'on the minimum' in every year between 1941 and 1944, and even in 1945 the figure was over 40 per cent (see Table 4.2).

The major cities were not the only areas heavily affected by wartime conditions. Coastal areas were especially hard hit, particularly those in eastern and southern England. Between 1918 and 1945, sixty-nine constituencies abutted the English south and/or east coasts, from St Ives in Cornwall to Berwick in Northumberland. The war, however, had a severe impact on these constituencies, thanks to enemy action, a greatly increased military presence, severe restrictions on freedom of movement, periodic invasion scares, partial evacuations, and voluntary removals, all of which played havoc with the kind of residential stability and ease of communication that were crucial to the effective maintenance of party organization and a mass membership (see Table 4.3). The effects of the intensification of the war, the fall of France, and the invasion scare can be seen in the figures for 1941, when 40 out of the 69 constituencies had little or nothing in the way of a functioning Labour party organization. The position could not get much worse in 1942, but it also took time to get better thereafter: it was only the return of peacetime conditions that allowed many of these parties effectively to revive. The disruption was greatest, unsurprisingly, in the south-eastern tip, covering Sussex, Kent, and Essex, and the east coast between there and the Humber. However, as the war situation eased, there was a degree of recovery, and the war's negative impact does not seem to have outlasted the end of hostilities:

Table 4.3. Labour party membership in English south and east coast constituencies, 1939–1945

Year	No DLP	240 or fewer	241 or more	Total
1938	0	11	58	69
1939	2	12	55	69
1940	1	23	45	69
1941	9	31	29	69
1942	6	36	27	69
1943	6	32	31	69
1944	5	29	35	69
1945	1	4	64	69

Source: LPAR 1939–46, passim.

by 1945, all 20 DLPs on the Sussex, Kent, and Essex coasts had memberships in excess of 240. The heaviest impact in the south-west came a little later: the areas was less vulnerable in 1940, but increasingly prone to aerial attack in 1941 and 1942, and often seriously disrupted by the build-up of Allied forces preparatory to D-Day in 1944. Here again, it is also noteworthy that all 23 constituencies had a functioning party, with membership above 240, by 1945. It is worth noting that the fall in Labour party membership was due, in large part, to problems that also faced the local Conservative and Liberal associations. It seems reasonable to suppose, therefore, that in these areas, their membership also suffered during the war.

Membership held up better in Wales than in Scotland. In Wales, a DLP was maintained in 34 of the 35 constituencies throughout the war, and although most DLPs suffered falling membership, at no point did more than a fifth of them drop to the 240 minimum membership. In Scotland, on the other hand, there were 70 constituencies (which elected 71 MPs); as early as 1940 there was no DLP at all in a tenth of them, and a further 34 were affiliating on the minimum. At the worst point, in 1942, only 15 DLPs had more than 240 members. This reflected, in part, the far-flung nature of many Scottish constituencies, but it was also down to Labour's ongoing weakness in Scotland, where the adverse effects of the split with the ILP were still being felt at constituency level, and which would not end with the Second World War.

Some DLPs did fare better. In 1941 and 1942, 30 still had more than 1,000 members. And, excluding parties that had been 'on the minimum' in 1938, 34 DLPs had the same or a higher membership in 1942 than in 1938. None was in Scotland. Three were scattered widely across Wales. In England, they included constituencies in the south and Midlands where the war had brought intensified industrialization and an influx of outside workers, like Yeovil (Somerset) and Wycombe (Buckinghamshire); constituencies where a modest gain was made on a very low 1938 figure; and areas where very conscious and devoted recruitment had continued despite the war. Notably, however, 20 of the 34 were located in the industrial north, and, of those 20, 13 were in Lancashire. Although it is important to remember that, even there, most parties lost members, it may be that this relative prosperity was not mere coincidence, and was due to factors such as physical distance from many of the war's worst impacts, solid levels of trade unionism, town patriotism in some of the constituencies, and lesser population movement than elsewhere. Some parts, at least, of such an interpretation would lend some support to the Conservative view that Labour benefited from the war organizationally, partly at least on the basis of the system of reserved occupations. However, as has also been demonstrated, such advantages were not, on the whole, as great as the Conservatives often claimed.

But Lancashire was not Britain, and the mood was gloomy in November 1941 when headquarters staff and regional organizers reviewed the national position. They agreed that the party's policy was not a major factor in the decline in membership. As Grace Taverner (Home and Southern Counties woman organizer) put it, '[a]fter the (roughly) 2 pacifists in each Division left the Party in the first weeks of the war, one heard no more of criticism of Party policy'. Indeed, the Scottish organizer, John Taylor, argued that to seek new members on the basis of policy was dangerous, as it might draw in Communists and other undesirable elements who agreed with Labour's present line on winning the war and increasing war production, but who would have no loyalty to Labour beyond that.[34] Instead, they identified three broad reasons for the fall in membership: first, '[g]eneral war time conditions', like the Blitz, the blackout, and so on; secondly, the '[a]bsence of normal Elections and Party rivalry' resulting from the Coalition and the lack of elections; and, finally, far-left mischief making, and especially the 'confusion created in the minds of ordinary members, by the repeated association of well known members with ad hoc and outside organizations, which tend to weaken and depreciate the value of Labour Party efforts'. To rectify matters, they suggested better publicity, the production of a short recruiting pamphlet, and, where possible, pilot membership drives in selected areas. There were hopes that the ongoing campaign to aid Russia had increased 'a "socialistic" interest' and would help provide a basis for future recruitment, especially among trade unionists.[35] It was also agreed that more should be done to try and replace departed collectors, and to develop contacts between DLPs and union branches. Taylor said that in Scotland he was 'plagued' by DLPs 'on the "minimum" and content to remain there, existing mainly as delegate bodies and covertly or overtly opposed to individual membership development', and he proposed special action to force such parties into active recruitment. However, there was

[34] LPNEC XIX, memo, 'Individual membership: resume of suggestions from district organizers and women organizers', to organization subcommittee 16 Dec. 1941.

[35] Ibid., memo, 'Individual membership', to organization subcommittee 18 Nov. 1941.

broad agreement that they could not be expected 'to turn all Constituencies into a Halifax at present'.[36]

As a result of these deliberations, 1942 saw recruitment schemes launched in Scotland, Wales, and the North-Western and Northern regions, while the publication of literature by headquarters was intensified.[37] One reason for the renewed emphasis on the development of regional councils of Labour at this point was the belief that they would prove to be effective vehicles for recruitment.[38] The campaign around *The Old World and the New Society* in early 1942 at least helped to shore up the existing membership, and some approaches were made to local trade union branches.[39] However, pressure from *Labour Organiser* and others to do more to revive the youth organization were brushed aside, not least for fear of opening a door to Communist infiltration.[40] Constituency parties also took their own initiatives. Most held their annual meetings in the first four months of 1942 and could hardly fail to notice how far their membership had fallen. Some did no more than try to contact lapsed members whose whereabouts were still known, but others were more enterprising: in London, Wandsworth Clapham DLP issued its own recruiting leaflet, while in the Lanarkshire coalfield, Hamilton DLP began a recruitment campaign that would lead to a significant increase in membership in 1943–4.[41] In many places, though, the situation remained dire. In Warwick and Leamington, for example, collections had virtually ceased due to long working hours and the blackout.[42] Such parties took in what came easily to them in terms of subscriptions, bought 240 party cards from headquarters, and did what they could while waiting for better times. It was clearer than ever that many parties affiliating on 240 members had far fewer members than that. East Grinstead (Sussex), for example, had only 116 'real' members in 1941 and just 91 in 1942; Gloucester had only 133 in 1943.[43] In addition, some parties that had been doing well now found the going tougher. Halifax, for example,

[36] LPNEC XIX, 'Notes on the discussions at the individual membership consultation between subcommittees of the national executive and members of the organizing staff', 19 Jan. 1942. For Halifax as exemplar, see *Labour Organiser*, Feb. 1942.

[37] LPNEC XIX, memo, 'Condition of the party', to NEC 25 Mar. 1942.

[38] See e.g. ibid., XX, memo, 'The Midland Counties and proposals for the establishment of regional councils of the Labour party therein', 30 June 1942.

[39] Labour party Wales records 3, South Wales regional council of Labour, executive committee 10 Mar. 1942; *Labour Organiser*, 1942, *passim* and especially Jan. 1942.

[40] LPNEC XIX, 'Notes on the discussions at the individual membership consultation between subcommittees of the national executive and members of the organizing staff', 19 Jan. 1942; organization subcommittee 18 Aug., 10 Nov. 1942; *Labour Organiser*, Jan., Feb. 1942; Taunton DLP papers, DD/TLP/1/1, annual meeting 28 Mar. 1942.

[41] See e.g. Blackpool DLP papers, DDX 2100/3/1, delegate meeting 15 Feb. 1942; Walsall DLP papers, Acc. 50/4, delegate meeting 17 Dec. 1942; Wandsworth Clapham DLP papers, IV/156/2/2, general committee 16 Apr. 1942; Hamilton DLP papers, BLPES film 211, reel 89, executive committee 25 Sept. 1942; annual report to annual general meeting 31 Mar. 1944.

[42] Warwick and Leamington DLP papers, MSS 133/1/1/4, annual meeting 11 July 1942.

[43] East Grinstead DLP papers, LA 2 MS 1/2/2, executive committee 8 Feb. 1943; Gloucester TLC papers, D3128/5/7, general committee 11 Nov. 1943.

came up against the law of diminishing returns in recruitment at just the point that it lost its agent and local working hours increased.[44]

Frustration continued to attend much recruitment activity. Tottenham South's hopes of launching 'a street by street campaign of recruitment to the Party', for example, were foiled when hardly anyone turned up to the launch meeting in November 1942.[45] In Lewisham West, the secretary considered mounting a membership drive, but had 'found it practically impossible to get the workers for such a campaign under present day conditions'.[46] When Norwich suffered air raids in May 1942, hundreds of party members who were bombed out and had to be rehoused lost touch with the party.[47] But where enthusiasts were willing and able to work hard through personal contact, new members could be brought in, even in difficult constituencies like Roxburgh and Selkirk in the Scottish borders.[48] In September 1942, a representative of Camberwell North West DLP claimed, on the basis of her own extensive experience, that, if collectors called, people would sign up to the party:

There was no resistance to membership appeals on policy grounds. She and her workers had been positively welcomed by the people they had visited. . . . Membership was there for the asking, but the job had to be done on the doorstep: there was no other way.[49]

By autumn 1942, many parties were planning fresh recruitment drives.[50] Some set specific targets: Pontypridd, for example, hoped to increase its membership from 747 in 1942 to 1,500 in 1943, and although the latter target was not reached, a figure of 1,222 was to be respectable, and higher than the 1938 level.[51] Even in London, a small campaign in war-ravaged Bethnal Green North-East that autumn brought in 40 new members.[52]

These efforts began to pay dividends in 1943, as decline ended and individual membership rose by 8 per cent. The number of constituencies without a DLP fell from 45 in 1942 to 32 in 1943, 29 in 1944, and just 10 in 1945. While this still left pre-1945 membership levels a long way short of peacetime expectations, it did reflect the fact that organization was becoming easier in many places, and showed the heightened interest in politics and party over post-war reconstruction.

---

[44] Halifax DLP papers, TU 28/2, executive committee minutes for 1942, *passim*.
[45] Tottenham South DLP papers, BLPES film 211A, reel 97564/2, general committee 25 Nov. 1942.
[46] Lewisham West DLP papers, A89/100/10, annual general meeting 15 Mar. 1943.
[47] Norwich DLP papers, SO 198/3/1, annual report 1942, n.d. [early 1943].
[48] Roxburgh and Selkirk DLP papers, Acc. 4145/1, quarterly meeting 13 Sept. 1942.
[49] London LP papers, Acc. 2417/A/26, conference of London DLPs, 12 Sept. 1942.
[50] See e.g. Lambeth North DLP papers, 1/3, special general committee 3 Sept. 1942; Brecon and Radnor DLP records 4, special meeting 7 Nov. 1942; Newport DLP papers, MNB/POL/6/A/8, executive committee 23 Nov. 1942; Scottish Labour party papers, TD 1384/1/2, executive committee 12 Dec. 1942.
[51] Labour party Wales records 3, South Wales regional council of Labour, executive committee 8 Sept. 1942.
[52] Bethnal Green North-East DLP papers, TH/8488/16, management committee 25 Feb. 1943.

Regional organizers and (where they existed) RCLs played an important role. The East Midlands regional organizer, J. T. Baxter, visited the DLPs in his area and set them specific targets for growth as part of a 'Two-Year Plan' which aimed to increase individual membership by 20 per cent.[53] Some parties reported impressive results. In Manchester Clayton, the secretary and six helpers, by following up a typewritten circular with personal calls, recruited 340 members in a few weeks in mid-1943; some inevitably fell away, but the party's overall membership rose from 1,113 in 1942 to 1,450 in 1943 and 1,800 in 1944.[54] In Loughborough (Leicestershire) later in the year, two members enrolled 173 and 103 new members respectively, part of a process that saw membership rise from 300 in 1942 to 550 in 1943, 1,050 in 1944, and 1,337 in 1945.[55] It was not just through conscious recruitment drives that new members were attracted, of course: other party activities, such as case work at advice bureaux, also helped.[56] In other places, though, things went less well. In Clapham, Communist activity hindered Labour recruitment; in Walsall, general disorganization saw membership collapse to such an extent that the NEC was forced to step in and reorganize the party; while in Cambridgeshire, a 1943 campaign saw much literature distributed, but only four new members recruited as a result.[57]

Increasing attention also began to be paid to the qualitative side of the party's individual membership. Concerns about an ageing membership had been expressed at a relatively early stage, but there were other factors, too.[58] In June 1943, the South Wales organizer spoke of the need to recruit abler members who could form 'a hard core of trained, experienced people'.[59] In response to concerns about the party's relative weakness among the middle classes, Derby DLP sent an envelope marked 'Personal' to every doctor in the town, enclosing a leaflet and a covering letter, in October 1942.[60] By 1943, increasing evidence of growing middle-class support for, and membership of, Common Wealth and the CPGB prompted Labour to firmer action. In the second half of the year *Labour Organiser* ran a series of five articles entitled 'Whom Do We Want in the Party?', emphasizing the importance of recruiting people from all ranks of the middle classes to the party. This was followed by a further series of five articles entitled 'How to Get Those Whom We Want into the Party', which ran from December 1943 until April 1944. These articles offered further advice on

[53] *Labour Organiser*, Sept. 1944; Northampton DLP papers, NLP 2, executive committee 7 Sept. 1943.

[54] *Labour Organiser*, Sept. 1943.   [55] Ibid., Nov. 1943.

[56] See e.g. Norwich DLP papers, SO 198/3/1, annual report 1943, n.d. [early 1944].

[57] Wandsworth Clapham DLP papers, IV/156/2/2, general management committee 21 May 1943; Walsall DLP papers, Acc. 50/15, annual report, 1943, n.d. [early 1944]; Cambridgeshire TCLP papers, 416/0.7, annual report for 1943–4, n.d. [early 1944].

[58] See e.g. *Labour Organiser*, Feb., Aug. 1942.

[59] Labour party Wales records 4, South Wales regional council of Labour, organization subcommittee 21 June 1943.

[60] Derby DLP papers, DL 116/1/1, executive committee 9 Oct. 1942.

recruitment, stressing inclusiveness and a broad appeal, and were very much in line with Transport House thinking.[61]

By October 1943, it was not unreasonable to take the view that the European war would end at some point in 1944. It was with this in mind that Labour launched 'A Year of Party Development' on 24 February 1944. The aim was to ensure 'a steady progressive enrolment of individual members', with an improvement in the overall 'quality' of the membership. All DLPs were to be set targets by their regional councils or district organizers.[62] The launch leaflet emphasized that 1944 would be 'a memorable year in our history' since, '[i]f our highest hopes are realised, it will be the year of victory in Europe'; if so, they were 'within measurable distance of a General Election' which it was 'imperative' that Labour won; and this could only be done if new and active members were recruited by 'a systematic and sustained effort, carried on with enthusiasm, efficiency, and drive'.[63] This emphasis on recruitment as a socialist act effectively yoked together ideological commitment and organizational zeal. Regional conferences were held all over Britain to get DLPs moving.[64] In some cases, this new push from Transport House simply confirmed the importance of the work they were already doing: some parties, indeed, had hardly stopped recruiting, while others had started afresh in the autumn of 1943.[65] What was different now was the unmistakable headquarters emphasis on recruitment as the necessary basis for electoral success. As a result, party members all over Britain began to show a new urgency in their recruitment activities. Many parties accepted their targets as a welcome challenge: Stockport started its campaign immediately, while Greenwich established recruitment 'canvassing squads', led by local councillors.[66] In February 1944 Ipswich set up a special committee to supervise a recruitment campaign, which included a big rally, the reinstitution of the party's political committee, and expenditure on leaflets, to get things moving, with some success.[67] Some foot dragging remained: Taunton (Somerset) complained that it lacked the resources to run a successful campaign.[68] But *Labour Organiser* could barely contain its astonishment when it reported news from Swindon that 'people are applying by post to join the Labour Party

[61] *Labour Organiser*, July–Dec. 1943, Jan.–Apr. 1944.

[62] LPNEC papers XX, 'Report of a consultation on individual membership', 20 Oct. 1943.

[63] Ibid., XXI, 'A Year of Party Development: Labour Must Prepare', Feb. 1944.

[64] See e.g. Blackpool DLP papers, DDX 2100/3/1, general committee 5 Mar. 1944.

[65] See e.g. Wansbeck DLP papers, NRO 527/A/3, executive committee 2 Oct. 1943.

[66] Stockport TCLP papers, B/MM/2/19A, political committee 3 Feb. 1944; Greenwich DLP papers, GLP 1.3, general committee 25 May 1944; see also e.g. Huddersfield DLP papers, BLPES film 211, reel 144, executive committee 6 June 1944; Hamilton DLP papers, BLPES film 211, reel 89, executive committee 30 June 1944.

[67] Ipswich TCLP papers, GK 400/1/1/4, executive committee 9 Feb. 1944, delegate meeting 16 Apr. 1944.

[68] Taunton DLP papers, DD/TLP/2/1, Taunton LLP meeting 22 May 1944; but see also DD/TLP/1/1, DLP general committee 1 July 1944.

without even being visited'; there was even improvement in Scotland.[69] These were new times indeed.

London remained something of an exception, although initially the 'Year of Party Development' began surprisingly well even there. In Clapham, for example, a meeting in June was told that canvassing was proceeding well, with 25 new members already made, although shortage of canvassers was a problem.[70] But a bigger worry was on the way, in the shape of the V-1 and, later, V-2 attacks. An emergency meeting on 6 July agreed to abandon the current campaign and close the DLP down until September.[71] However, with the worst raids apparently over, the party renewed its efforts, and by October its membership was rising.[72] Even though the headquarters of Wandsworth Central DLP suffered bomb damage no fewer than five times in 1944, individual membership was sustained fairly well thanks to the hard work of the collectors.[73] In Lewisham East, new members continued to be 'enrolled month by month despite the danger and difficulties': collectors 'often had to contact members in their shelters during the worst of the bombing—but contact them they did', enthused *Labour Organiser*.[74] But the raids often were disruptive. As in 1940–1, Bethnal Green North-East lost the membership, not only of those people who were killed, but also of those who were bombed out and had to go and live elsewhere.[75] After the event, the London Labour party concluded that the increase in individual membership in the capital would have been 'much greater' had there been no V-1 and V-2 attacks.[76] But elsewhere, where such attacks were much less of a concern, things were easier.

Some party members continued to argue that low membership was due to the party's moderate policy, and that 'the policy of the party was not sufficiently bold to attract new people to the Movement'.[77] But, as recruitment continued to increase, such attempts to beat the leadership using the membership figures lacked credibility. Organizational, rather than political, shortcomings had been largely to blame, and now they seemed to be under control. As early as June 1944, Transport House was already considering the campaign a success, Shepherd reporting that membership was up, and that the year would see 'a substantial' increase.[78] It was a sign of the continuing buoyancy of recruitment that there

---

[69] *Labour Organiser*, Sept. 1944; Scottish Labour party papers, TD 1384/3/1/1, executive committee report to 29th annual conference, 23–4 Sept. 1944.

[70] Wandsworth Clapham DLP papers, IV/156/2/2, general management committee 13 June 1944.

[71] Ibid., party officers' meeting 7 Aug. 1941.

[72] Ibid., general management committee 14 Sept. 1944, party officers' meeting 12 Oct. 1944, joint general and executive committees 19 Oct. 1944, annual report 1944 [early 1945].

[73] Bevin papers, BEVN II 8/1, Wandsworth Central DLP, annual report, 1944 [early 1945].

[74] *Labour Organiser*, May 1945.

[75] Bethnal Green North-East DLP papers, TH/8488/16, annual report 1944 [early 1945].

[76] London LP papers, Acc. 2417/A/27, 'The work of the London Labour party, 1944', Feb. 1945.

[77] Rother Valley DLP papers, 290/G1/1, special conference on organizing 15 July 1944.

[78] LPNEC papers XXI, organization subcommittee 21 June 1944.

was relatively little resistance to a change in the party's rules whereby a minimum individual membership fee (of 6*d*. per month) was set centrally for the first time, as opposed to 'a membership fee', the size of which had never been specified by the national party.[79]

Evidence as to the demographic profile of the new recruits is patchy. Many of them were young people. League of Youth branches began to be revived from mid-1944 onwards, and members of autonomous youth movements also began to gravitate towards the party.[80] In Cleveland, it was reported in March 1945 that the number of young people at party meetings was much higher than a year earlier.[81] In some areas, recruitment among women increased.[82] In South Wales, there were reports that numerous applications for membership had been received from members of the forces.[83] However, national and constituency records are largely silent on the matter of class composition, and there seems no reason to believe that there was a major change in this regard.

The approach of the end of the war and the general election brought other priorities for Labour's organizers and members in the first months of 1945, but recruitment continued all the same, and progress was encouraging: in Dulwich, for example, 44 new members joined in March 1945, 28 in April, and 25 in May.[84] After VE Day, there was a further intensification of effort. In Gloucester, two evenings' canvassing in a single ward led to the recruitment of 99 new members, a remarkable achievement given that the whole DLP's membership for 1944 had not exceeded 240.[85] The general election campaign itself was a very effective recruiting agent, with numerous reports of enthusiastic people, many of them young, coming forward to work for the party for the first time, and many DLPs registered significant increases in membership as a result.[86] And recruitment continued even more strongly after the election. Luton DLP (Bedfordshire), whose membership had been 656 in 1938 and 1,010 in 1944,

---

[79] Ibid., NEC 8 Dec. 1944; *LPACR* 1943, 220; *LPACR* 1944, 143, 196. For opposition, see e.g. Greenwich DLP papers, GLP 1.3, special general committee 7 Dec. 1944; Cambridgeshire TCLP papers, 416/0.7, annual general meeting 28 Apr. 1945.

[80] See e.g. Broxtowe DLP papers, DD/PP/6/6, council meeting 28 Oct. 1944; Newport DLP papers, MNB/POL/14/3, organizing subcommittee 23 Oct. 1944; Hendon DLP papers, BLPES film 211A, reel 97559/1, executive committee 20 Dec. 1944; Norwich DLP papers, SO 198/3/1, annual report 1944, n.d. [early 1945]; Halifax DLP papers, TU 28/2, secretary's report, Sept. 1944.

[81] Cleveland DLP papers, U/CDLP 1/1, annual report to annual meeting 10 Mar.1945; see also e.g. Wandsworth Clapham DLP papers, IV/156/2/2, annual general meeting of individual members 1 Mar. 1945.

[82] See e.g. Rother Valley DLP papers, 290/G1/1, executive committee 14 Oct. 1944.

[83] Labour party Wales records 4, meeting of election agents and CLP secretaries 3 Feb. 1945.

[84] See e.g. Stockport TCLP papers, B/MM/2/19, finance subcommittee 27 Feb. 1945; Dulwich DLP papers, A390/uncl., general management committee 29 Mar., 26 Apr., 17 May 1945.

[85] Gloucester TLC papers, D3128/5/7, executive committee 17 May 1945.

[86] See e.g. Derby DLP papers, DL 116/1/1, executive committee 13 July 1945; Lewisham West DLP papers, A89/100/10, general committee 16 July, 3 Sept. 1945; Great Yarmouth DLP papers, Acc. 2002/90, management committee 2 Aug. 1945.

soared to 4,218 members in 1945; Taunton, which had affiliated on the 240 minimum each year from 1938 to 1943, and had only managed a modest increase to 350 in 1944, now boomed to 1,536; and North Lanarkshire's membership rose from 240 to 1,313 in 1945. But some parties were in secular decline, and nowhere more so than in the depopulated areas of east London, where once thriving DLPs thrived no more. The most spectacular example was Stepney Mile End, whose officially declared membership in 1945—240—was only 11 per cent of the 1938 level of 2,169. A once-flourishing DLP was now no more than a shell, and it is scarcely surprising that the Communist Phil Piratin was able to take the seat in 1945.[87]

Elsewhere, Labour's managers realized that they must sustain the improvement. In his report on the election for the NEC, Phillips spoke of the need for a major membership drive after the November municipal elections; it duly took place in early 1946.[88] Problems remained, of course. In Scotland, there were still few parties that had much in the way of mass membership: in Glasgow, the very idea was little more than a joke, and there appears to have been little intention within the city party that things should change; it remained common for people to have 'a heck of a job' joining the party there.[89] That Barnsley DLP was still affiliating on 240 members even in 1945 was nothing short of abysmal. Overall, however, Labour was about to enter a new era. For the only time in its history, it stood on the verge of a truly mass membership. Although aspirations for a national individual membership of one million by 1947 were to prove overambitious (the actual figure achieved would be 608,487), that barrier was ultimately breached in both 1952 and 1953, before falling back to enter a fairly steady decline in the 1960s and 1970s.[90]

In numerical terms, of course, individual members were greatly outweighed by affiliated ones. Individual members were the ones who kept DLPs going, and there was a widespread feeling that 'Trade Unionists [did] not do their share in Labour Party machinery'.[91] But affiliated membership mattered, not least for financial reasons. Between the wars, it had fluctuated significantly, depending on the state of the economy (and hence the level of trade union membership) and the legal position of the political levy. The peak inter-war year had been 1920, when Labour's affiliated union membership had reached 4.3 million. It then fell back as unemployment rose, and the Conservatives' 1927 Trade Disputes Act,

---

[87] Bethnal Green North-East DLP papers, TH/8488/1, 'The Labour party: formation of new constituency party: particulars of Mile End Labour party', n.d. [1948].

[88] LPNEC XXI, Phillips, memo, 'General election, 1945: interim report by the secretary', n.d., to NEC 31 July 1945; Phillips papers, GS/1945/37, memo, 'Party development: report by general secretary', 26 Sept. 1945; *Labour Organiser*, Aug. 1945; LPNEC XXI, organization subcommittee 19 Sept., 17 Oct. 1945.

[89] D. Weinbren, *Generating Socialism: Recollections of Life in the Labour Party* (Stroud, 1997), 27.

[90] Wansbeck DLP papers, NRO 527/B/7, Newburn and District LLP, report for six months ending 30 June 1947, n.d. [1947]; *LPACR* 1978, 89–90.

[91] *Labour Organiser*, Oct. 1941.

which replaced 'contracting out' of the political levy with 'contracting in'—to place the power of inertia on the side of non-payment—led to a fall of about a third, from 3.2 million in 1927 to 2.0 million in 1928. The trade slump that followed saw a trough of 1.9 million reached in 1934, before a rather muted recovery to 2.1 million in 1938 and 2.2 million in 1939.[92]

The outbreak of war did not see a fall in Labour's affiliated membership, thanks in part to falling unemployment and an increasingly sympathetic state stance towards trade unionism. There was, however, sufficient in the past records of both Chamberlain and Churchill to remind trade unionists of the need for the Labour party, especially in the context of a war of production. Therefore affiliated membership did not undergo the same vicissitudes as the individual membership. Instead, it fluctuated around 2.2 million between 1938 and 1943, before rising slightly to 2.4 million in 1944 and 2.5 million the following year (see Table 4.1).

The identity of the affiliates changed little: the only significant new affiliation in the war years was that of the Association of Engineering and Shipbuilding Draughtsmen, which joined in 1944 with 14,438 members.[93] Much more importance was attached to increasing the proportion of union members paying the political levy. Much to the long-term vexation of Transport House, there was enormous variation in the extent of contracting in: in 1939, for example, 82.5 per cent of NUDAW's membership was contracting in to the political levy, but only 19.5 per cent of the AEU's. In January 1941, with individual membership falling and continuing concerns about money, the NEC began to take a closer look at the matter; some unions were already acutely conscious of the gap, and launched campaigns to try to close it; and DLPs did what they could to help.[94] But there was little improvement overall, and 1942's affiliated membership was slightly lower than 1939's. It was also clear by 1943 that, as union membership had risen in wartime, the contracted-in figure had not kept pace, so that only 39.9 per cent of union members were paying the levy, as opposed to 45.4 per cent in 1939. Worst of all, the number of contracted-in engineers had scarcely risen despite the AEU's huge rise in membership, which meant that now only about one in every seven AEU members was contributing to the Labour party.[95]

This was a problem, but also an opportunity. By late 1943, the NEC was talking seriously to union leaders about the issue. After all, if even half the remaining engineers started paying the levy, it would represent a major increase in membership and revenue. Little wonder that a committee of five leading trade

[92] *LPACR* 1940, 45.   [93] LPNEC papers XXI, NEC 26 Apr. 1944; *LPACR 1946*, 74.
[94] LPNEC papers XIX, finance and general purposes committee 16 Jan. 1941; Middleton papers, MID 65/61, A. Callighan, general secretary, National Union of Blastfurnacemen, etc., to J. S. Middleton, 1 May 1941; Cleveland DLP papers, U/CDLP 1/1, annual meeting 15 Feb. 1941.
[95] LPNEC papers XX, memo, 'Contracting-in membership of trade unions', Oct. 1943, to special conference of trade union officers, 12 Nov. 1943.

unionists was set up to look further into the matter.[96] A number of unions, and particularly the AEU, began to work very hard, and with some success, to increase their levels of contracting in.[97] Local campaigns were also important. A London Labour party effort in 1943–4 helped increase the party's affiliated membership in the year by 9,000 (about 7 per cent).[98] During 1944–5, DLPs and the regional councils also campaigned on the matter.[99] By 1945, there had been a modest, but significant, increase in Labour's affiliated membership to 2.5 million, the highest since before the 1927 Act; and, once the post-war Labour government had repealed that legislation in 1946, the figure rose to over 4.3 million. In 1952, it exceeded five million for the first time, and was to remain between five and six million between then and the 1980s. It was an expansion rooted in the Second World War.

As well as affiliating at national level, trade union branches could also affiliate to their local DLP. Here again there had been progress by 1945. The extent of such affiliation had always varied. In the best-organized parties with the most powerful local trade union movements, the results could be impressive. Derby DLP had 69 local union braches, totalling over 14,000 members, affiliated to it in 1939; Doncaster had 27.[100] But many DLPs had few, if any, such affiliations. These were not just in areas of Labour electoral weakness: indeed, an NEC report in 1943 suggested that the position was often worst in the large cities, either because of 'apathy', low levels of contracted-in membership, or because 'Subversive Movements ha[d] discouraged hard-working Trade Union representatives from attending meetings'.[101] Unions were asked bluntly to ensure that their branches were 'properly affiliated to the Constituency Parties', not least to 'ensure that Trade Union interests in [parliamentary] candidatures [were] not neglected'.[102]

From an early point in the war, many DLPs had begun to look at the possibilities of bringing in more affiliations, and there were some successes, but much remained to be done: in February 1942, for example, Epsom DLP noted that 17 of the constituency's 37 union branches were still not

    [96] LPNEC papers XX, special conference of trade union officers, 12 Nov. 1943.
    [97] Amalgamated Engineering Union papers, MSS 259/4/15/45, 'Report of the proceedings of the twenty-seventh national committee, 1945', 145, 167; AEU *Monthly Journal*, Jan., Feb. 1945.
    [98] London LP papers, Acc. 2417/A/3, executive committee 22 July 1943, A/27, 'The work of the London Labour party, 1943', Feb. 1944.
    [99] See e.g. Wolverhampton West DLP papers, D/LAB/1/9, executive committee 22 Apr. 1944; Labour party Wales records 4, South Wales regional council of Labour, organization subcommittee 23 May 1944.
    [100] Derby LP papers, Box 3, 18(a), DLP annual report 1939 [1940]; Doncaster DLP papers, DS 7/1/4, balance sheet, 1939, n.d. [early 1940].
    [101] LPNEC papers XX, memo, 'Report of the joint committee of the elections subcommittee of the national executive committee and representatives appointed by trade union officers', 5 Jan. and 23 Feb. 1943.
    [102] Ibid.

affiliating.[103] One tactic was to ask local branches to allow party officers to attend a branch meeting, and the intensity of such requests increased as the end of the war approached: in March 1945, Wolverhampton West DLP officers began a series of visits to such branches, recording very favourable receptions from all five branches visited (three of them AEU). Five further visits were planned for April and May 1945.[104] In part, this reflected increased pressure on branches from unions' headquarters. The AEU, Electricians (ETU) and Agricultural Workers (NUAW) all began to affiliate large numbers of branches to DLPs across the country.[105] Others, like the Woodworkers (ASW), also increased their presence, while there was also some tightening up of an already relatively strong position regarding railway union branches.[106] Even so, it often remained difficult to get large numbers of trade unionists to play a very active role in DLP life.[107]

Perhaps the greatest asset of the affiliated membership for Labour was its stability. Party managers, although concerned about individual membership for much of the war, could at least avoid panic. Without the affiliated membership, it might have been harder to resist those siren voices, like Laski's, that were keener to break with the Coalition and precipitate a very dangerous leap in the dark. So long as the union membership of the party was holding up, it was possible for the party to be held in a state of readiness for the post-war world, rather than making a premature, and potentially risky, move. It also meant that there was a strong base on which to build when, after the war, full employment and higher union membership, combined with a change in the law on the political levy, allowed much greater potential for expansion. In the face of this success, it is not surprising that those few who called for a more radical approach, such as moving over to a single membership fee for affiliated and individual members alike, got

---

[103] Epsom DLP papers, 2141/1, annual report for 1941 to annual general meeting 21 Feb. 1942; and see e.g. Northampton DLP papers, NLP 2, special executive committee 27 Aug. 1940; Wansbeck DLP papers, NRO 527/A/3, executive committee 30 Mar. 1940.

[104] Wolverhampton West DLP papers, D/LAB/1/9, executive committee 22 Apr. 1944, 22 Feb., 29 Mar. 1945.

[105] For the AEU, see e.g. Blackpool DLP papers, DDX 2100/3/2, general committee 16 Apr. 1944; Wolverhampton Bilston DLP papers, D/LAB/3/1, executive committee 7 Apr. 1945. For the ETU, see e.g. Doncaster DLP papers, DS 7/1/6, annual report for 1944 [early 1945]; Hamilton DLP papers, BLPES film 211, reel 89, annual report to annual general meeting 30 Mar. 1945. For the NUAW, see e.g. Cambridgeshire TCLP papers, 416/0.7, annual general meeting 28 Apr. 1945; Cleveland DLP papers, U/CDLP 1/1, annual report to annual meeting 10 Mar.1945.

[106] For the ASW, see e.g. Cambridge TCLP papers, 634/09, monthly meeting 11 July 1945. For the railway unions, see e.g. Lambeth North DLP papers, 1/3, management committee 6 Feb. 1944; South Shields DLP papers, BLPES film 211, reel 27, meeting 7 Sept. 1943; Taunton DLP papers, DD/TLP/1/1, annual meeting 14 Apr. 1945.

[107] LPNEC papers XX, memo, 'Report of the joint committee of the elections subcommittee of the national executive committee and representatives appointed by trade union officers', 5 Jan. and 23 Feb. 1943; Wrexham TCDLP papers, DD/DM/344/5, executive committee 4 Oct. 1944.

nowhere, and that the hybrid form of Labour party membership was left intact.[108]

THE CONSERVATIVES

The Conservative party compiled no national-level membership figures before 1946.[109] This makes it difficult to draw firm conclusions about wartime developments, but it does not render analysis impossible. In particular, constituency-level records, while rarely offering firm figures, are often highly suggestive. There is enough evidence to demonstrate at least the broad outlines of development.

In 1939, the Conservatives had every bit as much right to claim to be a mass-membership party as Labour did. As seen above, DLPs with 1,000 members were thought to be doing well, and those with 2,000 or more were exceptional. Compare that with the following Conservative figures for 1938 or 1939. The 11 constituencies that comprised Birmingham Unionist association (UA) had a total membership of 35,000 in March 1939, and Chelmsford CA (Essex) 3,000.[110] The parallel women's associations were often very large indeed: prior to the war Louth (Lincolnshire) had more than 4,300 members, Maidstone (Kent) almost 6,000, and Newbury (Berkshire) between 7,000 and 8,000.[111] Others were less fortunate: Mid-Bedfordshire, for example, had only 304 paid-up members in 1939.[112] But they could always try a membership drive: Honiton CA (Devon) recruited no fewer than 1,078 new members in 1938, while in July 1939 Epsom CA (Surrey) used 340 voluntary canvassers to recruit 1,120 new members.[113] Meanwhile, the membership of the party's youth movement, the Junior Imperial League (JIL), might have been as high as 100,000 in 1939.[114] Not all members were active, of course, but this was no different from Labour's experience, and even a passive membership, so long as it was large, was increasingly being seen as an asset, if only by ensuring a broader, and so more reliable, income base.[115]

One way of securing such a base was to introduce what Conservatives called the 'book system', whereby collectors called regularly on members and recorded

[108] NULOEA papers, uncl., annual conference, Blackpool, 20 May 1945.

[109] Ball, 'Local Conservatism', 290.

[110] Birmingham CA papers, uncat., management committee 10 Mar. 1939; Chelmsford CA papers, D/Z 96/13, annual general meeting 23 Feb. 1939.

[111] Heneage papers, HNC 2/48, Louth CA, annual report for 1938, to annual general meeting 23 Mar. 1939; Maidstone CA papers, U1634/A3/1/2, annual meeting 27 Mar. 1939; Newbury CA papers, D/EX 409/53, *Official Yearbook and Blotter* (Newbury, 1938), 5.

[112] Mid-Bedfordshire CA papers, Z 145/98, annual report for 1939, n.d. [1940].

[113] Western Conservative area council papers, ARE 11/1/1, annual report 1938, to annual meeting 31 Mar. 1939; South-East Conservative area council papers, ARE 9/11/4, finance committee 5 July 1939.

[114] CCO 500/1/10, 'Report of the youth committee', 14 Dec. 1943.

[115] See e.g. Blackpool CA papers, PLC 5/1/3, annual report to annual general meeting 31 Mar. 1939; Flint CA papers, D/DM/307/4, annual meeting 6 May 1939.

their subscriptions in a book. Such a system allowed the party to spread its membership, not least to the less well off who found small weekly payments easier than large quarterly or annual ones. This system, though far from universal, was spreading in the later 1930s, often producing good, and sometimes excellent, results: in Salisbury (Wiltshire), it was instrumental in the increase in the CA's membership by almost 300 in the year to April 1939.[116] It does not seem unreasonable to assume that, by and large, Conservative party membership was steady, and perhaps even increasing somewhat, down to the outbreak of war in 1939.[117]

Membership clearly fell once war broke out, however. Initially, this was a slow process. Many associations continued to try to collect subscriptions, following the advice that eventually emanated from Central Office; some, like Monmouth, justified this explicitly on the grounds that failure to collect during the Great War had led to severe organizational problems.[118] Some agreed to seek a reduced amount, to try and ensure that people remained members.[119] Evacuation areas were particularly hard hit, losing women members especially.[120] Efforts to chase lapsed members began to meet a poor response, and in some areas, collection was severely curtailed, or ceased altogether.[121] Some associations kept their membership better than others: in Harborough, for example, it was noted that all branches of the senior organization remained intact and that 'in most cases membership ha[d] been maintained'.[122] But membership in Glasgow began to fall in October, and the overall trend was clearly downwards by early 1940, with the war, and military service in particular, having a detrimental effect.[123] Significantly, the recruitment trophies customarily awarded by associations to

[116] Salisbury CA papers, 2639/1, annual general meeting 22 Apr. 1939; and see e.g. Gravesend CA papers,U1795/AD1/4, finance committee 18 July 1939; Bewdley CA papers, BA 956/8, special subcommittee on finance, 25 July 1939.

[117] See e.g. Stafford CA papers, D1289/1/3, finance committee 16 Jan. 1939; Reigate CA papers, 353/3/1/1, annual report to special meeting 6 May 1940; Ipswich CA papers, GK 401/1/1, annual report, 1938–9, to annual general meeting 6 Mar. 1939; Newport CA records 1, annual report of the women's section, for 1940, to annual meeting 17 Mar. 1939; Yorkshire Conservative area council papers, WYL 1856/1/3, annual report to annual meeting 17 Feb. 1940.

[118] Monmouth CA records 10, finance and general purposes committee 6 Sept. 1939; and see e.g. Fylde CA papers, DDX 1202/1/1, emergency committee 3 Oct. 1939.

[119] See e.g. Newbury CA papers, D/EX 409/3, finance and general purposes committee 18 Sept. 1939.

[120] See e.g. Southampton CA papers, D/STC/1/4, Shirley ward women's branch, report for 1939, n.d. [1940].

[121] See e.g. Chelmsford CA papers, D/Z 96/7, ways and means subcommittee, 11 Dec. 1939, 12 Feb. 1940; Watford CA papers, D/EX 901/3–11, collection books of Rickmansworth branch, 1923–43.

[122] Harborough CA papers, DE 1170/4, 46th annual report, for year to 31 Mar. 1940.

[123] Glasgow UA papers, Acc. 10424/74, general committee 23 Nov. 1939, 13 Mar. 1940; and see e.g. Western Conservative area council papers, ARE 11/7/3, Cornwall provincial division, annual report to annual meeting 20 Mar. 1940; Flint CA, papers, D/DM/307/4, annual general meeting 6 Apr. 1940; Fylde CA papers, DDX 1202/1/1, annual report 1943, to annual general meeting 25 Mar. 1943.

their branches had mostly been suspended by the spring of 1940.[124] As the war intensified, so did the decline. The main reasons appear to have been societal and organizational, rather than political. It may well be that some people left the party in disgust at the failure of Chamberlain to prevent the war, or because they opposed the war altogether, or, later, because they could not stomach Churchill as party leader; but there is little, if any, hard evidence of such actions, whereas there is considerable evidence that failures of organization played a large part. The chairman of Ealing CA argued in 1942 that the 'main' reason for the fall in membership there was the absence of collectors—'People would not come to the office to pay them but waited to be called upon'—and the Wessex area council found that '[w]here a real effort [was] made to collect subscriptions the response [was] satisfactory'.[125] The Blunsdon ward of Swindon had had a thriving association before the war, with 155 members in 1939, but it effectively collapsed in the spring of 1940—not due to any mass desertion, but simply because collectors could no longer be found. The lapsed members were probably no less Conservative than they had been when paying their subscriptions, and remained ready to return to the party once its organization began to revive in 1944–5.[126] Population movements and, as 1940 and 1941 wore on, the effects of enemy action were also significant, especially—but not only—in London and near the south and east coasts.[127] Hopes that area offices could be used as clearing houses to keep track of evacuated members were not fulfilled, any more than were Labour hopes of an efficient transfer system of members between DLPs.

A useful microcosm of the reasons for membership lapses can be seen in a detailed contemporary analysis of the position in the south London constituency of Clapham. Pre-war membership had stood at around 4,000, but when 1,356 members were lost between February and December 1941 alone, concerned officials decided to define the reasons why people had ceased to be members (see Table 4.4). Their findings demonstrated the extent to which societal, rather than political, reasons led people to abandon party membership. Only 7 out of the 1,356—0.5 per cent—cited political objections, namely the inactivity of the association and the MP; overwhelmingly, it was issues like air raids and evacuation that were responsible, a view supported by evidence from other cities.[128] There was some change in Clapham in 1942, when the war was going badly. Then, there were reports of male members, in particular, being 'critical

---

[124] See e.g. Salisbury CA papers, 2639/1, annual general meeting 27 Apr. 1940.

[125] Ealing CA papers, Acc. 1338/2, executive committee 15 Oct. 1942; Wessex Conservative area council papers, ARE 10/1/3, annual report to annual meeting 7 May 1941.

[126] Swindon CA papers, 2509/12, Blunsdon ward annual general meeting 16 Feb. 1939, 4 March 1940.

[127] Lambeth Norwood CA papers, IV/166/1/16, annual report 1940–1 to annual general meeting 15 Mar.1941, emergency committee 15 Aug. 1940; Wessex Conservative area council papers, ARE 10/1/3, annual report to annual meeting 27 May 1942.

[128] Clapham CA papers, BLPES film 548, finance committee 4 Dec. 1941; and see e.g. Sheffield Central CA papers, LD 2104, finance committee 27 Feb. 1942.

Table 4.4. Reasons given for ceasing membership of Clapham CA, 1941

Reason given	Number	%
Temporary evacuations, residential and business	507	37.4
Moved away	472	34.8
Bombed out and house demolished	246	18.1
Inability to afford subscription due to increased taxation, increased cost of living, illness, other calls and/or appeals, National Savings, and so on	66	4.9
Deceased	58	4.3
Refusal to continue supporting Conservative cause	7	0.5
Total	1,356	100.0

Source: Clapham CA papers, BLPES film 548, finance committee 4 Dec. 1941.

of political matters'.[129] Even at this stage, however, the bulk of the membership remained loyal, and associations which actively sought subscriptions tended to find that they came in satisfactorily.[130]

This fact led some associations to seek new members via recruitment drives at a relatively early stage of the war. In the first half of 1941, Manchester enrolled 90 new members, while Torquay CA (Devon) enrolled 350 new members in 1942.[131] From late 1941 onwards some associations were trying to contact and retrieve lapsed members, sometimes with positive results.[132] As early as June 1941, there were reports of JIL branches being re-established, albeit usually with very small memberships, and by 1942 there was increasing emphasis on the need to appeal to youth, in part because of concerns that young people were being drawn into bodies run by 'Pacifists and conscientious objectors', as one London Conservative put it in September 1942.[133]

The membership of most Conservative associations fell between 1940 and 1942.[134] But the military and domestic events of the winter of 1942–3 stimulated greater effort. They reminded Conservatives of the finite nature of the

[129] Clapham CA papers, BLPES film 548, finance and executive committee 29 May 1942.
[130] See e.g. Maidstone CA papers, U1634/A3/1/2, emergency subcommittee 9 Jan. 1942; Glasgow UA papers, Acc. 10424/75, general committee 23 Feb. 1942; Newport CA records 1, annual report 1941, to annual general meeting 20 Mar. 1942.
[131] Derby papers, 920DER(17)/16/4, T. H. Hewlett (Manchester CUA) to Earl of Derby, 14 July 1941; *Conservative Agents' Journal*, July 1943.
[132] See e.g. Dorset West CA papers, D399/4/1, finance committee 1 Sept. 1941; D399/3/2, war emergency executive committee 12 Dec. 1941.
[133] Lambeth Norwood CA papers, IV/166/1/16, emergency committee 20 June 1941, 25 Sept. 1942; Salisbury CA papers, 2639/1, annual general meeting 8 Aug. 1942; Middleton and Prestwich CA papers, PLC 1/3, finance and general purposes committee 28 June 1941.
[134] See e.g. Merionethshire CA papers, Z/M/4018/2, annual meeting 10 Feb. 1941.

war, and also that politics would remain contested after its end. Poor results in by-elections also acted as a spur, and a new tone of exhortation began to appear in the comments of some local officials to their parties' annual meetings in the spring of 1943.[135] Some associations continued to do little more than bemoan their falling membership, but others did something about it, and the book scheme was revived in a number of places with positive results.[136] By June 1943, the Scottish western divisional council was reporting 'a quickening of interest in a largely increased membership', the figure having increased by a quarter in the last year, and the improvement continued over the following year as well, while Salisbury CA recruited 'ever increasing' numbers of new members.[137] Some associations began to develop new lines of approach: Ealing, for example, held a 'very successful' recruitment lunch, attended by the MP and forty local businessmen and non-political 'local personalities'.[138]

In April 1944, Central Office staff decided to issue a recruitment leaflet, although the fact that they only updated a pre-war publication did not suggest a very wholehearted approach.[139] Some associations, like Chichester (West Sussex), began to advertise for members in the local press, although showing care not to be too combative in the wording of the notice for fear of upsetting the 'party truce'.[140] There were some impressive results: Northampton CA recruited 102 new members in 1944 (and a further 118 in 1945), while a single ward in Bolton recruited 45 new members in the year to May 1944.[141] The relaunch of the youth movement in autumn 1944 was also significant.[142] In Birmingham, a press advertisement in late 1944 attracted 300 applications for membership of the Young Conservatives; 200 people attended the inaugural meeting, and there were numerous successful launches elsewhere.[143] In early 1945, progress continued, with most associations checking over old membership lists and some engaging

---

[135] Chippenham CA papers, 2436/2, annual general meeting 20 Nov. 1943; Bolton CA papers, FDC/3/9, women's CA annual report 1942–3, to annual meeting 2 Apr. 1943.

[136] For moaning, see e.g. Norwich CA papers, SO 122/4, finance and general purposes committee 14 Apr. 1943; for doing, see e.g. Rushcliffe CA papers, DD/PP/3/1, West Bridgford CA general committee 30 Apr. 1943; *Conservative Agents' Journal*, Jan. 1945.

[137] Scottish UA papers, Acc. 10424/27(viii), western divisional council, annual report 1943, 1 July 1943; annual report 1944, 1 July 1944; Salisbury CA papers, 2639/1, annual general meeting 5 June 1943.

[138] Ealing CA papers, Acc. 1338/2, executive committee 8 June, 19 Oct. 1943.

[139] CCO 500/1/12, 'Report of the staff conference, 2 and 3 April 1944', 12 Apr. 1944.

[140] Chichester CA papers, CO/1CH/Add. MS. 12088, organization subcommittee 4 Dec. 1944.

[141] Northampton CA papers, NCCA/29, annual report 1945, 25 Mar. 1946; Bolton CA papers, FDC/3/9, women's CA annual report to annual meeting 1 May 1944.

[142] See e.g. Topping's speech to the NSCUA: NSCUA papers, Acc. 485/5, war emergency committee, 21 Sept. 1944.

[143] Birmingham CA papers, uncat., management committee 25 Jan. 1945; and see e.g. Norwich CA papers, SO 122/4, finance and general purposes committee 5 Feb. 1945; Western Conservative area council papers, ARE 11/1/1, annual meeting 9 Feb. 1945 (re Bristol); York CA papers, 156/22, executive committee 23 Feb. 1945.

paid collectors.[144] Press advertisements invited former members to come forward; they also showed a wider public that the association was reviving.[145] Another way of showing the party to the wider population was to collect and disseminate information on the war record of local party members, as in Gravesend, where branches were asked to compile a list of members lost or bereaved by enemy action, and any other particularly noteworthy items, such as 'decorations to members or their relatives'.[146] Recruitment continued up to the general election, although, as with Labour, other priorities temporarily came first.[147]

Defeat at that election provided a huge fillip to Conservative recruitment. Faced with the reality of a 'socialist' government, many lapsed members returned, and new ones came in for the first time.[148] It was now generally felt to be better to have large numbers of small subscribers than a small number of large ones, and this led associations like Hartlepool to place new emphasis on recruitment.[149] The launch of a national membership drive, 'Operation Knocker', in 1946 had a dramatic impact.[150] By the end of 1946, the 24 CAs in Middlesex had a combined membership of 49,544; in nearby Surrey, Guildford CA's membership rose from 3,000 in early 1946 to 10,717 in March 1947.[151] These were halcyon days for party recruitment, when, for example, 106 new members could be made in the small town of Chandlers Ford (Winchester constituency, Hampshire) in a single week's campaigning in 1947, or when a single member of Reigate CA (Surrey) could enrol a thousand members in the eighteen months to May 1948.[152] Ross McKibbin has argued that local Conservative associations were well networked with other voluntary organizations: this meant that lapsed members were probably quite easy to approach *en masse* once associations began seriously to revive, because they were relatively easy to find in chambers of commerce, golf and tennis clubs, masonic lodges, and the like.[153] Overall party membership totalled 911,000 when the first-ever national figures were collated in early 1946; it passed a million in 1947, and was to peak at 2.8 million in 1953.[154]

[144] See e.g. Bodmin CA papers, DDX 385/1, executive committee 16 Sept. 1944; Newbury CA papers, D/EX 409/20, memo, 'General election 1945', n.d. [Aug. 1945]; Ealing CA papers, Acc. 1338/2, executive committee 8 Feb. 1945.

[145] See e.g. Gravesend CA papers, U1795/AD1/4, executive committee 23 Mar. 1945.

[146] D/EX 409/53, U1795/AD5/1, women's advisory committee 11 May 1945.

[147] See e.g. Dorset West CA papers, D399/4/1, finance committee 14 Apr. 1945.

[148] See e.g. Tynemouth CA papers, Acc. 1633/2, special executive committee 3 Aug. 1945; Dorset West CA papers, D399/3/2, war emergency executive committee 19 Nov. 1945.

[149] City of Cardiff CA records 26, Llandaff and Barry CA finance and general purposes committee 20 Sept. 1945; The Hartlepools CA papers, D/X 327/2, executive committee 17 Aug. 1945.

[150] M. Pinto-Duschinsky, *British Political Finance, 1830–1980* (Washington, DC, 1981), 132.

[151] Essex and Middlesex Conservative area council papers, ARE 8/1/3, finance and general purposes committee 6 Aug. 1947; Guildford CA papers, 3960/7/2, annual report, 1946–7, 31 Mar. 1947.

[152] Winchester CA papers, 73M86W/52, women's branch, annual report 1947, Mar. 1948; Reigate CA papers, 353/3/1/3, annual report, 1947 to annual meeting 11 May 1948.

[153] R. I. McKibbin, *Classes and Cultures: England 1918–1951* (Oxford, 1998), 87, 96.

[154] Pinto-Duschinsky, *British Political Finance*, 185.

In the aftermath of defeat there was also much comment about the need for qualitative change. Here, there were to be areas of failure: efforts to increase the party's working-class membership met mixed results at best.[155] There was greater success in changing the membership's age profile. The party had aged in wartime; defeat at the general election, and a particular perception that the party had failed to win the support of younger voters, made the issue still more acute.[156] As one member of Loughborough (Leicestershire) CA put it in October 1945, 'the Party wanted not only fresh blood but young blood'.[157] A few days later, and a few miles to the west, the treasurer of Warwick and Leamington CA stated that it was 'vitally necessary for the younger generation to be encouraged to take a much more active part in combating this terrifying Socialism in our midst'.[158] A few days after that, a few miles further west still, the chief agent in Birmingham stressed that the 'outstanding need' was 'to rejuvenate our Organization from top to bottom'.[159] In fact, rejuvenation had begun before the end of the war, but it was undoubtedly accelerated by the general election defeat, not least through the impressive expansion of the Young Conservatives.

Conservative party membership endured many vicissitudes during the war. However, it did not collapse. Where associations continued to emphasize the need for people to pay subscriptions, and were prepared to go to the effort of collecting them, people were usually willing to maintain their membership. War service, population movements, and the like obviously played a major role in interrupting patterns of party membership. And yet the core of the party remained, ready to resume full activity in 1945. Some constituency associations began to try to recruit members from about 1943 onwards, although others were much slower, and overall the process was very ragged. But although it was only really in 1946 that the party's constituency organizations were firing on all cylinders where recruitment was concerned, the extent of the efforts made before then should not be underestimated.

THE LIBERALS

Evidence for Liberal party membership in this period is also thin on the ground: there are no aggregate figures, and even after the war, constituency totals were

[155] Wessex Conservative area council papers, ARE 10/25/4, Wessex area Conservative Agents' Association meeting 26 Sept. 1945; Dorset West CA papers, D399/3/2, war emergency executive committee 19 Nov. 1945.

[156] See e.g. Bolton CA papers, FDC/1/9, election committee 27 July 1945; Yorkshire Conservative area council papers, WYL 1856/1/3, council meeting 22 Sept. 1945; Henley CA papers, S. Oxon Con. II/1, finance and general purposes committee 5 Nov. 1945; Clapham CA papers, BLPES film 548, finance and executive committee 11 Feb. 1943.

[157] Loughborough CA papers, DE 2635/2, annual general meeting 13 Oct. 1945.

[158] Warwick and Leamington CA papers, CR 1392, executive committee 3 Nov. 1945.

[159] Birmingham CA papers, uncat., management committee 12 Nov. 1945.

regarded as 'unreliable', where they existed at all.[160] Comment must perforce be brief, but it is still possible to draw some conclusions.

One of the key aims of the 1936 Meston reforms had been the development of a 'modern' mass membership. However, the results had been mixed at best, and it was not unusual in the immediate pre-war years for Liberals to complain that membership was 'slowly diminishing'; in some places, a disproportionately old membership was literally dying out.[161] But it was not all bad news: in Paisley, for example, membership prior to the war was at least 'steady', while the more efficient associations, like Chester, were keen not only to maintain and improve quantity, but also to make a qualitative change, by making a stronger appeal to the professional classes, whom many saw as 'natural' Liberals.[162] Expectations could be high: in February 1939, for example, East Dorset LA had a total membership of 913, but it considered this 'most unsatisfactory', given that it was seen as a winnable seat.[163]

Although on the outbreak of war some associations curtailed their activities considerably, and others became dormant or worse (see Chapter 7), it was not all doom on the membership front. Headquarters and regional LFs told LAs to continue collecting subscriptions, and even to try to recruit new members: indeed, Chester's determination to continue collection and recruitment met an 'excellent' response, and optimism prevailed into 1940.[164] Initially, this proved justified, but membership was then hit, first by the call-up of increasing numbers of younger members to the forces, and later by the more general malaise that hit all parties' membership figures from spring 1940 onwards.[165] Such trends were not unique to Chester.[166] Until 1942, most associations could do little more than try to keep contact with existing subscribers.[167]

Stirrings in favour of more vigorous recruitment began in 1942, and came from two main directions. First, Liberal (later Radical) Action stressed the need for a larger membership. When one of its leading figures, Lancelot Spicer, was adopted as prospective candidate for Walthamstow West in May 1942, he called

[160] Women's LF, *Annual Report. . . 22 April 1947* (1947), 2.

[161] Western Counties LF papers, DM 1172, executive committee 8 Jan. 1938; see also DM 1172, executive committee 18 Feb. 1939; Walthamstow West LA papers, uncat., executive committee 25 May 1939.

[162] Paisley LA papers, ARC 67, annual report 1937–8, to annual meeting 21 Apr. 1938; Chester LA papers, CR159/5, executive committee 8 Dec. 1938.

[163] East Dorset LA papers, D1512/A1, annual report to annual general meeting 8 Feb. 1939.

[164] Lancashire, Cheshire, and North Western LF papers, M390/1/11, John A. Ormerod (chairman), circular, 4 Sept. 1939; Chester LA papers, CR159/5, emergency meeting of officers 5 Sept. 1939, council 21 Sept. 1939, coordinating committee 17 Jan. 1940.

[165] Chester LA papers, CR159/5, coordinating committee 21 Feb. 1940, annual meeting 13 June 1940; CR159/24, Chester League of Young Liberals, executive committee 4 Apr. 1940.

[166] See e.g. Westmorland LA papers, WDSo/174/9, women's LA annual meeting 6 Sept. 1939, WDSo/174/2, executive committee 28 Oct. 1939; R. Jarvis, *An Account of the Liberals in Walthamstow* (1968), 5; *Liberal Party Organisation Bulletin*, 6, Apr. 1940.

[167] Westmorland LA papers, WDSo/174/9, women's LA annual meeting 2 Sept. 1941; Manchester LF papers, M283/1/3/7, officers' meeting 18 Nov. 1941; Leeds LF papers, WYL 456/7, executive committee 1 Feb. 1941.

for the recruitment of 500 new members willing to pay £1 a year, to enable
the association 'to dictate to the "powers that be" [within the party] rather
than being dictated to, as had been the case in the past'.[168] Secondly, the LPO
also became more interested, not least as a way of countering Radical Action,
and also to draw in some of the people who were starting to drift towards
Common Wealth and, to some extent, the Communist party.[169] Thus far, most
Liberals had attributed falling membership to societal and organizational factors,
but there now seemed a chance that this might change.[170] Not surprisingly,
therefore, Roberts, as chairman of the LPO organization committee, toured the
country in 1942 emphasizing the need for more, and younger, members.[171]

By 1943, headquarters was imploring associations to be 'constantly on the
look-out for new recruits'.[172] The controversy over the Beveridge report proved
a useful recruiter, while also reminding associations of the need for a strong
membership to fight for the cause, and changing military fortunes brought the
post-war world into view. Increasing numbers of associations began to think
about recruitment and, as one MP put it, ' "roping in" the young people'.[173] By
late 1943, some associations were reporting improvements in membership, some
particularly amongst university students and other young people, and Chester
relaunched its youth movement in August 1943, although efforts in this direction
were often hampered by the demands of the armed forces.[174] Wider recruitment
drives were launched in Manchester and Leeds in the spring of 1944 and, on the
whole, Liberal party membership was clearly rising in late 1944 and early 1945.[175]

The general election campaign provided good recruitment opportunities.
Freed from the Coalition, headquarters finally produced some serious recruitment
literature, and the women's LF printed 100,000 copies of a pamphlet called *Why
Women should join and work for the Liberal Party*.[176] There is evidence that, in
some areas, progress was considerable. Candidates even in hopeless seats were
able to bring new people into the party, and meetings had lots of new faces.[177] In

        [168] Walthamstow West LA papers, uncat., general meeting 23 May 1942.
        [169] Harris papers, HRS/2, diary 4 Mar. 1943; Yorkshire LF papers, WYL 456/3, meeting of
constituency representatives with headquarters representatives, 18 July 1942.
        [170] Women's LF papers, DM 1193, report 1943 [covering Sept. 1942–July 1943].
        [171] Yorkshire LF papers, WYL 456/3, meeting of constituency representatives with headquarters
representatives, 18 July 1942.
        [172] Women's LF papers, DM 1193, report 1943 [covering Sept. 1942–July 1943].
        [173] Montgomeryshire LA records 3, LA executive committee 26 June 1943.
        [174] *Liberal Party Organisation Bulletin*, 45, Aug. 1943; LPO, *Seventh Annual Report* (1944), 17;
Chester LA papers, CR159/5, coordinating committee 13 Aug. 1943; Dundee LA papers, GD/DLA
1/1, annual general meeting 27 Oct. 1944.
        [175] Manchester LF papers, M283/1/1/4, annual meeting 6 May 1944; Leeds LF papers,
WYL 456/7, annual report, 1943–4, to annual meeting 22 Apr. 1944; Women's LF, *Annual
Report . . . 31 January 1945* (1945), 6.
        [176] Beveridge papers, VI/103, fos. 100–3, 'Why you should join the Liberal party', n.d. [*c*. May
1945]; Women's LF, *Annual Report . . . 8 May 1946* (1946), 2.
        [177] See e.g. Beveridge papers, VI/17, fo. 117, G. Granville Smith to Beveridge, 8 July 1945;
Westmorland LA papers, WDSo/174/2, annual meeting 20 July 1945.

Huddersfield, the Liberals recruited 'a great number of new members', 'younger, more intelligent people' who, it was thought, might form the 'nucleus' of a completely revivified Liberal party, while an internal party document spoke of 'the amazing number of new workers, most of them young' who had emerged in the election.[178] However, many associations ran the campaign on a skeleton membership and only really turned to recruitment later, albeit with positive results then.[179] To some extent, at least, the Liberals appear to have shared in the general increase in political party membership that characterized the later 1940s, although there remained concerns, not least about the party's inability to win over young women.[180]

The overall wartime trajectory of Liberal party membership was not dissimilar to that of the Conservatives or Labour. Some initial variability was followed in the period between May 1940 and early 1943 by a period of decline. This decline was largely due to war conditions and the lack of elections: as with their rivals, there is very little evidence of Liberals giving up their party membership for political reasons. From early 1943 onwards, increasing political polarization over post-war reconstruction, combined with pressure from Radical Action, persuaded the party that a more active recruitment policy was needed. However, efforts on the ground were patchy. Even in early 1945, when some LAs were working hard to recruit new members, others were delaying action and, in some cases, plainly procrastinating. The general election was a powerful stimulant, but in some areas the party was starting from such a low base that it was difficult to gain sufficient recruits to run an effective campaign. However, the period between 1944 and 1946 saw a large number of new members come into the party, and some of them would be important in the recovery that was to follow the depths of despair of the early 1950s. Whatever else the Liberal party had failed to achieve between 1939 and 1945, it had not lost its ability to recruit new members to its colours, and this would ensure that, even in the difficult days that were to follow, the party would not collapse, but would survive to fight another day.

CONCLUSION

Party membership was undoubtedly affected by the exigencies of wartime. It could hardly have been otherwise. Party membership as it had developed in Britain depended, above all, on residential stability: as long as people stayed

[178] Beveridge papers, VI/103, fos. 6–8, Elliott Dodds, 'Thoughts on the present discontents', 30 July 1945; fos. 10–13, anon., 'The future of Liberal party organization', n.d. [*c.* July 1945].
[179] Cambridgeshire LA papers, R93/73, executive committee 28 July 1945; LPO, *9th Report to Assembly* (1946), 13; Scottish LF papers, Acc. 11765/53, executive committee, 'Report to the general council', n.d. [Aug. 1946].
[180] Manchester LF papers, M283/1/1/4, annual meeting 25 May 1946; Women's LF, *Annual Report . . . 22 April 1947* (1947), 1.

in the same place, they could be called upon regularly for the contributions that would constitute their membership. If they moved and could not easily be traced, or if the collector stopped calling, their membership would lapse. Such eventualities became more likely when party organizations were losing staff and voluntary help to the demands of the war effort, and when people were moving about the country as never before. Even where people remained in the same place of residence as before the war, the blackout and enemy action meant that the most obvious time for many collectors to visit—the evening—was effectively off limits for a large part of the war.

This is not to say that some people did not give up their party memberships in protest against the line their party was taking. It is clear, for example, that a number of Labour party members left in the winter of 1939–40 in protest at the party's support for the war effort. These were not all hitherto 'secret' Communists, even if some of them did end up in the Communist party. But this did not represent a reaction against party *per se*. Because membership had declined largely due to what might be termed 'non-political' factors, there were few obstacles to its revival once the war began to draw towards a close and people began to return to their old routines. The intensified partisanship that accompanied reactions to the Beveridge report, and the increasingly shrill noises on all sides in 1944–5, served further to encourage people to join one or other of the parties. Meanwhile, the 'new movements'—Communists and Common Wealth—were unable to offer an alternative model to the mass membership party, or to recruit in the really large numbers that would have represented a serious challenge to the established system. For the CPGB to treble its membership to 56,000 between 1939 and 1942 was impressive, but it was starting from a very low base. It did represent some increase in influence at the workplace, particularly in engineering. But much of it was obviously the result of sympathy for the Soviet Union's struggle against Germany, and of support for the early opening of a second front. Therefore it was not a stable basis from which to expand in the future. Similarly, Common Wealth made recruits, but the total number involved—a maximum membership of 15,000—was nowhere near sufficient to challenge Labour. On the other hand, the core membership of the major parties had remained intact. The survival of those core memberships would allow Labour and the Conservatives, at least, to expand impressively beyond their cores in the late 1940s and early 1950s. Before then, it had also enabled constituency activities, at varying levels, to carry on during the war years, and it is to those activities that attention now turns.

5

Constituency Activities: The Conservatives

In 1939, Conservative organization in the constituencies was in a reasonably strong state. Each constituency had a Conservative association (CA), typically comprising a men's association, a parallel women's association, and a Junior Imperial League (JIL) organization. Political activity took place side by side with social activity, often on an impressive scale. In many areas, further bodies, such as Conservative clubs, also helped local Conservatism. The Second World War would hit constituency-level Conservative organization hard, but it would be an exaggeration to suggest that Conservative activity at this level ceased.

The coming of war did not take Conservative associations wholly by surprise, but there was initial confusion as to how they were to react: as seen in Chapter 1, early signs from both government and Central Office suggested closure, and it was only on 12 September that Hacking told associations clearly that they would be wrong to close down anything other than their JIL and Young Britons branches.[1] Legitimate activities included helping evacuees, establishing information bureaux, holding meetings 'to instruct members on the Government [*sic*] policy', and distributing government or Central Office literature. Membership should be maintained and, where possible, expanded.[2] Women's branches could form working parties to knit comforts for troops, help charities like the Red Cross, hold social events, and, while working, have a speaker 'on some matter of current interest'.[3] This message was repeated regularly, and although associations continued to be warned against overtly partisan behaviour, they were also told to remain intact, to work for 'war objects', and be ready to revive fully after the war, while in early 1941 Central Office was to produce a pamphlet on *War-time Activities in the Constituencies*, to help.[4]

Associations that met before 12 September 1939 often acted in good faith and closed down on the basis of what then appeared to be current advice. In

[1] CCO 500/1/9, Hacking to CA officers, 12 Sept. 1939.

[2] See e.g. ibid., Sir Eugene Ramsden (Chairman, NUEC) to CA chairmen, 23 Sept. 1939; Hacking to MPs, peers, prospective candidates, CA chairmen and women's section chairmen, 6 Oct. 1939, Topping to agents and women organizers, 13 Nov. 1939, Hacking to CA chairmen, 6 Feb. 1940, Ramsden to CA chairmen, 4 June 1940.

[3] Ibid., Hacking to CA chairmen and women's section chairmen, 26 Oct. 1939.

[4] NUA 4/1, NUEC 13 Nov. 1940; 4/2, card 149, NUEC report to NUCC 27 Mar. 1941.

Cornwall, Bodmin CA's officers met on 9 September and suspended all activity 'forthwith'; its executive was only to have two meetings between then and September 1944.[5] However, those associations that met after the initial flurry of correspondence from Central Office were more likely to remain active. Members of Middleton and Prestwich CA (Lancashire), meeting on 19 September, might have been bemused as the secretary read out the various Central Office letters; but as the most recent letters were clear that the association must carry on, they did so.[6]

Some constituency officials were nervous about remaining politically active in wartime, lest this be seen by their members and supporters as an unpatriotic act. Some were very cautious: York's executive only voted to continue its monthly meetings by 24 votes to 20.[7] Many associations took care to explain their actions. Northampton CA, for example, stressed that it was the party's opponents who, by refusing to join a coalition government and attacking the National government, were responsible: and '[t]his left us with no alternative but to meet the challenge' by remaining active, 'with the full approval of Mr Chamberlain'.[8] On the other hand, in Glasgow, where political polarities were fierce, and larded with religious and ethnic sectarianism, the city association agreed to do all it could to keep going.[9]

Which reaction was more typical? Some associations clearly did close down: had they not, then there would have been no need for Central Office to continue berating them for doing so.[10] The city party in Liverpool decided that 'the strictest level of economy' was imperative, with the result that it employed virtually no staff, and undertook virtually no activity, until after the war.[11] Chelmsford CA (Essex) was quick to cease most of its activities, save for knitting and whist drives for war charities, while Ipswich CA was effectively closed down, too, though its women members remained much more active.[12] In scattered rural constituencies, things were often very difficult indeed. In North Wales, Denbigh CA was effectively 'moribund for 6 years', while in Scotland, associations largely closing for the duration included those in the rural constituency of West Fife, the diffuse urban seat of Kirkcaldy Burghs, and the compact urban division

[5] Bodmin CA papers, DDX 385/1, meeting of officers 9 Sept. 1939, executive committee 11 Jan. 1941, 7 Nov. 1942, 16 Sept. 1944.
[6] Middleton and Prestwich CA papers, PLC 1/2, finance and general purposes committee 19 Sept. 1939.
[7] York CA papers, 156/22, executive committee 14 Sept. 1939.
[8] Northampton CA papers, NCCA/29, annual report for 1939–40, n.d. [1940].
[9] Glasgow UA papers, Acc. 10424/74, general committee 4 Sept. 1939.
[10] South-East Conservative area council papers, ARE 9/11/4, women's advisory council executive committee 12 Mar. 1940.
[11] Liverpool CA papers, 329/CON/1/3/1, Liverpool Constitutional association, 'Hon. Treasurer's report for the year 1942'; 329/CON/1/1/3, minute book.
[12] Chelmsford CA papers, D/Z 96/7, annual report for 1941, to executive committee 7 Mar. 1941; annual report for 1942, to executive committee 20 Mar. 1942; Ipswich CA papers, GK 401/1/3, women's divisional committee minute book 1937–46, *passim*.

of Glasgow Bridgeton.[13] In Warwick and Leamington, there were only three executive-level meetings in the whole of the war, in February 1940, May 1941, and March 1945, while in nearby Tamworth, the association closed down except for a few informal social gatherings.[14] In May 1940, when Berwick CA discussed whether it should close, it was suggested that, given the departure of the agent, the scarcity of petrol, the difficulty of finding speakers, and the impossibility of finding entertainments for social functions, they should 'bolt and bar [their] door, and stop the postman from putting letters in', leaving a sign 'just say[ing] "Gone away" '. Significantly, however, this was too much for the assembled members, and it was agreed instead to maintain the nucleus of an organization at the centre, and that local branches should continue to meet if possible.[15] It would admittedly be a very rusty machine that would swing into action against Beveridge in 1945, but it did exist—to such an extent, indeed, that the seat was gained for the party.

In fact most associations did not simply close down. In October 1939, surveying the party's Wessex area, the Central Office agent responsible reckoned that the majority of CAs were 'determined to keep their organizations in as high a state of efficiency as possible'.[16] In March 1941, the NUEC reckoned that only 'a small number' had 'either closed down or practically ceased to exist' in the first months of the war.[17] In Birmingham, there were unhappy memories of 1918, and a determination that the party machine there would 'not be found in the deplorable state it was [in] at the end of the last War'.[18] Manchester's recent thorough—and expensive—reorganization made party officials determined keep going, rather than let all their effort go to waste.[19] Tynemouth CA decided to continue with its activities, and for some time its only obvious concessions to the war were observance of the 'political truce' and the stipulation that no one should be admitted to any party event without a gas mask.[20] A number of women's branches in Wessex objected to handing over all the money they raised at social and other events to charity, and were ultimately allowed to keep some for party purposes, while Southampton CA's women were allowed to hold regular

[13] Denbigh CA papers, D/DM/80/6, finance and general purposes committee 21 June, 26 Sept. 1945; West Fife UA papers, MS 36593, annual general meeting 19 Mar. 1940, 11 Mar. 1947; Kirkcaldy Burghs UA papers, MS 36621, annual meeting 26 Jan. 1938, 15 Jan. 1946; Glasgow Bridgeton UA papers, Acc. 11368/50, special executive committee 19 Sept. 1939, annual general meeting 28 Jan. 1942, 30 Jan. 1945.

[14] Warwick and Leamington CA papers, CR 1392, executive committee 3 Feb. 1940, 13 May 1941, 2 Mar. 1945; Tamworth CA papers, CR 2430/14/1, W. E. Raybould, circular, 'October 1939'.

[15] *Alnwick Gazette*, 31 May 1940.

[16] Wessex Conservative area council papers, ARE 10/1/3, finance and general purposes committee 4 Oct. 1939.

[17] NUA 4/2, Card 149, NUEC report to NUCC 27 Mar. 1941.

[18] Birmingham UA papers, management committee 3 Nov. 1939.

[19] Derby papers, 920 DER(17)/16/4, Manchester CA, 'Report of the emergency committee to the annual meeting', 26 Apr. 1940.

[20] Tynemouth CA papers, Acc. 1633/2, executive committee 18 Sept., 24 Nov. 1939.

meetings with speakers on political subjects after protesting at being asked to forgo partisanship.[21]

Ultimately, therefore, most associations followed Central Office advice as finally determined by the 12 September letter: no overt party politics, but lots of war-related and social activity. In Lancashire, Bury CA eschewed political meetings as such because of 'the party political truce', but was determined otherwise to remain at 'the highest state of efficiency'.[22] Hertford CA agreed to maintain 'a minimum central organization', ready for 'any future emergency', while ensuring that Labour activities were closely watched.[23] In many constituencies, the merger of the hitherto separate men's and women's organizations broke down old gender divisions and also helped ensure that the men's organization did not collapse even when many of the men departed.[24] In Mid-Bedfordshire, there was hesitation as the association paused to make sure that it had understood headquarters' instructions correctly, but the pause was then followed by most branches resuming their activities 'in as near a normal manner as possible'.[25] In many areas, once the worst of the winter was out of the way, activity—albeit primarily social—increased significantly.[26]

The intensification of the war in 1940 brought new challenges. Shortly after the fall of France, Topping remained confident that most associations were still active in some way, but that summer saw some of those that had earlier decided to carry on now change their minds.[27] Subsequently, air raids often had a deleterious effect on activity. For example, Tynemouth CA's activity fell significantly after the town was bombed in April 1941; in particular, its labour advisory committee, which had met fortnightly until then, was disrupted by the raids and did not meet again until after the war.[28] Activity elsewhere often became increasingly difficult, for reasons seen in earlier chapters, such as fuel shortages, evacuation of members, and the like. Even so, however, numerous associations managed some form of activity. Attendance at Winchester CA's annual meeting in February 1941 was reckoned to be 'almost equal to the peace time average'.[29] That May, the Wessex area reported that the war effort 'ha[d] not prevented the maintenance of the Divisional Associations in a satisfactory state', and that branches were meeting regularly in 'numerous' constituencies, with members

---

[21] Wessex Conservative area council papers, ARE 10/1/3, executive committee 4 Oct. 1939.

[22] Bury CA papers, GCP/C/1/3, executive committee 27 Sept. 1939.

[23] Hertford CA papers, Acc. 3258, executive committee 25 Nov. 1939.

[24] See e.g. Northwich CA papers, LOP 1/1/4, chairman's advisory committee 22 Sept. 1939.

[25] Mid-Bedfordshire CA papers, Z 145/98, annual report for 1939, n.d. [1940].

[26] See e.g. Winchester CA papers, 73M86W/52, women's branch, annual report for 1939, n.d. [Feb. 1940].

[27] Chamberlain papers, NC 8/21/19, Topping to Hacking, 26 June 1940; Crookshank papers, MSS Eng. Hist. d. 360, diary 20 July 1940.

[28] Tynemouth CA papers, Acc. 1633/2, executive committee 23 May, 18 July 1941; Acc. 1633/5/2, labour committee minute book 1941–55, *passim*; O'Brien, *Civil Defence*, 418.

[29] Winchester CA papers, 73M86W/5, annual general meeting 15 Feb. 1940.

enjoying 'talks both upon the war and matters of domestic legislation'.[30] Two months later, the party's north-western area stated that 'reports from Divisions [were] most encouraging'.[31] Central Office helped by holding an extensive series of group conferences in 1941, addressed by Hacking or Topping and attended by constituency representatives. Six meetings were held in the North-Western area in the first half of 1941, while in Wessex, seven were held between March and May 1941, attracting 600 delegates.[32] Southend (Essex) held 'three days of "do's"' in December 1941; a year later, undeterred by the recent destruction of the association's offices and the Conservative club by German bombers, its MP, 'Chips' Channon, addressed three large meetings in the constituency.[33] In Hertford, the association chairman 'expressed his satisfaction' in March 1942 at the amount of work that local associations within the constituency were doing.[34] Inevitably, however, many associations found it increasingly difficult to carry on, especially in London, where extensive population movement began to disrupt Conservative activity at an early stage. In Lambeth, Norwood CA's three ward committees were not operating by early 1941 because their secretaries had all left the constituency.[35] In constituencies like Louth, abutting the Lincolnshire coast, activity came to be seen as impossible: even the women's organization appears to have fallen into decline, despite a bright start in September 1939.[36] It was, furthermore, one thing for associations to remain active at constituency level; quite another for all their subordinate branches to do likewise. In Tynemouth, for example, the Preston Ward committee did not meet at all during the war, while in Altrincham (Cheshire) 'the Branches [were] all out of action' by October 1940.[37]

In many places, the women's organization was the most obvious arena of continuing activity. In Birmingham, for example, most of the association's 100 peacetime women's branches remained in existence, 89 being reported as active in October 1939. The blackout, followed by the Blitz—in which Birmingham suffered eight major attacks between October 1940 and May 1941—hindered

[30] Wessex Conservative area council papers, ARE 10/1/3, annual general meeting 7 May 1941.

[31] Lancashire, Cheshire and Westmorland Conservative area council papers, ARE 3/1/2, annual meeting 26 July 1941.

[32] Ibid., annual meeting 26 July 1941; Wessex Conservative area council papers, ARE 10/1/3, finance and general purposes committee 26 Nov. 1941.

[33] H. Channon, *Chips: The Diary of Sir Henry Channon*, ed. R. Rhodes James (1967), 315, 340, 342, 15 Dec. 1941, 21 Oct., 14 Nov. 1942.

[34] Hertford CA papers, Acc. 3258, executive committee 28 Mar. 1942.

[35] Norwood CA papers, IV/166/1/16, annual report 1940–1 to annual general meeting 15 Mar. 1941.

[36] Louth CA papers, Misc. dep. 250/1, general meeting 21 Sept. 1944, reorganization committee 7 Dec. 1944; Heneage papers, HNC 2/48, Hilda Cordeaux (chairman, Louth CA women's branch) to A. P. Heneage, 2 Nov. 1939.

[37] Tynemouth CA papers, Acc. 1633/20/1, Preston ward committee minute book, 1923–69, *passim*; Grigg papers, Bodleian film 1005, reel 7, Mrs D. O'Neill (treasurer, Altrincham CA) to Sir Edward Grigg, 3 Oct. 1940.

activity, such that only 60 of the 100 branches were still active by April 1941. However, the fact that they were doing so was an achievement in itself, and between July 1941 and the autumn of 1944—when a more general revival began—around 70 branches were operating. It should be noted that the branches did become smaller, and their membership increasingly 'elderly'; even so, survival was a significant achievement.[38]

Central Office had advised the disbandment of the JIL on the outbreak of war. Some branches tried to carry on for a time, but the departure of members to military or other forms of national service made life increasingly difficult, and by late 1943, the Palmer committee (see Chapter 1) was reporting that the League had 'largely ceased to function'.[39] There were odd pockets of survival, even so. In Exeter, the JIL did 'first-class work' until the Baedeker raids of May 1942; the branches in north Devon and Richmond (Surrey) also remained very active.[40] Also in Devon, in March 1943 the Coly Vale branch of the JIL in the Honiton constituency had 96 members (27 of whom were serving in the forces), was distributing 80 copies a month of the *Onlooker*, was running a war savings group and a working party making comforts for the troops, and had held seven successful dances in the past year.[41] The survival of some branches might help to explain why the new Young Conservatives organization was able to develop so rapidly in the last nine months of the war—its branches were not all starting from scratch.

From an early stage of the war, some people held the truce responsible for inhibiting activity.[42] In October 1940, the chief agent for Birmingham acknowledged fears that Conservative interests were being damaged by letting opposition attacks go unanswered, but warned that 'the public' would not stand for a more partisan stance while Britain was 'engaged in a struggle for existence'.[43] Three months later, the Wessex area chairman, Sir Austin Low, criticized Central Office for forcing Conservatives 'to efface themselves in the constituencies', it being 'more than ever necessary that their Constituency Association[s] should be kept very much alive'. But although some agreed with him, others felt

[38] O'Brien, *Civil Defence*, 681, 404, 407–8; Birmingham UA papers, management committee 9 June, 3 Nov. 1939; 16 Apr., 29 July, 20 Nov. 1941; 25 Feb., 10 June, 16 Oct. 1942; 19 Mar., 23 Sept. 1943; 29 June 1944; 20 Apr. 1945.

[39] See e.g. Tamworth CA papers, CR 2430/14/3, Harold J. Merry (Dorridge) to W. E. Raybould, 20 Oct. 1939; Derby papers, 920 DER(17)/16/4, Manchester CA, 'Report of the emergency committee to the annual meeting', 26 Apr. 1940. Birmingham UA papers, management committee 3 Nov. 1939; Clitheroe CA papers, DDX 800/1/3, annual report 1939 to annual general meeting 28 Mar. 1940; annual report 1941 to annual general meeting 23 Mar. 1942; CCO 500/1/10, 'Report of the Youth Committee', 14 Dec. 1943.

[40] CCO 506/4/7, Miss N. H. Palmer (CCO agent, South-West area) to Topping, 11 June 1943; 506/4/11, P. Hornby-Smith to Lord Dunglass, 8 Apr. 1944.

[41] *Pulman's Weekly News*, 9 Mar. 1943.

[42] See e.g. CCO 4/2/142, Basil Steele (London) to Hacking, 6 Feb. 1940; 1922 committee minutes, 15 Nov., 1939, 5 Mar., 3 Dec. 1941, 25 Mar. 1942.

[43] Birmingham UA papers, management committee 4 Oct. 1940.

that 'it would not be playing the game if the Party encouraged Constituency Associations to undertake open political warfare'.[44] There were complaints elsewhere that Labour ministers' speeches were 'often *distinctly* [*sic*] political' and should be countered.[45] A particular grievance was that nothing was being done to rebut hostile allegations about the record of the pre-war government, or to expose Labour's pre-war failings on defence and foreign policy. On these points, however, nothing could be done: Churchill was hardly likely to favour any attempt to rehabilitate Chamberlain's policies when he himself had opposed them, and he saw that licensing Conservative attacks on Labour might well undermine his government. Accordingly, Central Office employees were reduced to sending out press cuttings of extracts from pre-war Labour speeches to Conservative activists who demanded stronger action.[46] By late 1942, grassroots pressure on Central Office over the truce was increasing significantly, with some Conservatives believing that, unless Labour propaganda was countered now, the party would be unable to win a post-war election; leading Conservatives in Birmingham and Liverpool were demanding a much stronger response, while in November 1943 the East Midlands area council voted unanimously for action 'to counteract the orgy of Socialist and Communist propaganda . . . against the Conservative Party', which was being carried on 'in spite of the fact that the Conservatives have observed the political truce both in the letter and spirit since the first day of the war'.[47]

The Scottish Unionist Association, which was responsible to the Scottish whip and not Central Office, was more actively critical of the truce from the outset. As early as March 1941, worried that Labour was taking the lead on post-war planning, the Scottish UA set up a reconstruction committee, which met regularly until early 1945.[48] The presence of the Communists in the west led to vigilance against the CPGB and other 'anti-war' bodies in 1940 and early 1941; by 1943, a close watch was being kept on Common Wealth, although it was felt—rightly, as it transpired—that the movement was unlikely to make much progress in Scotland.[49] Meetings with speakers were being held from a relatively early stage: by October 1943, meetings combining some kind of concert with a political speech were proving 'very popular', and by mid-1944 a series of lunchtime meetings had

[44] Wessex Conservative area council papers, ARE 10/1/3, executive committee 26 Nov. 1941.

[45] Flintshire CA papers, D/DM/307/4, P. J. Ashfield to T. F. James (agent), 3 Apr. 1941 (emphasis in the original). Apart from the period 1924–9, Flintshire had been represented by one or other form of Liberal since well before 1918.

[46] See e.g. Kennington CA papers, misc. coll. 463/3, Percy Cohen to J. Miller (agent), 1 Jan. 1942.

[47] Birmingham UA papers, management committee 16 Oct. 1942; Lancashire, Cheshire, and Westmorland Conservative area council papers, ARE 3/1/2, council meeting 20 Mar. 1943; NUA 4/1, card 65, NUEC 13 Jan. 1944.

[48] Scottish UA papers, Acc. 10424/64, central council executive committee 28 Feb., 18 Mar. 1941, 5 Mar. 1945.

[49] See e.g. ibid., Acc. 10424/33, western divisional council 10 Apr. 1940; western divisional council education and propaganda subcommittee 18 Feb. 1941, 5 Nov. 1942.

been held with speakers including Hogg, the MP Richard Law, and former party chairman Lord Davidson, with 'many other meetings' also taking place in the constituencies.[50] Scottish constituency associations did lapse occasionally, and it was recognized that it was easier for them to remain together in urban areas than in the often vast rural constituencies.[51] Nonetheless, the solid presence of the Scottish UA offered a continuing framework for activity and a basis for later revival.

A shortage of meeting places became a major impediment to many Conservative associations. The military and civil authorities went on a requisitioning spree at the start of the war, often taking all the premises suitable for meetings.[52] Sometimes, the CA's own premises were taken: the requisitioning of the headquarters of Waterloo CA (Lancashire) for the duration of the war went a long way towards explaining that association's lack of constituency-level activity during the conflict, while in North Wales, Wrexham lost its premises in similar fashion, and its occasional wartime committee meetings had to be held at a local brewery, courtesy of the proprietor, a leading local Conservative.[53] Where they were not requisitioned, party premises were sometimes rented out, sublet, or vacated to save money.[54] This helped the bank balance (see Chapter 8), but once premises had gone, the maintenance of an active organization became more complicated, and the limitations on any space remaining could be a positive disincentive to all but the most perfunctory activity. The Conservatives of Ipswich thought they were making a sensible financial move in giving up their offices in October 1939, but as a result they were still searching for suitable premises in 1946.[55]

There was widespread criticism that the Conservative clubs did not do more to help. There was nothing new about such complaints. They had not always been justified in the past, and they were not always justified now: relations in Lancashire appear to have remained fairly cordial, with the clubs in Manchester, for example, working hard to raise funds, providing meeting rooms, and so on.[56] But the war saw many of the joint committees that had bridged the gap between

[50] Scottish UA papers, Acc. 10424/32, western divisional council education and propaganda subcommittee 27 Oct. 1943; Acc. 10424/27(viii), western divisional council, annual report for 1944, 1 July 1944.

[51] See e.g. ibid., Acc. 10424/33, western divisional council 1 May 1942 Acc. 10424/27(viii), western divisional council, annual report for 1943, 1 July 1943; for 1944, 1 July 1944.

[52] Western Conservative area council papers, ARE 11/11/5, women's advisory council, Devon county committee 1 Nov. 1940.

[53] Waterloo CA papers, DDX 806/1/4, executive committee 16 Mar. 1945; Wrexham Conservative party records 2, special executive committee 21 Sept. 1939.

[54] See e.g. Henley CA papers, S. Oxon Con. I/3, finance and general purposes committee 7 Oct. 1940.

[55] Ipswich CA papers, GK 401/1/1, executive committee 5 Oct. 1939, 14 May 1943, 11 Jan. 1946.

[56] C. Stevens, 'The Conservative Club movement in the industrial West Riding, 1880–1914', *Northern History*, 38 (2001), 140; Birch, *Small-Town Politics*; and see e.g. Lancashire, Cheshire, and Westmorland Conservative area council papers, ARE 3/1/2, annual meeting 26 July 1941; Derby papers, 920 DER(17)/16/4, Manchester CA, 'Report of the emergency committee to the annual meeting', 26 Apr. 1940; annual report to annual meeting 15 June 1945.

the associations and the clubs fall into abeyance, and suspension of publication of the *Conservative Clubs Gazette* in 1941 did not help matters.[57] In 1942, party members in Flintshire (North Wales) felt that the clubs were 'not pulling their weight and [were] doing no political work', and that many club members 'were very critical of the conduct of the War and of certain Conservative leaders'; it was decided that the MP would go and speak in the clubs whenever he could, in order to draw the membership closer to the party.[58] At the party's Wales and Monmouthshire council in December 1945, lack of support from the clubs was identified as 'one of the main reasons' for the general election defeat—there needed to be 'immediate and drastic action in removing the Socialists from the Clubs'—while in Newbury (Berkshire), the Conservative agent felt that the club had been 'most unhelpful' and had 'contributed nothing to the campaign': most of its members, he went on, only joined 'for beer and billiards', and 'active steps [needed to be] taken to purge the Club', since it obviously had many Labour supporters among its members.[59]

The activity of some Conservative associations was almost entirely social for large parts of the war. The results could be spectacular: in 1942, Torquay CA organized 120 social gatherings to help with the war effort, and was running sixteen savings groups with investments totalling £50,000.[60] This was exceptional, but other associations tried to keep their members together through various social activities. High on the list were card games: whist drives were popular, and bridge drives by no means uncommon. Wilton women's branch in Northwich (Cheshire) was fairly typical in keeping together throughout the war by holding weekly whist drives and the occasional Christmas party.[61] In Kent, Maidstone CA stipulated that whist drives should be held in each village and ward to provide funds for war charities, and this proved a good way of keeping the core membership of the branches together.[62] In 1941, Ipswich women Conservatives held a whist drive and dance, with reduced admission prices for those in uniform.[63] Outings, very popular before the war, became more difficult to organize, as venues became less available, transport more difficult, and time more limited. However, some associations did their best, even if—as in the case of Sheffield Central women—it was simply a case of a short trip

[57] See e.g. Wessex Conservative area council papers, ARE 10/17/1, clubs advisory committee minute book, with no meeting between 3 June 1939 and 19 Oct. 1946; *Conservative Agents' Journal*, Oct. 1941.

[58] Flintshire CA papers, D/DM/307/4, management committee 9 May 1942, finance committee 6 Mar. 1943.

[59] Conservative party Wales records 4, Wales and Monmouthshire Conservative and Unionist council, annual general meeting 18 Dec. 1945; Newbury CA papers, D/EX 409/20, 'General election, 1945: agent's report', n.d. [Aug. 1945].

[60] *Conservative Agents' Journal*, July 1943.

[61] Northwich CA papers, LOP 1/2/4, women's branch executive committee 13 Nov. 1945; LOP 1/3/2, Wilton women's association branch committee meeting, 14 May 1940.

[62] Maidstone CA papers, U1634/A3/1/2, emergency subcommittee 16 Oct. 1939.

[63] Ipswich CA papers, GK 401/1/3, women's divisional committee 13 Feb. 1941.

out from the city centre into the glorious north-east Derbyshire countryside at Apperknowle.[64]

What is noticeable, however, is how soon apparently 'non-political' activities could take on a political tinge. This was certainly the case with the knitting parties that Conservative women formed in large numbers from September 1939 onwards. They were knitting 'comforts'—scarves, gloves, jumpers, and so on—for the troops and, occasionally, others. They bought the wool required by holding small social and other events, such as whist drives, jumble sales, coffee mornings, and American teas. Their output was impressive. The Conservative women of Sheffield Central had made more than 8,000 garments for the troops by December 1940, the Unionist women of Glasgow and district 12,000 items by July 1941.[65] A single branch of Gravesend CA (Kent) had produced 5,000 items by April 1943, despite its location in the German bombing corridor.[66] The Conservative women of Newport (South Wales) were also assiduous knitters. Between September 1939 and December 1941 they knitted a ton of wool, and by the end of 1943 a total of around 7,300 garments had been produced by 16 branches, all of them incorporating a label containing the words 'From the Newport Women's Conservative Association'. In December 1941, at the height of the German assault on Moscow, they decided to send 50 garments to the Red Army.[67] It is not known whether they reached the Eastern Front, but if they did, it is intriguing to consider whether Soviet soldiers really wore garments bearing the mark of the class enemy in distant South Wales.

Some associations brought comfort to the troops in other ways. For Christmas 1939, for example, Leeds West CA sent out 1,065 parcels to local men—the great majority of whom were not members of the party—who were serving in the forces. Each parcel comprised fifty cigarettes, fruit pastilles, liquorice allsorts, chocolate, chewing gum, and a detective novel, at a cost to the association of around five shillings each. The scale of the largesse was noteworthy; perhaps even more so was the fact that the association was able, through fund-raising, to bring in so much money in support of the scheme that it actually made a profit of £42 for association funds after the £262 cost of the parcels had been met.[68] That same Christmas, the Conservative women of Birmingham dispatched 6,880 garments, 105 plum puddings, and 14,000 cigarettes, while in February 1940, Llandenny

---

[64] Sheffield Central CA papers, LD 2104, women's association, 'Report 1940', n.d. [early 1941], 'Report 1941', n.d. [early 1942].

[65] Ibid., LD 2106, women's association, 'Report 1940', n.d. [early 1941]; Scottish UA papers, Acc. 10424/27(viii), western divisional council, annual report for year ending 30 June 1941, 1 July 1941.

[66] Gravesend CA papers, U1795/AD1/4, executive committee 20 Apr. 1944.

[67] Newport West CA records 1, Newport CA, report of comforts fund, 14 Mar. 1940; annual report for 1942, to annual general meeting 12 Mar. 1943; annual report for 1943, to annual general meeting 18 May 1944; 4, Newport CA women's branch executive committee 8 Dec. 1941.

[68] Leeds West CA papers, WYL 529/5, subcommittee 25 Nov. 1939, executive committee 29 Mar. 1940.

and Llansoy women's branch of Monmouth CA sent five shillings' worth of cigarettes to all local men serving in the forces.[69]

Supporting charities and various 'drives' was another activity in which CAs, and women's associations in particular, played a prominent part. Aid to Russia was one such cause, although given the political sensitivities of supporting a Communist regime, and in particular the dangers of becoming mixed up with that regime's domestic supporters, most Conservative aid was channelled through a special fund established under the Prime Minister's wife in association with the Red Cross.[70] In the South-East area, however, the women's advisory council chose instead to support a scheme in aid of British prisoners of war, which was a great success both in raising almost £3,000 and in helping to link branches together, 'so strengthening the organization'.[71] Meanwhile, many Conservative women became extremely active in war savings groups. Birmingham UA had 40 war savings groups as early as March 1940, while Newport established 17 such bodies which by 1943 had assets totalling £17,000.[72] In 1940, Sheffield Park CA canvassed 23,000 houses in connection with the Salvage Campaign.[73] In bombed areas, Conservative women sometimes visited to see what they could do to help those rendered homeless by enemy action.[74] Bolton women's CA decorated and furnished a house that was being provided for Channel Islands refugees who were coming to the town.[75]

The establishment of information or advice bureaux, as suggested by Hacking in October 1939, was another way of sustaining activity.[76] Clitheroe CA (Lancashire) established bureaux in the division's three main towns in October 1939. The agent would attend the Conservative club in each town on one day a week to listen to, and help with, the problems of anyone living in the constituency, whether Conservative or not; in the period to March 1940, 300 cases were dealt with; in 1940 as a whole, 1,100; and in 1941, over 2,000.[77]

---

[69] Birmingham UA papers, management committee 20 Mar. 1940; Monmouth CA records 5, Llandenny and Llansoy women's branch, meeting 5 Feb. 1940.

[70] See e.g. York CA papers, 156/22, executive committee 29 July 1942; Bolton CA papers, FDC/3/9, women's association 'Report of work done since . . . 18th April 1940', 16 July 1942.

[71] South-East Conservative area council papers, ARE 9/11/4, women's advisory council executive committee 30 Dec. 1941; women's advisory council finance committee 13 Jan., 19 May 1943.

[72] Birmingham UA papers, management committee 20 Mar. 1940; Newport West CA records 1, annual report for 1940, to annual general meeting 4 Apr. 1941; annual report for 1943, to annual general meeting 18 May 1944.

[73] Sheffield Park CA papers, LD 2116, women's association, annual report for 1940 to annual general meeting 8 Apr. 1941.

[74] See e.g. Norwood CA papers, IV/166/1/16, annual report 1940–1 to annual general meeting 15 Mar. 1941.

[75] Bolton CA papers, FDC/3/9, women's association 'Report of work done since . . . 18th April 1940', 16 July 1942.

[76] See e.g. Middleton and Prestwich CA papers, PLC 1/2, finance and general purposes committee 27 Feb., 5 Apr. 1940.

[77] Clitheroe CA papers, DDX 800/1/3, executive committee and subcommittee, 16 Oct. 1939, annual reports for 1939, 1940, 1941.

Bureaux were established in fifteen constituencies in western Scotland, many of them in Glasgow; at one stage in the winter of 1939–40, one bureau was dealing with up to sixty cases a week.[78] In South Wales, Llandaff and Barry CA established three bureaux in October 1939 in premises secured rent-free by its MP, Patrick Munro, and by May 1940, there were nine in operation, dealing with hundreds of cases. They did valuable work for ordinary people in the area, as well as helping to keep the constituency association active; nearby Cardiff South CA, which decided not to establish a bureau, struggled to maintain its identity during the war.[79]

A snapshot of Conservative women's activities in thirty-three constituencies in north-western England in late September 1940 shows the range of activities possible. All were meeting regularly. Ashton and Birkenhead had formed savings groups; the former was knitting for the Women's Voluntary Service (WVS) and the Army Comforts Depot, while the latter had undertaken 'the whole of the salvage scheme in the Borough', and was collecting Spitfire Funds. In Bolton, WVS work was attracting many Conservative women. In Bury, each ward branch had a working party. Women in Eccles were also knitting, as well as helping at the citizens' advice bureau and running two war savings groups. In Fylde, much was done to help incoming evacuees, and comforts were being made for the troops. In Salford, a Conservative information bureau had been established. Over 1,000 garments had been made in Accrington. Blackburn women were holding regular meetings with speakers on topical subjects, but were also engaged in national savings, salvage, and running a night canteen for the Home Guard. Heywood was helping with the WVS, Red Cross, and citizens' advice. Most of Liverpool's forty-plus women's branches were running working parties. Rochdale had produced 2,000 garments, and was actively raising money for the Red Cross and other charities. In the Wirral constituency, all but one of the twenty branches was doing 'active Conservative work'; the defaulting branch was about to be reorganized.[80]

Such activity enabled the women's organization of the party to remain largely intact. In February 1940, it had been reported that it was 'being maintained and . . . busily occupied with a variety of war work'; seventeen months later, reports showed that the women's organization 'was not only being maintained but that its scope was increasing'.[81] In London, Conservative women continued to meet even in the winter of 1940–1.[82] In September 1942, reports to Central

[78] Scottish UA papers, Acc. 10424/27(viii), western divisional council, annual report for year ending 30 June 1941, 1 July 1941.

[79] City of Cardiff CA records 26, Llandaff and Barry CA finance committee 31 Oct. 1939, 16 July 1941; 24, annual general meeting 3 May 1940; 12, Cardiff South CA finance committee 5 Dec. 1939.

[80] ARE 3/11/2, North-West area women's advisory council 24 Sept. 1940.

[81] CCO 170/1/1/2, central women's advisory committee 6 Feb. 1940, 9 July 1941.

[82] Ibid., central women's advisory committee 11 Apr. 1945.

Office showed that 'the Women's Organization was being well maintained'.[83] In March 1943, Rushcliffe CA (Nottinghamshire) reported that its women's branches were 'generally . . . flourishing', and doing valuable work maintaining the broader party organization.[84] Officers and members of Bury women's CA served in various roles during the war, including commandant, honorary secretary, and joint honorary treasurers of the Bury branch of the British Red Cross Society; county borough organizer, divisional representative, and salvage officer of Bury WVS; centre organizer of Totterington WVS; head of the Bury clothing depot; army welfare officer for Division 4 of the East Lancashire County area; and leaders of national savings committees and their street groups.[85] Not only did this reflect well on the association: it also brought new skills, and developed old ones, among those involved, to the benefit of the association. Meanwhile, the fact that Sunderland WVS was 'run . . . from the board room of the local Conservative Association' helped the latter in all kinds of ways.[86]

Such activity was obviously political in the sense that it was driven by ideas of patriotism that were inherent in Conservative ideology. But it was also political in another sense. For example, Bradford City CA achieved a great deal during the war. It raised almost £8,000 to provide 100,000 knitted articles to be sent to Red Cross hospitals and Bradfordians on active service; sent parcels to prisoners of war; presented a fully equipped mobile kitchen to the local authority, and a mobile resuscitation unit to the Bradford Royal Infirmary; ran an advice bureau; and also participated in war savings and war weapons weeks. This was sincerely patriotic activity, but it is nonetheless interesting that the association thought it worthwhile to publish all this information in a leaflet in April 1944. There was no reason why they should not have done so, but it is clear that the association was hoping that its charitable efforts would pay political dividends.[87] The fact that the Conservative women stitched a label into each garment they produced advertising the Newport CA was not a politically neutral act. Perhaps the most naked statement of the expected political benefits of all this knitting came from the city CA in Manchester, which declared as early as April 1940: 'Hundreds of letters of thanks and appreciation have been received, we believe the full value of this work will not be realized until the war is over and the electors once more go to the poll.'[88] As well as propaganda value, the work helped keep the party organization together: as the chairman of Bristol West CA put it in 1941, because the women's branches had been 'working at full pressure',

---

[83] Ibid., central women's advisory committee 30 Sept. 1942.

[84] Rushcliffe CA papers, DD/PP/1/1, annual meeting 20 Mar. 1943.

[85] Bury CA papers, GCP/D/2/1, Bury CA women's section, annual report 26 Mar. 1945.

[86] J. Hinton, 'Voluntarism and the welfare/warfare state: women's voluntary services in the 1940s', *Twentieth Century British History*, 9 (1998), 292.

[87] CCO 500/4/11, H. Lee (Secretary and Agent, Bradford CA) to Topping, 24 Apr 1944.

[88] Derby papers, 920 DER(17)/16/4, Manchester CA, 'Report of the emergency committee to the annual meeting', 26 Apr. 1940.

there would be 'a good foundation upon which to work' once full activities resumed.[89]

It was also possible to combine knitting with more overtly political activity. Bridport women's branch, in the constituency of West Dorset, on the Channel coast, was active throughout the war, running whist and bridge drives to raise money for wool, and knitting numerous comforts for the troops. In parallel with this activity, though, the meetings also listened to speakers. Indeed, in January 1941 it was agreed not to distribute the wool until after the speaker had performed, on the grounds that the click of knitting needles was 'most distracting' when people were trying to make, or listen to, a speech. The talks themselves were mostly given by men from the local CA, although the MP spoke occasionally. It is noticeable that the talks in 1941 and 1942 were either about military matters, or topics of general interest, but that from 1943 onwards, there was a much closer focus on issues like reconstruction, housing, education, health, and foreign and imperial policy.[90] In Monmouth, MoI speakers regularly addressed the knitting parties of one of the women's branches.[91] Meanwhile, the Southampton women who had been so keen to keep up their activities at the outbreak of war did so, except through the worst of the air raids. Knitting, whist drives, and American teas were accompanied by talks, although these did not take a really sharp party edge until later in the war. When a speaker did not turn up in September 1941, they turned to singing, recitations, an intelligence test, and whist.[92]

One form of activity undertaken by many associations was to distribute copies of the *Onlooker*, Central Office's only regular wartime publication. For some associations, distribution of the paper was one of their few overtly political acts prior to late 1944 or early 1945.[93] Maidstone and Monmouth CAs were both sending out 1,000 copies a month by 1941, when Merionethshire CA was distributing 400 copies a month across its large and sparsely populated patch of North Wales.[94] Circulation was often lower than before the war: in York, for example, the association was distributing 5,000 copies of the paper in May 1939, but only 300 by that November.[95] By the later part of the war, though, the Yorkshire area council was distributing almost 100,000 *Onlookers* a year to

[89] Bristol West CA papers, 38036/BW/2(b), annual general meeting 4 Apr. 1941.
[90] West Dorset CA papers, D399/6/1, Bridport women's branch, committee meeting 23 Sept. 1940, 6 Jan. 1941, and 1941–5, *passim*.
[91] Monmouth CA records 6, annual meeting 14 May 1941.
[92] Southampton CA papers, D/STC/1/4, Southampton CA papers, Shirley ward women's branch, monthly meeting 1 Sept. 1941, annual report for 1942, n.d. [1943].
[93] See e.g. Bolton CA papers, FDC/3/9, women's association 'Report of work done since . . . 18th April 1940', 16 July 1942; annual report to annual meeting 20 Apr. 1945.
[94] Maidstone CA papers, U1634/A3/1/2, 'Emergency subcommittee report up to April, 1941', to executive committee 28 May 1941; Monmouth CA records 6, annual meeting 18 May 1942; Merionethshire CA papers, Z/M/4018/2, finance and general purposes committee 13 Jan. 1941.
[95] York CA papers, 156/22, executive committee 15 May, 28 Nov. 1939.

Conservative associations across the county as a whole.[96] But the paper tended to be somewhat bland, for fear of upsetting the truce. To counter this, the city association in Manchester issued a duplicated *Manchester Supplement* with the Central Office publication. It was much livelier, and included attacks on shop stewards as lazy and Labour leaders as partisan, in an attempt to satisfy the demand for 'real' Conservative politics; indeed, it was so combative that it aroused some criticism inside and outside the party.[97] Some associations were assiduous in distributing other party literature, too. The Scottish UA western divisional council soon got through 22 dozen copies of Stelling's *Why I Am A Conservative*, while Middleton and Prestwich took a copy for each member of its leading committee, although other associations, like Flintshire, were much less enthusiastic.[98] Party education, meanwhile, was very much sidelined during the early part of the war, although it was returning to the agenda by the end of 1942, particularly in the north-west, where plans were laid for a one-day school for women Conservatives across the area to be held in March 1943.[99]

One initiative was the development of 'Looking Ahead' Circles, which were named after a National Union pamphlet publicizing the PWPCC's first report in 1941. The idea was that a party member would form a group with around eight or ten friends and acquaintances, at least some of whom should not be non-members of the party; they would meet regularly to discuss, and offer feedback to the PWPCC on, reconstruction matters; the groups would form a national network.[100] There was some progress. By 1943 a number of circles had been set up in the north and the north-west, and were proving successful in 'interesting people whose politics have not always been avowedly Conservative'; three 'Looking Ahead' conferences there, in March 1943, April 1944, and May 1945, attracted capacity crowds, and some new circles were formed as a result.[101] In Middlesex and Essex, the circles were reported to be 'going very well' in January 1944;[102] Ealing ran a successful discussion group, which ultimately

[96] Yorkshire Conservative area council papers, WYL 1856/1/3, annual meeting 19 Feb. 1944, 17 Feb. 1945.

[97] Derby papers, 920 DER(17)/16/4, *Manchester Supplement to the 'Onlooker'*, 9 (Apr. 1941), 16 (Mar. 1942), Joe Toole to Lord Derby, 20 June 1941; Derby to Toole, 21 June 1941.

[98] Scottish UA papers, Acc. 10424/32, western divisional council education and propaganda subcommittee 26 Aug. 1943; Middleton and Prestwich CA papers, PLC 1/3, finance and general purposes committee 21 Oct. 1943; Flintshire CA papers, D/DM/307/17, women's association annual meeting 24 July 1943.

[99] Lancashire, Cheshire, and Westmorland Conservative area council papers, ARE 3/11/2, women's advisory council general purposes committee 1 Dec. 1942.

[100] NUA 3/1, card 133, *Looking Ahead: An Account of the Proceedings of a Meeting of the Central Council of the National Union of Conservative and Unionist Associations, 2nd October 1941*; Northern Conservative area council papers, NRO 3303/2 ' "Looking Ahead" Circles: What Are They?', on verso of agenda for annual meeting 15 Apr. 1944.

[101] CCO 170/1/1/2, central women's advisory committee 8 July 1943, 6 Oct. 1943; Lancashire, Cheshire, and Westmorland Conservative area council papers, ARE 3/11/2, women's advisory council annual meeting 4 June 1943, 22 Sept. 1944, 18 Oct. 1945.

[102] Essex and Middlesex Conservative area council papers, ARE 8/1/2, council 15 Jan. 1944.

fed into the creation of a thriving branch of the Young Conservatives, from early 1942 onwards.[103] But these were not typical examples. Even where people showed interest, they were often too busy with work and other responsibilities to get involved; more general war conditions did not help, especially in the south-east and East Anglia; and there was often a failure to realize that non-members were meant to be central to the scheme.[104] In any case, such activity was not everyone's cup of tea: as the president of the JIL, Lord Dunglass, put it, ' "study circles" ' tended to feature 'grim and bespectacled female and serious minded man . . . whose company does not stir the pulse of the more ardent who want to be up and doing'.[105] Overall, therefore, Looking Ahead Circles were a disappointment. A firmer lead from the PWPCC might have helped, but the committee was in something of an eclipse when they were launched, with Butler having resigned as chairman. In any case, Churchill's obvious unwillingness to go too far with the PWPCC suggested that the circles would have limited purchase. By spring 1944, it was clear that there was unlikely to be further progress beyond the small number of circles already established, and ambitious plans for a separate headquarters department to coordinate them were accordingly scaled back.[106]

But not all political activity remained behind closed doors. From an early stage, for example, many Conservative associations were keeping a close eye on their opponents' activities. The MP Gerald Palmer expressly asked members of his association in Winchester to send him any pamphlets produced by 'outside bodies' that they came across.[107] Maidstone, which had virtually closed its branches at the outbreak of war, was by March 1940 calling upon them to remain in being so that they could counter 'subversive and defeatist propaganda and silly rumours', while party members in Birmingham remained deeply concerned about Communist activities throughout the war.[108] Such activity kept people politically engaged. However, the most obvious target of Conservative vigilance was Labour: and the obvious response of ordinary Conservatives to (sometimes considerable) Labour activity was to demand that they be allowed to expose and denounce it, which was not easily reconciled with the leadership's view of the 'political truce'. It also tended to lead to demands for more consideration of definite policies, especially on post-war reconstruction, which once again tended to fly in the face of the line coming from the top.[109] Some associations tested the water occasionally by

[103] Ealing CA papers, Acc. 1338/2, executive committee 24 Apr. 1942, 15 Jan., 19 Oct. 1943, 8 Feb. 1945.

[104] South-East Conservative area council papers, ARE 9/11/4, women's advisory council executive committee 2 Nov. 1943; Norwich CA papers, SO 122/4, annual report for 1942, 14 Mar. 1943; CCO 500/1/11, report of CCO staff conference, 18–20 Sept. 1943.

[105] CCO 506/4/4, Lord Dunglass to Dugdale, 23 Jan. 1943.

[106] CCO 500/1/12, report of CCO staff conference, 2–3 Apr. 1944.

[107] Winchester CA papers, 73M86W/5, special general meeting 27 Apr. 1940.

[108] Maidstone CA papers, U1634/A3/1/2, annual general meeting 9 Mar. 1940; Birmingham UA papers, management committee 20 Mar. 1940, 25 Feb. 1942.

[109] See e.g. Birmingham UA papers, management committee 20 Nov. 1941.

holding public meetings, but those held in 1939–41, in particular, were usually poorly attended and unsuccessful.[110]

By-elections could expose organizational decay savagely. The loss of Grantham (Lincolnshire) in March 1942 was a salutary lesson: as the Central Office agent responsible told the CA in nearby Horncastle, 'the chief cause' of the defeat had been that 'the organization and local officials had vanished into thin air'.[111] When Rugby (Warwickshire) was lost that April, the Central Office agent there felt that, although attitudes towards the pre-war ' "old gang" ' and discontent with the progress of the war had played their part, the chief problem had been the fact that the CA 'had been completely closed down since the outbreak of war', and a similar explanation was given for the (Liberal National) defeat at Eddisbury in 1943.[112] Although Windsor (June 1942) and Salisbury (July 1942) were held by decent majorities, the chairman of the Wessex area felt that both contests did the party 'a service' by showing the extent to which the local organization had decayed, and the same applied when Chippenham was almost lost to an Independent Liberal in August 1943.[113] The acting agent in Henley explicitly mentioned his experiences in the Chippenham by-election to drive the CA towards reorganization in May 1944, while Eddisbury was cited to stir up action in nearby Wrexham.[114] However, by-elections could also show the extent to which grassroots Conservatism remained vibrant, as the bitter contest between rival Conservative candidates at Brighton in February 1944 demonstrated.

Clearly, then, the Conservative party at the grassroots did not simply wither away during the war. But how far did grassroots attitudes change? This question can be studied briefly with reference to attitudes towards the party leadership, domestic policy, and foreign affairs.

Constituency records show no real evidence of grassroots dissatisfaction with Chamberlain prior to his fall from power. Annual meetings held in the first four months of 1940 were assiduous and unanimous in praising him and his colleagues.[115] The day before the start of the Norway debate that May, Leeds City CA passed a resolution of confidence in the government 'with acclamation'.[116] Shortly after he resigned from the premiership, Henley CA was one of a number

---

[110] See e.g. Bury CA papers, GCP/C/1/3, executive committee 6 Mar. 1940; York CA papers, 156/22, executive committee 18 Aug. 1941.

[111] Horncastle CA papers, Misc. dep. 268/1, annual general meeting 18 May 1942.

[112] CCO 1/3/312, Major H. H. Little (CCO agent, West Midlands area) to Topping, 1 May 1942; 170/2/1/3, Central Office women's organizers meeting, 23 July 1943.

[113] Wessex Conservative area council papers, ARE 10/1/3, annual general meeting 19 May 1943; Chippenham CA papers, 2436/2, annual general meeting 20 Nov. 1943; Wessex Conservative area council papers, ARE 10/1/3, executive committee 24 Feb. 1944.

[114] Henley CA papers, S. Oxon Con. I/3, finance and general purposes committee 4 May 1944; Wrexham Conservative party records 2, special executive committee 29 Apr. 1943.

[115] See e.g. Merionethshire CA papers, Z/M/4018/2, annual meeting 5. Feb. 1940; Bury CA papers, GCP/C/1/3, annual general meeting 3 Apr. 1940; Flintshire CA papers, D/DM/307/4, annual general meeting 6 Apr. 1940.

[116] City of Leeds CA papers, WYL 529/1, annual general meeting 6 May 1940.

to send him 'a message of appreciation for his past services'.[117] Later that year, his death brought forward many genuinely felt displays of sympathy. Members of his home association in Birmingham were far from being alone in feeling a 'deep personal loss'; the Scottish western divisional council stood in silence to remember 'a great statesman and a very great gentleman'; while the chairman of York CA 'paid a glowing testimony & tribute' to Chamberlain's memory.[118] At the end of 1940, Middleton and Prestwich CA ordered 200 copies of Central Office's memorial pamphlet for distribution at its annual meeting, while Welsh Conservatives' gift of an ambulance to Birmingham in October 1941 was sent 'in memory of our Late & Respected Prime Minister Mr Neville Chamberlain'.[119] As late as October 1944, the MP for Penryn and Falmouth, Maurice Petherick, was being 'cordially thanked' for presenting his association with a framed etching of Chamberlain, although a cynic might ask why he was then deciding to get rid of it.[120]

However, this did not mean that Churchill was unpopular. In May 1940, associations were usually quick to pledge their allegiance to him as premier, while declaring continued loyalty to Chamberlain as party leader. No evidence has been found of any CA supporting an alternative successor to Chamberlain, or calling for Churchill to stand down at any point in the war. If there were doubts, they remained private. When, in May 1941, Hertford CA passed a unanimous resolution of support for Churchill, it saluted his 'outstanding achievements' and expressed the association's complete faith in his 'indomitable and unconquerable spirit to wage war against the Enemy of Civilization, Liberty and Democracy until Victory is achieved', and pledged to support him 'to the last ounce, the last man and the last ditch'.[121] Norwich CA felt that the Baedeker raids on the city in spring 1942 only served to increase people's determination to win the war under Churchill's 'virile leadership'.[122] As Ramsden has shown, the parliamentary discontents of 1942 found no real echo in the associations, and at the height of the battle of El Alamein, the north-western area council passed a resolution 'deploring' the disloyalty of some Conservative MPs towards the premier, and pledging its own 'confidence in his policy, its unswerving loyalty and devoted gratitude for his inspiring and untiring leadership'.[123] By comparison,

[117] Henley CA papers, S. Oxon Con. I/3, annual general meeting 1 June 1940.

[118] Birmingham UA papers, management committee 24 Jan. 1941; Scottish UA papers, Acc. 10424/33, western divisional council education and propaganda subcommittee 18 Feb. 1941; York CA papers, 156/22, executive committee 12 Nov. 1940.

[119] Middleton and Prestwich CA papers, PLC 1/3, finance and general purposes committee 25 Jan. 1941; Merionethshire CA papers, Z/M/4018/2, executive committee 13 Oct. 1941.

[120] Penryn and Falmouth CA papers, DDX 551/16, finance and general purposes committee 21 Oct. 1944.

[121] Hertford CA papers, Acc. 3258, annual general meeting 17 May 1941.

[122] Norwich CA papers, SO 122/4, annual report for 1942, 14 Mar. 1943.

[123] Ramsden, *Age of Churchill and Eden*, 32; Lancashire, Cheshire, and Westmorland Conservative area council papers, ARE 3/1/2, council meeting 31 Oct. 1942.

Chamberlain's fate was sometimes retrospective damnation with faint praise, as in 1941, when Newport CA's annual report declared that they had all had 'such high regard', for him, but continued:

He was a peace loving Gentleman, and gave of his best and ablest to preserve peace without war [,] but war was unavoidable. To our new Leader, Mr Winston Churchill, we pledge our loyalty and admiration, he is an excellent and wonderful Prime Minister.
'The Right Man, in The Right Place, at The Right Time.'[124]

Where there was frustration with the higher echelons of the party, activists tended to speak not of Churchill, but of the party's *leaders*, in the plural.[125] In April 1945, the president of Bewdley CA told its first annual meeting for six years that the coming election would be 'a very puzzling one, because of the numbers of strange voters who would have votes in the constituency', but that 'the Association should keep before them the figure of the Prime Minister and sympathise with his burdens, and do all they could to lighten them by increase [*sic*] loyalty and confidence in him'.[126] The president of the CA, of course, was none other than Earl Baldwin of Bewdley, the former Conservative premier who, in the 1930s, had played a major part in obstructing Churchill's own return to office. It was symbolic of how their relative fortunes had changed that, contemporaneously, Hull East CA was changing the name of its headquarters from Baldwin House to Churchill House.[127]

Discontent did arise, however, from the reluctance of party leaders to visit the provinces to address meetings. In January 1942, for example, Newcastle-under-Lyme CA complained to the National Union that while Labour leaders like Attlee and Bevin were frequently to be found in the country, the same was not true of leading Conservatives; significantly, the NUEC concurred.[128] Wartime conditions clearly made matters worse here; it did not help, either, that relatively few ministers were 'orthodox party men'. However, it is also worth bearing in mind that such complaints had been heard regularly before the war.[129]

Where domestic policy was concerned, there was clearly some support for reform. The PWPCC's late 1942 interim report on education was widely welcomed, for example.[130] The Eastern area welcomed the Beveridge report in

[124] Newport West CA records 1, annual report for 1940, to annual general meeting 4 Apr. 1941.
[125] See e.g. Wessex Conservative area council papers, ARE 10/1/3, executive committee 9 Apr. 1942; Scottish UA papers, Acc. 10424/54, central council 27 Feb. 1942.
[126] Bewdley CA papers, BA 956/8, annual meeting 14 Apr. 1945.
[127] Chartwell papers, CHAR 2/545, W. M. McNicol to Churchill, 26 Apr. 1945.
[128] NUA 4/1, Card 63, NUEC 14 Jan. 1942.
[129] See e.g. Northern Conservative area council papers, NRO 3303/2, annual meeting 19 Mar. 1938; Bury CA papers, GCP/C/1/3, executive committee 10 May 1939; Chippenham CA papers, 2436/19, executive committee 26 July 1939; Scottish UA papers, Acc. 10424/44, eastern divisional council, 11 Jan. 1939.
[130] Essex and Middlesex Conservative area council papers, ARE 8/1/2, joint meeting of council and women's advisory committee 12 Dec. 1942; South-East Conservative area council papers, ARE 9/1/1, joint meeting of area council and women's advisory council 5 Nov. 1942.

principle, while also supporting Churchill's cool public attitude towards it.[131] But many Conservatives were much more sceptical. Clitheroe CA was told in December 1942 that 'undue stress had been laid upon the benefits conferred by the [Beveridge] Plan & little had been said about the obligations incurred', and its annual report in March 1943 suggested that the Beveridge, and other, reports 'contemplate[d] such fundamental alteration in the present social structure; involve[d] the spending of such large sums of money with a further extension of bureaucratic control if implemented, [*sic*] that the Conservative Party [was] bound to examine them closely in their cumulative effect upon the international position of this country as a competitive industrial, trading and agricultural nation'.[132] For its part, the Scottish western divisional council stated in February 1943 that 'little real interest was being shown by the public in the Beveridge Scheme'.[133]

There was, furthermore, evidence of resistance to those who wished to push reform too far. E. E. Gates, the MP for Middleton and Prestwich and a leading figure in the Tory Reform Committee (TRC), was increasingly criticized by his association for his activities, especially when he voted for equal pay for women teachers, against the government whip, in March 1944: it was only with some difficulty, and a dispute lasting almost a year, that relatively harmonious relations were restored.[134] Some associations were more enthusiastic about TRC MPs: in Stafford, Peter Thorneycroft was congratulated for the part that he was taking in wartime debates, even though his association took distinctly illiberal lines on issues like retaliatory bombing and the empire.[135]

Traditional Conservative themes remained much in evidence. Patriotism dictated a concern for service personnel and their families, and resolutions in favour of increased service pay were common.[136] There was also significant pressure against enemy aliens and perceived fifth columnists, especially in 1939–40. As early as January 1940, York CA was demanding 'a rigorous comb-out and the internment of all suspects' among 'the large number of enemy aliens who are at present allowed the freedom of this Country'.[137] That April, the women's advisory council of the North-Western area resolved with one dissentient that the government should take the 'strictest measures'

---

[131] Essex and Middlesex Conservative area council papers, ARE 8/1/2, council meeting 25 Mar. 1943; *The Times*, 22 Mar. 1943.
[132] Clitheroe CA papers, DDX 800/1/3, council meeting 12 Dec. 1942; annual report for 1942, to annual general meeting 27 Mar. 1943.
[133] Scottish UA papers, Acc. 10424/33, western divisional council education and propaganda subcommittee 25 Feb. 1943.
[134] Middleton and Prestwich CA papers, PLC 1/3, finance and general purposes committee 25, 29 Apr. 1944, 9 Feb. 1945.
[135] Stafford CA papers, D1289/1/3, combined finance and executive committee 7 Nov. 1944, annual general meeting 4 July 1942.
[136] See e.g. Wessex Conservative area council papers, ARE 10/1/3, annual general meeting 7 May 1941.
[137] York CA papers, 156/22, executive committee 23 Jan. 1940.

'to control—and if necessary to intern—all enemy aliens residing in the United Kingdom', and demanded action against 'dangerous and unpatriotic' and 'subversive' bodies like the Peace Pledge Union.[138] The Western area women's advisory council demanded bluntly in April 1940 'that more aliens should be interned'.[139] The following month, Ealing CA voted unanimously that 'all "Enemy Aliens" even though they may be refugees from Nazi oppression be [*sic*] interned for the duration of the War', while Henley CA demanded that 'all enemy aliens in Britain should be interned without delay and that during their internment they should be employed on useful national work'.[140] As late as April 1942, the Northern area council criticized excessive liberality towards enemy aliens, and demanded the internment of all Japanese people living in Britain and stern action against fifth columnists.[141] Religion also maintained a profile. The South-East women's advisory council was one of many bodies welcoming the inclusion of 'a sound Christian basis to education in schools' in Butler's Education Bill.[142] It remained customary, as well, for associations to attack what they saw as the left-wing bias of the BBC.[143]

On the economic front, hostility towards trade unionism continued. Any change to the 1927 Trade Disputes Act was resisted strongly, and there were calls for firmer action against strikes.[144] There was grumbling about slacking in war production: 'Stalin would not stand for that,' exclaimed the chairman of the Scottish Unionist association's central council in February 1942; 'why should we?'[145] There was also concern for the plight of the small trader, with particular criticism of the Ministry of Food's 1941 decision not to issue supplies to shopkeepers with fewer than twenty-five registered customers.[146] Agriculture retained a high profile in rural areas. The South-Eastern area called for a long-term plan for the industry in February 1941, while in some areas, like Lincolnshire, the National Farmers' Union (NFU) became more prominent in CA affairs.[147] Towards the end of the war, increasing disquiet was expressed at the plight of

[138] Lancashire, Cheshire, and Westmorland Conservative area council papers, ARE 3/11/2, women's advisory council 24 Apr. 1940.

[139] Western Conservative area council papers, ARE 11/11/5, women's advisory council 26 Apr. 1940.

[140] Ealing CA papers, Acc. 1338/2, executive committee 27 May 1940; Henley CA papers, S. Oxon Con. I/3, annual general meeting 1 June 1940.

[141] Northern Conservative area council papers, NRO 3303/2, annual meeting 18 Apr. 1942.

[142] South-East Conservative area council papers, ARE 9/11/4, women's advisory council annual general meeting 6 July 1943.

[143] Scottish UA papers, Acc. 10424/44, eastern divisional council, 10 July 1942; Bury CA papers, GCP/C/1/3, annual general meeting 27 Mar. 1945.

[144] See e.g. Wessex Conservative area council papers, ARE 10/1/3, annual general meeting 7 May 1941; Scottish UA papers, Acc. 10424/32, western divisional council 3 Sept. 1941.

[145] Ibid., Acc. 10424/54, central council 27 Feb. 1942.

[146] Ibid., Acc. 10424/44, eastern divisional council, 9 July 1941.

[147] South-East Conservative area council papers, ARE 9/1/1, annual meeting 21 Feb. 1941; Horncastle CA papers, Misc. dep. 268/1, general council 1 May 1944, finance and general purposes committee 18 May, 13 July 1942, 15 Nov. 1943, 6 Mar. 1944, executive committee 12 June 1944.

hoteliers and others in coastal areas whose businesses had been destroyed by wartime conditions and restrictions on the tourist trade.[148]

From early 1943 onwards, many Conservatives became increasingly preoccupied with the need for an early return to free enterprise after the war. Birmingham UA stated in March 1943 that 'an adequate standard of living after the war [could] only be obtained by the utmost encouragement of private enterprise both in commerce and in industry', and this was soon echoed by Leeds city CA, which declared that 'post-war prosperity and social progress' would be 'most speedily achieved by the removal at the earliest possible date of all unnecessary official control of trade, industry and personal liberty'.[149] When the Eastern area council demanded in July 1943 that a programme for the building of four million houses be developed, it added the proviso that this must be done 'using to the full the resources of Private Enterprise'.[150] It was important, agreed the Yorkshire area council in February 1945, that the end of the war should see the return of a Conservative government 'free from the belief that controls are desirable in themselves', and aiming to ensure that 'the greatest scope should be given to that free enterprise which has been the foundation of our national prosperity'.[151] Increasingly, indeed, this was seen as the fault line between the two major parties. As the Eastern area put it in April 1945, the last year had shown 'that, in the field of domestic politics, the issues separating the parties [were] genuine and deep-seated'. Labour's plans for nationalization were 'an approach to the totalitarian system which we are fighting to oppose': the Conservatives wanted 'an early return, over a large field, to the system of private enterprise'.[152] The South-East area was unanimous in April 1945 that there must be 'a policy of the maximum of Free Enterprise and the minimum of State Control as soon as practicable after the War'.[153] There was particular criticism of government waste.[154]

Not all local associations wanted a sudden return to unrestricted market forces, however. In March 1944, Norwood CA rejected a motion demanding 'the removal of all trade restrictions at the earliest possible moment', in favour of a milder statement calling for 'the removal of all unnecessary controls and restrictions as soon as post-war conditions permit'.[155] Emphases were sometimes inconsistent. The Northern area council, for example, thought nothing at its

---

[148] See e.g. Horncastle CA papers, Misc. dep. 268/1, general council 1 May 1944.

[149] Birmingham UA papers, management committee 19 Mar. 1943; City of Leeds CA papers, WYL 529/1, annual general meeting 27 May 1943.

[150] Essex and Middlesex Conservative area council papers, ARE 8/1/2, annual meeting 24 July 1943.

[151] Yorkshire Conservative area council papers, WYL 1856/1/3, annual meeting 17 Feb. 1945.

[152] Eastern Conservative area council papers, ARE 7/1/8, annual meeting 18 Apr. 1945.

[153] South-East Conservative area council papers, ARE 9/1/1, council meeting 19 Apr. 1945.

[154] Scottish UA papers, Acc. 10424/44, eastern divisional council, 9 July 1941.

[155] Norwood CA papers, IV/166/1/16, special emergency committee 13 Mar. 1944; annual general meeting 18 Mar. 1944.

annual meeting in April 1944 of following a resolution demanding a better policy on the location of industry after the war—which could only be effected by means of state intervention—with demands for the lifting 'as far as possible in the national interest' of all wartime controls once peace returned, and calling for the 'liberties of the citizen' to be upheld 'against the constantly increasing interference of the State'.[156]

In foreign affairs, no evidence surfaces in the records of the associations studied of any hostility towards the war as such, or of desire for a compromise peace. When the MP for Bristol West, C. T. Culverwell, made comments along these lines, he was rebuked, deselected as candidate, and subsequently ostracized by his constituency association, eventually retiring from parliament in 1945.[157] Such support as there may have been for his views remained private and inchoate. Overwhelmingly, attitudes towards Germany appear to have been taken for granted – it was the enemy and it must be defeated. Attitudes towards the Soviet Union emerge more explicitly. There were numerous examples of admiration for the Red Army's struggle on the Eastern Front, and, as stated above, many associations worked hard to raise funds to aid the Soviets. However, considerable suspicion remained. In November 1941 the party's Eastern area committee, 'while advocating wholehearted support of the Russian war effort, view[ed] with alarm the official film sponsored by the Ministry of Information called "Salute the Soviet", praising all aspects of the Russian social system'.[158] By 1945, distrust of the USSR was becoming widespread, and when, that March, the MP for Norwich, Henry Strauss, resigned as a junior minister over the Yalta agreement (which, he felt, betrayed the Poles to the Russians) his association gave him an overwhelming vote of confidence.[159] The chairman of Chippenham CA, launching his association on the general election campaign in June 1945, told his members they must work hard for Churchill because Britain 'must have the best FIGHTING LEADER [*sic*] to negotiate with Marshal Stalin'.[160] Attitudes towards America, meanwhile, were generally quite favourable, and the death of Roosevelt in April 1945 was met with expressions of sincere grief from many associations.[161]

For many Conservatives, therefore, politics never went away. Organization remained difficult, but not impossible. In April 1943, for example, even the party's Eastern area was able to report that, 'in the main, the Associations continue[d] to function', 'practically every' CA having held its annual meeting;

---

[156] Northern Conservative area council papers, NRO 3303/2, annual meeting 15 Apr. 1944.
[157] Bristol West CA papers, 38036/BW/2(b), special executive committee 15 Dec. 1939; *The Times*, 20 June 1944.
[158] Eastern Conservative area council papers, ARE 7/1/8, executive committee 13 Nov. 1941.
[159] Norwich CA papers, SO 122/4, executive committee 19 Mar. 1945.
[160] Chippenham CA papers, 2436/2, annual general meeting 9 June 1945.
[161] See e.g. Flintshire CA papers, D/DM/307/4, executive committee 14 Apr. 1945; Scottish UA papers, Acc. 10424/44, Eastern divisional council, 13 Apr. 1945.

there were even 'welcome signs of a limited revival of activities', such as increased demand for speakers, an increase in the circulation of the *Onlooker*, and the fact that many associations had discussed the PWPCC report on education and set up expert committees on post-war reconstruction.[162] Close to the Welsh border, meanwhile, the MP for Hereford, J. P. L. Thomas, was amazed at the 'series of fetes and house shows' put on by his association for his visit in August 1943: 'is there a war on?' he asked a friend sardonically.[163] Many activists were also greatly buoyed by the 1943 party conference, the first of the war, which, according to one delegate, showed 'how much more alive . . . the party were [*sic*] to the many subjects under consideration than at any previous meeting he had attended'.[164]

It was not entirely surprising, then, that some of the more forward-looking associations began to think about reorganization. Ealing CA identified two problem branches in 1943, and one of them was rapidly revived, although it said much for the patchiness of wartime experience that the other was still not functioning by VE Day.[165] Dugdale's new-year message for 1944 emphasized the need for redoubled effort in preparation for the post-war general election: such encouragement was increased after the West Derbyshire debacle that February, and, as the spring of 1944 approached, there were growing signs at the grassroots of 'an increasing desire for more activity' within the party.[166] Although renewed attention to military matters that summer led to a lull, by the autumn grassroots pressure began to be exerted on Central Office. It was now becoming easier to hold meetings as blackout restrictions were further relaxed.[167] Accordingly, when an exasperated MP asked Dugdale whether his association could hold political meetings to counteract their opponents' 'very busy' propaganda, Dugdale replied that it would be 'perfectly in order for Conservative political meetings to be held in your constituency'.[168] A few MPs had needed no Central Office imprimatur: Patrick Donner (Basingstoke) was making regular 'party political' speeches to Conservative branches in his constituency by mid-1944, while the junior minister Harry Crookshank felt able to give a general meeting of his CA in Lincolnshire 'a Conservative speech' that June.[169]

---

[162] Eastern Conservative area council papers, ARE 7/1/8, annual report to annual meeting 24 Apr. 1943.

[163] Emrys-Evans papers, Add. 58263, J. P. L. Thomas to Paul Emrys-Evans, 18 Aug. 1943.

[164] Middleton and Prestwich CA papers, PLC 1/3, finance and general purposes committee 8 July 1943; see also City of Cardiff CA records 26, Llandaff and Barry CA finance and general purposes committee 16 July 1943.

[165] Ealing CA papers, Acc. 1338/2, executive committee 8 June, 19 Oct. 1943, 11 May 1945.

[166] *Conservative Agents' Journal*, Jan. 1944; Birmingham UA papers, management committee 31 Mar. 1944.

[167] Tynemouth CA papers, Acc. 1633/2, executive committee 30 Sept. 1944.

[168] CCO 4/2/142, Sir Richard Wells to Dugdale, 6 Sept. 1944, Dugdale to Sir Richard Wells, 14 Sept. 1944.

[169] Winchester CA papers, 73M86W/17, Basingstoke CA, Broughton branch, meeting 9 June 1944; Crookshank papers, MSS Eng. Hist. d. 361, diary 24 June 1944.

But revival proved halting. The failure to reschedule the spring 1944 National Union conference cancelled due to D-Day preparations meant that an opportunity to draw associations together in the cause of organizational revival was lost.[170] Dugdale's 22 September appeal to associations to revive themselves—by filling vacant posts, and calling a meeting of all known members and supporters to be addressed by the MP or candidate—was a step in the right direction but, within days, the Allied advance on the Western Front was checked, and it was soon clear that the war would not end in 1944.[171] In other words, Conservative headquarters was forced to stand its battalions down just as they were getting ready to mobilize. Dugdale departed the party chairmanship shortly afterwards; Churchill, still toying with the possibilities of longer-term Coalition, told Assheton, his successor, to dampen grassroots expectations, saying he '[did] not want partisanship excited till we get nearer our political D Day'.[172]

Some associations continued to prepare regardless. Dugdale's letter was greeted with surprise in Monmouth, for example, because it only outlined activities that the CA there was already undertaking.[173] But others remained more torpid. In some cases, this was understandable. In particular, the V-1 and V-2 attacks severely depressed Conservative activity in many parts of southeastern England in the summer and autumn of 1944, at just the point that some associations had been getting back into their stride. Ealing—one of the better-organized associations—had no executive-level meeting for almost six months between April and October 1944, for example, while Norwood had none between March and October.[174] Nor was it just a metropolitan problem: Hertford CA's revival was pushed into the background once the attacks began in earnest.[175]

In other cases, however, continuing inertia was a good deal less explicable. In Lancashire, for example, Darwen was not suffering unduly from the pressures of war, and yet 'little of political [*sic*] or social character ha[d] been carried out by the Association' in the year to June 1945, and it would only be thanks to a severely split opposition vote that the seat would be held at the general election.[176] Chelmsford, which had remained largely inactive throughout the war, suddenly faced a by-election when its MP, Macnamara, was killed on active service in December 1944. Even though the by-election was delayed until April 1945, it was not long enough for the association to revive its organization fully,

[170] Ramsden, *Age of Churchill and Eden*, 50.
[171] Butler papers, H62, Dugdale circular, n.d., enc. with Dugdale to Butler, 22 Sept. 1944.
[172] Chartwell papers, CHAR 2/507, Churchill to Assheton, 7 Nov. 1944.
[173] Monmouth CA records 10, finance and general purposes committee 2 Oct. 1944.
[174] Ealing CA papers, Acc. 1338/2, executive committee 28 Apr., 3 Oct. 1944; Norwood CA papers, IV/166/1/16, annual general meeting 18 Mar. 1944, emergency committee 3 Nov. 1944.
[175] Hertford CA papers, Acc. 3258, annual report for 1944, to annual general meeting 1 June 1945; O'Brien, *Civil Defence*, 682.
[176] Darwen CA papers, PLC 2/2/2, annual report to annual general meeting 2 June 1945.

and the seat fell to Common Wealth.[177] Quick resuscitation usually proved difficult. In London, when Clapham CA's council met for the first time in four years in December 1943, it soon became clear that, due to enemy action, most of its members were no longer living in the constituency, and that some were no longer living at all.[178] What had been a safe seat in 1935 would be lost to Labour in 1945. In Oxfordshire, Henley CA's new agent, appointed in April 1945, found in his first two months in post that 'as a result of the war years and the political truce the pre-war organization had almost completely vanished': all that remained of the vibrant association of early 1939 was eight women's branches.[179]

By March 1945, Nazi Germany faced imminent defeat. At last, Central Office sent out an unequivocal message. Speaking to his own constituency association, Assheton 'referred to the strong Left-Wing propaganda which had been pouring out for some time despite the party truce. Now it would be our turn.'[180] Even so, some associations still hesitated. In November 1944, for example, a meeting of Wrexham CA branch chairmen was unanimous in urging that the association should hasten towards 'a fresh start', yet three and a half months later, 'the activity of the Association was practically non-existent', and it was only then that a proper reorganization committee was established.[181] Ongoing uncertainty, at least officially, as to whether or not the Coalition would survive the war had not helped grassroots Conservatives; it had, at the very least, given some of them an excuse for continuing inertia.

Distributing literature was one way of stimulating activity. In December 1944, Sowerby CA bought a hundred copies each of Stelling's *Why I Am A Conservative* and of *Current Political Affairs*, as well as 250 copies a month of the *Onlooker*; by April 1945, Glasgow UA had distributed 3,000 copies of the pamphlet *Principles and Aims of the Unionist Party* among the 15 constituency associations in the city.[182] A change in the procedure for electoral registration of the business premises vote offered another incentive to revival, although the extent to which associations took advantage of it varied: the deadline of 28 February fell too early for some. But a few were relatively successful: in Sheffield Central, where the association chairman unilaterally employed two canvassers to visit business people and get them to claim, 1,654 applications were made, while in Glasgow, the

---

[177] Chelmsford CA papers, D/Z 96/7, 'By-election 26th April 1945: election agent's report', 3 May 1945; E. R. Millington, *Was That Really Me?* (Palo Alto, Calif., 2006), 104–7.
[178] Clapham CA papers, BLPES microfilm 548 (reel 3), council 13 Dec. 1939, 15 Dec. 1943, 21 Sept. 1944.
[179] Henley CA papers, S. Oxon Con. I/3, finance and general purposes committee 16 June 1945.
[180] Rushcliffe CA papers, DD/PP/1/1, annual general meeting 24 Mar. 1945.
[181] Wrexham Conservative party records 2, meeting of chairmen of polling districts 8 Nov. 1944; meeting of executive committee with secretaries and chairmen of polling districts 21 Feb. 1945.
[182] Sowerby CA papers, executive committee 11 Dec. 1944; Glasgow UA papers, Acc. 10424/75, general committee 30 Apr. 1945.

registration of 6,000 out of a potential figure of 15,000 was seen as 'disappointing but much better than in other areas'.[183]

Some associations came back strongly. By April 1945, the Northern area council felt able to congratulate its associations—some of which had had no more than a 'nucleus' organization a year earlier—with the extent of their revival, although 'a great deal of hard work remain[ed] to be done'.[184] In Birmingham, all the constituencies were at least partly active in October 1944; by January 1945, there was 'a good deal of activity'; and by the following April, numerous meetings were being held.[185] Bolton, whose pre-war organization had been so formidable as to include a Conservative bowls league, had gone into cold storage during the war, except for the largely charitable activities of its women's association. However, its executive had begun to meet again in September 1944, and by the time of the election it had appointed a powerful and effective election committee, which had seven subcommittees to deal with various aspects of the campaign.[186] Even so, it would not be enough to stop both seats being lost to Labour in 1945.

Reviving the party at the lowest levels could be especially challenging. It was one thing to keep the central constituency organization going, after all: quite another to sustain the organization throughout all the wards, towns, and villages within a constituency. Reigate CA (Surrey) had had 32 branches in 1939, and although the main association was not totally inert in wartime, by early 1945 it was having difficulty in finding 'suitable "key" people, upon whom [it] could rely in many of the Polling Districts'.[187] Norwich CA officials worried throughout the war about the decline of ward organization, but failed to effect much improvement despite a determined effort in 1944, so that the association went into the 1945 election with a weak organization on the ground, and matters improved little in the year that followed.[188] Clitheroe CA underwent an organizational spring-cleaning in 1943, but had machinery in only half of the constituency's polling districts by mid-May 1945.[189] In June 1944, Wansbeck CA (Northumberland) began in earnest to try to revive its polling district organizations, employing an organizer

[183] Sheffield Central CA papers, LD 2104, finance committee 9 Mar. 1945; Glasgow UA papers, Acc. 10424/75, general committee 26 Mar. 1945.

[184] Northern Conservative area council papers, NRO 3303/2, annual meeting 11 Apr. 1945.

[185] Birmingham UA papers, management committee 6 Oct. 1944, 25 Jan., 20 Apr. 1945.

[186] Bolton CA papers, FDC/1/7, general purposes committee 24 Apr., 31 July 1939; then no further meeting until 31 May 1946; 1/8, executive committee 15 Sept. 1944, election committee 18 June to 27 July 1945.

[187] Reigate CA papers, 353/3/1/1, annual meeting 10 Mar. 1943; 353/3/2/3, emergency committee 22 Mar. 1945.

[188] Norwich CA papers, SO 122/4, annual report for 1939 to annual meeting 15 Mar. 1940; executive committee 14 Apr. 1943; finance and general purposes committee 20 Jan. 1944; annual report for 1944 to annual meeting 6 Apr. 1945; annual report for year ending March 1946, to annual general meeting 29 Mar. 1946.

[189] Clitheroe CA papers, DDX 800/1/3, annual general meeting 27 Mar. 1943, executive committee 16 May 1945.

for six months and getting the MP to make a series of speeches in villages across the constituency; but the seat was lost at the 1945 election, and even by that November, fifteen of the association's pre-war branches had still not resumed operations.[190] Meanwhile, in the Chichester division, it was impossible to revive the Slindon men's branch, since 'all the men in the village had left for the services or on war work'.[191]

Candidate selection usually stimulated greater activity: it could hardly be ignored, indeed, by those associations that lacked a candidate. More than a hundred Conservative and Liberal National candidates were adopted in the period between February and June 1945.[192] This is a useful indicator of the extent of grassroots Conservative revival at the very end of the war, but it was, by definition, localized: in particular, constituencies that already had MPs who were planning to stand at the election, or candidates of long standing, did not benefit. Finally, increasing numbers of associations were employing, or at least seeking to employ, agents by late 1944 (see Chapter 3). If they were successful, then the agent was a key promoter of greater activity. But even if they failed, the attempt was often sufficient to galvanize associations and take their activity to new levels.

The end of the Coalition came, essentially, at the hands of Labour, with the Liberals playing a supporting role. Although some Conservatives tried to make political capital out of these 'desertions', such outrage was largely synthetic: few Conservatives expected to lose the election that had now become inevitable, and the end of the Coalition also meant an end to any need to be polite about the party's opponents. After years of biting their tongues, in public at least, Conservatives could now really say what they felt; most believed that, once they did so, their party would be safely re-elected.

There was little that seemed 'normal' about the 1945 general election. Central Office agents' predictions of the result were qualified not only by the almost total uncertainty over the forces vote, but also because, as one put it, 'we have had practically no complete canvass anywhere'; some felt that Labour had greatly improved its organization.[193] Wartime population movements made prediction very tricky. In the south, for example, constituencies like the Isle of Wight, Winchester, Chippenham, and Fareham had all seen significant influxes of workers at various stages of the war, bringing with them earlier anti-Conservative commitments; many now remained to vote.[194] Winchester CA's chairman, speaking after the loss of the seat to Labour at the election, bemoaned this 'influx

[190] Wansbeck CA papers, Acc. 1633/35, executive committee 12 June 1944, special subcommittee of executive committee 9 Nov. 1945.

[191] Chichester CA papers, CO/1CH/Add. MS. 12088, organization subcommittee 4 Dec. 1944.

[192] Chartwell papers, CHAR 2/545, Assheton to Churchill, 24 Jan. 1945, Assheton to Beaverbrook, 9 Feb. 1945.

[193] CCO 4/2/61, J. W. Lancaster (CCO agent, East Midlands area) to Topping, 6 July 1945, Miss Cook (CCO woman organizer, South-East area) to Topping, 6 July 1945.

[194] Ibid., R. Homan (CCO agent, Wessex area) to Topping, 27 June 1945.

of new voters', 12,000 of whom were in 'a very Red District'.[195] A similar story came in The Wrekin, where a large ordnance factory at Donnington, built on the outbreak of war, was reckoned to be a reservoir of Labour votes; it was a similar story in other West Midlands constituencies, like Ludlow, Oswestry, Shrewsbury, Stourbridge, and Thornbury.[196] There was also concern that young people in factories would have been especially influenced by shop stewards while having heard 'little of the Conservative point of view'.[197]

There were some qualms about the party's reliance on its leader's prestige at the election. In Barkston Ash (West Yorkshire), for example, there were warnings that 'too much reliance [was] being placed upon Mr Churchill' when what was needed was a sound policy on housing.[198] Ealing CA's MP, Sir Frank Sanderson, took the view that 'the popularity of our Prime Minister would be such that he believed the Conservatives could win a General Election on that alone', but others in the association felt that a clear reconstruction policy would be of more value.[199] Conversely, however, Newbury CA showed its colours by timing the adoption of its candidate so that they had completed the business of the meeting in time to listen together to Churchill's first broadcast of the campaign on 4 June.[200] Meanwhile, old complaints about ministers resurfaced. Bury CA protested that Central Office was not sending any oratorical 'heavy artillery' to the town to counter opposition stars like Cripps, Bevin, Sinclair, and Beveridge.[201] Central Office replied that its efforts to get ministers to go to Bury had failed because they were busy, either with ministerial work or in their own constituencies (or, as Assheton put it in private, because 'every Minister has got to fight for his seat').[202] These explanations were not totally specious, but seemed rather feeble and unhelpful to many ordinary Conservatives. In fact, Central Office was appealing to ministers in such an apologetic and half-hearted manner that it is not surprising that few responded positively.[203] In Chelmsford, there were similar complaints, and Common Wealth held a seat that had produced a 16,000 Conservative majority in 1935.[204]

---

[195] Winchester CA papers, 73M86W/5, central executive committee 1 Dec. 1945.

[196] CCO 4/2/61, Major H. H. Little (CCO agent, West Midlands area) to Topping, 28 June 1945.

[197] Ibid.

[198] Barkston Ash CA papers, WYL 629/6, finance and general purposes committee 16 June 1945.

[199] Ealing CA papers, Acc. 1338/2, special executive committee 4 Mar. 1943, executive committee 19 Oct. 1943.

[200] Newbury CA papers, D/EX 409/3, council meeting 4 June 1945.

[201] Bury CA papers, GCP/C/1/3, Myles Kenyon and W. E. Rothwell to Topping, 14 June 1945; McCallum and Readman, *British General Election of 1945*, 135–6.

[202] Bury CA papers, GCP/C/1/3, Marjorie Maxse to Myles Kenyon, 16 June 1945; Avon papers, AP 11/4/68, Ralph Assheton to Anthony Eden, 15 June 1945.

[203] Emrys-Evans papers, Add. 58263, Marjorie Maxse to Paul Emrys-Evans, 29 May 1945.

[204] Chelmsford CA papers, D/Z 96/7, 'By-election 5th July 1945: election agent's report', n.d. [*c.* Aug. 1945].

Prior to the declaration of the results, few associations made adverse comment about the amount of voluntary help that they received. '[A]fter such a lapse of time, it was surprising and pleasing to find so many workers, again ready to drop into the General Election campaign,' said Sheffield Park's annual report for 1945.[205] Winchester CA had about 750 voluntary helpers at the election, including 160 who helped to address over 80,000 election communications and 40 car owners who took voters to the polls, while Bewdley CA had a 'magnificent' number of cars available on polling day.[206]

One case study illustrates many of the developments outlined above. Harborough (Leicestershire) was a county constituency with some significant urban areas. By 1935 it was a safe seat with a thriving Conservative association, which in early 1939 had 78 branches (18 men's, 34 women's, 20 joint, and 6 JIL), an active labour advisory committee, and a monthly magazine, *Progress*, with a circulation of around 900 copies.[207] Its first wartime meeting, on 23 September 1939, heard Hacking's various letters, before deciding to run down most of its activity, ending publication of *Progress* and dispensing with the agent and woman organizer. However, the Central Office area agent warned the association against too total a closure, especially in the light of continuing opposition activity and the need to fight an election after the war, and by January 1940 the CA were urging all branches to become more active: that March, all 78 branches were intact, with 'the great majority' having met since September 1939.[208] A year later, the women's and joint branches were still holding social meetings and whist drives; 24 out of 33 women's branches were functioning effectively, especially—but not solely—by knitting and helping war charities, while in 1942, the spectre of the Grantham by-election was raised to alert branches to the need to remain active.[209] By early 1943, the MP, Ronald Tree, was giving regular talks to branches on current affairs, discussion groups were being set up, and overtly political activity increasingly accompanied ongoing charitable activities.[210] A conference to discuss post-war reorganization was held in March 1944, and that December it was agreed to fill executive committee vacancies, revive branches, intensify fund-raising, seek a full-time agent, and find new offices.[211] By the end of the war there was significant revival, with both an agent appointed and new offices

[205] Sheffield Park CA papers, LD 2116, women's association, annual report for 1945 to annual general meeting 25 Mar. 1946.

[206] Winchester CA papers, 73M86W/5, central executive committee 1 Dec. 1945; Bewdley CA papers, BA 956/8, central council 22 Sept. 1945.

[207] Harborough CA papers, DE 1170/4, 45th annual report, to annual general meeting 29 Apr. 1939.

[208] Ibid., special executive committee 23 Sept. 1939, executive committee 13 Jan. 1940; 46th annual report, to annual general meeting 31 Mar. 1940.

[209] Ibid., 47th annual report, to annual general meeting 12 July 1941; 48th annual report, to annual general meeting 27 June 1942.

[210] Ibid., 49th annual report, to annual general meeting 26 June 1943.

[211] Ibid., special executive committee 11 Mar. 1944; 50th annual report, to annual general meeting 23 Sept. 1944; executive committee 16 Dec. 1944.

obtained. Tree was narrowly defeated in 1945, but the association responded with a vigorous reorganization plan.[212] Because the party had not fallen into desuetude during the war, there was a firm foundation upon which to build, and the association was soon back to a very strong position.

In the aftermath of defeat, nationwide opinions about the state of the party's wartime constituency organization were hastily revised. In July 1944, the *Conservative Agents' Journal* had singled out Thornbury CA as being in urgent need of reconstruction because it 'ha[d] NOT [*sic*] been one of the fortunate number to maintain extensive activity since the commencement of the war'.[213] This seemed to imply that it was unusual in being so dormant. In October 1945, however, the emphasis of the same publication was on the need to rebuild constituency machines which had, on the whole, been 'made derelict or partly derelict by the war'.[214] In May 1945, branch reports in Sowerby had shown that preparations for the election were going well; yet after the seat was lost, the constituency chairman blamed weak organization for the defeat.[215]

This was all part of coming to terms with Labour's victory, of course. Various reasons were put forward to try to explain the defeat. There was talk of a pendulum effect; of population movements; of the baleful influence of the Beaverbrook press; of poor party chairmen; of a failure to attract young people; even, for some, of the negative effects of Churchill's election broadcasts.[216] Yet the line that appears to have satisfied most people, and which enabled the party to avoid excessive internal recrimination and backbiting, was that which stressed the party's loyalty to the 'party truce' as against socialist perfidy. For the *Conservative Agents' Journal*, the election result could be 'summed up in a sentence—in organization and propaganda we had kept the Truce; our main opponents with the support of the Co-operative Societies and the Trades Unions had not; abuse was all that the great mass of electors had heard of the Conservative Party, and that over a period of years'.[217] This view was echoed by the party's North-Western area council in October 1945: 'It is some consolation to know that whilst during the whole of the war period our opponents continued their propaganda and their attacks on the Conservatives, the energies of the great masses in our Party were almost entirely devoted to war efforts in accordance with the desire of our great Leader, Mr Churchill.'[218] Similar verdicts came

[212] Ibid., executive committee 28 July, 20 Oct. 1945.
[213] *Conservative Agents' Journal*, July 1944.   [214] Ibid., Oct. 1945.
[215] Sowerby CA papers, executive committee 29 May, 27 Sept. 1945.
[216] See e.g. Bolton CA papers, FDC/1/9, election committee 27 July 1945; Clitheroe CA papers, DDX 800/1/3, executive committee and subcommittee, 16 Oct. 1939; Newbury CA papers, D/EX 409/20, 'General election, 1945: agent's report', n.d. [Aug. 1945]; Western Conservative area council papers, ARE 11/6/2, Somerset provincial division, annual meeting 18 Sept. 1945; Bury St Edmunds CA papers, GK 501/2/1, executive committee 10 Nov. 1945.
[217] *Conservative Agents' Journal*, Oct. 1945.
[218] Lancashire, Cheshire, and Westmorland Conservative area council papers, ARE 3/1/2, annual meeting 27 Oct. 1945.

from right across the party grassroots.[219] One effect of the growing Conservative consensus around this rather mythical view of the party's wartime experience was the exculpation of Churchill. Initially, there was some criticism, albeit veiled. At its first annual meeting after the war, for example, Barkston Ash CA demanded 'a bold declaration of policy by our leaders' which would 'lead to a much quicker revival of Conservatism than [would] any form of appeasement', and the need for 'inspired Leadership from the top'.[220] However, there remained considerable goodwill towards Churchill as 'one of the outstanding figures in the History of the World', and uniting around the myth of closure and socialist perfidy helped him to survive.[221]

Clearly, though, much remained to be done in revitalizing the party at constituency level. Even where they had been active, associations had been engaged in many types of activity that were hardly appropriate to peacetime. The cycle of elections had returned. So too had a more regular relationship with MPs and candidates, steadier membership collections, and the like. It was not surprising, therefore, that many associations spent the rest of 1945 and much of 1946 planning and executing further revival and reorganization.[222] Defeat in 1945 had only made imperative what would in any case have been urgent. A number of associations now decided to increase their party's profile in local government. There had been high-level pressure for party members to fight local elections under Conservative colours, rather than as 'independents' and the like, even before 1939; and, during the war, the PWPCC had favoured the formation of a local government advisory committee at Central Office.[223] By early 1945, some associations had decided that, in future, Conservatives needed to fight local elections as Conservatives, and that Conservative councillors should act as a caucus once elected. Defeat at the general election confirmed these views to many more.[224]

---

[219] See e.g. Scottish UA papers, Acc. 10424/27(viii), western divisional council, annual report for 1945, 31 Aug. 1945; Northern Conservative area council papers, NRO 3303/2, half-yearly meeting 6 Oct. 1945; Birmingham UA papers, management committee 12 Nov. 1945; Bolton CA papers, FDC/3/9, women's association, annual report to annual meeting 19 Mar. 1946.

[220] Barkston Ash CA papers, WYL 629/10, annual report 1945, to annual meeting 13 Apr. 1946; Scottish UA papers, Acc. 10424/44, eastern divisional council, 12 Oct. 1945.

[221] Blackpool CA papers, PLC 5/1/3, Harold Worden (chairman) to Churchill, n.d. [27 July 1945].

[222] See e.g. Gravesend CA papers, U1795/AD1/4, executive committee 31 Aug. 1945; Stafford CA papers, D1289/1/3, special meeting 1 Dec. 1945; Northampton CA papers, NCCA/29, annual report for 1945, 25 Mar. 1946; Pembrokeshire CA records 1, Ludchurch and Narberth South polling district, branch meeting 11 Feb. 1946.

[223] K. Young, *Local Politics and the Rise of Party: The London Metropolitan Society and the Conservative Intervention in Local Elections, 1894–1963* (Leicester, 1975), 181–3.

[224] See e.g. Worcester CA papers, BA 10925/3, meeting of executive council with Conservative aldermen and councillors, 2 May 1945; Essex and Middlesex Conservative area council papers, ARE 8/1/3, council meeting 27 July 1945; West Dorset CA papers, D399/3/2, war emergency executive committee 19 Nov. 1945; Flintshire CA papers, D/DM/307/4, annual general meeting 29 Sept. 1945.

Some objected.[225] But, for many Conservatives, Labour's success in 1945 owed much to perceptions of its record in local government, and to the fact that the Labour party's name was always being put before the electorate in local elections. If this was the recipe for success, then many Conservatives were happy to swallow their misgivings and take 'party' further into local government; in June 1946 Central Office appointed its first local government officer.[226]

There was a heavy turnover of constituency officials once the war and general election were over, with Central Office giving strong encouragement to rejuvenation.[227] Many older officials were probably exhausted by the travails of keeping their associations going through the war, and needed little encouragement. The process had begun even before the end of the war, annual general meetings in early 1945 seeing a significant number of retirements. To take just a few examples, April 1945 saw the retirement of Chelmsford's chairman and president, Bewdley's chairman and treasurer, and Louth's chairman, while the latter half of 1945 and the first months of 1946 saw the retirement of long-standing CA chairmen in North Cornwall, Darwen, Winchester, and Ipswich.[228] In October 1945 the president of Penryn and Falmouth CA retired because of deafness, and was joined by eight members of the finance and general purposes committee that had run the association through the war years.[229]

There can be no doubt that the activities of Conservative constituency organizations were curtailed by the war. In some cases, this curtailment was almost total, and remained such for the duration of the conflict. However, it is also clear that most Conservative associations did not simply shut up shop. For most, social activity of one kind or another continued, and such activity was often expected to have a political pay-off. Explicitly party political activity was heavily circumscribed by the natural inclination of many Conservatives to avoid issues of 'mere party' at a time of national peril (especially when that peril seemed gravest), and by the party's interpretation of the truce, reinforced by the realities of Coalition politics. However, such attitudes were not quite what they seemed: paradoxically, there were clearly hopes that an emphasis on 'nation before party' would bring party benefits. Furthermore, overt political

[225] See e.g. Chichester CA papers, CO/1CH/Add. MS. 12088, general purposes and finance committee 24 Sept. 1945; Bury St Edmunds CA papers, GK 501/2/1, executive committee 10 Nov. 1945.

[226] Young, *Local Politics and the Rise of Party*, 186

[227] Ramsden, *Age of Churchill and Eden*, 42; West Dorset CA papers, D399/4/1, finance committee subcommittee, 17 Dec. 1945.

[228] Chelmsford CA papers, D/Z 96/7, executive committee 5 May 1945; Bewdley CA papers, BA 956/8, executive committee 14 Apr. 1945; Louth CA papers, Misc. dep. 250/1, executive committee 18 Apr. 1945; North Cornwall CA papers, DDX 381/5, executive committee 15 Dec. 1945; Darwen CA papers, PLC 2/2/2, general meeting 21 Sept. 1945; Winchester CA papers, 73M86W/5, central executive council 1 Dec. 1945; Ipswich CA papers, GK 401/1/1, executive committee 11 Jan. 1946.

[229] Penryn and Falmouth CA papers, DDX 551/16, special finance and general purposes committee 27 Oct. 1945.

activity did not disappear totally from Conservative associations during the war, and increased as debates over reconstruction intensified from late 1942 onwards. Finally, it should be stressed that the extent to which Conservative associations remained active, or not, during the war also depended upon time and place: there were periods when activity was harder to sustain than others, and areas of the country where it was much more difficult than others to keep going. In this respect, there were significant similarities with the wartime experiences of Labour and Liberal constituency bodies, and it is to them that attention now turns.

6

Constituency Activities: Labour

The counterpart to the narrative of Conservative organizational decline at constituency level is the notion that Labour flourished. As will be seen in this chapter, this view is not entirely baseless, but it is an oversimplification, which masks both the extent to which Labour's constituency activity diminished at crucial stages of the war, and also the difficulties that attended the party's efforts to revive from 1943 onwards. It will also be shown that any wartime improvement in Labour's fortunes came about not as some inevitable benefit of 'total war', but very often as the result of hard work on the part of those Labourites whose view was, and remained, clearly fixed on the battle for power. If, by 1945, Labour's constituency parties stood on the brink of their most prosperous and expansive period, it was largely as a result of the work of party members at all levels during the preceding six years.

Constituency-level organization had been the cause of some concern for headquarters immediately prior to the war. Although they existed in almost all the territorial constituencies of Great Britain, DLPs' membership appeared stagnant, and there was a degree of organizational malaise with some. Worse still, continuing pessimism about the imminent general election had led a minority to favour some kind of electoral pact against the National government, in some cases even involving collaboration with the Communists. Indeed, Communist influence remained a concern in some constituencies up to the outbreak of war. Meanwhile, although most trade unions were by 1939 reasonably well disposed to the party at national level, at the local level union branches were often reluctant to affiliate to DLPs, and relations were often strained (see Chapter 4).

As has been seen, DLPs were not subjected to the conflicting signals that afflicted Conservative associations following the outbreak of war: the 4 September letter told them to carry on, and similar instructions continued to come (see Chapter 1). Most DLPs were happy to comply. On 3 September, Stockport TCLP's executive committee declared itself in 'constant session' for the duration of the conflict, although in the event their 'constant session' ended after only three days.[1] More typically, the City of Leeds LP decided on 8 September to continue meeting as normal (although earlier in the evening because of the blackout),

[1] Stockport TCLP papers, B/MM/2/19, executive committee 3, 11 Sept. 1939.

and four leading officials were nominated to act in case of emergency.[2] Hendon (Middlesex) DLP agreed that it was 'of the greatest importance', to keep the party intact by holding meetings, chasing subscriptions, and working to defend civil liberties and workers' interests. Participation in ARP and other war work was acceptable, but members 'should not become obsessed by this, and overlook their vital interest [*sic*] after the war'.[3] In Wansbeck (Northumberland) a series of public meetings scheduled for 10 to 20 September was cancelled, but the secretary was 'empowered to do all in his power to keep [the] Party organization intact during the period of the war', and he instructed local Labour parties (LLPs) within the constituency to meet as regularly as possible.[4] Many parties established new bodies to respond to the war situation, as a way of remaining active and helping their constituents. These included advice or information bureaux, and vigilance committees to look after working-class interests on issues like prices and rationing, while Bermondsey borough Labour party (BLP) offered the services of a sympathetic lawyer at the party offices free of charge for an hour a week.[5] Most parties accepted invitations to participate, along with other political and voluntary bodies, in MoI local committees, although there was suspicion of too close an involvement.[6] However, the mixed fate of local Labour newspapers showed that parties did not just carry on regardless. Leeds, Gloucester, Ipswich, and Reading did keep their publications going, although not without difficulty.[7] But Swansea abandoned its paper, while the London Co-operative Society's decision to suspend the *Citizen* service—a scheme whereby local parties were provided with a monthly newspaper with space in which to insert their own local news—was a blow to many London DLPs.[8]

There was much suspicion of the electoral truce, which was denounced by numerous DLPs and union branches, and protests continued despite repeated and vigorous headquarters responses.[9] These concerns showed that many Labourites were deeply unhappy about anything that implied supporting the National

[2] City of Leeds LP papers, WYL 853/4/16, special executive committee 8 Sept. 1939.

[3] Hendon DLP papers, BLPES film 211A, reel 97559/1, executive committee 13 Sept. 1939, general committee 23 Sept. 1939.

[4] Wansbeck DLP papers, NRO 527/A/3, executive committee 2 Sept. 1939.

[5] See e.g. Lewisham West DLP papers, A89/100/9, war emergency committee 7 Nov. 1939; Pontypridd TCLP papers, Birmingham microfilm 97137/5, meeting 4 Sept. 1939; Bermondsey Labour party papers, YL 254, *Bermondsey Labour Magazine*, Nov. 1939.

[6] See e.g. Bedford DLP papers, X494/2, executive committee 3 Oct., 28 Nov. 1939.

[7] Ibid., executive committee 12 Oct., 14 Dec. 1939; WYL 853/4/20, general committee 23 June 1943; Gloucester TLC papers, D3128/5/7, general committee 14 Sept. 1939; Ipswich TCLP papers, GK 400/1/1/3, executive committee 1 Oct. 1939, 5 June 1940, 3 Sept. 1941, 9 Aug. 1943; Mikardo, *Back-Bencher*, 58–9.

[8] Swansea LP papers, BLPES film 211A, reel 97580/11, Swansea Labour Association annual report to annual meeting 18 Apr. 1940; Bethnal Green North-East DLP papers, TH/8488/16, management committee 10 Oct. 1939.

[9] LPNEC XVIII, elections subcommittee 12 Dec. 1939; Middleton circular, 'The electoral truce', Feb. 1940; NEC emergency committee 28 Feb. 1940; Henley DLP papers, O4/1/A/1, general council 3 Feb. 1940.

government in the war. There was genuine concern about Labour jingoism and what the party's Scottish executive called the 'over-warlike tone' of the TUC-controlled *Daily Herald*.[10] There was a strong sense that a distinction must be drawn between Nazis and Germans.[11] Demands flooded into Transport House for an official statement of Labour's 'peace aims'.[12] Nelson and Colne (Lancashire) demanded a pan-European conference to discuss 'democratic terms for Peace',[13] which it circulated to other DLPs, gaining the support of some, while Greenwich DLP narrowly passed a motion calling on Labour's leaders to 'work for Peace and stop co-operating with the present Government, but work to overthrow Chamberlain and his Gangster Pack'.[14] It was in response to all this criticism (and the fear that the Communists might start to exploit it) that Attlee issued 'six points for peace' on 5 December 1939, that the party issued an official statement on 'Labour and the War' on 25 January 1940, and that a series of conferences was planned on the subject.[15]

But this was not enough to satisfy the more pacifistic Labour parties. On Armistice Day (11 November) 1939, Bermondsey West DLP (whose MP, Dr Alfred Salter, was a prominent pacifist) called on the NEC and PLP 'to exert all possible pressure on the Government to open negotiations for an honourable peace at the earliest possible moment', and the following month its magazine demanded 'Peace by Negotiation—Now!!! [*sic*]', a call endorsed by the Labour-controlled borough council. As late as April 1940, Salter was criticizing Britain for extending the war to Scandinavia, and calling on the British government to '[e]nd it all by a frank offer to negotiate an agreed peace', which was the only way to prevent bombs falling on Bermondsey.[16]

Most parties rejected such a line, of course. Derby DLP, on receiving a circular from twenty Labour MPs calling for a negotiated peace in December 1939, declared tersely that 'the opportunity for such a move had passed'.[17] But even among parties less pacifistically inclined than Bermondsey, debates over peace aims could provide a useful spur to action, as in Dulwich and Wansbeck, where lectures and a study circle on the subject helped to sustain activity over the

---

[10] Scottish Labour party papers, TD 1384/1/1, Scottish executive committee 29 Sept. 1939.

[11] See e.g. Hendon DLP papers, BLPES film 211A, reel 97559/1, general committee 23 Sept. 1939; Lewisham West DLP papers, A89/100/9, general committee 28 Apr. 1940.

[12] LPNEC XVIII, NEC 25 Oct., 20 Dec. 1939.

[13] Birmingham Deritend BLP papers, uncat., management committee 15 Oct. 1939.

[14] Darlington DLP papers, D/X 922/5, executive committee 24 Oct. 1939; Newport DLP papers, MNB/POL/6/A/8, meeting 20 Oct. 1939; Greenwich DLP papers, GLP 1.3, general committee 23 Nov. 1939.

[15] Clapham DLP papers, LMA/4284/02/001, C. R. Attlee, *Labour's Peace Aims* (London, 1939); LPNEC XVIII, Middleton circular to NEC members, 25 Jan. 1940, organization subcommittee 13 Dec. 1939; Scottish Labour party papers, TD 1384/3/1/1, executive committee report to 25th annual conference, 21 Sept. 1940.

[16] Bermondsey Labour party papers, YL 254, *Bermondsey Labour Magazine*, Nov., Dec. 1939, Jan., May 1940.

[17] Derby DLP papers, DL 116/1/1, executive committee 8 Dec. 1939.

winter of 1939–40.[18] And some parties continued to express concerns long into the 'Phoney War' period, as in February 1940, when Halifax DLP condemned the leadership's statement that there could be 'no cessation of hostilities until a military victory of a crushing character had been inflicted on Germany', and demanded instead that the NEC should exert unremitting pressure on 'the British Imperialist Government' to 'initiate and accept any and every opportunity for a negotiated peace, the risks of which even at their worst, cannot compare in disastrousness for the workers, to [*sic*] a Military Victory for this or any other Capitalist Government'.[19]

Divisional parties calling for statements of peace aims were an irritant to headquarters. Those talking about 'imperialist war' were a source of real alarm. The Communist party's change of line gave it a chance to exploit Labour discontent. Retrospective narratives focus on Labour unity, and argue for the unpopularity or irrelevance of the Communists' new approach. But this is to underestimate the extent to which it chimed in with what a minority of grassroots Labourites were thinking. On 20 September—*before* the CPGB's change of line—Huddersfield DLP defeated (by 29 votes to 25) a resolution supporting Labour's leadership, and instead demanded that Labour should 'expose the imperialist character of the war' and realize that the only acceptable outcome would be 'a Socialist peace based on freedom of all peoples from their own rulers'.[20] Three days later, again before the CPGB's line change, Brecon and Radnor DLP welcomed the action of the USSR 'in entering Poland and thus protecting the workers and inhabitants of that part of Poland from Nazi barbarity and savagery and in making them acquainted at first hand with the economic security of a classless socialist state'.[21] After the change of line, Cambridgeshire TCLP voted by 22 to 17 that the war was not one for democracy, 'but an Imperialist war', while parties like Epsom (Surrey) and Hendon lost members to the CPGB on the issue.[22] Bodies like the North London Anti-War Council sprang up with strong, but by no means universally Communist, involvement.[23] There were other examples of union branches or local Labour parties passing 'imperialist war' resolutions which, even if rejected by the constituency party, were a warning of the potential dangers of going too far in supporting the National government's line.[24]

---

[18] Dulwich DLP papers, A390/uncl., executive committee 17 Dec. 1939, 13 Feb. 1940; Wansbeck DLP papers, NRO 527/A/3, executive committee 11 Nov. 1939, 30 Mar. 1940.

[19] Halifax DLP papers, TU 28/1, annual meeting 29 Feb. 1940.

[20] Huddersfield DLP papers, BLPES film 211, reel 143, general committee 20 Sept. 1939.

[21] Brecon and Radnor LP records 4, DLP general meeting 23 Sept. 1939.

[22] Cambridgeshire TCLP papers, 416/0.7, general meeting 18 Nov. 1939; Epsom DLP papers, 2141/1, general committee 11 Nov. 1939; Hendon DLP papers, BLPES film 211A, reel 97559/1, executive committee 13 Sept. 1939; annual report for 1939 to annual meeting 16 Apr. 1940.

[23] Tottenham South DLP papers, BLPES film 211A, reel 97564/2, general committee 17 Jan. 1940, annual meeting 14 Feb. 1940.

[24] See e.g. Sheffield Brightside DLP papers, LP(B)7, executive committee 21 Oct. 1939.

In this context, by-elections were significant. Stern action, including expulsions and the disaffiliation of Bermondsey BLP, followed the Southwark Central by-election of January 1940, at which a Labour anti-war candidate opposed the official nominee man in a Labour-held seat.[25] West Ham Upton DLP was disaffiliated when it supported the Communist Harry Pollitt at the by-election in nearby Silvertown that February, while Glasgow Pollok DLP was also threatened with expulsion if it did not withdraw its anti-war candidate that April.[26] Indeed, the round of disaffiliations that continued into the spring and summer of 1940 was larger in scale than anything since the purges of the mid-1920s, further victims including Sheffield TLC and the BLPs in Hammersmith, Islington, and Paddington.[27]

Divisions at the top of the party over the Soviet attack on Finland were replicated further down. Some parties took a pro-Finnish view: the City of Leeds LP (influenced by the soon-to-be-proscribed, far left, but anti-Communist Militant Labour League) expressed its solidarity with the Finnish workers, and declared its 'indignation and disgust' at the Soviet action.[28] Kensington South DLP simultaneously deplored Soviet actions and called on the PLP to oppose the arming of Finland.[29] Finland so divided Blackpool DLP that no resolution was adopted on the grounds that any position taken would alienate one section or other of the party's membership.[30] The expulsion of Pritt also aroused protests: occasionally DLPs supported his views, but more often it was a case of them objecting to dissent being dealt with by expulsion.[31] In April 1940, the action of the French government in holding secret trials of Communists aroused similar divisions. Leeds took the line that 'in France, as elsewhere' the Communist party was 'the enemy of democracy and liberty' which had 'sought consistently the suppression of opinion contrary to its own'; although other parties were less unsympathetic, they still tended to base their criticisms of the French government on civil liberties grounds.[32] Others, however, were closer to the Communists. Bristol East, for example, raged against 'reactionary forces in Great Britain and France' whose aim was to use the

[25] LPNEC XVIII, elections subcommittee 11 Jan., 7 Mar. 1940.

[26] Ibid., elections subcommittee 10 Apr. 1940.

[27] Ibid., NEC emergency committee 3 July 1940; organization subcommittee 17 July 1940; NEC 25 Sept. 1940.

[28] City of Leeds LP papers, WYL 853/4/16, delegate meeting 17 Dec. 1939; for the MLL in Leeds, see e.g. ibid., WYL 853/4/17, executive committee 14 Mar., 11 Apr. 1940, general committee 17 Apr. 1940.

[29] Recorded in Epsom DLP papers, 2141/1, executive committee 26 Jan. 1940.

[30] Blackpool DLP papers, DDX 2100/3/1, delegate meeting 11 Feb. 1940.

[31] See e.g. East Grinstead DLP papers, LA 2 MS 1/2/2, executive committee 27 Mar. 1940; Gloucester TLC papers, D3128/5/7, general committee 11 Apr. 1940; Cambridgeshire TCLP papers, 416/0.7, annual general meeting 20 Apr. 1940; Pontypridd TCLP papers, Birmingham microfilm 97137/5, meetings 15, 29 Apr. 1940.

[32] City of Leeds LP papers, WYL 853/4/17, executive committee 11 Apr. 1940; Ipswich TCLP papers, GK 400/1/1/3, executive committee 4 Feb. 1940, delegate meeting 8 May 1940.

conflict 'to lead the workers into an attack on the great union of socialist republics'.[33]

Domestic policy concerns were also significant. A number of London DLPs complained about the large numbers of evacuated children who had now returned and who were left 'roaming the streets in the danger zones, in an undisciplined and uneducated state'; there were also widespread protests against high prices and profiteering.[34] Sheffield Hallam was among the parties that saw the importance of the politics of consumption, buying 200 copies of the Labour party pamphlet *The Shopping Basket in War Time* for free distribution to party members.[35] Many Labourites continued to fear that the war would be used as an excuse to screw down living standards: the Keynes plan for compulsory savings excited particular resistance on this score.[36] There were also increasing concerns about civil liberties.[37]

All this, added to the strong lead given at the start of the war by headquarters, meant that no DLPs ceased to operate at this stage, although it was a rather more mixed picture at the level of ward or local Labour parties: in south-east London, for example, only two out of seven of Greenwich DLP's ward Labour parties were still running normally by February 1940.[38] Many DLPs tried to sustain pre-war levels of activity. Social events like whist drives often remained successful; many advice bureaux were extremely busy.[39] In November 1939 the secretary of Lewisham West DLP noted that the organizational position 'appeared to be very gradually returning to normal', as wards began to meet again, and by January 1940 he was suggesting that party affairs were 'in [a] sound condition', although he admitted that this might change 'if the war speeded up considerably'.[40] On the other hand, when the agent for Bethnal Green North-East wrote to 600 party members in January 1940 suggesting regular members' meetings, he received

---

[33] Bristol East DLP papers, 39035/19, general committee 10 Mar. 1940; see also C. Mayhew, *A Time to Explain* (1987), 52.

[34] Lewisham West DLP papers, A89/100/9, general committee 22 Oct. 1939; Frome DLP papers, A/AAW 28, annual general meeting 10 Feb. 1940; Cambridge TCLP papers, 634/08, monthly meeting 3 Apr. 1940.

[35] Sheffield Hallam DLP papers, LD 1564/2, management committee 10 Mar. 1940.

[36] See e.g. Tottenham North DLP papers, BLPES film 211A, reel 97564/4, general committee 25 Apr. 1940; Huddersfield DLP papers, BLPES film 211, reel 143, general committee 30 Apr. 1940; R. Toye, 'Keynes, the Labour movement, and "how to pay for the war"', *Twentieth Century British History*, 10 (1999).

[37] See e.g. Hendon DLP papers, BLPES film 211A, reel 97559/1, general committee 10 Feb. 1940.

[38] Greenwich DLP papers, GLP 1.3, annual meeting 23 Feb. 1940; and see e.g. Bishop Auckland DLP papers, D/BAL 1/1, Bishop Auckland LLP women's section annual meeting 6 Dec. 1939; meeting 6 July 1944; Birmingham Deritend BLP papers, uncat., management committee 10 Dec. 1939, annual management committee 11 Mar., 1940, DLP meeting 8 July 1940.

[39] See e.g. Dulwich DLP papers, A390/uncl., executive committee 10 June 1940; Frome DLP papers, A/AAW 28, general committee 16 Mar. 1940.

[40] Lewisham West DLP papers, A89/100/9, war emergency committee 7 Nov. 1939, 9 Jan. 1940.

only one reply, and no meeting of any kind was held before March 1941, although literature distribution and an advice bureau did continue; the women's section closed early in the war, and only reopened in 1943.[41]

In this latter respect, Bethnal Green was unusual: in most places, Labour women's activity continued and, in some ways, expanded. Many sections formed or joined vigilance committees. A 'very large number' established work parties, although, as well as knitting for the forces, they also produced garments for evacuated children or refugees, or, later in the war, for children in liberated countries.[42] As with the Conservatives, many also became involved in salvage, billeting, and similar activities. In Scotland, Greenock DLP women's section ran a 'successful' canteen for the troops who were stationed in the town.[43] Educational conferences continued, especially on 'Labour and the War', and 'Protection of Women and Children in Wartime'.[44]

The 1940 party conference was due to open in Bournemouth on 13 May, and a number of DLPs were looking forward to using it as a platform from which to attack the perceived weakness and failure of the parliamentary leadership. Penistone DLP was ready to denounce the leadership's 'unqualified support for the National Government'; Gloucester specifically mandated its delegate to vote against any coalition government; and Windsor did likewise, also telling its delegate to abstain if a motion were put offering 'unqualified appreciation of the work of the Parliamentary Labour Party', and to oppose 'any move of the National Executive Committee to join a Government under Tory leadership'.[45] On Friday, 10 May, the day that was to see Chamberlain's resignation, Derby DLP agreed that Labour should only take office if it were offered some 'major posts', including 'finance and supply'.[46] In the event, however, the conference took place in completely changed circumstances, and the NEC's strong support for entry into government under Churchill could be presented as a *fait accompli*. Indeed, the leadership could not have had a more favourable context in which to discuss the issue: even so, there was some resistance to Attlee's resolution approving participation in the new government. Chelsea and Chislehurst (Surrey) DLPs both demanded 'a Socialist Government . . . as the only way of extracting the country from its present disastrous position', while Edinburgh and District

[41] Bethnal Green North-East DLP papers, TH/8488/16, management committee 9 Mar. 1941, '1943 report' to management committee 20 Jan. 1944.

[42] *Report of the Twentieth National Conference of Labour Women*, 15–16 Oct. 1940; Derby DLP papers, Box 3, 18(a), annual report 1940, 1941; Hendon DLP papers, BLPES film 211A, reel 97559/1, annual report for 1939 to annual meeting 16 Apr. 1940; Scottish Labour party papers, TD 1384/3/1/1, executive committee report to 29th annual conference, 23–4 Sept. 1944.

[43] Scottish Labour party papers, TD 1384/3/1/1, executive committee report to 25th annual conference, 21 Sept. 1940.

[44] *Report of the Twentieth National Conference of Labour Women*, 15–16 Oct. 1940.

[45] Penistone DLP papers, BLPES Film 211A, reel 97135/1, executive committee 16 Mar. 1940; Gloucester TLC papers, D3128/5/7, special general meeting 25 Apr. 1940, general committee 9 May 1940; Windsor DLP papers, D/EX 832/3, general committee 2, 7 May 1940.

[46] Derby DLP papers, DL 116/1/1, executive committee 10 May 1940.

LP put forward a straight 'imperialist war' resolution. However, Greenwood, in a powerful speech, attacked Chelsea and Chislehurst as 'twittering sparrows' in safe Conservative seats, whereas 'the most powerful Trade Union organizations in this country'—who did know something about real life—were supporting the leadership. 'If they trust us,' he added, 'Chislehurst and Chelsea ought to trust us.' The critical resolutions were defeated by 'overwhelming' majorities, while Attlee's motion was passed by 2,413,000 votes to 170,000. With conference in this mood, motions criticizing the party leadership's ' "Fight to the Finish" attitude', and attacking the electoral truce, were easily defeated. Some constituency delegates, though, noticed Greenwood's dismissive line towards DLPs, helping to stoke later resentment.[47] Some criticism persisted: there were resignations from the party in, among other places, Tottenham South, Epsom, and Northampton at this point, precisely on this issue, with some of the defectors joining the Communist party.[48] But most DLPs offered strong support for Labour's entry into government. In Nottinghamshire, Broxtowe DLP, which in November 1939 had demanded 'the immediate cessation of hostilities', now came out strongly for the war effort, while even Bermondsey switched its attention from calling for peace to protecting civil liberties in wartime.[49] Although there would be very real strains, the presence of Labour ministers at the heart of the government considerably assisted the incorporation of the party's grassroots organizations and members into the war effort.

The continuing presence of the 'Men of Munich' in the government did arouse grassroots Labour criticism, however, especially once party members had absorbed the arguments of the contemporaneous best-seller *Guilty Men*. Blackpool DLP demanded the ousting of Chamberlain, Hoare, Wood, Simon, and 'other Lordly Pro-Fascists', while Penistone DLP (south Yorkshire) attacked them as 'Pro-Fascist' and 'Friends of Hitler'.[50] The strong criticism that emanated from many DLPs at the closure of the Burma Road in July 1940, although originating in a circular from the China Campaign Committee, owed much to the notion that closure represented the appeasement of Japan.[51] Other parties, however, were more moved by ideas of national unity, and rejected calls to seek the

---

[47] *LPACR 1940*, 126–43.

[48] Tottenham South DLP papers, BLPES film 211A, reel 97564/2, general committee 29 May 1940; Epsom DLP papers, 2141/1, executive committee 7 June 1940; Northampton DLP papers, NLP 2, executive committee 11 June 1940.

[49] Broxtowe DLP papers, DD/PP/6/6, executive committee 27 Nov. 1939; DD/PP/6/4, council meeting 16 Dec. 1939, 1 June 1940; Bermondsey Labour party papers, YL 254, *Bermondsey Labour Magazine*, Sept. 1940; and see e.g. Gloucester TLC papers, D3128/5/7, special general committee 23 May 1940; South-West Norfolk DLP papers, Acc. 2001/145/1, executive committee 20 July 1940.

[50] Blackpool DLP papers, DDX 2100/3/1, delegate meeting 14 July 1940; Penistone DLP papers, BLPES Film 211A, reel 97135/1, general meeting 6 July 1940.

[51] See e.g. Barrow DLP papers, BLPES film 211A, reel 97566/1, general meeting 25 July 1940; Leeds Central DLP papers, WYL 853/63/6, meeting 19 Sept. 1940; Tottenham North DLP papers, BLPES film 211A, reel 97564/4, general committee 28 Sept. 1940.

removal of Chamberlain and others.[52] West Derbyshire went so far as to reject the Burma Road resolution, on the grounds that 'they were confident that our Party Leaders in the War Cabinet would not have concurred without fullest justification'.[53]

Many Labour parties remained vibrant. In June 1940, for example, it was reported that all five of Hertfordshire's DLPs had been affected by the war, but that all were thriving nonetheless.[54] Many parties campaigned for better air raid shelters and post-raid facilities, and others continued to purchase and distribute headquarters literature, while many advice bureaux continued to flourish: thirty such bodies were being run by DLPs and LLPs in Scotland alone by September 1940.[55] Some parties continued with activities which might, in retrospect, seem almost reckless, as when over 100 members of Halifax DLP went on an outing to Scarborough and Whitby, on the east coast of Yorkshire, on Sunday, 30 June.[56]

But this was not the whole story. In early May, Frome DLP had planned a major revitalization of its organization at all levels, but the subsequent transformation of the military and political position, allied to the agent's departure for the army, meant the plans were left in abeyance, and in the mid-war years the DLP would prove relatively inactive.[57] Successful social events held by Leeds Central DLP in the summer of 1940 were not repeated once enemy bombing began, and by early October there was a significant 'falling off' of attendance at all party meetings in the constituency.[58] Faversham, on the north Kent coast, was hit hard: after the fall of France the constant threat of invasion and 'incessant air raids' severely hampered Labour party activities, while fear of invasion led to a significant fall in political activity in much of Norfolk and Suffolk: DLPs there were briefed by the party's regional organizers on the actions they should take to safeguard party interests in the case of invasion, which included duplicating party records and membership details and sending to them to headquarters.[59] The significant civilian evacuation that followed shortly afterwards offered further potential for disruption.[60] In London, Lambeth Brixton DLP explicitly authorized its secretary

[52] See e.g. Sheffield Hallam DLP papers, LD 1564/2, management committee 8 May 1940; Lewisham West DLP papers, A89/100/9, general committee 8 July 1940.

[53] West Derbyshire DLP papers, D1650 G/M2, executive committee 30 July 1940.

[54] Hertfordshire Labour Federation papers, D/EX 273Z1, quarterly council 15 June 1940.

[55] See e.g. Gloucester TLC papers, D3128/5/7, special general committee 24 Oct. Apr. 1940; Swansea LP papers, BLPES film 211A, reel 97580/11, Swansea Labour Association annual report to annual meeting 24 Apr. 1941; Scottish Labour party papers, TD 1384/3/1/1, executive committee report to 25th annual conference, 21 Sept. 1940.

[56] Halifax DLP papers, TU 28/1, executive committee 20 June, 18 July 1940.

[57] Frome DLP papers, A/AAW 28, executive committee 30 Apr., 22 June 1940.

[58] Leeds Central DLP papers, WYL 853/63/6, executive committee 4 June, 19 Sept., 1 Oct. 1940.

[59] Faversham DLP papers, U3272, annual report for 1940, to annual meeting 19 Jan. 1941; Ipswich TCLP papers, GK 400/1/1/3, executive committee 3 July 1940.

[60] Ibid., delegate meeting 11 Sept., 8 Dec. 1940.

'to obliterate all records which would give information to the enemy should he reach this country', while at the other end of the country, Orkney and Shetland DLP had no choice but to shut down, since 'meetings were impractical in the present conditions'.[61] Even in less unfavourable locations, some parties began to curtail their activities significantly.[62]

The onset of the Blitz in September 1940 affected London Labour parties badly. On 14 September, indeed, Greenwich DLP's executive had to curtail its meeting when the air raid siren sounded, to enable various members to go on ARP duty.[63] Across the capital, there was 'serious dislocation' of women's sections once the raids began in earnest: 'In one area after another, Sections disappeared, officers were temporarily "lost", members scattered.'[64] Some officials of Southwark North DLP were killed when its headquarters took a direct hit in November 1940, and the offices of Tottenham South and Hendon DLP were also bombed out.[65] Clapham DLP's premises were bombed twice, although they were not rendered uninhabitable, and its shrewd secretary negotiated a rent reduction.[66] Some women's sections in the blitzed areas of London were beginning to meet again as early as March 1941, but overall recovery was patchy and often slow.[67] If, as Dan Weinbren has argued, '[n]eighbourhood links rather than workplace links were central' to Labour's constituency organization in the capital, then it is the extent, rather than the scarcity, of local Labour activity at this period which is most remarkable.[68]

On the night of 14–15 November 1940, 554 people were killed and 865 seriously injured in air raids on Coventry.[69] The DLP lost all its office furniture and equipment, and most of its records. The party's membership was 'scattered' by the evacuation that followed, and party organization 'largely collapsed'. However, the secretary did what he could from his own house; the candidate, Richard Crossman, replaced some of the equipment; and a number of nearby DLPs offered assistance. Because the party's financial records had mostly survived, there was a basis for retaining existing members, and the party's sound financial position meant that revival was possible. In the aftermath of the raid there was

---

[61] Lambeth Brixton DLP papers, IV/156/1/1, executive committee 1 July 1940; Scottish Labour party papers, TD 1384/1/1, Scottish executive committee 18 Apr. 1942.

[62] See e.g. F. Bealey, J. Blondel, and W. P. McCann, *Constituency Politics: A Study of Newcastle-under-Lyme* (1965), 90–1.

[63] Greenwich DLP papers, GLP 2.4, executive committee 14 Sept. 1940.

[64] *Report of the Twenty-First National Conference of Labour Women* (1942), 5.

[65] LPNEC XVIII, NEC 27 Nov. 1940; Tottenham South DLP papers, BLPES film 211A, reel 97564/2, general committee 10 Nov. 1940, annual general meeting 23 Feb. 1941; Hendon DLP papers, BLPES film 211A, reel 97559/1, executive committee 2 Mar. 1941.

[66] Wandsworth Clapham DLP papers, IV/156/2/2, general management committee 8 May 1941.

[67] *Report of the Twenty-First National Conference of Labour Women* (1942), 5.

[68] D. Weinbren, 'Building communities, constructing identities: the rise of the Labour party in London', *London Journal*, 23 (1998), 53.

[69] O'Brien, *Civil Defence*, 404–5.

a determination to carry on, with 'cottage meetings' being held and a reunion of members acting as a springboard to recovery.[70] In the short term, this was an excellent example of optimism in the face of adversity, reflecting 'the spirit of the blitz'. However, after this initial rally, Coventry DLP's experiences were not dissimilar to those of many other constituency parties: its immediate reaction to adversity was impressive, but it was insufficient to restore the party quickly to its pre-raid strength, and propaganda efforts often fell flat, while ward-level organization only really revived from November 1944 onwards.[71]

The 1940–1 air raids also disrupted Labour activity elsewhere in the provinces. By July 1941, the effects of enemy action in Salford had left only one of its three DLPs functioning seriously.[72] Southampton was heavily bombed in December 1940; although the DLP itself soon returned to action, it took some ward parties the rest of the war to start recovering.[73] Air raids on Birmingham led to 'an entire lack of political activity' in the inner-city Deritend constituency.[74]

The dramatic and sudden impact of air raids can be contrasted with the unheroic, gradual deflation of activity and enthusiasm that most DLPs were experiencing by the first half of 1941. The number of local party resolutions submitted to headquarters each month had dwindled to 'only a few' by the middle of the year, and there were reports of a minority of parties ceasing to meet.[75] A spring 1941 revival of women's sections would prove short-lived, and by May 1943 the number of live women's sections would be 'the lowest for a number of years'.[76] In March 1941, the NEC's organization subcommittee was told that there was now a 'very restricted' scope for public meetings; even so, there were 'signs of life', and when in May 1941 headquarters reviewed the series of conferences that had taken place across the country over recent months, it emerged that interest in them 'had been remarkable despite the circumstances', and planning proceeded apace on a new series of policy conferences on 'Democracy and Reconstruction'.[77] But great difficulties remained. One was the curtailment of local transport services, which inhibited attendances at party and public meetings alike, especially in rural and semi-rural

[70] Coventry DLP papers, MSS 11/1/4, executive committee 8 Dec. 1940.

[71] Ibid., MSS 11/1/3/4, women's section, annual report 1942; MSS 11/1/4, executive committee 23 Feb., 7 Sept., 4 Oct. 1941; MSS 11/1/5, organization and redevelopment committee, 6 Nov. 1944, 7 Jan., 4 Feb. 1945.

[72] Salford BLP papers, BLPES film 211A, reel 97555/2, executive committee 25 Sept. 1940, delegate meeting 4 Dec. 1940, joint policy committee 13 Dec. 1940, executive committee 23 June 1941.

[73] Southampton DLP papers, D/LAB/box 2, executive committee minutes, *passim.*

[74] Birmingham Deritend DLP papers, uncat., annual report for 1941, to annual management committee 29 Mar. 1942, 15 Oct. 1939.

[75] LPNEC XVIII, NEC emergency committee 23 Oct. 1940; XIX, NEC 25 June 1941; memo, 'Burslem and Tunstall DLP', n.d. [*c.* Feb. 1941].

[76] *Report of the Twenty-Second National Conference of Labour Women* (1943), 8.

[77] LPNEC XIX, 'Memorandum on [*sic*] propaganda section of the organization department in response to a request of the organization subcommittee meeting [*sic*] at its February meeting, 1941 [*sic*]', 24 Mar. 1941; organization subcommittee 28 May 1941.

constituencies.[78] At least the steady flow of headquarters literature throughout the war was a boon to those DLPs, like Derby, Halifax, and Newport, that had the money to buy it and the will and personnel to sell or distribute it, while *Labour Woman* remained crucial in encouraging and stimulating the work of women's sections.[79]

Somewhat paradoxically, 1940–1 was a period when many people detected a significant radicalization of the population, or, at least, sections of it. Many Labourites shared the view articulated contemporaneously by George Orwell: that the war would be lost unless its whole basis were shifted and radicalized.[80] One of the best examples of this mood was a resolution passed by Bournemouth DLP in October 1940 and circulated to all constituency parties. Bournemouth argued that the fundamental determinant of the war effort was the full support of the workers. To secure that support, the government must repeal the 1927 Trade Disputes Act, abolish the household means test, extend social services, and prepare a class-neutral education system for implementation at the end of the war. More immediately, it should also nationalize transport, power, coal, arms production, and the Bank of England. It should also unite with all anti-Nazis and anti-fascists the world over, and adopt a statement of peace aims committing Britain to the restoration of democracy across Europe, and its introduction to India and the colonies.[81] A number of DLPs were quick to adopt it, although, predictably, it cut no ice with the party leadership.[82]

There was less DLP enthusiasm for the NEC's decision to make the June 1941 party conference largely a plebiscite on the leadership, with no opportunity for DLPs or other affiliated organizations to put forward resolutions of their own; many DLPs stayed away, some explicitly on these grounds.[83] Perhaps it was their absence that gave the NEC such an easy ride: in the two main votes at the conference, on 'The War' and 'The Peace', the party leadership's line was endorsed, with almost 2.5 million votes in favour in each case, and, respectively, only 19,000 and 30,000 against.[84]

---

[78] See e.g. Penistone DLP papers, BLPES Film 211A, reel 97135/1, general meeting 16 Sept. 1939; Greenwich DLP papers, GLP 1.3, general committee 22 May 1941.

[79] Derby DLP papers, DL 116/1/1, executive committee 13 Oct. 1939, 12 Jan. 1940, 10 Jan., 14 Mar. 1941; Newport DLP papers, MNB/POL/6/A/8, general committee 18 Apr. 1941; Halifax DLP papers, TU 28/1, executive committee 22 May 1941; *Report of the Twenty-First National Conference of Labour Women* (1942), 5–6.

[80] See e.g. Lambeth Brixton DLP papers, IV/156/1/1, special general management committee 15 Jan. 1940.

[81] Wansbeck DLP papers, 527/A/3, executive committee 16 Nov. 1940.

[82] See e.g. ibid., executive committee 16 Nov. 1940; Darlington DLP papers, D/X 922/5, executive committee 26 Nov. 1940; Wolverhampton West DLP papers, D/LAB/1/8, executive committee 3 Nov. 1940.

[83] LPNEC XIX, NEC 21 Jan. 1941; and see e.g. Bristol East DLP papers, 39035/19, general committee 11 May 1941; Cambridgeshire TCLP papers, 416/0.23, John Kearsey to J. S. Middleton, 5 May 1941; Northampton DLP papers, NLP 2, Labour council 13 Mar. 1941.

[84] *LPACR* 1941, 144, 166.

Meanwhile, the Communists remained a concern. After June 1940, the CPGB moved increasingly towards agitating against the concrete adverse effects of the war on working-class people. This allowed them to find common ground with many Labourites, and the result was the people's vigilance movement of autumn 1940, which culminated in the People's Convention, held in London in January 1941. Transport House took a stern line (see Chapter 4). Party members were expelled, and Waterloo (Lancashire), Newbury (Berkshire), and Canterbury (Kent) DLPs were all disaffiliated and reorganized.[85] Protests against the government's ban on the Communist *Daily Worker* in January 1941 aroused the sympathy of some DLPs, although others rejected the opportunity to attack the ban.[86] Most of those protesting, however, would have agreed with the line of Cambridge TCLP, which protested against the 'infringement' of press freedom involved, while stressing that it 'in no way associat[ed] itself with the anti-war policy of the "Daily Worker" '.[87] Things were to become worse, in some ways, after the German invasion of the Soviet Union on 22 June 1941. Numerous pro-Communist bodies emerged in the guise of supporting the Soviet war effort, and Transport House had to work very hard to discourage DLPs from becoming involved in them, though many DLPs were now so tired of disruption that they needed no prompting to deal with Communist sympathizers.[88] DLPs which threatened the truce, meanwhile, were put under considerable pressure: Birmingham King's Norton was subjected to a full and lengthy headquarters investigation, and then suspended, for merely suggesting that Labourites should abstain from voting for the (Conservative) government candidate in the May 1941 by-election there, and it was only readmitted to the party in January 1942 after formally submitting to NEC authority.[89]

By late 1941 it was becoming apparent that Labour's grassroots organization was in difficulty. Membership was falling, while the lack of halls, fears about money, unavailability of speakers, population movements, and ongoing problems of the blackout and air raid warnings, were all making it very difficult for DLPs to conduct any 'platform propaganda'.[90] The enfeebled state of many DLPs was one of the main reasons why the NEC suspended the adoption of new parliamentary

---

[85] LPNEC XVIII, NEC 26 Feb. 1941; organization subcommittee 25 Mar., 22 Apr. 1941.

[86] Greenwich DLP papers, GLP 1.3, general committee 23 Apr. 1942 and Bristol East DLP papers, 39035/19, general committee 23 Feb. 1941; cf. Ipswich TCLP papers, GK 400/1/1/3, delegate meeting 9 Feb. 1940 and South Shields DLP papers, BLPES film 211, reel 26, meeting 4 Mar. 1941.

[87] Cambridge TCLP papers, 634/08, monthly meeting 12 Mar. 1941.

[88] LPNEC XIX, 'Individual membership: resume of suggestions from district organizers and women organizers', n.d. [to organization subcommittee 16 Dec. 1941]; Hendon DLP papers, BLPES film 211A, reel 97559/1, executive committee 27 Aug. 1941.

[89] LPNEC XIX, NEC 30 May 1941, 24 Sept. 1941; organization subcommittee 20 Jan. 1942.

[90] Ibid., 'Memorandum on platform propaganda under war conditions now prevailing', 16 Dec. 1941.

candidates in October 1941. There were good reasons for this—the remoteness of a general election, many potential candidates' inability to attend selection conferences, and a fear of Communist infiltration—but, whatever its merits, the ban, which remained formally in place until 1944, removed one good reason for DLPs to remain active, and so it helped to weaken some of them still further.[91] In Glasgow, things reached a very low ebb indeed. The trial of a number of Labour councillors for corruption in autumn 1941 did not help matters, but the problems ran deeper: as the party's Scottish organizer reported that December, only seven of the city's fifteen DLPs were meeting regularly and functioning 'reasonably well according to local standards'; a further five met 'spasmodically' and 'd[id] not function effectively'; the remainder met 'seldom or not at all' and were 'devoid of any planned activity'. There was, he concluded, need for 'a general "clean-up" involving the entire structure of the Party in the city'.[92] But it was much easier said than done.

Parties in areas where Labour was traditionally weak suffered very badly indeed. By late 1941, Shepherd was reporting confidentially that the Gainsborough division of Lincolnshire 'ha[d] lost Labour Party organization almost entirely', while 60 miles to the south, Rutland and Stamford DLP 'ha[d] not been called together for a considerable time'.[93] Meanwhile, sub-constituency-level organizations often struggled. There was, perhaps, no 'typical' experience: in Northampton, for example, St John's ward party closed down in October 1939, not to meet again until March 1946, whereas Kingsley ward party met monthly throughout the war, its activity and politicization evident in the number of resolutions it sent to the DLP executive.[94] But in many places, even where meetings were still held, attendances were falling, with 'the same old members' turning up but nobody else.[95] In many places, women were 'the backbone of the party': in order to keep going, many women's sections met in members' houses, and some sections combined to pool their strength, rather than letting them go out of existence.[96] These were not wholly unproblematic expedients, but they allowed sections to remain alive, and to form nuclei from which expansion could follow in better times. But the League of Youth was in poor shape, its young members prime targets for military service and war work, and its organization

    [91] LPNEC XIX, elections subcommittee 15 Oct. 1941.

    [92] Ibid., John Taylor, Scottish organizer, 'Memorandum to the national agent on the present position of the Labour Movement in Glasgow', n.d. [*c.* Dec. 1941]; see also A. McKinlay, 'Labour and locality: Labour politics on Clydeside, 1900–39', *Journal of Regional and Local Studies*, 10 (1990), 56–7.

    [93] MS Attlee dep. 4, fo. 103, Shepherd to Attlee, 25 Nov. 1941.

    [94] Northampton DLP papers, NLP 6, St John's ward LP, minute book 1929–55, *passim*; 7, Kingsley ward LP, minute book 1929–43, *passim*.

    [95] LPNEC XIX, 'Individual membership: resume of suggestions from district organizers and women organizers', n.d. [to organization subcommittee 16 Dec. 1941]; Sheffield Hallam DLP papers, LD 1564/3, annual meeting 14 Dec. 1941.

    [96] Lewisham West DLP papers, A89/100/10, general committee 8 May 1944.

collapsing all over Britain, although a few did linger longer, and a handful continued throughout the war.[97]

Labour's constituency organizations were inhibited from total inertia, however, by the fact that they had a number of regular triggers to action. One was the need to declare a membership figure to headquarters. A second was local government. Although there were often complaints about councillors ignoring party meetings, many did attend, and often gave very full accounts of their council activities.[98] This was important because it offered an important standing item for discussion, and kept to the fore the idea of Labour in government at local level. For many Conservative associations, on the other hand, local government was not a matter of 'party politics', so a key element forcing continuing organization was absent. A third trigger was provided by Labour movement ritual and custom. In particular, May Day was a traditional highpoint of the year which many parties tried to maintain.[99] All this gave a framework into which other meetings on issues like post-war reconstruction could be placed.

Public meetings tended to be of limited value, even where they could be held. There were exceptions: in Northumberland, Wansbeck DLP held 'satisfactory' public meetings fairly regularly from late 1941 onwards.[100] On the whole, though, they remained difficult to organize and financially draining. Attendances were rarely such as to encourage a repetition. Party after party looked into restarting public meetings in 1942, only to be discouraged either before or after the event was held.[101] In July 1942, Rother Valley (South Yorkshire) DLP responded enthusiastically to the NEC's suggestion that parties should hold public meetings addressed by Allied international speakers, and initially planned to hold five or six such meetings in different parts of the constituency, but LLP responses were so poor that the only ultimate outcome was a speech by a Polish socialist to a private meeting of the DLP executive committee that November.[102] Free French speakers often went down well; some DLPs felt that Soviet speakers would be even more of a draw, but met resistance from headquarters which feared that Russian speakers 'would probably have communist tendencies'.[103] Bristol East might reasonably have expected a healthy interest in a public meeting addressed by its MP, Cripps, in November 1942, but in fact the attendance

[97] See e.g. Stafford DLP papers, D1371/1, divisional management committee 16 Dec. 1939; Bristol East DLP papers, 39035/19, general committee 23 Feb. 1941.

[98] See e.g. Southampton DLP papers, D/LAB/box 2, executive committee 10 Oct. 1941; Hamilton DLP papers, BLPES film 211, reel 89, quarterly meeting 30 June 1944.

[99] See e.g. Norwich DLP papers, SO 198/1/3, executive committee 9 Apr. 1940, 8 Apr. 1941; Colne Valley DLP papers, BLPES Film 211, reel 5, annual reports 1940–5, *passim*.

[100] Wansbeck DLP papers, NRO 527/A/3, executive committee 13 Dec. 1941, 7 Feb. 1942, 8 Aug. 1942.

[101] See e.g. Blackpool DLP papers, DDX 2100/3/2, executive committee 30 Aug. 1942.

[102] Rother Valley DLP papers, 290/G1/1, executive committee 25 July, 17 Oct., 14 Nov. 1942.

[103] Newport DLP papers, MNB/POL/6/A/8, general committee 12 June 1942; Norwich DLP papers, SO 198/1/3, executive committee 19 Aug. 1943.

was 'disappointing', and it was agreed not to repeat the experiment for the time being.[104]

Other activities could be less circumscribed. Social events were important. In spring 1941, Derby DLP held weekly whist drives, and ran a dance where servicemen were admitted at a reduced price; in 1942, its activities included a boxing tournament, a very successful vegetable show, and a bazaar.[105] In August 1941, 200 people went on a Southampton DLP outing to the nearby New Forest.[106] And in May 1942, the worst of its torment from the bombers apparently over, Faversham (Kent) DLP organized a reunion of members for the first time since the outbreak of war, and was delighted when more than 500 members and friends turned up for the celebration at Sheerness.[107]

The USSR provided a much-needed stimulus to activity from June 1941 onwards. Labour supporters had very widely divergent views of the Communist party in Britain, and indeed of its Soviet counterpart, but they were just about united in coming to admire the Red Army's efforts, although a small but active minority in Leeds remained strongly critical of Soviet policy.[108] Really gushing pro-Soviet effusions were made only rarely.[109] There were, though clear signs that enthusiasm for Russia was starting to help the CPGB by 1942, as DLPs which had earlier supported the ban on the *Daily Worker* now called for it to be lifted.[110] This call was endorsed by the May 1942 party conference, albeit by a very narrow margin.[111] Sympathy for Russia had a pale reflection in campaigns for China; Salford BLP was one of a number of parties that held a successful China Week in autumn 1942.[112]

Domestic politics also continued to agitate DLPs. Strong feeling was frequently expressed against the 1927 Trade Disputes Act.[113] Some parties took a strong line on gender issues: Huddersfield, for example, passed resolutions calling for the local authority to establish crèches (April 1941) and in favour of equal compensation and against sex discrimination (December 1942).[114] State control was generally favoured, and advances in it welcomed, while profiteering was

[104] Bristol East DLP papers, 39035/19, general committee 29 Nov. 1942.

[105] Derby DLP papers, DL 116/1/1, executive committee 9 May, 11 July 1941, 8 May, 11 Sept., 12 Dec. 1942.

[106] Southampton DLP papers, D/LAB/box 2, executive committee 20 Aug. 1941.

[107] Faversham DLP papers, U3272, annual report for 1942, to annual meeting 14 Feb. 1943.

[108] City of Leeds LP papers, WYL 853/4/18, general committee 16 July 1941.

[109] See e.g. Liverpool TCLP papers, BLPES film 211A, reel 97572/9, TCLP meeting 21 Dec. 1941.

[110] See e.g. Ipswich TCLP papers, GK 400/1/1/3, delegate meeting 9 Feb., 13 Aug. 1941; special executive committee 18 Feb. 1942.

[111] *LPACR* 1942, 157–60.

[112] Salford BLP papers, BLPES film 211A, reel 97555/2, executive committee 23 Oct. 1942, delegate meeting 1 Nov. 1942; and see also e.g. Blackpool DLP papers, DDX 2100/3/2, general committee 25 Oct. 1942.

[113] Hendon DLP papers, BLPES film 211A, reel 97559/1, general committee 21 Feb. 1942.

[114] Huddersfield DLP papers, BLPES film 211, reel 143, general committee 20 Apr. 1941, 8 Dec. 1942.

frequently condemned, and parties continued to press for better service pay and allowances.[115] Opinions about the military side of the war effort varied significantly. In September 1941, a number of DLPs debated a Labour Pacifist Fellowship resolution denouncing retaliatory bombing of Germany, and calling on Churchill to offer the Germans a convention outlawing the bombing of civilians. Although some parties rejected it out of hand, others passed it, suggesting that the desire for revenge was not always as strong as might have been thought.[116] Events in India during 1942 also brought a response from many DLPs, with some DLPs demanding that it be granted freedom, or at least democracy.[117] Meanwhile, criticism of the electoral truce continued. In May 1942, with the war going badly, the government relatively unpopular, and independent candidates making inroads at by-elections, the party conference only defeated a resolution denouncing the truce by the narrow margin of 1,275,000 votes to 1,209,000.[118] A few days later, Jim Griffiths had to be sent by the NEC to his native South Wales to persuade Llandaff and Barry DLP, with difficulty, to remain neutral in the by-election there.[119]

By-elections in Labour seats could expose the weakness of divisional parties very sharply, as in the safe east London seat of Poplar South in August. The DLP's membership had fallen from 2,375 in 1939 to only 414 (very few of whom were active) in 1942.[120] The London organizer reported that it was 'unable to undertake even the routine work of a By-election', and local members contributed very little to the campaign. Whole streets had been destroyed or rendered uninhabitable by bombing, and 'it was a rare thing to find an elector resident at his 1939 Register address'. The party's office was a single room of nine feet by four. Only two 'sparsely attended' indoor election meetings could be held. The gloomy conclusion was that 'the conditions for conducting a test of electoral opinion do not exist in an area where the electorate has become dispersed and disorganized'. In effect, the DLP was virtually useless, and irrelevant to victory at the by-election. It made no rapid recovery: its real membership in January 1945 was to be just 70.[121] Of course, Poplar South was not typical of the country as a whole; but the extent of its decline demonstrated graphically one extreme that faced some DLPs.

Just a few miles to the south-east it was a different story, however. Woolwich BLP, which oversaw the borough's East and West divisions, had always been

[115] City of Leeds LP papers, WYL 853/4/18, special executive committee 20 May 1942; Wansbeck DLP papers, NRO 527/A/3, annual meeting 21 Feb. 1942; Halifax DLP papers, TU 28/1, general meeting 30 Oct. 1941.

[116] For rejection, see e.g. Leeds Central DLP papers, WYL 853/63/6, meeting 21 Aug. 1941; Norwich DLP papers, SO 198/1/3, executive committee 9 Sept. 1941; for support, see e.g. Dulwich DLP papers, A390/uncl., DLP meeting 24 Sept. 1941.

[117] See e.g. Wansbeck DLP papers, NRO 527/A/3, annual meeting 21 Feb. 1942; Windsor DLP papers, D/EX 832/3, general committee 19 Feb. 1942.

[118] *LPACR* 1942, 150.   [119] LPNEC XIX, NEC 5 June 1942.

[120] *LPACR* 1940, 108; *LPACR* 1943, 102.

[121] LPNEC XX, Hinley Atkinson, 'Report', n.d. [to NEC 28 Oct. 1942]; Poplar South DLP papers, TH/8488/17, ward committee 25 Jan. 1945, West ward meeting 1 Aug. 1945.

very well run. The borough suffered considerably in air raids, though, and the problem faced in 1940 can be seen in the fact that two of the five women's sections ceased to meet. However, the remaining three were extremely active with knitting and other social service functions, while the advice bureau dealt with hundreds of enquiries. Collectors continued to call on members, despite frequent air raids. Social activities were difficult to organize because 'all halls in the Borough were commandeered for Civil Defence and other war purposes', but although this lack of halls ruled out the resumption of regular ward meetings in 1941, some successful aggregate meetings took place, and 1942 saw ward gatherings resumed 'in practically all wards', while successful study classes were also held. By 1943, the average attendance at general committee meetings had increased to 65; all wards were meeting regularly; 290 new members were made in the first six months of the year; the MP for Woolwich East was visiting all parts of the borough; and a series of lectures on local government had attracted an average attendance of 50. By the end of the year, a Woolwich Labour Choir and a Woolwich Labour Cycling Club had been formed.[122] This was a well-organized party facing the war with confidence, and meeting its challenges very effectively.

But Woolwich was exceptional, and the state of the party in the country at large was giving Transport House considerable concern by mid-1942. The government's establishment of a Committee on Electoral Machinery suggested that there was some desire to opening up at least the possibility of a wartime general election, and senior Labour officials at least claimed to be concerned at the possibility of a snap election. Shepherd, for example, travelled to Scotland in both August and September 1942 to stress the need to be ready for such a poll.[123] How far he really believed this, and how far it was a ploy to urge greater grassroots activity, is unclear, but, either way, his actions suggest that he was far from sanguine about the state of the party.

It took the talk of post-war reconstruction at the turn of 1942–3, and a realization that the nature of that reconstruction was likely to be seriously contested, to inject more urgency into the work of many constituency parties. Conservative resistance to a fuel rationing scheme in mid-1942 had already suggested that Labour's opponents had changed little, if at all, and such concerns seemed to be amply confirmed by Conservative reactions to the Beveridge report, which had been eagerly awaited at the Labour grassroots.[124] Ironically, there was some disappointment with it when it appeared: Broxtowe DLP (Nottinghamshire) focused on its 'weaknesses' in February 1943, especially in

---

[122] Woolwich BLP papers, WLP 40.3, annual report, 1940, to annual general meeting 23 Mar. 1941; 1941, to annual general meeting 11 Apr. 1942; 1942, to annual general meeting 3 Apr. 1943; 1943, to annual general meeting 25 Mar. 1944; WLP 6, 'Agent's report for half-year ending June 30th, 1943', n.d. [July 1943].

[123] Scottish Labour party papers, TD 1384/1/1, Scottish executive committee 3 Aug., 18 Sept. 1942.

[124] See e.g. Darlington DLP papers, D/X 922/5, executive committee 22 May 1942; Broxtowe DLP papers, DD/PP/6/4, council meeting 21 Nov. 1942.

relation to workmen's compensation and old age pensions, while the Leeds City party agreed that it was a welcome recognition of certain social evils, but that 'Socialism [was] the only real cure for economic injustice'.[125] For the president of Penistone DLP, it was 'nothing to write home about', while in nearby Huddersfield, it was agreed that, while the report represented an advance, Labour must resist attempts to let it replace 'a genuine Socialist Plan'.[126] But others were more favourable from the outset, and, within weeks, Conservative reactions had consolidated Labour opinion behind Beveridge, at least in the short term.[127] Indeed, after February's parliamentary debate, DLPs were often quick to claim Labour ownership of the report, and to recognize that it was 'an excellent starting place for a greater effort in Propaganda'.[128] A week after damning the 'weaknesses' of the report, Broxtowe decided to send a letter of congratulation to the Labour MPs who had voted against the government on the subject, and asked the PLP 'to sever its connections' with the government; still more remarkably, a year later it would be calling on the government to introduce a new and simplified Workmen's Compensation Act 'based on the lines of the Beveridge Report'.[129] Just two months after damning Beveridge with faint praise, Huddersfield DLP was congratulating the PLP on its stance in voting for the report in the Commons, and by the end of March 1943, the majority of resolutions being received by Transport House were along similar lines.[130] By now, some saw the report as 'an immense step forward'; most saw it as, at least, a valuable first instalment of reform.[131] This shift of mood was undoubtedly helped by contemporaneous Conservative backbench resistance to the Catering Wages Bill and the Uthwatt report on land, and by the series of well-attended conferences run across the country by Transport House in support of the Beveridge report.[132]

The shape of post-war Europe was also exercising Labour minds. There was criticism of the rabidly anti-German views of the former diplomat Lord Vansittart

[125] Broxtowe DLP papers, DD/PP/6/4, special council meeting 13 Feb. 1943; City of Leeds LP papers, WYL 853/4/20, general committee 17 Jan. 1943.
[126] Penistone DLP papers, BLPES Film 211A, reel 97135/1, annual general meeting 6 Feb. 1942; Huddersfield DLP papers, BLPES film 211, reel 143, executive committee 5 Jan. 1943.
[127] Pontypridd TCLP papers, Birmingham microfilm 97137/5, meeting 7 Dec. 1942.
[128] Rother Valley DLP papers, 290/G1/1, special executive committee 27 Feb. 1943; see also e.g. Coventry DLP papers, MSS 11/1/4, executive committee 10 Feb. 1943, annual meeting 21 Feb. 1943.
[129] Broxtowe DLP papers, DD/PP/6/4, council meeting 20 Feb. 1943, 26 Feb. 1944.
[130] Huddersfield DLP papers, BLPES film 211, reel 143, executive committee 2 Mar. 1943; LPNEC XX, NEC 24 Mar. 1943.
[131] Salford BLP papers, BLPES film 211A, reel 97555/2, annual meeting 4 Apr. 1943; Greenwich DLP papers, GLP 1.3, general committee 17 Dec 1942, 22 Apr. 1943.
[132] Blackpool DLP papers, DDX 2100/3/2, general committee 14 Feb. 1943; Swansea LP papers, BLPES film 211A, reel 97580/11, Swansea Labour Association annual report to annual meeting 22 Apr. 1943; LPNEC XX, social insurance conference arrangements committee 5 Jan. 1943; memo, 'Suggested centres for conferences and demonstrations on Beveridge Report, 1943', n.d. [to NEC 27 Jan. 1943].

('Vansittartism').[133] However, there was some support for Vansittart within the party; and opinion against Germany hardened as more became known about the fate of European Jewry at the hands of the Nazis. In November 1942, for example, Salford BLP passed a resolution condemning Nazi atrocities, and demanding the establishment of 'the Jewish National Home in Palestine'.[134] In Leeds, where there was a relatively large Jewish population, Labour calls for a national homeland had begun earlier in 1942, and later in the year 'stern justice' was demanded against the perpetrators of Nazi atrocities. In December 1942, a speaker from Paole Zion, the Zionist party affiliated to Labour, spoke about the deportation and mass murder of Jews, and Alderman Brett, one of the party's leaders, broadened the issue to cover discrimination at home as well as on the continent: 'In this city the term "yid" is used derisively. We must stamp this out.'[135] In October 1944, Leeds welcomed the NEC's support for a Jewish state in Palestine, adding that non-Jews already living there would not suffer because they would have a 'free choice of remaining and sharing in the benefits which Jewish colonisation brings in its wake or be assisted to participate in the development of the vast resources of undeveloped land in the neighbouring Arab countries'.[136] Birmingham BLP passed two resolutions on 10 January 1943, first denouncing leading Labourites for supporting Vansittart, and secondly expressing 'horror' at the Nazis' 'organized mass slaughter' of Jews in occupied Europe, and demanding that the British government do more to help, for example by lifting restrictions on Jewish immigration to Britain; in April 1945, Rotherham TLC condemned the atrocities at Belsen and Buchenwald, and demanded that the perpetrators be brought to justice.[137]

The increase in party political controversy put renewed focus on relations with the Communists and the newly formed Common Wealth. Some parties including Rotherham, Norwich, and Walsall, supported Communist affiliation at this point, but they had to be careful not to associate with Communist bodies in doing so: Weston-super-Mare (Somerset) was disaffiliated in January 1943 when it failed to be careful enough.[138] But there was also a good deal of hostility towards the idea. Parties like Hendon and Epsom, which had suffered significant disruption early in the war due to Communist activities, were firmly opposed, Red Army or no Red Army; Darlington DLP denounced the CPGB as 'sworn

---

[133] Ipswich TCLP papers, GK 400/1/1/4, delegate meeting 8 Nov. 1942; Tottenham South DLP papers, BLPES film 211A, reel 97564/2, general committee 23 Sept. 1943.

[134] Salford BLP papers, BLPES film 211A, reel 97555/2, delegate meeting 1 Nov. 1942.

[135] City of Leeds LP papers, WYL 853/4/19, general committee 15 Mar., 16 Sept., 20 Dec. 1942; see also e.g. Wansbeck DLP papers, NRO 527/A/3, annual meeting 27 Feb. 1943.

[136] City of Leeds LP papers, WYL 853/4/21, general committee 20 Oct. 1944.

[137] Birmingham BLP papers, uncl., meeting 10 Jan. 1943; Rotherham TLC papers, 443/G, meeting 24 Apr. 1945.

[138] Ibid., meeting 27 Apr. 1943; Norwich DLP papers, SO 198/1/3, special executive committee 22 Apr. 1943; Walsall DLP papers, Acc. 50/4, delegate meeting 17 Jan. 1943; LPNEC XX, organization subcommittee 19 Jan. 1943.

to a policy of dictatorship'.[139] Islington North DLP tried to exploit leadership fears to lever a more radical policy stance, circulating widely its resolution that the NEC should 'give a virile and fighting policy on socialism to enable us to combat the Communist menace'.[140] The 1943 party conference's decisive vote removed Communist affiliation from the agenda, but did not entirely dispose of DLPs' problems with Communists. There would be concerns about growing Communist influence in South Wales in the summer of 1944, for example.[141] But constant Transport House monitoring left the Communists little room to gain real influence; pressure for cooperation with the Communists was coming by mid-1944 mainly from a few trade unions, most notably the AEU, the ETU, and the Fire Brigades Union, rather than the constituency parties.[142]

The development of Common Wealth also gave Labourites pause for thought, and a few DLPs dabbled with Acland's ideas and writings at various times.[143] However, there was little grassroots Labour enthusiasm for the new organization beyond *Schadenfreude* at the difficulties it caused the Conservatives. The NEC's proscription of CW on 24 March 1943 made DLPs even more wary of it.[144] In January 1944, Dulwich DLP leaders agreed to meet local representatives of CW to discuss cooperation at the post-war general election, but rapidly changed their minds on the advice of the national agent, and although they were to welcome the help of CW members at the 1945 election, it would be very much as individuals, and not as representatives of CW as such.[145]

By the second half of 1943, most Labour parties were reviving, in some cases strongly. Many fulfilled social service functions, some on behalf of service personnel. Such activity had begun in 1940 with occasional social events for locally-stationed troops.[146] Hendon LLP sent parcels to 76 of its members serving in the forces for Christmas 1942, while a year later the DLP there sent 2,000 cigarettes to a section of the forces serving in the Middle East, and greetings cards

---

[139] Hendon DLP papers, BLPES film 211A, reel 97559/1, general committee 10 June 1943; Epsom DLP papers, 2141/1, special general committee 29 Apr. 1943; Darlington DLP papers, D/X 922/5, general committee 28 Mar. 1943.

[140] Reported in Lewisham West DLP papers, A89/100/10, general committee 16 Feb. 1943; see also Huddersfield DLP papers, BLPES film 211, reel 143, executive committee 2 Feb. 1943; Bedford DLP papers, X494/3, executive committee 12 Jan. 1943.

[141] Labour party Wales records 4, joint meeting of South Wales regional council of Labour executive committee and Welsh MPs 24 July 1944

[142] LPNEC XX, elections subcommittee 10 Nov. 1943; memo, 'Kirkcaldy by-election', n.d. [to NEC 24 Nov. 1943]; XXI, elections subcommittee 6 Jan. 1944; NEC 28 June 1944; joint meeting of elections and organization subcommittees 5 July 1944; NEC 25 Apr. 1945.

[143] East Grinstead DLP papers, LA 2 MS 1/2/2, executive committee 27 Mar. 1940; Hendon DLP papers, BLPES film 211A, reel 97559/1, executive 26 Aug., 8 Nov. 1942.

[144] LPNEC XX, NEC 24 Mar. 1943; Wimbledon DLP papers, 1/2, Merton and Morden LLP, general committee 20 May, 17 June 1943.

[145] Dulwich DLP papers, A390/uncl., general management committee 17 Jan., 24 Feb. 1944, 28 May 1945.

[146] Gloucester TLC papers, D3128/5/7, executive committee 7 Nov. 1940.

from the candidate and the party were sent to every serving member of the DLP whose address could be found.[147] In rural Cambridgeshire, little direct party activity was possible for much of the war, but increasing numbers of members were involved in various forms of war charity and civil defence work, and the party's secretary was not slow to point out that this was 'practical propaganda for socialism which cannot be overestimated & of which the Party will reap the fruits at the next General Election'.[148] This kind of reaction echoed the comments of the secretary of Coventry DLP in the aftermath of the November 1940 raids there, that 'despite the fact that straight party organization was hampered, the Party had gained in prestige by the public work of its members'.[149] As with the Conservatives, discussion circles became increasingly important. Clapham DLP started a small but successful weekly group in September 1942, which continued through to 1945, while Ipswich launched a successful study circle, originally for younger members but rapidly catering for a wider constituency, in July 1943; in the winter of 1944–5 alone it met twenty-four times, with good attendances and a high quality of discussion.[150]

Organization at sub-constituency organization level remained a concern. In the mining constituency of Hamilton, activists built on the enthusiasm that had been evident in the by-election of January 1943 (which had seen Labour retain the seat against an independent), to consolidate the main branch in Hamilton town and establish three new LLPs elsewhere in the division.[151] Derby's success in reviving its wards earned it much praise.[152] In August 1943, Norwich DLP adopted a reorganization plan which supplemented ward meetings with monthly aggregate meetings that could be attended by all party members in the city; the first, that October, featured a speech on post-war town planning by a local councillor followed by discussion, and was a valuable stimulus to activity.[153] In autumn 1943, meanwhile, new DLPs were formed in the Scottish constituencies of Argyll, and Kinross and West Perthshire.[154] Elsewhere, and especially in London, things remained more difficult.[155]

---

[147] Hendon DLP papers, BLPES film 211A, reel 97559/1, executive committee 3 Jan. 1943, annual report for 1943, to annual meeting 25 Mar. 1944.

[148] Cambridgeshire TCLP papers, 416/0.7, annual report for 1943–4, n.d. [early 1944].

[149] Coventry DLP papers, MSS 11/1/4, executive committee 26 Jan. 1941.

[150] Wandsworth Clapham DLP papers, IV/156/2/2, annual report for 1943, n.d. [Feb. 1944], annual report for 1944, n.d.; Ipswich TCLP papers, GK 400/1/1/4, executive committee 7 July 1943, 4 Apr. 1945.

[151] Hamilton DLP papers, BLPES film 211, reel 89, 3 Feb. 1943, annual general meeting 26 Mar. 1943, executive committee 30 Apr., 28 May, 25 June 1943, annual general meeting 31 Mar. 1944.

[152] Derby DLP papers, DL 116/1/1, executive committee 11 June, 10 Sept. 1943, 14 Apr. 1944.

[153] Norwich DLP papers, SO 198/1/3, reorganization committee 17 Aug., 14 Sept., 12 Oct., 21 Nov. 1943.

[154] Scottish Labour party papers, TD 1384/1/1, Scottish executive committee 11 Dec. 1942.

[155] London LP papers, Acc. 2417/A/26, D. H. Daines to Labour MPs, prospective parliamentary candidates, and LCC members, 14 July 1943.

It was perhaps inevitable that, as DLPs revived in organizational terms, there should be renewed questioning of the utility and future of the electoral truce. In advance of the June 1943 party conference, Windsor DLP circularized DLPs with a resolution demanding the immediate restoration of local government elections. This was a clever tactic, both because some parties which might have baulked at the threat to the Coalition implied in an attack on the parliamentary truce could see the potential benefits of a resumption of local elections, and also because it was hard for the leadership to portray a call for the restoration of *local* elections as egregiously rebellious or disloyal.[156] A number of DLPs supported it, some even while opposing suggestions of an end to the electoral truce, but it was easily defeated at conference.[157] However, this subtler approach influenced Newport DLP, which sent out a questionnaire to DLPs in November 1943. It asked whether parties supported an immediate end to the truce, a general election immediately the war in Europe ended, and votes at the age of 18, rather than the usual 21, for those who had served in the war (as had been done after the Great War).[158] The questions received a mixed response, but showed that support for the truce was conditional and often grudging, and that it might not take much to stretch it beyond the limits of its endurance.[159] Those limits were severely tested in January and February 1944 at the West Derbyshire by-election, where there was considerable Labour hostility towards the actions of the party leadership in supporting Hartington, and still more towards Muff and Walkden for going to speak in his favour. Resolutions of condemnation abounded; Muff would be ultimately deselected as candidate by his DLP in Hull East.[160] Halifax DLP entered an 'emphatic protest', demanded an immediate end to the truce, and reversed its earlier opposition to Communist affiliation.[161] Even here, though, many Labourites were reluctant to be too critical of their leaders, whom they saw to be in a very difficult position, and some DLPs rejected motions attacking the party's line, not least because they recognized that their own unpreparedness and the relatively good progress of the war would make a general election very tough going.[162]

---

[156] Windsor DLP papers, D/EX 832/3, general committee 11 June 1943.

[157] See e.g. Ipswich TCLP papers, GK 400/1/1/4, special meeting 6 June 1943; Darlington DLP papers, D/X 922/5, general committee 21 Apr. 1943; for the latter position, see e.g. Lewisham West DLP papers, A89/100/10, general committee 7 June 1943; *LPACR* 1943, 132–3.

[158] Newport DLP papers, MNB/POL/6/A/8, executive committee 8 Nov. 1943.

[159] See e.g. Dulwich DLP papers, A390/uncl., general management committee 6 Jan. 1944; Rhondda LP records 4, Rhondda West DLP executive committee 7 Dec. 1943; Gloucester TLC papers, D3128/5/7, general committee 13 Jan. 1944; Halifax DLP papers, TU 28/2, general meeting 30 Dec. 1943; Wansbeck DLP papers, NRO 527/A/3, executive committee 8 Jan. 1944, annual meeting 26 Feb. 1944.

[160] See e.g. Huddersfield DLP papers, BLPES film 211, reel 143, executive committee 14 Mar. 1944; Dalton, *Second World War Diary*, 855, 26 Apr. 1945.

[161] Halifax DLP papers, TU 28/2, annual meeting 24 Feb. 1944.

[162] See e.g. Greenwich DLP papers, GLP 1.3, general committee 24 Feb. 1944.

Increasingly, however, Labour activists were demanding greater levels of activity because debates over reconstruction were showing still more clearly that the Conservatives had not changed very much. As the secretary of Woolwich BLP put it in March 1944:

Victory for the Allies in the military field is now certain. Victory in the economic, the social and the political spheres cannot yet be foreseen. . . . During [1943] the vested interests have begun to show their hands in various ways, and from their pronouncements it is clear that the leopard has not changed its spots. High profits and big dividends will still be first in their thoughts and the interests of the country and the workers are still to be in second place.[163]

Similar sentiments were expressed later that year by the executive of the Scottish Council of the Labour party:

The opponents of public ownership and an organized international economy, who were silent during the anxious times following Dunkirk, are vocal and active again, and, their confidence growing with every Allied victory, they seek to re-establish the old pre-war set-up which would, we firmly believe, lose the peace, betray those workers now fighting, create mass unemployment, and set the stage for another global war.[164]

As was seen briefly in Chapter 1, three matters aroused particular grassroots Labour anger. The release of Mosley from internment in October 1943 shook the confidence of many Labourites very strongly, 'crystallising' the 'deepening anxiety about the future' that Mass-Observation had perceived to be growing in the previous twelve months: if the war was being fought against fascism, it seemed to make little sense to release Britain's most prominent fascist from detention, and condemnation was widespread, although not unanimous.[165] Secondly, Bevin's Defence Regulation 1AA (April 1944), outlawing unofficial strikes, was seen widely as a serious restriction of free trade unionism. By late June, Transport House had received no fewer than 111 resolutions protesting against it: Halifax DLP denounced it as 'a serious blow at the rights of the workers', Penistone as 'a flagrant transgression of everything that the rank and file of the Labour and Trade Union Movement have fought for', Huddersfield as 'anti-working class', and Broxtowe as simply 'vicious'.[166] Finally, there were increasing concerns about post-war Europe. In 1944, many parties began to focus

---

[163] Woolwich BLP papers, WLP 40.3, annual report, 1943, to annual general meeting 25 Mar. 1944.

[164] Scottish Labour party papers, TD 1384/3/1/1, executive committee report to 29th annual conference, 23–4 Sept. 1944.

[165] Mass-Observation papers, FR 1990, 'Mosley and after', 1 Jan. 1944; and see e.g. Wimbledon DLP papers, 1/2, Merton and Morden LLP, general committee 18 Mar. 1943; Doncaster DLP papers, DS 7/2/8, executive committee 1 Dec. 1943.

[166] LPNEC XXI, NEC 28 June 1944; Halifax DLP papers, TU 28/2, monthly meeting 29 June 1944; Penistone DLP papers, BLPES Film 211A, reel 97135/1, committee of management 20 May 1944; Huddersfield DLP papers, BLPES film 211, reel 143, executive committee 9 May 1944; Broxtowe DLP papers, DD/PP/6/4, council meeting 13 May 1944.

on the third pre-war 'fascist' state, Spain; when, on 24 May, Churchill appeared to praise it for its neutrality, Labourites were outraged, and numerous resolutions were passed demanding the withdrawal of all 'diplomatic, political and economic support' from Franco's regime.[167] Events in Greece that December led numerous DLPs and trade unions to record their anger and dismay at government policy, and while the crisis was soon over, it further cemented the sense that the Coalition must end as soon as victory in Europe had been secured.[168] On the whole, however, the December 1944 party conference was probably less divided than one held in June would have been, especially given Labour's October commitment to fighting the next election independently. Grassroots attention was turning increasingly towards issues like housing.[169] There was growing concern, too, about how the post-war world might look *without* a Labour government. As unemployment began to return fleetingly into view in some places that winter, there were calls for the government to help establish new industries in the pre-war depressed areas, to avert any return to mass joblessness there.[170]

Activities increased. A major campaign of almost forty conferences on post-war planning, held in a wide range of locations between September 1943 and January 1944, helped.[171] Women's sections across the country showed a 'a great revival of notable political activity' from January 1944 onwards.[172] Greenwich DLP ran a series of local government forums, which aimed to stimulate activity by bringing councillors face to face with activists to talk about local post-war planning.[173] In Sheffield Brightside, wards were being revived by a combination of political activities and social events from late 1943 onwards, while on D-Day (6 June 1944), Huddersfield DLP called on the secretaries of inert ward parties to organize regular meetings, and removed those who failed to do so.[174] After years without local government elections, some parties began in 1943 or early 1944 to resurrect their panels of approved municipal candidates.[175] The calling of an unofficial 'Victory for Socialism' (VfS) conference at Birmingham for September 1944 acted as a stimulus to some DLPs, despite Transport House's

---

[167] Greenwich DLP papers, GLP 1.3, general committee 14 Nov. 1944.

[168] See e.g. ibid., general committee 28 Dec. 1944; Salford BLP papers, BLPES film 211A, reel 97555/2, delegate meeting 6 Dec. 1944; Thorpe, ' "In a rather emotional state" '.

[169] See e.g. Sheffield Brightside DLP papers, LP(B)8, executive committee 17 Jan. 1945; Wolverhampton Bilston DLP papers, D/LAB/3/1, executive committee 9 Dec. 1944.

[170] Hamilton DLP papers, BLPES film 211, reel 89, annual general meeting 30 Mar. 1945; Cleveland DLP papers, U/CDLP 1/1, annual meeting 11 Mar.1944.

[171] LPNEC XX, 'Report on policy conferences on Labour and post war planning', n.d. [to organization subcommittee 15 Nov. 1943].

[172] *Report of the Twenty-First National Conference of Labour Women* (1942), 7.

[173] Greenwich DLP papers, GLP 1.3, general committee 27 Jan. 1944.

[174] Sheffield Brightside DLP papers, LP(B)8, annual report for 1943; Huddersfield DLP papers, BLPES film 211, reel 144, executive committee 6, 20 June 1944.

[175] See e.g. Darlington DLP papers, D/X 922/5, general committee 19 May 1943; City of Leeds LP papers, WYL 853/4/21, special executive committee 15 May 1944.

rapid anathematization of the event as Communist inspired.[176] Social events also remained important. Whist retained its unique hold. Dances were also held, if suitable halls could be found: in November 1943, for example, Darlington DLP began a series of dances at the Labour hall, led by Dan Sorrento's Band.[177] 'Brains trusts' were also popular, and provided a combination of the social and the political, in that they were informative but entertaining, and could be combined with other activities.[178] In London, by late 1943, '[t]he number of social efforts [was] limited only by lack of facilities'.[179]

It was not a linear process of improvement, however. Public meetings remained rather hit and miss affairs, and many of those held before mid-1944 were disappointing, which was doubly frustrating given the difficulties that remained in finding halls in which to hold them.[180] In the immediate aftermath of D-Day, 'preoccupation with Invasion [*sic*] news and worries' led to DLPs 'damping down meeting activity', while the further decline of transport facilities made MPs increasingly resistant to travelling long distances to speak.[181]

The threat of V-weapon attacks, particularly in the south-east, had a dampening effect. The summer of 1944 was to have seen a major party development campaign, but the London Labour party found that the arrival of the flying bombs placed a serious obstacle in the place of increased activity.[182] In February 1944, Clapham DLP decided to spend the next year building on 'definite signs of renewed activity', but had to admit in February 1945 that the V-weapons had 'blasted [their] good intentions'.[183] Greenwich DLP had planned to open a twelve-month party propaganda and development campaign on 1 July 1944, but the raids meant that the party had to be closed down completely between 22 June and 28 September.[184] Bethnal Green North-East had its premises seriously damaged by a flying bomb on 22 August, and shortages of repair materials, plus a further bomb, meant that the office could only be reopened on 18 December,

[176] Woolwich BLP papers, WLP 6, leaflet, 'Victory for Socialism', n.d. [1944]; LPNEC XXI, elections subcommittee 1 Sept. 1944; Middleton, circular 'to secretaries of affiliated organizations', 2 Aug. 1944; Dulwich DLP papers, A390/uncl., general management committee 15 June, 10 Aug., 27 Sept. 1944.

[177] Bedford DLP papers, X494/3, annual meeting of individual members 13 Mar. 1945; Darlington DLP papers, D/X 922/5, general committee 24 Nov. 1943.

[178] See e.g. Windsor DLP papers, D/EX 832/ZA/11, annual report for 1942, 16 Feb. 1943; Newport DLP papers, MNB/POL/6/A/8, organization subcommittee 12 Mar. 1944.

[179] London LP papers, Acc. 2417/A/27, 'The work of the London Labour party, 1943', Feb. 1944.

[180] See e.g. Norwich DLP papers, SO 198/3/1, annual report 1943, n.d. [early 1944]; Gloucester TLC papers, D3128/5/7, general committee 14 Oct. 1943; Windsor DLP papers, D/EX 832/3, executive committee 25 July 1944.

[181] LPNEC XXI, 'Report on propaganda', 21 June 1944; organization subcommittee 21 June 1944.

[182] London LP papers, Acc. 2417/A/27, memo, 'The work of the London Labour party, 1944', Feb. 1945.

[183] Wandsworth Clapham DLP papers, IV/156/2/2, annual report for 1943, n.d. [Feb. 1944]; meeting of officers 6 Mar. 1944; annual report for 1944, n.d. [Feb. 1945].

[184] Greenwich DLP papers, GLP 1.3, general committee 25 May, 28 Sept. 1944.

while Wandsworth Central's premises were hit on five separate occasions.[185] The wider south-east was also affected, a number of DLPs reporting that the V-weapon attacks severely impeded their work in the summer of 1944.[186] Away from the south-east, however, the summer of 1944 was often a productive time. On 1 July, Taunton DLP launched a major campaign to revive its branches: within four months a number of new LLPs had been formed, and the party was making 'good progress in the villages' and looking well set for the post-war election. When it came, '[a]ll but a few Polling Stations were manned'; there was a lot of campaigning, and plenty of transport on polling day; and '[w]hile the organization was not perfect it was a very great improvement on our past efforts'.[187] So too was the result: in a straight fight with the Conservatives, Labour won the seat for the first time. New ward parties and LLPs were formed in constituencies as different as Rotherham, Cambridgeshire, and, with the help of the NUAW, East Grinstead (Sussex).[188] In King's Lynn (Norfolk), a locally stationed soldier almost single-handedly raised an LLP at Hunstanton.[189]

Election preparations provided a strong spur to activity. With the ban on the adoption of prospective candidates coming to an end in 1944, selections proceeded apace. It was by no means unusual for twenty candidates a month to be adopted from autumn 1944 onwards: 461 were in place by February 1945.[190] Headquarters gave particular attention to the West Midlands, long an area of Labour weakness, where special efforts were made to pick promising younger candidates.[191] Meetings to train election workers were launched all over Britain: 600 delegates attended one such London LP event in November 1944, and a similar gathering followed in February 1945.[192] By now, public meetings were often getting a better response. Star speakers could expect a good audience: when Bevan spoke at Hamilton on 29 October 1944, 948 tickets were sold and the event was a success in financial, as well as propaganda, terms.[193] But it was not all good news: Halifax DLP was encouraged by good attendances at a series

[185] Bethnal Green North-East DLP papers, TH/8488/16, annual report 1944 to annual meeting of management committee 18 Jan. 1945; Bevin papers, BEVN II 8/1, Wandsworth Central DLP, annual report for 1944, n.d. [early 1945].

[186] Epsom DLP papers, 2141/1, annual report for 1944, to annual general meeting 3 Mar. 1945.

[187] Taunton DLP papers, DD/TLP/1/1, general committee 1 July, 28 Oct., 30 Dec. 1944, 21 July 1945.

[188] Rotherham TLC papers, 443/G, meeting 28 Nov. 1944; Cambridgeshire TCLP papers, 416/0.7, annual report for 1944–5, n.d. [Apr. 1945]; East Grinstead DLP papers, LA 2 MS 1/2/2, executive committee 27 Jan., 16 Apr., 10 Aug. 1945.

[189] Weinbren, *Generating Socialism*, 9.

[190] LPNEC XXI, elections subcommittee 4 Oct. 1944, 14 Feb., 23 Apr. 1945.

[191] Dalton, *Second World War Diary*, 748–9, 19, 24 May 1944; Birmingham BLP papers, uncl., meeting 14 June 1944; LPNEC XXI, elections subcommittee 1 Aug. 1944.

[192] LPNEC XXI, organization subcommittee 18 Oct. 1944; London LP papers, Acc. 2417/A/27, memo, 'Conference on organization and electoral matters, Beaver Hall, Saturday, November 4', 9 Nov. 1944; London LP papers, Acc. 2417/A/27, memo, 'A second special conference on party organization and electoral matters', 17 Feb. 1945.

[193] Hamilton DLP papers, BLPES film 211, reel 89, executive committee 24 Nov. 1944.

of Sunday-evening meetings in November 1944, it being seen as a particularly good sign that the majority of those attending were not party members, but attendances soon began to tail off, leaving the secretary to lament that 'in this matter of Public Meetings the vagaries and aberations [*sic*] of the public are past all understanding'.[194] And halls could still be scarce, especially in areas like Sussex, which still had a high military presence.[195]

As VE Day approached, many DLPs were in reasonable shape. In Salford, for example, all three DLPs were functioning effectively once again by January 1945, with ward parties meeting regularly.[196] But many remained less healthy. The MP for Tottenham South stated in March 1945 that 'the [constituency] Party organization was practically non-existent'; Bermondsey Rotherhithe DLP, which had been bombed out in 1940, was relaunched, in theory, in September 1943, but essentially 'started from scratch in the [1945] Election'; and in Lewisham West, the party secretary felt that it was fortunate that 'helpers had sprung from nowhere' in the general election campaign, because the organization had been 'at a low ebb'.[197] And, in reality, a number of DLPs had struggled throughout the war. Warwick and Leamington DLP became inactive early on; its executive committee met only rarely until 1943, due to war conditions, the blackout, and the secretary's difficult working hours; and its main LLP, at Stratford-upon-Avon, only met infrequently until spring 1944.[198] The tempo then quickened somewhat: a new local *Labour Bulletin* was published, and LLPs were formed or revived in Kenilworth, Warwick, and Claverdon.[199] However, by March 1945 the *Bulletin* had collapsed because the authorities refused to allocate sufficient paper to the party, a planned day school at Leamington had to be abandoned because of 'a poor response & difficulties in transport', and hopes of holding public meetings ahead of the dissolution of parliament were stymied by a lack of money.[200] Warwick LLP did not become fully operational until September 1945, while Kenilworth's first recorded meeting after 1939 was in December 1945.[201] Any idea that Labour was pulling effortlessly ahead of the Conservatives organizationally in this constituency was some way from the truth.

---

[194] Halifax DLP papers, TU 28/2, executive committee 23 Nov., 21 Dec. 1944.
[195] East Grinstead DLP papers, LA 2 MS 1/2/2, executive committee 1 Dec. 1944.
[196] Salford BLP papers, BLPES film 211A, reel 97555/2, executive committee 31 Jan. 1945.
[197] Tottenham South DLP papers, BLPES film 211A, reel 97564/2, meeting of party officers 4 Mar. 1945; Bermondsey Rotherhithe DLP papers, A54/A/1, management committee 12 Sept. 1943, 22 Feb. 1945, 15 Aug. 1945; Lewisham West DLP papers, A89/100/10, general committee 16 July 1945.
[198] Warwick and Leamington DLP papers, MSS 133/1/1/4, executive committee 1 June 1940 and *passim*; Stratford LLP papers [Warwick and Leamington DLP], CR 14091/12, minute book 1937–51, *passim*.
[199] Warwick and Leamington DLP papers, MSS 133/1/1/4, executive committee 11 Nov. 1944, 27 Jan. 1944.
[200] Ibid., executive committee 17 Mar., 5 May 1945.
[201] Ibid., executive committee 21 July, 15 Sept. 1945; 133/6/3/1, Kenilworth LLP minute book 1933–48, *passim*.

Labourites celebrated victory in Europe but also recognized that a new fight awaited them. Meeting on 10 May, members of Gloucester TLC stood in silence in respect for those who had 'made the supreme sacrifice in the war against fascism', but went on to make plans for the election campaign that was expected imminently.[202] There was no recorded grassroots Labour opposition to the end of the Coalition: the party's activists clearly welcomed the return to more overtly partisan politics as much as their Conservative counterparts. Very few DLPs were unable to run a candidate in 1945, although some selections had to be rushed through; Orkney and Shetland DLP, which had only been revived in late 1944, contested a parliamentary election for the first time.[203] Where DLPs could not run candidates, Common Wealth sometimes could. Some Labour candidates accepted the help of individual Communists, while rebuffing the local Communist party as such; but most such advances appear to have been rejected.[204] Even where DLP organization was felt to be lacking, impressive efforts were made: in Lewisham West, for example, ten out of twelve committee rooms worked well, and 4,000 posters, 7,000 window cards, 30,000 leaflets, 45,000 poll cards, and 52,000 election addresses were distributed.[205] Orders for *Let Us Face the Future* often ran into the hundreds.[206] Labour did not win Windsor, held by the Conservatives by a substantial majority; but the DLP could at least report that '[t]here was no doubt that we had by far the best organization'.[207] In Derby, the agent reported 'one of the most strenuous [campaigns] in the history of the Party', but added that he had had 'a wonderful band of helpers', and that 'in some of the Wards where the organization for some time had been rather poor, it had been surprising to see that there had been quite a revival'.[208]

Victory was greeted ecstatically. All across Britain, Labourites danced, sang, and ate victory suppers in celebration of their party's first parliamentary majority.[209] The prospect of the first local government elections since 1938, to be held in November 1945, also drove DLPs forward. Strong membership recruitment continued, and ward and local parties continued to be revived or created. All

---

[202] Gloucester TLC papers, D3128/5/7, general committee 10 May 1945.

[203] *Labour Organiser*, Nov. 1944; Labour party Wales records 5, South Wales regional council of Labour executive committee 28 May 1945.

[204] See e.g. Dulwich DLP papers, A390/uncl., general management committee 29 Mar. 1945; Frome DLP papers, A/AAW 26, executive committee 2 June 1945; Stafford DLP papers, D1371/2, divisional management committee 26 May 1945. For rejections, see e.g. Derby DLP papers, DL 116/1/1, executive committee 11 May 1945.

[205] Lewisham West DLP papers, A89/100/10, general committee 16 July 1945.

[206] See e.g. Batley and Morley DLP papers, MS 146/2, executive committee 26 May 1945.

[207] Windsor DLP papers, D/EX 832/3, general committee 21 July 1945.

[208] Derby DLP papers, DL 116/1/1, executive committee 13 July 1945.

[209] See e.g. Hamilton DLP papers, BLPES film 211, reel 89, executive committee 10 Aug. 1945, victory dance at the Hamilton Salon, 7 Sept. 1945; Stafford DLP papers, D1371/2, divisional management committee 11 Aug.1945; South Shields DLP papers, BLPES film 211, reel 27, executive committee 27 July 1945.

seven of Lewisham West's ward parties were fully operational by September 1945, while in Derbyshire, Belper DLP could report by early 1946 that twelve new LLPs had been formed in the past year, some of them in places where there had been no previous Labour organization.[210] A number of parties carried on with their advice bureaux into peacetime, that in Clapham still proving 'very successful' in September 1945.[211] But recovery could be slow: Bermondsey BLP was only able to relaunch the *Bermondsey Labour Magazine* in November 1946.[212] Similarly, although a few League of Youth branches had operated throughout the war, and some others were being revived by May 1945, it was still common in early 1946 for parties to be lamenting the weakness of their youth work.[213] The Labour party, therefore, was a long way from being fully rebuilt by the time of the 1945 election.

Lambeth North DLP (London) illustrates many of the themes of this chapter. On 1 September 1939, it accepted the London Labour party's advice to carry on if war came.[214] Its leading committees were to continue meeting throughout the war, except for a short hiatus in the summer of 1944 as a result of the flying bomb attacks. Women's sections remained particularly active, though with low attendances at times. During the Phoney War, social activities continued, an advice bureau was set up, and pressure on issues like the continuing closure of local schools was sustained.[215] Demands were made for a clear definition of Labour's war aims; the party was not united behind the leadership's line on the war, Labour's statement about Finland was deplored as legitimizing the capitalist countries' desire to attack the Soviet Union, and a number of members were expelled for supporting the anti-war Independent at the January 1940 Southwark Central by-election.[216] Consequently there was resistance to Communist overtures in the winter of 1940–1 over the People's Convention, but enthusiasm for the Soviet war effort after June 1941 changed that: the DLP protested against Labour headquarters issuing anti-Communist propaganda at such a time, especially when paper was short, and its attitudes ultimately changed so much that it voted in favour of Communist affiliation in March 1943.[217] Protests against the electoral truce began early (and the party was to vote against it as late as April 1943, though discussion of the Newport questionnaire in February

[210] Lewisham West DLP papers, A89/100/10, general committee 3 Sept. 1945; Belper DLP papers, D2064/3/7, annual report for 1945 [early 1946].

[211] Wandsworth Clapham DLP papers, IV/156/2/2, executive committee 13 Sept. 1945. See also Greenwich DLP papers, GLP 8, 28th annual report, 1945, n.d. [Jan. 1946].

[212] Bermondsey Labour party papers, YL 254, *Bermondsey Labour Magazine*, Nov. 1946.

[213] Sheffield Brightside DLP papers, LP(B)8, executive committee 16 May 1945; Norwich DLP papers, SO 198/3/1, annual report 1945, n.d. [early 1946].

[214] Lambeth North DLP papers, 1/3, meeting of party members 1 Sept. 1939.

[215] Ibid., emergency subcommittee 27 Oct., 8 Sept., 6 Oct. 1939.

[216] Ibid., general committee 15 Dec. 1939, 19 Jan., 9 Feb. 1940.

[217] Ibid., general committee 19 Jan., 12 Oct. 1941, 11 Feb 1943; management committee 27 Sept. 1942, 12 Mar. 1943.

1944 ended in agreement that ending the truce was not 'practicable').[218] But the DLP gave unanimous approval to Labour's entry into government in May 1940, in the belief that 'the war was now a People's war for liberty and social progress against the powers of reaction and monopoly power', and the party participated willingly in the MoI local committee formed in May 1940.[219] The onset of the Blitz initially unsettled the DLP, but the women's sections were soon back in action, and the raids offered new opportunities for activism, with the party demanding better air raid shelters and post-raid facilities.[220] The party also remained closely concerned with local issues like venereal disease and housing, while there were also periodic complaints about the failure of councillors to attend DLP committee meetings regularly.[221] Inevitably, post-war planning became increasingly important. A rather cautious initial reception awaited the Beveridge report, but the local MP, G. R. Strauss, was congratulated for voting against the government on the subject, and any signs that the party leadership was conniving in 'compromise schemes' for post-war Britain were condemned; there was, meanwhile, great enthusiasm for the County of London Plan, and overall the party called for 'the maintenance of, and indeed the strengthening of State Controls' after the war.[222] Disillusionment increased over Mosley's release, DR1AA, and Greece, but by early 1945, Lambeth North DLP was politically united, and in a healthy organizational state: its standing 'had never been higher', according to the borough's Labour mayor.[223] That March, a panel of potential municipal election candidates was established, and the secretary began a series of lectures on party organization.[224] That the party faced the 1945 general election with confidence said a great deal about the resilience, but also the political ardour, of its members and officers. It was little surprise when Strauss was re-elected with a much-increased majority.

The Second World War provided as stiff a challenge to Labour's constituency parties as it did to the constituency Conservative associations. Some DLPs did not cope well, and struggled more or less throughout. Most experienced decline in the period between 1940 and late 1942, but then began to recover, although revival after that point was no more inevitable or linear than decline had been before it. The very clear instructions that came from the party headquarters from the outbreak of war onwards clearly helped; so too, in a different way, did the presence of the Communist party which, while not always very strong, acted as

[218] Ibid., management committee 28 Apr. 1943, 6 Feb. 1944.
[219] Ibid., annual general meeting 24 May 1940, general committee 21 June, 16 Aug. 1940.
[220] Ibid., general committee 27 Oct., 16 Nov. 1940.
[221] Ibid., executive committee 30 Dec. 1942, management committee 11 June 1943, 22 Sept. 1944, executive committee 8 July 1942.
[222] Ibid., party meeting 17 Jan. 1943; management committee 12 Mar. 1943; executive committee 28 Feb. 1944; annual general meeting 5 Sept. 1943, 22 Sept. 1944.
[223] Ibid., management committee 21 Nov. 1943, 18 May 1944, 8 Dec. 1944; annual general meeting 16 Feb. 1945.
[224] Ibid., management committee 16 Mar. 1945.

a reminder of what might happen if Labour local organizations were allowed to collapse altogether. Labour also had advantages such as the regular publication of membership figures and the party's ritual calendar as prompts to activity that were denied to the Conservatives. Early in the war, Labourites were often sustained in their activity by the belief that only 'socialism' could win the war. Later, when it became clear that the war was going to be won without a socialist transformation, they carried on because they could see that their Conservative rivals had only been winded by the events of 1939–40. This realization that the peace settlement was going to be bitterly contested, combined with 'memories' of what had happened when Labour had had no input into peacemaking in 1918–19, or into government for most of the two decades thereafter, spurred Labourites all over Britain to action. It would be fair to say that most DLPs were closer, at the end of the European war, to their normal pre-war state than most Conservative associations were to theirs; but they had not had it easy. They had had to work very hard to survive the war, and to prosper in its aftermath. At the same time, however, their overall organizational form was not significantly changed. Most DLPs were on the verge of a new period of growth and prosperity in 1945, but they would be in many ways quite similar to their earlier forms.

7

Constituency Activities: The Liberals

By the later 1930s, the Conservatives and Labour had organizations in practically every parliamentary constituency. Some of them were weak, and a few very weak; but they existed. It was different for the Liberals, who faced the challenge, not only of sustaining the activities of existing organizations, but also of trying to relaunch constituency associations in places where they had died out. The fact that, ultimately, they would only run 306 candidates for 640 seats in 1945 suggests that they achieved only limited success, but it is also important to note the extent to which the Liberals did try to sustain their activities in wartime. Although they were weaker than the Conservatives and Labour, they remained the third party in British politics, and were not prepared to be written off as a historical footnote. Indeed, the maintenance of grassroots Liberal activity in wartime was crucial to the ability of the party to survive and, eventually, to make a revival from the later 1950s onwards.

In the later 1930s, Liberals were still very active in many parts of Britain, and Liberal associations (LAs) across the country ran petition campaigns on the rising cost of living in 1938 and old age pensions in 1939.[1] But elsewhere, splits, financial problems, personnel deficiencies, and political weaknesses had all served to weaken or destroy Liberal organization. The 1936 Meston reforms had been intended to stem the tide, but the results had not been as impressive as had been hoped. At the end of 1937, 292 constituency Liberal associations (LAs) were affiliated to the LPO, which covered England and Wales, where there were 520 territorial seats. A year later, the figure had risen to 305, but this was still less than 60 per cent of constituencies. It is true that some associations existed but did not affiliate, for a number of reasons, and that, in some places (like County Durham), many associations had gone over to the Liberal Nationals. But, overall, Liberal constituency organization was patchy: in Manchester, for example, only four of the ten constituencies had an active association in 1939.[2] Many associations were struggling, and, like Dundee, finding particular difficulty in sustaining organization at sub-constituency

---

[1] See e.g. Dundee LA papers, GD/DLA 1/1, executive committee 10 Feb. 1938; Manchester LF papers, M283/1/3/7, executive committee 26 Apr. 1939; Manchester Exchange LA papers, M283/4/1/2, executive committee 24 May 1939.

[2] Manchester LF papers, M283/1/3/7, executive committee 28 June 1939.

level.[3] Some regional federations were beginning to do more to help the constituency associations in their areas: the Lancashire, Cheshire, and North Western Liberal federation (LCNWLF), for example, had grouped its 83 constituencies into 11 district councils, which helped to stimulate activity and strengthen the bonds between federation and constituencies.[4] In some places, like Lewisham, new associations were being formed after many years of Liberal dormancy.[5] On the whole, however, such manifestations were occasional rather than typical, and there was little to suggest a major grassroots Liberal revival in the first eight months of 1939.

War, therefore, merely compounded an already difficult situation. At least Liberal headquarters did not add to those difficulties once war came, showing none of the equivocation that characterized Conservative Central Office in September 1939. Liberal associations were left in no doubt that they were meant to carry on with all but 'purely Party activities' (see Chapter 1).[6] The response was initially favourable. East Dorset LA agreed that it would be 'disastrous to close down'; Chester decided, not only to carry on with regular meetings and activities, but also to proceed with the planned launch of a new magazine, whose first edition duly appeared in November; Walthamstow East and West LAs, which in any case shared headquarters, agreed to pool their resources and secretaries for the duration of the war; the London LF cancelled a fund-raising bazaar and a major demonstration planned for October, but agreed otherwise to remain active; Manchester Exchange LA called off its annual weekend school in Derbyshire, but continued its normal meetings with only a short hiatus; and Westmorland LA cancelled a garden fête and sale of work planned for September, and a public meeting arranged for October, but otherwise decided to try to carry on as best it could in a very scattered and largely rural constituency.[7] The message continued to be pressed from the centre, although clearly the fact that it was deemed to require repetition suggested anxieties about the extent to which it was being heeded.[8]

[3] Montgomeryshire LA records 3, reorganization committee 10 Dec. 1938; Dundee LA papers, GD/DLA 1/1, executive committee 3 Nov. 1938.

[4] Lancashire, Cheshire and North Western LF papers, M390/1/11, annual report 1938, to annual meeting 4 Feb. 1939.

[5] T. Jeffery, 'The suburban nation: politics and class in Lewisham', in D. Feldman and G. Stedman Jones (eds.), *Metropolis, London: Histories and Representations since 1800* (1989), 202.

[6] *Liberal Magazine*, Sept. 1939; LPO, *Fourth Report* (1941), 7.

[7] Dorset East LA papers, D1512/A1, executive committee 20 Sept. 1939; Chester LA papers, CR159/5, coordinating committee 31 Oct. 1939; Walthamstow LA papers, uncat., joint executive committee 9 Sept. 1939; London LF papers, Acc. 1446/7, general purposes committee 6 Sept., 10 Oct. 1939; Manchester Exchange LA papers, M283/4/1/2, annual report to annual meeting 11 Mar. 1940; executive committee 24 May 1939, 13 Feb. 1940; Westmorland LA papers, WDSo/174/2, executive committee 2 Sept., 28 Oct. 1939.

[8] *Liberal Party Organisation Bulletin*, 6, Apr. 1940; LPO, *Fourth Report* (1941), 8; Yorkshire LF papers, WYL 456/3, executive committee 25 Nov. 1939; Lancashire, Cheshire, and North Western LF papers, M390/1/11, John A. Ormerod, circular, 4 Sept. 1939.

Most Liberals were fully behind the war effort. Only in North Wales was there serious public dissension. Here, Lloyd George's influence remained strong, and during October 1939 he was suggesting that Britain should not close the door on the idea of a negotiated peace. The annual meeting of the North Wales LF on 28 October became 'rather disorderly' as it discussed a proposal that the Liberal parliamentary party should 'press upon the Government that the time was opportune for convening a world conference with a view to putting an end to the arbitrament of war'. After 'a strong conflict of opinion', the resolution was carried by 34 votes to 14. However, this is perhaps best regarded as the federation rallying behind a local hero, whom many believed to have been misrepresented; and it was significant that he himself had felt the need, a week earlier, to trim severely a speech in his constituency (Caernarvon Boroughs) because of the pro-war views of his audience.[9] Far more typical of Liberal opinion in the country at large was the Yorkshire LF's view of March 1940, that '[t]o most Liberals to day the war that is being fought is a war for things that Liberalism and the Liberal Party gave to the people of Britain'.[10] But this did not prevent Liberals being critical of the government. Manchester Exchange LA declared no confidence in the ministry, 'with the honourable exception of Mr Churchill [once a Liberal MP for the city]', and there were also early demands for a clear statement of peace aims.[11] One Liberal aim rapidly enunciated by headquarters and associations alike was electoral reform, but nothing was to come of it.[12]

Headquarters worked hard to encourage Liberals to carry on. It sent senior figures like Lords Samuel and Meston to spread the message to the annual meetings of the regional federations early in 1940, and encouraged Liberal women to come together to knit for the war effort, with some success: Manchester WLA knitting parties sent 'several parcels' of garments to forces depots, lifeboat stations, and HMS *Manchester*.[13] The regional federations also stimulated the constituencies. In December 1939, for example, more than 60 constituency officers and candidates representing 31 LAs met under the aegis of the London LF to discuss ways to remain active, while six days later the Western Counties LF agreed that it had been 'too precipitate' in suspending many of its activities,

[9] *The Times*, 23 Oct. 1939; *Manchester Guardian, Liverpool Post*, 30 Oct. 1939; *Western Mail*, 31 Oct. 1939; P. Rowland, *Lloyd George* (1975), 766.

[10] Yorkshire LF papers, WYL 456/3, annual report 1939, to annual meeting 16 Mar. 1940.

[11] Manchester Exchange LA papers, M283/4/1/2, annual report to annual meeting 11 Mar. 1940; and see e.g. Lancashire, Cheshire, and North Western LF papers, M390/1/11, executive committee 15 Sept. 1939.

[12] Western Counties LF papers, DDM 1172, executive committee 17 Feb. 1940; Lancashire, Cheshire, and North Western LF papers, M390/1/11, executive committee 6 May 1941, 24 Sept. 1943.

[13] Manchester LF papers, M283/1/3/7, executive committee 31 Jan. 1940; see also e.g. LPO, *Fourth Report* (1941), 9; *Liberal Party Organisation Bulletin*, 7, May 1940; Edinburgh South LA papers, Acc. 12038/5, women's association executive committee 7 Dec. 1939.

and agreed to reopen its office as soon as possible; by February 1940 it was busy exhorting LAs to 'meet from time to time and thus help to keep Liberal comradeship alive'.[14] Responses were often favourable. The early spring of 1940 saw high levels of activity in big cities like Liverpool, metropolitan suburbs like Finchley, smaller centres such as Chester, mixed urban-rural areas like Yeovil (Somerset), and rural areas like the Isle of Ely. In Derbyshire, High Peak LA had its 'most successful annual meeting for many years', while Sheffield city LA, long in the doldrums, was about to open new premises.[15] Chester was particularly active, holding a successful public meeting for grassroots favourite Mrs Corbett Ashby in February 1940, running regular whist drives, and planning a series of lectures in the summer.[16]

There were already countervailing trends, however. The Scottish LF, which had decided to carry on, not least to combat Communist and fascist anti-war propaganda, found by January 1940 that 'very little political work was . . . being done'.[17] In the north-west, the decision of all but one of the eleven divisional committees not to hold their annual meetings in early 1940 effectively ended their activities for the duration of the war: unsurprisingly, the one council to remain in being was West Cheshire, which included the powerful Chester association.[18] Paisley LA, lethargic before the war, descended into virtual dormancy between April 1940 and 1944.[19] This was a poor performance for a party which had a Liberal MP, and the party was to pay a heavy price in 1945, losing the seat to Labour with only a tenth of the votes cast. Garry Tregidga has argued that, in the south-west, most LAs became 'virtually moribund'.[20]

Liberal organizations in the country had no say in the developments that saw a change of government in May 1940, but the LPO council, delighted to see Liberals once more in office, declared its support for the new administration, while calling on 'every Liberal Association in the country' to 'maintain . . . without controversy its Liberal activities, and to show to the world that men and women, by being Liberals, are all the better patriots'.[21] Federations and associations also responded positively: the Scottish LF executive welcomed the new government, praised Sinclair, lauded the 'unexampled valour' of the British armed forces, denounced Mussolini's 'treachery' in declaring war, and welcomed Roosevelt's

[14] London LF papers, Acc. 1446/7, general purposes committee 13 Nov., 11 Dec. 1939; Western Counties LF papers, DDM 1172, finance and general purposes committee 8 Dec. 1939, executive committee 17 Feb. 1940.

[15] *Liberal Party Organisation Bulletin*, 6, 7, Apr., May 1940.

[16] Chester LA papers, CR159/5, coordinating committee 21 Feb., 1 Apr. 1940.

[17] Scottish LF papers, Acc. 11765/14, executive committee 22 Nov. 1939, joint finance committee 24 Jan. 1940.

[18] Lancashire, Cheshire, and North Western LF papers, M390/1/11, executive committee 2 Feb. 1940.

[19] Paisley LA papers, ARC 67, minute book, *passim*.

[20] G. Tregidga, *The Liberal Party in South-West Britain since 1918: Political Decline, Dormancy and Rebirth* (Exeter, 2000), 102–3.

[21] LPO, *Fourth Report* (1941), 9.

statement in favour of the Allied cause.[22] In the face of all this, less was said than might have been expected about the government's distinctly illiberal policy of internment without trial. When Westmorland LA called for the release of 'friendly aliens' in July 1940, for example, the call itself was perhaps less remarkable than the fact that it was unaccompanied by any expression of concern for other internees.[23]

As with the other parties, there was no sudden collapse of grassroots activity in 1940. As late as September, the north-western Liberal agents were noting that 'many Associations were meeting the changed circumstances successfully', and the regional secretary could report that, although narrowly party activity had been 'practically abandoned', Liberals remained very active in war-related work, many women's LAs were thriving, and he had 'not found a single instance of the closing down of any Liberal Organization'; indeed, the revival of MoI local committees in June 1940 had given him a chance 'of re-awakening Liberals in some derelict Constituencies'; indeed, MoI lectures and films were a good way of bringing members together.[24] Social activity also helped. Dundee Liberal women held weekly whist drives throughout the war, and knitting remained important.[25] The women of Edinburgh South LA held regular sales of work from autumn 1940 onwards, keeping members together, creating a profile for the association with the wider public, and making some money for association funds, while in April 1941 they held 'a very happy evening' comprising music, tea, and a whist drive.[26] In some cases, there were clear efforts to politicize those women drawn into the social side by the chance to knit and talk, as in Chester, where in September 1941 it was decided that one political committee meeting a month should be held in the party office, but with the door open so that the women knitting in the adjoining main room would be able to listen to—although, perhaps significantly, not join in with—the discussion.[27]

Activity did decline over time, however. There had been ill omens even before May 1940. Associations in rural areas, where transport was increasingly difficult, were the earliest and hardest hit. In rural Wales, Cardiganshire LA

[22] Scottish LF papers, Acc. 11765/14, executive committee 12 June 1940; see also e.g. Lancashire, Cheshire, and North Western LF papers, M390/1/11, executive committee 24 May 1940.

[23] Westmorland LA papers, WDSo/174/2, annual meeting 27 July 1940. See also Manchester LF papers, M283/1/3/7, executive committee 31 July 1940; Lancashire, Cheshire, and North Western LF papers, M390/1/11, executive committee 21 Feb. 1941.

[24] Society of Certificated and Associated Liberal Agents (North-Western district) papers, annual meeting 7 Dec. 1940; Lancashire, Cheshire, and North Western LF papers, M390/1/11, executive committee 27 Sept. 1940; Manchester LF papers, M283/1/3/7, executive committee 25 Sept. 1940.

[25] Dundee LA papers, GD/DLA 1/1, executive committee 5 Dec. 1939, 19 May 1941; Manchester Withington LA papers, M283/9/2/6, Didsbury women's LA, annual reports 1940, 1940–1, 1941–2.

[26] Edinburgh South LA papers, Acc. 12038/5, women's association executive committee 28 Nov. 1940, 2 Dec. 1941, 18 May 1943; Acc. 12038/1, special executive committee 26 Apr. 1941.

[27] Chester LA papers, CR159/19, women's LA coordinating committee 16 Sept. 1941.

held no meetings at all in the three years from October 1939, while the LA in the unwieldy Devon constituency of Tiverton held no meetings between May 1939 and August 1942, and met only very rarely thereafter: only the Tiverton town women's association remained active.[28] Cambridgeshire LA held no meetings at all between July 1939 and December 1944.[29] The London LF was forced to abandon its outdoor meetings in Hyde Park, and its women's committee collapsed, while hopes of holding an 'At Home' at the National Liberal Club in September 1940 were thwarted by German bombers; one of the more active London associations, Hampstead, moved towards a series of 'drawing room' meetings, which helped to keep a core membership together but did not suggest a very expansive approach.[30] By November 1941 the capital's associations were 'steadily deteriorating'.[31] Chester, which published its magazine throughout the war, ran highly successful discussion groups from 1940 onwards, and created a new Liberal library in August 1941, was unusual.[32] By March 1942, Manchester Exchange LA was reporting that 'in the stress of war less and less political activity is possible'.[33] And, as with the Conservatives and Labour, constituency organizations in coastal towns and rural areas in the south and east were especially hard hit, with major shifts of population involving the departure of many officers and members, and most of those remaining being preoccupied with war work of one kind or another.[34]

LPO affiliation figures offer some indication of wartime fluctuations (see Table 7.1). They need to be qualified somewhat: after all, they only reflect those associations that paid affiliation fees to the LPO in any given year, and it is clear that some LAs, though existing, failed, for one reason or another, to pay their subscriptions at various times.[35] Still, the figures do indicate trends. In December 1938, 305 associations were affiliated, but this figure had fallen by almost 20 per cent (to 247) by August 1942. The lack of figures for the intervening period is frustrating; so too is the fact that the 1942 figures are those for August, since they fail to show the handful of associations that would have paid their subscriptions between then and December. However, it is noteworthy that south and east

---

[28] Cardiganshire LA records 1, annual meetings 21 Oct. 1939, 31 Oct. 1942; Tiverton LA papers, 4996G/A2, minute book, *passim*; executive committee 31 Mar. 1944.

[29] Cambridgeshire LA papers, R93/73, selection committee 8 July 1939, executive committee 30 Dec. 1944.

[30] London LF papers, Acc. 1446/7, general purposes committee 4 Mar., 1 Apr., 3 Sept. 1940; *Liberal Party Organisation Bulletin*, 7, May 1940.

[31] London LF papers, Acc. 1446/7, general purposes committee 26 Nov. 1941.

[32] *Liberal Party Organisation Bulletin*, 10, Aug. 1940; Chester LA papers, CR159/5, e.g. coordinating committee 13 Aug. 1941, council 15 Jan. 1942, coordinating committee 13 Aug. 1943.

[33] Manchester Exchange LA papers, M283/4/1/2, annual report to annual meeting 18 Mar. 1942.

[34] Home Counties LF papers, DM 668, executive committee report, 1 Apr. 1940–30 June 1941.

[35] See e.g. Yorkshire LF papers, WYL 456/3, executive committee 3 May 1941.

Table 7.1. Constituencies affiliated to the
Liberal Party Organization, 1937–1950

Date	Number affiliated
31 December 1937	292
31 December 1938	305
19 August 1942	247
31 December 1943	272
31 December 1945	266
31 December 1946	317
31 December 1947	383
31 December 1949	406
31 December 1950	399

Source: LPO, *Annual Reports*, 1938–51.

coast constituencies accounted for 21, and London 14, of the 78 constituencies which affiliated in 1938 but not in 1942. Although the number of affiliations in 1943 rose to 272, the figure did not then rise appreciably until well after the end of the war: only 266 associations would be affiliated as late as December 1945. In short, the decline in the number of affiliated associations bottomed out, but the Liberals remained well adrift of their Conservative and Labour rivals.

The continuing activity of 'an encouraging number' of women's organizations behind the façade of apparently inert constituency associations meant that things were not always as bad as they seemed.[36] The association in the vast Westmorland constituency became dormant early in the war due to sheer logistics and the departure of the agent and candidate. No LA meetings of any kind were held between October 1940 and February 1945, but the women's organization, based in the main town, Kendal, remained active.[37] On the first Wednesday of the war, they met and agreed to carry on, holding social meetings every Tuesday afternoon, 'with music & knitting etc.', and monthly social evenings, the first of which, in November 1939, saw the room 'filled to capacity' for supper, a speech by the candidate's wife on war aims, songs by a soloist, and community singing.[38] Soon, Wednesday afternoon knitting meetings were being held as well.[39] Activities in 1940 included a general knowledge quiz, a jumble sale, and speeches by various people, including Austrian and Czech refugees.[40]

[36] Women's LF papers, DM 1193, report 1942 [covering Sept. 1939–Sept. 1942].
[37] Westmorland LA papers, WDSo/174/2, finance and general purposes committee 19 Oct. 1940, general committee 3 Feb. 1945; 'Secretary's report to AGM held 22nd June 1946'.
[38] Westmorland LA papers, WDSo/174/9, women's LA annual meeting 6 Sept. 1939, women's LA monthly social 13 Nov. 1939.
[39] Ibid., women's LA annual meeting 30 Aug. 1940.
[40] Ibid., women's LA socials 8 Jan., 12 Feb., 11 Mar., 6, 25 May, 11 Nov. 1940.

This level of activity continued through the remainder of the war. There was particular delight in February 1941, when the captain of the troopship SS *Nerissa*, Gilbert Watson (a Kendal man), came to thank the working party personally for its efforts on his crew's behalf, amounting to the production of 92 pairs of socks, 13 scarves, 22 helmets, 9 pairs of gloves, 18 pairs of mittens, and 14 jumpers; tragically, Watson and 200 others were to be killed just ten weeks later when the *Nerissa* was torpedoed by a German U-boat off the coast of Ireland.[41]

They were not alone in their activity. Many Liberal women enrolled in the WVS, salvage schemes, and national savings. There were some noteworthy special efforts. In Edinburgh South, what had begun in October 1940 as an idea for 'a knife and fork tea' for a few troops ended up as a major event, when on 30 December the women's association organized a Christmas party for locally stationed Canadian troops, comprising a sit-down supper of beef, steak pie, potatoes, and peas, followed by pudding and mince pies. The Canadians, who were collected by a coach organized by the association, were joined by another group of 'overseas' troops who had only arrived in Edinburgh that day. After the meal, young Liberals and their friends joined the soldiers for a dance, the whole event ending at midnight.[42] The Liberal women of Yorkshire raised £850 to buy a mobile canteen which they presented to the West Riding County Council in early 1942 for use in the aftermath of air raids.[43] As with the other parties, there were hopes that all this activity would pay political dividends. Indeed, in December 1942 Manchester LF decided to organize a high-profile charity event expressly for the purposes of party propaganda.[44]

There were lacunae: the women's area committee in the Western Counties lapsed completely between 1940 and mid-1942, although it recovered quite well thereafter; the inactivity of Cardiganshire LA was in no way counteracted by its WLA, which was to hold only one meeting (October 1940) between June 1939 and February 1946; and, overall, 'many WLAs suspended activities'.[45] And youth organization declined, on the whole. Conscription rapidly depleted the ranks of Manchester Exchange Young Liberals, while even Chester's Young Liberals were in very dire straits by early 1941.[46] But the pattern was by no means uniform,

[41] Westmorland LA papers, WDSo/174/9, women's LA social 10 Feb. 1941; <http://www.ssnerissa.com/> (accessed 15 Aug. 2007).

[42] Edinburgh South LA papers, Acc. 12038/5, women's association executive committee 14 Oct., 28 Nov., 30 Dec. 1940.

[43] Yorkshire LF papers, WYL 456/3, executive committee 31 Jan. 1941; annual report 1941, to annual meeting 28 Mar. 1942.

[44] Manchester LF papers, M283/1/3/7, executive committee 1, 29 Dec. 1942.

[45] Western Counties LF papers, DDM 1172, finance and general purposes committee 25 July, 16 Nov. 1943; Cardiganshire LA records 2, Aberystwyth women's LA minute book, *passim*; Women's LF papers, DM 1193, annual report 1947 [covering May 1946–Apr. 1947].

[46] Manchester Exchange LA papers, M283/4/1/2, annual reports to annual meetings 11 Mar. 1940, 2 Apr. 1941, 18 Mar. 1942; Chester LA papers, CR159/5, annual meeting 15 May 1942.

with activity being well maintained in Dewsbury and Bradford in January 1942, while there was also a revival of student interest, with the Union of Universities Liberal Societies, which had become 'inactive' soon after the outbreak of war, being revived in April 1941.[47]

The new emphasis on the small trader in the second half of 1941 (see Chapter 1) boosted grassroots activity. Following the establishment of the Dodds committee in 1941, a series of largely successful conferences was held in venues across northern England.[48] The LCNWLF organized successful conferences at Liverpool and Manchester, while Rochdale LA conducted a private 'fact-finding' conference among local traders, and when two reports were made available by the committee in March 1942, the Liverpool Fruiterers ordered 1,200 copies of each for circulation to their members.[49] However, not all associations were so favourable: Dodds himself was 'depressed' by the hostility shown at the 1942 assembly by more left-wing bodies like North Cornwall LA.[50]

The importance invested in this committee by the Liberal party in 1941 is a timely reminder that many Liberals remained anything but pale imitations of socialists. In April 1942, Philip Oliver, a former MP and current president of Manchester LF, told the latter's annual meeting that 'the underlying principles of modern Liberalism' were 'Freedom and Security', adding: 'Each is equally important and each is necessary to the other. . . . Only when property is diffused will there be Security; only when power is diffused will there be Freedom.'[51] Yorkshire Liberals were well known for their long-standing hostility towards socialism, and when Wilfrid Roberts visited the federation there in July 1942 to encourage activity, he was told that nationalization was 'the high road to Fascism' and that 'the most important thing the party c[ould] strenuously work for [was] Free Trade'.[52] Later that year, East Grinstead (Sussex) LA circularized Liberal organizations with a statement stressing the post-war importance of free trade and demanding resistance to the clamour for a planned economy, but although Yorkshire LF supported it, most other Liberal organizations were less keen.[53]

[47] Yorkshire LF papers, WYL 456/3, executive committee 31 Jan. 1942; annual report 1941, to annual meeting 28 Mar. 1942; LPO, *Fifth Annual Report* (1942), 13.

[48] LPO, *Fifth Annual Report* (1942), 16; Yorkshire LF papers, WYL 456/3, executive committee 29 Nov. 1941.

[49] Lancashire, Cheshire, and North Western LF papers, M390/1/11, executive committee 6 Nov 1941, 20 Mar. 1942.

[50] Yorkshire LF papers, WYL 456/3, executive committee 3 Oct. 1942.

[51] Manchester LF papers, M283/1/1/4, annual meeting 23 Apr. 1942.

[52] See K. Laybourn and J. Reynolds, *Liberalism and the Rise of Labour, 1890–1918* (1984); Yorkshire LF papers, WYL 456/3, meeting of constituency representatives with headquarters representatives, 18 July 1942.

[53] Yorkshire LF papers, WYL 456/3, executive committee 3 Oct. 1942; and see e.g. Manchester LF papers, M283/1/3/7, executive committee 29 Dec. 1942; Chester LA papers, CR159/5, coordinating committee 8 Jan. 1943.

From early 1941, indeed, there was significant rank-and-file pressure for the leadership to do something about post-war reconstruction.[54] Partly for this reason, headquarters organized a series of eight area policy conferences in southern and central England between August 1941 and February 1942; these were followed, between June and September 1942, by eleven organizational conferences, where headquarters officials met area federation representatives.[55] However, these were not always very satisfactory: although the LCNWLF was pleased that 221 representatives from 61 of its 83 constituency LAs attended a meeting with head office representatives that September, it also felt that headquarters' representatives offered a 'disappointing and unconvincing' lead.[56] Some associations continued to place themselves in the public eye. Hampstead LA loyally observed the truce at the by-election of 27 November 1941 (which the Conservative won comfortably against opposition from three Independents), but it ensured that there was a press announcement of its decision, to show to voters that it still existed, and a questionnaire was sent to all four candidates; Nuneaton LA organized a petition demanding a Speaker's conference on electoral reform.[57] Immediately after the 1942 assembly, Roberts gave detailed instructions to associations about the need to remain active, write to the local press, hold discussion meetings, and seek new members; and, during the year, LAs were revived in a few constituencies, such as Eccles (Lancashire).[58]

Grassroots complaints about the electoral truce soon mounted; unlike Labour, the Liberals could not even console themselves that they were well represented in the Coalition. At the first Liberal assembly of the war, in June 1941, a motion was proposed attacking the truce as 'harmful to Parliamentary democracy', although it was opposed by the party leadership and withdrawn without a vote.[59] When Roberts met constituency representatives in Yorkshire in July 1942, a Young Liberal from Bradford told him that the truce had led to apathy in the party, with the result that increasing numbers of young Liberals 'were responding to the call of Sir Richard Acland'. Roberts replied that the truce was only an arrangement about by-elections, that '[p]olitical activity and propaganda should be continued', and that Acland's line 'may be right or wrong but it is not Liberalism'.[60] However, concerns about the truce, and indeed about Common Wealth, were not that easily dismissed.

[54] See e.g. Lancashire, Cheshire, and North Western LF papers, M390/1/11, executive committee 21 Feb. 1941.

[55] LPO, *Fifth Annual Report* (1942), 12–13.

[56] Lancashire, Cheshire, and North Western LF papers, M390/1/11, executive committee 25 Sept. 1942.

[57] *Liberal Party Organisation Bulletin*, 26, Dec. 1941.

[58] LPO, *Sixth Annual Report* (1943), 16–17; Lancashire, Cheshire, and North Western LF papers, M390/1/11, executive committee 22 Jan. 1943.

[59] LPO, *Fifth Annual Report* (1942), 9.

[60] Yorkshire LF papers, WYL 456/3, meeting of constituency representatives with headquarters representatives, 18 July 1942.

Closely linked to concerns about the truce were grumbles about the party leader. There was some feeling, for example, that he ought to have battled harder to get a place in the war cabinet.[61] In March 1941 the Scottish LF executive was alarmed by his statement that a general election might not take place until three years after the end of the war, and wrote demanding that he clarify his comments; on receiving his reply, they declared that the general election must come soon after the armistice.[62] The chairman of Edinburgh South LA, Colonel Ross, denounced Sinclair's 'dictatorship', while Lancaster LA, where Ross was the prospective candidate, refused to affiliate to the LPO until it received satisfactory guarantees about the future independence of the party, and supported him in his by-election fight that October when he came second as an independent Liberal.[63] Ross's position was, admittedly, somewhat extreme: but although Manchester Exchange LA attacked him and declared its full faith in Sinclair's leadership, criticism of Sinclair continued elsewhere.[64]

Other issues also exercised Liberal minds in 1941 and 1942. Nazi atrocities against the Jews were denounced roundly, and the demand made that the British government should grant asylum to any Jews who escaped from the continent.[65] There was pressure on the government to do more to resolve India's problems, although no expressions of support for independence.[66] In 1941, the Scottish LF urged the government to investigate the possibilities of Scottish home rule, and agreed to cooperate with the Scottish National party in pressing for a post-war referendum on home rule.[67] In parts of Wales, there was much support for the 1942 Welsh Courts Act, which allowed the use of the Welsh language in legal proceedings in Wales for the first time since the 1536 Act of Union, and which Cardiganshire LA hoped would be the prelude to the creation of a Parliamentary Secretaryship for Wales (a year later they would be calling for a full Secretaryship of State).[68]

The Beveridge report was warmly welcomed by Liberal associations all over Britain.[69] Rank-and-file Liberals made rapid moves to claim the report and its author as their own. The chairman of Paisley LA enthused that it had been

---

[61] See e.g. Lancashire, Cheshire, and North Western LF papers, M390/1/11, executive committee 17 Dec. 1940.

[62] Scottish LF papers, Acc. 11765/14, executive committee 26 Mar. 1941, emergency executive committee 16 Apr. 1941.

[63] Edinburgh South LA papers, Acc. 12038/1, annual meeting 5 Apr. 1941; Lancashire, Cheshire, and North Western LF papers, M390/1/11, executive committee 6 May, 2 Sept. 1941.

[64] Manchester Exchange LA papers, M283/4/1/2, annual meeting 2 Apr. 1941; Lancashire, Cheshire, and North Western LF papers, M390/1/11, executive committee 20 Mar. 1942.

[65] See e.g. Manchester LF papers, M283/1/3/7, executive committee 29 Dec. 1942; Western Counties LF papers, DDM 1172, finance and general purposes committee 27 Feb. 1943.

[66] See e.g. Manchester LF papers, M283/1/3/7, executive committee 29 Dec. 1942.

[67] Scottish LF papers, Acc. 11765/14, executive committee 18 June 1941. Home Rule remained a key claim of the Scottish Liberals: see e.g. Scottish LF papers, Acc. 11765/14, executive committee 6 Dec. 1944.

[68] Cardiganshire LA records 1, annual meeting 21 Oct. 1942, 16 Oct. 1943.

[69] See e.g. Dorset East LA papers, D1512/A1, annual general meeting 31 Mar. 1943.

'compiled by a man, who throughout his political life had been a strong and influential member of the party'.[70] This was, to say the least, an exaggeration: Beveridge had had little formal relationship with the party for many years. But what mattered, of course, was the perception, rather than the reality. The report came at a crucial juncture for ordinary Liberals. They believed that the war had come about due to 'Tory' failings in the period since the end of the Great War.[71] Now, at last, the tide was turning. From west and east, there appeared to be encouraging signs. Roosevelt was 'the greatest Liberal of us all'; the Anglo-American partnership, and the Soviets' struggle for survival, were sure signs that the war was 'part of a world revolution' for 'some new vision'; the war would go on 'until all the evils and dross of the past ha[d] been burnt away'.[72] Beveridge was the domestic counterpart of these struggles. As the secretary of Manchester Exchange LA put it in March 1943, '[a]fter three years of great danger and many disasters we meet at last in an atmosphere of hope'. This meant that Liberals had much to do: 'The world is in travail and needs our help and our counsel. Let us see that we do not fail it.'[73] The WLF claimed that Liberal women were excited by the Beveridge report, 'a truly Liberal plan' which 'Liberals must continue to work for'.[74] By mid-1943 the women's area committees were 'holding many more meetings than at the beginning of the war', while there was some limited revival of the youth organization.[75] In response to the call of the 1942 Liberal Assembly for LAs to meet more regularly, Walthamstow LA began to meet bimonthly, very much encouraged to do so by Walthamstow West's prospective candidate, Radical Action chairman Lancelot Spicer.[76] A new association was formed at Richmond (Surrey), where there had been no Liberal candidate since 1929, and associations were also re-formed in Newbury, Watford, and Bournemouth.[77] Chislehurst (Kent) LA campaigned successfully to get Liberal publications placed in the reading rooms of local libraries.[78] And a further series of policy conferences followed in 1943, in the Western Counties and Midlands LF areas, the main topics discussed being international affairs and the Beveridge report.[79] Public meetings were also held,

---

[70] Paisley LA papers, ARC 67, annual meeting 21 May 1943.

[71] Manchester Exchange LA papers, M283/4/1/2, annual report to annual meeting 27 Mar. 1939.

[72] Ibid., annual report to annual meeting 18 Mar. 1942.

[73] Ibid., annual report to annual meeting 17 Mar. 1943. For further praise of Roosevelt, see e.g. Paisley LA papers, ARC 67, annual report 1940–1, to annual meeting 30 Apr. 1941; Cardiganshire LA records 1, annual meeting 2 Dec. 1944.

[74] Women's LF papers, DM 1193, annual report 1942 [covering Sept. 1942–June 1943].

[75] See e.g. Chester LA papers, CR159/5, annual meeting 15 May 1942, coordinating committee 19 Mar., 24 Sept. 1943, 28 Jan. 1944.

[76] Walthamstow LA papers, uncat., joint executive committee 24 Nov. 1942.

[77] Home Counties LF papers, DM 668, executive committee report, 1 July 1941–30 Apr. 1943; *Liberal Party Organisation Bulletin*, 41, Apr. 1943.

[78] *Liberal Party Organisation Bulletin*, 41, Apr. 1943.

[79] *Liberal Party Organisation Bulletin*, 42, May 1943; LPO, *Sixth Annual Report* (1943), 20.

although constraints on the availability of halls affected the Liberals as much as anyone else.[80]

It would be rash, however, to get too carried away by signs of progress. Manchester Exchange agreed to revert to monthly meetings in October 1943, but nothing happened.[81] Some associations did manage to secure good attendances at meetings despite the increasing problems of transport, but others were not so fortunate, and parties in coastal areas, in particular, found their efforts at greater activity frequently stymied, not least in the run-up to D-Day in June 1944.[82] A useful corrective to too optimistic a view of Liberal associations in this period is provided by a look at the attendance figures at East Dorset LA's annual meetings. Although no meetings were held in 1941, 1942, or 1945, we can still get a sense of the situation from the attendance data of those meetings that were held. At the last peacetime annual meeting, in February 1939, 77 people attended. In January 1940, the figure was 60—lower, but not remarkably so. In March 1943, however, only 35 attended, and in April 1944 the figure was only 27. This suggests little sign of significant revival prior to the second half of 1944. (The figure for the first post-war annual meeting was to be around 100.[83]) Beneath the constituency level, meanwhile, Liberal organization became patchier, although conscious efforts at revival from late 1943 onwards did bring some positive results, for example in Walthamstow.[84]

Discontent with Sinclair's leadership continued. In October 1943, Paddington LA circularized associations asking them to join it in protesting against Sinclair's signing letters of support to government candidates in by-elections.[85] Two months later, Radical Action passed a resolution suggesting that the Liberal ministers should have resigned after the Beveridge debate in February 1943, and that, had they done so, they would have won four or five by-elections since. This demand went too far for most Liberals, but continuing suspicions that there would be an attempt to sustain the Coalition after the war, coupled with misgivings about Sinclair's leadership, were important in helping Beveridge and Radical Action to make as much progress as they did.[86] One reason why some Liberals were prepared to contemplate reunion with the Liberal Nationals in 1944 was as an alternative to participation in a post-war coalition, not a supplement to it: in Scotland, for example, it was hoped that it would retrieve the

---

[80] For unsuitability, see e.g. Harris papers, HRS/2, diary 30 Apr. 1943.

[81] Manchester Exchange LA papers, M283/4/1/2, general divisional meeting 6 Oct. 1942, executive committee 17 June 1943, 23 Mar. 1944.

[82] Cardiganshire LA records 1, annual meeting 16 Oct. 1943; Tiverton LA papers, 4996G/A2, executive committee 31 Mar. 1944.

[83] Dorset East LA papers, D1512/A1, annual general meetings 8 Feb. 1939, 24 Jan. 1940, 31 Mar. 1943, 19 Apr. 1944, 30 Apr. 1946.

[84] Walthamstow West LA papers, uncat., joint wards meeting 12 Oct. 1943.

[85] Reported in Walthamstow LA papers, uncat., joint executive committee 7 Oct. 1943.

[86] See e.g. Lancashire, Cheshire, and North Western LF papers, M390/1/11, executive committee 3 Dec. 1943, 14 Jan. 1944.

eight Liberal National constituency associations, thus buttressing the Liberals' grassroots organization.[87] Coded criticism of Sinclair was not hard to find, even though the traditional resolutions of support for the party leader continued to be passed at annual meetings up and down the country.[88] In February 1944, for example, there was strong resistance when the Scottish LF executive sent a message of support to the leader, while that July, disappointment was expressed at the executive of the LCNWLF that Sinclair had not found more time for big public meetings, and it was agreed that 'it was time we had some real Liberal speeches as distinct from Service speeches'.[89] Even after the party had made it clear that it would be fighting the next election independently, fears about Sinclair's true intentions, and concern that the leadership was not taking sufficient note of the views of the rank and file, remained.[90]

Meanwhile, Beveridge began to overshadow everything and everybody else. Some Liberals attempted to integrate, and even subsume, Beveridge's proposals into the wider mix of Liberalism. The Yorkshire LF's statement supporting Beveridge also stressed its commitment to securing full employment through the restoration of free trade, and its support for the taxation of land values: as seen above, free trade, in particular, remained a core concern for Liberals all over Britain.[91] However, the careful balance of freedom and security demanded by Philip Oliver began to be lost, as the 'security' offered by Beveridge became a more immediate concern than fears about the implications of his proposals for liberty. Other, older elements of Liberalism were increasingly seen as potentially damaging: temperance advocates, for example, were treated as an embarrassment.[92] This line risked alienating traditional Liberal voters in the futile quest for the votes of those who had already decided to vote Labour or Conservative.

Some old-style Liberals fought back. On 10 July 1943, a meeting of Yorkshire LF heard its honorary secretary, Ashley Mitchell, denounce the Beveridge scheme as 'unacceptable', because, by increasing taxation, it would 'cause unemployment', and, above all, because '[t]he increased regimentation inherent in the scheme would further extend an already inflated bureaucracy and make a serious attack on the liberty of the individual'. He criticized 'the overplanned planning policy of the Party', and stated baldly that 'Beveridge was a Socialist' whose report 'contained a number of very ill-liberal [*sic*] ideas'. However, he faced strong opposition: a counter-resolution declared Beveridge 'a very great man' and expressed full support for his report. Crucially, Mitchell's ardour was such as to

[87] Scottish LF papers, Acc. 11765/14, special executive committee 28 June 1944.
[88] See e.g. Glasgow Hillhead LA papers, TD 480, annual general meeting 11 Mar. 1944.
[89] Scottish LF papers, Acc. 11765/14, executive committee 9 Feb. 1944; Lancashire, Cheshire, and North Western LF papers, M390/1/11, executive committee 28 July 1944.
[90] Western Counties LF papers, DDM 1172, executive 4 Nov. 1944.
[91] Yorkshire LF papers, WYL 456/3, annual report, 1942 to annual meeting 27 Mar. 1943; see also e.g. Dorset East LA papers, D1512/A1, annual general meeting 19 Apr. 1944.
[92] Walthamstow LA papers, uncat., joint executive committee 5 Sept. 1944.

alienate even those with some sympathy towards his line: Dodds, for example, stated that '[t]here was nothing in the Beveridge Report which Liberals could not support'. Ultimately, only 4 out of the 35 people present supported Mitchell, who resigned as secretary shortly afterwards; but his stance did demonstrate the existence of Liberal disquiet.[93] By January 1944 the federation was welcoming Spicer as a speaker, but it also continued to look the other way, as when it held a favourable discussion of 'Gladstonian finance' (in which both Mitchell and Dodds participated) in August 1944.[94]

There were other pockets of resistance. The publication of the Dodds report on the independent trader in July 1943 was followed by the formation of an Independent Traders' Alliance which, although ostensibly non-party, had Dodds as chairman and a former Liberal MP as president.[95] At first, it developed well, particularly in Lancashire, Yorkshire, and the Western Counties.[96] The London Liberal party ran a well-attended conference at Grosvenor House of 24 November 1943 on 'London's Stake in Overseas Trade', addressed by Harris and a dozen leading business figures; there was significant press interest, the speeches were published as a pamphlet, and a similar event followed in Birmingham on 30 March 1944.[97] That February, meanwhile, a policy committee established by Leeds Liberals in response to the Beveridge report published 'Liberalism: The Leeds Declaration'. This stated that 'the Liberal Party declares itself for liberty' ('economic security is not enough'), declared its support for the rule of law, and its opposition to regulations unless specifically made by parliament, and emphasized that the test of all policy must be moral. 'Recognising that the party system is necessary to parliamentary democracy', the party invited all 'progressively-minded' men and women to join it. It was agreed further to send a copy to every LA in the country, and '[t]hat propaganda for Liberalism and the Liberal Party be inaugurated forthwith'.[98] Some associations, like Manchester Exchange, responded favourably.[99]

But Beveridge and his report seemed to offer Liberals a bridge to the general public such as they had not had since the late 1920s; and it took a very self-denying Liberal not to be tempted. The LCNWLF passed a resolution in favour of the report and organized meetings supporting it in thirteen towns across its area, leading many LAs into an upswing in activity.[100] The federation also ran other activities, such as a series of lunchtime lectures in Manchester on issues like trade, the state and industry, land and housing, women's work, money and

[93] Yorkshire LF papers, WYL 456/3, executive committee 10 July, 18 Sept. 1943; see also Scottish LF papers, Acc. 11765/14, executive committee 28 Oct. 1942.
[94] Yorkshire LF papers, WYL 456/3, executive committee 22 Jan., 10 Aug. 1944.
[95] LPO, *Sixth Annual Report* (1943), 21.   [96] LPO, *Seventh Annual Report* (1944), 28.
[97] Ibid. 19–20; London LF papers, Acc. 1446/7, general purposes committee 7 Dec. 1943.
[98] Leeds LF papers, WYL 456/7, executive committee 6 Feb. 1943, 12 Feb., 5 Apr. 1944.
[99] Manchester Exchange LA papers, M283/4/1/2, annual meeting 12 Apr. 1944.
[100] Lancashire, Cheshire, and North Western LF papers, M390/1/11, executive committee 22 Jan., 30 Mar., 21 May 1943.

banking, health, and, inevitably, Elliott Dodds on 'Fair play for the small man', but Beveridge increasingly crowded out other topics.[101] In March 1944, 1,350 people packed into a thousand-seater hall in Bolton to hear a speech by the LPO president, Lady Violet Bonham Carter.[102] This suggested that the party might have a future without a celebrity recruit; and yet Bonham Carter was to be among those most anxious to bring Beveridge into the party late in the year. And Beveridge's election to parliament, and his subsequent accession to the position of virtual joint leader with Sinclair, stymied attempts to head off his brand of Liberalism, especially since Radical Action was now flexing its muscles. At the December 1943 meeting of the LPO council, Spicer had demanded that it do more to interest activists in its work, and to ensure that there was 'healthy competition for seats on the Council'. This push for renewal and a sweeping away of older Liberal traditions was complemented by the growing strength of the Liberals' student organization.[103]

As the end of the war approached, a hard task faced the party's grassroots: in May 1944, the LPO reported that some constituency organizations were 'scarcely functioning'.[104] There were some encouraging signs, though. As early as June 1943, Manchester Gorton LA, which had expired around 1930, was re-formed, although it appears to have lapsed once more by the spring of 1944. Manchester Moss Side LA, 'which had not been active for some years', was relaunched at a meeting attended by forty people in April 1944. It proved longer lived than Gorton, partly because it had longer to 'bed in' before the greater organizational challenges of winter, partly because there was more encouragement and incentive to remain active in 1944 than in 1943, and partly because, unlike Gorton, it adopted a parliamentary candidate immediately it was formed.[105] Organizational revival had begun in Liverpool in February 1944, thanks partly to the independent trader campaign (see Chapter 3).

The London Liberals had begun to revive some associations in mid-1943. In Lambeth North, letters were sent to known supporters, and women members conducted a canvass of 'supposed Liberal electors'. By mid-1944, each meeting of the London executive was responding positively to requests for help from one or more LAs, and in the final six months of the war the London party was closely overseeing the development of around twenty associations. But planning was often haphazard, depending at times simply on the chance emergence of willing individuals, and the party's attempts to help associations did not always amount to much.[106] In Walthamstow, however, the party began seriously to

---

[101] Lancashire, Cheshire, and North Western LF papers, leaflet, 'LCNWLF: The 5th series of mid-day meetings', n.d. [c. Sept. 1943].
[102] LPO, *Seventh Annual Report* (1944), 17.   [103] Ibid. 14, 17–19.   [104] Ibid. 30.
[105] Manchester LF papers, M283/1/3/7, executive committee 28 June 1943, 25 Jan., 28 Mar., 25 Apr. 1944.
[106] London LF papers, Acc. 1446/7, general purposes committee 22 July to 20 Mar. 1945, *passim*.

revive from June 1944 onwards, starting with press advertisements, posters at railway stations, extensive pamphlet distribution, and, from that November, publication of a local newsletter.[107] The north-west also witnessed revival. Six of the LCNWLF's eleven district councils had met by early October 1944, and extensive reorganization soon followed in a number of constituencies, including Crewe (Cheshire) and Leigh (Lancashire). The federation decided to contest as many seats as possible, thus rejecting Roberts's attempt to steer them towards fighting a limited number of seats with strong potential as part of a more realistic aim of securing fifty or sixty seats nationally to secure 'a beachead [*sic*] in the Reconstruction period'; Young Liberal organization had been revived in fifteen of the federation's constituencies, while a newly formed local LA at Droylesden (in the Mossley division of Lancashire) opened a Liberal bookshop.[108] In November 1944 Stockport LA, which had collapsed in 1936, was revived, with energetic new officers and plans; by April 1945, ward organizations had been formed, and at the election two candidates were run in; although heavily defeated, they were not humiliated.[109] In February 1945, Westmorland LA elected a new 26-strong general purposes committee, and began to plan public meetings and seek an agent; by May, it also had new offices, a publicity committee, and a panel of speakers.[110] The Home Counties LF began a series of public conferences in April 1944, addressed by leading Liberals like Harris and Dingle Foot, and preceded by private meetings of LA officers and candidates to discuss organization and election preparations; Yorkshire followed suit in June.[111] Sub-constituency-level organizations were also revived, although even more patchily than in the case of the Conservatives or Labour.[112] University students provided teams of campaigners for around twenty LAs—usually with Radical Action candidates—in the winter of 1944–5; for example, teams from Oxford helped at Walthamstow, Elland, and Leeds North.[113]

In that final winter of the war, the failure of Liberal reunion (which broke few grassroots hearts), coupled with Beveridge's election to parliament, helped to propel the party further leftwards; so too did Lloyd George's return to the news, first by the award of a peerage in January 1945 and then by his death

[107] Walthamstow LA papers, uncat., joint executive committee 6 May, 15 Nov. 1944.

[108] Lancashire, Cheshire, and North Western LF papers, M390/1/11, executive committee 25 Aug., 1 Dec. 1944.

[109] Stockport LA papers, B/NN/2/10, executive committee 21 Nov. 1944, 19 Apr. 1945.

[110] Westmorland LA papers, WDSo/174/2, general committee 3 Feb. 1945, general purposes and finance committee 10 Feb. 1945, executive committee 24 Mar., 17 May 1945.

[111] Home Counties LF papers, DM 668, executive committee report, 1 May 1943–31 Dec. 1944; Yorkshire LF papers, WYL 456/3, executive committee 3 June 1944.

[112] See e.g. Dundee LA papers, GD/DLA 1/2, finance committee 11 Jan. 1945; Cardiganshire LA records 1, special meeting 22 Feb. 1945.

[113] LPO, *Report to the Assembly* (1946), 13; Walthamstow LA papers, uncat., joint executive committee 15 Nov. 1944, 2 Jan. 1945; Yorkshire LF papers, WYL 456/3, executive committee 16 Dec. 1944.

that March.[114] One Glasgow Liberal pronounced him '[o]ne of the greatest Statesmen . . . who have lived. Worthy to rank with Julius Ceasar [*sic*].'[115] While most Liberals might not have gone that far, the high profile Lloyd George thus received helped once more to highlight the kind of social reform that Beveridge was advocating. Beveridge himself helped matters, of course. His willingness to travel, and to speak at meetings large and small, was a great boon to grassroots Liberals more accustomed to being unable to secure the services of 'big name' speakers. Even in the dry cadences of federation and association minute books, the excitement generated by an offer by Beveridge to come and speak is palpable.[116] The Scottish LF, having met him for the first time on 7 May, elected him as chairman of their new campaign committee despite his admission that he would be unable to attend many of their meetings.[117] Traditionalist associations like East Grinstead were now seen by headquarters as problem cases to be saved from themselves.[118]

Grassroots Liberals generally welcomed the end of the Coalition, and looked forward with some confidence to an electoral fight as an independent party.[119] In March 1945, Glasgow Hillhead LA decided to run its first candidate since 1923 after receiving a euphoric report from its delegates to the previous month's Liberal assembly; nearby Paisley LA believed it was 'a time of opportunity for all true Liberals', although the break with Churchill did lead some senior party members to protest, or even resign from the party.[120] Sometimes the signals from the grassroots were confusing. In April 1945, for example, the leading Liberal in Liverpool, Alderman William Denton, communicated to Sinclair two resolutions which had been passed the previous day. One, passed by the Liberal members of the city council, was strongly critical of the decision to withdraw from the Churchill government; but the other, agreed upon by the Liberal area council, declared 'wholehearted support' for the party's decision to fight the election as an independent party. As Denton concluded, there was 'a considerable difference of opinion', with 'many of our most influential Liberals believ[ing] that the Party [was] committing a tactical mistake by not promising support to the Prime Minister', while 'the majority particularly the keen and hardened campaigners adhere[d] to the Party programme enunciated

---

[114] See e.g. London LF papers, Acc. 1446/7, general purposes committee 30 Nov. 1944; Yorkshire LF papers, WYL 456/3, executive committee 16 Dec. 1944; Cardiganshire LA records 1, annual meeting 2 Dec. 1944; Manchester LF papers, M283/1/3/7, executive committee 2 Jan., 27 Mar. 1945.

[115] Glasgow Hillhead LA papers, TD 480, William M. Elder to Miss MacNeill, 2 Mar. 1945.

[116] See e.g. Western Counties LF papers, DDM 1172, finance and general purposes committee 3 Mar. 1945.

[117] Scottish LF papers, Acc. 11765/14, special executive committee 7 May 1945.

[118] Beveridge papers, VI/13, fo. 148, Sir John Stewart-Wallace to Beveridge, 30 Apr. 1945.

[119] See e.g. Mitchell, *Election '45*, 30, 50; Tregidga, *Liberal Party in South-West Britain*, 95.

[120] Glasgow Hillhead LA papers, TD 480, annual meeting 2 Mar. 1945; Paisley LA papers, ARC 67, annual report 1944–5, to annual meeting 30 Apr. 1945; Samuel papers, SAM/A/155(XI), Lord Reading to Samuel, 31 May 1945; Lord Hamilton of Dalzell to Samuel, 19 Apr. 1945.

at the Assembly and [did] not forget the previous disaster of the "coupon" election'.[121]

The star of the Liberals' general election campaign, so far as associations were concerned, was Beveridge. Like the grassroots Liberals who heard them, he regarded his numerous speeches as hugely successful: '[i]f meetings are any test', he wrote to one candidate, 'the Liberal revival everywhere is immense.'[122] In retrospect, however, he was to feel that the election had come too soon for the Liberals, and the evidence would seem to support him.[123] They were unable to run more than 306 candidates. All existing seats were defended, and almost all of the stronger associations did run candidates. But time and again, regional federations spoke as though running candidates in about half their constituencies was some kind of success, when ultimately the failure to run candidates in more than half the constituencies nationally would be seen as a root cause of the Liberals' 1945 debacle. London LF, for example, felt that the fact that it had managed to adopt 30 candidates for the 62 London seats was 'satisfactory, having regard to the many difficulties encountered', but it was nothing of the kind—the Conservatives and Labour faced many of the same problems, yet were running candidates in virtually every seat.[124] Yorkshire Liberals heard plenty about their energetic candidate in Elland, in the west of the county, but might have directed their attention more profitably southwards, and reflected on why they would end up being unable to run more than two candidates in the fourteen constituencies of south Yorkshire.[125] The secretary of the LCNWLF reported 'slow progress' in adopting candidates for its 92 constituencies in December 1944; he was right, because only 34 had been adopted by mid-May 1945.[126] But this was not for want of trying on his part. The federation had to do 'everything within [its] power to persuade Associations to adopt Candidates', because all too many LAs sheltered behind excuses—usually challenged by younger members of the party—that time or money were too short. Even so, and despite personal meetings with representatives of each of the area's 85 LAs, only 45 candidates ultimately ran.[127] The vain idea that more candidates would be put up somewhere else to offset the lack in one's own area was noticeable. In some places, the optimism of headquarters or regional federations overcame a more cautious approach in the constituency. For example, headquarters virtually forced Cambridgeshire LA to run a candidate against its better judgement; he

[121] Thurso papers, THRS II 85/4, Denton to Sinclair, 6 Apr. 1945.

[122] Walthamstow LA papers, uncat., joint executive committee 5 June 1945; Beveridge papers, VI/17, fo. 173, Beveridge to Joan Gaved, 27 June 1945.

[123] Lord Beveridge, *Power and Influence: An Autobiography* (1953), 344.

[124] London LF papers, Acc. 1446/7, general purposes committee 20 June 1945.

[125] For Elland, see e.g. Yorkshire LF papers, WYL 456/3, executive committee 16 Dec. 1944, 22 Jan. 1945.

[126] Lancashire, Cheshire, and North Western LF papers, M390/1/12, executive committee 1 Dec. 1944, 11 May 1945.

[127] Ibid., 'Report on the election, July 1945', 26 July 1945.

managed to take only 15 per cent of the poll.[128] But even some associations which had carried on throughout the war nonetheless felt they were too weak to run a candidate: for example, Edinburgh South, organizer of the impressive supper and dance for the troops at the end of 1940, was reduced to helping the party's candidates in the city's North and West divisions.[129] Occasional candidates in seas of straight fights were treated as pioneers; but parties of pioneers do not win power.

Even so, some Liberals were genuinely optimistic. This optimism meant that, in some places, candidates appeared at the last moment virtually from nowhere, and although LAs were often enthusiastic and keen to do what they could, they had little hope of success.[130] Beveridge wrote privately that he was pleased to see a Liberal candidate standing at Acton (Middlesex), since it was 'precisely in constituencies of this kind that we shall see many Liberal victories'.[131] In the event, Labour gained the seat from the Conservatives, with the Liberal taking fewer than 10 per cent of the votes cast. Some candidates were more realistic, and spoke merely of 'put[ting] Liberalism on the map' and 'laying the foundations for a permanent organization'.[132]

The election results, though, were terrible. The last two remaining seats in Scotland, and the last four remaining seats in urban England, were all lost. Two losses in rural North Wales included Lloyd George's former seat. After the election, the party held only five widely dispersed and very rural constituencies in England (three by less than 1,000 votes, and only one won in opposition to a Labour candidate), and seven seats in Wales, six of which were overwhelmingly rural and the seventh of which—the University of Wales, won in a straight fight with Plaid Cymru—the incoming Labour government was pledged to abolish.[133] For all the efforts of the London LF, all 30 of its candidates had been defeated, and 10 had lost their deposits (for polling fewer than an eighth of the votes cast); 11 of the 23 candidates in Scotland had also lost their deposits, while the 66 candidates in the 100 seats of the Home Counties LF area did not win a single seat between them.[134] For the lively Walthamstow Liberals, defeat was 'a bitter blow', because, both in the borough and in the party nationally, '[h]ope had run so high, signs of success had been so many, that a disaster of that magnitude had never been envisaged'. But although they resolved to take it

---

[128] Cambridgeshire LA papers, R93/73, meeting and conference 17 Mar. 1945.

[129] Edinburgh South LA papers, Acc. 12038/1, annual meeting 2 Apr. 1945, executive committee 12 June 1945.

[130] See e.g. Cleveland LA papers, U/GLA 3, Guisborough local LA meeting 2 June 1945.

[131] Beveridge papers, VI/17, fo. 140, Beveridge to Brian Goddard, 4 June 1945.

[132] Ibid., fo. 117, G. Granville Slack to Beveridge, 8 July 1945.

[133] J. G. Jones, 'The Liberal party and Wales, 1945–79', *Welsh History Review*, 16 (1993), 354–5.

[134] Thurso papers, THRS VII 1/1, Scottish LF, 'Report of the election committee', n.d. [Aug. 1945]; Home Counties LF papers, DM 668, executive committee report for year ended 31 Dec. 1945.

'not as a defeat, but as a challenge', a further challenge then followed with dismal results in the first post-war municipal elections in November 1945.[135] Over the past generation, Liberals had become accustomed to comforting themselves about the 'real' significance of general election results. It was the same story in 1945: as the LPO's annual report put it, '[t]he general public [had] displayed a keen and searching interest in Liberal ideals during the election, and reports from all parts of the country amply demonstrate[d] that the total Liberal sentiment [was] much in excess of the Liberal poll'. The need, therefore, was to cure the party's *organizational* weakness.[136] There was considerable feeling that the party had suffered from being able to run candidates in only about half the seats, which had ruled out even a theoretical prospect of a Liberal government and therefore swayed potential Liberal voters into voting Labour or Conservative. The lesson was that the party must put up more candidates next time.[137] There was, as usual, little recognition of the fact that the organizational weakness might be the effect, and not the cause, of the party's *political* weakness.

The city of Leeds illustrates many of the trends discussed in this chapter. Once a Liberal stronghold, it had turned from the party between the wars, to such an extent that the Liberals had not run a single candidate for any of the six seats in 1935, when even the fringe Social Credit party of Great Britain had managed one. However, the Leeds LF and six constituency LAs remained in being. When war broke out, plans for a big dance in February 1940 were abandoned, but there was no thought of giving up. The federation's central committees continued to meet throughout the war, and knitting and social service work carried on.[138] The federation congratulated Sinclair on refusing to enter Chamberlain's government in 1939, and offered fierce criticism of Chamberlain's leadership the day before the Norway debate opened in May 1940.[139] In May 1941, it set up a discussion group, and a year later it had five active subcommittees, the social committee was busy organizing events, and the organization committee was working to help the six LAs, albeit with very mixed results.[140] Politically, there was conflict between Beveridgism and more traditional forms of Liberalism; as seen above, the 'Leeds Declaration' of February 1944 showed that the former did not simply carry all before it.[141]

---

[135] Walthamstow East LA papers, Acc. 10208/4, executive committee's report for 1945, to annual general meeting 28 Mar. 1946; C. Cook, 'Liberals, Labour and local elections', in G. Peele and C. Cook (eds.), *The Politics of Reappraisal, 1918–1939* (1975), 185.

[136] LPO, *Report to the Assembly* (1946), 22–3. See also McCallum and Readman, *British General Election of 1945*, 141, Rasmussen, *The Liberal Party*, 13.

[137] Westmorland LA papers, WDSo/174/2, 'Secretary's report to AGM [*sic*]', 22 June 1946.

[138] Leeds LF papers, WYL 456/7, annual report for 1943–4, to annual meeting 22 Apr. 1944; executive committee 6 Feb. 1943.

[139] Ibid., executive committee 28 Oct. 1939, 6 May 1940.

[140] Ibid., executive committee 24 May 1941, 24 Oct. 1942, 30 Aug. 1945; annual report for 1941–2, to annual meeting 25 Apr. 1942.

[141] Ibid., executive committee 13 Dec. 1941; annual report for 1941–2, to annual meeting 25 Apr. 1942, annual meeting 25 Apr. 1942, 10 Apr. 1943.

The declaration also helped to revive the city's Liberal organization, and by April 1944 three of the six constituencies had candidates. There were obstacles, of course, particularly in finding halls for public meetings, but by October 1944, four of the LAs were reporting 'splendid' levels of activity; by February 1945, plans for the general election, and the municipal elections expected in November, were well advanced.[142] But the election brought little joy; the party contested all six seats for the first time since 1922, but came a poor third in all of them. The federation put on a brave front: at a post-election meeting, there were lots of young people and 'new faces' present, and sixteen seats were fought at the municipal elections; by April 1946, there was a live association in each constituency, the Young Liberals were reviving strongly, and the ward organizations were working hard.[143] The Liberals might be the third party in Leeds, but they remained a party nonetheless.

If any party might have been thought vulnerable to a wartime *coup de grâce*, it would have been the Liberals. Yet their organization in the constituencies often survived, and in a few cases prospered. For all the turmoil of the war years, there was a significant continuity about grassroots Liberalism in this period. Organization had been patchy in 1939; it still was so in 1945. In some parts of the country, there had been no Liberal organization before the war, and there was none after it. In other places, organization came and went: in common with the Conservatives and Labour, Liberal associations in places especially affected by the war, like coastal regions and London, often found it hardest to survive. In a few places, though, like Chester and Walthamstow, local organization remained relatively strong, if not strong enough to deliver parliamentary victory in 1945. That the Liberal headquarters acted decisively at the outbreak of war helped, although this must be set against Sinclair's rather pusillanimous leadership. An ability to blame the old enemy, Conservatism, for the war, the nature of the war effort, and a belief that the Americans and Roosevelt, in particular, were fighting for Liberal causes all helped to boost grassroots morale. From 1943 onwards there was some revival, and in places this was impressive. However, the lure of celebrity, in the person of Beveridge, proved too much for many Liberals, and he was able to assume an unhealthy prominence in the last year of the conflict. Even so, he did offer a short-term morale boost to the grassroots, and the party survived his retirement after the 1945 election defeat. That defeat was in some ways crushing, but for many ordinary Liberals the response was not despair, but a desire to fight back, a fact that could be seen in the impressive increase in affiliations to the LPO in the second half of the 1940s. Many Liberals had hoped that

---

[142] Leeds LF papers, annual meeting 22 Apr. 1944, executive committee 26 July, 14 Nov. 1944, 13 Feb. 1945.

[143] Ibid., executive committee 30 Aug. 1945; annual report for 1945–6, to annual meeting 29 Apr. 1946.

the war would see a powerful revival of British Liberalism. They were wrong; but so too were those who had expected the war to finish the Liberal party off. In fact, the party's survival at all levels was impressive. Furthermore, the experience of that survival would help the party cope with renewed setbacks in the early 1950s.

8

Money

INTRODUCTION

The history of party finance in twentieth-century Britain has been somewhat neglected, despite the fact that raising and spending money were prime functions of political parties.[1] In the context of the present study, however, money can be seen as a key indicator of the health, or otherwise, of the established parties in wartime. This chapter is primarily concerned to assess the financial state of the Conservative, Labour, and Liberal parties at national and local levels during the conflict. It will assess how far their sources of income changed, and look at changing patterns of expenditure, as well as attempting to assess the relative changes in their overall financial positions. Finally, it will also comment on how far the war affected longer-term patterns of funding.

THE CONSERVATIVES

Most commentary on Conservative wartime finances has suggested a story of struggle. Woolton, who took over as party chairman in 1946, later recalled that the party had 'had very little money' by the end of the war.[2] The long-time party official Sir Joseph Ball suggested that the party had only a tenth as much to spend at the 1945 election as it had had in 1935; John Ramsden has suggested that this was an exaggeration, but he agrees that the party's finances had 'virtually withered away' by 1945, while Michael Pinto-Duschinsky has estimated that real-terms Central Office expenditure in 1945 was only between 6.2 and 12.5 per cent of the figure for 1935.[3]

Information about the state of Conservative finances in this period is scanty, but in 1938 the party chairman, Hacking, was saying privately that they were

---

[1] A. Ware, *Political Parties and Party Systems* (Oxford, 1996), 111. For serious treatments of the subject see Pinto-Duschinsky, *British Political Finance*; M. Dawson, 'Money and the real impact of the Fourth Reform Act', *Historical Journal*, 35 (1992).

[2] R. Rhodes James, *Anthony Eden* (1986), 314; Earl of Woolton, *The Memoirs of the Rt. Hon. the Earl of Woolton* (1959), 374.

[3] Ramsden, *Age of Balfour and Baldwin*, 359; idem, *Age of Churchill and Eden*, 4, 73; Pinto-Duschinsky, *British Political Finance*, 127, 143.

'not too healthy', and in July 1939 Topping was stressing that the party was living in 'days of financial stringency', which meant severe limitations on Central Office subsidies to local organizations.[4] The apparent permanence of the National government, and Labour's continuing electoral weakness, had led to complacency among potential donors, who saw no reason to fund a party that would win elections anyway.[5] This state of affairs was hardly likely to be improved by the outbreak of war.

By the late 1930s, the national party organization had four main sources of funding. First, there were large subscriptions and donations from wealthy individuals.[6] Secondly, business funding had increased significantly since 1918, as firms came to see the value of contributing to an anti-socialist party. Thirdly, the Conservatives continued to receive support from the National Publicity Bureau (NPB), which had been created in 1934 to raise cash in support of the National government: the Conservatives, as by far the largest National party, had benefited most. The NPB had spent lavishly in the 1930s, getting through as much as £300,000 in the thirteen months leading up to the 1935 general election, and would have spent heavily in any 1939 or 1940 election campaign.[7] Finally, a trade in honours continued. Although the worst excesses of Lloyd George's time in office were long past, it is clear that the distribution of honours to 'suitable' people who had contributed generously to party funds continued: for example, Cecil Harmsworth, brother of the press baron Lord Rothermere, was awarded a peerage in 1939 in return for a payment of £25,000 to Conservative party funds.[8]

Some of these sources were adversely affected by the war. Big individual donations did not disappear, and in June 1945 the motor manufacturer Lord Nuffield gave a 'generous cheque'.[9] But, for those less well off, high levels of wartime taxation might well have made the difference between a pre-war subscription and a wartime refusal to give.[10] Similarly, honours sales appear to have died off. Names continued to be exchanged between leading politicians and

[4] C. Brooks, *Fleet Street, Press Barons and Politics: The Journals of Colin Brooks, 1932–1940*, ed. N. Crowson (1998), 206, 4 May 1938; CO 4/1/86, Topping circular to Central Office agents, 28 July 1939.
[5] J. W. B. Bates, 'The Conservative party in the constituencies, 1918–39', University of Oxford D.Phil. thesis, 1994, esp. 259; see also Davidson papers, DAV/273, Davidson memo, 'Secret', 25 Jan. 1940.
[6] Derby papers, DER(17)/31/6, Hacking to Derby, 2 July 1937.
[7] Pinto-Duschinsky, *British Political Finance*, 119–23; Woolton papers, 21, fo. 16, Sir J. Ball, 'Brief summary of the memorandum entitled "The last general election"', 29 Mar. 1946; Yorkshire Conservative party papers, WYL 1856/1/3, provincial area council annual report to annual meeting, 17 Feb. 1940.
[8] Derby papers, DER(17)/31/6, Hacking to Derby, 2 July 1937; Chamberlain papers, NC 8/21/8, Ball to Chamberlain, 1 June 1938; *The Times*, 2 Jan., 8 Feb. 1939; Brooks, *Fleet Street*, 206, 222, 225, 238, 243, 247–8, 4 May, 5, 13 Oct. 1938, 16 Jan., 15 Feb., 22 May 1939.
[9] Chartwell papers, CHAR 2/545, Assheton to Churchill 9 June 1945.
[10] Ramsden, *Age of Churchill and Eden*, 50.

officials under Chamberlain, but Attlee's parsimonious attitude towards the award of honours once in Coalition (see below) probably inhibited the Conservatives, while Churchill's often distant relationship towards Central Office can hardly have facilitated matters.[11] On the other hand, business donations may have been hit less hard. They certainly appear to have recovered somewhat from 1943 onwards, as suggested by the formation of British United Industrialists (BUI) late in the war to channel money from private companies to the Conservative party.[12] The timing of BUI's formation also fits well with the notion that party politics became more polarized as issues of post-war reconstruction arose strongly from 1943 onwards.[13] The NPB, for its part, shut up shop in 1939–40, but it continued to exist, and was, in fact, to assist the party with 'substantial funds' in 1945.[14] Its expenditure in the latter year was to be less than it had been in 1935, but it had spent with considerable extravagance in that election, and in 1945—when there was less on which to spend money, in any case—it did not stint in helping the party.[15]

Whatever they said in retrospect, Conservative officials did not express much anxiety about money during the war years. Central Office did call for reductions in the legal maximum that candidates could spend at elections, but not because the party was impoverished; rather, Topping hoped that a lower maximum would reduce the appeal of rich candidates to local associations, thus opening up candidatures to the ablest, rather than the wealthiest.[16] The Downing Street emergency meeting of February 1944, called in the aftermath of West Derbyshire, identified nine reasons for the party's crisis, but money—or lack of it—was not among them.[17] The fact that the Tory Reform Committee appeared to Butler to be 'heavily backed and financed' suggests that money was available for Conservative causes.[18] Other party reformers like Henry Brooke also doubted that lack of cash was a real problem, while Assheton did not regard finance as being likely to damage Conservative prospects at the 1945 election.[19]

Party officials showed more concern about the future shape of the party's finances. In November 1942, the NUEC set up a special finance committee under Major Richard Proby. Its March 1944 report suggested that the party would not be able to rely so much upon 'wealthy candidates and wealthy

[11] See e.g. Davidson papers, DAV/273, Davidson to Earl Baldwin, 12 Apr. 1940.

[12] Cockett, *Thinking the Unthinkable*, 73.

[13] See Johnman, 'The Labour party and industrial policy', 29–53; Harvie-Watt, *Most of my Life*, 166.

[14] Chartwell papers, CHAR 2/548B, Assheton to Churchill, 28 Apr. 1945.

[15] Pinto-Duschinsky, *British Political Finance*, 121.

[16] D. E. Butler, *The Electoral System in Britain since 1918* (Oxford, 1963), 95; CO 4/1/86, Topping to Hacking, 14 Nov. 1939.

[17] Chartwell papers, CHAR 2/507, meeting at 10 Downing Street, 17 Feb. 1944.

[18] Butler papers, H61, Butler to Dugdale, 23 Dec. 1943.

[19] Ibid., H62, Brooke memo, 'Organizing to win elections', 8 June 1944; Avon papers, AP 11/4/68, Assheton to Eden, 15 June 1945.

individuals' after the war: 'princely subscriptions from wealthy peers or from industrial magnates' were 'drying up'. But this offered a chance to develop more robust sources of income. These included an expansion of the existing central subscriptions list, with special collectors being appointed to concentrate on obtaining 'substantial subscriptions from the wealthier members of the community'. The report referred enviously to Labour's ability to access small regular payments from its individual and affiliated members, and clearly wanted associations to develop their fund-raising in this direction, although the idea of Central Office quotas levied on constituency associations was shelved as being too controversial an imposition on local autonomy. To oversee the new scheme, the report recommended the formation of a National Board of Finance, chaired by the party treasurer, and including a number of MPs, peers, provincial party officials, and expert fund-raisers from the business world.[20] The report was approved unanimously by the NUEC and the area chairmen and treasurers, but the hopes of Proby and Topping for early action were dashed. Churchill's approval was vital, but by spring 1944 he was, once more, fully occupied with the war effort, and his first reaction on seeing the report was to ask Beaverbrook to see if Central Office was trying to trick him.[21] It was only in mid-August, after Beaverbrook had given his grudging approval, that Churchill finally accepted it; by then, the V-1 attacks had started, and Dugdale was about to be replaced as party chairman, condemning the report to oblivion for the time being.[22] As in other areas, however, the power of Churchill and others to block reform was greatly weakened by the 1945 election defeat, and a new central board of finance was created in 1946, while in 1948 the Maxwell-Fyfe committee went further than Proby in recommending constituency quotas, which were subsequently introduced very successfully.[23]

Constituency-level funding came from a variety of sources prior to 1939. Some associations relied on large donations from MPs and candidates, or big subscriptions from a handful of wealthy donors. Stuart Ball has suggested that large numbers of CAs were in this position, which resulted in 'a perilously narrow financial base, vulnerable to the effects of defeat and the absence of a candidate and to the death, removal, or resignation of the few large subscribers'.[24] Between

[20] Beaverbrook papers, BBK/D/422, special finance committee, 'Report', 16 Mar. 1944.

[21] Chartwell papers, CHAR 2/507, James Stuart to Churchill, 14 June 1944; CO 500/1/12, Central Office memo, enc. with Topping to Central Office agents, 20 Apr. 1944; Butler papers, H62, Brooke memo, 'Organizing to win elections', 8 June 1944; Beaverbrook papers, BBK/D/422, Churchill to Beaverbrook, 3 July 1944.

[22] Beaverbrook papers, BBK/D/422, Beaverbrook to Churchill, 5, 11 July 1944; Chartwell papers, CHAR 2/507, Churchill to Stuart, 18 Aug. 1944.

[23] Pinto-Duschinsky, *British Political Finance*, 128, 130; D. E. Butler and M. Pinto-Duschinsky, 'The Conservative elite, 1918–78: does unrepresentativeness matter?', in Z. Layton-Henry (ed.), *Conservative Party Politics* (1980), 189; NUA 6/2/6, 'Interim report of the committee on party organization', 28 July 1948.

[24] Ball, 'Local Conservatism', 286.

a quarter and a third of associations in the later 1930s, however, were dependent on small subscriptions from large numbers of relatively 'ordinary' people, plus quota payments from women's and JIL branches; such sources were increasingly important for many more CAs, too.[25] For the very worst off, there might also be subsidies from an area or city party, or from Central Office itself. The results were not always very favourable. In agricultural Louth, subscriptions were proving elusive because of hostility toward the government's farming policy, leaving CA finances in a 'rotten state', with an overdraft of £225 at the end of 1938, while South Derbyshire CA was running a £400 deficit in May 1939.[26]

Most associations were faring rather better than this prior to September 1939, but the war has been seen as bringing severe challenges. First, it has been suggested, wartime taxation had a 'crushing impact' on middle-class incomes, with consequent effects on CA finances, as constituency treasurers were often 'too embarrassed to "bother" people with demands for money'; on this model, recovery only began late in the war, around the autumn of 1944, and, even then, income remained well below pre-war levels.[27] Secondly, significant, if hesitant, moves towards reform of local party funding—most notably on the question of candidates' contributions—were effectively put on ice for the duration of the conflict.[28]

Some Conservative associations did face enormous financial problems. Those of Lambeth Kennington CA (London) began in March 1939, when the death of its MP and loss of the seat at the consequent by-election meant the end of a £700 annual subsidy. Suddenly without any significant source of income, the association virtually ceased activities that summer. A new candidate was adopted in September 1939, and he at least paid the office rent; but, of course, when he resigned in 1942 the office had to be vacated. By May 1945, with no election fund, they needed to find a candidate who could finance his or her campaign in full. They managed to do so, but Central Office rules now prohibited new candidates from footing the whole bill. Unsurprisingly, the Conservative candidate was heavily defeated by a Labour candidate who outspent him, while the association itself was left in debt.[29] Warwick and Leamington CA's pre-war hopes of developing a large list of small subscribers had come to little, and matters were made worse by the death of a large (£300 a year) benefactor days after the outbreak of war. By March 1945, the association had a deficit of £350, and

[25] Harrison, *Transformation of British Politics*, 185.
[26] Heneage papers, HNC 2/48, R. H. Helmer to Sir A. P. Heneage, 4 Jan. 1939; Louth CA, annual report, 1938; Charles Webb (CA agent) to Heneage, 11 Apr. 1939; Emrys-Evans papers, Add. 58250, fo. 96, J. A. Perks to Paul Emrys-Evans, 4 May 1939.
[27] Ramsden, *Age of Churchill and Eden*, 50.   [28] Ibid. 2.
[29] Kennington CA papers, Coll. Misc. 463/3, general purposes committee 12 July 1939; executive committee 15 July 1939; selection committee 19 Sept. 1939; meeting of officers and ward chairmen, 23 Sept. 1939; executive committee 17 Jan. 1942; special meeting of members 23 June 1943; special committee meeting 15 Jan. 1944; D. S. Flatman (Hon. Treasurer) to Mr Armstrong (Central Office), 12 May 1945; CA meeting, 24 May 1945.

ultimately Eden (the MP) had to pay the whole of his election expenses (£800), which would have been against Central Office rules if he had been a newly adopted candidate. After the war the association did take to heart its treasurer's plea to move beyond its 'ridiculously small' number of pre-war subscriptions, and built up a substantial list of small subscribers, but the war itself had been a period of indubitable financial failure.[30] Elsewhere, Lanark CA collected no subscriptions at all between May 1940 and the end of the war; Chester-le-Street CA (Durham) had no money at all in 1945; while in the summer of 1944, the chairman of Wandsworth, Balham, and Tooting CA was telling potential candidates that it 'had neither money nor effective organization'.[31]

All this suggests general financial impoverishment, but caution is needed. After all, the notion of general financial impoverishment played a significant role in Conservative mythologizing about the Second World War, because Conservatives needed 'memories' of financial ruin in wartime to help them to rationalize their 1945 defeat, and to pave the way for the financial reforms that followed it. Other evidence suggests a more complex picture. In Essex, Chelmsford CA found subscriptions difficult to collect early in the war, and its MP cut his annual subscription from the pre-war £300 to just £25; by April 1945 it would be sending out begging letters to local MPs in its vain by-election fight against Common Wealth.[32] Yet its financial position was regarded by its treasurer as 'highly satisfactory'. Subscriptions continued to arrive, especially those paid by banker's order, which did not rely on the availability of collectors and where inertia tended to be on the side of the payments continuing. Expenditure also fell—salaries, for example, cost £582 in 1938 but nothing at all between 1941 and 1943. This was not an association in a disastrous financial position, especially when its reserves of more than £3,000 are taken into account.[33] In Manchester, a pre-war deficit of over £2,000 had been transformed into a surplus of £6,500 by early 1946, in part due to the wartime recruitment of new subscribers.[34] Birmingham UA, despite its grim expectations, found that most subscriptions continued to come in, and was able to make new investments amounting to at least £11,500 in the war years.[35] In East Norfolk, increased subscriptions, plus parsimonious expenditure, turned a 1939 deficit of £170 into a surplus of £800

[30] Warwick and Leamington CA papers, CR1392, annual meeting 6 May 1938, 3 May 1939, executive committee 2 Mar. 1945, finance committee 3 Nov. 1945; Avon papers, AP 11/1/27A, A. J. Gibbs (agent) to Eden, 3 Mar. 1945; AP 11/1/36, Eden to Gibbs, 13 June 1945; AP 11/1/52B, Gibbs to Mrs Jephson, 24 July 1945; AP 11/1/52F, Gibbs to Mrs Jephson, 30 July 1945.

[31] Thorpe, *Alec Douglas-Home*, 119; Mitchell, *Election '45*, 36; Lord Hill of Luton, *Both Sides of the Hill* (1964), 5.

[32] Butler papers, H62, Richard Magor (chairman, Chelmsford CA) to R. A. Butler, 9 Mar. 1945.

[33] Chelmsford CA papers, D/Z 96/3, executive committee 29 Mar. 1939; ways and means subcommittee 22 Feb. 1940, 11 Dec. 1939, 24, 25 Jan. 1941; D/Z 96/26, annual report, 1945.

[34] Derby papers, 920DER(17)/16/4, T. H. Hewlett to Derby, 15 Nov. 1940, 14 July 1941, 26 Feb. 1942; James Watts to Derby, 11 Jan. 1946.

[35] Birmingham UA papers, unclassified, minute books 1939–45, *passim* and officers' subcommittee 18 July 1945.

by January 1945.[36] In Newport, the association's finances had been the cause of 'much concern' before the war, but by January 1944, with a Reconstruction Fund that stood at £850 in 3 per cent Defence Bonds, such concerns were a vague memory.[37] Clitheroe CA (Lancashire) entered the war £54 in debt, but had moved into credit by May 1942, when subscriptions were 'coming in very satisfactorily', and the association eventually invested £370 in Defence Bonds in 1944, and raised an election fund of £800 in 1945.[38] Indeed, the myth of Conservative closure ignores the commitment that was shown by many ordinary Conservatives to ensuring that their associations continued to bring in at least some regular income: such efforts were, in turn, often driven by 'memories' of financial problems caused by inertia during the Great War.[39]

Cutting expenditure was usually the first step towards a better overall position. Associations that virtually ceased activity reaped financial benefits, because at least some money continued to come in, if only through uncancelled bankers' orders. North Cornwall CA closed down on 11 September 1939 with a deficit of £143, but reopened in June 1945 with a credit balance of £237.[40] In Denbigh (North Wales) the association's income fell significantly, but spending fell so dramatically (less than £3 was spent in 1944) that the net effects were positive (see Table 8.1). There, as elsewhere, the departure of agents and other employees was the major factor, because salaries and wages had often accounted for between 50 and 75 per cent of associations' pre-war expenditure. If an agent left early in 1939 or 1940, therefore, massive savings could be made, allowing both income to fall and profits to rise.[41] The need to make up the pay of agents who had gone into some form of national service initially diluted the financial benefits, but such subsidies became less onerous as their former agents' pay in their new positions rose.[42] Sharing agents also helped reduce outgoings (see Chapter 3). Without an agent, offices could be given up, which also meant savings could be made.[43] Of course, all this brought potential problems of inactivity, but, ideally, it left associations solvent and free to revive towards the end of the war.

On the income side, experiences varied. As seen above, many associations had been highly dependent upon contributions from MPs or candidates before the war, and money had remained a central consideration in candidate selection.

---

[36] East Norfolk CA papers, SO 92/1, joint executive committee 22 July 1939, 13 Jan. 1945.

[37] Newport CA records 1, annual report for 1937; 22, account book 1938–46, *passim*.

[38] Clitheroe CA papers, DDX 800/1/3, minute book 1939–45, *passim*.

[39] See e.g. Reigate CA papers, 353/3/1/2, annual report for 1945; York CA papers, 156/22, executive committee 14 Sept. 1939; Monmouth CA records 10, finance and general purposes committee 6 Sept. 1939.

[40] North Cornwall CA papers, DDX 381/5, executive committee 11 Sept. 1939, 2 June 1945; annual meeting 29 Mar. 1941.

[41] See e.g. City of London CA papers, Acc. 487/28, annual general meeting minute book 1900–45; Middleton and Prestwich CA papers, PLC 1/4, ledger 1934–57; Northampton CA papers, NCCA/29, secretary's reports, 1936–57.

[42] See e.g. Sheffield CA papers, LD 2104, finance committee 9 Mar. 1945.

[43] See e.g. Harborough CA papers, DE 1170/4, executive committee 12 July 1941.

Table 8.1. Denbigh CA: income and expenditure, 1938–1945

Year	Income (£)	Expenditure (£)	Overall credit (+)/debit (−)
1938	537	537	—
1939	590	567	+23
1940	146	155	−9
1941	101	33	+68
1942	165	11	+154
1943	231	39	+192
1944	247	3	+244
1945	518	330	+188

Source: Denbigh CA papers, DD/DM/80/6, finance and general purposes committee minute book 1928–48.

Although some associations were starting to take a new line by the late 1930s, there were limits, and even Central Office, which claimed to want more candidates of modest means, showed doubts in practice.[44] Roger Conant, elected as MP for Bewdley (Worcestershire) in 1937, spent £1,600 on election expenses and support for the CA in the two years to the outbreak of war in one of the safest Conservative seats in the country, and an academic study suggested in 1943 that most Conservative MPs and candidates before the war had been paying between £320 and £600 a year to their CAs, as well as subscriptions to other local bodies.[45] The selection process could certainly become something of a bidding war; this could irritate the wealthy and deter others from trying in the first place.[46] The outbreak of war tended to restrict candidates' financial contributions, for a number of reasons. One was sheer opportunism: there would never be a better chance to break the cycle of contributions, given plausible excuses about either financial hardship (arising from increased taxation or loss of income) or CA inactivity. In the period between 1940 and 1942, sheer remoteness of the next election was another factor. The MP for Altrincham (Cheshire), Sir Edward Grigg, cut his payment by half to £100 in early 1940, but then, due to his 'awful' financial position, cut it further, making a final payment of £50—which he described as 'blood from a stone'—that October.[47] Even a reduced subscription could still represent a significant amount of money: when Tree halved his annual contribution in Harborough the new figure, at £250, was still substantial.[48] But many simply stopped contributing, and

[44] Brooks, *Fleet Street*, 238, 16 Jan. 1939.
[45] Bewdley CA papers, BA 956/8, executive committee 9 June 1939; J. F. S. Ross, *Parliamentary Representation* (1943), 131–5.
[46] See e.g. Middleton and Prestwich CA papers, PLC 1/2, selection committee 19, 23, 27 June 1939; finance and general purposes committee 30 June 1939, 8 July 1943.
[47] Grigg papers, Bodleian Library film 1005, reel 7, Sir E. Grigg to Mrs D. O'Neill, 29 Mar., 29 June, 14 Oct. 1940.
[48] Harborough CA papers, DE 1170/4, special executive committee 23 Sept. 1939.

although some associations showed understanding, an amicable outcome was far from inevitable.[49] In Fylde (Lancashire), news that the MP planned to reduce his subscription for the duration was 'not favourably received'. He was reminded of his promise when adopted to contribute £200 a year, and told 'that he would be expected to honour this pledge'.[50] Some MPs who initially cut their contributions restored them as party politics intensified after 1942 and the end of the war approached, as was the case in Swindon (Wiltshire) and Henley (Oxfordshire).[51] And some MPs and candidates continued paying up regardless. The wartime strength of Maidstone CA (Kent) was due partly to the continuing generosity of its MP, Alfred Bossom, who contributed £300 annually throughout the conflict, while in York, Lord Irwin's annual contributions remained at their pre-war £100.[52] Other large benefactors varied similarly.[53]

Subscriptions more generally did not dry up completely. A few associations did decide explicitly not to collect in wartime.[54] But this was contrary to advice of Central Office as eventually determined, and in fact most associations did approach their subscribers, and expected to receive a positive response.[55] Ramsden is correct to say that there was some coyness about such approaches, especially early in the war, but initial reserve often gave way to something bolder.[56] Stafford CA was rather tentative and doubtful when it decided to seek the renewal of subscriptions in November 1939; by late 1941 it was chasing defaulters for payment.[57] Also in 1941, West Dorset CA forced out its MP, Sir Philip Colfox, precisely on the grounds that he was an obstacle to the collection of subscriptions (and was proved right when money came in rapidly once he had gone).[58] Many, and in some places most, subscribers continued to pay, where they were asked to do so. In the spring of 1940, the Northern area council found that 'where an

Clapham CA papers, BLPES film 548, finance committee 26 June 1941; Stafford CA papers, D1289/1/3, finance committee 2 Nov. 1939.

[50] Fylde CA papers, DDX 1202/1/1, emergency committee 2 Oct. 1940.

[51] Swindon CA papers, 2509/9, account book 1936–68; South Oxon CA papers, I/3, Henley CA finance and general purposes committee 4 May 1944.

[52] Maidstone CA papers, U1634/A3/2/2, subscriptions register 1943–5; York CA papers, Acc. 156/50–1, subscription books 1937–46.

[53] For cuts, see e.g. Merioneth CA papers, Z/M/4018/2, executive committee 14 Feb. 1944; Derby papers, 920DER(17)/16/4, G. Beattie (Manchester) to Derby, 15 Jan. 1940, 13 Jan. 1941; for generosity, see e.g. Beaverbrook papers, BBK/D/423, Beaverbrook to Churchill, 26 Apr. 1945.

[54] Sheffield CA papers, LD 2109, City of Sheffield Conservative women's advisory committee, emergency committee 13 Sept. 1939.

[55] See e.g. Central Office 500/1/9, Hacking to CA officers, 12 Sept. 1939; Chamberlain papers, NC 4/4/1, Chamberlain, speech at NUEC meeting, 27 June 1940; NUA 4/2, card 149, NUEC report to NUCC, 27 Mar. 1941; NUA 4/1, card 65, NUEC 27 July 1944.

[56] Northwich CA papers, LOP 1/11/5, J. L. S. Steel to Mr Poole, 2 Apr. 1940.

[57] Stafford CA papers, D1289/1/3, finance committee 2 Nov. 1939, 23 June, 2 Dec. 1941.

[58] West Dorset CA papers, D399/3/1, war emergency executive committee 27 Sept. 1940, 10 Jan. 1941, D399/4/1, finance committee 23 Apr. 1941, 25 Apr. 1942, 15 May 1943; D399/3/2, war emergency executive committee 12 Dec. 1941.

approach has been made [by associations] to subscribers, support has generally been forthcoming'; Winchester CA (Hampshire) found that annual subscriptions 'had come in well'; and subscriptions to Lambeth Norwood CA (London) had come in 'better than anticipated'.[59] Naturally, the worst of the air raids in the winter of 1940–1 brought some disruption, and 1941 was an especially lean year.[60] By early 1942, however, things were changing for some associations. Maidstone reported a 'most satisfactory response' to its appeal for subscriptions that January, while in April Henley CA found that its subscriptions had been coming in 'excellently'.[61] Some associations became more aggressive: in July 1943, Bradford city CA launched a book scheme for collecting, which within eighteen months had produced £1,500 in new subscriptions.[62] In April 1944, the treasurer of Salisbury CA (Wiltshire), which also used the book scheme, could report that the subscription list had increased by £500 over the past year, adding—ironically, in view of customary interpretations of the Conservative party at war—that '[h]ard cash in the future may not be so plentiful nor so easy to collect'.[63] Overall, subscription income, having fallen in the early part of the war, expanded from about 1942 onwards in a large number of constituencies. This offered a clear basis for a scheme of party finance based on small subscriptions to be developed after the war.

In peacetime, Conservative women had been significant fund-raisers. Wartime saw them otherwise engaged, to some extent (see Chapter 5). But, in many places, support continued.[64] And even where the money they were raising was going to other causes, like war charities, the fact that they were still fund-raising meant that they continued to hone their skills, ready for the time when they would be raising money for the party once more. It was, in one sense, a loss to Conservatism that the £694 raised by Newcastle West women's branch during the war went to charities and not the party. But it did demonstrate what a valuable weapon the party would have once peace returned.[65] Social activities also raised money. In London, for example, Norwood CA's annual report for 1940–1 stated that a whist drive and bring and buy tea had produced 'a substantial profit', and subsequent events were also successful, a 1944 Christmas Draw clearing £567.[66]

[59] Northern area Conservative council papers, NRO 3303/2, council annual report for 1940, 3 May 1941; Winchester CA papers, 73M86W/5, special general meeting 27 Apr. 1940; Norwood CA papers, IV/166/1/16, emergency committee 15 Aug. 1940.
[60] See e.g. Leek CA papers, D1358/A/1/1/1, subscription book 1914–45.
[61] Maidstone CA papers, U1634/A3/1/2, emergency subcommittee 28 May 1941, 9 Jan. 1942; South Oxon CA papers, I/3, Henley CA finance and general purposes committee 13 Apr. 1944.
[62] *Conservative Agents' Journal*, Jan. 1945.
[63] Salisbury CA papers, 2639/13, annual general meeting 22 Apr. 1944.
[64] See e.g. Barkston Ash CA papers, WYL 629/6, finance and general purposes committee 5 Apr. 1941; West Dorset CA papers, D399/6/1, Bridport women's branch CA, committee meeting 7 Apr. 1941, 2 Feb. 1942, 3 May 1943, 28 Feb. 1944, 26 Feb. 1945.
[65] Newcastle West CA papers, Acc. 1579/8, women's branch annual meeting 23 Mar. 1945.
[66] Norwood CA papers, IV/166/1/16, annual report 1940–1, emergency committee 20 Nov. 1942, 11 Dec. 1944.

A few CAs benefited from central or area subsidies in the war years, but they were very much the minority. They tended to be confined to marginal seats like Oxford and Swindon, and the amounts involved were small.[67] In Glasgow, selected constituency associations continued, as before the war, to benefit from small subsidies of up to £40 a year, distributed by the city association out of funds provided by the major Unionist clubs in the city.[68] In the Eastern area, meanwhile, bulk copies of the *Onlooker* were sent to selected constituency associations at the area's expense.[69]

Finally, the specific conditions of wartime brought a few novel ways to make money. Some associations were able to rent out all or part of their premises to the military and civil authorities, or to private firms. The War Office paid Salisbury CA £250 a year, and Newbury (Berkshire) and West Dorset £100 each, for the rent of their halls; Northwich (Cheshire) rented its offices to the Employment Exchange for £141 a year; and Ealing rented three of its rooms to the Ministry of Works for £80.[70] Henley CA rented two rooms to a private firm for £75 a year.[71] This was all useful income, but it could backfire if, as the end of the war approached, tenants proved difficult to move despite the imminent return of electoral politics.

From mid-1944 onwards, Conservative associations were increasingly looking to revive their activities. Agents, refurbishment, and, in some cases, new premises all cost money.[72] With Central Office encouragement, associations began to organize fighting funds to meet these costs.[73] Such funds were often successful. In southern England, Clapham raised £500 between February and June 1945, and Newbury and Gravesend (Kent) £688 and £305 respectively between May and July; while, further north, Harborough raised £1,164 in the three months prior to the election, Wansbeck (Northumberland) raised enough to meet heavy election expenses of £1,262 and still have a small surplus as the basis for a new election fund, and Merioneth (North Wales), despite having little wartime activity to its name, raised almost £900.[74] In other cases, however, wartime

[67] ARE 10/1/3, Wessex area Conservative council, finance and general purposes committee 28 Feb., 15 Nov. 1940, 28 Feb., 26 Nov. 1941, 24 Nov. 1943.

[68] Glasgow Unionist Association papers, 11368/11, joint executive committee minute book 1939–46, *passim.*

[69] ARE 7/1/8, Eastern area of the Conservative party, finance committee 14 Mar., 12 Nov. 1940.

[70] Salisbury CA papers, 2639/1, annual general meeting 27 Apr. 1940; Newbury CA papers, D/EX 409/20, finance and general purposes committee 9 June 1942; West Dorset CA papers, D399/3/2, finance committee 25 Apr. 1942; Northwich CA papers, LOP 1/1/4, executive committee 2 Apr. 1941; Ealing CA papers, Acc. 1338/2, executive committee 20 July 1942.

[71] South Oxon CA papers, I/3, Henley CA finance and general purposes committee 7 Oct. 1940.

[72] See e.g. Harborough CA papers, DE 1170/4, executive committee 25 Jan., 9 June 1945; Tynemouth CA papers, Acc. 1633/6/1, finance committee 26 Jan. 1945.

[73] Norwood CA papers, IV/166/1/16, executive committee 6 Apr. 1945.

[74] Clapham CA papers, BLPES film 548, finance and executive committee 13 June 1945; Newbury CA papers, D/EX 409/20, finance and general purposes committee 27 Nov. 1945; Gravesend CA papers, U1795/AD1/4, executive committee 1 June, 31 Aug. 1945; Harborough

inactivity could not be rectified rapidly: North Cornwall CA entered the 1945 campaign with no election fund, and emerged from it defeated and £350 in debt to its candidate.[75]

Fighting funds were, in any case, only an emergency response; and there was a widespread, although as yet far from unanimous, view that aspects of CA funding would have to change once peace returned. The first proposition, on which there was near-universal agreement, was that more money would be needed, given that prices and wages had risen, and that Labour was now better funded (see below). There was much talk of the need for a minimum annual income of between £1,000 and £1,500.[76] The traditional way of raising these amounts would have been to seek more from the MPs, candidates, and wealthy benefactors, but high taxation would have inhibited such an approach even if the desire to democratize the party had not.[77] Working-class, and many middle-class, people, as well as the young, would be ruled out if candidatures were closely tied to funding; and, in the context of a war fought 'for democracy', such practices were still further discredited.

Topping had been keen on reform even before the war, and the establishment of the standing advisory committee on candidates (SACC) in 1935 had been intended to regulate candidates' contributions.[78] In 1941, the National Union formally denounced the purchase of candidatures, while the 1922 Committee also took an interest in the matter, and from 1942 onwards SACC became increasingly interventionist.[79] The Proby report proposed that candidates and MPs should be allowed to contribute no more than £100 a year and half their election expenses, because candidates should be selected 'on merit and merit alone, without regard to their bank balances', and some associations were coming to the same conclusions by 1945.[80] In the run-up to the election, SACC applied Proby's maximum limits and refused to approve new candidates who were proposing to pay more, although it had no control over MPs and

CA papers, DE 1170/4, executive committee 20 Oct. 1945; Wansbeck CA papers, Acc. 1633/35, executive committee 13 Sept. 1945; Conservative party Wales records 2, Wales and Monmouthshire Conservative and Unionist Council, finance and general purposes committee 18 Dec. 1945.

[75] North Cornwall CA papers, DDX 381/5, executive committee 15 Sept. 1945.

[76] See e.g. York CA papers, 156/22, annual general meeting 23 Mar. 1945; Chichester CA papers, CO/1CH Add. MS 12089, executive committee 14 May 1945.

[77] I. Harvey, memo, 'A plutocratic system: facts regarding the selection and adoption of candidates for parliament in the Conservative interest', 1 Jan. 1939, reprinted in Ross, *Parliamentary Representation*, 236–8.

[78] Chamberlain papers, NC 8/21/18, London organization committee, 'Summary of report', n.d. [15 June 1938]; CO 4/1/86, Topping to Hacking, 14 Nov. 1939; Criddle, 'Members of Parliament', 151–3.

[79] Criddle, 'Members of Parliament', 153; CPA 1922/4, 1922 Committee meeting 21 May 1941.

[80] Beaverbrook papers, BBK/D/422, special finance committee, 'Report', 16 Mar. 1944; and see e.g. Salisbury CA papers, 2639/1, annual general meeting 14 Apr. 1945; Williams, *Politics Grave and Gay*, 129.

candidates already selected.[81] This process culminated after the war in the Maxwell-Fyfe reforms, whereby all election expenses had to be paid by the association, annual payments were limited to a maximum of £50 for MPs and £25 for candidates, and pre-selection questions about money were prohibited.[82] The second aspect of funding reform, as stated above, was an increased emphasis on small subscriptions, as the wartime resilience of CAs' lists of small subscribers convinced many doubters that book systems and the like had a future. It was the rapid expansion of such schemes between 1944 and 1947 that would pave the way for the introduction of compulsory CA quota payments to Central Office.

The financial side of the Conservative party at war was rather more complicated than has sometimes been suggested. The position was neither so strong in 1939, nor so dire in 1945, as conventional wisdom has had it. During the war, constituency association treasurers in their dozens had pronounced their part of the party's finances to be at least 'satisfactory', and this meant that the party remained in a potentially strong position from which to face the post-war world. However, the shock of an unprecedentedly well-financed Labour party scoring an unprecedented electoral success in 1945 changed perceptions, and led to the development of a false memory of wartime impoverishment. Although the reality was somewhat different, the perception was a significant feature in uniting the party after the 1945 defeat, and in pushing it towards reform later in the decade. That reform was largely prefigured by wartime developments, but 1945 was nonetheless significant in removing, or at least disabling, most of the remaining opposition to change.

LABOUR

The Labour party had been underfunded throughout the inter-war period. The expansive plans that had accompanied financial good fortune in 1917–19 had been hampered by the end of the post-war boom in 1920, persistently high levels of unemployment (which dampened trade union membership), the effects of the 1927 Trade Disputes Act, and the failure to develop mass individual membership. At every inter-war general election, the average Labour candidate was able to spend less, not just than the average Conservative, but also than the average Liberal. Labour remained vulnerable to periodic financial crises. In early 1939 a predicted deficit of £7,000 was seen as 'extremely serious', and the financial outlook remained very gloomy, not least because the party conference seemed unlikely to accept increased affiliation fees, which seemed to be the only

[81] Butler papers, RAB H62, standing joint advisory committee on candidates: agenda, 10 May 1945.
[82] NUA 6/2/6, 'Interim report of the committee on party organization', 28 July 1948.

Table 8.2. Labour party, receipts and payments, 1939–1945 (£)

Year	Balance b/f	In-year recpts	Total	Expenditure	Balance c/f
1939	−6,046	76,677	70,631	66,683	3,948
1940	3,948	56,313	60,261	53,749	6,512
1941	6,512	63,900	70,412	50,574	19,838
1942	19,838	63,192	83,030	59,401	23,629
1943	23,629	65,646	89,275	64,741	24,534
1944	24,534	104,561	129,095	64,145	64,950
1945[a]	64,950	190,149	255,099	114,927	140,173

[a] Figures include general election fund of £90,969 (in-year receipts), £40,615 (expenditure), and £84,954 (balance c/f).

Source: LPNEC XXI, memorandum, 'The Labour party: statement of receipts and payments for years 1939 to 1943', finance and general purposes committee, 17 Feb. 1944; *LPACR 1939*, 126–9; *LPACR 1945*, 22–5; *LPACR 1946*, 40–3.

way out of the crisis; swingeing cuts—including the slashing of the agricultural campaign planned for that summer—followed.[83] By July 1942, however, the party was to have £20,000—equivalent to about five months' income before the war—invested in 3 per cent Savings Bonds, and the following March, the NEC would be pronouncing that 'the financial position of Constituency Parties [was] generally much better than in Peace [*sic*] time', while a senior Labour figure would be reassuring the national agent that Labour could afford to launch a strong campaign against Communist affiliation because '[t]he Party funds are no longer an anxiety'.[84] By May 1945, indeed, Transport House would be sitting on a substantial surplus and building up a formidable fighting fund for the general election (see Table 8.2).

This remarkable transformation began immediately war broke out. As in 1931, crisis loosened union purse-strings: party officials' pleas regarding Labour's 'precarious' finances were met with donations of £6,750, and some unions paid their 1940 affiliation fees in advance, while the May 1940 party conference finally agreed to increase affiliation fees by 11 per cent from $4\frac{1}{2}d$. to $5d$. per member.[85] Union–party financial relations remained positive, affiliated membership remained steady and then rose, and growing numbers of union

[83] Labour party NEC papers, box XVII, anon. memo, 'The Labour party: financial position of the party', 18 May 1939, finance and general purposes committee, 20 Apr. 1939; C. V. G. Griffiths, *Labour and the Countryside: The Politics of Rural Britain 1918–1939* (Oxford, 2007), 124.

[84] LPNEC XX, finance and general purposes committee, 16 July 1942, organization subcommittee, 3 Mar. 1943; Attlee papers, MS Attlee dep. 7, fos. 198–200, George Ridley to G. R. Shepherd, 10 Mar. 1943.

[85] LPNEC XVIII, finance and general purposes committee, 26 Sept., 16 Nov. 1939; NEC 20 Dec. 1939, 20 Mar., 22 May 1940; MFGB papers, MNA/NUM/1/1/37, fo. 379, executive committee 14 Sept. 1939; *LPACR 1940*, 155.

branches affiliated to DLPs (see Chapter 4). Many unions also continued to sponsor parliamentary candidatures (126 candidates would be sponsored by 23 different unions in 1945).[86] A further boost came when the June 1943 party conference accepted Preston TLC's resolution demanding improvements in the party's financial position and management: a series of positive meetings between party officials and union leaders followed.[87] One outcome was a strong response to the election fund appeal launched early in 1944: the MFGB promised £20,000, and the fund raised £56,000 in its first four months and £101,181 in its first year.[88] A DLP quota scheme requiring parties to pay between £10 and £50 according to their strength was expected to raise a further £10,000 to £12,000, and there were also plans for further approaches to unions and individuals.[89] The appeal raised just about double the highest previous yield from an election appeal (£49,200 in 1929); the most recent (in 1935) had raised only £21,800.[90] Repeal of the 1927 Act would have made matters still better, but despite cross-party talks in 1943, no progress was made on this question, largely because of Conservative resistance from Churchill downwards.[91] This left it to the post-war Labour government to repeal the legislation (in 1946), but the Coalition's failure to act helped Labour by reminding the unions—which were bitterly hostile towards the 1927 Act—of the merits of a purely Labour government.

Some Labourites, like Barbara Betts (later Castle), criticized the party's reliance on union money, not least because it entrenched union power at conference through the bloc vote system.[92] But there was no viable alternative. Individual membership, even by 1945, was nowhere near sufficient to fund the party by itself. Labour had dabbled in other areas, such as business funding, but they were neither very lucrative nor politically acceptable to the mass of party members.[93] Trade in honours, an avenue which appears to have interested Middleton, was rendered impossible by Attlee's decision not to make any such awards other than privy counsellorships and 'such peerages as are required for the efficient working of the Upper House'.[94] Headquarters did try to tap wealthy individuals, but such contributions as came in were not sufficient to threaten the primacy of

---

[86] Cole, *History of the Labour Party*, 441.

[87] *LPACR 1943*, 134–5; LPNEC XX, memo, 'The Labour party', 6 Oct. 1943; special conference of trade union officers, 12 Nov. 1943.

[88] LPNEC XXI, NEC 22 Mar. 1944; joint meeting of trade union representatives and the finance and general purposes committee, 28 Apr. 1944; finance and general purposes committee, 10 Aug. 1944; joint meeting of trade union officers and NEC finance committee, 6 Mar. 1945.

[89] Phillips papers, GS/45AP/1, draft letter, 'The Labour party: fighting fund', n.d. [Mar. 1945]; LPNEC XXI, joint meeting of trade union officers and NEC finance committee, 6 Mar. 1945.

[90] McHenry, *Labour Party in Transition*, 50–1.   [91] LPNEC XX, NEC 23 June 1943.

[92] LPNEC XXI, NEC 26 Apr. 1944; Phillips papers, GS/1945/3, Willesden BLPTC, 'Memorandum on party reorganization', 30 Jan. 1945.

[93] The best available estimate suggests that in the period 1932–7, out of an estimated average global income at all levels of the party of £330,000 a year, industry and miscellaneous sources together contributed no more than £5,000: see McHenry, *Labour Party in Transition*, 54.

[94] Attlee papers, MS Attlee dep. 4, fo. 85, Attlee to Middleton, 21 Nov. 1941.

Table 8.3. Labour party, by-election fund, 1939–1945 (£)

Year	Income	Expenditure	Surplus for year	Assets
1939	5,137	4,484	653	653
1940	4,964	2,120	2,844	3,497
1941	5,637	1,170	4,467	7,964
1942	5,622	957	4,665	12,629
1943	5,680	543	5,137	17,766
1944	6,355	1,242	5,113	23,058
1945	6,222	3,297	2,925	25,401

Source: LPNEC XXI, memorandum, 'The Labour party: statement of receipts and payments for years 1939 to 1943', presented to finance and general purposes committee, 17 Feb. 1944; *LPACR 1945*, 22–3; *LPACR 1946*, 40–1.

union funding, and would have come in for severe criticism had they done so.[95] The party's By-Election Insurance Fund was a notable source of profit, though. Set up in 1932 to cover by-election candidates' costs, it comprised compulsory flat-rate payments from all DLPs, as well as payments from unions according to size.[96] Transport House insisted that DLPs and unions continued to pay into the fund throughout the war, even though expenditure from it was severely curtailed because of the electoral truce.[97] This meant that the fund, which had generally broken even before the war, became little more than a high-yielding levy on DLPs and unions, and its assets rose from virtually zero in 1939 to £23,000 in 1944 (see Table 8.3). It seems improbable that this was not a consideration in Labour managers' firm ongoing commitment to the truce.

This new-found prosperity allowed the party to move in new directions. First, large amounts were spent on major campaigns, such as those supporting the Beveridge report or opposing Communist affiliation.[98] Secondly, new staff were employed; leading office holders like Phillips and Young were paid significantly more than their predecessors; and money was spent forcing ineffectual staff to retire early, as in the case of the head of the International Department, William Gillies.[99] Finally, Labour was also able to develop its regional organization, to

[95] See LPNEC XVII, 'Report of the sub-committee appointed to investigate ways and means of increasing and stabilising normal party income', May 1938; finance and general purposes committee, 18 May 1939, memo, 'The Labour party: financial position of the party', Mar. 1939; XX, finance and general purposes committee, 8 Nov. 1943; XXI, organization subcommittee, 21 Feb. 1945; London LP papers, Acc. 2417/A/3, executive committee, 27 Nov. 1941; Phillips papers, GS/45AP/1–42, e.g. H. Wickham to Morgan Phillips, 20 Mar 1945.

[96] McHenry, *Labour Party in Transition*, 52.

[97] LPNEC XIX, finance and general purposes committee, 22 May, 20 Feb. 1941.

[98] LPNEC XXI, memo, 'The Labour party', to finance and general purposes committee, 17 Feb. 1944.

[99] LPNEC XIX, executive committee of NEC, 12 Mar. 1941; policy committee, 29 May 1941; XX, NEC 24 Nov. 1943; XXI, policy committee, 23 Jan. 1945; Dalton, *Second World War Diary*, 497, 673, 845, 25 Sept. 1942, 17 Nov. 1943, 28 Mar. 1945.

supersede the ineffectual county federations. The first such body, the South
Wales regional council of Labour (RCL), had been established in 1937, largely as
an anti-Communist measure, and a Lancashire and Cheshire RCL had followed
in 1938.[100] Financial constraints prevented further pre-war progress, but by
1941 those constraints were easing; two new regional councils (Northern and
Yorkshire) were established early in 1942, to be followed that December by two
more (East Midlands and West Midlands).[101] This gave Labour six regional
councils as well as the Scottish and London party organizations, and it was
planned to extend the scheme to the rest of the country. The annual cost of
the RCLs, once they were all in position, was expected to be £22,080; this was
almost half of headquarters' total expenditure in the 1930s, and a significant
increase on the £13,113 spent on regional organization in 1942.[102] No more
councils were formed before the end of the war, but this was not due primarily
to financial considerations: the remaining regions—East Anglia, the south-east,
and the south-west—were all still very much affected by war conditions, and
so best left until peacetime.[103] Even so, the wartime expansion of Labour's
regional organization was ambitious and impressive, and its achievement due
directly to the new possibilities that were opened up by the war's impact on party
finances.

Labour's national finances had never been healthier than they were in 1945.
The same was true, on the whole, at local level. The overwhelming majority of
DLPs whose records have been consulted showed a significant improvement in
their financial position over the war period, largely irrespective of geographical
location. In London, Bethnal Green North-East DLP moved from a small surplus
of £23 for 1938–9 to one of £200 for 1945; Woolwich BLP (which covered
two constituencies) built on an already strong position in 1939 to reach a credit
balance of almost £1,000 by 1945.[104] Relatively safe Labour seats in the north,
like Wansbeck (Northumberland) or Sheffield Attercliffe, saw very significant
increases in their balances, to around £1,000 in each case by the end of the war.[105]
In Derbyshire, Belper DLP moved from a very modest pre-war credit balance
to a surplus of £402 by 1945, while in nearby Nottinghamshire, Mansfield

[100] K. O. Morgan, *Rebirth of a Nation: Wales, 1880–1980* (Oxford, 1981), 297; C. Prothero,
Recount (Ormskirk, 1982), 40.

[101] D. J. Wilson, *Power and Party Bureaucracy in Britain: Regional Organization in the Conservative
and Labour Parties* (Farnborough, 1975), 35–6; LPNEC XIX, finance and general purposes
committee, 17 July 1941; XX, G. R. Shepherd, memo, 'Regional organization', 11 July 1942.

[102] LPNEC XX, national agent's department, memo, 'Extension of regional councils', 15 Nov.
1943.

[103] See e.g. ibid., XIX, finance and general purposes committee, 19 Mar., 16 Apr. 1942; XX,
finance and general purposes committee, 16 Dec. 1943. The Southern and Eastern RCLs were
ultimately established in 1947, and the South-West RCL in May 1948.

[104] Bethnal Green North-East DLP papers, TH/8488/16, minute book 1938–46, *passim*;
Woolwich BLP papers, WLP 40.3, annual reports, 1938–45, *passim*.

[105] Wansbeck DLP papers, NRO 527/A/3, minute book 1935–50, *passim*; Hynd papers, HYND
2/4, Sheffield Attercliffe DLP, annual report, 1944.

DLP turned a £2 surplus in 1940 into one of £102 in 1944.[106] In southern England, Epsom (Surrey) moved from an £85 credit balance in 1939 to one of £393 in 1944, while Southampton DLP, already prosperous in 1939, boomed to such an extent that by 1945 it was able to spend £3,000 on the purchase of a new Labour hall which included two flats and two lock-up shops.[107] At the outbreak of war, the party in Wrexham (North-East Wales) was in debt, but, by March 1943, its treasurer was able to report that 'the financial position was far better than at any period he could remember', while even Roxburgh and Selkirk DLP, a weak party in the Scottish borders, was able to run a profit and build up an election fund which stood at £720 by 1945.[108] The retention of an agent—as in Colne Valley—could eat into funds and prevent such a dramatic transformation, but it was a sign of financial health that when the NEC declared an agents' war bonus of £39 per annum in 1942, it was accepted by DLPs with scarcely a murmur.[109] A few parties did struggle. The DLP in the safe seat of Sheffield Brightside had to rely on a headquarters subsidy to fight the 1945 election, while Birmingham Deritend was able to spend less on its campaign then than it had ten years earlier.[110] But these were exceptions to a generally rosy picture.

Such an outcome had appeared unlikely in September 1939. Then, there was gloom in Gloucester, where a 'serious' deficit was now unlikely to be alleviated by fund-raising social events; it was not alone, and some DLPs began to appeal to headquarters for help, although the NEC was resolute in demanding that parties support themselves.[111] However, as the government allowed cinemas and other places of entertainment to reopen, it became clear that social events could also go ahead, and Gloucester had soon reinstated its whist drives and football competition, so that by the end of October revenue 'of fairly large proportions' was coming in.[112] But collecting remained difficult, and fund-raising in general was affected by longer working hours and the invasion scare that followed the intensification of the war in May 1940.[113] Air raids inhibited activity generally,

---

[106] Belper DLP papers, D 2064/3/6–9, annual reports, 1939–46, *passim*; LP East Midlands Regional Organizer papers, DD/PP/14/7/5, C. Davey, circular, 3 May 1944.

[107] Southampton DLP papers, D/LAB/Box 2, executive committee 9 June 1945; Box 3, account book, 1930–51.

[108] Wrexham TCLP papers, annual meeting, 10 Mar. 1943; Roxburgh and Selkirk DLP papers, Acc. 4145/1, annual general meetings 21 Jan., 4 Feb. 1945; party meeting 19 Aug. 1945.

[109] Colne Valley DLP papers, BLPES film 211, reel 5, annual reports, 1937–47, *passim*; Newport DLP papers, MNB/POL/6/A/8, executive committee, 1 June 1942.

[110] Sheffield Brightside DLP papers, LP(B)8, executive committee, 16 May, 18 July 1945; *Returns of Election Expenses*, 1935 and 1945.

[111] Gloucester TLC papers, D3128/5/6, executive committee 31 Aug. 1939; LPNEC XVIII, finance and general purposes committee, 14 Dec. 1939, 22 Feb., 11 July 1940.

[112] Gloucester TLC papers, D3128/5/6, special party meeting 4 Sept. 1939; special finance subcommittee 26 Oct. 1939.

[113] See e.g. *Labour Organiser*, 'Blitz 1940, second issue' [Nov. or Dec. 1940]; South-West Norfolk DLP papers, 2001/145/1, executive committee, 20 July 1940.

but also had a very direct impact on some DLPs. Bermondsey West DLP was bombed out in late 1940.[114] Its requests for financial help from other DLPs met a mixed response; DLPs which refused to help often demanded that Transport House should do something, and it was a similar story when Birmingham Yardley DLP suffered the loss of its premises through enemy action in early 1941.[115] In response, headquarters decided to use the By-Election Insurance Fund to pay moderate grants of up to £40 to parties affected by raids.[116] This was never going to be enough to rebuild blitzed premises, of course, but it would cover some immediate and urgent costs. The larger expenses were ultimately to be covered by state action, with the inclusion of party premises in the compensation scheme.[117] So far as the NEC was concerned, all this had one further, and very useful, aspect: they could argue that all DLPs should continue to pay into the By-Election Fund, even though it was spending little on by-elections, because the money was needed to help blitzed DLPs. But not all parties were content to rely on handouts. When their joint premises were destroyed in 1941, Fulham East and West DLPs set up a huge prize draw, and invited other DLPs to participate, the proceeds being split half and half between Fulham and the participating DLP. The scheme was a great success, running for a number of years thereafter.[118]

It was in 1943 that most DLPs' finances began to improve significantly. While expenditure remained quite flat, income began to expand. Collecting, and with it individual membership, increased. Many parties found that hitherto-unaffiliated union branches now wanted to join them, and social activities became more feasible. This financial outlook allowed DLPs to start planning for the post-war general election. Some DLPs already had election funds, but many others—as at Birmingham and Southampton—were brought into being by the sharpening of politics in early 1943.[119] A steady succession of parties followed thereafter.[120] Parties' financial efforts were increasingly centred on such funds in the months leading up to the end of the war, and still more so in the period between VE Day and polling day. The only serious disruption to

---

[114] F. Brockway, *Bermondsey Story: The Life of Alfred Salter* (1949), 228.

[115] For Bermondsey, see e.g. Darlington DLP papers, D/X 922/5, executive committee 26 Nov. 1940; Bristol East DLP papers, 39035/19, general committee, 24 Nov. 1940; for Yardley, see e.g. Walsall DLP papers, Acc. 50/4, executive committee 13 May 1941; Clapham DLP papers, IV/156/2/2, general management committee 30 Mar. 1941.

[116] LPNEC XVII, finance and general purposes committee, 20 Feb. 1941.

[117] Coventry DLP papers, MSS 11/1/4, divisional meeting 9 Nov. 1941.

[118] See e.g. Hendon DLP papers, BLPES Film 211A reel 97559/1, executive committee 2 July 1941.

[119] See e.g. Norfolk South-West DLP papers, Acc. 2001/145/1, annual meeting 6 Apr. 1940; Bedford DLP papers, X494/2, annual meeting 14 Mar. 1939, annual meeting 23 Mar. 1943; Birmingham BLP papers, unclassified, annual meetings 14 Mar. 1943, 8 Mar. 1944; Southampton DLP papers, D/LAB/Box 2, executive committee 12 Mar. 1943.

[120] See e.g. Sorensen papers, SOR 194, Leyton West DLP, *Labour News*, 42, Oct. 1943; Wansbeck DLP papers, NRO 527/A/3, executive committee, 13 May 1944.

the upsurge in fund-raising activity came in the summer of 1944, with the start of the V-weapon attacks, which particularly affected London and the south-east.[121]

Overall, then, the financial position of most DLPs was unprecedentedly strong by early 1945. The reasons for this were numerous. First, as with the Conservatives, war meant lower expenditure. The departure of an agent was significant for some parties: Belper DLP was paying £220 in wages and salaries in 1938, but only £30 by 1943.[122] The lack of elections, and fewer public meetings, meant lower costs, although they also inhibited fund-raising. Subletting of premises reduced rental outlay: Bristol East DLP rented its headquarters to the ARP for £200 a year, while in nearby Frome (Somerset), the military authorities' requisitioning of a room in the DLP offices brought in enough rent to allow the party to pay the rent on the remainder of the building, rather than seeking alternative, inferior, accommodation.[123] (Of course, things could work the other way: Darlington DLP struggled to pay the rent because it was harder to rent out their hall to outside bodies for social events in wartime, and neither the military nor the civil defence authorities were interested in taking it over.[124]) The amount spent on motoring also diminished for those DLPs that had owned a car in 1939. In Wansbeck (Northumberland) the agent's van and loudspeaker equipment were rented to the Ministry of Information.[125]

Reduced expenditure was only part of the story, however. Many parties maintained existing income streams and even developed new ones. The first of these was individual membership. Most members who did not move to a different area, and on whom collectors called, continued to pay their subscriptions (see Chapter 4). Even where individual membership fell significantly, it was often not financially disastrous, because such payments did not make up the bulk of the income of most DLPs. In 1938, only 8.5 per cent of Derby DLP's income had come from this source; this was, admittedly, unusually low, but the 1939 figure for Ipswich (22 per cent) was fairly typical.[126] Trade unions also played an important role. The minority of DLPs that had a union-sponsored candidate were fortunate, although payments varied: the NUGMW, for example, was lavish in its payments, funding Cleveland DLP to the tune of £200 a year, whereas the

[121] See e.g. Woolwich BLP Papers, WLP 40.3, annual report 1944 (to annual meeting 7 Apr. 1945).

[122] Belper DLP papers, D2064/3/6–9, annual reports, 1938–46.

[123] Bristol East DLP papers, 39035/19, general committee 26 Apr., 28 June 1939; Frome DLP papers, A/AAW 28, executive committee 14 June 1941.

[124] Darlington DLP papers, D/X 922/5, general committee 28 Dec. 1941, special executive committee 14 Jan. 1942.

[125] Wansbeck DLP papers, NRO 527/C/5, M. Rowntree (Ministry of Information) to D. Dawson (agent), 20 Mar. 1941.

[126] Derby DLP papers, Box 3, 18(a), annual report 1938; Ipswich TCLP papers, GK 400/1/1/3, executive committee minute book 1936–42, *passim*.

Lanark Miners' Union only paid Hamilton DLP £45.[127] Other DLPs received small ad hoc grants, while shortly before the 1945 election, the South Wales region of the National Union of Mineworkers granted £1,000 to help non-mining constituencies in the area.[128] The war period also saw an increase in trade union affiliations at the local level (see Chapter 4). By 1941, for example, affiliation fee income to Faversham DLP (Kent) was the highest since the party's formation.[129] The Co-operative movement also made important contributions. The Royal Arsenal Co-operative Society (RACS) paid annual affiliation fees of around £600, plus organization grants, to Woolwich BLP throughout the war; in broad terms it was contributing about a third of the income of a party responsible for two important constituencies.[130] The RACS was providing a quarter of Lewisham West DLP's income by 1941.[131] Some provincial parties, like Derby, benefited from Co-operative party affiliation, while 34 Labour and Co-operative candidates were funded by the Co-operative party at the 1945 general election, 23 of them being elected.[132]

In some constituencies, personal contributions from the MP or candidate remained significant. The 1933 Hastings Agreement had limited such contributions (and those of the unions) to a maximum of £150 in a borough constituency or £200 in a county seat, and no more than 80 per cent of the legal maximum of election expenses, but this still left considerable scope for wealthy candidates.[133] George Strauss gave his DLP at Lambeth North £180 a year, paid the rates on the party's premises, and, when they decided to liquidate their long-standing debt in 1942, he promised to match anything they raised pound for pound.[134] Noel-Baker paid his DLP at Derby £100 annually throughout the war; Lady Noel-Buxton, the prospective candidate for Norwich, paid hers £150 a year, and others gave more modest, but still significant, amounts.[135] Some well-off MPs

[127] Cleveland DLP papers, U/CDLP 1/5, balance sheets 1938–45; Hamilton DLP papers, BLPES film 211, reel 89, special executive committee 8 Jan. 1943, executive committee 24 Dec. 1943, annual general meeting 30 Mar. 1945, executive committee 10 Aug. 1945.
[128] Labour party Wales records 5, South Wales regional council of Labour, executive committee 18 July 1945; Prothero, *Recount*, 56; and see e.g. Darlington DLP papers, D/X 922/5, general committee 20 Dec. 1942; City of Leeds LP papers, WYL 853/63/6, executive committee 13 June 1940, 13 Apr. 1944.
[129] Faversham DLP papers, U3272, annual report 1941, to annual general meeting 22 Feb. 1942.
[130] Woolwich BLP Papers, 40.3, annual reports 1938–45.
[131] Lambeth North DLP papers, 1/3, general committee 27 Oct. 1940; Lewisham West DLP papers, A89/100/10, annual general meeting 13 Mar. 1939, general committee 11 Aug. 1941, 13 Nov. 1943.
[132] Derby DLP papers, Box 3, 18(a), annual reports 1938–46; Co-operative Union Ltd., *Co-operative Party Report to the Annual Conference, 1946*, 11, 43–7.
[133] Pinto-Duschinsky, *British Political Finance*, 79.
[134] Lambeth North DLP papers, 1/3, executive committee 8 July 1942, management committee 27 Sept. 1942, annual general meeting 5 Sept. 1943.
[135] Derby DLP papers, Box 3, 18(a), annual reports 1938–46; Norwich DLP papers, SO 198/3/1, annual reports, 1938–47; Gloucester TLC papers, D3128/5/6, minute book 1939–45.

and candidates contributed towards their election expenses, with sums between £50 and £100 being by no means unusual; Charles White, populist Independent victor in the famous West Derbyshire by-election of February 1944, belied his common man image with a £100 contribution towards his own election expenses as the Labour candidate at the 1945 election.[136] Some MPs and candidates also contributed towards the more specific needs of their parties. In Brecon and Radnor, the MP paid the typist's wages, and also gave 50 guineas towards the purchase of loudspeaker equipment, while in Taunton, the candidate paid £50 towards office refurbishment in 1944.[137]

Such reliance could cause problems, of course. Some candidates cut their payments: Reginald Paget paid Northampton DLP £110 in 1939 but only £10 in 1940, and nothing at all in 1941.[138] He got away with it, but others were not so fortunate. When, in October 1939, the MP for Doncaster, John Morgan, proposed that his contributions should cease, the DLP appealed immediately to the regional organizer, who forced Morgan to keep paying, and when G. R. Mitchison asked Elland (West Yorkshire) DLP in 1942 whether it might be willing to accept for the duration of the war £100 a year rather than the usual £200, the affronted DLP 'responded by cancelling his candidature'.[139] Problems also arose when candidates left: when Mackay abandoned Frome (Somerset) to fight Llandaff and Barry as an independent in 1942, the DLP was left in financial difficulties from which it only emerged thanks to the arrival of a TGWU-sponsored candidate in time for the 1945 general election.[140]

The party's improving financial position and high wartime taxation combined to help shift the party's culture away from this kind of funding, however. When a potential candidate offered to pay Stockport TCLP £150 a year plus £150 towards his election expenses in November 1944, he was rebuffed, while Leah Manning recalled that, in 'a reversal of all [her] previous experience', she was selected as candidate in Epping (Essex) precisely because she offered nothing, in contrast to her rival's offer to pay all his own expenses.[141] One of those previous experiences had been at Bristol East in 1931, where she had been outbid by Cripps, who had gone on to fund the DLP to the tune of at least £300 a year

[136] See e.g. Ipswich TCLP papers, GK 400/1/1/4, special finance committee 7 Jan. 1945; Batley and Morley DLP papers, MS 146/2, executive committee 26 May 1945; Newport DLP papers, MNB/POL/6/A/8, finance subcommittee 27 Aug. 1945; West Derbyshire DLP papers, D1650 G/M2, executive committee 2 June 1945.

[137] Brecon and Radnor DLP records 4, executive committee 17 May 1941, general meeting 24 Feb. 1945; Taunton DLP papers, DD/TLP/1/1, general committee 28 Oct. 1944.

[138] Northampton DLP papers, NLP 2, minute book 1938–44 *passim*.

[139] LPNEC XVIII, organization subcommittee, 18 Oct. 1939; XIX, elections subcommittee, 15 Apr. 1942.

[140] Frome DLP papers, A/AAW 28, annual general meeting 22 Jan. 1939, executive committee 14 June 1941.

[141] Stockport TCLP papers B/MM/2/19A, political executive committee 22 Nov. 1944; L. Manning, *A Life for Education: An Autobiography* (1970), 163.

throughout the 1930s, but when Bristol officials tried to tease some money from him in April 1945, following his return to the Labour party, Cripps replied bluntly that, although he would help with his election expenses, he would be 'unable in future to make any financial contribution towards the maintenance of the Constituency organization', and that if it wanted an agent it would have to pay his or her salary.[142] Evan Durbin's failure to secure nomination as prospective candidate for Clay Cross (Derbyshire) in 1944 was put down by a peeved Dalton partly to financial considerations.[143]

More general fund-raising efforts were often anything but lacklustre. Writing in 1938, Dean McHenry had suggested that bazaars, jumble sales, and the like were very effective at raising money for local Labour parties.[144] Some activists had feared that such schemes were losing appeal to the cinema, and to 'Woolworth's and Mark's and Spencer's'.[145] But wartime experience was to suggest otherwise. Although war conditions made large events difficult to organize, many DLPs experienced success. In late 1941, for example, a Halifax women's section's 'At Home' raised £100; in late 1942, Derby DLP made a profit of £87 at its bazaar, while Woolwich women's section cleared £148 at a Christmas novelty sale.[146] Hendon (Middlesex) DLP managed to hold a Christmas bazaar in every year of the war, and profits over the period 1939–43 alone totalled around £400.[147] Dancing, cards, and competitions also brought in money. Fairly typical levels of profit on dances were realized in Bedford in July 1940 (£24), Newport in June 1941 (£25), and Batley and Morley in April 1943 (£26).[148] Norwich was even more successful. Its pre-war income from dances fell from £53 in 1938 to £31 in 1939, and no dances could be held at all in 1940. Thereafter, however, income soared, reaching £546 in 1943 and £558 in 1944, before falling back to £269 in 1945: doubtless the presence of so many relatively well-paid American servicemen in the area helped. This meant that dances, which had accounted for a twelfth of Norwich DLP's income in 1938, made up half in 1943, and still stood at a third in 1945.[149] Meanwhile, whist drives remained important. In London alone, more than 10 per cent of Lewisham West's income came

---

[142] P. Clarke, *The Cripps Version: The Life of Sir Stafford Cripps* (2002), 67; Bristol East DLP papers, 39035/54, general committee, 24 Nov. 1940; 39035/61, memo, 'Consultations with Sir Stafford Cripps in London', n.d. [Apr. 1945].

[143] Dalton, *Second World War Diary*, 722, 14 Mar. 1944; see also P. Gordon Walker, *Political Diaries, 1932–1971*, ed. R. Pearce (1991), 165, 8 Aug. 1945.

[144] McHenry, *Labour Party in Transition*, 103.

[145] Chichester DLP papers, LA/1CH 1/1/1, executive committee 26 Feb. 1939.

[146] Halifax DLP papers, TU 28/2, executive committee 18 Dec. 1941; Derby DLP papers, Box 3, 18(a), annual report 1942; Woolwich BLP Papers, 40.3, annual report 1943.

[147] Hendon DLP papers, BLPES film 211A, reel 97559/1, executive committee 14 Feb., 22 Dec. 1940, 4 Jan. 1942; annual reports, 1942, 1943.

[148] Bedford DLP papers, X494/3, executive committee 9 July 1940; Newport DLP papers, MNB/POL/6/A/8, executive committee, 23 June 1941; Batley and Morley DLP papers, MS 146/2, executive committee 17 Apr. 1943.

[149] Norwich DLP papers, SO 198/3/1, annual reports, 1938–45.

from this source in 1942; Greenwich and Lambeth North also found them very lucrative.[150] Prize draws and sweepstakes were also effective fund-raisers. Southampton's huge profit of £275 on its 1941 Christmas draw was exceptional, but other parties also posted good results.[151] Profits rose as the war went on: Windsor, which was reasonably content with £17 at Christmas 1940, found it was clearing £70 four years later.[152] Some parties also raised funds through draws and sweepstakes based on major horse races. Southampton (again) achieved the remarkable profit of £305 in its Manchester November Handicap Draw in 1942; perhaps more typical was Newport's profit of £25 from its Derby Draw in 1941.[153] Overall pride of place, though, probably goes to Ipswich's pontoon competition, which had built up assets of over £1,500 by early 1945: its generous prizes (35 per cent of gross receipts) ensured that it had a very wide appeal in the town.[154] Another ingenious, if less lucrative, means of raising money was adopted by South Norfolk DLP, which retailed tea bought wholesale from the CWS.[155]

Reflecting on the 1945 election campaign in the long interval between polling day and the counting of the votes, one Labour official in the East Midlands enthused that most parties there had 'tackled the money-raising job in fine style'; one DLP had been 'almost embarrassed with the response it secured to its appeal for money at meetings, and in factories etc'.[156] But Labour's financial success during the election campaign could only come about because of its positive performance in this area over the war years as a whole. In 1938, McHenry had remarked that '[m]any of the Labour Party's pressing problems remain[ed] unresolved because of the lack of adequate funds'.[157] By 1945, this excuse was no longer valid. Of course, problems did remain, not least in what McHenry had called the 'spotted and unbalanced' allocation of funds within the party; and, as Pinto-Duschinsky has suggested, this misallocation was, if anything, to intensify over the post-war period.[158] But in 1945, funds were usually abundant, locally as well as nationally. If a DLP like Chichester, in a safe Conservative seat on the war-ravaged Sussex coast, could spend £633 on its election campaign in 1945 (as

---

[150] Lewisham West DLP papers, A89/100/10, general committee minute book 1941–6; Greenwich DLP papers, GLP 1.3, general committee 25 Apr. 1940, 26 Aug. 1943; Lambeth North DLP papers, 1/3, executive committee 8 July 1942, management committee 9 July 1942, 28 Apr. 1943.

[151] Southampton DLP papers, D/LAB/Box 2, executive committee 31 Jan. 1942; and see e.g. Derby DLP papers, Box 3, 18(a), annual report 1941.

[152] Windsor DLP papers, D/EX 832/3, general committee 17 Jan. 1941, 18 Jan. 1945.

[153] Newport DLP papers, MNB/POL/6/A/8, executive committee, 23 June 1941; Southampton DLP papers, D/LAB/Box 2, executive committee 30 Jan. 1943.

[154] Ipswich TCLP papers, GK 400/1/1/3, annual meeting 11 Feb. 1945, finance committee 29 Apr. 1942.

[155] Mayhew, *Time to Explain*, 41.

[156] LP East Midlands Region, Women's Organizer papers, DD/PP/14/8/5, memo, 'From the East Midlands front', n.d. [*c*. mid-July 1945].

[157] McHenry, *Labour Party in Transition*, 44.

[158] Ibid. 56; Pinto-Duschinsky, *British Political Finance*, 155.

opposed to just £291 in 1935), and still have £200 left in its election account, then Labour's finances were buoyant indeed.[159]

THE LIBERALS

Money, or the lack of it, is usually cited as a factor in the Liberal party's decline. Yet tales of Liberal impoverishment are often exaggerated. Even though the 1945 general election was to be the first at which the average Liberal candidate was outspent by his or her average Labour rival, the former still spent 89 per cent of the amount of the latter, and Liberal candidates collectively spent over £160,000. This alone suggests a more complicated story than is usually told.

The party had relied for some years on the proceeds of honours sales. Between 1916 and 1924, it drew mainly on the proceeds of such sales made during the years of Liberal government between 1905 and 1916. Thereafter, it relied to a large extent on subsidies from the fund that had been built up by Lloyd George's sale of honours as Coalition premier between 1916 and 1922.[160] However, his lavish spending ended in early 1930, and his estrangement from the party in the early 1930s, the defection of the Liberal Nationals in 1931–2, and the death of a very generous benefactor, Lord Cowdray, in 1934 all hit funds hard.[161] Partly as a result, the party could only run 161 candidates in 1935; things might have been worse still if Lloyd George had not subsidized a number of Liberal candidates who supported his 'Council of Action'.[162] After the 1935 election, the Meston committee aimed to resolve the party's financial difficulties; its report nodded in the direction of modernization, for example by demanding that constituency associations pay affiliation fees to the new Liberal Party Organization. However, the LPO continued to subsidize regions and constituencies, while the continued existence of the secretive Liberal Central Association, which was in charge of candidates and which had its own funds, continued to confuse matters.[163] The £50,000 annual income estimated by Meston as the LPO's minimum requirement remained a distant target, with £11,000–12,000 the usual figure reached: but this was not a disastrous start, it did not presage the party's imminent collapse, and the LPO remained solvent.[164] The gloomy tones of Liberal officials on finance can to some extent be explained by the fact that they were seeking to increase revenue, and that they were hardly likely to achieve this if they told the party at large that, although

[159] *Return of the Expenses of Each Candidate at the General Election of July, 1945*, PP 128, 1945–46; Chichester DLP papers, LA/1CH 1/1/2, executive committee 26 Aug. 1945.
[160] Pinto-Duschinsky, *British Political Finance*, 49, 83–4.
[161] Baines, 'The survival of the British Liberal party', 23.
[162] Stannage, *Baldwin Thwarts the Opposition*, 219.
[163] Baines, 'The survival of the British Liberal party', 43; Harris, *Forty Years*, 183.
[164] *Liberal Assembly 1946*, 25; Baines, 'The survival of the British Liberal party', 43.

more money would be welcome, the LPO was balancing its books and had investments amounting to a few thousand pounds. It was certainly propping up grassroots organization, because, as Malcolm Baines has shown, '[v]ery little local [Liberal] organization was self-supporting'.[165]

The onset of war did bring some problems for Liberal headquarters, but, again, they have tended to be exaggerated. Percy Harris claimed that, when he took over the LCA in late 1940, he 'found an overdraft at the bank and less than seventy candidates fixed'; but Harris was desperate to show his predecessor, Johnstone, in the worst possible light, and in 1940 the LPO found its finances strong enough to increase its investments.[166] The June 1944 comment of Lloyd George's secretary, A. J. Sylvester, that 'the Central Fund of the Liberal Party at the moment consists of an overdraft of £500' must have referred to the LCA, because at that time the LPO was running a surplus.[167] Unfortunately, evidence regarding the LCA remains elusive, but we do know that, although the LPO's income fell in 1940 and 1941, it then rose annually until 1946. Expenditure fell even faster than income at first, roughly halving in the first year, but then recovered again from a wartime low of £6,223 in 1940 to £17,925 in 1945 and £21,523 in 1946. It should also be noted that the LPO had an in-year profit every year except 1943 and 1944, that it remained in credit throughout the war, and that its investments increased through the purchase of Defence Bonds and the like from £2,579 in 1938 to £9,277 in 1945 and £12,179 in 1946.[168] This was not a party on the verge of bankruptcy.

As with the Conservatives and Labour, improved balances were built, in part, on economies in expenditure. There were limited savings on salaries and wages as staff joined up or retired and were not replaced; but even in 1941, wage spending was still at 88 per cent of its pre-war level, and it then expanded to reach 171 per cent of the pre-war level in 1944 and 262 per cent in 1945. Larger savings were made in expenditure on organization—mainly in terms of the limitation of grants to regions and constituencies—and expenditure here fell from almost £5,000 in 1939 to around £1,000 in 1940 and 1941. As late as 1944, expenditure only amounted to 57 per cent of the 1939 figure. Rent costs fell heavily with the move to Sutton, but the return to London in December 1941 meant they rose once more. Finally, significant savings were also made on publications, with spending falling from £3,320 in 1939 to £1,747 in 1941, and only recovering significantly in 1944, when it rose to over £3,000.[169]

---

[165] Ibid., 23.
[166] Harris, *Forty Years*, 183; Harris papers, HRS/1, diary 6 Dec. 1940; LPO, *4th Report to Assembly* (1941), 28.
[167] Lloyd George papers, LG/G/25/3/93, Sylvester to Lloyd George, 15 June 1944; LPO, *8th Report to Assembly* (1946), 44–5.
[168] Figures taken from LPO *Reports to Assembly*, 1941–6.
[169] Calculated from figures in LPO *Reports to Assembly*, 1941–6, *passim*.

The party was not on the verge of bankruptcy, but it was not on the verge of a new approach to funding, either. It is notable that the leaders of Radical Action, for their part, left their forward-looking ideas at home when it came to cash: Lloyd George and City sympathizers were their first ports of call when seeking funding.[170] In 1939, constituency affiliation fees had only amounted to £679—just 6 per cent of LPO income. By 1945 the proportion was just 4 per cent. Therefore subscriptions and donations paid directly to headquarters remained the LPO's main source of income. Around 90 per cent of the LPO's money came from this source in 1939 and throughout the war, with the proportion exceeding pre-war levels in 1943, and peaking at 96 per cent in 1945; wealthy sympathizers like the Rowntrees and Lord Leverhulme remained crucially important and, as Mark Egan has argued, the party 'was financed at all levels primarily by a small number of rich benefactors'.[171] But existing benefactors were often quite advanced in years, and thus had a propensity to die at inconvenient times, and it is noteworthy that the LPO's annual reports devoted two pages to a 'Form of Bequest' ready for completion by those Liberals eager to leave something to the party in their wills.[172] Harris and Sinclair clearly hoped to make some money from honours sales, but were stymied by Churchill's decision—as Harris put it—'to give no Political [*sic*] honours—only rewards for service arising out of the war'; without honours to offer, new donors were hard to find.[173] Business donations probably increased in wartime, but the amounts involved were probably not all that large.[174] Direct appeals to delegates at the annual Liberal assemblies from 1942 onwards brought in a couple of thousand pounds a time, and a big appeal for the 1945 election was reasonably successful, although it did not reach the rather ambitious initial target of £250,000.[175]

At the local level, the Liberals' wartime experiences were not dramatically different from those of their Conservative and Labour rivals. On the outbreak of war, LAs were told to continue collecting money, and the message was repeated frequently thereafter.[176] A handful of associations, like Hackney Central, did finally fold under the financial strain, but they had been virtually moribund anyway, and others struggled along: Dundee LA began and ended the war in

---

[170] Lloyd George papers, LG/G/25/3/93, Sylvester to Lloyd George, 15 June 1944.

[171] Ibid.; M. Egan, 'The grass-roots organization of the Liberal party, 1945–64', Oxford University D.Phil. thesis, 2000, 39.

[172] LPO, *4th Report to Assembly* (1941), 21, 24–5.

[173] Harris papers, HRS/1, diary 28 Nov. 1940, HRS/2, diary 1 Apr. 1943.

[174] De Groot, *Liberal Crusader*, 210; Pinto-Duschinsky, *British Political Finance*, 179–80.

[175] *Liberal Party Organisation Bulletin*, 22, Aug. 1941; LPO, *Report to Assembly 1943* (1943), 24–5; LPO, *Report to Assembly 1944* (1944), 30; Lancashire, Cheshire, and North-Western LF papers, M390/1/12, executive committee 16 Feb., 11 May 1945; LPO, *8th Report to Assembly* (1946), 46–7.

[176] *The Times*, 7 Sept. 1939; Yorkshire LF papers, WYL 456/3, executive committee 25 Nov. 1939; LPO, *4th Report to Assembly* (1941), 12, 20–2.

debt, despite remaining relatively active in fund-raising activities; in 1946 it would be forced to sell off part of its premises in order to meet its liabilities.[177] But some associations had a good war. After years of penury, Glasgow Hillhead LA felt able in March 1941 to offer its prospective candidate 'a hopeful, if not glowing, account of the resources at the disposal of the Association', while Leeds LF entered the war in debt, but ended it with a credit balance 'for the first time in many years'.[178]

As with the Conservatives and Labour, improvement was usually due to the fact that, although income fell, expenditure fell further. Cuts in salaries, cuts in staff, removal to cheaper premises, giving up premises altogether and running association business from the home of a paid or unpaid official, and having the telephone removed from the office, all helped.[179] Of course, all of these were potentially detrimental to the party's performance, but the difficulties faced could be mitigated if local officials showed commitment. Some associations achieved a better financial state via a state of near-dormancy: Paisley LA had income of only £176 in 1944 but spent just £18.[180] Subscription income fluctuated, falling when collecting was difficult, though some LFs and LAs found it holding up quite well, and various expedients, including organizational changes and the payment of commission to collectors, were employed to ensure the maintenance and development of this income stream.[181] Finally, social events remained important fund-raisers. These revived particularly from 1942 onwards. A dance at Cheetham Liberal Club (Manchester) in October 1942 raised £15 for the Manchester LF; Walthamstow's whist drives, interrupted by air raids in 1941, were resumed in early 1943, and made a small net contribution to LA funds; and in December 1944, a 'Christmas Fayre' in the Scottish LF's Edinburgh office raised £250.[182]

But central, top-down grants remained much more important for the Liberals than for their main rivals. Initially, headquarters had intended to suspend such payments, but the tide of regional federation protests that followed persuaded it

[177] London Liberal party papers, Acc. 1446/4, general purposes committee 26 Nov. 1941; Dundee LA papers, GD/DLA/1/2, finance committee minute book 1939–46, *passim*; GD/DLA/1/1, executive committee 1 July 1946.

[178] Glasgow Hillhead LA papers, TD 480, council meeting 14 Oct. 1940; subcommittee meeting, 14 Mar. 1945; Leeds LF papers, WYL 456/7, executive committee 28 Oct. 1939; annual meeting 24 Mar. 1945.

[179] See e.g. East Dorset LA papers, D1512/A1, executive committee 20 June 1940; London Liberal party papers, Acc. 1446/7, general purposes committee 13 Nov. 1939; Scottish LF papers, Acc. 11765/14, joint finance committee 25 Feb. 1942.

[180] Paisley LA papers, ARC 67, minute book 1922–47, *passim*.

[181] Chester LA papers, CR159/5, minutes 1939–43, *passim*; Manchester LF papers, M283/1/3/7, executive committee 17 Sept. 1941; East Dorset LA papers, D1512/A1, executive committee 16 Jan. 1942.

[182] Manchester LF papers, M283/1/3/7, executive committee 22 Sept., 2 Nov. 1942; Walthamstow LA papers, unclassified, joint executive committee 10 July 1941, 9 Feb. 1943; Scottish LF papers, Acc. 11765/14, executive committee 6 Dec. 1944.

to offer reasonably generous grants, conditional upon federations retaining their secretaries on current terms, and on the maintenance of the 'utmost possible activity': London was awarded £50 for its secretary's salary for the remainder of 1939, plus £200 for 1940, as well as £100 to meet its general expenses; the Western Counties LF was given £200 or £250 annually throughout the war; and in 1943, the Lancashire, Cheshire, and North-Western was awarded a total of £275.[183] These significant sums also enabled grants to be passed further down the line to some LAs, while headquarters support helped ensure the running of many candidates in 1945.[184]

Associations had few qualms about accepting money, when it was available, from MPs, candidates, and rich benefactors. Clement Davies contributed generously to Montgomeryshire LA, while Beveridge paid virtually the whole of his by-election expenses (more than £500) at Berwick in October 1944, and funded the local association lavishly in the nine months between then and the general election.[185] East Dorset's choice of J. A. H. Mander as its candidate in 1944 was greatly influenced by his promise to pay £500 into its election fund.[186] By that time, and in stark contrast to the modernizing efforts of Conservative Central Office, Liberal headquarters was asking potential candidates explicitly how much they would be prepared to pay towards their election expenses, and towards the annual costs of their associations.[187] Wealthy donors remained important: in June 1944, for example, Henry Kenyon, a party member, offered to lend Manchester LF £100 if nineteen others would do the same, and to increase his annual subscription to five guineas if twenty others would follow suit.[188] The problem, though, as at national level, was that the stock of wealthy donors was dying off, and although this could lead to (sometimes generous) bequests, the latter were, by definition, 'one-off' payments.[189]

Appeals provided a final major source of income for local Liberalism. Those launched early in the war were not terribly successful: the LCA's 1941–2 Victory Candidates Scheme, which aimed to establish an election fund in every

[183] London Liberal party papers, Acc. 1446/4, Chairman, LPO, and Treasurer, LCA, to Harold Glanville (Chairman, London LF), 31 Aug. 1939; Acc. 1446/7, general purposes committee 10 Oct. 1939; Western Counties LF, DDM 1172, finance and general purposes committee 8 Dec. 1939, 17 Feb. 1941, 18 Apr. 1942, 2 Feb. 1944.

[184] Walthamstow LA papers, unclassified, Walthamstow West LA emergency committee 13 Aug. 1943; Cambridgeshire LA papers, R93/73, meeting and conference 17 Mar. 1945; selection committee 28 Apr. 1945.

[185] Montgomeryshire LA records 6, account book 1934–70, *passim*, Beveridge papers, VI/1, fo. 12, W. J. Belcher to Beveridge, 1 Nov. 1944; VI/20 (part 2), fo. 7, James Froud (Berwick LA) to Miss M. E. Grigson (Berwick), 27 July 1945.

[186] East Dorset LA papers, D1512/A1, annual meeting 19 Apr. 1943; finance and general purposes committee 5 Oct. 1944, 4 Jan. 1945.

[187] Pinto-Duschinsky, *British Political Finance*, 209.

[188] Manchester LF papers, M283/1/3/7, executive committee 6 June 1944; see also e.g. East Dorset LA papers, D1512/A1, executive committee 22 Apr. 1940.

[189] Scottish LF papers, Acc. 11765/14, joint finance committee 22 Nov. 1939; London Liberal party papers, Acc. 1446/7, general purposes committee 6 May 1940.

constituency, made little impact even though fronted by Lady Sinclair; and more localized *ad hoc* efforts proved little more lucrative.[190] The election appeals that opened in 1944 had rather better results, however. The LCNWLF's fighting fund, launched in November 1944, amounted to £2,131 by March 1945, and the 85 constituency associations in the federation area raised £10,500 by mid-May, allowing them to run candidates in more than half of the constituencies in the region.[191] Yorkshire LF's fund raised £1,400 between February and April 1945, while Cardiganshire LA raised £388 between February and July.[192] Many LAs, however, were slower off the mark. Many did not start serious appeals until after VE Day, which gave them problems in finding candidates, let alone running effective campaigns.[193]

The failure of the Liberals to run more candidates in 1945 was not due solely, or even mainly, to financial considerations. In the aftermath of defeat, however, doing something about money was seen as a positive step towards reviving the party. Accordingly, the reconstruction committee which was appointed in September 1945 made radical proposals on funding, and these were accepted by the Liberal Assembly in March 1946.[194] A Liberal Foundation Fund was established with the aim of raising £25,000 a year for five years. Individual Liberals were asked to sign a 'Liberal Compact', pledging to pay £50 annually over that period; if they could not afford that much, they were asked to take out a 'Liberal Bond', guaranteeing to make a smaller regular payment. The worst off could subscribe 3*d*. a week through a newsagent to receive a Liberal *Newscard*, carrying very brief party news; the newsagent would deduct a handling fee and send the remainder on to party headquarters. Headquarters would share the proceeds from all these schemes with the constituencies and regional federations concerned.[195] This scheme helped to secure Liberal finances for a time: £58,000 was received in the first eight months, income was healthier by 1948 than for many years, and it was in no small part due to the success of the scheme that the party was able to run 475 candidates at the 1950 general election. However, dismal failure at that election helped to kill the revival and any chance of modernizing the party's finances. As party membership fell 'to an all-time low' in 1953, Liberal income again became dominated by a relatively small number

---

[190] LPO, *Report to Assembly 1942* (1942), 13; Manchester LF papers, M283/1/3/7, executive committee 30 Dec. 1941, 27 Jan. 1942; Montgomeryshire LA records 3, executive committee 26 June 1943.

[191] Lancashire, Cheshire, and North Western LF papers, M390/1/12, executive committee 29 Sept., 20 Oct., 1 Dec. 1944, 16 Mar., 11 May, 27 July 1945.

[192] Yorkshire LF papers, WYL 456/3, executive committee 10 Feb. 1945, annual meeting 6 Apr. 1946; Cardiganshire LA records 1, special executive committee 22 Feb. 1945, executive committee 29 Sept. 1945.

[193] See e.g. Westmorland LA papers, WDSo/174/2, executive committee 17 May 1945; Stockport LA papers, B/NN/2/10, executive committee 4 May 1945; Walthamstow LA papers, unclassified, Walthamstow West LA emergency committee 5 June 1945.

[194] Rasmussen, *The Liberal Party*, 14–15; LPO, *8th Report to Assembly* (1946), 24–5.

[195] Ibid., 26–8.

of large donors.[196] But even the 1946 scheme had betrayed some traces of older attitudes: it looked first for big subscriptions, and money was to be collected by headquarters and only then disbursed to lower party organs in top-down fashion. Ultimately, money was a symptom, and not the cause, of the Liberal party's problems. And this was as much the case after the war as it had been before it.

MONEY AT THE 1945 GENERAL ELECTION

Analysis of candidates' 1945 election expenses, and comparison of them with the election that had taken place a decade earlier, is very revealing (see Table 8.4). These were the total figures that were spent by candidates in the constituencies, and declared as such by law. They did not include the amounts spent on national-level campaigning, which were subject to no legal restrictions. But the figures given are highly suggestive. First, there appears to have been a significant increase in the amount spent as compared with 1935, in absolute terms, both overall and on average. Pinto-Duschinsky argued, however, that, in real terms, the 1945 figure was lower than that for 1935 (£10,400,000 as opposed to £12,400,000 at 1980 prices). But a real-terms drop of this order was not cataclysmic—indeed, the real-terms figure for 1945 would be higher than that for 1950.[197] This would suggest that there was still plenty of money available for expenditure by parliamentary candidates in 1945.

The second point to note is that, in 1945, the Conservatives—and their allies, the Liberal Nationals and the Nationals—remained the highest spenders, both overall and per candidate. This reflected the continuing underlying financial strength of the Conservative party. However, there was then a change in that Labour spent more per candidate than the Liberals in 1945, whereas its candidates had been significantly outspent by Liberals a decade earlier. This shows the extent to which Labour's finances had improved since 1935, and especially during the war. Conversely, the Liberals had put their finances under some pressure by fighting on a much broader front than in 1935; but, even so, few of their candidates were working on a shoestring. It is also worth noting that, by running a relatively small number of candidates, both Common Wealth and, still more, the Communist party were able to spend significant amounts of money where they did fight.

Finally, Conservative candidates outspent Labour ones in 1945, as they had done at every previous general election. But Labour had never before come so close to the Conservatives. In 1929, the average Labour candidate had spent only 50 per cent as much as the average Conservative; in 1935, the figure had

---

[196] Rasmussen, *The Liberal Party*, 14–15; Pinto-Duschinsky, *British Political Finance*, 180–1.
[197] Pinto-Duschinsky, *British Political Finance*, 27.

Table 8.4. General elections, 1935 and 1945: candidates' election expenses (£)

	1935			1945		
	Opposed candidates	Total expenditure	Average per candidate	Opposed candidates	Total expenditure	Average per candidate
Conservative	492	375,204	762.61	558	439,336	787.34
Liberal National	41	32,155	784.27	49	36,732	749.63
National	4	3,409	852.25	10	7,251	725.10
National Labour	20	18,669	933.45	—	—	—
(Total National)	557	429,437	770.98	617	483,319	783.34
Labour	539	196,244	364.09	601	357,596	595.00
Liberal	161	78,893	490.02	306	163,186	533.29
ILP	17	2,200	129.41	5	1,589	317.80
Communist	2	663	331.50	21	14,255	678.81
Common Wealth	—	—	—	23	14,184	616.70
SNP	8	1,355	169.38	8	2,414	301.75
Plaid Cymru	1	324	324.00	7	2,239	319.86
Other	24	8,915	371.46	92	34,434	374.29
Total opposed	1309	718,031	548.34	1680	1,073,216	638.82
Unopposed	39[a]	4,062	104.15	3[b]	132	44.00
Grand total	1348	722,093	535.68	1683	1,073,348	637.76

[a] 23 Conservative, 3 Liberal National (26 National government); 13 Labour.
[b] 1 Conservative, 2 Labour.

Source: Return of the Expenses of Each Candidate at the General Election of November, 1935, PP 150, 1935–6; Return of the Expenses of Each Candidate at the General Election of July, 1945, PP 128, 1945–6.

dropped to 48 per cent.[198] Now, it stood at 75 per cent. Furthermore, in 1935, the Labour candidate had outspent the Conservative in only 26 constituencies, whereas in 1945, the figure was 97. In some seats the imbalance was spectacular, and nowhere more so than in Lewisham East, where Herbert Morrison spent £1,540 as opposed to his Conservative opponent's £722. Such changes clearly made an impression on many Conservatives, and perhaps help to explain why the Conservative 'myth of 1945' took hold so strongly in so many Conservative hearts and minds.

CONCLUSION

Money did not buy political success. However, it could be a reflection of the success of political organization. As this chapter has shown, the respective parties' financial trajectories had some commonalities during the war. All suffered most in the early part of the conflict, especially between mid-1940 and late 1942. However, even then, the major parties' finances were far from collapsing, and Labour's, in particular, were beginning to show real promise. From early 1943 onwards, all parties began to make financial progress, as it became increasingly plain that the issues that would dominate the peace were ones well suited to the medium of party. Labour made the running at this point, and it entered the final phase of the war, and the 1945 election, in better financial shape than ever before. The Conservatives could not match that level of progress, but their finances held up quite impressively overall, and plans for reform were taking shape that would ultimately help to redesign the post-war party. The Liberals, for their part, were never in quite such dire straits as they liked to claim; nonetheless, they were unable, at least before the end of the war, to start modernizing their finances. All three parties had moments of financial difficulty between 1939 and 1945. But, as will be seen in the Conclusion, there was little in the funding of the Communists or Common Wealth to suggest that they had anything to teach the established parties; and, overall, the existing parties and party system were largely confirmed and vindicated by the financial experience of war.

[198] Butler, *Electoral System in Britain*, 170.

Conclusion

The election of the first majority Labour government in 1945 was one of twentieth-century Britain's most sensational political events, all the more so for being won in opposition to the war hero, Churchill. Long years of Conservative ascendancy in national politics came to an end, and for the next twenty-five years general elections would be overwhelmingly two-party contests, with power swinging from Labour to the Conservatives and then back again. This book has not sought to deny the significance of the 1945 general election. At the same time, though, it has tried to show that the experience of British wartime politics cannot simply be reduced to the question of how far events between 1939 and 1945 contributed to that election's outcome. There was more to it than that.

Perhaps most significant of all was the resilience of party. In retrospect, there were few points more likely to see an 'Ostrogorskian moment' in twentieth-century Britain than the first half of the Second World War. Historians have pointed to other times when the future of party as the main organizing concept in British politics seemed to be in doubt (1911–14, 1930–1, and the mid-1970s), but there was never more of such talk than in the years 1940–2. With all the major parties apparently struggling to sustain their organizations, a Coalition government in office, 'new' political movements and 'non-party' figures coming to the fore, and apparent evidence of a shift in public opinion, it seemed that the time had come for a dramatic change in British politics, and perhaps a permanent move away from party altogether.[1]

Much of this talk was exaggerated. There was nothing particularly new in popular distrust of party and party politicians. It went back well into the nineteenth century, and had been taken as read by those who had periodically called for 'national government' in the first four decades of the twentieth.[2] It was hardly surprising that it should become more noticeable at this point. With

[1] S. Fielding, 'The Second World War and popular radicalism: the significance of the "movement away from party"', *History*, 80 (1995).

[2] J. Lawrence, 'Popular politics and the limitations of party: Wolverhampton, 1867–1900', in E. F. Biagini and A. Reid (eds.), *Currents of Radicalism: Popular Radicalism, Organised Labour and Party Politics in Britain, 1850–1914* (Cambridge, 1991), 71, 75–7, 84; J. Vernon, *Politics and the People: A Study in English Political Culture, c.1815–1867* (Cambridge, 1993), 172–7; G. R. Searle, *Country before Party: Coalition and the Idea of 'National Government' in Modern Britain, 1885–1987* (1995).

the country facing a struggle for survival, a Coalition government in office, and (most) elections uncontested, it was natural that people should ask questions about the future of party. The organizational problems faced by all three major parties contributed to the mood, of course. But, as has been demonstrated, those problems were largely contingent: there was nothing inherently permanent or inevitable about them.

And, crucially, the challenge was relatively weak, even at this stage. The Communist party aroused more suspicion than enthusiasm, even at the height of 'Russomania' in 1941–4. Two decades of suspicion, fear, and hatred did not simply evaporate. The party did advance at various points of the war: its anti-war line during the Phoney War mopped up support from dissident Labourites and others on the left who were alarmed at Britain's involvement in a new world war; the campaign that led to the People's Convention of January 1941 exploited popular discontent with some of the war's effects on civilian life; and, most substantially, its membership rose dramatically in 1941–2 due to sympathy for the USSR, admiration of the Red Army, and the CPGB's advocacy of a second front in Western Europe. But even then, its peak membership (December 1942) was only 56,000, and even though that represented a quarter of Labour's individual membership at that time, it was the closest the two figures would ever come, as Labour's recovered and the Communists' proved unsustainable, falling to just over 45,000 by March 1945.[3] Affiliation to Labour would have created new opportunities, but that door was kept resolutely closed, and even after the abolition of the Comintern in 1943, the party's Soviet links were a source of suspicion, and became more so as concerns about current and future Soviet policy grew towards the end of the war. The CP was an integral part of British political life, but it did not break into the mainstream, and its failure to elect more than two MPs in 1945 told its own story. Many people admired the Red Army, and some developed great enthusiasm for Stalin, but those emotions did not make any more than a very small minority yearn for a Soviet Britain led by Harry Pollitt.

Unlike the Communist party, Common Wealth was a product of the war. At first, its expansion appeared significant, and its by-election performances were impressive, with three seats gained from the Conservatives or Liberal Nationals, the last, at Chelmsford, less than a fortnight before VE Day. Acland's writings sold well, and CW made a lot of noise: its basic message, of the need for a shift from the material to the ethical, played well to certain sections of public opinion.[4] In reality, though, Common Wealth had much more style than substance: it made headlines, but ultimately lacked the impetus or energy to

---

[3] A. Thorpe, 'The membership of the British Communist party, 1920–45', *Historical Journal*, 43 (2000), 781.

[4] See esp. R. Acland, *Unser Kampf: Our Struggle* (1940); idem, *The Forward March* (1941); idem, *What it will be Like in the New Britain* (1942).

make serious incursions into the territory of mainstream politics. Its membership was very limited, peaking at just under 15,000 in early 1945.[5] It was unable to expand at all in Scotland or Wales, and remained very weak in many parts of England. Its by-election victories were impressive, but they said as much about the organizational decay of some constituency Conservative and Liberal National machines as about Common Wealth's attractions, and relied on a 'bandwagon', involving campaigners from all over the country, that could not possibly be replicated at a general election. The party's finances, meanwhile, were chaotic. Attempts to fund it on the basis of membership subscriptions failed dismally, and it was almost entirely dependent on a handful of wealthy men, and especially its treasurer, the wealthy businessman Alan Good, and Acland himself, who between them contributed 84 per cent (£17,000) of its income in 1943, and 63 per cent (£16,250) the following year.[6] CW's failure was ultimately political, but the financial failure was symptomatic of the movement's essentially limited potential, and there was nothing in its financial practices worthy of emulation by its more established political rivals.[7] There was some Labour and Liberal concern about Common Wealth at first, but by the second half of 1944 neither was paying it much heed. By the end of that year, it was in crisis; by the time of the 1945 election, it would be in terminal decline.

Beyond the Communists and Common Wealth, perhaps the most discussed option was Cripps, in 1942; but even though some earlier views of him had been revised, such revisions were based on a largely bogus view of his importance in securing the Anglo-Soviet alliance. For most people, Cripps's previous career remained a warning that he was untrustworthy, and made him especially suspicious to most of the Conservative MPs who still comprised a large majority in the House of Commons. Cripps could not have led a post-party, post-Churchill coalition, in a parliament elected in 1935.

The only alternative to a return to the politics of party in 1945 would have been the continuation of the Coalition. This was seen by some as a practical proposition: Churchill himself made the case for it at various points, and was joined in his enthusiasm by people as varied as Sir Archibald Sinclair and Harry Pollitt. Labour leaders also appear, at times, to have considered the possibility. But it all came to nothing. Sinclair's party would have overthrown him if he had not finally declared against the continuation of the Coalition in 1944. The Labour party leadership made a similar declaration that October, mindful that otherwise it would face rebellion at the approaching party conference. And

---

[5] Calder, 'Common Wealth', i. 77.

[6] Ibid., i. 286, 305; ii. 123. For Good, see e.g. Churchill papers, CHAR 2/480, Churchill to Dugdale, 18 Apr. 1943; Lloyd George papers, LG/G/25/3/40, A. J. Sylvester to Lloyd George, 9 Mar. 1944; for Acland, see Hilson and Melling, 'Public gifts and political identities'.

[7] Calder, 'Common Wealth', i. 321. The same was often true of Independent by-election candidates during the war, who were often reliant on subventions from wealthy individuals: see e.g. Reakes, *Man of the Mersey*, 106–10; Hollis, *Jennie Lee*, 106.

few Conservatives wept anything other than crocodile tears when the Coalition came to an end. There was considerable appetite for a return to the politics of party by 1945. This could be seen in the way that those who had given up on, or tried to supersede, party were rushing back to it by 1944–5: witness the admission or readmission of Cripps, Driberg, and Mackay to the Labour party, or Morris-Jones's earlier return to the Liberal Nationals. Indeed, the further decline of the Liberals, the assimilation of the Conservatives' erstwhile 'National' partners, the decline of fringe parties like the Communists, and the increasing partisan visibility of the Conservatives in the arena of local government would all make party—in the form of the 'two-party system'—even more dominant after 1945 than it had been in the years prior to 1939.[8] Only five years after the war's end, indeed, two sociologists would be writing, as if stating a law of nature, that in Britain 'the party is the chief instrument of political power, locally as well as nationally: it is through the party that all political aspirations must find fulfilment or frustration'.[9]

If talk of a wartime movement from party was exaggerated, however, we must ask why it gained some credence. There were, perhaps, five key reasons. First, the early years of the war gave rise to a rather apocalyptic mood. In the context of 1940–1, it really did not seem altogether outlandish to say that the war must become a revolutionary war or else it would be lost, and that in this process the old parties must be swept away.[10] As the military tide turned, however, such talk came to seem increasingly outlandish, even bizarre. Here, the entry of the USSR and the USA into the war, and the turn of the military tide, were crucial; so too was the realization, from late 1942 onwards, that, contrary to earlier expectations, the established parties remained reasonably effective, indeed essential, vessels of political argument. Secondly, Churchill's apparent ambivalence towards party was taken a little too literally at times. As Prime Minister of a Coalition, it made sense for him to downplay party. But he had no doubt that the Conservative party would be of central importance to the future of the country once the war was won. Thirdly, many people, particularly on the left, underestimated the extent to which Labour and its image would change during the war. A key complaint against Labour in the later 1930s had been its inability to transcend the 'sectional' politics of trade unionism and socialism, an obstacle to the creation of a 'national' party of the left; by 1945 it had, to all intents and purposes, become that party. Fourthly, the wish was often father to the thought. This was particularly the case with Mass-Observation, one of the most-cited sources of evidence for the 'movement away from party'. Its leading figure, Tom Harrisson, was a Liberal who desperately wanted to see evidence that Conservative–Labour

---

[8] P. Norris, *Electoral Change in Britain since 1945* (Oxford, 1997), 62, 66.

[9] M. Benney and P. Geiss, 'Social class and politics in Greenwich', *British Journal of Sociology*, 1 (1950), 316.

[10] See e.g. D. R. Costello, '*Searchlight Books* and the quest for a "People's War", 1941–42', *Journal of Contemporary History*, 24 (1989), 258, 264, 272–3.

dominance was breaking up. The file reports that he and his colleagues prepared on the basis of raw material submitted to M-O were certainly not biased towards the notion that the established parties had a bright future. Although it is beyond the scope of this study, it would be interesting to see a detailed analysis of the methodology whereby Harrisson and his co-workers produced their reports, on the basis of information from fewer than 3,000 volunteers.[11]

Underlying all this, however, was a further reason: that, in the first half of the war, the parties themselves appeared to be in headlong organizational decline. This could be seen especially in the area of party membership, which fell for all three main parties in the period to 1942. However, the decrease was largely due to wartime disruption. This is not to say that there were no resignations on political grounds. But such departures were not the main cause of falling membership. Much more important were the lack of collectors and the difficulties of collecting. But the people who ceased being members because their subscriptions were no longer being collected were always liable to resume membership once the collector came back. There was a reserve army of dormant party members waiting to be re-recruited, and it is clear that many of them were brought back into the fold in increasing numbers after 1942. They had not turned their backs permanently on parties or party: even without formal institutional support, party attachment remained strong.

None of this is to deny that the war posed severe challenges to all three main parties. Political organization required personnel, money, paper, and other consumable goods, printing and other consumable services, premises in which to hold meetings, and efficient transport. War made them all scarcer. Personnel were lost to the forces, to other forms of national service, and to the increasing demands of work and family. Money was a problem early in the war, at least until expenditure had been reined in, often with the help of much-decreased levels of activity. Rationing affected the amount of paper and other consumables that were available. Printing capacity in the country as a whole was reduced, and that which remained was in heavy demand, with the result that parties often encountered difficulties in getting material printed at all. The requisitioning of premises was a factor affecting many constituency organizations from an early stage of the war, and the reluctance of the authorities to release premises was an obstacle to some even at the 1945 election. Wartime restrictions on movement, the inconveniences of the wartime railway and bus systems, and draconian petrol rationing, all conspired to make transport very difficult, to the extent that in many larger constituencies it became virtually impossible to organize at all. Parties also required residential stability. There was nothing more disconcerting to political organizers than rapid or frequent shifts of population, and yet the war

---

[11] P. Summerfield, 'Mass-Observation: social research or social movement?', *Journal of Contemporary History*, 20 (1985), 443; J. M. Heimann, *The Most Offending Soul Alive: Tom Harrisson and his Remarkable Life* (2002), esp. 197.

saw many areas characterized by very significant changes in this respect. Even in the inter-war period, migration had had political effects, and the increased population shifts of the war years had even more of an impact.[12]

Place could be more significant than party in determining levels of activity. All parties in London were affected by the heavy air raids suffered at various points of the war. The south and east coasts of England were also hit very hard by war conditions, and party activity in many such areas fell away to a considerable extent. In most rural areas, organization was a problem for all parties, given transport problems, military activity, and the like. Time was also an important factor. Speaking generally, the three parties were less active by mid-1940 than they had been a year earlier; and all were less active still a year after that. However, things began to change around the end of 1942. This was in part because the turn in the military tide discredited arguments that political controversy should be avoided for fear of causing defeat in the war; but it was also because it brought into view the prospect of the post-war world, which was bound to cause political dissension between the parties. Nowhere was this represented more starkly than in the controversy over the Beveridge report. It was not the first wartime event to highlight continuing political polarization—earlier chapters have shown clearly how the attitudes of the various parties' activists differed on a wide range of issues from 3 September 1939 onwards—but it was, in many ways, the most significant. It is notable how Labour consciously decided to attach itself to the report despite some early misgivings. For many Conservatives, on the other hand, Beveridge came increasingly to be seen as symbolic of the dangers of a permanent wartime state, drifting towards totalitarianism on 'the road to serfdom'. At this stage, Labour probably moved quicker than the Conservatives. Peace, however, was still some distance away, and all parties were adversely affected by the V-1 and V-2 attacks. By late 1944, though, all were reviving fairly strongly and looking towards the post-war general election; and, by then, politics was very obviously polarized around parties once again.

At the grassroots level, the overwhelming majority of constituency-level bodies that had entered the war did not go out of existence. This was due to pressure from headquarters and regional-level bodies, but also to the conscious commitment of thousands of voluntary party workers up and down Britain. Their continuing hard work with the minutiae of grassroots politics was at the core of the survival of the three parties. This level of commitment came partly from habit, but it cannot be understood entirely without reference to the importance of politics and political ideology. It becomes obvious, after reading hundreds of constituency minute books, that activists saw their activity at least partly in ideological terms. For sure, there were associational and other benefits to being politically active;

---

[12] See e.g. P. Scott, 'The state, internal migration, and the growth of new industrial communities in inter-war Britain', *English Historical Review*, 115 (2000); S. Bussy, 'The Labour victory in Winchester in 1945', *Southern History*, 8 (1986), 149–50.

but that was not the whole story. Knitting endless 'comforts', walking miles to collect subscriptions, and organizing whist drives and dances were all, in part at least, ideological acts.

It is true that some Conservative associations did close down, but even they usually possessed a core of people who could be relied upon to revive them once peace approached. Many of them kept up some social activity, at least; and many expected such 'non-political' activity to pay distinctly political dividends once the war ended. Constituency Labour parties were much less likely to close down altogether, and did so only in extreme circumstances. Below the constituency level, however, ward branches and local parties/associations did often fizzle out. But there was little uniformity to the process, and although the Conservatives and Liberals were probably more affected than Labour, it was also a factor for the latter. Organizational factors were not the chief cause for the outcome of the 1945 general election, but it would probably be fair to say that, at constituency level, Labour was closer to its 'normal' state than were the Conservatives.

There were some significant divergences between the wartime experiences of the three parties. The strongest party at the outbreak of war, the Conservatives, were clearly damaged by early indecision, and Central Office's mixed messages led to grassroots confusion. Calls to abandon party activity owed much to genuine patriotism; but, like the party's exaggerated interpretation of the electoral truce, they also aimed to obtain political advantage by appearing to relinquish the quest for it. There was certainly a significant decline in Conservative activity at all levels in the early years of the war. This was due largely to war conditions, although it may also have owed something to a collective loss of confidence following the failure to prevent war and the subsequent fall of Chamberlain. Churchill's succession to the party leadership left the party in the hands of someone who, while committed to Conservative ends and recognizing the party's importance in the longer term, was also concerned primarily to keep his Coalition government together so that the war could be won. This meant that there was a sense of organizational and political drift for much of the war: the party enjoyed little in the way of 'joined-up government' in this period, and Churchill's periodic lapses towards a charismatic model of politics did not help matters. Even so, he was not indifferent to the fate of his party. And, even at its nadir, the party's officials, MPs, remaining agents, and activists had kept it going. The intensification of party battles from late 1942 onwards began to stir Conservative passions and restore a degree of confidence, and by late 1944 the party was planning a robust campaign, including a vigorous reassertion of the party's commitment to free-market economics. By then, the party organization was recovering quite strongly, although considerable patchiness remained, and the lack of full-time agents—far more vital to the pre-war Conservatives than to any other party—was keenly felt.

The Conservatives recovered surprisingly quickly after 1945. This can be attributed to a number of factors, but perhaps the most important of all was the way in which the party closed ranks in the aftermath of defeat. Its means of doing so was to agree on a narrative of wartime politics that stressed Conservative self-sacrifice against socialist self-interest. A typical, if unusually extended, exposition of this view was given to leading Conservatives in Birmingham, where 10 of the 13 seats had been lost to Labour, in November 1945 by the city association's chief agent:

> The public were in the mood for a change, they had largely been influenced through the incessant propaganda of the Socialists during the War, the young voters particularly had heard little about the Unionist Party except in the nature of attacks from our opponents. We had observed the political truce and we paid the penalty for putting the Nation's interests before the Party [sic] interests. During the War we were without Agents and we had to face the Election with a mere skeleton of an Organisation [sic]. The Socialists on the other hand reaped advantage from the fact that during the War thousands of people entered factories and came into touch with the Trade Union Movement and under the sway of shop stewards. Whilst our Agents were in the Forces the T.U. Officials and Co-op Socialist Officials remained at home and continued their political work, and when the Election came, these full time paid officials were switched in [sic] the Election machine. We had only seven experienced Agents in the thirteen Divisions and we had to be satisfied with untrained and inexperienced men as Election Agents in several Divisions. A swing to the Left was anticipated and we feared the loss of four or five seats but the sweeping loss of ten seats was an unexpected disaster.[13]

By then, few of those present would have been unfamiliar with this argument, but what is most impressive is the extent to which Conservatives came to choose to believe it, often despite their own actual experiences. Repeated again and again in minutes, reports, tracts, this myth of wartime closure and self-sacrifice was to become as much a part of Conservative party folklore as Disraeli's primrose and Churchill's cigar. Its great virtue was that it allowed 'closure' in a different sense. There was no need for recriminations about what had happened between 1939 and 1945: the party had had no alternative but to follow its patriotic duty, and, given that it had, socialist perfidy had made the outcome (electoral defeat) inevitable. This tacit agreement to 'forget' the past and move on—amounting almost to an unwitting conspiracy to cultivate false memory—was to be a crucial factor in allowing the party to recover as quickly as it did in the later 1940s. It is as powerful an example of political myth construction as any in twentieth-century British history.[14]

This book has shown, of course, that the myth was not without foundation. Such myths rarely are: it is why they are able to take hold. From the perspective of 1945, indeed, it was clear that Labour was the major beneficiary of the Second World War. Labour headquarters was very much geared up for the post-war election, when its campaign was far more professional, and in particular better

[13] Birmingham UA papers, uncat., chief agent's report on general election, to management committee 12 Nov. 1945.
[14] For more on the construction of such myths see R. Gerwarth, *The Bismarck Myth: Weimar Germany and the Legacy of the Iron Chancellor* (Oxford, 2005), esp. 4–7.

financed, than any it had previously run. In a sense, the Labour machine that emerged from the Second World War was the ultimate vindication of Arthur Henderson, the architect of the of the party's 1918 constitution, although he had not lived to see it. But this positive outcome was neither inevitable nor painless; it was one for which Labour people had had to work very hard. It was the result of leaders and headquarters consciously developing a close working relationship, a carefully crafted unity which had been tried and tested over issues like resistance to Communist affiliation. At various points, the relationship had appeared to be under threat; and its maintenance was a major achievement. It was to be the basis of the very harmonious intra-Labour movement period that would follow under the Attlee government, and would only really start to break down in the early 1950s. However, success in 1945 bred a degree of complacency at headquarters: unlike the Conservatives, Labour had no strong incentive to take a long, hard look at its organization, and indeed this may have become still more the case once the onset of the Cold War increased the Communists' difficulties.

The war also brought longer-term beneficial effects for Labour. If David Marquand was right to argue that that the inter-war Labour party outgrew its strength like an adolescent in the years prior to 1931, then the war years were the period when it put on the flesh and muscle that would allow it to become an 'adult' party capable of rivalling the Conservatives on equal terms.[15] Before the war, the party had been chronically underfunded; that was now emphatically no longer the case. Membership also moved onto a new plane. Affiliated membership was buoyant, and would increase still more after the repeal of the 1927 Trade Disputes Act in 1946; individual membership was, by 1944, on the strong upward trajectory that would take it to over a million in 1952. Labour party agents finally achieved their superannuation scheme, giving them more security and enabling the party to compete for more able people. The overhaul of the party's regional structure that had begun in the mid-1930s was brought close to completion. However, to focus solely on the picture in and after 1945 is to miss a lot. Before 1943, in particular, it had often been a different story, with membership falling and some local parties struggling to sustain themselves. Although most DLPs had continued to exist, a few had slipped in and out of a comatose state, while organization at subdivisional level had often dried up.

In short, the Conservative view greatly underestimated the extent to which Labour had shared many of the same problems. However, four factors helped Labour at all levels, and DLPs in particular, to remain active to at least a basic extent. First, Labour had a ritual calendar that was fuller than the Conservatives', demanding action, or at least action to justify inaction, at various points of the year. Such triggers included May Day, the annual purchase of membership cards from Transport House, consideration of resolutions in the run-up to the party conference, and so on. Secondly, the formal system of accountability enshrined

---

[15] D. Marquand, *Ramsay MacDonald* (1977), 794–5.

in affiliation fees and the like demanded continuing activity from officials and party bodies at all levels from headquarters downwards—unions, in particular, demanded value for their members' money. Similarly, party meetings could be used to call Labour local councillors to account, whereas the much lower 'party' profile of the Conservatives in local government made them far less likely to use meetings for this purpose. Thirdly, Labour faced more political competition for its constituency of support during the war: the existence of the Communist party, and later of Common Wealth, warned it not to lower its guard, or to leave activity to others. There was no serious movement to the right of the Conservatives seeking to soak up their supporters, at least once the state had effectively smashed most Fascist organizations in May 1940. Finally, 'memory' played a part here, too. Labourites 'remembered' that the last war had ended in the 'betrayal' of those who had fought it, and the domination of inter-war Britain by Conservative-led governments incapable of producing (or sustaining) economic prosperity, social progress, or peace. The most extended exposition of this myth of betrayal, the 1940 best-seller *Guilty Men*, was hugely influential in this respect. The only way to avoid a repetition, it was argued, was to ensure the election of a Labour government at the war's end, and the only way to achieve that was to sustain the party organization in wartime.

The Liberals, for their part, entered the war in a rather fragile organizational state, and little that happened in the next six years improved matters. Unlike Labour and the Conservatives, they did not have nationwide coverage in 1939. Their leadership was weakened by the war, with Sinclair preoccupied with his Air Ministry work and hankering after long-term coalition. However, those hankerings were ultimately defeated, with results that included the failure of tentative moves towards Liberal reunion; and, overall, the party did not collapse. Even in the depths of the war, interesting work was being done on policy, although that work was then largely overcome by the party's lurch leftwards, as first Radical Action and then Beveridge began to take the initiative. Beveridge, indeed, was crucial in redefining Liberalism in the last year of the war. Once he had joined the party and won a seat in parliament, he emerged to rival the lacklustre Sinclair as the public face of Liberalism. His celebrity status guaranteed him a high profile, but this may not have been a wholly positive development, in that it set the Liberals up to try and rival Labour in the language of collectivism and security, when they might have been better off trying to rival the Conservatives in the language of individualism and freedom. But Beveridge did play an important role in pulling the Liberal organization back to life. The 1945 election ruthlessly exposed the naive optimism of some Liberals for what it was, but the party did then set out to reform itself, and the seeds of its survival through the dark days of the early 1950s were sown in and immediately after the Second World War. And, here again, political mythology was a factor: years of setbacks had enabled Liberals to develop their own comforting false consciousness—that Liberalism remained popular, that electoral defeat was due to the malfeasance of the electoral and political systems, and that the Liberal party would rise again.

In some aspects of party organization, the war did act as a harbinger of change. The Labour agents' superannuation scheme is one example; its development of strong regional organization, another. For the Conservatives, restrictions on candidates' financial contributions—already in the air before the war—were further entrenched. MPs were increasingly expected to play a significant role in their constituencies and constituency organizations, although the process had not begun in wartime and it would be rash to exaggerate the extent of change that took place in the period 1939–45 alone. The Conservatives relaunched their youth operation on more dynamic lines, with the formation of the Young Conservatives, although there was less change here for Labour or the Liberals, despite the fact that both parties appear to have recruited quite well among younger people later in the war. More broadly, there were widespread calls for rejuvenation of local parties and associations by 1945, and there does seem to have been significant turnover in personnel, if only because deferred retirements could now take place, given the increasing pool of potential replacements.

On the other hand, some wartime changes proved to be temporary. Particularly significant here were issues of gender. Women had never been anonymous in constituency-level politics prior to 1939, but the events of the war years did bring them to greater prominence in many local party organizations. As has been seen, it was often women who came to the fore when officers and others left. It was quite common for women organizers, wives, or even daughters to fill in for agents who had joined the armed forces, for example. Women played a very significant role in maintaining the political activities of the constituency parties and associations of all three parties; in the social sphere, where they had been more prominent before 1939, their activity sometimes took on new and exciting forms. This was not, however, the prelude to a permanent breakthrough. The return of men in the period following the end of the war led to a comb-out of many women. Meanwhile, it was as difficult as ever for women to gain nomination to stand for parliament, let alone be elected to it, and the rapid falling from favour in the eyes of all the main parties of the Women for Westminster movement merely confirmed the fact. Much of this was not consciously designed, by men or women, but the fact that, to a large extent, it 'just happened' says much for what a later age would have called the 'institutionalized sexism' of mid-twentieth-century British politics.

The practice of constituency politics changed less than might have been expected in other ways, too. A combination of political and social events still prevailed; whist did not lose its popularity overnight. Indeed, in many ways the social/political mix was vindicated by the fact that it helped organizations stay together in wartime. Many of the more ambitious plans for radical organizational change, such as Topping's scheme for the central employment of Conservative agents, were thwarted. In many ways, all three parties were recognizably very similar in 1945 to what they had been in 1939. However, change did not stop in 1945; in particular, defeat in 1945 shifted the balance of power within the Conservative party very much in favour of the reformers, who were able to make significant changes through the Maxwell-Fyfe report in 1948. Those changes were now acceptable to Churchill, given the shock of defeat in 1945 and the realization that he could best sustain his position as leader by allowing his younger colleagues to make the running on organization and policy.[16]

Ever since they began to develop, modern political parties have been much criticized, even derided. The demise of 'party' has often been predicted, and even more frequently wished. Yet many of these arguments have been based on shaky theoretical premisses, and a utopian vision of how politics can operate. They have also been based, crucially, on an inadequate understanding of the extent to which 'party' was rooted in the political soil of twentieth-century Britain. This is because, in particular, historians have tended to fight shy of the detailed empirical engagement with the sources available for the study of party at the grassroots. By failing to engage with what are often, in themselves, perceived to be quite obscure and unexciting sources, they have made assumptions about the fragility of party that turn out, on deeper investigation, to be seriously flawed, or even unsustainable. If ever there was a chance for party to be ousted from the core of British politics, it came in the period of the Second World War. Party's emergence from that conflict not weaker, but stronger, than in 1939 was a testimony to its immense reserve powers, but also to the commitment and hard work of politicians, agents, officials, activists, and members to see that it was so. They believed that politics mattered, and that party was the best way to make a difference. If they were wrong, then it can be said in their defence that no more convincing solution to the problem of organizing power in liberal democracies has ever been demonstrated.

---

[16] Ramsden, *Appetite for Power*, 316–17.

General Election Results, 1935 and 1945

1935 (TURNOUT 71.1 PER CENT)

	Votes	% share	Candidates	MPs	Unopposed
Conservative	10,496,300	47.8	515	387	23
National	53,189	0.3	4	1	—
Liberal National	866,354	3.7	44	33	3
National Labour	339,811	1.5	20	8	—
Total National	11,755,654	53.3	583	429	26
Labour	8,325,491	38.0	552	154	13
Liberal	1,443,093	6.7	161	21	—
ILP	139,577	0.6	17	4	—
CPGB	27,117	0.1	2	1	—
Irish Nationalist	101,494	0.3	2	2	—
Other	204,628	1.0	31	4	1
Grand total	21,997,054	100.0	1,348	615	40

1945 (TURNOUT 72.8 PER CENT)

	Votes	% share	Candidates	MPs	Unopposed
Conservative	9,101,099	36.2	559	197	1
National	133,179	0.5	10	2	—
Liberal National	737,732	2.9	49	11	—
Total National	9,972,010	39.6	618	210	1
Labour	11,967,746	48.0	603	393	?
Liberal	2,252,430	9.0	306	12	—
ILP	46,769	0.2	5	3	—
CPGB	102,780	0.4	21	2	—
Common Wealth	110,634	0.5	23	1	—
Irish Nationalist	148,078	0.4	3	2	—
Other	494,748	1.9	104	17	—
Grand total	25,095,195	100.0	1,683	640	3

Bibliography

Place of publication is London unless otherwise specified.

ABBREVIATIONS

AC	Archive Centre
AD	Archives Department
ALS	Archives and Local Studies
AO	Archive Office
AS	Archive Service
BLPES	British Library of Political and Economic Science (London School of Economics)
CA	Conservative association
DLP	Divisional Labour party
LA	Liberal association
LHASC	Labour History Archive and Study Centre
LHL	Local History Library
LLP	Local Labour party
LSL	Local Studies Library
MRC	Modern Records Centre
NLS	National Library of Scotland
NLW	National Library of Wales
RO	Record Office
UL	University Library

PRIMARY SOURCES

1. National-level party papers

1.1. Conservative party

Conservative party (Bodleian Library, Oxford)
1922 Committee (Bodleian Library, Oxford)
National Society of Conservative and Unionist Agents (Westminster AO)
Conservative party, *Annual Conference Reports*

1.2. Labour party

Labour party (LHASC, Manchester)
Parliamentary Labour party (LHASC, Manchester)
Labour party, *Annual Conference Reports*
Labour party, *Report of the National Conference of Labour Women*

1.3. Liberal party

Liberal party (BLPES, London)
Society of Certified and Associated Liberal Agents (West Yorkshire AS, Leeds)

Women's Liberal federation (Bristol UL)
Liberal Party Organization, *Reports to Assembly*
Women's Liberal federation, *Annual Reports*

2. *Regional-level party papers*
2.1. *Conservative party*

Eastern area (Bodleian Library, Oxford)
Home Counties North area (Bodleian Library, Oxford)
Northern area (Northumberland RO, Newcastle-upon-Tyne)
North Wales committee (Denbighshire RO, Ruthin)
North-West area (Bodleian Library, Oxford)
Scottish Conservative and Unionist association (NLS, Edinburgh)
South-East area (Bodleian Library, Oxford)
Wales and Monmouthshire Conservative and Unionist council (NLW, Aberystwyth)
Wessex area (Bodleian Library, Oxford)
Western area (Bodleian Library, Oxford)
Yorkshire area (West Yorkshire AS, Leeds)

2.2. *Labour party*

Durham County Labour women's advisory council (Durham RO, Durham)
East Midlands regional Labour party (Nottinghamshire RO, Nottingham)
Hertfordshire Labour federation (Hertfordshire ALS, Hertford)
London Labour party (London Metropolitan Archives)
Northumberland Labour women's advisory council (Northumberland RO, Newcastle-upon-Tyne)
Scottish Council of the Labour party (Mitchell Library, Glasgow)
South Essex Labour women's advisory council (Essex RO, Chelmsford)
South Wales regional council of Labour (NLW, Aberystwyth)

2.3. *Liberal party*

Home Counties Liberal federation (Bristol UL)
Lancashire, Cheshire, and North-Western Liberal federation (Manchester ALS)
Leeds Liberal federation (West Yorkshire AS, Leeds)
London Liberal federation [party from 1943] (London Metropolitan Archives)
Manchester Liberal federation (Manchester ALS)
Scottish Liberal federation (NLS, Edinburgh)
Society of Certified and Associated Liberal Agents, North-Western District (Manchester ALS)
Western Counties Liberal federation (Bristol UL)
Yorkshire Liberal federation (West Yorkshire AS, Leeds)

3 *Constituency-level party papers*
3.1. *Conservative party*

Ayrshire, Central UA (NLS, Edinburgh)
Bedfordshire, Bedford CA (Bedfordshire and Luton AS, Bedford)
Bedfordshire, Mid CA (Bedfordshire and Luton AS, Bedford)
Berkshire, Newbury CA (Berkshire RO, Reading)
Birmingham city UA (Birmingham City Archives)

Bolton CA (Bolton AS)
Bradford Central CA (West Yorkshire AS, Bradford)
Bradford East CA (West Yorkshire AS, Bradford)
Bristol West CA (Bristol RO)
Bury CA (Bury AS)
Bury St Edmunds CA (Suffolk RO, Bury St Edmunds)
Cardiff Central CA (NLW, Aberystwyth)
Cardiff East CA (NLW, Aberystwyth)
Cardiff South CA (NLW, Aberystwyth)
Cheshire, Northwich CA (Cheshire RO, Chester)
City of London CA (Westminster AO)
Cornwall, Bodmin CA (Cornwall RO, Truro)
Cornwall, North CA (Cornwall RO, Truro)
Cornwall, Penryn and Falmouth CA (Cornwall RO, Truro)
Denbighshire, Denbigh CA (Denbighshire RO, Ruthin)
Denbighshire, Wrexham CA (NLW, Aberystwyth)
Derby CA (Derbyshire RO, Matlock)
Dorset, West CA (Dorset RO, Dorchester)
Durham, Stockton CA (Durham RO, Durham)
Ealing CA (London Metropolitan Archives)
Essex, Chelmsford CA (Essex RO, Chelmsford)
Fife West UA (St Andrews UL)
Flintshire CA (Flintshire RO, Hawarden)
Glasgow, Bridgeton UA (NLS, Edinburgh)
Glasgow city UA (NLS, Edinburgh)
Hampshire, Winchester CA (Hampshire RO, Winchester)
The Hartlepools CA (Durham RO, Durham)
Herefordshire, Leominster CA (Herefordshire RO, Hereford)
Hertfordshire, Hertford CA (Hertfordshire ALS, Hertford)
Hertfordshire, Watford CA (Hertfordshire ALS, Hertford)
Ipswich CA (Suffolk RO, Ipswich)
Kent, Gravesend CA (Centre for Kentish Studies, Maidstone)
Kent, Maidstone CA (Centre for Kentish Studies, Maidstone)
Kirkcaldy Burghs UA (St Andrews UL)
Lambeth, Brixton CA (BLPES, London)
Lambeth, Kennington CA (BLPES, London)
Lambeth, Norwood CA (Lambeth AO)
Lancashire, Blackpool CA (Lancashire RO, Preston)
Lancashire, Clitheroe CA (Lancashire RO, Preston)
Lancashire, Darwen CA (Lancashire RO, Preston)
Lancashire, Fylde CA (Lancashire RO, Preston)
Lancashire, Middleton and Prestwich CA (Lancashire RO, Preston)
Lancashire, Waterloo CA (Lancashire RO, Preston)
Leeds Central CA (West Yorkshire AS, Leeds)
Leeds West CA (West Yorkshire AS, Leeds)
Leicestershire, Bosworth CA (Leicestershire RO, Leicester)

Leicestershire, Harborough CA (Leicestershire RO, Leicester)
Leicestershire, Loughborough CA (Leicestershire RO, Leicester)
Lincolnshire, Horncastle CA (Lincolnshire Archives, Lincoln)
Lincolnshire, Louth CA (Lincolnshire Archives, Lincoln)
Liverpool Constitutional Association (Liverpool RO)
Llandaff and Barry CA (NLW, Aberystwyth)
Merionethshire CA (Gwynedd AO, Dolgellau)
Monmouthshire, Monmouth CA (NLW, Aberystwyth)
Newcastle West CA (Tyne and Wear AS, Newcastle-upon-Tyne)
Newport CA (NLW, Aberystwyth)
Norfolk East CA (Norfolk RO, Norwich)
Northampton CA (Northamptonshire RO)
Northumberland, Berwick CA (Northumberland RO, Berwick-upon-Tweed)
Northumberland, Wansbeck CA (Tyne and Wear AS, Newcastle-upon-Tyne)
Norwich CA (Norfolk RO, Norwich)
Nottingham, South CA (Nottinghamshire RO, Nottingham)
Nottinghamshire, Rushcliffe CA (Nottinghamshire RO, Nottingham)
Oxfordshire, Henley CA (Oxfordshire RO, Oxford)
Pembrokeshire CA (NLW, Aberystwyth)
Sheffield city CA (Sheffield Archives)
Sheffield Central CA (Sheffield Archives)
Sheffield Ecclesall CA (Sheffield Archives)
Sheffield Park CA (Sheffield Archives)
Southampton CA (Southampton AS)
Staffordshire, Leek CA (Staffordshire RO, Stafford)
Staffordshire, Stafford CA (Staffordshire RO, Stafford)
Staffordshire, Stone CA (Staffordshire RO, Stafford)
Surrey, Guildford CA (Surrey History Centre, Woking)
Surrey, Reigate CA (Surrey History Centre, Woking)
Sussex East, Rye CA (East Sussex RO, Lewes)
Sussex West, Chichester CA (West Sussex RO, Chichester)
Tynemouth CA (Tyne and Wear AS, Newcastle-upon-Tyne)
Wandsworth, Clapham CA (BLPES, London)
Warwickshire, Tamworth CA (Warwickshire RO, Warwick)
Warwickshire, Warwick and Leamington CA (Warwickshire RO, Warwick)
Wiltshire, Chippenham CA (Wiltshire and Swindon History Centre, Chippenham)
Wiltshire, Salisbury CA (Wiltshire and Swindon History Centre, Chippenham)
Wiltshire, Swindon CA (Wiltshire and Swindon History Centre, Chippenham)
Wolverhampton, West CA (Wolverhampton ALS)
Woolwich West CA (Greenwich Heritage Centre)
Worcester CA (Worcestershire RO, Worcester)
Worcestershire, Bewdley CA (Worcestershire RO, Worcester)
York CA (York City Archives)
Yorkshire West Riding, Barkston Ash CA (West Yorkshire AS, Leeds)
Yorkshire West Riding, Sowerby CA (West Yorkshire AS, Calderdale, Halifax)

3.2. *Labour party*

Barrow-in-Furness DLP (on microfilm at BLPES, London)

Batley and Morley DLP (Sheffield UL)

Bedfordshire, Bedford DLP (Bedfordshire and Luton Archives and Record Service, Bedford)

Bedwellty DLP (Swansea UL)

Berkshire, Windsor DLP (Berkshire RO, Reading)

Bermondsey, Rotherhithe DLP (Southwark Local Studies Library)

Bethnal Green, North-East DLP (Tower Hamlets AO)

Birkenhead TCLP (Liverpool RO)

Birmingham BLP (Birmingham City Archives)

Birmingham, Deritend DLP (Birmingham City Archives)

Birmingham, King's Norton DLP (MRC, University of Warwick)

Blackpool DLP (Lancashire RO, Preston)

Bolton TC (on microfilm at BLPES, London)

Brecon and Radnor DLP (NLW, Aberystwyth)

Brighouse and Spenborough DLP (West Yorkshire AS, Calderdale, Halifax)

Bristol East DLP (Bristol RO)

Camberwell, Dulwich DLP (Southwark Local Studies Library)

Cambridge TCLP (Cambridgeshire RO, Cambridge)

Cambridgeshire TCLP (Cambridgeshire RO, Cambridge)

Carmarthenshire, Llanelli DLP (Carmarthenshire AS, Carmarthen)

Coventry DLP (MRC, University of Warwick)

Coventry, East DLP (MRC, University of Warwick)

Darlington DLP (Durham RO, Durham)

Denbighshire, Wrexham TCLP (Denbighshire RO, Ruthin)

Derby DLP (Derby LSL)

Derbyshire, Belper DLP (Derby LSL; Derbyshire RO, Matlock)

Derbyshire, West DLP (Derbyshire RO, Matlock)

Durham, Bishop Auckland DLP (Durham RO, Durham)

Durham, Seaham DLP (Durham RO, Durham)

East Ham South DLP (London Metropolitan Archives)

Glamorgan, Pontypridd TCLP (on microfilm at Birmingham Central Library)

Gloucester TLC (Gloucestershire RO, Gloucester)

Great Yarmouth DLP (Norfolk RO, Norwich)

Greenwich DLP (Greenwich Heritage Centre)

Halifax DLP (West Yorkshire AS, Calderdale, Halifax)

Hendon DLP (on microfilm at BLPES, London)

Hendon, South DLP (on microfilm at BLPES, London)

Huddersfield DLP (on microfilm at BLPES, London)

Ipswich TCLP (Suffolk RO, Ipswich)

Kent, Faversham DLP (Centre for Kentish Studies, Maidstone)

Lambeth, Brixton DLP (Lambeth AO)

Lambeth, North DLP (BLPES, London)

Lanarkshire, Hamilton DLP (on microfilm at BLPES, London)

Lancashire, Farnworth DLP (Bolton AS)
Lancashire, Heywood and Radcliffe DLP (Bury AS)
Leeds Central DLP (West Yorkshire AS, Leeds)
Leeds city LP (West Yorkshire AS, Leeds)
Lewisham, West DLP (Lewisham ALS)
Liverpool TCLP (on microfilm at BLPES, London)
Manchester, Gorton DLP (Manchester ALS)
Merthyr Tydfil, Aberdare DLP (Swansea UL)
Middlesex, Uxbridge DLP (London Metropolitan Archives)
Newcastle-under-Lyme DLP (Staffordshire RO, Stafford)
Newport DLP (Swansea UL)
Norfolk, South West DLP (Norfolk RO, Norwich)
Northampton DLP (Northamptonshire RO)
Northamptonshire, Peterborough DLP (on microfilm at BLPES, London)
Northumberland, Berwick DLP (Northumberland RO, Berwick-upon-Tweed)
Northumberland, Wansbeck DLP (Northumberland RO, Newcastle-upon-Tyne)
Norwich DLP (Norfolk RO, Norwich)
Nottingham city LP (Nottinghamshire RO, Nottingham)
Nottinghamshire, Broxtowe DLP (Nottinghamshire RO, Nottingham)
Nottinghamshire, Newark DLP (Nottinghamshire RO, Nottingham)
Oxfordshire, Banbury DLP (Oxfordshire RO, Oxford)
Oxfordshire, Henley DLP (Oxfordshire RO, Oxford)
Poplar, South DLP (Tower Hamlets AO)
Reading DLP (Berkshire RO, Reading)
Rhondda, West DLP (NLW, Aberystwyth)
Rotherham TLC (Rotherham ALS)
Roxburgh and Selkirk DLP (NLS, Edinburgh)
Salford BLP (on microfilm at BLPES, London)
Sheffield Brightside DLP (Sheffield Archives)
Sheffield Hallam DLP (Sheffield Archives)
Sheffield TLC (Sheffield Archives)
Somerset, Frome DLP (Somerset RO, Taunton)
Somerset, Taunton DLP (Somerset RO, Taunton)
Somerset, Yeovil DLP (Somerset RO, Taunton)
Southampton DLP (Southampton AS)
South Shields DLP (on microfilm at BLPES, London)
Staffordshire, Stafford DLP (Staffordshire RO, Stafford)
Stepney, Mile End DLP (Tower Hamlets AO)
Stockport TCLP (Stockport AS)
Suffolk, Sudbury DLP (Suffolk RO, Bury St Edmunds)
Sunderland DLP (Tyne and Wear AS, Newcastle-upon-Tyne)
Surrey, Epsom DLP (Surrey History Centre, Woking)
Sussex West, Chichester DLP (West Sussex RO, Chichester)
Sussex West, East Grinstead DLP (West Sussex RO, Chichester)
Swansea Labour association (on microfilm at BLPES, London)

Tottenham, North DLP (on microfilm at BLPES, London)
Tottenham, South DLP (on microfilm at BLPES, London)
Walsall DLP (Walsall Local History Centre)
Walthamstow BLP (Waltham Forest ALS, Walthamstow)
Wandsworth, Clapham DLP (London Metropolitan Archives; Lambeth AO)
Warwickshire, Warwick and Leamington DLP (MRC, University of Warwick; Warwick-
     shire RO, Warwick)
Wimbledon DLP (BLPES, London)
Wolverhampton, Bilston DLP (Wolverhampton ALS)
Wolverhampton, West DLP (Wolverhampton ALS)
Woolwich BLP (Greenwich Heritage Centre)
Worcester DLP (Worcestershire RO, Worcester)
York DLP (York City Archives)
Yorkshire (North Riding), Cleveland DLP (Teesside AO, Middlesbrough)
Yorkshire (West Riding), Colne Valley DLP (on microfilm at BLPES, London)
Yorkshire (West Riding), Doncaster DLP (Doncaster AD)
Yorkshire (West Riding), Penistone DLP (on microfilm at BLPES, London)
Yorkshire (West Riding), Rother Valley DLP (Rotherham ALS)

3.3. Liberal party
Blackpool LA (Lancashire RO, Preston)
Cambridgeshire LA (Cambridgeshire RO, Cambridge)
Cardiganshire LA (NLW, Aberystwyth)
Chester LA (Cheshire RO, Chester)
Derbyshire, Chesterfield LA (Derbyshire RO, Matlock)
Devon, Tiverton LA (Devon RO, Exeter)
Dorset, East LA (Dorset RO, Dorchester)
Dorset, South LA (Dorset RO, Dorchester)
Dorset, West LA (Dorset RO, Dorchester)
Dundee LA (Dundee City Archives)
Edinburgh South LA (NLS, Edinburgh)
Flintshire LA (Flintshire RO, Hawarden)
Glasgow, Hillhead LA (Mitchell Library, Glasgow)
Hampshire, New Forest and Christchurch LA (Hampshire RO, Winchester)
Huddersfield LA (West Yorkshire AS, Kirklees, Huddersfield)
Leicestershire, Harborough LA (Leicestershire RO, Leicester)
Manchester, Exchange LA (Manchester ALS)
Manchester, Withington LA (Manchester ALS)
Montgomeryshire LA (NLW, Aberystwyth)
Paisley LA (Paisley LSL)
Stockport LA (Stockport AS)
Walsall LA (Walsall Local History Centre)
Walthamstow East LA (Waltham Forest ALS, Walthamstow)
Walthamstow West LA (Waltham Forest ALS, Walthamstow)
Westmorland LA (Cumbria RO, Kendal)
Yorkshire (North Riding), Cleveland LA (Teesside AO, Middlesbrough)

3.4. Other parties

Bradford ILP (West Yorkshire AS, Bradford)
Bradford Liberal National Association (West Yorkshire AS, Bradford)
Huddersfield Liberal Association [Liberal Nationals] (West Yorkshire AS, Kirklees, Huddersfield)

4. Other organizations

Amalgamated Engineering Union (MRC, University of Warwick)
Common Wealth (Sussex UL)
Fabian Society (BLPES, London)
Mass-Observation Archive (Sussex UL)
Metropolitan Union of Conservative and Unionist Agents (BLPES, London)
Miners' Federation of Great Britain (Swansea UL)
South Wales Miners' Federation (Swansea UL)
Transport and General Workers' Union (MRC, University of Warwick)

5. Politicians' papers
5.1. Conservative

Adams papers (BLPES, London)
Avon papers (Birmingham UL)
Beaverbrook papers (Parliamentary Archives, London)
Butler papers (Trinity College Library, Cambridge)
Chamberlain papers (Birmingham UL)
Chartwell papers (Churchill AC, Cambridge)
Chelwood papers (East Sussex RO, Lewes)
Crookshank papers (Bodleian Library, Oxford)
Davidson papers (Parliamentary Archives, London)
Derby papers (Liverpool RO)
Elliot papers (NLS, Edinburgh)
Emrys-Evans papers (British Library)
Glyn papers (Berkshire RO, Reading)
Grigg, Sir Edward, papers (Bodleian Library, Oxford)
Hailes papers (Churchill AC, Cambridge)
Hannon papers (Parliamentary Archives, London)
Heneage papers (Lincolnshire Archives, Lincoln)
Margesson papers (Churchill AC, Cambridge)
Templewood papers (Cambridge UL)
Winterton papers (Bodleian Library, Oxford)
Woolton papers (Bodleian Library, Oxford)

5.2. Labour

Addison papers (Bodleian Library, Oxford)
Ammon papers (Hull UL)
Attlee papers (Bodleian Library, Oxford; Churchill AC, Cambridge)
Bevin papers (Churchill AC, Cambridge)

Chuter-Ede papers (British Library)
Citrine papers (BLPES, London)
Dalton papers (BLPES, London)
Durbin papers (BLPES, London)
Greenwood papers (Bodleian Library, Oxford)
Hynd papers (Churchill AC, Cambridge)
Laski papers (Hull UL)
Lawson papers (Durham UL)
Lees-Smith papers (Hull UL)
Mathers papers (NLS, Edinburgh)
Middleton papers (Ruskin College, Oxford)
Noel-Baker papers (Churchill AC, Cambridge)
Parker papers (BLPES, London)
Phillips papers (LHASC, Manchester)
Pritt papers (BLPES, London)
Shinwell papers (BLPES, London)
Sorenson papers (Parliamentary Archives, London)
Stansgate papers (Parliamentary Archives, London)
Stokes papers (Bodleian Library, Oxford)
Woodburn papers (NLS, Edinburgh)

5.3. Liberal

Beveridge papers (BLPES, London)
Foot papers (Churchill AC, Cambridge)
Harris papers (Parliamentary Archives, London)
Haydn Jones papers (NLW, Aberystwyth)
Lloyd George papers (Parliamentary Archives, London)
Mander papers (Bristol UL)
Rhys Williams papers (BLPES, London)
Samuel papers (Parliamentary Archives, London)
Thurso papers (Churchill AC, Cambridge)

5.4. Liberal National

Mabane papers (West Yorkshire AS, Kirklees, Huddersfield)
Morris-Jones papers (Flintshire RO, Hawarden)
Simon papers (Bodleian Library, Oxford)

5.5. National Labour

Malcolm MacDonald papers (Durham UL)
Nicolson papers (Balliol College Library, Oxford)

5.6. Fascist

Robert Sanders papers (Sheffield UL)

6. Public records

CAB 65	War cabinet conclusions
CAB 66	War cabinet memoranda
HLG 71	Ministry of Health, Planning Division

HO 45   Home Office papers
KV 2   Security Service: personal files
PREM 2   Prime Minister's Office: honours lists and papers
PREM 4   Prime Minister's Office: confidential correspondence and papers
T 172   Chancellor of the Exchequer's Office: miscellaneous papers

7. Parliamentary sources

House of Commons Debates, 5th series
Return of the Expenses of each Candidate at the General Election of November, 1935, PP 150,
    1935–6
Return of the Expenses of each Candidate at the General Election of July, 1945, PP 128,
    1945–6

8. Newspapers

AEU Monthly Journal
Alnwick Gazette
Bermondsey Labour Magazine
Bury Times
Conservative Agents' Journal
Fabian Quarterly
Forward
Labour Candidate
Labour Organiser
Liberal Magazine
Liberal Party Organisation Bulletin
Liverpool Post
Manchester Guardian
Northampton Independent
Onlooker
Pulman's Weekly News
The Times
Western Mail
West Leyton Labour News

9. Contemporary works

Acland, R., *The Forward March* (1941).
_____ *Unser Kampf: Our Struggle* (1940).
_____ *What it will be Like in the New Britain* (1942).
'Cassius' [M. Foot], *The Trial of Mussolini* (1943).
_____ *Brendan and Beverley* (1944).
'Cato' [F. Owen, M. Foot, and P. Howard], *Guilty Men* (1940).
'Celticus' [A. Bevan], *Why Not Trust the Tories?* (1944).
Citrine, W. M., *My Finnish Diary* (Harmondsworth, 1940).
Erskine-Hill, A. G., *The Future of the Small Trader* (1944).
'Gracchus' [T. Wintringham], *Your MP* (1944).
Greenwood, A., *Why We Fight: Labour's Case* (1940).

Haxey, S., *Tory MP* (1939).

Hogg, Q., *The Left was Never Right* (1945).

_____ *The Times We Live In* (1944).

Labour party, *Stalin's Men: About Turn* (1940).

Laski, H., *The Labour Party, the War and the Future* (1939).

Liberal independent trader committee, *Fair Play for the Small Man* (1943).

Liberal party committee on reconstruction, *Coats off for the Future!* (1946).

'Licinius' [authorship uncertain], *Vote Labour? Why?* (1945).

Morrison, H., *Looking Ahead: War-Time Speeches* (1943).

Orwell, G., *The Lion and the Unicorn: Socialism and the English Genius* (1941).

Shinwell, E., *The Britain I Want* (n.d. [1943]).

Stelling, D., *Why I am a Conservative* (1943).

10. Diaries

Amery, L. S., *The Empire at Bay: The Leo Amery Diaries 1929–1945*, ed. J. Barnes and D. Nicholson (1988).

Bonham Carter, V., *Champion Redoubtable: The Diaries and Letters of Violet Bonham Carter, 1914–1945*, ed. M. Pottle (1998).

Brooks, C., *Fleet Street, Press Barons and Politics: The Journals of Colin Brooks, 1932–1940*, ed. N. Crowson (1998).

Channon, H., *Chips: The Diary of Sir Henry Channon*, ed. R. Rhodes James (1967).

Colville, J., *The Fringes of Power: Downing Street Diaries, 1939–1955* (1985).

Dalton, H., *The Political Diary of Hugh Dalton, 1918–40, 1945–60*, ed. B. Pimlott (1986).

_____ *The Second World War Diary of Hugh Dalton, 1940–45*, ed. B. Pimlott (1986).

Ede, J. C., *Labour and the Wartime Coalition: From the Diary of James Chuter Ede, 1941–1945*, ed. K. Jefferys (1987).

Gordon Walker, P., *Political Diaries, 1932–1971*, ed. R. Pearce (1991).

King, C. H., *With Malice toward None: A War Diary*, ed. W. Armstrong (1970).

Last, N., *Nella Last's War: A Mother's Diary, 1939–45*, ed. R. Broad and S. Fleming (Bristol, 1981).

Reith, J., *The Reith Diaries*, ed. C. Stuart (1975).

Sylvester, A. J., *Life with Lloyd George: The Diary of A. J. Sylvester, 1931–45*, ed. C. Cross (1975).

11. Memoirs

Avon, Earl of, *The Eden Memoirs: The Reckoning* (1965).

Benn, J., *Something in the City* (1959).

Beveridge, Lord, *Power and Influence: An Autobiography* (1953).

Bevins, R., *The Greasy Pole: A Personal Account of the Realities of British Politics* (1965).

Boothby, Lord, *Recollections of a Rebel* (1978).

Brabazon of Tara, Lord, *The Brabazon Story* (1956).

Brown, G., *In my Way: The Political Memoirs of Lord George-Brown* (1971).

Butler, Lord, *The Art of the Possible* (1971).

Callaghan, J., *Time and Chance* (1987).

Carrington, Lord, *Reflecting on Things Past* (Glasgow, paperback edn., 1989).

Castle, B., *Fighting All the Way* (1993).

Chandos, Viscount, *The Memoirs of Viscount Chandos* (1962).

Churchill, W. S., *The Second World War* (6 vols., 1948–54).

Croft, Lord, *My Life of Strife* (n.d. [1948]).

Dalton, H., *The Fateful Years: Memoirs 1931–1945* (1957).

Deedes, W. F., *Dear Bill: W. F. Deedes Reports* (1997).

Donner, P., *Crusade: A Life against the Calamitous Twentieth Century* (1984).

Driberg, T., *Ruling Passions* (1977).

Duff Cooper, A., *Old Men Forget* (1953).

Fletcher of Islington, Lord, *Random Reminiscences* (1986).

Gallacher, W., *Last Memoirs* (1966).

Griffiths, J., *Pages from Memory* (1969).

Grigg, P. J., *Prejudice and Judgment* (1948).

Grimond, J., *Memoirs* (1979).

Hailsham, Lord, *The Door Wherein I Went* (1975).

_____ *A Sparrow's Flight: The Memoirs of Lord Hailsham of St Marylebone* (1990).

Halifax, Earl of, *Fulness of Days* (1957).

Harris, Sir P., *Forty Years in and out of Parliament* (n.d. [1947]).

Harvie-Watt, G. S., *Most of my Life* (Windlesham, 1980).

Healey, D., *The Time of my Life* (1989).

Heath, E., *The Course of my Life: An Autobiography* (1998).

Hemingford, Lord [Sir Dennis Herbert], *Back-Bencher and Chairman* (1946).

Hill of Luton, Lord, *Both Sides of the Hill* (1964).

Hollis, C., *Along the Road to Frome* (1958).

Horner, A., *Incorrigible Rebel* (1960).

Hyde, D., *I Believed* (1950).

Jenkins, R., *A Life at the Centre* (1991).

Kilmuir, Earl of, *Political Adventure: The Memoirs of the Earl of Kilmuir* (1964).

Lee, J., *This Great Journey* (1942).

MacEwen, M., *The Greening of a Red* (1991).

Macmillan, H., *Tides of Fortune, 1945–1955* (1969).

_____ *Winds of Change, 1914–1939* (1966).

McShane, H., and Smith, J., *Harry McShane: No Mean Fighter* (1978).

Manning, L., *A Life for Education: An Autobiography* (1970).

Mayhew, C., *A Time to Explain* (1987).

Mikardo, I., *Back-Bencher* (1988).

Millington, E. R., *Was That Really Me?* (Palo Alto, Calif., 2006).

Morris-Jones, H., *Doctor in the Whips' Room* (1955).

Mosley, O., *My Life* (1968).

Pakenham, Lord, *Born to Believe: An Autobiography* (1953).

Parker, J., *Father of the House: Fifty Years in Politics* (1982).

Piratin, P., *Our Flag Stays Red* (1948; new edn., 1978).

Prothero, C., *Recount* (Ormskirk, 1982).

Reakes, G. L., *Man of the Mersey* (1956).

Samuel, Viscount, *Memoirs* (1945).

Stuart, J., *Within the Fringe: An Autobiography* (1967).

Teeling, Sir L. W. B., *Corridors of Frustration* (1970).

Thatcher, M., *The Path to Power* (1995).

Thomas, G., *Mr Speaker: The Memoirs of Viscount Tonypandy* (1985).

Tiptaft, N., *The Individualist* (Birmingham, 1954).

Westacott, F., *Shaking the Chains: A Personal and Political History* (Chesterfield, 2002).

Wigg, Lord, *George Wigg* (1972).

Williams, F., *A Prime Minister Remembers: The War and Post-War Memoirs of the Rt. Hon. Earl Attlee* (1961).

Williams, Sir H. G., *Politics Grave and Gay* (1949).

Winterton, Earl, *Orders of the Day* (1953).

Woolton, Earl of, *The Memoirs of the Rt. Hon. The Earl of Woolton* (1959).

SECONDARY SOURCES

1. Handbooks, guides, etc

Bellamy, J., and Saville, J. (eds.), *Dictionary of Labour Biography* (11 vols., 1972–2003).

Brack, D. (ed.), *Dictionary of Liberal Biography* (1998).

Butler, D., and Butler, G., *Twentieth Century Political Facts* (Houndmills, 2000).

Craig, F. W. S., *British Electoral Facts, 1832–1987* (1987).

_____ *British Parliamentary Election Results 1918–49* (1969).

Dear, I. C. B., *The Oxford Companion to the Second World War* (rev. edn., Oxford, 2001).

Oxford Dictionary of National Biography.

Stenton, M., and Lees, S., *Who's Who of British Members of Parliament* (4 vols., Brighton, 1976–81).

2. Biographies

Addison, P., *Churchill on the Home Front, 1900–1955* (2nd edn., 1993).

Allen, W. G., *The Reluctant Politician: Derick Heathcoat Amory* (1958).

Beckett, F., *Clem Attlee* (1997).

Best, G., *Churchill: A Study in Greatness* (2001).

Birkenhead, Lord, *Walter Monckton: The Life of Viscount Monckton of Brenchley* (1969).

Blake, R., and Louis, W. R. (eds.), *Churchill* (1993).

Boyle, A., *Poor, Dear Brendan: The Quest for Brendan Bracken* (1974).

Brittain, V., *Pethick-Lawrence: A Portrait* (1963).

Brivati, B., *Hugh Gaitskell* (1996).

Brockway, F., *Bermondsey Story: The Life of Alfred Salter* (1949).

Brown, G., *Maxton* (Edinburgh, 1986).

Bryant, C., *Stafford Cripps: The First Modern Chancellor* (1997).

Bullock, A., *The Life and Times of Ernest Bevin*, ii: *Minister of Labour, 1940–1945* (1967).

Burridge, T., *Clement Attlee: A Political Biography* (1985).

Callaghan, J., *Rajani Palme Dutt* (1993).

Campbell, J., *Edward Heath: A Biography* (1993).

_____ *Lloyd George: The Goat in the Wilderness* (1977).

_____ *Nye Bevan and the Mirage of British Socialism* (1987).

Carlton, D., *Anthony Eden: A Biography* (1981).

Charmley, J., *Churchill: The End of Glory* (1993).

Chisholm, A., and Davie, M., *Beaverbrook: A Life* (1992).

Clarke, P., *The Cripps Version: The Life of Sir Stafford Cripps* (2002).

Cooke, C., *The Life of Richard Stafford Cripps* (1957).

Cosgrave, P., *The Lives of Enoch Powell* (1989).

Crosland, S., *Tony Crosland* (1982).

Cross, J. A., *Lord Swinton* (Oxford, 1982).

——— *Sir Samuel Hoare: A Political Biography* (1977).

Dalyell, T., *Dick Crossman: A Portrait* (1989).

De Groot, G. J., *Liberal Crusader: The Life of Sir Archibald Sinclair* (1993).

Donoughue, B., and Jones, G. W., *Herbert Morrison: Portrait of a Politician* (1973).

Dutton, D., *Anthony Eden: A Life and a Reputation* (1997).

——— *Neville Chamberlain* (2001).

——— *Simon: A Political Biography of Sir John Simon* (1992).

Eastwood, G. G., *George Isaacs: Printer, Trade-Union Leader, Cabinet Minister* (n.d.).

Estorick, E., *Stafford Cripps: A Biography* (1949).

Feiling, K., *The Life of Neville Chamberlain* (1946).

Fisher, N., *Harold Macmillan: A Biography* (1982).

——— *Iain Macleod* (1973).

Gilbert, M., *Winston S. Churchill*, v: *Prophet of Truth 1922–1939* (1976).

——— *Winston S. Churchill*, vi: *Finest Hour, 1939–1941* (1983).

——— *Winston S. Churchill*, vii: *Road to Victory, 1941–1945* (1986).

——— *Winston S. Churchill*, viii: *Never Despair, 1945–1965* (1988).

Grigg, J., *Nancy Astor: Portrait of a Pioneer* (1980).

Harris, J., *William Beveridge* (rev. edn., Oxford, 1997).

Harris, K., *Attlee* (1982).

Harrod, R. F., *The Prof: A Personal Memoir of Lord Cherwell* (1959).

Heffer, S., *Like the Roman: The Life of Enoch Powell* (1998).

Heimann, J. M., *The Most Offending Soul Alive: Tom Harrisson and his Remarkable Life* (2002).

Hollis, P., *Jennie Lee: A Life* (Oxford, 1997).

Horne, A., *Macmillan, 1894–1956: Volume I of the Official Biography* (1988).

Howard, A., *Crossman: The Pursuit of Power* (1990).

——— *RAB: The Life of R. A. Butler* (1987).

Jefferys, K., *Anthony Crosland* (1999).

Jones, M., *Michael Foot* (1994).

Jones, T., *Lloyd George* (1951).

Kramnick, I., and Sheerman, B., *Harold Laski: A Life on the Left* (1993).

Macleod, I., *Neville Chamberlain* (1961).

Marquand, D., *Ramsay MacDonald* (1977)

Minney, R. J., *The Private Papers of Hore-Belisha* (1960).

Morgan, K., *Harry Pollitt* (1993).

Morgan, K. O., *Callaghan: A Life* (Oxford, 1997).

——— *Labour People: Leaders and Lieutenants from Hardie to Kinnock* (Oxford, 1987).

——— and Morgan, J., *Portrait of a Progressive: The Political Career of Christopher, Viscount Addison* (Oxford, 1980).

Newman, M., *Harold Laski: A Political Biography* (1993).

Pearce, R., *Attlee* (1997).

Pelling, H., *Winston Churchill* (2nd edn., 1989).

Pimlott, B., *Harold Wilson* (1992).

___ *Hugh Dalton* (1985).

Reynolds, D., *In Command of History: Churchill Fighting and Writing the Second World War* (2004).

Rhodes James, R., *Anthony Eden* (1986).

___ *Bob Boothby: A Portrait* (1991).

Robbins, K., *Churchill* (1992).

Roberts, A., *'The Holy Fox': A Life of Lord Halifax* (1991).

Rose, N., *Churchill: An Unruly Life* (1994).

Roth, A., *Enoch Powell: Tory Tribune* (1970).

Rowland, P., *Lloyd George* (1975).

Self, R. C., *Neville Chamberlain: A Biography* (Aldershot, 2006).

Shepherd, R., *Iain Macleod* (1994).

Skidelsky, R., *Oswald Mosley* (1975).

Slowe, P., *Manny Shinwell* (1993).

Thomas, H., *John Strachey* (1973).

Thorpe, D. R., *Alec Douglas-Home* (1997).

Vernon, B. D., *Ellen Wilkinson* (1982).

Walker, G., *Thomas Johnston* (Manchester, 1988).

Wasserstein, B., *Herbert Samuel: A Political Life* (Oxford, 1992).

Wheeler-Bennett, J. W., *John Anderson: Viscount Waverley* (1962).

Wheen, F., *Tom Driberg: His Life and Indiscretions* (1990).

Williams, P. M., *Hugh Gaitskell: A Political Biography* (1979).

Young, K., *Churchill and Beaverbrook: A Study in Friendship and Politics* (1966).

___ *Sir Alec Douglas-Home* (1970).

Ziegler, P., *Wilson: The Authorized Life* (1993).

3. Other books

Addison, P., *The Road to 1945: British Politics and the Second World War* (1975).

Alderman, G., *London Jewry and London Politics, 1889–1986* (1989).

Alexander, A., *Borough Government and Politics: Reading, 1835–1985* (1985).

Andrews, G., et al. (eds.), *Opening the Books: Essays on the Cultural and Social History of the British Communist Party* (1995).

Ball, S., *Baldwin and the Conservative Party: The Crisis of 1929–1931* (New Haven, 1988).

Barnsby, G. J., *A History of the Wolverhampton, Bilston and District Trades Union Council, 1865–1990* (Wolverhampton, 1994).

Bealey, F., Blondel, J., and McCann, W. P., *Constituency Politics: A Study of Newcastle-under-Lyme* (1965).

Beckett, F., *Enemy Within: The Rise and Fall of the British Communist Party* (1995).

Beer, S. H., *Modern British Politics: A Study of Parties and Pressure Groups* (2nd edn., 1969).

Berger, S., *The British Labour Party and the German Social Democrats, 1900–1931: A Comparative Study* (Oxford, 1994).

Biagini, E. F., and Reid, A. (eds.), *Currents of Radicalism: Popular Radicalism, Organised Labour and Party Politics in Britain, 1850–1914* (1991).

Birch, A. H., *Small-Town Politics: A Study of Political Life in Glossop* (Oxford, 1959).

Blake, R., *The Conservative Party from Peel to Thatcher* (1985).

Blondel, J., *Voters, Parties and Leaders: The Social Fabric of British Politics* (Harmondsworth, 1963).

Branson, N., *History of the Communist Party of Great Britain 1927–41* (1985).

—— *History of the Communist Party of Great Britain 1941–51* (1997).

Brennan, T., Corney, E. W., and Pollins, H., *Social Change in South-West Wales* (1954).

Brivati, B., and Heffernan, R. (eds.), *The Labour Party: A Centenary History* (Houndmills, 2000).

—— and Jones, H. (eds.), *What Difference did the War Make?* (1993).

Brooke, S., *Labour's War: The Labour Party during the Second World War* (Oxford, 1992).

Butler, D. E., *The Electoral System in Britain since 1918* (Oxford, 1963).

—— and Stokes, D., *Political Change in Britain: The Evolution of Electoral Choice* (2nd edn., 1974).

Calder, A., *The Myth of the Blitz* (1991).

—— *The People's War: Britain 1939–1945* (1969).

Callaghan, J., *The Far Left in British Politics* (1987).

Campbell, A., et al. (eds.), *Miners, Unions and Politics 1910–47* (1996).

Carroll, W. S., *92 Years in Richmond and Barnes: A Chronicle of the Richmond and Barnes Conservative Association, 1880–1972* (Richmond, 1972).

Charmley, J., *A History of Conservative Politics, 1900–1996* (1996).

Clegg, H. A., *A History of British Trade Unions since 1889*, iii: *1934–51* (1994).

Cockett, R., *Thinking the Unthinkable: Think-Tanks and the Economic Counter-Revolution, 1931–1983* (rev. edn., 1995).

—— *Twilight of Truth: Chamberlain, Appeasement and the Manipulation of the Press* (1989).

Cole, G. D. H., *A History of the Labour Party from 1914* (1948).

Cole, M., *The Story of Fabian Socialism* (1961).

Cook, C., *A Short History of the Liberal Party, 1900–2001* (6th edn., Houndmills, 2002).

—— and Ramsden, J. (eds.), *By-Elections in British Politics* (2nd edn, 1997).

—— and Taylor, I. (eds.), *The Labour Party* (1980).

Cowling, M., *The Impact of Hitler: British Politics and British Policy, 1933–1940* (Cambridge, 1975).

Coxall, W. N., *Parties and Pressure Groups* (1981).

Crang, J. A., *The British Army and the People's War, 1939–1945* (Manchester, 2000).

Crosby, T. L., *The Impact of Civilian Evacuation in the Second World War* (1986).

Crowson, N. J., *Facing Fascism: The Conservative Party and the European Dictators, 1935–1940* (1997).

Davies, S., *Liverpool Labour: Social and Political Influences on the Development of the Labour Party in Liverpool, 1900–1939* (1996).

Dean, K., *Town and Westminster: A Political History of Walsall* (Walsall, 1972).

Donnachie, I., Harvie, C., and Wood, I. S. (eds.), *Forward! Labour Politics in Scotland, 1888–1988* (Edinburgh, 1989).

Donnelly, M., *Britain in the Second World War* (1999).

Douglas, R., *The History of the Liberal Party 1895–1970* (1971).

Dutton, D., *A History of the Liberal Party* (Houndmills, 2004).

Duverger, M., *Political Parties: Their Organization and Activity in the Modern State* (1954).

Eckstein, H., *Pressure Group Politics: The Case of the British Medical Association* (1960).

Feldman, D., and Stedman Jones, G. (eds.), *Metropolis, London: Histories and Representations since 1800* (1989).

Field, W., *Regional Dynamics: The Basis of Electoral Support in Britain* (1997).

Fielding, S., Thompson, P., and Tiratsoo, N., *England Arise! The Labour Party and Popular Politics in 1940s Britain* (Manchester, 1995).

Finer, S. E., *The Changing British Party System, 1945–1979* (Washington, DC, 1980).

Finlay, R. J., *Independent and Free: Scottish Politics and the Origins of the Scottish National Party, 1918–45* (Edinburgh, 1994).

Fishman, N., *The British Communist Party and the Trade Unions, 1933–45* (1995).

Francis, M., and Zweiniger-Bargielowska, I. (eds.), *The Conservatives and British Society 1880–1990* (1996).

Freeden, M., *Liberalism Divided: A Study in British Political Thought, 1914–39* (Oxford, 1986).

Gallagher, T., *Glasgow, The Uneasy Peace: Religious Tension in Modern Scotland* (1987).

Gash, N., *Politics in the Age of Peel: A Study in the Technique of Parliamentary Representation, 1830–1850* (1953).

Gerwarth, R., *The Bismarck Myth: Weimar Germany and the Legacy of the Iron Chancellor* (Oxford, 2005).

Gledhill, C., and Swanson, G. (eds.), *Nationalising Femininity: Culture, Sexuality and British Cinema in the Second World War* (1996).

Goodhart, P., with Branson, U., *The 1922: The Story of the Conservative Backbenchers' Parliamentary Committee* (1973).

Gottlieb, J., *Feminine Fascism: Women in Britain's Fascist Movement, 1923–45* (2000).

Green, E. H. H., *Ideologies of Conservatism: Conservative Political Ideas in the Twentieth Century* (Oxford, 2002).

Griffiths, C. V. J., *Labour and the Countryside: The Politics of Rural Britain, 1918–1939* (Oxford, 2007).

Griffiths, R., *Patriotism Perverted: Captain Ramsay, the Right Club and British Anti-Semitism, 1939–40* (1998).

Griffiths, T., *The Lancashire Working Classes, c.1880–1930* (Oxford, 2001).

Hall, J. E. D., *Labour's First Year* (Harmondsworth, 1947).

Hanham, H. J., *Elections and Party Management: Politics in the Time of Disraeli and Gladstone* (1959).

Harrison, B., *The Transformation of British Politics, 1860–1995* (Oxford, 1996).

Hills, J., Ditch, J., and Glennerster, H. (eds.), *Beveridge and Social Security: An International Retrospective* (1994).

Hindess, B., *The Decline of Working Class Politics* (1971).

Hinton, J., *Labour and Socialism: A History of the British Labour Movement, 1867–1974* (Brighton, 1983).

—— *Shop Floor Citizens: Engineering Democracy in 1940s Britain* (Aldershot, 1994).

—— *Women, Social Leadership, and the Second World War: Continuities of Class* (Oxford, 2002).

Hoffman, J. D., *The Conservative Party in Opposition, 1945–51* (1964).

Holroyd-Doveton, J., *Young Conservatives: A History of the Young Conservative Movement* (Edinburgh, 1996).

Howe, A., *Free Trade and Liberal England 1846–1946* (Oxford, 1997).

Hutchison, I. G. C., *Scottish Politics in the Twentieth Century* (Houndmills, 2001).

Inwood, S., *A History of London* (1998).

Janosik, E. G., *Constituency Labour Parties in Britain* (1968).

Jarvis, R., *An Account of the Liberals in Walthamstow* (1968).

Jefferys, K., *The Churchill Coalition and Wartime Politics, 1940–1945* (Manchester, 1991).

—— (ed.), *Leading Labour: From Keir Hardie to Tony Blair* (1999).

Jones, G. W., *Borough Politics: A Study of the Wolverhampton Town Council, 1888–1964* (1969).

Jupp, J., *The Radical Left in Britain, 1931–41* (1982).

King, F., and Matthews, G. (eds.), *About Turn* (1990).

Kinnear, M., *The British Voter: An Atlas and Survey since 1885* (1968).

Kirkby, A., *In the Cause of Liberty: Exeter Trades Council, 1890–1990* (Exeter, 1990).

Kushner, T., *The Persistence of Prejudice: Anti-Semitism in British Society during the Second World War* (1989).

Lancaster, B., and Mason, T. (eds.), *Life and Labour in a Twentieth-Century City: The Experience of Coventry* (1986).

Lawlor, S., *Churchill and the Politics of War, 1940–1941* (Cambridge, 1994).

Laybourn, K., and Reynolds, J., *Liberalism and the Rise of Labour, 1890–1918* (1984).

Layton-Henry, Z. (ed.), *Conservative Party Politics* (1980).

Lee, J. M., *The Churchill Coalition, 1940–1945* (1980).

Leonard, R. L., *Elections in Britain* (1968).

Lewis, D. S., *Illusions of Grandeur: Mosley, Fascism and British Society* (1987).

Lindsay, T., and Harrington, M., *The Conservative Party 1918–79* (1979).

Linehan, T., *British Fascism, 1918–1939: Parties, Ideology and Culture* (2000).

—— *East London for Mosley: The BUF in East London and South West Essex 1933–40* (1996).

Lipset, S. M., *Political Man* (1960).

—— and Rokkan, S. E. (eds.), *Party Systems and Voter Alignments: Cross-National Perspectives* (New York, 1967).

Lukacs, J., *Five Days in London: May 1940* (New Haven, 1999).

Lunn, K., and Thurlow, R. (eds.), *British Fascism: Essays on the Radical Right in Inter-War Britain* (1980).

Lynch, P., *SNP: The History of the Scottish National Party* (Cardiff, 2002).

McCallum, R. B., and Readman, A., *The British General Election of 1945* (1947).

McCrillis, N. R., *The British Conservative Party in the Age of Mass Suffrage: Popular Conservatism, 1918–1929* (Columbus, Oh., 1998).

McHenry, D. E., *The Labour Party in Transition, 1931–1938* (1938).

Mackay, R., *Half the Battle: Civilian Morale in Britain during the Second World War* (Manchester, 2002).

—— *The Test of War: Inside Britain 1939–45* (1999).

McKenzie, R. T., *British Political Parties: The Distribution of Power within the Conservative and Labour Parties* (rev. 2nd edn., 1964).

—— and Silver, A., *Angels in Marble: Working Class Conservatives in Urban England* (1968).

Mackenzie, S. P., *The Home Guard: A Military and Political History* (Oxford, 1995).

McKibbin, R. I., *Classes and Cultures: England 1918–1951* (Oxford, 1998).

_____ *The Ideologies of Class: Social Relations in Britain, 1880–1950* (Oxford, 1990).

McLaine, I., *Ministry of Morale: Home Front Morale and the Ministry of Information in World War II* (1979).

Macnicol, J., *The Movement for Family Allowances 1918–45* (1981).

Marwick, A., *War and Social Change in the Twentieth Century* (1974).

Michels, R., *Political Parties: A Sociological Study of the Emergence of Leadership, the Psychology of Power, and the Oligarchical Tendencies of Organisation* (1915).

Minkin, L., *The Labour Party Conference: A Study in the Politics of Intra-Party Democracy* (rev. edn., Manchester, 1980).

Mitchell, A., *Election '45: Reflections on the Revolution in Britain* (1995).

Morgan, K., *Against Fascism and War: Ruptures and Continuities in British Communist Politics 1935–41* (1989).

Morgan, K. O., *Labour in Power, 1945–1951* (Oxford, 1984).

_____ *Rebirth of a Nation: Wales, 1880–1980* (Oxford, 1981).

Noakes, L., *War and the British: Gender and National Identity, 1939–1991* (1998).

Norris, P., *Electoral Change in Britain since 1945* (Oxford, 1997).

O'Brien, T. H., *Civil Defence* (1955).

Ostrogorski, M., *Democracy and the Organisation of Political Parties* (2 vols., 1902).

Payton-Smith, D. J., *Oil: A Study in War-Time Policy and Administration* (1971).

Peele, G., and Cook, C. (eds.), *The Politics of Reappraisal, 1918–1939* (1975).

Pelling, H., *A Short History of the Labour Party* (8th edn., 1986).

_____ *The British Communist Party* (1958).

Pimlott, B., *Labour and the Left in the 1930s* (Cambridge, 1977).

Pinto-Duschinsky, M., *British Political Finance, 1830–1980* (Washington, DC, 1981).

Pugh, M., *The Making of Modern British Politics, 1867–1939* (2nd edn., Oxford, 1993).

Ramsden, J., *The Age of Balfour and Baldwin, 1902–1940* (1978).

_____ *The Age of Churchill and Eden, 1940–1957* (1995).

_____ *An Appetite for Power: A History of the Conservative Party since 1830* (1998).

_____ *The Making of Conservative Party Policy: The Conservative Research Department since 1929* (1980).

_____ *The Winds of Change: Macmillan to Heath, 1957–1975* (1996).

Rasmussen, J. S., *The Liberal Party: A Study of Retrenchment and Revival* (1965).

Ray, J., *The Night Blitz, 1940–41* (1996).

Renton, D., *Fascism, Anti-Fascism and Britain in the 1940s* (Houndmills, 2000).

Reynolds, D., *Rich Relations: The American Occupation of Britain, 1942–45* (1996).

Reynolds, J., and Laybourn, K., *Labour Heartland: The History of the Labour Party in West Yorkshire during the Inter-War Years, 1918–1939* (1987).

Riddell, N., *Labour in Crisis: The Second Labour Government, 1929–31* (Manchester, 1999).

Roberts, A., *Eminent Churchillians* (1994).

Ross, J. F. S., *Parliamentary Representation* (1943).

Rossiter, D. J., Johnston, R. J., and Pattie, C. J., *The Boundary Commission: Redrawing the UK's Map of Parliamentary Constituencies* (Manchester, 1999).

Salmon, P., *Electoral Reform at Work: Local Politics and National Parties, 1832–1841* (2002).

Savage, M., *The Dynamics of Working-Class Politics: The Labour Movement in Preston 1880–1940* (1987).

Scarrow, S. (ed.), *Perspectives on Political Parties: Classic Readings* (Houndmills, 2002).

Searle, G. R., *Country before Party: Coalition and the Idea of 'National Government' in Modern Britain, 1885–1987* (1995).

Seldon, A., and Ball, S. (eds.), *Conservative Century: The Conservative Party since 1900* (Oxford, 1994).

Sheppard, F., *London: A History* (Oxford, 1998).

Smart, N., *British Strategy and Politics during the Phony War* (2003).

—— *The National Government 1931–40* (1999).

Smith, H. L. (ed.), *War and Social Change: British Society in the Second World War* (1986).

Smith, M., *Britain and 1940: History, Myth and Popular Memory* (2000).

Srebrnik, H. F., *London Jews and British Communism, 1935–1945* (Ilford, 1995).

Stacey, M., *Tradition and Change: A Study of Banbury* (1960).

Stammers, N., *Civil Liberties in Britain during the Second World War: A Political Study* (1983).

Stannage, T., *Baldwin Thwarts the Opposition: The British General Election of 1935* (1980).

Stewart, G., *Burying Caesar: Churchill, Chamberlain and the Battle for the Tory Party* (1999).

Stewart, J. D., *British Pressure Groups: Their Role in Relation to the House of Commons* (Oxford, 1959).

Summerfield, P., *Reconstructing Women's Wartime Lives: Discourse and Subjectivity in Oral Histories of the Second World War* (Manchester, 1998).

—— *Women Workers in the Second World War: Production and Patriarchy in Conflict* (1984).

Sutcliffe, A., and Smith, R., *History of Birmingham*, iii: *Birmingham 1939–1970* (1974).

Swift, J., *Labour in Crisis: Clement Attlee and the Labour Party in Opposition, 1931–40* (2001).

Sykes, A., *The Rise and Fall of British Liberalism* (1997).

Tanner, D., Thane, P., and Tiratsoo, N. (eds.), *Labour's First Century* (Cambridge, 2000).

—— Williams, C., and Hopkin, D. (eds.), *The Labour Party in Wales, 1900–2000* (Cardiff, 2000).

Taylor, A. J. P., *English History, 1914–1945* (Oxford, 1965).

Thompson, W., *The Good Old Cause: A History of the Communist Party of Great Britain 1920–91* (1992).

Thorpe, A. (ed.), *The Failure of Political Extremism in Inter-War Britain* (1989).

—— *A History of the British Labour Party* (3rd edn., 2008).

—— *Britain in the 1930s* (1992).

—— *The British Communist Party and Moscow 1920–1943* (2000).

Thurlow, R., *Fascism in Britain 1918–85* (Oxford, 1987).

Tiratsoo, N. (ed.), *The Attlee Years* (1991).

—— *Reconstruction, Affluence and Labour Politics: Coventry 1945–60* (1990).

Titmuss, R. M., *Problems of Social Policy* (1950).

Tregidga, G., *The Liberal Party in South-West Britain since 1918: Political Decline, Dormancy and Rebirth* (Exeter, 2000).

Vernon, J., *Politics and the People: A Study in English Political Culture, c.1815–1867* (Cambridge, 1993).

Waller, P. J., *Democracy and Sectarianism: A Political and Social History of Liverpool, 1868–1939* (Liverpool, 1981).

Waller, R. J., *The Dukeries Transformed: The Social and Political Development of a Twentieth Century Coalfield* (Oxford, 1983).

Ware, A., *Political Parties and Party Systems* (Oxford, 1996).

Weinbren, D., *Generating Socialism: Recollections of Life in the Labour Party* (Stroud, 1997).

White, J., *The Worst Street in North London: Campbell Bunk, Islington, between the Wars* (1986).

Whiting, R. C., *The View from Cowley: The Impact of Industrialization upon Oxford, 1918–1939* (Oxford, 1983).

Williams, C., *Democratic Rhondda: Politics and Society, 1885–1951* (Cardiff, 1996).

Wilson, D. J., *Power and Party Bureaucracy in Britain: Regional Organisation in the Conservative and Labour Parties* (Farnborough, 1975).

Winter, J. M. (ed.), *The Working Class in Modern British History* (Cambridge, 1983).

Wootton, G., *Pressure Groups in Britain, 1720–1970* (1975).

Young, K., *Local Politics and the Rise of Party: The London Metropolitan Society and the Conservative Intervention in Local Elections, 1894–1963* (Leicester, 1975).

Young, M., and Willmott, P., *Family and Kinship in East London* (1957).

Zweiniger-Bargielowska, I., *Austerity in Britain: Rationing, Controls and Consumption, 1939–1955* (Oxford, 2000).

4. Articles

Addison, P., 'By-elections of the Second World War', in C. Cook and J. Ramsden (eds.), *By-Elections in British Politics* (2nd edn., 1997) 130–50.

——— 'Churchill and the price of victory: 1939–1945', in N. Tiratsoo (ed.), *From Blitz to Blair: A New History of Britain since 1939* (1997) 53–76.

——— 'Journey to the centre: Churchill and Labour in coalition, 1940–5', in A. Sked and C. Cook (eds.), *Crisis and Controversy: Essays in Honour of A. J. P. Taylor* (1976), 165-93.

——— 'The road from 1945', in P. Hennessy and A. Seldon (eds.), *Ruling Performance: British Government from Attlee to Thatcher* (Oxford, 1987) 5–27.

Arnstein, W. L., ' "The Liberals and the general election of 1945": a sceptical note', *Journal of British Studies*, 14 (1975), 120–6.

Aubel, F., 'The Conservatives in Wales, 1880–1935', in M. Francis and I. Zweiniger-Bargielowska (eds.), *The Conservatives and British Society 1880–1990* (1996), 96–110.

Baines, M., 'The Liberal party and the 1945 general election', *Contemporary Record*, 9 (1995), 48–61.

——— 'The survival of the British Liberal party, 1933–59', in A. Gorst, L. Johnman, and W. S. Lucas (eds.), *Contemporary British History 1931–1961: Politics and the Limits of Policy* (1991) 17–32.

Ball, S., 'Churchill and the Conservative party', *Transactions of the Royal Historical Society*, 5th series, 11 (2001), 307–30.

——— 'Local Conservatism and the evolution of the party organisation', in A. Seldon and S. Ball (eds.), *Conservative Century: The Conservative Party since 1900* (Oxford, 1994), 261–311.

——— 'National politics and local history: the regional and local archives of the Conservative party, 1867–1945', *Archives*, 22 (1996), 27–59.

Ball, S., 'The national and regional party structure', in A. Seldon and S. Ball (eds.), *Conservative Century: The Conservative Party since 1900* (Oxford, 1994), 169–220.

——— 'The 1922 Committee: the formative years, 1922–45', *Parliamentary History*, 9 (1990), 129–57.

Beaven, B., and Griffiths, J., 'The blitz, civilian morale and the city: Mass-Observation and working-class culture in Britain, 1940–41', *Urban History*, 26 (1999), 71–88.

Bennett, G. H., 'The wartime political truce and hopes for post-war coalition: the West Derbyshire by-election, 1944', *Midland History*, 17 (1992), 118–35.

Benney, M., and Geiss, P., 'Social class and politics in Greenwich', *British Journal of Sociology*, 1 (1950), 310–27.

Bentley, M., '1931–1945', in A. Seldon (ed.), *How Tory Governments Fall* (1996) 285–314.

——— 'Party, doctrine and thought', in M. Bentley and J. Stevenson (eds.), *High and Low Politics in Modern Britain: Ten Studies* (Oxford, 1983), 123–53.

Black, A., and S. Brooke, 'The Labour party, women, and the problem of gender, 1951–1966', *Journal of British Studies*, 36 (1997), 419–52.

Black, L. ' "Still at the penny-farthing stage in a jet-propelled era": branch life in 1950s socialism', *Labour History Review*, 65 (2000), 202–26.

Brooke, S., 'The Labour party and the 1945 general election', *Contemporary Record*, 9 (1995), 1–21.

——— 'The Labour party and the Second World War', in A. Gorst, L. Johnman, and W. S. Lucas (eds.), *Contemporary British History 1931–1961: Politics and the Limits of Policy* (1991) 1–16.

——— 'Revisionists and fundamentalists: the Labour party and economic policy during the Second World War', *Historical Journal*, 32 (1989), 157–75.

Brookshire, J. H., ' "Speak for England", act for England: Labour's leadership and British national security under the threat of war in the late 1930s', *European History Quarterly*, 29 (1999), 251–87.

——— 'The National Council of Labour, 1921–1946', *Albion*, 18 (1986), 43–69.

Bruley, S., ' "A very happy crowd": women in industry in south London in World War Two', *History Workshop Journal*, 44 (1997), 58–76.

Bussy, S., 'The Labour victory in Winchester in 1945', *Southern History*, 8 (1986), 145–52.

Butler, D. E., and Pinto-Duschinsky, M., 'The Conservative elite, 1918–78: does unrepresentativeness matter?', in Z. Layton-Henry (ed.), *Conservative Party Politics* (1980), 186–209.

Callaghan, J., 'Common Wealth and the Communist party and the 1945 general election', *Contemporary Record*, 9 (1995), 62–79.

Callcott, M., 'The nature and extent of political change in the interwar years: the example of County Durham', *Northern History*, 16 (1980), 215–37.

Charmley, J., 'Churchill as war hero', *International History Review*, 13 (1991), 96–104.

Clark, J. C. D., 'A general theory of party, opposition and government, 1688–1832', *Historical Journal*, 23 (1980), 295–325.

Cockett, R. B., 'Ball, Chamberlain and *Truth*', *Historical Journal*, 33 (1990), 131–42.

——— 'The party, publicity and the media', in A. Seldon and S. Ball (eds.), *Conservative Century: The Conservative Party since 1900* (Oxford, 1994), 547–77.

Cook, C., 'Liberals, Labour and local elections', in G. Peele and C. Cook (eds.), *The Politics of Reappraisal, 1918–1939* (1975), 166–88.

Corfield, T., 'Why Chamberlain really fell', *History Today*, 46/12 (1996), 22–8.

Costello, D. R., '*Searchlight Books* and the quest for a "People's War", 1941–42', *Journal of Contemporary History*, 24 (1989), 257–76.

Crang, J. A., 'Politics on parade: army education and the 1945 general election', *History*, 81 (1996), 215–27.

Criddle, B., 'Members of Parliament', in A. Seldon and S. Ball (eds.), *Conservative Century: The Conservative Party since 1900* (Oxford, 1994), 145–67.

Crowson, N., 'Conservative parliamentary dissent over foreign policy during the premiership of Neville Chamberlain: myth or reality?', *Parliamentary History*, 14 (1995), 315–36.

Cullen, S. M., 'Another nationalism: the British Union of Fascists in Glamorgan, 1932–40', *Welsh History Review*, 17 (1994), 101–14.

Dawson, M., 'Money and the real impact of the Fourth Reform Act', *Historical Journal*, 35 (1992), 369–82.

Denver, D., and Hands, H. T. G., 'Politics 1929–74', in J. D. Marshall (ed.), *The History of Lancashire County Council, 1889 to 1974* (1977), 194–244.

Dickie, M., 'Town patriotism in Northampton, 1918–39: an invented tradition?', *Midland History*, 17 (1992), 109–17.

Donnison, D. V., and Plowman, D. E. G., 'The functions of local Labour parties', *Political Studies*, 2 (1954), 154–67.

Dutton, D., 'Power brokers or just "glamour boys"? The Eden group, September 1939–May 1940', *English Historical Review*, 118 (2003), 412–24.

_____ 'William Mabane and Huddersfield politics, 1931–1947: "By any other name a Liberal" ', *Northern History*, 43 (2006), 137–53.

Epstein, L., 'British MPs and their local parties: the Suez cases', *American Political Science Review*, 54 (1960) 374–90.

Fair, J. D., 'The Norwegian campaign and Winston Churchill's rise to power in 1940: a study of perception and attribution', *International History Review*, 9 (1987), 410–37.

Fielding, S., 'Activists against "affluence": Labour party culture during the "Golden Age", circa 1950–1970', *Journal of British Studies*, 40 (2001), 241–67.

_____ 'Labourism in the 1940s', *Twentieth Century British History*, 3 (1992), 138–53.

_____ 'The good war: 1939–1945', in N. Tiratsoo (ed.), *From Blitz to Blair: A New History of Britain since 1939* (1997) 25–52.

_____ 'The Second World War and popular radicalism: the significance of the "movement away from party" ', *History*, 80 (1995), 38–58.

_____ 'What did "the people" want? The meaning of the 1945 general election', *Historical Journal*, 35 (1992), 623–40.

Finlay, R. J., 'Pressure group or political party? The nationalist impact on Scottish politics, 1928–45', *Twentieth Century British History*, 3 (1992), 274–97.

_____ 'Scottish Conservatism and Unionism since 1918', in M. Francis and I. Zweiniger-Bargielowska (eds.), *The Conservatives and British Society 1880–1990* (1996), 111–26.

Fishman, N., 'No home but the trade union movement: Communist activists and "reformist" leaders, 1926–56', in G. Andrews et al. (eds.), *Opening the Books: Essays on the Cultural and Social History of the British Communist Party* (1995), 102–23.

Franklin, M., and Ladner, M., 'The undoing of Winston Churchill: mobilization and conversion in the 1945 realignment of British voters', *British Journal of Political Science*, 25 (1995), 429–52.

Fry, G. K., 'A reconsideration of the British general election of 1935 and the electoral revolution of 1945', *History*, 76 (1991), 43–55.

Fyrth, J., 'Days of hope: the meaning of 1945', in idem (ed.), *Labour's Promised Land? Culture and Society in Labour Britain 1945–51* (1995), 3–15.

Gilbert, B. B., 'Third parties and voters' decisions: the Liberals and the general election of 1945', *Journal of British Studies*, 11/2 (1972), 131–41.

——— ' "The Liberals and the general election of 1945": a modest rejoinder', *Journal of British Studies*, 14/2 (1975), 127–8.

Gliddon, P., 'The political importance of provincial newspapers, 1903–1945: the Rowntrees and the Liberal press', *Twentieth Century British History*, 14 (2003), 24–42.

Goodlad, G., 'The Liberal Nationals 1931–40: the problems of party in a "partnership government" ', *Historical Journal*, 38 (1995), 133–43.

Gorman, J., 'The Labour party's election posters in 1945', *Labour History Review*, 61 (1996), 299–308.

Gould, J., 'Riverside: a Labour constituency', *Fabian Journal* (November 1954), 12–18.

Hamilton, C. I., 'The decline of Churchill's "garden suburb" and the rise of his private office: the Prime Minister's Department, 1940–45', *Twentieth Century British History*, 12 (1992), 133–62.

Harris, J., 'Beveridge's social and political thought', in J. Hills, J. Ditch, and H. Glennerster (eds.), *Beveridge and Social Security: An International Retrospective* (Oxford, 1994), 23–36.

——— 'War and social history: Britain and the Home Front during the Second World War', *Contemporary European History*, 1 (1992), 17–36.

Harvie, C., 'Labour in Scotland during the Second World War', *Historical Journal*, 26 (1983), 921–44.

——— 'The recovery of Scottish Labour, 1939–51', in I. Donnachie et al. (eds.) *Forward! Labour Politics in Scotland, 1888–1988* (Edinburgh, 1989) 66–83.

Hastings, R. P., 'The Birmingham Labour movement, 1918–1945', *Midland History*, 5 (1979–80), 78–92.

Hennessy, P., 'Churchill and the premiership', *Transactions of the Royal Historical Society*, 6th series, 11 (2001), 295–306.

Hilson, M., and Melling, J., 'Public gifts and political identities: Sir Richard Acland, Common Wealth, and the moral politics of land ownership in the 1940s', *Twentieth Century British History*, 11 (2000), 156–82.

Hinton, J., 'The Communist party, production and Britain's post-war settlement', in G. Andrews et al. (eds.), *Opening the Books: Essays on the Cultural and Social History of the British Communist Party* (1995), 160–75.

——— 'Voluntarism and the welfare/warfare state: women's voluntary services in the 1940s', *Twentieth Century British History*, 9 (1998), 274–305.

——— 'Women and the Labour vote, 1945–50', *Labour History Review*, 57 (1992), 59–66.

Hollins, T. J., 'The Conservative party and film propaganda between the wars', *English Historical Review*, 96 (1981), 359–69.

Hooson, E., 'Clement Davies: an underestimated Welshman and politician', *Transactions of the Honourable Society of Cymmrodorion, 1997*, new series, 4 (1998), 168–86.

Howard, C., 'Expectations born to death: local Labour party expansion in the 1920s', in J. M. Winter (ed.), *The Working Class in Modern British History* (1983), 65–81.

Howkins, A., 'A country at war: Mass-Observation and rural England, 1939–45', *Rural History*, 9 (1998), 75–98.

Ismay, T. C., 'A reassessment of Anglo-French strategy during the Phony War, 1939–40', *English Historical Review*, 119 (2004), 333–72.

Jarvis, D., ' "Behind every great party": women and Conservatism in twentieth-century Britain', in A. Vickery (ed.), *Women, Privilege, and Power: British Politics, 1750 to the Present* (Stanford, Calif., 2001) 289–314.

_____ 'The shaping of the Conservative electoral hegemony, 1918–39', in J. Lawrence and M. Taylor (eds.), *Party, State and Society: Electoral Behaviour in Britain since 1820* (Aldershot, 1997), 131–52.

Jeffery, T., 'The suburban nation: politics and class in Lewisham', in D. Feldman and G. Stedman Jones (eds.), *Metropolis, London: Histories and Representations since 1800* (1989), 189–216.

Jefferys, K., 'British politics and social policy during the Second World War', *Historical Journal*, 30 (1987), 123–44.

_____ 'May 1940: the downfall of Neville Chamberlain', *Parliamentary History*, 10 (1991), 363–78.

_____ 'R. A. Butler, the Board of Education and the 1944 Education Act', *History*, 69 (1984) 415–31.

Johnman, L., 'The Labour party and industrial policy, 1940–45', in N. Tiratsoo (ed.), *The Attlee Years* (1991), 29–53.

Johnstone, M., 'The CPGB, the Comintern and the war, 1939–41: filling in the blank spots', *Science and Society*, 61 (1997), 27–45.

Jones, J. G., 'The Liberal party and Wales, 1945–79', *Welsh History Review*, 16 (1993), 326–55.

Kandiah, M. D., 'Television enters British politics: the Conservative party's Central Office and political broadcasting, 1945–55', *Historical Journal of Film, Radio and Television*, 15 (1995), 265–84.

_____ 'The Conservative party and the 1945 general election', *Contemporary Record*, 9 (1995), 22–47.

Kelly, R., 'The party conferences', in A. Seldon and S. Ball (eds.), *Conservative Century: The Conservative Party since 1900* (Oxford, 1994), 221–60.

Knox, W. W., and MacKinlay, A., 'Remaking Scottish Labour in the 1930s', *Twentieth Century British History*, 6 (1995), 174–93.

Lawrence, J., 'Popular politics and the limitations of party: Wolverhampton, 1867–1900', in E. F. Biagini and A. Reid (eds.), *Currents of Radicalism: Popular Radicalism, Organised Labour and Party Politics in Britain, 1850–1914* (Cambridge, 1991), 65–85.

Layton-Henry, Z., 'The Young Conservatives, 1945–70', *Journal of Contemporary History*, 8 (1973), 143–56.

Lovenduski, J., Norris, P., and Burness, C., 'The party and women', in A. Seldon and S. Ball (eds.), *Conservative Century: The Conservative Party since 1900* (Oxford, 1994), 611–35.

Lowe, R., 'The Second World War, consensus, and the foundation of the welfare state', *Twentieth Century British History*, 1 (1990), 152–82.

McCulloch, G., 'Labour, the left and the British general election of 1945', *Journal of British Studies*, 24 (1985), 465–89.

McKenzie, R. T., 'Parties, pressure groups and the British political process', *Political Quarterly*, 29 (1958), 5–16.

McKibbin, R. I., 'Classes and cultures: a postscript', *Mitteilungsblatt des Instituts für soziale Bewegungen*, 27 (2002), 153–65.

McKinlay, A., 'Labour and locality: Labour politics on Clydeside, 1900–39', *Journal of Regional and Local Studies*, 10 (1990), 48–59.

Marwick, A., 'Middle opinion in the thirties: planning, progress and political "agreement" ', *English Historical Review*, 79 (1964), 285–98.

Mason, T., 'Looking back on the blitz', in B. Lancaster and T. Mason (eds.), *Life and Labour in a Twentieth Century City: The Experience of Coventry* (1986) 321–41.

Middlemas, K., 'The party, industry, and the City', in A. Seldon and S. Ball (eds.), *Conservative Century: The Conservative Party since 1900* (Oxford, 1994), 445–97.

Morell, J., 'Arnold Leese and the Imperial Fascist League: the impact of racial fascism', in K. Lunn and R. Thurlow (eds.), *British Fascism: Essays on the Radical Right in Inter-War Britain* (1980), 57–75.

Morgan, K., 'The Communist party and the *Daily Worker*, 1930–56', in G. Andrews et al. (eds.), *Opening the Books: Essays on the Cultural and Social History of the British Communist Party* (1995) 142–59.

Morgan, K. O., 'Power and glory: war and reconstruction, 1939–1951', in D. Tanner, C. Williams, and D. Hopkin (eds.), *The Labour Party in Wales, 1900–2000* (2000), 166–88.

Morris, J., 'Morale under air attack: Swansea, 1939–41', *Welsh Historical Review*, 11 (1982), 358–87.

Nicholas, S., ' "Sly demagogues" and wartime radio: J. B. Priestley and the BBC', *Twentieth Century British History*, 6 (1995), 247–66.

—— 'From John Bull to John Citizen: images of national identity and citizenship on the wartime BBC', in R. Weight and A. Beach (eds.), *The Right to Belong: Citizenship and National Identity in Britain, 1930–1960* (1998) 36–58.

Norton, P., 'The growth of the constituency role of the MP', *Parliamentary Affairs*, 47/4 (1994), 705–20.

—— 'Winning the war but losing the peace: the British House of Commons during the Second World War', *Journal of Legislative Studies*, 4 (1998), 33–51.

Oram, A., ' "Bombs don't discriminate!" Women's political activism in the Second World War', in C. Gledhill and G. Swanson (eds.), *Nationalising Femininity: Culture, Sexuality and British Cinema in the Second World War* (1996), 53–69.

Owen, N., 'The Conservative party and Indian independence, 1945–1947', *Historical Journal*, 46 (2003), 403–36.

Parker, J., 'After a year of coalition', *Fabian Quarterly*, 30 (1941) 5–9.

Pateman, M., 'Mancunians' perceptions of Labour in the Second World War', *Manchester Region History Review*, 14 (2000), 91–102.

Pelling, H., 'The 1945 general election reconsidered', *Historical Journal*, 23 (1980), 399–414.

Pelling, H., 'The impact of the war on the Labour party', in H. L. Smith (ed.), *War and Social Change: British Society in the Second World War* (1986) 129–48.

Pimlott, B., 'The Labour left', in C. Cook and I. Taylor (eds.), *The Labour Party: An Introduction to its History, Structure and Politics* (1980), 163–88.

Pollock, J. R., Jr., 'British party organization', *Political Science Quarterly*, 45 (1930), 161–80.

Pugh, M., 'The *Daily Mirror* and the revival of Labour, 1935–1945', *Twentieth Century British History*, 9 (1998), 420–38.

_____ 'Popular Conservatism in Britain: continuity and change, 1880–1987', *Journal of British Studies*, 27 (1988), 254–82.

_____ 'The rise of Labour and the political culture of Conservatism, 1890–1945', *History*, 87 (2002), 514–37.

Ramsden, J., 'How Winston Churchill became "The Greatest Living Englishman"', *Contemporary British History*, 12/3 (1998), 1–40.

_____ 'Winston Churchill and the leadership of the Conservative party, 1940–51', *Contemporary Record*, 9 (1995), 99–119.

Redfern, N., 'Winning the peace: British Communists, the Soviet Union and the general election of 1945', *Contemporary British History*, 16 (2002), 29–50.

Rix, K., 'Hidden workers of the party: the professional Liberal agents, 1885–1910', *Journal of Liberal History*, 52 (2006), 4–13.

Rolf, D., 'Birmingham Labour and the background to the 1945 General Election', in A. Wright and R. M. Y. Shackleton (eds.), *Worlds of Labour: Essays in Birmingham Labour History* (1981) 127–55.

Rowe, A., 'Conservatives and trade unionists', in Z. Layton-Henry (ed.), *Conservative Party Politics* (1980), 210–30.

Scott, P., 'The state, internal migration, and the growth of new industrial communities in inter-war Britain', *English Historical Review*, 115 (2000), 329–53.

Seldon, A., 'Conservative century', in A. Seldon and S. Ball (eds.), *Conservative Century: The Conservative Party since 1900* (Oxford, 1994), 17–65.

Sibley, R., 'The swing to Labour during the Second World War: when and why?', *Labour History Review*, 55 (1990), 23–34.

Skidelsky, R., 'Reflections on Mosley and British fascism', in K. Lunn and R. Thurlow (eds.), *British Fascism: Essays on the Radical Right in Inter-War Britain* (1980), 78–99.

Smart, N., 'Four days in May: the Norway debates and the downfall on Neville Chamberlain', *Parliamentary History*, 17 (1998), 215–43.

Smith, H. L., 'The effect of the war on the status of women', in H. L. Smith (ed.), *War and Social Change: British Society in the Second World War* (1986) 208–29.

_____ 'The womanpower problem in Britain during the Second World War', *Historical Journal*, 27 (1984), 925–45.

Stevens, C., 'The Conservative Club movement in the industrial West Riding, 1880–1914', *Northern History*, 38 (2001), 121–44.

_____ 'The electoral sociology of modern Britain reconsidered', *Contemporary British History*, 13 (1999), 62–94.

Stevens, R., 'Containing radicalism: the Trades Union Congress Organisation Department and trades councils, 1928–1953', *Labour History Review*, 62 (1997), 5–21.

_____ '"Disruptive elements"? The influence of the Communist party in Nottingham and district trades council, 1929–1951', *Labour History Review*, 58 (1993), 22–37.

_____ ' "Rapid demise or slow death?" The Independent Labour party in Derby, 1932–1945', *Midland History*, 22 (1997), 113–30.

Stevenson, J., 'Planner's moon? The Second World War and the planning movement', in H. L. Smith (ed.), *War and Social Change: British Society in the Second World War* (1986) 58–77.

Summerfield, P., ' "The girl that makes the thing that drills the hole that holds the spring . . .": discourses of women and work in the Second World War', in C. Gledhill and G. Swanson (eds.), *Nationalising Femininity: Culture, Sexuality and British Cinema in the Second World War* (1996), 35–52.

_____ 'Mass-Observation: social research or social movement?', *Journal of Contemporary History*, 20 (1985), 439–52.

_____ 'The "levelling of class" ', in H. L. Smith (ed.), *War and Social Change: British Society in the Second World War* (1986) 179–207.

Tanner, D., 'The Labour party and electoral politics in the coalfields', in A. Campbell et al. (eds.), *Miners, Unions and Politics, 1910–47* (Aldershot, 1996), 59–92.

_____ 'The pattern of Labour politics, 1918–1939', in D. Tanner, C. Williams, and D. Hopkin (eds.), *The Labour Party in Wales, 1900–2000* (2000), 113–39.

Taylor, A., 'The politics of labourism in the Yorkshire coalfield, 1926–1945', in A. Campbell et al. (eds.), *Miners, Unions and Politics 1910–47* (1996), 223–49.

Taylor, I., 'Labour and the impact of war, 1939–45', in N. Tiratsoo (ed.), *The Attlee Years* (1991) 7–28.

Thane, P., 'Visions of gender in the making of the British welfare state: the case of women in the British Labour party and social policy, 1906–45', in G. Bock (ed.), *Maternity and Gender Policies: Women and the Rise of the European Welfare States, 1880s–1950s* (1991) 93–118.

_____ 'The women of the British Labour party and feminism, 1906–45', in H. L. Smith (ed.), *British Feminism in the Twentieth Century* (Aldershot, 1990), 126–43.

Thorpe, A., 'Britain', in J. D. Noakes (ed.), *The Civilian in War* (Exeter, 1992) 14–34.

_____ 'Comintern "control" of the Communist party of Great Britain, 1920–43', *English Historical Review*, 113 (1998), 637–62.

_____ ' "In a rather emotional state"? The Labour party and British intervention in Greece, 1944–45', *English Historical Review*, 121 (2006), 1075–1105.

_____ 'J. H. Thomas and the rise of Labour in Derby, 1880–1940', *Midland History*, 15 (1990), 111–28.

_____ 'Stalinism and British politics', *History*, 83 (1998), 608–27.

_____ 'The Communist International and the British Communist party', in T. Rees and A. Thorpe (eds.), *International Communism and the Communist International, 1919–43* (1998) 67–86.

_____ 'The membership of the British Communist party, 1920–45', *Historical Journal*, 43 (2000), 777–800.

Thurlow, R. C., 'The evolution of the mythical British fifth column, 1939–46', *Twentieth Century British History*, 10 (1999), 477–98.

Todd, N., 'Labour women: the Bexley branch of the British Labour party, 1945–50', *Journal of Contemporary History*, 8 (1973), 159–73.

Tombs, I., 'The victory of socialist "Vansittartism": Labour and the German question, 1941–5', *Twentieth Century British History*, 7 (1996), 287–309.

Toye, R., 'Keynes, the Labour movement, and "how to pay for the war"', *Twentieth Century British History*, 10 (1999), 255–81.

—— 'The Labour party and the economics of rearmament, 1935–39', *Twentieth Century British History*, 6 (2001), 303–26.

Trythall, A. J., 'The downfall of Hore-Belisha', *Journal of Contemporary History*, 16 (1981), 391–412.

Vincent, J., 'Chamberlain, the Liberals and the outbreak of war, 1939', *English Historical Review*, 113 (1998), 367–83.

Webber, G., 'Patterns of membership and support for the BUF', *Journal of Contemporary History* (1984), 575–606.

Weight, R., 'State, intelligentsia and the promotion of national culture in Britain, 1939–45', *Historical Research*, 69 (1996), 83–101.

Weinbren, D., 'Building communities, constructing identities: the rise of the Labour party in London', *London Journal*, 23 (1998), 41–60.

Williams, C., '"The hope of the British proletariat": the South Wales miners, 1910–1947', in A. Campbell et al. (eds.), *Miners, Unions and Politics, 1910–47* (Aldershot, 1996), 253–71.

Williamson, P., 'Christian Conservatives and the totalitarian challenge, 1933–40', *English Historical Review*, 115 (2000), 607–42.

Witherell, L., 'Lord Salisbury's "Watching Committee" and the fall of Neville Chamberlain, May 1940', *English Historical Review*, 116 (2001), 1134–66.

Wrigley, C. J, 'The Second World War and state intervention in industrial relations, 1939–45', in idem. (ed.), *A History of British Industrial Relations, 1939–79* (1996), 12–41.

Zweiniger-Bargielowska, I., 'Rationing, austerity and the Conservative party recovery after 1945', *Historical Journal*, 37 (1994), 173–97.

5. Theses

Baines, M. I., 'The survival of the British Liberal party, 1932–59', University of Oxford D.Phil., 1990.

Bates, J. W. B., 'The Conservative party in the constituencies, 1918–39', University of Oxford D.Phil., 1994.

Calder, A. L. R., 'The Common Wealth party, 1942–45', University of Sussex D.Phil., 1968.

Egan, M., 'The grass-roots organization of the Liberal party, 1945–64', University of Oxford D.Phil., 2000.

Griffiths, C. V. J., 'Labour and the countryside: rural strands in the British Labour movement, 1900–39', University of Oxford D.Phil., 1997.

Johnson, J. E., 'From defeat to victory: the Conservative party in the constituencies, 1945–59', University of Oxford D.Phil., 2001.

Kandiah, M. D., 'Lord Woolton's chairmanship of the Conservative party, 1946–51', University of Exeter Ph.D., 1992.

Index